5TH EDITION

Industrial and Organizational Psychology

Research and Practice

PAUL E. SPECTOR

Department of Psychology University of South Florida

BICENTENNIAL
1807
WILEY
2007
BICENTENNIAL

JOHN WILEY & SONS, INC.

PUBLISHER	Jay O'Callaghan
ACQUISITIONS EDITOR	Christopher Johnson
ASSISTANT EDITOR	Eileen McKeever
SENIOR PRODUCTION EDITOR	Valerie A. Vargas
MARKETING MANAGER	Jeffrey Rucker
CREATIVE DIRECTOR	Harry Nolan
PRODUCTION MANAGEMENT SERVICES	PineTree/Laserwords
SENIOR PHOTO EDITOR	Tara Sanford
EDITORIAL ASSISTANT	Carrie Tupa
MEDIA EDITOR	Allison Morris
COVER DESIGN	Michael St. Martine
COVER PHOTO	© Jonathan Evans/Getty Images

Bicentennial Logo Design: Richard J. Pacifico

This book was set in Times by Laserwords Private Limited and printed and bound by RRD-JC. Cover printed by Phoenix Color, Corp.

This book is printed on acid free paper. ⊗

To order books or for customer service please, call 1-800-CALL WILEY (225-5945).

ISBN-13 978-0-470-12918-0

Library of Congress Cataloging-in-Publication Data

Spector, Paul E.
  Industrial and organizational psychology : research and practice / Paul E.
Spector.–5th ed.
      p. cm.
  Includes bibliographical references and index.
  ISBN 978-0-470-12918-0
  1. Psychology, Industrial. 2. Personnel management. I. Title.
  HF5548.8.S625 2008
  158.7–dc22

                                                          2007039262

Printed in the United States of America

10 9 8 7 6 5 4 3 2

To Gail and Steven Spector

Preface

Industrial/organizational, or I/O, psychology is an exciting field that has enjoyed continual growth in the United States and the industrialized world throughout its almost 100 year history. What began as a tiny subspecialty of psychology, known only to a few practitioners and professors, has grown to be one of the major applied specialties in psychology worldwide. This attention is due to two factors. First, I/O is concerned with the workplace, so its findings and principles are relevant to everyone who has held a job. Second, I/O has developed proven methods that organizations find of value. I/O psychologists are often called upon to help organizations have a more efficient and healthier workforce.

The field of I/O psychology has a dual nature. First, it is the science of people at work. This aspect ties it to other areas of psychology, such as cognitive and social. Second, I/O psychology is the application of psychological principles in organizational and work settings. There is no other area of psychology in which a closer correspondence between application and science exists, making I/O a good example of how society can benefit from the study of psychology.

The field of I/O is a large and diverse one. Many topics are covered, ranging from methods of hiring employees to theories of how organizations work. It is concerned with helping organizations get the most from their employees, or human resources, as well as helping organizations take care of employee health and well-being. For this reason a single text can provide only an overview of the major findings and methods that I/O psychologists use. The goal of this book is to provide such an overview, as well as a comprehensive understanding of the field. Each of the major areas that comprise I/O is covered.

Part One of this book provides an overview of the I/O field. Chapter 1 covers the nature of the field and its history. I/O is discussed as both a practice and a science. The chapter describes what a career in I/O involves, and what it takes to become an I/O psychologist. Chapter 2 is an overview of the basic principles of I/O research methods.

The remainder of the book is divided into four major sections. In Part Two, Chapter 3 discusses job analysis, or the assessment of jobs. Chapter 4 focuses on the assessment of employee job performance. Chapter 5 explores the way in which employee characteristics are measured. Part Three contains two chapters. Chapter 6 deals with the methods that organizations use to hire new employees. Chapter 7 follows those new employees, as well as experienced ones, through their training programs.

The four chapters in Part Four discuss the relationship between the individual and the organization. Chapter 8 covers theories of motivation. Chapter 9 focuses on how people feel about their jobs—their attitudes about the job and the emotions they experience at work. The topic of Chapter 10 is productive and counterproductive work behavior. Chapter 11 deals with occupational health psychology, a rapidly emerging new field that is concerned with worker health, safety, and well being.

The final part of the book, Part Five, is concerned with the social context of work. Chapter 12 explores small work groups or work teams and their effect on the individual. Chapter 13 discusses leadership and supervision in the workplace. Chapter 14, the last chapter, takes an organization perspective. It covers organizational development and organizational theory.

► SPECIAL FEATURES

In each chapter of the book there are "Learning by Doing" exercises that actively engage the student with the material in the chapter. All of the exercises ask the student to address an I/O issue or answer a particular question. Some involve interviewing working individuals about an aspect of their work experience. Others require observations of a public work setting, such as a retail store or a restaurant. Still others are accomplished through the Web. These experiences are designed to enhance the student's knowledge of how information can be used to address a problem.

In all but the first two chapters, there are three special features. First, there is a detailed summary of a research study from one of the major I/O journals. Each "Research in Detail" was chosen to give added insight through a study that is relevant to topics covered in the chapter. The implications of each study for the practice of I/O are also discussed. Second, there is a detailed summary of a research study conducted outside the United States. Most I/O research until relatively recently was conducted in the United States and a handful of culturally similar Western countries, such as Canada and Britain. These "International Replications" explore the extent to which American research does or doesn't generalize to other countries and cultures. Third, a case study describes how a practicing I/O psychologist was able to help an organization with a problem. These "I/O Psychology in Practice" cases were chosen to represent the wide variety of settings and applied work that involve I/O psychologists.

At the end of each "I/O Psychology in Practice" case are discussion questions. The purpose of these questions is to encourage students to think about the principles discussed in the book. They require the student to apply the chapter principles to a real situation. The questions can be used in a variety of ways. They can be assigned to groups of students or to individuals. They can be used for in-class debates, discussions, oral presentations, or written assignments. The cases themselves are provided to help show students the connections between practice and research in the I/O field. Students often have a difficult time seeing the relevance to their lives of much of what they study in college. I/O psychology is a field that is relevant to almost everyone.

► CHANGES TO THE FIFTH EDITION

My goal with all five editions has been to provide a text as current and up-to-date as possible, covering both the traditional core material of the field and the exciting new emerging areas and findings. The first major task I had with the revision was to update the material and add important new developments. The science of I/O psychology is rapidly developing, with new findings and insights emerging almost daily. I added more than 150 new references, with 98% published in 2004 or later. The overall organization of the book retains the original 14 chapters.

Although the early development of I/O was primarily in the United States, in the 21st century I/O psychology is international in scope. Across all the editions of this book there has been material concerning the international nature of the I/O field, and the book attempts a broader focus than just the United States. For example, Table 1.2 in Chapter 1 lists I/O graduate programs outside the United States, and it has grown from edition to edition of the book. In addition, with the third edition came the "International Replication" feature.

Another characteristic of I/O psychology during most of the twentieth century was that its major concern was with employee performance and productivity, and how they contributed to organizational well being. Much of this was driven by the applied job market and the sorts of services organizations were willing to purchase from consultants or hire psychologists to do. In recent years there has been rapidly advancing interest in the well being of employees themselves, independent of their organizations. This can be seen in the emerging new field of occupational health psychology (OHP) that is developing in large part out of I/O psychology. OHP is a multidisciplinary field that is concerned with the health, safety, and well being of employees. These topics have been in this book since the first edition, but the fifth provides more balance between issues of employee performance and well being.

Content Changes in the Fifth Edition

Although all of the topics covered in the first four editions are still here, some have been expanded or modified, and some are new. Of particular note are the following new topics:

Blended learning

Dysfunction mentoring

Effects of mentoring on mentors

Executive coaching

Goal orientation (learning versus performance)

Mediator and moderator variables

Political skill

Racial differences in performance appraisal

Team innovation

Team KSAOs

Virtual teams

Web-based tests

As in the fourth edition there is an appendix that contains a guide for students interested in applying to I/O graduate school. It begins with tips on preparing for an I/O career, and offers advice about how to apply, what programs look for, and how to choose the right program. A discussion of etiquette in dealing with student recruitment is also provided.

Textbook Internet Support Site (http://shell.cas.usf.edu/~spector)

One of the biggest problems with textbooks is that much of their information is quickly outdated or time sensitive. It isn't feasible for publishers to update more often than the three- to five year revision cycle of most upper level texts. The Internet, however, provides a means of doing just that. My Web site continues to be a resource for both instructors and students to support this textbook. The "Industrial and Organizational Psychology: Research and Practice" section will contain updated information, as well as other supplemental features.

PowerPoint lecture slides for each chapter are available on my Web site. I have also included some Internet exercises that are tied to particular topics. At present there is at least one exercise per chapter. All require the student to find information on one or more Internet sites and either answer questions or write a report. These exercises can be used in a variety of ways, including as the basis for class discussions. Most exercises are tied to particular portions of the text and make use of the links on my site. Students can use these links to find more background information that can help put the case in context.

Students tell me that the practice exams for each chapter are the most useful feature. These contain short-answer questions that do not overlap in format with the testbank for the book. The questions and answers are provided separately. The best way for the student to use these exams is to take them a few days before an in-class exam. They provide guidance about whether preparation has been sufficient. A student who can answer all or almost all the questions has mastered the material. If the student does poorly on the practice, additional preparation and study are needed.

Outside the textbook section are additional Web site features. Perhaps of most interest is the extensive links part. This list contains descriptions and links to sites that are relevant to I/O psychology. These includes professional associations, not all of which are in the United States, including Academy of Management, American Psychological Association, Association of Psychological Science, British Psychological Society, International Association of Applied Psychology, and Society of Industrial and Organizational Psychology (SIOP). Links to I/O journals are also provided, many of which contain abstracts and tables of contents for recent issues. A section includes sites that have I/O related information, such as the Gallup Organization and the U.S. Bureau of Labor Statistics. Another section has links to I/O consulting firms, whose sites explain the services the companies provide. As I learn of relevant new sites, they will be added. Students can be referred to the links for additional information; for example, I regularly suggest that students try the SIOP link for information about graduate schools in the United States and Canada. A student curious about what the large consulting firms do could check out their extensive and interesting Web sites.

▶ ACKNOWLEDGMENTS

In writing all five editions of this book, I was lucky to have had advice and assistance from many people. I express my sincere thanks to the many colleagues and students who provided such help, as well as to the Wiley people, who did a superb job.

First are the members of the USF I/O group:

Tammy Allen

Walter Borman

Michael Brannick

Michael Coovert

Russell Johnson

Edward Levine

Carnot Nelson

Herb Meyer

Steve Stark

There are colleagues and friends from around the world who provided feedback and information:

Seymour Adler, Assessment Solutions, Inc.

Julian Barling, Queens University, Canada

John Bernardin, Florida Atlantic University

Stephen Bluen, South Africa

Peter Chcn, Colorado State University

Yochi Cohen-Charash, Baruch College, City University of New York

Steven Cronshaw, University of Guelph, Canada

Donald Davis, Old Dominion University

Dov Eden, Tel Aviv University, Israel

Barbara Ellis, Charleston, South Carolina

Michael Frese, University of Giessen, Germany

Yitzhak Fried, Wayne State University

Barbara Fritzsche, University of Central Florida

Joan Hall, Naval Air Warfare Center Training Systems Division

Paul Jackson, University of Sheffield, England

Richard Jeanneret, PAQ Services, Inc.

Steve Jex, Bowling Green State University

Boris Kabanoff, University of New South Wales, Australia

Filip Lievens, University of Ghent, Belgium

John C. Munene, Makere University, Uganda

Lakshmi Narayanan, Florida Gulf Coast University

Brian O'Connell, ICF International

Richard Perlow, University of Lethbridge

Mark Peterson, Florida Atlantic University

Ivan Robertson, University of Manchester Institute of Science and Technology, England

Juan Sanchez, Florida International University

Oi-Ling Siu, Lingnan University, Hong Kong

Arie Shirom, Tel Aviv University, Israel

Dirk Steiner, Université de Nice Sophia Antipolis, France

Paul Taylor, University of Waiko, New Zealand

Richard Vosburgh, MGM Mirage Resorts

In addition, twelve I/O psychologists provided the "Psychology in Practice" cases:

Joan Brannick, Brannick HR Connections

Jonathan Canger, Marriott Vacation Club International

Janis Cannon-Bowers, University of Central Florida

Amy Carver, Wachovia Bank

Jeanne Carsten, JP Morgan Chase

Stephen Cohen, Carlson Inc.

Anna Erickson, Questar

Chuck Evans, Jackson Leadership Systems

Charles Michaels, University of South Florida

Stacey Moran, St. Paul Travelers Insurance Co.

Lynn Summers, North Carolina State Personnel

Tom White, Changelink, Australia

The reviewers of the various drafts of the book did a superb job, and the comments of every one of them were a tremendous help.

Robert B. Bechtel, University of Arizona

David V. Day, Pennsylvania State University

Janet Barnes Farrell, University of Connecticut

M. Jocelyne Gessner, University of Houston

Sigrid Gustafson, American Institutes for Research

Jane Halpert, De Paul University

Leslie Hammer, Portland State University

Joseph Horn, University of Texas at Austin

David Kravitz, George Mason University

Marjorie Krebs, Gannon University

Karl Kuhnert, University of Georgia

Dan Landis, University of Mississippi

Terese Macan, University of Missouri–St. Louis

Karen Maher, California State University at Long Beach

Patrick McCarthy, Middle Tennessee State University

John Meyer, University of Western Ontario

Susan Mohammad, Pennsylvania State University

George Neuman, Northern Illinois University

Gerald L. Quatman, Xavier University

Ann Marie Ryan, Michigan State University

Steven Scher, Eastern Illinois University

Susan Shapiro, Indiana University East

Kenneth Shultz, California State University at San Bernardino

Steven Stern, University of Pittsburgh at Johnstown

Ladd Wheeler, University of Rochester

H. A. Witkin, Queens College

My editor, Maureen Clendenny, solicited lots of good feedback and made sure I stayed on track and on time. Eileen McKeever picked up as editor once the initial revision was completed and oversaw the production stage. The psychology editor, Chris Johnson, was always responsive in making sure things ran smoothly.

The production staff at Wiley did an outstanding job of turning my manuscript into the final book form. They were my production editor, Valerie A. Vargas, photo editor, Tara Sanford, and copyeditor, Robert Milch.

Finally, I would like to thank my wife, Gail Spector, for helping in many ways, including helping me make the hundreds of little decisions involved in writing a book.

Paul E. Spector
May 16, 2007

Brief Contents

Contents

INTRODUCTION

(*Photo Disc*)

Introduction

Most people in the industrialized world come into direct or indirect contact with organizations every day. If you go to a supermarket to buy groceries, that store is part of an organization. On a given day you might encounter a few employees, such as the produce manager who helps you find some fresh grapes, the checker who rings up your order, and the bagger who puts all your items in bags. The organization, however, might employ thousands and even tens of thousands of individuals who are collectively responsible for seeing to it that the products you wish to purchase are continually available at each of its stores. This requires the coordinated action of many individuals, likely cutting across many countries. Needless to say, managing such a complex enterprise is extremely difficult. The managers responsible hire a great many specialists to assist them. They often turn to industrial/organizational (I/O) psychologists for help with many of their employee-related problems. For example, I/O psychologists have helped

AT&T develop assessment centers to choose the best managers

General Electric (GE) develop systems to provide job performance feedback to employees

The U.S. Army use psychological tests to place recruits in the appropriate jobs

The U.S. Postal Service develop procedures to reduce assaults by employees

If you go to work for a large organization, there is a good chance that your work life will be affected by industrial/organizational (I/O) psychology. An I/O psychologist may have designed the application form that you will fill out to get the job, the salary, and that benefit package that you will be offered, the training that you will receive, and the structure of the tasks that will comprise your job. I/O psychologists are involved in issues related to employee health, job performance, motivation, safety, selection (hiring), and training. They can also deal with the design of equipment and job tasks. This book discusses all of these areas, and more.

There are two equally important aspects of the I/O psychology field. First, I/O involves the scientific study of the human side of organizations. Many I/O psychologists, particularly those who are professors at universities, conduct research about people at work. Second, I/O includes the application of the principles and findings of the research. Most I/O psychologists are involved in practice, either as consultants or as employees of organizations. What distinguishes the practice of I/O from many other practice fields is that I/O is an evidence-based field, meaning that the things practitioners do are based on scientific methods and principles. This book reviews the major findings from I/O science and explores how practicing I/O psychologists apply those findings in organizational settings.

Industrial/organizational psychology is an eclectic field that has borrowed concepts, ideas, techniques, and theories from many other disciplines. Experimental psychology provided the historical basis of the I/O field. Its principles and techniques, such as psychological testing, were applied by several early experimental psychologists to problems of organizations. As we will discuss later in this chapter, psychologist Robert Yerkes convinced the army to use psychological tests during World War I. Other influences on the I/O field have come from industrial engineering, management, social psychology, and sociology. Although I/O psychology had its beginnings largely in the United States, it has become an international activity, especially in industrialized countries.

This chapter contains an overview of the I/O field. It covers the major activities and employment settings for I/O psychologists and presents a brief history of the field. The chapter discusses the training needed to become an I/O psychologist and where that training is offered, not only in the United States but throughout the world. The research process will be discussed, and the major publication outlets for I/O research will be listed. I/O psychologists are very concerned with the ethical treatment of people. The ethical principles of I/O psychology will be summarized.

Chapter 2 contains a discussion of the research methods used in I/O psychology. Chapters 3 to 14 cover the major topics of the field, and begin with a focus on the assessment of jobs and people. Next they cover two major areas that are relevant to developing productive employees—selecting good people and training them to do their jobs well. Chapters 8 to 11 are concerned with the individual in the context of the organization and cover motivation, how people feel about their jobs, employee behavior, and employee health and safety. Chapters 12 to 14 deal with the individual employee in the social context of the organization. Major topics discussed include groups, leadership, techniques to change organizations, and theories of organizations.

Objectives: The student who studies this chapter should be able to:

▶ Define I/O psychology.
▶ Describe the major activities of I/O psychologists.

▶ Summarize the history of the I/O field.

▶ Explain the importance of research and how it relates to practice.

▶ WHAT IS I/O PSYCHOLOGY?

Psychology is the science of human (and nonhuman) behavior, cognition, emotion, and motivation. It can be subdivided into many different specializations, some of which are concerned primarily with psychological science (experimental psychology) and others of which are concerned with both psychological science and the application of that science (applied psychology). I/O psychology falls into the latter category of being concerned with both psychological science and its application to issues of people in organizations.

As its two-part name implies, the field of I/O psychology contains two major divisions: the industrial (or personnel) and the organizational. Although the content of the two major divisions overlaps and cannot be easily separated, each grew out of different traditions in the history of the field. Industrial psychology, which was the original name for the field, is the older branch and tended to take a management perspective of organizational efficiency through the appropriate use of human resources, or people. It is concerned with issues of efficient job design, employee selection, employee training, and performance appraisal. Organizational psychology developed from the human relations movement in organizations. It focuses more than industrial psychology on the individual employee. It is concerned with understanding behavior and enhancing the well-being of employees in the workplace. Organizational topics include employee attitudes, employee behavior, job stress, and supervisory practices. The major topics of the field, however, cannot easily be characterized as strictly industrial (I) or organizational (O). Motivation, for example, is relevant to the I concerns of employee efficiency and performance, but it is also relevant to the O concern with the happiness and well-being of employees. Even though the I and O areas cannot always be clearly distinguished, together they suggest the broad nature of the field.

The applied area with the largest number of psychologists is the more widely known clinical psychology. Clinical psychologists deal with the study and treatment of psychological disorders and problems. **Industrial/organizational psychology** is a smaller, but more rapidly growing, applied field that is concerned with the development and application of scientific principles to the workplace. I/O psychologists do not deal directly with employees' emotional or personal problems. This activity falls in the domain of clinical psychology. An I/O psychologist, however, might recommend hiring a clinical psychologist to help with such problems as employee alcoholism or post-traumatic stress disorder (PTSD).

▶ ACTIVITIES AND SETTINGS OF I/O PSYCHOLOGISTS

I/O psychologists do many different jobs in a wide variety of settings. We often divide I/O settings into those that are concerned with practice and those that are concerned with scientific research. The practice activities involve the use of psychological principles to solve real-world problems, such as excessive job stress or poor job performance. Research provides principles that can be applied in practice. Both practice and research are equally important within the I/O field. One major objective of I/O is to help organizations function more effectively. In order to do so, the field must have research findings on which to base practice. Not all research is done with practice in mind, however. Some psychologists study work behavior just to learn why people do the things they do at work. As with all forms of basic research, often the findings of such activities can be applied to important human problems.

Although settings can be classified as either practice or research, there is considerable overlap in activities across the two. Many I/O psychologists in research settings get involved in practice, and psychologists in practice settings sometimes do research. Furthermore, some practice activities require research to determine the best approach to solve the problem at hand. Principles might not exist in all cases. In fact, I/O psychologists often don't have ready made answers, but rather they have the means of finding answers.

Most research settings are the colleges and universities in which I/O psychologists are professors. Practice settings include consulting firms, government, the military, and private corporations. Consulting firms provide I/O services to organizations that hire them. Large consulting firms might have hundreds of employees providing services to organizations throughout the world. I/O psychologists often work for governments (city, county, state, or national), the military (usually as civilian specialists), and private corporations. I/O psychologists in each of these practice settings might be doing the same sorts of activities. Figure 1.1 shows the percentage of I/O psychologists found in each of the major settings.

Many I/O psychologists are college or university professors. Most are in psychology departments, but frequently they can be found in colleges of business administration or other places on campus. Although they spend much of their time doing research and teaching students, they do far more than that. Many are involved in practice as consultants to organizations, and some have started their own consulting firms to pursue this interest. The following list describes the major activities of professors:

Teach courses

Do research

Write research papers and present them at meetings

Publish articles in scientific journals

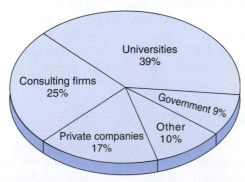

Figure 1.1   Percentage of I/O Psychologists Who Work in Various Settings
Source: Society for Industrial and Organizational Psychology 2006 Member Survey: Overall Report. [Online] Available: www.siop.org/reportsandminutes/survey_results06.aspx.

Provide consulting services to organizations

Write textbooks

Mentor students

Provide information to the public

Develop courses

Keep up with their field

Help administer the teaching function of their university

The basic functions of a professor are to create and disseminate knowledge. Each activity on this list is concerned with one or both of these functions.

Practicing I/O psychologists do many of the same things as their academic colleagues, including conducting research and teaching college courses. The major focus of a practice job, however, is the application of the findings and principles of the field. The following list of activities shows what practicing I/O psychologists do:

Analyze the nature of a job (job analysis)

Conduct an analysis to determine the solution to an organizational problem

Conduct a survey of employee feelings and opinions

Design an employee performance appraisal system

Design an employee selection system

Design a training program

Develop psychological tests

Evaluate the effectiveness of an activity or practice, such as a training program

Implement an organizational change, such as a new reward system for employees who perform well

Much of the effort of I/O psychologists is directed toward enhancing the effectiveness and functioning of organizations. They do so by focusing on several aspects, including the selection of people who can do the job better, training people to do the job better, designing jobs that can be done better, or designing organizations to function better. I/O psychologists also attempt to change organizations to make them healthier and safer places for people to work, even if the effectiveness of the organization is not improved.

► I/O PSYCHOLOGY AS A PROFESSION

I/O psychology is a profession in many ways like the profession of accounting or law. Some states in the United States require that I/O psychologists be licensed; but in most states, only clinical psychologists must be licensed. Many I/O psychologists work for consulting firms that provide services for a fee to client organizations. These services are provided in much the same way that an accounting firm or law firm provides them.

I/O psychologists belong to several professional/scientific societies. The Society for Industrial and Organizational Psychology (SIOP), which is a division of the American Psychological Association (APA), is the largest organization in the United States that is comprised entirely of I/O psychologists. It has about 6,000 members, with about

38% of them student affiliates, and about 6% foreign (non-American) affiliates. All members of SIOP are also members of APA or the Association For Psychological Science (APS), which split from APA several years ago. The Academy of Management is a larger organization than SIOP, but the majority of its members are not psychologists. It is comprised of people who have interests in the broad field of management, mostly professors from colleges of business administration. Many I/O psychologists, primarily those who are college professors, are active members of this organization.

In addition to the national associations, there are many regional and city associations of I/O psychologists. These smaller local associations can be found in many areas, including central Florida, Michigan, New York City, Ottawa, San Francisco, and Washington, DC. Professional associations of I/O psychologists can be found in many countries throughout the world. Australia has the College of Organisational Psychologists, Canada has its own Society for Industrial and Organizational Psychology, the British Psychological Society has its Division of Occupational Psychology, and many similar associations exist throughout Europe. Over a dozen of them have formed the European Association of Work and Organizational Psychology (EAWOP). Also very relevant to I/O psychologists is the International Association of Applied Psychology, Division of Organizational Psychology, which is the largest division. I/O psychologists from around the world are members, especially those with interests in cross-cultural and international issues. The newest American organization relevant to I/O is the Society for Occupational Health Psychology (SOHP), which began in 2006. About half of this society's members are I/O psychologists who are interested in issues concerning employee health, safety, and well-being.

▶ I/O PSYCHOLOGY AS A SCIENCE

Research is one of the major activities of I/O psychologists. Research can develop new methods and procedures for such activities as selecting or training employees. Often such research is conducted for specific organizations to solve a particular problem. Other research focuses on understanding some organizational phenomenon, such as the causes of employee theft or the effects of job attitudes. Results of these sorts of research studies are presented at professional meetings and published in scientific journals.

The national and international associations noted earlier all have conferences, usually annually, where results of research are presented. The annual meeting of the Academy of Management, for example, attracts several thousand practitioners and researchers who can share and discuss their research findings and ideas. Practitioners often find such meetings to be a good place to learn about new solutions to their organizational problems. Researchers can find out about the latest findings before they are published in the scientific journals.

Scientific journals of the field represent the major outlet for research results. Some major journals are produced by professional associations, whereas others are published privately. For example, the *Journal of Applied Psychology* is published by APA, and the *Journal of Occupational and Organizational Psychology* is published by the British Psychological Society. Table 1.1 lists the major journals that publish research on I/O topics. Most are like magazines that are published in four to six issues per year. One, the *International Review of Industrial and Organizational Psychology*, is published once per year and summarizes the state of knowledge on various topics.

TABLE 1.1   **Journals That Publish I/O Research and Theory**

Academy of Management Journal	*Journal of Applied Psychology*
Academy of Management Review	*Journal of Business and Psychology*
Administrative Science Quarterly	*Journal of Management*
Applied Psychology: An International Review	*Journal of Occupational and Organizational Psychology*
Group and Organization Studies	*Journal of Occupational Health Psychology*
Human Factors	*Journal of Organizational Behavior*
Human Relations	*Journal of Vocational Behavior*
Human Resources Management Review	*Organizational Behavior and Human Decision Processes*
International Journal of Selection and Assessment	*Organizational Research Methods*
International Review of Industrial and *Organizational Psychology*	*Personnel Psychology* *Work & Stress*

I/O researchers, most of whom are college professors, submit articles for possible publication to these journals. Their work is then sent to experts in the field for a critique. Articles are revised based on the critiques, and often several rounds of revision and resubmission will be necessary before an article is accepted for publication. Only the 10 to 20% of submitted articles that survive a rigorous peer review process will be published in the best journals. Peer review helps maintain high standards for published work so that the best research makes it into print.

Publication of research papers is a competitive and difficult endeavor. College professors, particularly those without tenure, are under tremendous pressure to be successful at publication. I/O programs at most universities have a "publish or perish" philosophy that requires professors to be active researchers who contribute to the knowledge base of the field. This is true of all scientific disciplines in most universities. A publication record in the best journals is a major determiner of career success for a professor, as reflected in the ability to find a job, earn tenure, get promoted, and receive raises. Keep in mind, however, that one of the major functions of a university is to create and disseminate new knowledge for the benefit of society, so there is a good reason to emphasize research.

► HISTORY OF THE FIELD OF I/O PSYCHOLOGY

I/O psychology is a twentieth century invention, with roots in the late 1800s and early 1900s.[1] It has existed almost from the beginning of the psychology field. The first psychologists to do I/O work were experimental psychologists who were interested in applying the new principles of psychology to problems in organizations. Early work focused on issues of job performance and organizational efficiency. As the field matured during the first half of the century, it expanded into the areas that it covers today. Figure 1.2 shows the major events in the development of I/O psychology that occurred in the United States.

Two psychologists are credited with being the main founders of the field. Hugo Münsterberg and Walter Dill Scott were both experimental psychologists and university

---

[1]Unless otherwise noted, most of this section is based on Katzell and Austin's (1992) history of the I/O field.

1991	Americans with Disabilities Act passes
1970	APA adopts the name, Division of Industrial and Organizational Psychology
1964	Civil Rights Act passes
1941	World War II war effort begins
1924	Hawthorne studies begin
1921	First I/O Ph.D. is awarded; Psychological Corporation is founded
1917	Mental tests for job placement are developed
1913	First I/O textbook is published

Figure 1.2   A timeline of major events in the history of I/O psychology

professors who became involved in applying psychology to problems of organizations. Münsterberg, who came to the United States from his native Germany, was particularly interested in the selection of employees and the use of the new psychological tests. Landy (1997) posits that Münsterberg's inability to gain the respect of colleagues at Harvard University was the motivation for his shift to the new emerging field of industrial psychology. Scott was interested in many of the same things as Münsterberg, as well as the psychology of advertising. Scott wrote a pioneering textbook, *The Theory of Advertising* (1903), and Münsterberg wrote the first I/O textbook, *Psychology and Industrial Efficiency* (1913).

A major influence on the I/O field was the work of Frederick Winslow Taylor, an engineer who studied employee productivity throughout his career during the late nineteenth and early twentieth centuries. Taylor developed what he called "Scientific Management" as an approach to handling production workers in factories. Scientific Management included several principles to guide organizational practices. In his writings Taylor (1911) suggested the following:

1. Each job should be carefully analyzed so that the optimal way of doing tasks can be specified.

2. Employees should be selected (hired) according to characteristics that are related to job performance. Managers should study existing employees to find out what personal characteristics are important.

3. Employees should be carefully trained to do their job tasks.

4. Employees should be rewarded for their productivity to encourage high levels of performance.

Though refined over the years, these same ideas are still considered valuable today.

Another influence from the field of engineering can be seen in the work of Frank and Lillian Gilbreth, a husband and wife team who studied efficient ways of performing tasks. They combined the fields of engineering and psychology (Frank was an engineer, and Lillian a psychologist) in studying how people perform tasks. Their best known contribution was the time and motion study, which involved measuring and timing people's motions in doing tasks with the goal of developing more efficient ways of working.

Hugo Münsterberg
(*Archives of the History of American Psychology*)

Walter Dill Scott
(*Archives of the History of American Psychology*)

Frederick Winslow Taylor
(*Samuel C. Williams, Library of Stevens Institute of Technology in Hoboken, NJ*)

Robert Yerkes
(*Archives of the History of American Psychology*)

Although the basic ideas were Taylor's, the Gilbreths refined and used their new technique to help many organizations (Van De Water, 1997). Some historians claim that Lillian, in 1915, was the first person to receive an I/O Ph.D. (Koppes, 1997), although most historians give this distinction to Bruce V. Moore in 1921. The Gilbreths' work served as the foundation of what would later become the field of human factors, which is the study of how best to design technology for people. In later years, Lillian turned her attention to designing consumer products and invented the foot-pedal trash can and refrigerator door shelves, among other things (Koppes, 1997). However, the Gilbreths themselves are best known as the subjects of the autobiographical 1950 movie *Cheaper by the Dozen*, which chronicled their lives as the working parents of 12 children.

World War I saw the beginning of the use of I/O psychology by the U.S. military, which gave a boost to the development of the field. When the United States entered the

Frank and Lillian Gilbreth
(*UPI/Corbis Images*)

war in 1917, a number of psychologists, led by Robert Yerkes, offered their services to the army. The best-known accomplishment of the group was the development of the Army Alpha and Army Beta group tests for mental ability. One of the biggest problems for the army was placing new recruits in jobs for which they were best suited. The newly invented psychological tests seemed to the psychologists to be an efficient way to solve that problem. This was the first large-scale application of psychological testing to place individuals in jobs. It provided a foundation for mass testing that has been used ever since in educational (e.g., the Scholastic Aptitude Test, or SAT) and employment settings.

During the decades between the two world wars, I/O psychology expanded into most of the areas in which it is used today. As organizations grew in size, they began hiring I/O psychologists to address many of their increasing employee problems, particularly those that were relevant to productivity. As suggested earlier, in 1921 Penn State University awarded what many consider the first Ph.D. in what was then called industrial psychology to Bruce V. Moore. I/O psychologists began organizing into consulting firms that would provide services to organizations for a fee. The most well known of these was the Psychological Corporation, founded in 1921 by James McKeen Cattell, which today is called Harcourt Assessment. One of the most important events of this period was the Hawthorne studies, which continued for more than 10 years at the Western Electric Company.

Before the Hawthorne studies, I/O psychologists focused almost exclusively on issues of employee productivity and organizational efficiency, including the assessment of employee abilities and the efficient design of jobs. Although the Hawthorne researchers set out to study these topics, they quickly discovered that many social aspects of organizational life affected employee behavior and performance. Their study of supervision and work groups helped launch the O, or organizational, side of the field.

The best known of the Hawthorne studies was the investigation of lighting-level effects (Roethlisberger & Dickson, 1939). The objective of this study was to determine the lighting level that would produce optimal performance on a factory task. The researchers conducted an experiment in which a group of employees was taken to a special room where lighting levels were changed. Lights were made brighter and dimmer from day to day to see the effects on productivity. The researchers were surprised to find that over the course of the experiment, productivity increased and seemed to have little to do with lighting levels. Many explanations of these results have been advanced and debated. The most frequently discussed is that knowledge of being in an experiment, or what has come to be called the **Hawthorne Effect**, caused increases in performance. Whatever the reason, it seems clear that social factors can be more important than physical factors in people's job performance.

World War II had a tremendous stimulating effect on the development of the I/O field. Hundreds of psychologists from all specializations contributed to the war effort. Psychologists dealt with problems that spanned the entire scope of both I and O work, including the selection of recruits, placement of recruits in different jobs, training, morale, performance appraisal, team development, and equipment design. Prior to World War II, the American Psychological Association (APA) limited its interests to experimental psychology and rejected attempts by I/O psychologists to make practice, which was considered nonscientific, part of its mission. As a result of the war, however, the APA opened its doors to applied psychology, and Division 14 of Industrial and Business Psychology was formed in 1944 (Benjamin, 1997). After the war, the two areas of industrial and organizational psychology continued to expand. For example, Arthur Kornhauser conducted research on how work conditions can have effects on both employee mental health and personal life, thus producing some of the early work on what is now called occupational health psychology (Zickar, 2003). In 1970 the Industrial Psychology Division 14 of the American Psychological Association changed its name to the Division of Industrial and Organizational Psychology, and it is today called the **Society for Industrial and Organizational Psychology (SIOP)**. The society's Web site (www.siop.org) is an important resource for information about the field, including information about graduate school, job postings, and society business.

Another event in the United States that helped shape the field of I/O psychology was the passage of the Civil Rights Act of 1964. This act set into motion forces that have had a tremendous impact on how organizations hire and treat employees, and not only in the United States. When discrimination against minorities and women became illegal, organizations had to change many of their employment practices. I/O psychologists were called upon to help develop procedures that would eliminate discrimination in the workplace. The passage of the Americans With Disabilities Act (ADA) in 1990 extended protection against discrimination to the disabled. Here again I/O psychologists have been called upon to find ways to eliminate unfair discrimination.

The history of the field is full of examples of how I/O psychologists have helped improve organizations and work conditions for employees. The field has grown from its initial concern with productivity to the many diverse areas we find today. I/O psychology has much to contribute to the operation of organizations and the well-being of employees. Its future looks bright as organizations continue to need help with employee issues, as discussed throughout this book.

▶ I/O PSYCHOLOGY AROUND THE WORLD

So far our discussion of I/O psychology has focused on the United States, where the field had its beginnings and most (but not all) of its early development. However, I/O psychology exists throughout the world, and many of its findings and principles have come from other countries. In addition, the practice of I/O psychology differs somewhat among countries. For example, the techniques used to select employees vary among countries (Clark, 1993; Shackleton & Newell, 1991). Until recently I/O psychology in the United States focused more attention to the I side than the O side of the field. This tendency was reinforced by increasing legal requirements that organizations avoid discriminatory hiring practices, as we will discuss in Chapter 6. Employers, feeling government pressure, turn to I/O psychologists to help design legally defensible hiring procedures. I/O psychology in other countries—for example, in Canada and Europe—focused more on the organizational direction. In part this is because of the stronger labor union movements in these countries, which puts greater emphasis on employee rights and well-being than is true in the United States. Thus, much of the early research on topics of employee attitudes, health, safety, and well-being comes from Canada and Europe.

These differences in research interests among scholars of I/O psychology in various countries are illustrated by a study of topic popularity in the major research journals conducted by Miriam Erez (1994) of the Israel Institute of Technology. She tabulated the number of articles published in psychological research journals for each of 25 topics by

TABLE 1.2   Most Frequently Studied I/O Research Topics in Eight Countries Listed in Order of Popularity Within Country

Country	Topics	Country	Topics
Britain	Employee selection	Japan	Job stress
	Turnover		Leadership
	Leadership		Career issues
	Gender differences		Motivation
	Job stress		
Canada	Employee selection	Israel	Career issues
	Job stress		Values
	Leadership		Cross-cultural issues
	Career development		Motivation
			Performance appraisal
			Job satisfaction
Germany	Job Stress	Scandinavia	Job stress
	Motivation		Shift work
	Training		Gender differences
	Work environment		Unemployment
India	Job satisfaction	United States	Employee selection
	Motivation		Career issues
	Job level in organization		Performance appraisal
	Job stress		Leadership

Note: From Erez, M. (1994). Toward a Model of Cross-cultural Industrial and Organizational Psychology. In H. C. Triandis, M. D. Dunnette, and L. Hough (eds.), *Handbook of Industrial and Organizational Psychology*. Vol. IV. *Theory in Industrial and Organizational Psychology*. Palo Alto, CA: Consulting Psychologists Press.

country of author. Table 1.2 lists the most frequently studied topics for each country. The differences are quite striking. For example, in Scandinavian countries (Finland, Norway, and Sweden), 53 percent of studies were concerned with employee health and stress, with additional studies covering related issues. In the United States these topics were found in only 5 percent of studies. Conversely, in the United States employee selection was the most popular topic, but it was unstudied in Scandinavia. This difference in focus on employee health versus selection mirrors societal differences in the value placed on employee productivity versus well-being.

As Erez's results show, job stress is a research area that is international in scope. Many of the major developments have come from outside the United States. For example, there has been an important program of job stress research at the University of Stockholm in Sweden, and the journal *Work & Stress*, which is devoted to work in this area, is published in England. Much of the research concerning job stress that we will discuss in Chapter 11 was not conducted in the United States but comes from a variety of countries. On the other hand, most of the research we will discuss on employee selection is from the United States.

In the twenty-first century, I/O psychology will almost certainly continue to develop and prosper throughout the world. The practice is spreading rapidly as our I/O techniques gain acceptance in more and more places. The international interest in I/O is well indicated by the rapid spread of I/O master's and Ph.D. programs outside the United States (see Table 1.3). Although an I/O psychologist's focus can differ across countries, just as we saw with research topics, the field has available a wide variety of methods and techniques that can be helpful in dealing with employee issues in organizations. Although most of the research once came almost exclusively from the United States, more and more research is originating in other countries, including Australia, Canada, China (including Hong Kong and Taiwan), Britain, Germany, Israel, and New Zealand, just to mention a few. Cross-cultural research comparing different countries or replicating results from Western cultures in other contexts is becoming increasingly popular. This work is important because principles used in the West will not necessarily work in other countries or cultures. We will discuss some of these studies throughout the book.

▶ WHAT IT TAKES TO BECOME AN I/O PSYCHOLOGIST

The most common route to becoming an I/O psychologist is to earn a graduate degree (master's or Ph.D.) in I/O psychology from one of the many I/O psychology graduate programs in the United States and other countries. Many people who do I/O work have other backgrounds, such as in other areas of psychology or in business administration. Some of these people consider themselves to be I/O psychologists and may hold jobs with that title. In the United States, most I/O psychologists hold a Ph.D. degree. Although it is possible to be an I/O psychologist with a master's degree in the I/O field, such people are often referred to as master's level I/O psychologists to reflect their lower degree status. One can have a successful career as an I/O psychologist with a master's degree, but opportunities and salaries are better with the Ph.D.

In some countries, such as Canada, the situation is similar to that in the United States. However, in other places, including most of Europe, the Ph.D. is not as common as the master's degree. Rather, the master's degree is considered a practice degree, whereas the Ph.D. is a research credential. An individual who wishes to be a practitioner will likely have only the master's degree. Someone who continues on to earn a Ph.D. is most likely to be interested in research and will be found in a research institute or a university. It is possible for a practitioner to have a Ph.D., but it is not considered as important as in the United States and Canada.

Table 1.3 lists master's and Ph.D. programs throughout the United States, and Table 1.4 lists a sample of graduate programs (both master's and Ph.D.) in other countries. As the size of the lists may suggest, the United States is the world leader in terms of the number of programs, but there are many fine I/O programs throughout the rest of the world. I/O may have begun in the United States, but it has spread throughout the world, especially wherever there are large profit-making organizations.

Admission to American graduate programs is quite competitive, especially for the well established Ph.D. programs (see the appendix for a graduate school application guide). Most base admission largely, but not exclusively, on undergraduate grade point average (usually just the junior and senior years) and Graduate Record Exam (GRE) scores. Prior applied and research experience can be helpful, especially for top Ph.D. programs. Letters of recommendation from faculty members are usually required. I/O graduate programs are challenging and require both communication (verbal and written) and mathematical skills. Thus, to do well, a student should properly prepare as

TABLE 1.3   Universities in the U.S. with Graduate Programs in I/O Psychology

State	M.A. Program	Ph.D. Program
Alabama		Auburn University
California	California State University	Alliant University
	Long Beach	Claremont Graduate University
	Sacramento	University of California Berkeley
	San Bernadino	
	Golden Gate University	
	National University	
	San Diego State University	
	San Francisco State University	
	San Jose State University	
	Sanoma State University	
Colorado		Colorado State University
Connecticut	Fairfield University	University of Connecticut
	University of Hartford	
	University of New Haven	
Florida	Carlos Albizu University	Florida Institute of Technology
	University of West Florida	Florida International University
		University of Central Florida
		University of South Florida
Georgia	Valdosta State College	Georgia Institute of Technology
		University of Georgia
Idaho	University of Idaho	
Illinois	Adler School of Professional Psychology	Chicago School of Professional Psychology
	Elmhurst College	DePaul University
	Illinois State University	Illinois Institute of Technology
	Roosevelt University	Northern Illinois University
	Southern Illinois University at Edwardsville	University of Illinois, Urbana-Champaign
Indiana	Indiana University–Purdue University at Indianapolis	Purdue University
Iowa	University of Northern Iowa	
Kansas	Emporia State University	Kansas State University
Kentucky	Eastern Kentucky University	
	Northern Kentucky University	
	Western Kentucky University	
Louisiana	Louisiana Technological University	Louisiana State University
Maryland	University of Baltimore	University of Maryland
Massachusetts	Springfield College	
Michigan	Springfield College	Central Michigan University
	University of Detroit-Mercy	Michigan State University
		University of Michigan
		Wayne State University
		Western Michigan University
Minnesota	Minnesota State University	University of Minnesota
	St. Cloud State University	
Mississippi	William Carey College on the Coast	

(Continued)

TABLE 1.3 *(Continued)*

State	M.A. Program	Ph.D. Program
Missouri	Missouri State University	St. Louis University
		University of Missouri–St. Louis
Montana	Montana State University	
Nebraska		University of Nebraska at Omaha
New Jersey	Fairleigh Dickinson University	Rutgers University (Psy.D.)
	Kean University	
	Montclair State University	
New York	City University	Baruch College, CUNY
	Iona College	Columbia University, Teachers College
		Hofstra University
		New York University
		SUNY at Albany
North Carolina	Appalachian State University	North Carolina State University
	East Carolina University	University of North Carolina–Charlotte
Ohio	Cleveland State University	Bowling Green State University
	Xavier University	Ohio University
		Union Institute
		University of Akron
		Wright State University
Oklahoma	University of Oklahoma Tulsa	University of Oklahoma
		University of Tulsa
Oregon	Southern Oregon University	Portland State University
Pennsylvania	St. Joseph's University	Penn State University
	West Chester University	Temple University
South Carolina		Clemson University
Tennessee	Autin Peay State University	University of Memphis
	Middle Tennessee State University	University of Tennessee–Knoxville
	University of Tennessee–Chattanooga	
Texas	Angelo State University	Rice University
	Lamar University	Texas A & M University
	St. Mary's University	University of Houston
	Stephen F. Austin State University	University of Texas Arlington
Virginia	Christopher Newport University	George Mason University
	Radford University	Old Dominion University
		Virginia Technological University
Washington	Central Washington University	Seattle Pacific University
		Washington State University
Washington, DC		George Washington University
West Virginia	Marshall University	
Wisconsin	University of Wisconsin–Oshkosh	
	University of Wisconsin–Stout	
Distance Programs	Kansas State University	Capella University
		Saybrook Graduate School

Note: Includes applied psychology, organizational psychology, and other psychology programs that are similar.

Source: SIOP Web site, www.siop.org/GTP/gtplookup.asp, December 21, 2006.

TABLE 1.4 Sample of Universities Outside the U.S. That Offer Graduate Degrees in I/O Psychology

Country	University	Country	University
Australia	Curtin University	Germany	Technical University of Dresden
	Griffith University		University of Frankfurt
	Macquarie University		University of Giessen
	Monash University		University of Konstanz
	Murdoch University		University of Mainz
	University of New South Wales		University of Munich
	University of Queensland		University of Potsdam
Belgium	Free University of Britain	Hong Kong	Chinese University of Hong Kong
	Exeter University		Lingnan University
	University of Hull	Ireland	University College Dublin
	University of London	Israel	Bar-Ilan University
	University of Manchester Institute of Science and Technology		Technion–Israel Institute of Technology
	University of Nottingham		
	University of Sheffield	Italy	University of Verona
	University of Surrey	Korea	Kwang-Woon University
Brussels	University of Ghent	Latvia	University of Latvia
	University of Leuven	Netherlands	Free University of Amsterdam
	University of Liége		University of Amsterdam
Canada	Queen's University		University of Groningen
	St. Mary's University		University of Nijmegen
	University of Calgary		University of Tilburg
	University of Guelph	New Zealand	University of Canterbury
	University of Moncton		University of Massey at Auckland
	University of Montreal		University of Waikato
	University of Quebec in Montreal		Victoria University of Wellington
	University of Waterloo	Nigeria	University of Jos
	University of Western Ontario		University of Nsuka
China	Beijing University		University of Legos
	Beijing Normal University	Portugal	ISCTE Institute of Management and Social Sciences–Lisbon
	China Eastern Normal University		
	Zhejiang University	Puerto Rico	Carlos Albizu University
	Institute of Psychology, Chinese Academy of Science		Interamerican University of Puerto Rico
Costa Rica	Latin University of Costa Rica		Pontifical Catholic University
	Autonomous University of Monterrey	Romania	Babes-Bolyai University
France	University of Provence Aix-Marseille		University of Bucharest
	University of Bordeaux		West University
	University of Metz		
	University of Paul Valéry Montpellier	Russia	Moscow State University

(Continued)

TABLE 1.4   *(Continued)*

Country	University	Country	University
Scotland	Heriot-Watt University/ University of Strathclyde	Sweden	Stockholm University
	University of Aberdeen		University of Lund
Singapore	National University of Singapore	Switzerland	University of Bern
			University of St. Gallen
South Africa	University of Stellenbosch	Turkey	Koc University
	University of the Witwatersrand		Middle East Technical University
Spain	Complutense University		
	University of Barcelona	Uganda	Makerere University
	University of Santiago		
	University of Valencia	Zimbabwe	University of Zimbabwe

an undergraduate. A solid background in basic mathematics (i.e., algebra) and statistics is a good start. Good basic communication skills, especially writing, is also valuable. It is always wise to take a course in I/O before making the choice to pursue this career. Interestingly, many students enter graduate school without having taken this course. Finally, a good background in basic psychology will make things easier. Students who have other undergraduate majors and don't have this background find they have a lot of catching up to do, especially in the first year.

The training of I/O psychologists includes both the practice and research sides of the field. An I/O psychologist is trained to be a scientist-practitioner, meaning someone who is able both to conduct scientific research and to apply principles to problems of organizations. Students are exposed to procedures for applying principles of the field as well as to research methodology. The specific content and emphasis can differ among graduate programs, especially when comparing these programs across countries. There are many excellent programs offering terminal master's degrees to people who do not wish to spend the extra years it would take to earn the Ph.D. These programs offer training that is usually oriented more toward practice than science, in part because they do not have sufficient time to cover each side of the field in depth and in part because they are intended to train practitioners. The Ph.D. programs tend to offer a better balance between practice and science in part because they take more than twice as long to complete. These programs train people to be both practitioners and researchers.

A master's degree can be completed in about two years, while a Ph.D. can be completed in about four to five years by a person who has a bachelor's degree. Programs vary, but a master's program will include coursework on research methodology and the various areas of the I/O field that will be discussed in this book. A Ph.D. program covers the same areas, as well as general psychology and more extensive research methodologies. For this degree, the Society for Industrial and Organizational Psychology (1985) suggests areas that should be covered that include each of the chapters in this book. In addition, there is practicum experience working in an organizational setting with a practicing I/O psychologist, and research experience (e.g., a master's thesis or doctoral dissertation) done under the supervision of a committee of I/O faculty members.

The job market for I/O psychologists in the United States has been excellent, although it does fluctuate with general economic conditions. Surveys of I/O psychologists done by the American Psychological Association over the years have generally found less than 1% unemployment among those who wish to work. Khanna and Medsker (2007) reported the results of a salary survey of American I/O psychologists in 2006. The median salary was $72,000 per year for individuals with a master's degree, and $98,500 per year for those with a Ph.D. Median starting salaries for nonacademic applied positions was $73,750, which is higher than the median salaries for the beginning rank assistant professors of psychology ($55,600). College professors working in psychology departments, however, made less than college professors in colleges of business administration. Women made considerably less than men ($100,000 versus $85,000 median salary per year), but women were less likely to have a Ph.D. and tended to have less job experience, in large part due to their relatively recent entry into the I/O field. Finally, it should be kept in mind that these are median salaries, meaning that half the people make more and half less than these numbers. Salaries can range considerably among I/O psychologists who live in different places, and even among psychologists in the same organization.

The field of I/O psychology was at one time a predominantly male profession. In the 1960s only about 8% of Ph.D.s in I/O were awarded to women. Interestingly, prior to 1930 women comprised a much higher proportion of practicing I/O psychologists than they did in 1960. Although accurate estimates of numbers are impossible to make (Koppes, 1997), women may have comprised as many as 25% of I/O psychologists in the 1920s. In the past few decades women have entered the field in increasing numbers, and today they earn about half or more of the Ph.D.s awarded in the United States. The membership of SIOP in 2006 was 36.7% female, which represents a sizable increase over the 1960s. This trend can also be found elsewhere in the world.

► INTERNET RESOURCES FOR I/O PSYCHOLOGISTS AND STUDENTS

Over the past few years, the Internet has become an increasingly important medium for sharing ideas and information. E-mail facilitates communication, especially among people spread around the world. SIOP has its own Web site containing its publication, *The Industrial/Organizational Psychologist*, or *TIP*, as well as other useful information. Of perhaps most interest to students is detailed information on most of the I/O graduate programs in Canada and the United States, and a sample from overseas. All I/O-related societies have their own Web sites. One of the most useful is the American Psychological Association Web site, which in addition to information about APA also contains abstracts of articles from all its journals and links to many psychology related sites. The addresses of these and other useful sites are in Table 1.5, and can be found on my own Web site, which is also listed. This Web site contains updated information about I/O psychology, including a section that supplements the textbook.

► ETHICS OF THE I/O FIELD

Psychology has had a long tradition of concern with ethical behavior and the welfare of people. I/O psychologists in the United States follow an ethical code that has been developed over the years by the American Psychological Association. The code includes

TABLE 1.5   I/O Psychology Internet Resources

Web Address	Description
http://shell.cas.usf.edu/spector	Paul Spector's Web site: Contains updated information to supplement the textbook as well as links to many I/O sites. The author's own class notes are included.
www.aom.pace.edu	Academy of Management (AOM): Contains information about this I/O-related association and the field itself.
www.apa.org	American Psychological Association (APA): Contains information about the association, lots of psychology links, and abstracts of articles in APA journals.
www.psychologicalscience.org	Association for Psychological Science (APS): Another major psychological association focused mainly on science.
www.hr-software.net/EmploymentStatistics	Mostly selection oriented information and links.
www.hfes.org	Human Factors and Ergonomics Society (HFES): Contains information about the association and its publications.
http://allserv.rug.ac.be/~pcoets/div/home.htm	International Association of Applied Psychology (IAAP) Organizational Psychology Division: Contains information and links about the field in Europe.
http://online.onetcenter.org	Occupational Information Network, O*NET. The U.S. Department of Labor job-information site.
www.siop.org	Society for Industrial and Organizational Psychology (SIOP): Contents of *TIP* and lots of information about the field and about graduate programs.
www.piop.net	PIOP.NET is a student-run resource for information about the I/O field.

both ethical principles and statements of appropriate professional conduct. Although the association has little enforcement power other than to terminate a psychologist's membership, most I/O psychologists are guided by the principles in their professional work.

The basic philosophy of the ethical code is that psychologists should do their best to avoid harming other people through their professional work. This means that a psychologist should avoid committing any illegal or immoral act that might harm someone either physically or psychologically. On the other hand, psychologists have a social

TABLE 1.6   Six Ethical Principles from the American Psychological Association Code

Competence:
A psychologist only does work that he or she is competent to perform.
Integrity:
Psychologists are fair and honest in their professional dealings with others.
Professional and Scientific Responsibility:
Psychologists maintain high standards of professional behavior.
Respect for People's Rights and Dignity:
Psychologists respect the rights of confidentiality and privacy of others.
Concern for Others' Welfare:
Psychologists attempt to help others through their professional work.
Social Responsibility:
Psychologists have a responsibility to use their skills to benefit society.

Source: From "Ethical Principles of Psychologists and Code of Conduct," by the American Psychological Association, 1992, *American Psychologist, 47*, pp. 1597–1611.

responsibility to use their talents to help other people. In other words, the goal of the profession is to improve the human condition through the application of psychology. For the I/O psychologist, this means helping to improve organizations so that they function better and helping to improve the well-being of employees.

The APA ethical code contains six principles, each of which is listed in Table 1.6. As you can see from the table, these principles are concerned with basic ethical standards of honesty, integrity, respect for others, and responsibility. The code also contains a detailed list of appropriate and inappropriate behaviors; too long to reprint here, it can be found on the APA Web site at www.apa.org/ethics.

Many psychologists follow the code of ethics of the Academy of Management. Although somewhat different from the APA code, the two codes are compatible. The Academy of Management code deals with standards of behavior in three domains of organizational work by its members—practice, research, and teaching. It, too, is based on the principles that one does not harm others and that one has talents to benefit society.

▶ CHAPTER SUMMARY

The field of industrial/organizational (I/O) psychology is one of the major applied areas of psychology. It is a diverse field concerned with the human side of organizations. The I/O field can be divided into two major areas. The industrial side is concerned with organizational efficiency through the appraisal, selection, and training of people and the design of jobs. The organizational side is concerned with understanding the behavior of people on the job and protecting their health, safety, and well-being.

I/O psychology is both a practice and a science. Most I/O psychologists can be found working for organizations to address issues and problems involving people. They are practitioners who work either as consultants to many organizations or as employees of a single organization. A little over a third of I/O psychologists are college professors (see Figure 1.1), most of whom conduct research to develop better methods and procedures for dealing with employee problems at work or to understand behavior.

An I/O psychologist needs to earn a graduate degree from an I/O psychology program in a university. Many such programs may be found throughout the United States and the rest of the industrialized world, including Australia, Canada, China, Europe, Israel, New Zealand, and South Africa, with new programs being added in other places. Although the field began in the United States, it has rapidly expanded throughout most of the world. Many of the findings discussed in this book have come from studies done with organizations and people throughout the world.

There are many associations of I/O psychologists (and others with similar interests) that allow for the dissemination of ideas and research findings of the field. This is done by holding conventions and by publishing scientific journals. These associations also have developed codes of ethical conduct for their members. The basic philosophy in these ethical codes is that I/O psychologists should take care not to harm anyone and that I/O psychologists have a social responsibility to use their skills to benefit others. Both the Academy of Management and the American Psychological Association have published ethical standards.

LEARNING BY DOING

Graduate Study In I/O Psychology

Go to the SIOP Web site, www.siop.org. Go to the "Graduate Training Program University Listing" and choose the program of your choice (they are listed by university). Click on the university name and review the information provided here, as well as on the program's own site. Answer the following questions.

1. What is the focus of the program, i.e., what does the description say the program is about?

2. How many faculty are in the program?
3. How many students are there?
4. How many of the faculty are cited in this textbook (check the author index)?

Advantages of Association Membership

Go to the SIOP Web site, www.siop.org. From the material there, list the advantages to psychologists and students of being a member of the association.

Research Methods in I/O Psychology

CHAPTER 2 OUTLINE

Imagine that you are a practicing I/O psychologist working for a company. You are assigned the task of determining if a new training program is effective in producing better performance in employees. Perhaps employees are being trained in the use of a new computer system that is supposed to increase employee productivity. How would you go about finding out if the training works? Would you review the program and see if it looks as if it should be effective, or would you conduct a research study to determine its effects?

The problem with the first approach is that a training program that looks as if it should be effective is not always effective. The only way to be certain that training accomplishes its purpose is to conduct a research study. To conduct a study to determine training effectiveness requires knowledge of research methodology, a topic in which I/O psychologists today are extensively trained. Whether an I/O psychologist is in a job that primarily involves practice or research, he or she needs to know the methods that are used for conducting studies.

Research is the foundation of both the practice and science of I/O. In many practice jobs, I/O psychologists are hired to provide research skills so that questions concerning whether or not programs work can be answered scientifically. This is important for evaluating the success of organizational practices (such as training programs). Research is also important for the development of new practices, such as procedures for hiring people.

I/O psychology is a science because the methods used to expand knowledge of organizational phenomena are scientific methods. This means that the I/O psychologist gathers data or information in a systematic way to address research questions of interest, such as:

Does the training program work?

Will the new absence policy result in better employee attendance?

Each scientific study begins with a research question that defines the purpose of the study. An investigation is planned using a particular design or structure in which data are collected. For example, in a simple experiment to test a training program, you might divide a sample of employees into two groups, only one of which receives the training. After the training has been completed, the two groups would be compared on their job performance. The basic experiment defines one of the simplest designs for an investigation. Data would be collected on performance and analyzed using a statistical test, which in this case would probably be a t test. (See the discussion of inferential statistics later in this chapter.) Conclusions would be drawn concerning the effects of the training by considering the statistical results in the context of the investigation's design. With the training program, it is hoped that the trained group will perform better than the nontrained group after the training has been completed. If this were the finding, one feasible conclusion would be that the training worked. In any given study, however, there can be many competing explanations for results that must be addressed with further research. In the training study, perhaps the trained people performed better just because they knew they were in an experiment and not because the training worked, an example of the Hawthorne Effect. With organizational studies (as with studies in any science), one cannot always be certain why results occurred, but with proper research design competing explanations can be eliminated.

This chapter covers the four major components of a research study. First, it discusses the nature of research questions and how they are refined into testable research hypotheses. Second, it reviews several types of research designs and how they are used as the basis of organizational research studies. Third, it addresses the basic principles of measurement, which define how observations of the phenomena of interest are collected. Fourth, it shows how statistics are used to draw conclusions from the data of an investigation. In addition, this chapter reviews the major principles of research ethics.

Objectives: The student who studies this chapter should be able to:

▶ Explain the major concepts of design.

▶ Describe the major types of designs and list their advantages and limitations.

▶ Discuss the types of reliability and validity.

▶ Explain how inferential statistics can be used to make conclusions about data.

▶ State the major principles of research ethics.

▶ RESEARCH QUESTIONS

Every study begins with a research question. This is true for studies done by practicing I/O psychologists, whose questions address an immediate issue for an organization, such as the effectiveness of a procedure or program. It is just as true for the I/O scientist whose research is addressing a question he or she believes is scientifically important, even if it is not of immediate concern to any particular organization.

Research questions can be general or specific. A general question would be:

What causes people to like or dislike their jobs?

The problem with this sort of question is that it is not sufficiently specific to provide the basis of a study. Too many different factors could be studied as possible influences on liking the job. To be useful, the question should specify exactly what is being studied. A better question that is more specific is:

Does level of pay affect how much people like their jobs?

This question specifies a particular influence on liking the job. It tells the researcher exactly what to study as a possible cause of liking the job. To address this question, the researcher needs to assess people's pay levels and their feelings about their jobs.

As we will see in Chapter 9, pay itself is not as important as the fairness of pay policies. People tend to be satisfied when they believe that they have been treated fairly when it comes to pay. They will be dissatisfied if they believe they have been unfairly treated, even if their pay is very high. Thus, the amount of pay is not necessarily the most important factor.

Many investigations go beyond raising questions by stating specific theoretical hunches or hypotheses about the outcomes of a study. A **hypothesis** is the researcher's best guess about what the results of a study will be. Rather than merely raising the question, the hypothesis is a theoretical answer. Thus, one might hypothesize that

People who are well paid will like their jobs better than people who are not.

or

People who are fairly paid will like their jobs more than people who are not.

The hypothesis is a statement of the results that the researcher expects to find. Research studies are conducted to confirm hypotheses. In other words, do the results come out the way they were predicted?

Most hypotheses and research questions come from prior research and theory. Although occasionally a researcher will have a sudden inspirational research idea, most studies and theories come from hard work in studying the research literature of an area. This is the way that all sciences advance and evolve, with individual studies becoming the foundations for later work. The best advice one can give a new researcher is to look to other people's research for new hypotheses and research questions.

The hypothesis and research question are the basis of the study and in some ways its most critical aspect. Without a specific and well-formulated question, it is difficult to design a study that will adequately address it. The question defines the goal or objective of the study, as well as the phenomena of interest. When both are known, the design of the study and the choice of measurement techniques can be relatively easy and straightforward.

▶ IMPORTANT RESEARCH DESIGN CONCEPTS

The design of an investigation specifies the structure of the study. A large number of common designs are used in organizational research. Each has its own particular strengths and weaknesses, so that no design is necessarily superior to the others. Before discussing the various types of designs, we will define several concepts that must be understood first.

Variables

Variables are the basic building blocks of a design. A **variable** is an attribute or characteristic of people or things that can vary (take on different values). People's abilities (e.g., intelligence), attitudes (e.g., job satisfaction), behavior (e.g., absence from work), and job performance (e.g., weekly sales) are all common variables in organizational research. Each subject's standing on each variable is quantified (converted to numbers) so that statistical methods can be applied.

Variables can be classified into one of two types. In experiments, **independent variables** are those that are manipulated by the researcher, while **dependent variables** are those that are assessed in response to the independent variables. In other words, the independent variables are assumed to be the cause of the dependent variables. In the training program example, employees were assigned to either a group that was trained or a group that was not trained. Group assignment (trained or not trained) is the independent variable. It is manipulated because the researcher created the training and decided who does and does not get trained. Subsequent job performance would be the dependent variable, because it is not manipulated by the researcher but is merely assessed after training.

Research Setting

The research setting can be classified as either field or laboratory. A **field setting** is one in which the phenomenon of interest occurs naturally. Organizations are field settings in which to study employee behavior. **Laboratory settings** are artificial environments in which phenomena of interest do not normally occur. They occur only because the researcher created them in that setting. The same physical location can be the setting for either a field or a laboratory study, depending on what is studied. A university classroom is a field setting in which to study student learning but a laboratory setting in which to study reactions to job conditions.

Most I/O research occurs in organizational field settings, but much of it takes place in the laboratory as well. Dipboye (1990) reported that 29% of I/O studies published in major journals of the field are laboratory studies. Laboratory studies can involve any aspect of work. For example, many researchers have created simulated job conditions to test people's reactions. Taken together the results of both field and laboratory studies help enhance our understanding of organizational phenomena (Dipboye, 1992).

Generalizability

Generalizability of results means that the conclusions of a study can be extended to other groups of people, organizations, settings, or situations. Generalizability is often a concern with laboratory studies because we cannot be certain that the results will hold for organizational settings. The more dissimilar the study is to the organizational setting in terms of both conditions and subjects, the less confidence there can be in the generalizability of the results. The only sure way to be certain about generalizability is to replicate the study in the field setting. If the results in the laboratory are also found in the field, we can have confidence in the generalizability of the laboratory findings.

Generalizability can also be a concern in field studies, for studies done in one organization or with one group of subjects might not have the same results in other places or with other groups of subjects. For example, a study done with nurses in a hospital might have different results from the same study done with physicians. Furthermore, results found in a hospital might be different from results found in a university. Of even greater concern is generalizability across countries and cultures. We cannot be certain that the findings from all of our American and Western research will generalize to countries with different cultures, such as China or India. Finally, even if we only wish to generalize within a single occupation in a single organization, conditions of the study might hold only for the setting in which the study is conducted. A training program that is conducted as part of a study might differ somewhat from the program that is implemented throughout the organization. Trainees and trainers can be affected by knowing they are participants in a research study, just as in the Hawthorne studies we discussed in Chapter 1. This knowledge can motivate the trainers to perform their training tasks in a more effective way than they would if the training was for other purposes. Thus, a training program might work well in the research phase but not in the implementation phase of a training development project.

Control

Every study offers several possible explanations for why the results occurred. **Control** refers to procedures that allow researchers to rule out certain explanations for results other than the hypotheses they wish to test. For example, suppose we wish to find out if salary affects how much people like their jobs. We could conduct a survey of employees in various organizations, asking them how much they are paid and how much they like their jobs. We might find that the higher the salary the greater the liking. However, with this sort of design, there are many uncontrolled variables that might be the real cause of liking. For example, perhaps the higher paid people are in different types of jobs than the lower paid people. If the higher paid people are all professional athletes and the lower paid people are sales clerks, it will be difficult to conclude that the pay caused the liking. This is because the type of job was uncontrolled, and it is a possible alternative explanation for results.

Control can be achieved by a number of procedures. For the most part, these involve either holding constant or systematically varying the levels of one or more variable. With the pay survey example, one might hold constant the type of job by limiting the survey to people of only one occupation. If the subjects of the study all had the same job, job type could not have accounted for the results because it was controlled. One could also control for job type by systematically varying it. Or one could choose a group of subjects that included equal numbers of higher and lower paid people in each of several job types. For example, the study might be limited to groups of actors and athletes that had about the same mix of higher and lower paid people.

Control can be achieved in experiments by the use of a **control group**. A control group is a collection of people who receive a condition or manipulation different from the one of interest. In determining the effectiveness of a training program, the group that does not get trained and is compared to the group that did get trained is called the *control group*. A control group can sometimes be exposed to some manipulation that is used to control specific variables of concern. For example, with a training study it is possible that training has a nonspecific or Hawthorne Effect. A person who knows he or she has been trained might perform better because of increased effort rather than increased skills. This is important to know because there is no need to send someone through expensive and time-consuming training if it does not have the intended effect. The control group can be given bogus or placebo training to control for the Hawthorne Effect. If individuals who are told they are being trained but receive little actual training perform as well as the trained group, the researcher will know that the training did not achieve its intended results.

Laboratory experiments are often conducted in I/O psychology because they provide the strongest control over many variables that might affect results. Even though they may lack the generalizability of a field study, a researcher might choose this more controlled approach. It is common for research on new topics to begin in the laboratory, so that a researcher can see, under highly controlled conditions, if a hypothesis might hold. If it does, field studies can follow to be sure the results generalize to the settings of ultimate interest—organizations.

Random Assignment and Random Selection

The term *random* refers to a process that eliminates systematic influences on how subjects are treated in a study. It is used in two ways—random assignment and random selection.

Random assignment occurs when people are assigned to various treatment conditions or levels of an independent variable in a nonsystematic way. This means that every subject of a study has an equal chance of being assigned to every condition. In a training study, each employee who participates would have an equal chance of being assigned to the trained group or to the control group. The random assignment process is a means of controlling for subject variables that are not of interest in the study. We expect that on average subjects in both groups will be more or less equivalent in their characteristics. For example, they should be of approximately the same ability, age, motivation, and tenure.

Random selection means that we choose the subjects of our investigation by a nonsystematic method: Every possible subject of our study has an equal chance of being chosen to participate. Random selection is important if we wish to draw accurate conclusions about the entire group of interest. If we wish to find out how the employees of a given organization feel about their jobs, unless we are going to study all of them, we want to be sure that the group we choose is a random sample. Otherwise we run the risk of choosing employees who do not feel the same way about their jobs as the majority of employees. It would not be a good idea to conduct a survey of a large organization and only get the views of top management. Their feelings are not likely to reflect those of employees at the lower levels of the organization.

Random assignment is used as a means of control by which groups of subjects can be made more or less equivalent to one another on variables not being studied. This is a powerful means of control used in experimental studies such as our training study example. Random selection enhances generalizability by choosing subjects who represent the people of interest. This might mean choosing a sample from all employees of a given organization or from all working people in an entire country.

Confounding

Confounding occurs when two or more variables are intertwined in such a way that conclusions cannot be drawn about either one. For example, age is confounded with job tenure (how long people have been on their jobs). This is because one cannot be on the job a long time unless one is relatively old. A 25-year-old cannot have been on the job for 20 years. If you were to find that age was associated with job performance, you could not be certain that it was not job tenure that was the important variable. Age might relate to performance only because the older employees had longer job tenure.

With commission sales jobs, pay is determined by job performance. Employees who sell the most product have the highest pay. This confounds pay and performance. If you wished to relate either variable to another variable of interest, you could not easily know which was the more important factor. For example, if job satisfaction related to performance, you could not be certain if pay or performance was the reason for satisfaction.

Often control procedures can be used to unconfound variables. For example, one might study the age-performance connection in only a sample of newly hired employees. Control would have been achieved over tenure by limiting the study to those people with approximately the same low level of job tenure. You might study the performance-satisfaction connection by limiting the study to employees who were not on commission or other pay-for-performance systems.

Statistical procedures can also be used to control for confounding. Although it is beyond our scope here, there are many complex statistics that allow for statistical control of unwanted confounding variables. Much of the research in the literature of I/O psychology is concerned with testing for the confounding effects of variables. Often this helps us understand why two variables, such as performance and satisfaction, are related.

► RESEARCH DESIGNS

A **research design** is the basic structure of a scientific study. Research designs can be classified along a continuum from those that involve active manipulation of conditions (experimental) to those that involve relatively passive observation of people. The various designs have their strengths and weaknesses, and rarely will a particular design allow us to draw definitive conclusions about a research question. To do so requires the use of a variety of designs that produce similar results.

The Experiment

An **experiment** is a design in which there are one or more independent variables and one or more dependent variables, as well as random assignment of subjects. An independent variable contains two or more levels or conditions of interest. The following have been independent variables in organizational experiments:

Length of daily work shift (in hours)

Pay categories (in dollars)

Availability or nonavailability of training

Setting or nonsetting of job goals

The dependent variable is measured but not manipulated by the researcher and is presumed to be caused by the independent variable. Examples of some frequently studied dependent variables in organizational research are:

Frequency of absences from work

Satisfaction with the job

Job performance

Turnover (quitting the job)

The experiment can be distinguished from other designs by two particular features. First, in an experiment subjects are assigned at random to two or more conditions that represent the levels of the independent variable or variables. Even though other research designs may have levels of independent variables, to be a true experiment there must be random assignment. Second, the experiment usually involves the creation of the independent variable levels by the researcher. For example, a researcher might design experimental training programs. Sometimes, however, the independent variable levels may occur naturally, and the researcher merely assigns subjects to those levels. In an organization, for example, there might be ongoing training programs that the researcher assigns people to at random.

Most experiments in the I/O literature have taken place in the laboratory (Schaubroeck & Kuehn, 1979). However, experiments can be conducted in more naturalistic settings. The **field experiment** is conducted within an organization rather than the laboratory. The many field experiments that have been conducted are often only approximations to true experiments and are called *quasi-experiments* (Cook & Campbell, 1988). In a **quasi-experiment design**, one or more of the features of a true experiment have been compromised. Very often there is not random assignment to the levels of the independent variable. In a training study, members of one work group might be given the training, while members of another serve as the control group. Observed differences between the trained and untrained employees might result from the work group itself rather than the training, because of the lack of random assignment.

The major advantage of the experiment is the ability to draw causal conclusions. If the experiment is done properly, one can be reasonably certain that the independent variable is the cause of the dependent variable. If the experiment is conducted in the laboratory, however, one cannot be certain that the results will generalize to the field. With field experiments, generalizability is more likely.

Even with the experiment, however, there can be alternative explanations for results. Often the independent variable will be confounded with another variable. For example, suppose you are interested in determining whether the number of training sessions employees receive affects their job performance. One group might get five sessions and the other ten sessions. However, the total training time is confounded because the second group gets twice the time of training as the first. You could control total time by making the sessions for the five-session group twice as long as those for the ten-session group. Unfortunately, now the length of session is confounded with the number of sessions. Disentangling the effects of session length, session number, and total training time can be difficult. It can require several experiments to reach a definitive conclusion.

Survey Designs

The survey design is one of the simplest and easiest to conduct of all the major designs. A **survey design** uses a series of questions compiled to study one or more variables of interest. These questions are then asked of a sample of respondents at a single point in time. Most surveys are presented as paper-and-pencil **questionnaires** that respondents complete and return to the researcher. Other means of conducting surveys can involve computers, face-to-face interviews, telephone interviews, and even the Internet via e-mail or the World Wide Web. In recent years, the Web-based approach has been gaining in popularity as a means for organizations to survey their employees.

The most common version of the survey involves collecting all data directly from the respondent, but some studies use other data sources as well. For example, one can survey employees about their jobs and get additional information from co-workers or supervisors. Studies of job performance often get performance data from supervisors rather than the employees who are being studied. It is also common to ask customers or peers to provide assessments of job performance. For example, some restaurants ask customers to fill out a card indicating how good the service was. This can be used as a measure of performance if the waiter or waitress is identified.

Most surveys are **cross-sectional**, meaning that all data were collected at a single point in time. A **longitudinal design** is one in which data are collected at more than one point in time. For example, one might collect data on people's feelings about the job when they are first hired and on their performance a year later. This design allows one to see if initial feelings predict later job performance. Many studies of employee turnover are longitudinal, with turnover assessed a year or more after the initial survey. This sort of study involves both a survey and one other type of data, turnover assessed from organizational records.

Using a survey design to study organizational phenomena has two advantages. First, the survey is a quick and relatively inexpensive way to find out how people feel about the job. Second, surveys are usually conducted on employees who are asked about their own jobs. This means that generalizability is not as big a problem as it is with laboratory experiments.

Surveys have two major disadvantages. First, employees are not always good sources of information about the variables of interest. For example, self-appraisals of job performance are usually biased in favor of the employee (Harris & Schaubroeck, 1988). In other words people overrate their own performance. Second, the cross-sectional nature of most surveys makes it difficult to draw conclusions about which variables were likely to be the cause of which other variables. For example, a survey of teachers might find that their reports of their job stress relate to their reports of their job performance. From this alone it could not be determined that stress caused performance, performance caused stress, or a third variable (e.g., job tenure) caused both. The use of longitudinal designs can be more helpful in drawing causal conclusions. Studies in which employee feelings about their jobs predict their later turnover, for example, have provided convincing evidence that job attitudes are a causal factor in turnover (Gerhart, 1990).

Perhaps the biggest problem in conducting a survey is assuring a sufficiently high response rate. **Response rate** is the percentage of those surveyed who agree to participate. If the response rate is low because only a small percentage of people are willing to provide data, the generalizability of results could be questioned, especially if you wish to determine the average level of a variable, such as mean level of motivation. The responses of these few people might not be the same as those of the people who did not participate. Procedures have been developed to increase response rates, such as avoiding threatening questions and sending reminder letters (Fowler, 1988; Kalton, 1983).

Observational Designs

In an **observational design**, the researcher observes employees in their organizational settings. Observations can be done either with (obtrusive) or without (unobtrusive) the employees' knowledge. With obtrusive methods, the researcher might watch individual employees conducting their jobs for a period of time. Employees would know that the observer was conducting research about a particular aspect of their jobs.

With **unobtrusive methods**, the subjects of study might be aware that the researcher was present, but they would not know that they were being studied.

In some obtrusive studies, observers assess specific behaviors or events of interest. For example, observers might record the number of times workers take breaks. In other obtrusive studies, the observer might be asked to rate the person's job conditions or reactions to their jobs. For example, Glick, Jenkins, and Gupta (1990) asked observers to estimate how much employees liked their jobs after watching them for about two hours.

The unobtrusive observational study can be conducted in many ways. A well-designed study can be quite simple but requires creativity and ingenuity to think of a reasonable way to assess the variables of interest. Often such studies are done by having a person pretend to be doing something other than recording people's behavior. The guard at the entrance of an office building can keep track of the arrival times of employees in a study of tardiness. Such data might also be gathered from a videotape of the entrance that has the time recorded on the picture.

One disadvantage of the obtrusive study is that the researcher can affect the phenomenon being studied. Remember how in the Hawthorne study job performance kept going up no matter what lighting levels were chosen (see Chapter 1). Employee motivation was affected by the research process, making it seem that lighting had no effect on performance. This is why unobtrusive methods can be valuable, although it is not always possible to use them because of ethical and legal requirements to respect people's privacy.

Qualitative Studies

Over the past decade there has been increasing interest in the use of nonquantitative methods to study organizational phenomena. These **qualitative methods** (Strauss & Corbin, 1990) offer an alternative to the highly quantitatively oriented approaches of most I/O psychologists. There are many different approaches to conducting a qualitative study, including case studies, participant observations (the researcher spends time in an organization observing employees), and interviewing. In pure form, the qualitative approach involves observing behavior in an organization and then recording those observations in a narrative form. Conclusions and generalizations can be drawn from repeated observations of the same phenomenon without quantifying the results. The qualitative approach can be a good means of generating hypotheses and theories from observations of what happens in organizational settings.

Other qualitative methods involve content analysis of interviews, responses to open-ended questions, or written materials. In this sort of qualitative study, trained judges are asked to sort materials into categories that are then given a descriptive name. The frequency of each category is then calculated. An example of this approach is a cross-national comparative study of job stress by Liu, Spector, and Shi (1992). Both American and Chinese employees were asked to describe a stressful incident at work. Judges read the incidents and placed them into categories. The frequencies with which types of stressful incidents were mentioned were compared across countries, showing that Americans are more likely than Chinese to mention lack of control and less likely to mention making mistakes as being stressful.

▶ MEASUREMENT

Measurement is the process of assigning numbers to characteristics of people or things. Variables in every study must be measured or quantified so that data analysis can be conducted to draw conclusions. One of the most critical steps in planning a research study is deciding how each variable will be measured. The nature of measurement determines in part the type of data analysis that can be done.

Measurement can be classified as either categorical or continuous. With **categorical measurement**, the values of the variable represent discrete categories and not the amount of the characteristic of interest. Numbers are assigned arbitrarily to people or things so that low values do not represent less of the characteristic than high values. Player numbers on a sports team and job titles are categorical because (in most cases) they are arbitrary substitutes for the name of the person in the former case and the name of the job in the latter.

Continuous measurement is used when the numbers represent the amount of the characteristic in question. Higher numbers represent more of the characteristic than lower numbers, so that inferences can be made based on the value of a variable. Dependent variables are usually continuous in large part because continuous measurement allows for a variety of sophisticated data analytic methods. Much of the work of both the I/O practitioner and researcher involves the assessment or measurement of jobs and people. Number of training sessions or total sales per month would be continuous measures.

In experiments, the levels of the independent variables are often categorically measured by numbering them arbitrarily when the levels do not represent an underlying characteristic that can be measured continuously. For example, the independent variable of the method of information presentation in a training program would not represent a continuously quantified dimension. There might be four levels of presentation. For example,

1 = Book   3 = Lecture
2 = Computer   4 = Videotape

These are four discrete items that are numbered arbitrarily.

Classical Measurement Theory

According to **classical measurement theory**, every observation of a variable can be divided into two components: true score and error. The true score is assumed to represent the variable of interest. The error comprises random influences on the observed score that are independent of the true score. Because errors are random, they are as likely to deflate as inflate the observed values of the variable. Thus, if multiple observations of a variable are taken on the same person or thing, the errors will average out to approximately zero and disappear. Suppose you wish to weigh yourself on a bathroom scale with a needle that tends to stick, randomly indicating a too high or too low weight on successive attempts. If you weigh yourself several times and average the observations, the resulting mean is likely to be close to your true weight. For example, suppose you weigh 120 pounds and the observed scores are

116, 118, 122, 124.

Each of these observed weights is inaccurate because of an error component. The magnitudes of the error components are

−4, −2, 2, 4, respectively.

The average of the four error components is zero. This means that if you average the four observations of weight, the errors will disappear and the resulting mean will be the correct weight of 120 pounds.

Psychological tests use multiple items to increase accuracy of measurement by averaging out error. Each item of the test contains both a true score and an error component. By combining the items with random errors, the errors should cancel each other out. This leaves a more accurate measurement of the true score.

Even the elimination of error with multiple measures, however, does not guarantee that what was assessed reflects what was intended to be assessed. Depending on the measurement process, many factors may affect the observed score beyond the intended variable and error. For example, rating scales that ask people to indicate the characteristics of their jobs can be affected by the responder's cognitive processes, feelings about the job, mood, and personality (Spector, 1992). The multitude of influences on an observed score is one factor that makes it difficult to interpret the meaning of results from a single study.

Most I/O research is conducted in the workplace.
(*Renee Lynn/Photo Researchers*)

Reliability

Reliability is the consistency of measurement across repeated observations of a variable on the same subject. In classical measurement theory terms, it reflects the relative size of the error to true score components. When the error component is small, there will be little variation from observed score to observed score on the same subject. As the error component increases, observations will differ each time the subject is assessed.

There are several types of reliability that can be classified as either internal consistency or test-retest. We often take multiple measurements of each subject on the variable of interest to increase the accuracy of measurement by averaging out the error components, as we discussed in the previous section. **Internal consistency reliability** refers to how well the multiple measures on the same subject relate to one another. Measures presumed to assess the same true score should be highly correlated with one another. A lack of perfect correlation among multiple measures of the same construct reflects error or unreliability, and in practice no measure is perfectly reliable.

The instrument that uses multiple measures most often is a psychological test that combines multiple items into a total score for the variable of interest. The items must be interrelated for the test to have internal consistency reliability. Usually the more items there are in a test, the better will be its internal consistency. Multiple-item measures are used to assess many of the variables discussed throughout this book, including abilities, job attitudes, perceptions of the job environment, and personality.

Multiple measures are also used when we ask people to rate variables of interest. For example, employee job performance can be assessed by asking supervisors to rate the performance of subordinates. Supervisors are asked to indicate how well subordinates perform by using a rating scale, such as the following:

How would you rate the performance of your staff assistant?

_____ Excellent

_____ Good

_____ Fair

_____ Poor

Performance ratings are very much like grades given to students by teachers. For research purposes, two or more people might be asked to rate each employee's performance. The ratings can be combined in the same way that multiple items on a test are combined. **Inter-rater reliability** is the extent to which the ratings of two or more raters are correlated with one another.

Test-retest reliability refers to the consistency of measurement when it is repeated over time. If you were to assess a person's job satisfaction several times in a row, a reliable scale would give you the same score each time. This assumes, of course, that the satisfaction remained constant. Similarly, a psychological test or other measuring device should give you the same value for a subject each time, unless the true score changes. The time span over which test-retest reliability is assessed is dependent on how stable the variable is assumed to be. With tests of some human attributes, such as intelligence, high levels of reliability have been found over time spans of decades.

Both internal consistency and test-retest reliability are necessary properties for a useful measuring device. If a measure contains too much error, it will not give a sufficiently accurate measurement to be useful. The first required property of a measure is reliability. Reliability is not enough, however. Just because a measuring device is consistent does not mean that it actually assesses the variable of interest. The interpretation of scores from any measuring device represents its validity, which we discuss next.

Validity

Validity has to do with the inferences that are made about what an observed score measures or represents. In classical measurement theory, it refers to our interpretation of the true score component. Thus, validity refers to the inferences made about a measuring device rather than the device itself. For example, an intelligence test is considered valid if people who score high do better than people who score low on tasks that in theory require intelligence. **Construct validity** means that we are able to give an interpretation to scores on a measure. To say that a measure has construct validity is to say that we have confidence in our interpretation of what that measure represents. We attribute construct validity to standard intelligence tests because we have decades of research showing that scores on these tests predict expected performance in school and on the job.

There are several different ways to assess validity, all of which involve inferences that can be made about measures. **Face validity** means that a measure appears to assess what it was designed to assess. An item from a scale to assess how people feel about their jobs, such as,

Do you like your job?

might be considered to have face validity because it appears to assess what was intended. An issue of concern with face validity is the perspective of those judging it. Sometimes experts in a domain are asked to judge the face validity of a measure. I/O psychologists can be used as experts for measures of organizational variables.

Face validity does not provide particularly strong evidence to support construct validity. Often a measuring device might appear to have face validity, but it does not assess what was intended. The question "Have you stolen from your employer?" might appear to be a face valid measure of honesty, but if dishonest employees lie in their answers, the question will not be a valid measure of honesty. Although we sometimes rely on face validity to interpret our measures, it is far from sufficient for establishing construct validity.

TABLE 2.1   Four Types of Validity For a Measure and What Each One Means

Type	Meaning
Face	Measure looks like what it assesses
Content	Measure assesses entire variable
Criterion-related	Measure relates to what is expected
Construct	Interpretation of a measure's meaning

Content validity means that a multiple-item measure of a variable does an adequate job of covering the entire domain of the variable. This is best seen in determining whether or not the questions on a course examination do a good or poor job of adequately covering the entire body of material students were assigned. A single question would generally be inadequate to cover all the material in a single chapter of a textbook. The question

What is content validity?

would not represent an adequate and content valid examination on this chapter. A content-valid exam would ask many questions that cover a good sampling of the topics in the chapter. As with face validity, experts are used to judge the content validity of a measure.

Criterion-related validity means that scores on a measure of interest relate to other measures that they should relate to in theory. As noted earlier, scores on an intelligence test that is considered valid should relate to performance on tasks that in theory should require intelligence, such as taking examinations in college courses. Intelligence tests have been shown to relate to many variables, including job and school performance, lending confidence to the interpretation of what they represent. The ability of intelligence tests to predict performance makes them valuable tools for the practitioner who wishes to select employees for jobs (see Chapter 5). Although criterion-related validity is important for building a case for construct validity, it is not sufficient. Sometimes we can find support for our predictions for reasons other than what we expect.

The four types of validity are summarized in Table 2.1. The first three—face, content, and criterion-related—represent ways to assess validity. Combined they provide evidence for the fourth, construct validity of a measure. Construct validity is inferred based on research evidence. It is our best guess about what a measure represents.

► STATISTICS

Most studies carried out by I/O psychologists require statistical methods for the data analysis. Two types of statistics are used. Descriptive statistics summarize the results of a study, and inferential statistics help interpret the results using a variety of statistical tests. In this section, we review descriptive statistics and the purpose of several inferential statistics tests.

Descriptive Statistics

The study designs discussed in this chapter result in the collection of data on samples of several individuals or jobs. When such data are collected in a study, it is all but impossible to make sense of them without some sort of summary analysis. **Descriptive statistics** provide ways of reducing large amounts of data to summary statistics, such as means or variances. These statistics can be interpreted much more easily than the original data.

Measures of Central Tendency and Dispersion

Several different statistics measure the center of a group of scores. The **arithmetic mean** is the sum of the observations divided by the number of observations. For example, suppose we have the following numbers of absences in a year for five employees:

2, 3, 4, 5, 6

The mean of these five numbers is four absences per year. It is computed by taking the sum of the five numbers (20) and dividing it by the number of employees (5). The **median** is the middle number when the observations are rank ordered from lowest to highest. In this case, 4 is also the median because there are two observations below and two above this value.

The measure of central tendency might indicate the middle score, but it does not give any indication about how much the observations differ from one another in value. For example, the following five observations:

48, 49, 50, 51, 52

have the same mean of 50 as

0, 1, 50, 99, 100

even though there is a larger difference among observations in the second case. Measures of dispersion indicate the degree to which the observations differ from one another.

The **variance** is a dispersion measure that is the arithmetic mean of the squared differences between each observation and the arithmetic mean of the same observations. For example, the arithmetic mean of the following absence frequencies:

2, 3, 4, 5, 6

is 4. The differences between each observation and the mean of 4 are

−2, −1, 0, 1, 2

I/O researchers analyze their data by computer.

(*LWA-JDC/Corbis Stock Market*)

Each of these differences squared results in

4, 1, 0, 1, 4

The arithmetic mean of these numbers is 2 (10 divided by 5), which is the variance. The **standard deviation** is the square root of the variance, which is 1.4 in this example. It is frequently reported in research papers as the measure of dispersion.

Correlation

Measures of central tendency and dispersion are useful for summarizing groups of observations from a single variable. **Correlation** is a statistic used to indicate the degree to which two continuous variables are related (magnitude) and the direction of the relation. This is important because many research questions concern the relations among variables. For example, a question such as,

Does level of pay relate to job performance?

is likely to be answered by computing a correlation statistic between a measure of pay and a measure of job performance.

The most commonly used descriptive statistic to assess correlation is the **Pearson product-moment correlation coefficient**. This statistic can be computed when there are two observations, each representing a different variable, on every subject in a given sample. Table 2.2 contains hypothetical observations of pay and job performance for 12 employees of an organization. Each employee has an observation for each variable. The table contains three possible associations reflected in how the observations of the two variables are paired. Each of the three cases is plotted in Figure 2.1.

TABLE 2.2   Hypothetical Data Showing Three Possible Associations Between Pay and Job Performance

Positive Association		Negative Association		No Association	
Job Performance	Pay	Job Performance	Pay	Job Performance	Pay
1	1	1	12	1	1
2	2	2	11	2	12
3	3	3	10	3	3
4	4	4	9	4	10
5	5	5	8	5	5
6	6	6	7	6	8
7	7	7	6	7	7
8	8	8	5	8	6
9	9	9	4	9	9
10	10	10	3	10	4
11	11	11	2	11	11
12	12	12	1	12	2

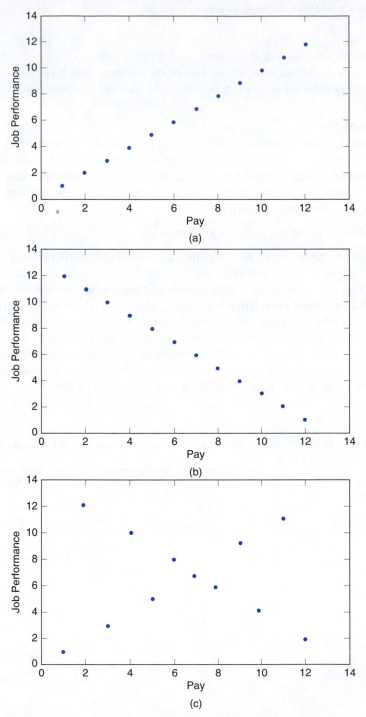

Figure 2.1 Three possible associations between income and job performance: (a) positive association; (b) negative association; (c) no association.

In the first case, a positive association or correlation exists between pay and job performance. Employees who have low pay also have low job performance, and employees who have high pay have high job performance. In Figure 2.1a the two variables are plotted with performance on the vertical axis and pay on the horizontal axis. The observations form a straight line from the lower left to upper right portion of the graph. This means that pay and performance are positively correlated, with a value of 1.0.

Figure 2.1b illustrates negative association or correlation. Employees who have low pay have high job performance, and employees who have high pay have low job performance. The observations form a straight line from the upper left to the lower right on the graph. This indicates a negative correlation between pay and job performance. This time the value for the correlation coefficient is −1.0.

Figure 2.1c illustrates little association between pay and performance. Some employees with low pay have low job performance, and some have high job performance. Some employees with high pay have low performance, and some have high performance. The observations do not form a straight line but are scattered widely throughout the graph, meaning that the value for the correlation coefficient is approximately zero (0).

Figures 2.1a and 2.1b illustrate perfect correlation because the observations form a straight line. In almost all studies, there is likely to be a much smaller association between variables, reflected in correlation coefficients that are closer to 0 than the upper limit of 1 in absolute value. In I/O research, correlation coefficients rarely exceed .50. In many domains correlations can be considerably smaller. Figure 2.2 is a plot of 50 observations on two variables that have a correlation between them of approximately .50. The points form an elliptical shape from the lower left to the upper right. The direction of the plot indicates a positive association. If the observations had lined up from the upper left to the lower right, the magnitude of the correlation would have been the same, but it would have been negative in sign (−.50).

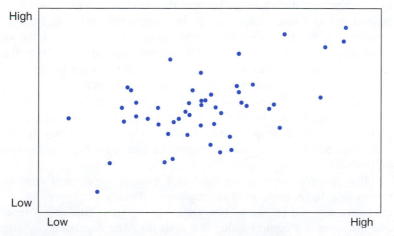

Figure 2.2　Plot showing 50 observations of two variables that were correlated at approximately .50.

Regression

An important by-product of correlated variables is that you can use one to predict the other. With the case illustrated in Figure 2.1a, we can predict that employees with low pay will have low performance, and employees with high pay will have high performance. Precise predictions can be made when the numerical value for performance is predicted from the numerical value for pay. This calculation is done using a regression equation that is computed from a set of data.

The **regression equation** provides a mathematical formula that allows for the prediction of one variable from another. If you enter the value of one variable (called the **predictor**) into the equation, it will give you the value for the other variable (called the **criterion**). In almost all cases, the two variables will not be perfectly correlated, so prediction of the criterion from the predictor will not be completely accurate. However, even relatively imprecise predictions can be helpful in many situations in which predictions are made. For example, psychological tests (e.g., the Scholastic Aptitude Test, or SAT) are used to select students for admission to colleges and universities because they have been shown to predict grade point average. Even though predictions are imperfect, use of the test can result in better average performance by the students, who are admitted based on test scores.

It is also possible to combine data from two or more predictor variables in order to predict a criterion variable. **Multiple regression** is a technique that enables the researcher to combine the predictive power of several variables to improve prediction of a criterion variable. For example, both high school grades and scores on the SAT could be combined to predict college grades. An equation can be developed from a sample of subjects that can plug in values of the predictor variables (e.g., high school grades and SAT) to predict a criterion variable (e.g., college grades).

Inferential Statistics

The hypotheses and research questions of most studies cannot be adequately addressed by descriptive statistics alone because data from a limited sample of people must be generalized to a much larger group. In other words, the data from a small sample of employees who is studied is generalized to all employees of the organization or to all employees of all organizations. We are not satisfied to just note the results with the subjects studied. We wish to draw conclusions about larger groups of people so that we can make general statements about the variables of interest.

Inferential statistics allow us to draw conclusions that generalize from the subjects we have studied to all the people of interest by allowing us to make inferences based on probabilities. The descriptive statistics from a small group of subjects from a research study are extended to the findings to other subjects by using statistical tests that are based on probability.

For example, suppose we conduct a training experiment and wish to extend the results to a larger population of employees. Twenty employees of an organization are randomly assigned to one of two groups of 10 each. One group receives the training, and the other is a control group that does not. The dependent variable is performance on the job. Table 2.3 contains hypothetical data from the study. The performance scores of subjects within each group varied from one another, even though every subject in

TABLE 2.3 Hypothetical Data for an Experiment Comparing a Trained Group to a Control Group

Control Group Performance	Trained Group Performance
1	2
1	4
2	5
2	5
3	6
3	6
4	7
4	8
5	8
10	9
Mean 3.6	6.0

each of the two groups had the same treatment assigned to that group. This variability among subjects who receive the same treatment in an experiment is called **error variance**, which makes it difficult to draw conclusions just by looking at descriptive statistics. This is because the variability among subjects treated the same will produce differences in means between groups. If we were to place subjects into groups randomly, it is unlikely that the groups would have the same mean on the variable of interest. If many different groups of subjects are taken at random from the same organization, it is unlikely that the mean performance of many of them will be the same. There will be variability from sample to sample. Interpreting the results of a study means deciding if observed differences between means are due to error variance or the treatment in question.

If the performance scores in each group are equivalent and produce the same mean, it would be obvious that the training was ineffective. On the other hand, if the performance scores of the trained subjects were all higher than the performance scores of the control group subjects, it would be obvious that the training worked as expected. Neither case is likely to occur in an actual study, making the interpretation of results difficult based on inspection of means alone. The data illustrated in Table 2.3 are typical of the results usually found. Even though the trained group's mean is higher than the control group's mean, there is overlap in the scores of subjects across the two groups. Some control group subjects performed better than some trained group subjects, and the best performer was in the control group. To interpret these results, you must decide if there is enough difference between the groups to conclude that the training worked or that the differences were due to error variance.

Inferential statistics or *statistical tests* are procedures that help you decide if the results can be attributed to error variance or the experimental treatment. The tests allow you to calculate the probability that the observed results, the differences between means in this case, were not due to error variance. If the probability of finding the mean difference by chance is less than 1 in 20 (.05), the conclusion is reached that the difference was likely due to the training rather than error variance. This is called **statistical significance**,

TABLE 2.4   Five Commonly Used Inferential Statistics Tests and Their Usage

Independent Group *t* test: Used to determine whether two groups of subjects differ significantly on a dependent variable.

Analysis of Variance (ANOVA): Used to determine whether two or more groups of subjects differ significantly on a dependent variable.

Factorial ANOVA: Used to determine the significance of the effects of two or more independent variables on a dependent variable.

***t* test for Correlation:** Used to determine whether the correlation between two variables is significantly greater than zero.

Multiple Regression: Used to determine whether two or more predictor variables can significantly predict a criterion variable.

meaning that the probability of finding the observed value of the statistical test by chance alone is less than .05.

There are dozens of different statistical tests, each used for a different situation. Some are used for various experimental designs, whereas others are used for nonexperimental designs, and many can be used for both. Some are limited to two variables, such as the one independent variable and one dependent variable in the present example. Others can be used with an unlimited number of variables. Table 2.4 lists several of the statistical tests most commonly used in I/O research. Although they may have different purposes, all are based on the same underlying principle of determining if the probability of the test statistic is statistically significant.

An independent group *t* test is used in the present example to see if the two groups differ significantly on a dependent variable. If there are two or more groups, the analysis of variance (ANOVA) would be used. This would allow you to compare two different training methods to a control group. In most experiments, however, there are two or more independent variables. For example, suppose you wish to compare the trained group to the control group separately for men and women. You could randomly assign 10 men to the control group and 10 men to the trained group. Similarly, you could randomly assign 10 women to the control group and 10 women to the trained group. This would produce a factorial design consisting of the training variable and the gender variable, each of which had two levels. A **factorial design** has two or more independent variables. **Factorial ANOVA** is a statistical test that is used to analyze the data from a factorial design. It tells us if the subjects in the various groups differed significantly on the dependent variable.

The correlation coefficient can be tested to see if it is significantly different from zero. This is done with a variation of the *t* test. A significant correlation means that there is significant association between two variables and that you can predict one variable from the other better than by chance. When more than two variables are related to a third, multiple regression is used. There are significance tests to show that two or more predictor variables in the regression analysis are related significantly to the criterion variable. Again, significance means that the criterion can be predicted by the predictors better than by chance.

Meta-Analysis

A single study is never considered to offer a definitive answer to a research question. To achieve confidence in a conclusion about a phenomenon of interest, we need to conduct several studies. It is not unusual, however, for different studies to yield somewhat different results. The same sampling error that produces differences among means taken from the same population will produce differences in the results of inferential statistical tests. To make sense of conflicting results across studies requires the use of a special type of analysis called meta-analysis.

A **meta-analysis** is a quantitative way of combining results of studies, much as our statistics summarize the results across individual subjects (Hunter & Schmidt, 1990; Rosenthal, 1991). A meta-analysis can summarize statistically the results of different studies in the domains of interest to I/O psychologists. Such analyses can be simple descriptive summaries of results or very complex mathematical and statistical procedures.

Perhaps the simplest form of meta-analysis summarizes the results of multiple studies with means of descriptive statistics. A meta-analysis might report that the mean correlation between two variables has been found to be a particular value, such as .40. For example, suppose you found five studies that reported the following correlations between job satisfaction and pay level:

.20, .22, .24, .26, .28

A simple meta-analysis of these five studies would conclude that the mean correlation between these two variables was .24. More complex analyses could also be conducted to explore other aspects of these studies. If some studies were conducted on managers and others on nonmanagers, one could test to see if the correlations were different for the two types of employees.

In this book, the results of studies are often summarized by referring to meta-analysis. These analyses have become popular in the I/O research literature. It can be difficult to read several studies and make sense of the findings without the use of some sort of method such as meta-analysis. In most areas that have been frequently studied, meta-analyses can be found to help interpret and summarize what those individual studies have found.

Mediator and Moderator Variables

Regardless of the design, experimental or nonexperimental, studies help us determine the extent to which two or more variables are related to one another. Other studies, however, are intended to explore more complex relationships among variables. A **mediator** is a variable that is part of the intervening process between two other variables. In other words it explains why two variables relate to one another. For example, we know that ability relates to performance, so if you score well on the quantitative portion of the SAT, you will likely do well in statistics classes. This fact alone does not really tell us why these variables are related. One possibility is that ability enhances motivation, and motivation results in greater effort and thereby better performance. Thus students who score well on the SAT have more confidence in their abilities and are motivated to work hard in quantitative courses. They work harder in their statistics classes, and that effort leads to better performance. In this example, motivation is a mediator.

A **moderator** is a variable that affects the relationship between two other variables. Participants at one level of the moderator variable will have a different relationship between two other variables than participants at another level. College major would serve as a moderator if the relationship between two variables is different among students of different majors. For example, suppose the correlation between the quantitative SAT score and grade point average is .50 for mathematics majors, but only .10 for fine arts majors. Major would be said to moderate the relationship between SAT and grades. Continuous variables can also be moderators. For example, it might be that the SAT versus grade relationship is stronger for older than younger students. In this case age would have moderated the relationship.

Mediation and moderation are frequently confused, even in journal articles. Remember that a mediator is an intervening variable that explains the relationship between two other variables. It is concerned with the causal chain of events that one variable causes the mediator which in turn causes another variable. A moderator is a variable that changes the relationship between two other variables. That is, the relationship is different at one level of the moderator than another.

▶ ETHICS OF RESEARCH

The ethical principles of I/O psychologists hold for research as well as for practice. The overriding ethical consideration is that the researcher must protect the well-being of subjects. This means that manipulations, such as an experimental training procedure, should not be used if they are known to cause harm. Even with nonexperimental studies, such as surveys, the researcher must take care to protect identities when appropriate. If respondents to a survey provide negative feedback about their supervisors, supervisors should not be able to find out who provided the feedback. This way there can be no retaliation against a subordinate for saying something that the supervisor did not like.

At times, however, conflicting demands can make it difficult to decide what is correct ethically. It would be considered unethical to violate confidentiality and disclose the identities of surveyed employees. On the other hand, a psychologist who works for an organization has an ethical responsibility to that organization much as he or she would have to an individual client. That responsibility might extend to identifying disgruntled employees who might cause trouble or need help. A psychologist might have to weigh the well-being of individuals against the well-being of the organization. This responsibility to two parties creates an ethical dilemma because two conflicting demands are placed on the psychologist. It is difficult to know what is the right thing to do in all such situations. An I/O psychologist must carefully weigh the costs to everyone involved in taking different actions. An ethical psychologist will discuss the issue with other psychologists and with superiors in the hope of reaching an ethical and satisfactory decision. In some cases the psychologist might be forced to take the organization's side or risk being fired.

It is a good idea to try to foresee these situations and avoid them. If you suspect that supervisors might demand to know employee identities, conduct surveys anonymously. If you do not know the identities, you cannot disclose them. Even so, ethical dilemmas can arise in both practice and research. They can be difficult to resolve because someone might be harmed no matter what action is taken. For example, a psychologist might become aware that an employee has violated company policy. If the psychologist says nothing, the company might suffer harm, but if the psychologist reports it, the employee might be fired.

Another ethical principle is that subjects of studies should be informed about the nature and purpose of a study before they participate. If there is even a slight possibility that participation has some drawbacks, each subject should be asked to sign an **informed consent form**. These forms explain the nature of the study and what is expected of subjects, and alerts them that they can withdraw from the experiment at any time. Although using these forms can be awkward in field settings, informed consent means that the subjects understand the possible risks. This protects the researcher from legal action if someone claims that harm, either real or imagined, occurred from participation. Keep in mind that I/O practitioners also are concerned about ethics, but informed consent is not typically used when employees are asked to do things that are part of their jobs or are required as part of their employment rather than for research itself.

► CHAPTER SUMMARY

I/O psychology is a science because the methods used in research are scientific methods. This means that I/O psychologists collect and analyze data to address organizational issues and questions. An I/O research study begins with a research question, which defines the purpose of the study. The question leads to a research hypothesis, which is the researcher's best guess about how a study will turn out. A specific hypothesis will serve as the basis for the design of a study.

An I/O study can take place in either a field or laboratory setting. In a field setting, the phenomenon in question occurs naturally; in a laboratory, it is created. Generalizability means that the results of a given study can be extended to other settings and situations. Control is an important component of research studies in that it allows one to rule out alternative explanations for results. There are many different approaches to achieving control in studies. Random assignment refers to choosing subjects in a nonsystematic way so that every individual has an equal chance of being assigned to different treatment conditions. Random selection means that every possible subject has an equal chance of being chosen to participate in the study. Confounding occurs when two or more variables are intertwined and related in a way that makes it difficult to draw conclusions about either one.

Research designs can be divided into experimental and nonexperimental forms. In experimental designs, the researcher randomly assigns subjects to conditions that are constructed for the study. Nonexperimental designs involve observation without assignment of subjects or construction of conditions.

Measurement is the process by which characteristics of people or things are quantified. Reliability refers to the consistency of measurement, whereas validity means that inferences can be drawn about the meaning of a measure. The data generated by a study are analyzed with statistical methods. Descriptive statistics summarize the data from a study, and inferential statistics allow for the interpretation of findings.

Ethical principles of I/O psychologists apply to research studies. In general, researchers should ensure that their studies do not harm anyone. This is accomplished by taking care that procedures are not dangerous or harmful. Subjects should be informed about the nature of a study by having them read and sign an informed consent form.

They should be allowed the opportunity to decline participation. Care should be taken to protect the identities of subjects when information they provide could be used against them in a detrimental way.

LEARNING BY DOING

Methods Used In I/O Research

Find an article that describes a research study from one of the I/O journals listed in Table 1.1. Answer the following questions about that article:

1. What is the research question being addressed?
2. State one hypothesis from the paper.
3. What kind of research design was used?
4. What does the study tell us about the reliability of its measures?
5. Note one inferential statistic reported in the study.
6. What is the most important conclusion from the study?

PART II

ASSESSMENT OF JOBS, PERFORMANCE, AND PEOPLE

(*Eye Wire*)

Job Analysis

CHAPTER 3 OUTLINE

How would you describe the job of a police officer? What are the different tasks that police officers do, and how much time do they spend doing each one? How difficult is it to learn the various tasks, and how long does it take? What personal characteristics does it take to do each task, as well as the entire job? These questions are addressed by a variety of techniques that I/O psychologists refer to as job analysis.

Even for the most familiar jobs, a job analysis is necessary to provide an accurate picture of all the details of the job and all the characteristics required of the people who will do it. For example, everyone is somewhat familiar with the job of a police officer. However, the public perception of the job is based to a large extent upon depictions in popular movies and television programs, such as *Law and Order* and *CSI*. Television programs focus on the more dramatic aspects of the job, which may be rarely performed. Most police officers spend more time on routine patrol duties and paperwork than on apprehending criminals (Bernardin, 1988). The firing of a weapon is a common occurrence on television, but it is rarely done by most police officers on the job. A thorough job analysis would provide an accurate picture of what police officers do all day on the job. The police officer's job has been thoroughly studied with many different job analysis methods and procedures. We look at some of them throughout this chapter.

There are two different categories of job analyses—the job oriented and the person (or employee) oriented. The job-oriented job analysis focuses on the tasks that are done on the job, whereas the person-oriented analysis is concerned with the personal characteristics needed for a job. In other words, the job-oriented procedures describe jobs, and the person-oriented procedures describe the characteristics people need to perform jobs. Both are important tools for describing jobs and their requirements.

In this chapter we discuss the job-oriented and person-oriented approaches, and the particular methods that are used for each. In addition, we discuss the uses and purposes of job analysis information, the sources of the information that goes into a job analysis, and the reliability and validity of job analysis methods. Finally, we discuss job evaluation, which is a job analysis technique used to set salary levels.

Objectives: The student who studies this chapter should be able to:

▶ List the uses of job analysis information.
▶ Describe the sources and ways of collecting job analysis information.
▶ Discuss the different job analysis methods.
▶ Describe the evidence for reliability and validity of job analysis methods.
▶ Explain how job evaluation is used to set salary levels for jobs.

▶ WHAT IS JOB ANALYSIS?

Job analysis is a method for describing jobs and/or the human attributes necessary to perform them. According to Brannick, Levine, and Morgeson (2007, p. 8) there are three elements that comprise a formal job analysis:

1. The procedure must be systematic. This means that the analyst specifies a procedure in advance and follows it.

2. A job is broken into smaller units. We describe components of jobs rather than the overall job.

3. The analysis results in some written product, either electronic or on paper.

There is no one way to do a job analysis. Many methods provide different types of information about jobs and the human attributes needed for jobs. As noted earlier, job analysis techniques can be used to collect information that is job oriented or person oriented, depending on the purpose of the job analyst.

The Job-Oriented Approach

The **job-oriented job analysis** provides information about the nature of tasks done on the job. Some methods describe the tasks themselves. Other methods provide information about characteristics of tasks. For example, a task for a police officer would be:

Completes report after arresting a suspect

This describes something a police officer does. A characteristic of an officer's job would be:

Uses pencils and pens

Photograph 1: A job analysis is needed to describe what a police officer does at work.
(*Richard Hutchings/Photo Researchers*)

The characteristic isn't a specific task but describes common features that cut across tasks. A police officer performs many tasks involving writing, such as completing reports of many types and giving citations to motorists. The purposes of the job analysis determine which type of approach would be most useful. The task descriptions provide a picture of what people do on a job. Characteristics of tasks can be used to compare the nature of tasks across different kinds of jobs. Police officers and teachers share the characteristic of using pencils and pens to do tasks, so there can be some similarities in types of tasks, even though the specific tasks themselves may vary.

Tasks can be divided into a hierarchy in which higher level descriptions are broken down into smaller and smaller pieces of the job. For example, one of the major tasks performed by police officers is apprehending suspects. This police function can be broken down into the specific actions that are involved, such as

Go to suspect's house to make arrest

Knock on door and identify self

Inform suspect of legal rights

Handcuff suspect

Put suspect in car

Drive suspect to police station

Brannick et al. (2007) discuss a hierarchy that contains five levels of specificity:

1. Position
2. Duty
3. Task
4. Activity
5. Element

A *position* is a collection of duties that can be performed by a single individual. Typically each employee has a single position, although it is possible for one individual to hold more than one position. Furthermore, a number of similar positions might be given the same title; for example, several police officers in a department might have the title of "patrol officer," although each has a separate position and collection of tasks. One position might be assigned to patrol an area of the city by car, another patrols on foot, and a third is assigned to desk work in the station.

A *duty* is a major component of a job. For a police officer, a duty would be

Enforce the law

Each duty is accomplished by performing one or more associated tasks. A *task* is a complete piece of work that accomplishes some particular objective. One of the tasks involved in enforcing the law is

Arrest suspects who violate the law

Each task can be divided into *activities*, which are the individual parts that make up the task. In this case activities would include

Driving to a suspect's house to perform an arrest

To accomplish this activity, a number of very specific *actions* or elements are involved, such as

Place handcuffs on suspect

For most jobs there are several duties; each duty is associated with several tasks; each task is associated with several activities; and each activity can be broken down into several elements. This means that a job analysis can contain a great deal of very specific information about what happens on a particular job. A job analysis that goes to the level of job actions produces a long and detailed report.

The Person-Oriented Approach

A **person-oriented job analysis** provides a description of the characteristics, or KSAOs, necessary for a person to successfully perform a particular job. **KSAOs** are the *knowledge*, *skills*, *abilities*, and *other characteristics* necessary for a job. The first three characteristics focus mainly on job performance; the "other" characteristics relate to job adjustment and satisfaction, as well as performance.

Knowledge is what a person needs to know to do a particular job. For example, a carpenter should have knowledge of local building codes and power tool safety.

Skill is what a person is able to do on the job. A carpenter should have skill in reading blueprints and in using power tools.

Ability is a person's aptitude or capability to do job tasks or learn to do job tasks. It is a person's potential to develop skills. Most skills require one or more abilities. The skill of using power tools requires several abilities, including hand-eye coordination. In order to build the roof on a house, a carpenter should have good balance and ability to work quickly.

Finally, **other personal characteristics** include anything relevant to the job that is not covered by the other three. A carpenter should have a willingness to do manual tasks and to work outdoors.

Although they might seem to overlap, KSAOs and tasks are very distinct. A task is something a person does. A KSAO is an attribute or characteristic required of the person to do a particular task or tasks. Tasks define what is done on a job, whereas KSAOs describe the sort of person needed. Table 3.1 provides some examples of tasks and associated KSAOs.

Many job analysis methods have been developed to do both job- and person-oriented analyses. Some are specific to one of the two major types of analyses, whereas others can be used for either one or both. The appropriateness of a particular method is determined by its purpose, the next topic we discuss.

TABLE 3.1　Examples of KSAOs and Associated Tasks

KSAO	Task
Knowledge of legal arrest procedures	Arrest suspects
Skill in using a firearm	Practice shooting firearm on firing range
Ability to communicate with others	Mediate a dispute between two people to prevent violent incident
Courage (as other personal characteristic)	Enter dark alley to apprehend suspect

TABLE 3.2   Eleven Uses of Job Analysis Information

Use	Description
Career development	Define KSAOs necessary for advancement
Legal issues	Show job relevance of KSAOs
Performance appraisal	Set criteria to evaluate performance
Recruitment and selection of employees	Delineate applicant characteristics to be used as basis for hiring
Training	Suggest areas for training
Setting salaries	Determine salary levels for jobs
Efficiency/safety	Design jobs for efficiency and safety
Job classification	Place similar jobs in groupings
Job description	Write brief descriptions of jobs
Job design	Design content of jobs
Planning	Forecast future need for employees with specific KSAOs

Source: Based on "A Framework for Evaluating Job Analysis Methods," by R. A. Ash and E. L. Levine, 1972, *Personnel*, 57, 53–59.

▶ PURPOSES OF JOB ANALYSIS

Job analysis information has many purposes. It can serve as the foundation on which many other activities and functions are built. Ash and Levine (1980) outlined 11 common uses of job analysis information, five of whch we discuss in this section of the chapter. A sixth, the use of job analysis information for setting salary levels, will be discussed later under the heading "Job Evaluation." The 11 uses are listed in Table 3.2.

Career Development

Many organizations have systems that allow employees to move up through the ranks to higher and higher positions. This is referred to as a **career ladder**: A progression of positions is established for individuals who acquire the necessary skills and maintain good job performance. Perhaps the best known career ladder system is in the military. Personnel move up through the ranks from lieutenant to captain to major to colonel to general. Not everyone can climb to the top of the ladder because of limited opportunities for promotion and inability to achieve the necessary KSAOs.

In recent years **competency systems** have become popular in organizations to reward employees for acquiring the knowledge and skills needed to both improve performance and be promoted (Levenson, Van der Stede, & Cohen, 2006). Such systems require the identification of critical competencies, availability of the means of learning and developing competencies, and a procedure for evaluating progress.

Job analysis contributes to career development by providing a picture of the KSAO requirements for jobs at each level of the career ladder, and by identifying the key competencies. Knowledge of KSAO requirements can be incorporated into employee development and training programs that can focus on skills necessary for career advancement. This benefits employees, because they are told exactly what they need to be eligible for promotion. It benefits organizations, because they develop a readily available supply of candidates for upper level positions.

Legal Issues

Most industrialized countries have laws prohibiting discriminatory employment practices, especially in the hiring of employees. In Canada and the United States, for example, it is illegal to discriminate on the basis of age, color, disability, gender, race, or religion. Although the specific groups that are protected against discrimination vary from country to country, the basic idea that decisions affecting people should be fair is almost universal. Fairness in employment means that decisions should be based on job performance or job potential rather than irrelevant personal characteristics. Job analysis provides a list of relevant KSAOs as the basis for hiring rather than irrelevant personal characteristics.

An important legal concept in U.S. employment law is that of **essential functions**, which are actions that must be done on a job. A receptionist must answer the telephone, for example. A nonessential function might be done occasionally but is not important for a person in that position to do. A custodian might receive an occasional phone call, but answering the phone is not an important part of the job.

The concept of essential function is important in deciding whether or not to hire a disabled person. In the United States, an organization may be able to legally deny employment to a disabled person who cannot perform essential functions under certain conditions (see Chapter 6). It is illegal to refuse to hire disabled individuals because they cannot perform nonessential functions, because these functions can easily be done by someone else, or they do not need to be done at all. With nonessential functions, and at times with essential functions, an organization is required to make reasonable accommodations so that the disabled person is able to do the job (Cleveland, Barnes-Farrell, & Ratz, 1997), as we will discuss at greater length in Chapter 5.

"So, Jim, where do you see yourself in ten minutes?"

(© *The New Yorker Collection (2001) Matthew Diffee from cartoonbank.com*)

Job analysis is used to identify essential functions and KSAOs (Mitchell, Alliger, & Morfopoulos, 1997). This can help ensure that decisions about actions that affect people are based on personal factors that are job relevant. For example, a legally defensible system to hire people should be based on KSAOs that have been shown to be relevant to the job in question. Promotion decisions should be based at least in part on the KSAOs of the possible candidates for the position. Only those individuals who possess the established characteristics that are necessary for the job should be considered. When KSAOs are derived from a properly conducted job analysis, employment actions based on those KSAOs are likely to be legal. Furthermore, employees and job applicants will probably believe that they were fairly treated, and will be unlikely to file lawsuits claiming discrimination.

Performance Appraisal

A well-designed performance appraisal system will be based on a job analysis. Criterion development—determining the major components of job performance to be evaluated—is one of the major uses of job analysis information. A job-oriented analysis provides a list of the major components of a job, which can be used as dimensions for performance evaluation.

The behavior-focused performance appraisal methods to be discussed in Chapter 4 are based on a job analysis. The specific behaviors contained in such instruments are collected with **critical incidents** from a job analysis (Flanagan, 1954). These critical incidents are instances of behavior that represent different levels of job performance from outstanding to poor, and they become an important part of the assessment of performance. A poor incident would describe how someone actually did something that was ineffective, such as a police officer getting into an argument with a citizen that resulted in violence. A good incident would describe how someone did something that worked well, such as a police officer defusing a potentially violent encounter by allowing a person to explain his or her side of the story.

Selection

The first step in deciding who to hire for a job is determining the human attributes, or KSAOs, necessary for success on that job. This means that a person-oriented job analysis should be the first step in the design of an employee selection system. Once the KSAOs for a job are identified, procedures can be chosen to determine how well job applicants fit the requirements for the job. This is done by using methods to assess individual characteristics, such as interviews and psychological tests (see Chapter 5).

A person-oriented job analysis produces a list of the KSAOs for a particular job. These KSAOs include both the characteristics that a job applicant is usually expected to have at the time of hiring and the characteristics that will be developed on the job through experience and training. Most accountant positions in large organizations, for example, require a college degree in accounting. This ensures that most applicants will have a reasonable level of knowledge about accounting principles and procedures. Specific knowledge about the organization's own policies and practices are learned on the job. This leads us to the next use of job analysis information—training.

Training

The KSAOs for a job suggest the areas in which training efforts should be directed. The KSAOs that applicants do not have when they apply for a position are areas for training after they are hired. An effective training program in an organization should be based on a thorough analysis of the KSAO requirements for a job. The KSAO requirements can be compared to the KSAOs of applicants or employees. Deficiencies on the part of applicants or employees are the areas in which training efforts should be directed if the characteristics can be acquired. For example, one can teach a person to use a tool, but one cannot train a person to be taller if there is a height requirement for a job.

Vocational Counseling

A major function of schooling, including at the university level, is to assist students in making vocational choices about their future careers. A number of vocational counseling tools exist to help individuals match their KSAOs to the KSAO requirements of jobs. Some of these tools attempt to match individual preferences and personalities to occupations that they would enjoy. Other approaches match individual capabilities to job requirements. Job analysis is particularly useful for matching KSAOs of people with occupations.

Converse, Oswald, Gillespie, Field, and Bizot (2004) provided an example of how job analysis can be used for vocational counseling. They used job analysis to determine KSAO requirements for specific occupations. A battery of ability tests was administered to a sample of individuals, and their ability profiles were matched to the requirements for each of the available jobs. Scores of how well the individual KSAOs matched job requirements were computed in order to demonstrate the best and worst fitting occupation for each person. For example, one person's abilities were a good match for occupations involving driving, such as truck driver or subway operator, but were a poor match for health-related occupations, such as physician assistant or physician. Another person was a good match for factory machine operator but was a poor match for biologist.

Research

An additional use of job analysis information is in research. Many researchers are interested in determining the role of job requirements or task characteristics in many organizational phenomena that we will discuss in this book, ranging from employee motivation and performance to health and safety. For example, Elovainio and Kivimäki (1999) used job analysis data in their study of individual differences in job stress. In this Finnish study, it was shown that people who had an aversion to change and uncertainty were likely to experience high levels of emotional strain (anxiety and tension) at work, but only if their jobs were complex, as determined by job analysis. If their jobs were simple, these individuals were no more likely to experience strain than were people who enjoy change and uncertainty.

▶ HOW JOB ANALYSIS INFORMATION IS COLLECTED

Job analysis information is collected in several ways. All of them use people who are trained in quantifying job characteristics and the KSAOs necessary to accomplish the different aspects of jobs. These people either survey the employees who do the jobs in question or experience the job firsthand by doing it themselves or observing it being done.

Who Provides the Information?

Most job analysis information comes from one of four different sources:

Job analysts   Supervisors
Job incumbents   Trained observers

Job analysts and trained observers actually do the job or spend time observing employees doing the job and translate these experiences into a job analysis. Incumbents and supervisors are considered to be **subject matter experts** (SMEs), people with detailed knowledge about the content and requirements of their own jobs or the jobs that they supervise. They are asked to provide information about jobs either in interviews or by completing job analysis questionnaires.

INTERNATIONAL REPLICATION

Psychologists have long recognized that there are vast individual differences in what people find to be stressful—what one person finds unpleasant another finds enjoyable. The authors of this study were interested in exploring a personality variable's role in occupational stress and in seeing if the job context plays a role as well.

This study was conducted in Finland with a sample of 734 local government employees from six health care facilities. A questionnaire was used to assess the personality characteristics of need for structure and emotional strain at work. Job complexity was assessed with data from the *Dictionary of Occupational Titles* database. The personality variable was related to strain in the entire sample—individuals who were high in need for structure tended to be high in strain at work. However, when job complexity was added to the analysis, this was found to be true only for individuals in highly complex jobs. For individuals with simple jobs, there was no relation between personality and strain.

The authors concluded that job context was an important element in job stress. Individual differences alone do not account for strain, but only do so under certain circumstances. In this case, when jobs are simple, there is presumably high structure, and so there is little reason for those high in need for structure to experience the job any differently than those who are low. However, when jobs are complex and structure is low, the effects of this personality variable emerge.

As noted in Chapter 1, Scandinavian research is almost all concerned with employee well-being, and this study is no exception. Whereas in the United States a job analysis study would most likely be concerned with employee selection or performance appraisal, in Finland such a technique is used to study occupational stress.

Source: Elovainio, M. and Kivimäki, M. (1999). Personal need for structure and occupational strain: An investigation of structural models and interaction with job complexity. *Personality and Individual Differences*, 26, 209–222.

Approaches to Collecting Job Analysis Information

People can provide job analysis information in many ways. The four most commonly used are:

Perform the job
Observe employees on the job

Interview subject matter experts

Administer questionnaires to subject matter experts

Perform Job

One way to collect job analysis information is for the job analyst to actually do some of the job tasks or the whole job. The job can be performed as an employee would, or the tasks can be performed under simulated conditions. By doing the job, the analyst gains insight into the nature of the job tasks and how the job tasks interrelate. It also provides an appreciation for the context in which employees do their jobs. Both an insurance salesperson and a police officer, for example, operate an automobile, but the conditions under which they do so can be very different.

Although this method can provide good information, it is not often used. Experiencing the job by doing it can be costly and time-consuming. It can require extensive training before the analyst can do the job. Some jobs are dangerous, particularly for an inexperienced person. Finally, this approach does not clearly indicate that tasks can differ among employees with the same job title.

Observe

Another way to collect information about a job is to observe people doing it. Observers can be job analysts or people trained to observe others. Observers are often given forms to complete about the jobs they observe. The form might contain a list of activities, and the observer indicates how often the observed employee does each one. As with the prior technique, observing employees can give insights into the context in which job tasks are performed. It can also be expensive and time-consuming. Furthermore, employees might not behave in the usual manner when they know they are being observed.

Interview

One of the most popular ways to collect information about jobs is by interviewing subject matter experts who are familiar with them. The SMEs are usually job incumbents and their supervisors. Interviews are carried out by job analysts or trained interviewers. Interviews are often used to generate lists of all tasks and activities done by everyone who has the same job title. Some tasks might be performed by few employees. Other tasks might be performed by every employee but only on rare occasions.

Questionnaire

The questionnaire is the most efficient means of collecting job analysis information. It can contain hundreds of questions about the job and can be administered easily to thousands of employees. No other technique can provide as much information about jobs with as little effort on the part of the job analyst. The same questionnaire can be given to every employee with the same job title. Comparisons can be made among groups that have the same job title but may differ on some characteristics, such as location.

Multiple Approaches

Each of the four ways of collecting job analysis information has its own set of advantages and limitations in providing a picture of what a job is like. Table 3.3 lists the advantages and limitations of each method. In practice, multiple ways are often used so that the

TABLE 3.3   Advantages and Limitations of Four Techniques for Collecting Job Analysis Information

Job Analyst Performs the Job

Advantages:	Provides context in which job is done
	Provides extensive detail about the job
Limitations:	Fails to show differences among jobs with same title
	Expensive and time-consuming
	Can take extensive training of analyst
	Can be dangerous to analyst

Interview

Advantages:	Provides multiple perspectives on a job
	Can show differences among incumbents with same job
Limitations:	Time-consuming as compared to questionnaires
	Fails to show context in which tasks are done

Observe Employees Doing the Job

Advantages:	Provides relatively objective view of job
	Provides context in which job is done
Limitations:	Time-consuming
	Employees might change their behavior because they know they are being observed

Questionnaires

Advantages:	Efficient and inexpensive
	Shows differences among incumbents in same job
	Easy to quantify and analyze statistically
	Easy to compare different jobs on common job dimensions
Limitations:	Ignores context in which job is done
	Limits respondent to questions asked
	Requires knowledge of job to design questionnaire
	Easy for job incumbents to distort to make their jobs seem more important

limitations of one are offset by the strengths of another. For example, a job analyst might do the job to get a feel for the context and then administer questionnaires to get detailed information from a wide cross section of employees with the same job title.

▶ METHODS OF JOB ANALYSIS

Many methods have been developed to conduct job analysis. These methods use the different sources of information and the different ways of collecting information. Some of the methods focus on either the job or the person, whereas others focus on both. The methods vary in their use of the four sources of job analysis information and the four ways of collecting information. Many of these methods use more than one source and more than one way of collecting information. One reason that so many methods exist is that they are not all suited to the same purposes. Levine, Ash, Hall, and Sistrunk (1983) found that job analysts rated different methods as being best suited to different purposes.

In this section we discuss four of the many job analysis methods. The Job Components Inventory, Functional Job Analysis, and the Position Analysis Questionnaire are general methods that can be used to compare different jobs; task inventories are used to provide a description of the specific components and tasks of individual jobs. Each method has its own particular strengths and was developed to address a particular purpose.

Job Components Inventory

The **Job Components Inventory (JCI)** was developed in Great Britain to address the need to match job requirements to worker characteristics (Banks, Jackson, Stafford, & Warr, 1983). This method allows for the simultaneous assessment of the job requirements and a person's KSAOs. In other words, the KSAOs for a job and for an individual are listed. The degree of correspondence of the lists is used to determine if an individual is suited to a particular job or needs additional training in order to perform a job adequately. The JCI has been used in school settings for both curriculum development and vocational guidance.

The JCI covers over 400 features of jobs that can be translated into skill requirements. Five components of job features are represented in the JCI:

1. Use of tools and equipment
2. Perceptual and physical requirements
3. Mathematics
4. Communication
5. Decision making and responsibility

Examples of the skill requirements for each of the five components for clerical jobs in Great Britain can be found in Table 3.4. Just about any job can be analyzed with the

TABLE 3.4 Examples of Frequently Needed Skills for British Clerical Occupations Grouped by the Five Components of the Job Components Inventory

Component	Skill
Use of tools and equipment	Use of pens
	Use of telephone
Perceptual and physical requirements	Selective attention
	Wrist/finger/hand speed
Mathematics	Use decimals
	Use whole numbers
Communication	Advise or help people
	Receive written information
Decision-making and responsibility	Decide on sequencing of work
	Decide on standards of work

Source: From "Skills Training for Clerical Work: Action Research Within the Youth Opportunities Programme," by M. H. Banks and E. M. Stafford, 1980, *BACIE Journal*, 37, 57–66.

TABLE 3.5   First and Last Entries in *Dictionary of Occupational Titles*, 4th Edition, 1977 Index*

ABALONE DIVER: Gathers or harvests marine life, such as sponges, abalone, pearl oysters, and geoducks from sea bottom wearing wet suit and scuba gear, or diving suit with air line extending to surface.

ZYGLO INSPECTOR: Applies iron oxide and zyglo solutions to ferrous metal parts and examines parts under fluorescent and black lighting to detect defects, such as fissures, weld breaks, or fractures.

*Condensed.

JCI, matching its skill requirements to those of potential employees. An existing database of job requirements for many jobs can be used with people who wish to know how well their own skills match those of a chosen career.

Functional Job Analysis

Functional Job Analysis (FJA) (Fine & Wiley, 1971) uses both observation and interviews with SMEs to provide a description of a job and scores on several dimensions concerning the job and potential workers. The dimensions are applicable to all jobs, so that the procedure can be used to make comparisons among jobs. FJA was the job analysis method used by the U.S. Department of Labor to produce the **Dictionary of Occupational Titles**, or DOT (U.S. Department of Labor, 1977, 1991). The DOT is a rather large document that contains job analysis information for more than 20,000 jobs. The index from the 1977 edition lists jobs from abalone diver to zyglo inspector, both of which are described in Table 3.5. The DOT description for the job of police officer is shown in Table 3.6. The DOT has been replaced with an expanded, electronic resource, O*NET.

Occupational Information Network, O*NET

Enlisting the help of many I/O psychologists from both research firms and universities, the **Occupational Information Network**, or **O*NET**, was launched by the U.S. Department of Labor in the 1990s, but its development and refinement is an ongoing process (Dorsey, 2001). This information system is a computer-based resource for job-related information on approximately 1,100 groups of jobs sharing common characteristics (Peterson, Mumford, Borman, Jeanneret, Fleishman, Levin, Campion, Mayfield, Morgeson, Pearlman, Gowing, Lancaster, Silver, & Dye, 2001). It is available in a number of forms, including a CD-ROM for the personal computer and via the World Wide

TABLE 3.6   Description of Police Officer Job From *Dictionary of Occupational Titles*, 4th Edition, 1977*

Patrols assigned beat to control traffic, prevent crime and arrest violators. Notes suspicious persons and establishments and reports to superior officer. Disperses unruly crowds at public gatherings. Issues tickets to traffic violators. May notify public works department of location of abandoned vehicles to tow away. May accompany parking meter personnel to protect money collected.

*Condensed.

TABLE 3.7   Sample of Information Provided By O*NET for Police Patrol Officer Job

Domain	Contents of Domain	Examples of Patrol Officer Information
Experience Requirements	Training, Learning, Licensing	Training in vocational schools, related on-the-job experience, or an associate's degree. May require a bachelor's degree
Worker Requirements	Basic skills, cross-functional skills, general knowledge, education	Skill in problem identification and speaking. Knowledge of public safety and law
Worker characteristics	Abilities, interests, work styles	Quick reaction time and far vision. Interested in work activities that assist other. Achievement oriented.
Occupation requirements	Generalized work activities, work context, organizational context	Working with the public, operating vehicles or equipment
Occupation-specific information	Occupational knowledge, occupation skills, tasks, machines, tools and equipment	Patrols specific area, maintains order, arrests perpetrator, monitors traffic
Occupation characteristics	Labor market information, occupation outlook, wages	Employment projects suggest an increase of 17.8% from 1996 to 2006, national median wages are $34,632.

Source: O*NET98 Database Files accessed with O*NET98 Viewer Version 1.0, U.S. Department of Labor.

Web (http://online.onetcenter.org). The idea is to make this database widely available to individuals and organizations.

O*NET began with much of the raw material that went into the DOT, but the contents of the O*NET are far more extensive than anything yet attempted. It provides a tremendous amount of information about the content of jobs and the KSAOs needed by individuals in those jobs. The *O*NET98 Data Dictionary* (U.S. Department of Labor, 1998) lists over 450 separate dimensions along which jobs are described and rated. Table 3.7 (column 1) shows the six domains of the O*NET content model. Half of the domains (Experience Requirements, Worker Requirements, and Worker Characteristics) list KSAOs. Occupation Requirements and Occupation Specific Information are concerned with characteristics of job tasks. Occupation Characteristics deal with other kinds of information concerning the labor market and wages for a job.

With O*NET it is possible to lookup a particular job and get a description and detailed information about the six domains. Although the underlying data are the same, the version for personal computers and the online version provide information in a somewhat different format. Table 3.7 shows a sample of the information provided for a police officer, organized by the six domains. The officer information overlaps with that provided by the Position Analysis Questionnaire (compare the third column of Table 3.7 with Table 3.9), which isn't surprising, because as Jeanneret and Strong (2003) showed, corresponding O*NET and PAQ dimension scores are strongly related.

TABLE 3.8   Major Categories of the PAQ

Category	Example
Information input	Collecting or observing information
Mediation processes	Decision-making and information processing
Work output	Manipulating objects
Interpersonal activities	Communicating with other people
Work situation and job context	Physical and psychological working conditions
Miscellaneous aspects	Work schedule

Source: From "A Study of Job Characteristics and Job Dimensions as Based on the Position Analysis Questionnaire (PAQ), by E. J. McCormick, P. R. Jeanneret, and R. C. Mecham, 1972, *Journal of Applied Psychology*, 56, 347–368.

Position Analysis Questionnaire

The **Position Analysis Questionnaire (PAQ)** (McCormick, Jeanneret, & Mecham, 1972) is an instrument that can be used to analyze any job. The questionnaire itself contains 189 items dealing with the task requirements or elements of jobs. A KSAO profile for a job can be developed from the elements. The elements of the PAQ are general and allow comparisons of different jobs on a common set of dimensions or KSAOs.

The elements of the PAQ are organized into six major categories, each of which is further divided into several minor categories (Table 3.8). The elements cover a wide variety of task requirements, including the inputting and processing of information, the use of equipment and tools, general bodily movements, interpersonal interaction, and work context. The elements can be translated into KSAOs for any job. A job that involves using mathematics, for example, requires skill in this area. Because the PAQ generates a standard list of KSAOs, jobs can be compared on their KSAO requirements.

The PAQ produces a profile of the task elements and KSAOs for a job. The profile compares a given job to the hundreds of jobs in the PAQ database. It indicates the percentile score for each element and KSAO in comparison to all jobs. A low score means that the element or KSAO is a less important part of the target job than it is for jobs in general. A high score means that the element or KSAO is a more important part of the target job than of jobs in general. A percentile of 50 means that the job is average on the element or dimension in question.

Table 3.9 contains a sample of the most important elements and KSAOs for the job of police officer. As the table shows, a police officer job involves engaging in general personal contact and wearing specified versus optional apparel. Table 3.9 also contains several sample KSAOs for the job of police officer. The two most important are far visual acuity and simple reaction time. Note that both of these were identified by O*NET as well.

Task Inventories

A **task inventory** is a questionnaire that contains a list of specific tasks that might be done on a job that is being analyzed. The inventory also contains one or more rating scales for each task. Ratings might be made on such dimensions as

Amount of time spent doing the task

Criticality of the task for doing a good job

TABLE 3.9   PAQ KSAOs, and Task Elements for a Police Officer

KSAOs	Task Elements
Far visual acuity	Interpreting what is sensed
Simple reaction time	Being aware of environmental conditions
Movement detection	Controlling machines and/or processes
Rate control	Engaging in general personal contact
Auditory acuity	Wearing specified versus optional apparel

Source: Job Profile, PAQ Number 003127, used by permission of PAQ Services.

Difficulty of learning the task

Importance of the task

Job incumbents usually are asked to complete the inventory for their own job. Results are compiled across incumbents to give a picture of the average importance or time spent for each task in a particular job.

When several people complete a task inventory, they are certain to give somewhat different ratings on the same dimensions for each task. This can reflect differences in how individuals make judgments about their jobs. In other words, if two people spend the same amount of time on a task, one might give it a higher time-spent rating than the other. An alternative possibility is that differences in ratings across people reflect real differences in tasks (Harvey & Wilson, 2000; Sanchez & Levine, 2000). There can be large differences in the content of jobs with the same title in the same organization. For example, Lindell, Clause, Brandt, and Landis (1998) found that the number of employees in the work unit (an emergency preparedness department) affected the ratings concerning amount of time spent in various tasks. It seems likely that the smaller the work group, the larger the number of tasks each person must perform.

Most task inventories are used for purposes in which differences among people with the same job are of no particular interest, but there are two notable exceptions. Conte, Dean, Ringenbach, Moran, and Landy (2005) showed that feelings about the job related to job analysis ratings. Individuals who were satisfied with their jobs reported spending more time on various tasks than people who were dissatisfied. Similarly, in a study of stockbrokers, ratings of time spent in several tasks predicted the individual's sales performance (Borman, Dorsey, & Ackerman, 1992). For example, stockbrokers who spent more time away from the office with clients sold more than their counterparts who spent less time (see the Research in Detail box). Whether the time spent is the cause or the result of good performance and satisfaction with the job is not totally clear in these studies. Further study is needed to determine why task inventory ratings vary among people.

A task inventory for even a fairly simple job can contain hundreds of tasks. To make interpretation easier, tasks are often placed into dimensions that represent the major components of a job. The dimensions for a police officer job that came from a task inventory are shown in Table 3.10. Each of these dimensions was associated with several specific tasks, and each task was rated by subject matter experts on a variety of different scales. A better understanding of this job can be gained by considering the individual tasks in the context of the major dimensions.

TABLE 3.10   Major Dimensions of Police Officer Job from a Task Analysis

Driving a car or other police vehicle	Investigating accidents and related problems
Making arrests	Issuing tickets and citations, such as those for traffic violations
Interviewing witnesses and other people	
Maintaining vigilance during routine patrol	Responding to disturbances, such as family quarrels
Writing reports	Providing service to citizens

Source: From *Selection of Police Officers, Report Supplement No. 1: Job Analysis*, by R. M. Guion and K. M. Alvares, 1980. Bowling Green, OH: Bowling Green State University.

RESEARCH IN DETAIL

Lack of agreement among raters of a task inventory is usually interpreted as lack of reliability. In this study the authors viewed disagreement from a different perspective. They believed that people in the same job would differ in the amount of time they spent on various tasks. Furthermore, the researchers believed that the time-spent differences might relate to sales performance of stockbrokers. In other words, people who are high performers might spend their time differently on the job than people who are low performers.

To test this idea, the authors conducted a job analysis with 580 stockbrokers as subject matter experts. Each one completed a task inventory with 160 tasks. Ratings of amount of time spent were made for each task. In addition, data were collected for each stockbroker's sales performance (dollars sold) for the prior year.

The amount of time spent in some of the tasks correlated significantly with sales performance. For example, the following tasks were associated with high sales:

Dealing with corporate clients and clients in non-business settings

Advising and helping other stockbrokers

The authors noted that it was tempting to conclude that their results suggest effective strategies for stockbrokers to adopt for good sales performance. They believed, however, that the strategies might be the effect rather than the cause of good performance. A stockbroker with many clients is likely to have many opportunities to spend time with them away from the office setting. He or she is also likely to have high sales volume because of the number of clients. A stockbroker with few clients has fewer opportunities for client contact outside the office setting or for sales. Thus, the activity of spending time with clients away from the office may not be the cause of high sales volume, but just the by-product of having many clients. The major contribution of this study is that it shows that there can be important differences among people in the same job. It might prove useful for job analysts to provide information to organizations about employee differences in time spent doing tasks.

Source: Borman, W. C., Dorsey, D. and Ackerman, L. (1992). Time-spent responses as time allocation strategies: Relations with sales performance in a stockbroker sample. *Personnel Psychology*, *45*, 763–777.

A task inventory often is a major component of an extensive job analysis project that collects several different types of information about jobs and people. Edward Levine's **Combination Job Analysis Method** (C-JAM) (Brannick et al., 2007) is one such approach. C-JAM uses both interviews and questionnaires to collect information about KSAOs and tasks. It produces a detailed picture of the KSAOs for a job and the tasks performed. Table 3.11 contains an example of several KSAOs for a police officer job analyzed with C-JAM.

TABLE 3.11 Examples of KSAOs for a police officer job analyzed with C-JAM

Knowledge of laws, statutes, ordinances (including types of crimes)	Skill in handling/maintaining handgun/shotgun
	Ability to enforce laws, statutes, ordinances
Knowledge of where/when to conduct interview/interrogation	Ability to take charge of a situation
	Integrity (moral/ethical/honesty)
Skill in operating special equipment (helicopter, boat, MDT, voice radio, etc.)	Courage

Source: From Job Analysis of Deputy Sheriff in the Pinellas County Sheriff's Office, by E. L. Levine and D. P. Baker, 1987, unpublished paper, University of South Florida, Tampa.

Choosing a Job Analysis Method

We have discussed only a few of the many available job analysis methods. With such a wide variety of methods, how can one choose? Each method has its own advantages and limitations, and not every method is appropriate for every application. Levine et al. (1983) asked job analysis experts to rate the effectiveness of seven job analysis methods for eleven purposes. Each method was better suited for some purposes than others. Functional Job Analysis was seen as being relatively effective for almost all purposes; however, it was also seen as one of the most time-consuming to complete. Choice of method requires consideration of several factors, including cost and purpose.

Job Analysis Methods for Work Teams

So far we have discussed job analysis methods that are designed for jobs done individually. However, more and more work in organizations is being done by teams rather than individuals, requiring the use of special job analysis methods. As pointed out by Brannick et al. (2007), team job analysis is similar to the other methods we have already discussed in that the same sources and data collection approaches can be adapted. However, there are specific KSAOs and tasks necessary for communication and coordination among team members. For example, Stevens and Campion (1999) note that teamwork requires special KSAOs related to communication, conflict resolution, goal setting, problem solving, and task coordination among team members.

► RELIABILITY AND VALIDITY OF JOB ANALYSIS INFORMATION

Job analysis information depends on the judgment of people who either do a job or observe others do it. People's judgments are imperfect, so it is important to determine how reliable and valid each job analysis method is. Many studies have addressed this issue for some methods. In general, results suggest that ratings of jobs by different people are often reasonably reliable. In other words, there will be a relatively high correlation among the ratings of the same job by different people for at least some job analysis methods. Validity is a more difficult question, and some researchers have begun to study the question of what job analysis ratings actually represent. In other words, are they accurate representations of task characteristics and KSAO requirements?

Reliability

Dierdorff and Wilson (2003) used meta-analysis (see Chapter 2) which allowed them to summarize the results of 46 studies that reported reliabilities for various job analysis methods. They found a mean test-retest reliability of .83, suggesting that people are quite consistent over time in making their job analysis ratings. Inter-rater agreement (whether or not different job analysts agree in their ratings) was somewhat lower, depending upon the types of raters (e.g., analysts vs. SMEs) and the dimensions being rated. Correlations among ratings by different people ranged from .48 to .81.

Several studies have examined the reliability of task inventory ratings. Wilson, Harvey, and Macy (1990) found that test-retest reliabilities varied considerably for different rating scales, such as amount of time spent doing the task or importance of the task. Although some reliabilities were very high, others were unacceptably low. Sanchez and Fraser (1992) found that inter-rater reliabilities among job incumbents varied across different rating scales and also across different jobs.

Taken together, the studies suggest that job analysis ratings can be reasonably reliable. As noted here, there are exceptions with task inventory ratings. Care should be taken in deciding which scales to use for rating tasks when job incumbents are the subject matter experts. The next question is whether or not job analysis ratings are valid.

Validity

The best evidence for the validity of job analysis ratings comes from studies that compared different methods or sources of information, such as incumbents versus supervisors. Spector, Brannick, and Coovert (1989) summarized the results of nine studies that reported correlations among methods or sources that ranged from .47 to .94. These results are suggestive of validity for job analysis ratings, but an intriguing study raises some doubts about the interpretation of source agreement. Smith and Hakel (1984) compared the PAQ ratings of trained job analysts with college students who were given only job titles. The students' ratings correlated very well with the ratings of the analysts. This seemed strange, because the analysts conducted in-depth interviews with incumbents, whereas the students were given limited information about the job. Smith and Hakel wondered if the analyst ratings reflected preconceived notions about the job rather than the information gathered with the job analysis procedures. If this is the case, then job analysis ratings might be less valid than I/O psychologists usually assume.

Other researchers who have studied the correspondence between ratings by students and trained job analysts have reached different conclusions. Cornelius, DeNisi, and Blencoe (1984) believe that students have accurate knowledge about many jobs; therefore, both job analysts and students can provide valid indicators of job information. Although students have accurate knowledge, more extensive information can be gathered in a thorough job analysis conducted by trained analysts (Cornelius et al., 1984).

Green and Stutzman (1986) conducted a job analysis in which they had job incumbents complete a task inventory. The task inventory included tasks that no one did on the job the researchers were analyzing. Over half of the incumbents indicated that they did at least one fake task. This finding suggests that many people are either careless or not completely honest when they complete task inventories. Whether or not this reduces the accuracy of the task inventory was not determined by this study. Hacker (1996), however, followed up on this research by conducting a similar study and comparing incumbents who endorsed fake tasks with those who did not. He found that the groups did not differ in their ratings of all other tasks or in the reliability of their ratings of all other tasks. His results suggest that this phenomenon does not affect job analysis results.

The research on the validity of job analysis ratings suggests that they can provide useful information, but they are not perfect and are potentially subject to some biases because they are based on human judgment (Morgeson & Campion, 1997; Morgeson Delaney-Klinger, Ferrara, Mayfield, & Campion, 2004). Green and Stutzman's (1986) results emphasize that incumbents are not necessarily accurate in making their ratings. Sanchez and Levine (1994) attempted to improve job analysis results by training incumbents in how to rate their jobs. Although their results were only partially successful, such training might prove useful in the future. Even though there is a need to improve job analysis procedures, the various methods are important tools used by I/O psychologists.

► JOB EVALUATION

Job evaluation refers to a family of quantitative techniques that are used to scientifically determine the salary levels of jobs (Morgeson, Campion, & Maertz, 1979). These techniques are very much like the job analysis methods we have already discussed. In fact, job analysis methods are sometimes used to conduct job evaluation. For example, Robinson, Wahlstrom, and Mecham (1974) used the PAQ to conduct a job evaluation. The major difference between job analysis and job evaluation is that job evaluation determines the relative salaries for different jobs by mathematically combining job information.

Perhaps the most popular job evaluation method is the **point method** (Treiman, 1979). There are four steps involved in conducting a point method job evaluation. First, a panel, often managers or other organization members, determines the compensable factors for the job. **Compensable factors** are characteristics that will serve as the basis for the evaluation. They include

Consequences of error on the job	Responsibility
Education required	Skill Required

Second, a panel (comprised of new people or the same people) judges the degree to which each job has each compensable factor. This is done on a quantitative scale so that each job gets points for each factor. A particular job, for example, might get 2 points out of a possible 20 for consequences of errors made and 20 points out of a possible 20 for education. This means that the job would be low on consequences for error and high on education level required. Third, the points for the factors are summed for each job to provide a total score. In this example, the job would get a total of 22 points (2 + 20) for the two factors. These numbers are not in dollar units, and so they do not indicate the actual salary level. Rather, the numbers are relative, so that the higher the number, the higher the salary the job should have.

The fourth and final step is to plot the actual salaries for each job against the point totals for each job. If the salary system is fair according to the compensable factors, the plot should be a straight line. This means that the higher the points, the higher the salary. If the point for a particular job is not on the straight line, the job is either overpaid (point is above the line) or underpaid (point is below the line). Steps can then be taken to bring the job in line with the other jobs with similar totals. Jobs that are paid too much according to the system can have salaries frozen. Jobs that are paid too little can be given salary increases.

Although the job evaluation can indicate the relative value of a job, other factors enter into salary levels. One of the biggest influences is the market wage for a job. A hospital is likely to find, for example, that physicians are overpaid in relation to nurses. However, it would not be feasible for a hospital to set salaries completely according to compensable factors. The cost of paying nurses much higher salaries would be prohibitive. Paying physicians much lower wages would result in not being able to hire or retain them. Thus, the wages paid throughout the area or country must be considered. A salary survey can be conducted to find out what other organizations pay each position. To conduct such a survey, all hospitals in the area could be contacted to determine their salary levels for nurses and physicians.

The point system is just one of many different job evaluation methods. There are also several varieties of point systems. They are all used to determine the pay levels of jobs by estimating their comparative worth. Research on the various methods suggests that they may be interchangeable. Studies have shown that the results of different methods are often quite similar (e.g., Gomez-Mejia, Page, & Tornow, 1982).

Comparable Worth

It is well known that in the United States and other countries women's salaries are lower on average than men's. Some of the differences are attributable to the fact that jobs held primarily by women, such as secretary, are paid less than jobs held primarily by men, such as electrician (Allen & Sanders, 1985). Although the Equal Pay Act of 1963 made it illegal to pay a woman less than a man for the same job, there is no law preventing an organization from paying a woman less than a man in a different job.

The concept of **comparable worth** means that different but comparable jobs should be paid the same. If jobs that are held predominantly by women contribute as much to the organization as jobs held primarily by men, the jobs should be paid the same. The difficulty is finding a common measure by which to gauge the comparable worth of jobs. Job evaluation provides a means of doing so.

To do a comparable worth study with job evaluation, one would first apply one of the methods to the jobs of an organization. Those jobs that are held primarily by men would be compared to those held primarily by women. In many instances, the women's jobs would likely be underpaid according to the compensable factors. Using mathematical procedures, it would be possible to calculate how much adjustment each of the underpaid jobs should receive. If made, those adjustments could accomplish comparable worth between the predominantly female and predominantly male jobs.

The use of job evaluation to establish comparable worth has not been without critics (e.g., Eyde, 1983). Part of the difficulty is that the judgments used in a job evaluation can be biased in ways that perpetuate the lower salaries of women. For example, Schwab and Grams (1985) found that people who assign points to jobs in organizations are influenced by knowledge of current salaries. As a result, lower paid jobs are given fewer points than they deserve, and higher paid jobs are given more points than they deserve. Job evaluations might undervalue lower paid predominantly female jobs and overvalue the higher paid predominantly male jobs.

Perhaps the biggest impediment to achieving comparable worth is not bias in job evaluation, but the cost of substantially raising salaries in predominantly female occupations, such as clerk and elementary school teacher. Adjusting these salaries would be extremely expensive unless it was accompanied by reductions in the salaries of other jobs. In addition, there is the issue of market wages, which is a major influence on the salary levels set by organizations. Although some progress has been made in the United States, it seems unlikely that comparable worth will be achieved in the near future.

► FUTURE ISSUES AND CHALLENGES

Job analysis is one of the most frequently used tools of practicing I/O psychologists. Therefore, we might expect that a lot of research has been conducted on its accuracy and validity. This is not the case, however; on the contrary, most research on job analysis has been concerned with developing new methods rather than studying the validity of old methods. There is a need for more research on the validity of methods, for the existing research has raised some alarming questions. The human judgments on which job analysis is based are imperfect. To understand job analysis better and to improve it, we need to understand the judgment process (Morgeson & Campion, 1997).

Several approaches could be taken to improve the accuracy of job analysis judgments. Morgeson and Campion (1997) provide a number of suggestions for reducing bias and inaccuracy. For example, they suggest that job incumbents will be more motivated to distort their ratings than job analysts. Incumbents might inflate their ratings of how often important tasks are performed (arrest suspects) and deflate ratings of seemingly less important tasks (take a coffee break). Although many of their propositions have never been tested, Morgeson and Campion provide a reasonable prescription for maximizing job analysis accuracy.

Rater training is another area of possible research. A better understanding of how people make their ratings would suggest useful ways of training raters. It may be that accuracy could be increased with training. Perhaps the inaccurate raters who endorse tasks they do not do on task inventories could benefit from training.

In the future, there are likely to be increased calls to help organizations keep actions that affect employees, such as promotions and selection, job relevant. The present worldwide trend toward fairness in actions that affect people will require the use of job analysis. A job analysis can help ensure that decisions about who to hire or promote will be based on the KSAOs for a job rather than arbitrary or discriminatory criteria. Job analysis is being used for this purpose extensively, especially in the United States. This use is likely to spread throughout the world in the future.

It is surprising that so far little use has been made of electronic tools for conducting job analysis (Sanchez, 2000). Sanchez points out that in many organizations, many employee functions that are done by computer are monitored electronically. These electronic records can be used to get a more accurate picture of the time spent in various activities than is obtained using SME ratings. Sanchez also suggests that Web-based approaches can be used to facilitate both job analysis interviews and questionnaires.

A final trend is a shift toward focusing more on describing competencies (attributes that distinguish high from low performers) rather than on what are often minimum KSAO requirements found in a typical job analysis. The competency modeling trend, although fitting our definition of job analysis, represents a somewhat new direction. As noted by Schippmann, Ash, Battista, Carr, Eyde, Hesketh, Kehoe, Pearlman, Prien, and Sanchez (2000), the increasingly competitive corporate environment has challenged the field to pay attention not just to the KSAOs a person needs at a minimum, but to the characteristics that describe the outstanding employee who is able to maximize performance.

▶ **CHAPTER SUMMARY**

Job analysis is a method for describing jobs and the personal attributes necessary to do jobs. The job-oriented approach provides information about the nature of a job and the tasks involved in a job. The person-oriented approach describes the KSAOs (knowledge, skills, abilities, and other personal characteristics) a person must have for a job. There are dozens of job analysis methods that provide information about either the job, the person, or both.

Job analysis information has many purposes. It can be used for

Career development of employees

Legal issues, such as ensuring fairness in actions affecting employees

Performance appraisal

Selection

Training

Vocational counseling

Research

Most job analysis information comes from one of four different sources:

Job analysts   Supervisors
Job incumbents   Trained observers

They obtain information in one of the following ways:

Performing the job themselves

Interviewing people who do the job

Observing people doing the job

Giving questionnaires to people who do the job

Many different methods can be used to conduct a job analysis; no one method stands out as being superior to the others. Each has its particular advantages and limitations. The job analyst's purpose should be to determine which method is chosen. Four popular methods are:

Job Components Inventory

Functional Job Analysis

Position Analysis Questionnaire

Task Inventories

Most job analysis methods have been found to be reasonably reliable. Inadequate research attention has been given to exploring their validity. Existing research has shown promise, but there is evidence that people are not always accurate in their job analysis ratings. More attention should be directed to studying ways to increase the accuracy of job analysis information.

Job evaluation is one of a family of techniques that are used to set salary levels. Job evaluation procedures are much like job analysis, and often job analysis methods are used to conduct job evaluations. Research suggests that many of the different job evaluation techniques give similar results when applied to the same jobs. Job evaluation has been used in an attempt to reduce the salary inequities between men and women. The concept of comparable worth means that jobs that make equivalent contributions to organizations should be paid the same.

I/O PSYCHOLOGY IN PRACTICE

(*Courtesy Joan Brannick*)

This case deals with a job analysis conducted by Dr. Joan Brannick as part of a collaborative effort to validate a selection test for supermarket warehouse employees. Brannick received her Ph.D. in I/O psychology in 1987 from Bowling Green State University. She is currently president of Brannick HR Connections, a human resources consulting company based in Tampa, Florida. The company helps organizations improve employee retention by working with organizations to create, implement, and evaluate selection and promotion processes that assess job-fit and culture-fit. Prior to starting Brannick HR Connections in 1995, Brannick worked for Eckerd Corporation, which at the time was one of the largest drugstore chains in the United States. It is a common career path for I/O psychologists to work for several years for a private corporation and then start their own consulting business.

A national supermarket chain hired Brannick to be part of a team that developed and validated a selection test for warehouse workers. A testing company that specializes in physical agility testing actually designed the test. The client wanted an independent consultant to do the initial job analysis that would indicate what sort of test was needed, and then to do the validation to show whether the test worked. The client was concerned about potential conflict of interest if the testing company were to do the entire project, especially the validation. Brannick was hired to provide an objective expert's point of view. It is quite common for I/O consultants from different companies to work together, each doing a separate piece of a complete job.

The job in question involved the filling of orders received from individual stores. Each day supermarkets would submit orders for various products. Warehouse employees filled these orders by loading products into large plastic tote boxes at the warehouse and shipping these totes by truck to the stores. The job required physical agility, because various items had to be taken from shelves and put into totes by hand. Brannick used an observational method of job analysis. She took a tour of the warehouse, and then spent many hours watching employees and recorded the specific physical motions required. There were three in particular that were important: grasping (picking up an item with all fingers and thumb of one hand), lifting (picking up an item with both hands), and pinching (picking up an item with index finger and thumb only). After the specific motions were determined, the testing company designed the actual psychomotor test (see Chapter 5) to determine how well applicants were able to perform the required motions.

Once the test was developed, it was administered to 350 employees. Brannick trained supervisors to rate the quality of their employees' job performance. Objective performance data were also collected on absenteeism and the number of totes per day each employee filled. She then conducted statistical data analysis to see if the test could predict how well employees performed their jobs. This study was successful in showing that the test was valid; in other words, test performance significantly predicted job performance. The test is being used today to help select warehouse workers.

Discussion Questions

1. Why was it important to conduct a job analysis before developing the test?

2. Would a questionnaire job analysis method of asking employees or supervisors what motions were needed have been as effective?

3. How would this job analysis help a company if it was sued for discriminating against a disabled person?

4. Why was it important to conduct a validation study?

LEARNING BY DOING

Conducting a Job Analysis Interview

One way to conduct a job analysis is to interview employees who hold the job in question. During the interview you would ask them to describe their jobs, the specific tasks involved in their jobs, and the KSAOs needed to do the job. Choose a person you know (acquaintance, family member, or friend) who is currently employed in a job you have never held yourself. Interview this person about the job, taking careful notes of what you are told. You might ask them to provide the following information:

1. Job title
2. The general function and purpose of the job.
3. Brief description or overview of the job.
4. The most important tasks involved in the job.
5. The most important KSAOs needed for the job.

Write a brief report that provides an overview of what you learned about the job.

Using O*NET

The O*NET is a good place to find job analysis information about a job. This free resource can be found on the Web at www.online.onetcenter.org. It allows you to enter the name of a job, and provides information about tasks, KSAOs and more.

Choose a job that you think you might like to do once you graduate from college. Go to the O*NET Web site and enter the job. Find the summary report that lists information about the job. Write a brief report that describes the major tasks for the job, the KSAOs that are needed, and the context. Answer the following questions about the job.

1. What preparation is needed for the job?
2. Is a college degree necessary?
3. What work values are addressed by the job?
4. What is the future outlook for employment growth in this occupation?

4

Performance Appraisal

CHAPTER 4 OUTLINE

Imagine that you are a manager for a large organization and you are given the task of determining how well your subordinates are doing their jobs. How would you go about appraising their job performance to see who is and who is not doing a good job? Would you watch them as they perform their jobs? If you did watch them, how would you know what to look for? Some people seem to work very hard but in fact accomplish little that contributes to the organization's objectives. For many jobs it might not be readily apparent how well a person is doing just by observing, unless you have a good idea of what constitutes good job performance. Performance is best appraised by measuring a person's work against a criterion or standard of comparison.

In this chapter we are concerned with issues involved in the appraisal of employee job performance. First, there is the issue of the criterion, or standard of comparison, by which performance is judged and measured. Before we can appraise performance, we must have a clear idea of what good performance is. Once we know that, we can address the second issue of developing a procedure to assess it. Performance appraisal is a two-step process of first defining what is meant by good performance (criteria development) and then implementing a procedure to appraise employees by determining how well they meet the criteria. Before we discuss criteria and procedures for appraising performance, we look at the major reasons for engaging in this potentially time-consuming activity.

Objectives: The student who studies this chapter should be able to:

▶ List the uses of job performance information.

▶ Discuss the importance of criteria for performance appraisal.

▶ Describe the various methods of performance appraisal, as well as their advantages and limitations.

▶ Discuss how to conduct a legally defensible performance appraisal.

▶ WHY DO WE APPRAISE EMPLOYEES?

The first question that we address is the rationale for organizations to appraise the performance of their employees. Performance appraisal can be a time-consuming chore that most managers and their subordinates dislike. Why then do most large organizations appraise employee job performance at least once per year? The reason is that job performance data can benefit both employees and organizations. Performance data can be used for administrative decisions, employee development and feedback, and research to determine the effectiveness of organizational practices and procedures.

Administrative Decisions

Many administrative decisions that affect employees are based, at least in part, on their job performance. Most large organizations use job performance as the basis for punishments and rewards. Punishments can include both demotion and termination (firing), and some organizations have policies that require the firing of employees whose performance is unsatisfactory. Rewards can include promotion and pay raises, and many organizations have merit pay systems that tie raises to the level of job performance.

The basis for using job performance data for administrative decisions can be found in both contract and law. A union contract will often specify that job performance is the basis for particular administrative decisions, such as pay raises. A contract can also state that performance appraisals will not be done. Civil service (government) employees in the United States can be fired only for unsatisfactory job performance or violation of work rules. Rule violations include assaulting a co-worker, being convicted of a felony, falling asleep on the job, or not showing up for work when scheduled. Even so, many fired government employees have been reinstated because of long records of satisfactory performance on the job. The United States is not the only country that has laws requiring administrative decisions to be based on job performance. In Canada, for example, the legal requirement that employee firing must be based on job performance has been extended to private companies as well as the government.

Employee Development and Feedback

In order for employees to improve and maintain their job performance and job skills, they need job performance feedback from their supervisors. One of the major roles of supervisors is to provide information to their subordinates about what is expected on the job and how well they are meeting these expectations. Employees need to know when they are performing well so that they can continue to do so, and when they are not so that they can change what they are doing. Even employees who are performing well on the job can benefit from feedback about how to perform even better. Feedback can also be helpful in telling employees how to enhance their skills to move up to higher positions. A new trend is for companies to go beyond the once per year evaluation by designing a comprehensive performance management system. In addition to the annual appraisal, such systems can include goal setting and periodic coaching and feedback sessions between employee and supervisor. Whereas the annual review might be used for administrative purposes, the interim reviews would be used only for feedback, thus reducing some of the anxiety and defensiveness employees experience when being evaluated for raises and promotions. The performance management system at Wachovia Bank is described in the I/O in Practice case in this chapter.

Criteria for Research

Many of the activities of practicing I/O psychologists concern the improvement of employee job performance. The efforts of I/O psychologists can be directed toward designing better equipment, hiring better people, motivating employees, and training employees. Job performance data can serve as the criterion against which such activities are evaluated. To do so, one can conduct a research study. A common design for such a study involves comparing employee performance before and after the implementation of a new program designed to enhance it. A better design would be an experiment in which one group of employees receives a new procedure while a control group of employees does not. The two groups could be compared to see whether the group receiving the new procedure had better job performance than the control group. Better job performance by the trained group would serve as good evidence for the effectiveness of the training program.

▶ PERFORMANCE CRITERIA

A criterion is a standard against which you can judge the performance of anything, including a person. It allows you to distinguish good from bad performance. Trying to assess performance without criteria is like trying to help a friend find a lost object when the friend will not tell you what it is. You cannot be of much help until you know what it is you are looking for. In a similar way, you cannot adequately evaluate someone's job performance until you know what the performance should be.

Characteristics of Criteria

Actual Versus Theoretical Criteria

Criteria can be classified as either actual or theoretical. A theoretical criterion is a definition of what good performance is rather than how it is measured. In research terminology, a **theoretical criterion** is a theoretical construct. It is the idea of what good performance is. An **actual criterion** is the way in which the theoretical criterion is assessed or operationalized. It is the performance appraisal technique that is used, such as counting a salesperson's sales.

Table 4.1 contains theoretical and corresponding actual criteria for five different jobs. As can be seen, both types of criteria can be quite different for some jobs. For others, the correspondence between the theoretical and actual criteria is quite close. For example, for an insurance salesperson, the theoretical criterion is to sell, and the actual criterion is a count of the sales the person made. For an artist, the correspondence is not as close. The theoretical criterion of producing great works of art is matched to the actual criterion of asking art experts for an opinion about the person's work. In this case there is room for subjectivity about who is deemed an art expert and about the expert judgments of what is and is not good art. As these cases illustrate, the criteria for different jobs may require quite different assessment approaches.

Contamination, Deficiency, and Relevance

Our actual criteria are intended to assess the underlying theoretical criteria of interest. In practice, however, our actual criteria are imperfect indicators of their intended theoretical performance criteria. Even though an actual criterion might assess a piece of the intended theoretical criterion, there is likely some part of the theoretical criterion that is left out. On the other hand, the actual criterion can be biased and can assess something other than the theoretical criterion. Thus, the actual criterion often provides only a rough estimate of the theoretical criterion it is supposed to assess.

Three concepts help explain this situation: criterion contamination, criterion deficiency, and criterion relevance. **Criterion contamination** refers to that part of the actual criterion that reflects something other than what it was designed to measure. Contamination can arise from biases in the criterion and from unreliability. Biases are common when people's judgments and opinions are used as the actual criterion. For example, using the judgments of art experts as the actual criterion for the quality of someone's art work can reveal as much about the biases of the judges as it does about the work

TABLE 4.1   Examples of Theoretical and Actual Criteria for Five Jobs

Job	Theoretical Criterion	Actual Criterion
Artist	Create great works of art	Judgments of art experts
Insurance salesperson	Sell insurance	Monthly sales
Store clerk	Provide good service to customers	Survey of customer satisfaction with service
Teacher	Impart knowledge to students	Student achievement test scores
Weather forecaster	Accurately predict the weather	Compare predictions to actual weather

itself. Because there are no objective standards for the quality of art, experts will likely disagree with one another when their judgments are the actual criteria for performance.

Unreliability in the actual criterion refers to errors in measurement that occur any time we try to assess something. As discussed in Chapter 2, measurement error is part of the measurement process and consists of random errors that make our measurements inaccurate. It is reflected in the inconsistency in measurement over time. If we were to repeatedly assess the job performance of someone over time, the measure of performance would vary from testing to testing even if the performance (theoretical criterion) remained constant. This means that our actual performance criterion measures will have less than perfect reliabilities.

Criterion deficiency means that the actual criterion does not adequately cover the entire theoretical criterion. In other words, the actual criterion is an incomplete representation of what we are trying to assess. This concept was referred to in Chapter 2 as content validity. For example, the mathematics achievement test scores of their students could be used as an actual performance criterion for elementary school teachers. It would be a deficient criterion because elementary school teachers teach more than just mathematics. A less deficient criterion would be student scores on a comprehensive achievement test battery, including mathematics, reading, science, and writing.

Criterion relevance is the extent to which the actual criterion assesses the theoretical criterion it is designed to measure, or its construct validity (see Chapter 2). The closer the correspondence between the actual and theoretical criteria, the greater the relevance of the actual criterion. All of the actual criteria in Table 4.1 have some degree of relevance for assessing their intended theoretical criterion. Theoretical criteria can be quite abstract, such as producing great works of art; therefore, it can be difficult to determine the relevance of a criterion. As with the validity of any assessment device, relevance concerns the inferences and interpretations we make about the meaning of our measurements of performance.

Criterion contamination, deficiency, and relevance are illustrated in Figure 4.1. The actual criterion is represented by the lower circle, and the theoretical criterion is represented by the upper circle. The overlap between the two circles (shaded area) represents the extent to which the actual criterion is assessing the theoretical, which is criterion

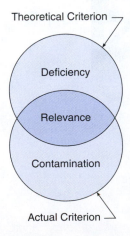

Theoretical Criterion

Deficiency

Relevance

Contamination

Actual Criterion

Figure 4.1 Criterion contamination, relevance, and deficiency. The lower circle represents the actual criterion, and the upper circle represents the theoretical criterion. Contamination is the part of the actual criterion (nonshaded area) that does not overlap the theoretical criterion. Deficiency is the part of the theoretical criterion that is not overlapped by the actual criterion (nonshaded area). Relevance is represented by the overlap between the actual and theoretical criteria (shaded area).

relevance. The part of the lower circle that does not overlap the theoretical criterion (unshaded area) is either contamination, if the actual criterion is assessing something else, or measurement error. The part of the upper circle that does not overlap the lower (unshaded area) is criterion deficiency because part of the theoretical criterion is not assessed.

Level of Specificity

Most jobs are complex and involve many different functions and tasks. Job performance criteria can be developed for individual tasks or for entire jobs. For some purposes, it may be better to assess performance on an individual task, such as making arrests for a police officer, or selling products for a salesperson, whereas for other purposes the person's entire job performance is of interest. For developing an employee's skills, it is better to focus at the individual task level so that feedback can be specific. The employee might be told that he or she types too slowly or makes too many errors. This sort of specific feedback can be helpful for an employee who wishes to improve performance. For administrative purposes, overall job performance might be of more concern. The person who gets promoted might be the one whose overall performance has been

It takes close observation to see how well an employee is doing the job.

(*Arvind Garg/Photo Researchers*)

the best. The particular methods used to assess performance should be based on the purposes of the assessment information.

Criterion Complexity

Because most jobs involve multiple tasks, and most tasks can be evaluated from several perspectives, criteria can become quite complex. Job performance even on a single task can usually be assessed along a quality dimension (how well the worker does the job) and a quantity dimension (how much or how quickly the worker does the job). The complexity of job performance means that multiple criterion measures are necessary to assess performance adequately. These might involve only quality, only quantity, or both. The measures can be at the level of specificity of a single task or at the level of the entire job. The nature of the job and the purposes of the assessment information determine the nature of the criteria that are used as well as the level of specificity.

The nature of some jobs requires that quality be the major focus, whereas for others quantity may take priority. In athletics, sometimes one or the other serves as the criterion for winning a competition. In gymnastics, quality is the criterion used. Judges score each gymnast's performance along a quality dimension, and the athlete with the highest score wins. In track and field events, the criterion is concerned with quantity—jumping farthest, jumping highest, running fastest, or throwing farthest. The quality of jumping form or running style form is not relevant, and so there are no judges to rate performance in these events. With jobs there can be an emphasis on quality or on quantity, often depending on the nature of the tasks involved. For a sales job, the emphasis is usually on the quantity of sales, whereas for a teacher it is on the quality of instruction.

There are many other possible criteria beyond work quality and quantity. Table 4.2 contains a performance appraisal form that has eight rather general criteria that are relevant to many jobs. For example, maintaining a professional appearance on the job is relevant when public image is important. Many organizations expect employees who meet the public to display a certain image. This might involve a dress code that specifies the sort of clothing that is appropriate for work, such as a business suit. Factories can have dress codes that are concerned not with public image but with safety. Ties are often

TABLE 4.2   Example of a Performance Appraisal form with Eight Criterion Dimensions

Dimension	Rating Categories				
	Poor	Fair	Adequate	Good	Outstanding
Attendance	_____	_____	_____	_____	_____
Communicating with others	_____	_____	_____	_____	_____
Following directions	_____	_____	_____	_____	_____
Instructing others	_____	_____	_____	_____	_____
Motivating others	_____	_____	_____	_____	_____
Professional appearance	_____	_____	_____	_____	_____
Work quality	_____	_____	_____	_____	_____
Work quantity	_____	_____	_____	_____	_____

forbidden because they could get caught in machinery, resulting in a serious accident and injury.

There are two ways to deal with the complex nature of criteria. The **composite criterion approach** involves combining individual criteria into a single score. If employees receive a number to represent performance on each of four dimensions, a composite would be the sum of the four dimension scores for each employee. An employee who received the following performance scores on a 1 to 5 scale:

Attendance = 5	Work quality = 4
Professional appearance = 4	Work quantity = 5

would have a composite performance score of 18—the sum of the dimension scores (5 + 4 + 4 + 5). A grade point average would be a composite score for school performance. The **multidimensional approach** does not combine the individual criterion measures. In the previous example, there would be four scores per employee.

The composite approach is preferred for comparing the performance of individual employees. It is easier to compare employees when each has a single performance score. The multidimensional approach is preferred when feedback is given to employees. It gives specific information about the various dimensions of performance rather than general feedback about overall performance.

Dynamic Criteria

Criteria are usually considered to be constant or static standards by which employee performance can be judged. Some I/O psychologists believe, however, that job performance itself is variable over time. This means that the best performer on the job at one point in time will not be best at another point in time. Performance variability makes assessment difficult because the performance would not have been the same throughout the entire measurement time period. How should we assess the performance of someone who performs well for part of the year and not well for the other part?

Variability of performance over time is referred to as the **dynamic criterion**, although it is the performance and not the standard that changes. The dynamic criterion idea has generated some controversy among I/O psychologists: Some believe that performance is stable, and others suggest that it is not (Schmitt & Chan, 1998). On the one hand, Deadrick and Madigan (1990) provide data with sewing machine operators in a clothing factory showing that performance was stable over short periods of time (weeks) but was not very consistent over long periods of time (months). On the other hand, Vinchur, Schippmann, Smalley, and Rothe (1991) found that job performance of manufacturing employees was reasonably stable over a five-year time span. Deadrick, Bennett, and Russell (1997) pointed out that employee performance tends to improve over time, at least early in an employee's tenure, and that the factors that determine performance of new employees are not necessarily the same as those that determine later performance improvement. Furthermore, Hofmann, Jacobs, and Baratta (1993) showed that different people have different patterns of performance over time. Some of their newly hired insurance salespeople tended to increase performance over the entire three-year study, whereas others increased at first and then leveled off. Looking at all these studies leads to the conclusion that people's performance over time can be variable, and that people differ in their patterns of performance variability.

Contextual Performance

Criteria for most jobs concern tasks that are specifically required and are certainly listed in a job analysis of the job. However, it has been recognized that employees do a great deal more for organizations than what is required, and these extra behaviors are essential for organizations to function smoothly. **Contextual performance** consists of extra, voluntary things employees do to benefit their coworkers and organizations, such as volunteering to carry out extra tasks or helping a coworker (Borman, Buck, Hanson, Motowidlo, Stark, & Drasgow, 2001). Although not specifically required, contextual performance is noticed and appreciated by managers, and their ratings of subordinate performance will be affected by it (Johnson, 2001). This all suggests that contextual performance should be considered in developing criteria for jobs. We will return to the issue of contextual performance in Chapter 10 when we discuss organizational citizenship behavior.

► METHODS FOR ASSESSING JOB PERFORMANCE

The job performance of individuals can be assessed in many ways. The most common procedures can be divided into two categories—objective performance measures and subjective judgments. **Objective measures** are counts of various behaviors (e.g., number of days absent from work) or the results of job behaviors (e.g., total monthly sales). **Subjective measures** are ratings by people who should be knowledgeable about the person's job performance. Usually supervisors provide job performance ratings of their subordinates. Both types of measures can be useful, but studies in which both are assessed on the same employees have shown that they don't always agree on the level of performance (Sundvik & Lindeman, 1998; see International Replication), suggesting that they reflect different aspects of job performance. Both objective and subjective measures will be presented in the following discussion.

INTERNATIONAL REPLICATION

An important issue in performance appraisal concerns the accuracy of supervisor ratings. In this study the researchers had available not only supervisor ratings but data on objective performance with which to compare them.

This study was conducted in Finland in a state-owned company that provided banking and transportation services. Participants were 208 supervisors who together rated the performance of 268 female salespersons. For each salesperson, data were collected on the actual sales productivity during the prior year.

In addition, each salesperson was rated by her supervisor on a five point rating scale ranging from poor (1) to very good (5). Because the nature of each measure was different, each was standardized to a mean of zero and standard deviation of 1. Thus a salesperson with average productivity should have a score of zero, and her supervisor rating would also be expected to be zero. By comparing the scores for each salesperson, the researchers were able to determine whether the supervisor underrated, overrated, or accurately rated the salesperson.

The results found that roughly a third of the ratings fell into each of the accuracy categories, although there were somewhat more overratings than underratings. This should not be surprising, because rating leniency is quite common. Supervisors had a tendency to overrate those employees they knew best, perhaps suggesting there was some favoritism toward subordinates who had developed good working relationships with their supervisors. Furthermore, the study found that female supervisors gave more accurate ratings than male supervisors.

These findings show that most ratings of performance are not accurate when compared to objective performance, and that the relationship a supervisor has with a subordinate affects ratings. However, it should be kept in mind that this was a case in which performance had an objective and quantifiable outcome—sales. In cases in which there is no such standard, we might expect accuracy to suffer even more. Furthermore, the ratings here were done solely for the purposes of the research, and are likely to be more accurate than ratings done for administrative purposes, where subordinates might suffer consequences from less than outstanding evaluations.

Source: Sundvik, L., and Lindeman, M. (1998). Performance rating accuracy: Convergence between supervisor assessment and sales productivity. *International Journal of Selection and Assessment*, 6, 9–15.

Objective Measures of Job Performance

Organizations keep track of many employee behaviors and results of behavior. Human resource departments record the number of absences, accidents, incidents, and latenesses for each employee. Some organizations also keep track of the productivity of each employee. Productivity data must be collected if an organization has an incentive system that pays employees for what they produce, such as a commission or piece-rate.

Five common objective measures of job performance are listed in Table 4.3. Each is an objective count of the number of behaviors or amount of work produced. Such data are usually found in organization records, but they can be collected specifically to assess performance. Two of the measures are concerned with attendance—number of times absent and number of times late for work. Accidents can be either automotive or nonautomotive, such as being injured by a machine in a factory. Incidents are the number of times the individual is involved in a work incident that is considered important for the particular job. For example, in a psychiatric inpatient facility, the number of times a staff person is assaulted by a patient is recorded in an incident report. For police officers, shooting incidents become part of the employee's record. Productivity is the amount of work produced by an individual.

Attendance measures are almost always applicable because the majority of jobs have scheduled work hours. For jobs that are unstructured in terms of work schedule (e.g., college professor), attendance is not a criterion for job performance. The other three

TABLE 4.3   Examples of Objective Measures of Job Performance

Absences	Days Absent Per Year
Accidents	Number of accidents per year
Incidents at work (e.g., assaults)	Number of incidents per year
Latenesses	Days late per year
Productivity (e.g., sales)	Dollar amount of sales

TABLE 4.4 Examples of Objective Productivity Measures for Several Jobs

Job	Measure
Assembly line worker	Number of units produced
College professor	Number of publications
Lawyer	Number of cases won
Salesperson	Amount of sales
Surgeon	Number of operations performed

objective measures are specific to a particular job. For example, the type of incidents recorded is a function of the nature of the job and the job environment. Records of assaults by students might be kept for urban public school teachers, but they are not likely to be kept for college professors. Teachers are assaulted relatively frequently in large American cities, but college professors are rarely the target for violence. The productivity measure chosen must match the nature of the work done. Specific productivity measures for some common jobs are listed in Table 4.4. As you can see, the nature of productivity can be very different from job to job. This makes it difficult to compare the performances of people who hold different jobs.

Using objective measures to assess job performance has several advantages. First, it can be easy to interpret the meaning of objective measures in relation to job performance criteria. For example, it is obvious that no absences in the past year is a good indicator of satisfactory attendance, but four work-related traffic accidents in the prior six months is an indicator of unsatisfactory driving performance. Second, the quantitative nature of objective measures makes it easy to compare the job performance of different individuals in the same job. For attendance measures, comparisons can be made of individuals across different jobs, as long as all the jobs require that employees work on a particular schedule. Third, objective measures can be tied directly to organizational objectives, such as making a product or providing a service. Finally, objective measures can often be found in organizational records, so that special performance appraisal systems do not have to be initiated. These data often are collected and stored, frequently in computers, for reasons other than employee performance appraisal, making performance appraisal a relatively easy task to accomplish.

Unfortunately, objective performance measures also have several limitations. Many of the objective measures are not appropriate for all jobs. When jobs do not involve countable output, productivity is not a feasible measure of performance. Also, it is not always obvious what number is considered satisfactory performance. For example, how many absences per year should be considered good performance? Data taken from records can be contaminated and inaccurate. Sometimes behaviors and productivity are attributed to the wrong person or are never recorded. People can also distort records by omitting bad incidents for individuals who are being favored, and employees might fail to report accidents and injuries.

Objective measures are often deficient as indicators of job performance criteria. They tend to focus on specific behaviors, which may be only part of the criterion, and they may ignore equally important parts. Measures of productivity focus on work quantity rather than quality. Although quantity might be more important in some jobs, it is difficult to imagine a job in which quality is not also somewhat important. Finally, what is reflected in an objective measure is not necessarily under the control of the individual being assessed. Differences in the productivity of factory workers can be caused by differences in the machinery they use, and differences in the sales performance of salespeople can be caused by differences in their sales territories. A person who is assaulted at work may have done nothing wrong and may have been unable to avoid the incident. A police officer who uses a weapon might have been forced into it by circumstances rather than poor job performance. In using objective measures to assess individuals, these other factors should be taken into account.

Subjective Measures of Job Performance

Subjective measures are the most frequently used means of assessing the job performance of employees. Most organizations require that supervisors complete annual performance appraisal rating forms on each of their subordinates. There are many types of rating forms that different organizations use to assess the performance of their employees. In this section, we discuss several different types.

Graphic Rating Form

The most popular type of subjective measure is the **graphic rating form**, which is used to assess individuals on several dimensions of performance. The graphic rating form focuses on characteristics or traits of the person or the person's performance. For example, most forms ask for ratings of work quality and quantity. Many include personal traits such as appearance, attitude, dependability, and motivation.

A graphic rating form, as illustrated in Table 4.2, consists of a multipoint scale and several dimensions. The scale represents a continuum of performance from low to high and usually contains from four to seven values. The scale in the table contains five scale points, ranging from "poor" to "outstanding," with "adequate" in the middle. The form also contains several dimensions of job performance along which the employee is to be rated. This form includes attendance and work quality. To use the form, a supervisor checks off a rating for each of the dimensions.

Behavior-Focused Rating Forms

The graphic rating forms just discussed focus on dimensions that are trait oriented, such as dependability, or general aspects of performance, such as attendance. **Behavior-focused forms** concentrate on specific instances of behavior that the person has done or could be expected to do. Behaviors are chosen to represent different levels of performance. For attendance, an example of a good behavior would be "Can be counted on to be at work every day on time," whereas a poor behavior would be "Comes to work late several times per week." The rater's job is to indicate which behaviors are characteristic of the person being rated. The way the form is scored is dependent on the particular type of form.

There are several different types of behavior-focused rating forms. We will discuss three of them:

Behaviorally Anchored Rating Scale (BARS) (Smith & Kendall, 1963)

Mixed Standard Scale (MSS) (Blanz & Ghiselli, 1972)

Behavior Observation Scale (BOS) (Latham & Wexley, 1977).

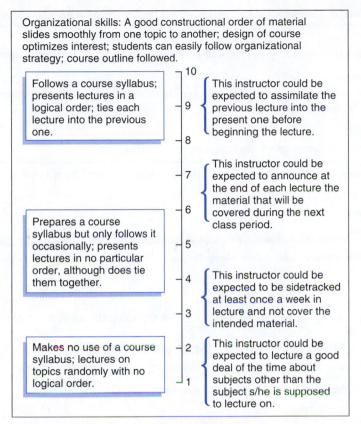

Figure 4.2 An example of a behaviorally anchored rating scale for a college professor.

Source: From *Performance Appraisal: Assessing Human Behavior at Work* by H. J. Bernardin and R. W. Beatty, 1984, Boston, MA: Kent. Reprinted with permission.

All three of these scales provide descriptions of behavior or performance rather than traits, but they differ in the way they present the descriptions and/or the responses.

The **Behaviorally Anchored Rating Scale (BARS)** is a rating scale in which the response choices are defined in behavioral terms. An example for the job of college professor is shown in Figure 4.2. This scale is designed to assess performance on the dimension of Organizational Skills in the Classroom. The rater chooses the behavior that comes closest to describing the performance of the person in question. The behaviors are ordered from bottom to top on the scale along the continuum of performance effectiveness.

A BARS performance evaluation form contains several individual scales, each designed to assess an important dimension of job performance. A BARS can be used to assess the same dimensions as a graphic rating form. The major difference is that the BARS uses response choices that represent behaviors, and the graphic rating form asks for a rating of how well the person performs along the dimension in question. Thus, both

TABLE 4.5   Three Items for a Mixed Standard Scale to Assess the Dimension of Relations with Other People

Good Performance

Is on good terms with everyone. Can get along with people even when he or she doesn't agree with them.

Satisfactory Performance

Gets along with most people. Only very occasionally does he or she have conflicts with others on the job, and these are likely to be minor.

Poor Performance

Has the tendency to get into unnecessary conflicts with other people.

Note: Each item is rated on the following scale: For each item on the scale, indicate if the employee is

Better than the item

As good as the item

Worse than the item

Source: From "The Mixed Standard Scale: A New Rating System," by F. Blanz and E. E. Ghiselli, 1972, *Personnel Psychology*, 25, 185–199.

types of rating forms can be used to assess the same dimensions of performance for the same jobs.

The **Mixed Standard Scale (MSS)** provides the rater with a list of behaviors that vary in their effectiveness. For each statement, the rater is asked to indicate whether

1. the ratee is better than the statement
2. the statement fits the ratee
3. the ratee is worse than the statement

There are several dimensions of performance in a Mixed Standard Scale, and each dimension has several behaviors associated with it. An example of three statements that reflect performance for the dimension of Relations with Other People is shown in Table 4.5. The three statements represent good, satisfactory, and poor job performance along the dimension.

In a Mixed Standard Scale, the statements for the various dimensions are presented in a random order. The rater is not told the specific dimensions associated with each behavior, although the nature of the behaviors is certainly clear. The original idea of Blanz and Ghiselli (1972) was that the mixed order of presentation of the statements would make it more difficult for the raters to bias their ratings than is true of the other types of rating forms. When Dickinson and Glebocki (1990) compared responses to both the mixed and sorted (by dimension) orders, they found that subjects responded similarly in their ratings with both orders. Thus, it does not seem to matter if the dimensions are identified or the statements are mixed up.

The **Behavior Observation Scale (BOS)** contains items that are based on critical incidents, making it somewhat like a Mixed Standard Scale. A **critical incident** is an event reflecting either effective or ineffective behavior by an employee (Flanagan, 1954). An example of a poor incident for a teacher would be "slapping a child who made a disrespectful comment." With the BOS, raters are asked to indicate for each item the amount of time the employee engaged in that behavior. The developers of the scale recommend having raters indicate the percentage of time the employee does each behavior by using the following percentage options:

0 percent to 64 percent

65 percent to 74 percent

75 percent to 84 percent

85 percent to 94 percent

95 percent to 100 percent

This scale is different from the MSS in that the raters indicate frequency rather than comparisons of employee behavior with the item. In theory, it should indicate how often employees engage in performance-relevant behavior.

Use of the frequency ratings has been criticized by Kane and Bernardin (1982). They point out that frequency of a behavior is not a good indicator of performance in many instances because the specific behavior in question determines the criterion for good performance in terms of frequency. They give as examples two behaviors for police officers. An 85 to 94% frequency of occurrence would be outstanding for obtaining arrest warrants but abysmal for being vindicated in the use of lethal force. Thus, considerable judgment can be required in interpreting the meaning of frequency ratings with the BOS. Of course, judgment is required in interpreting many measures of job performance.

Development of Behavior-Focused Forms

Development of behavior-focused forms takes considerable effort from several people in an organization. Because it focuses on specific behaviors, a form must be developed for a specific job or family of jobs. The process involves four steps and can take a long time to complete. The four steps are listed in Table 4.6.

Step 1 is a job analysis that identifies the specific dimensions of performance, such as making arrests or writing reports for a police officer. Step 2 involves writing the descriptions of behaviors that vary in their effectiveness or ineffectiveness on the job. This can be done by collecting critical incidents from people who are knowledgeable about the job in question, such as employees who do the job or their supervisors. Critical incidents can provide examples that vary from extremely effective to extremely ineffective performance.

Step 3 involves having judges (knowledgeable people) sort the descriptions of behavior into dimensions to verify that the descriptions reflect the intended dimensions. The final step is to have judges rate the descriptions of behavior along a continuum of effectiveness. With a BARS, these ratings allow for the placement of the descriptions along

TABLE 4.6   Four Steps in Developing a Behavior-Focused Rating Form to Assess Job Performance

Step 1: Perform job analysis to define job dimensions

Step 2: Develop descriptions of effective and ineffective job performance from critical incidents

Step 3: Have knowledgeable judges place descriptions into job dimensions

Step 4: Have knowledgeable judges rate the effectiveness of the descriptions the scale for each dimension, as in Figure 4.2. With the MSS, the ratings are used to place statements into the three categories of good, satisfactory, and poor.

Cognitive Processes Underlying Ratings

The development of sound performance appraisal methods requires that we understand the cognitive processes that affect rating behavior. I/O psychologists have studied these processes and have devised several models to explain ratings. Some of these models focus on how people utilize information to make judgments. Others are concerned with how people's views of job performance influence their evaluations of employees.

Models of the Rating Process

There are several competing models of the cognitive processes that influence ratings of performance (e.g., DeNisi, Caferty, & Meglino, 1984; Feldman, 1981). These models suggest that the rating process involves several steps (see Ilgen, Barnes-Farrell, & McKellin, 1993), including:

Observing performance

Storing information about performance

Retrieving information about performance from memory

Translating retrieved information into ratings

The process begins with observation of the employee by the supervisor. Next, observations of performance are stored in the supervisor's memory. When asked to rate performance, the supervisor must retrieve information about the employee from his or her memory. The information is then used in some manner to decide what performance rating to give for each dimension of job performance.

The various models describe how humans process information at each step. One idea is that people use **schemata** (categories or frames of reference) to help interpret and organize their experiences (Borman, 1987). Perhaps the best-known schema is the *stereotype*—a belief about characteristics of the members of a group. The characteristics can be favorable or unfavorable. For example, one stereotype might be that private sector managers are hard working.

Another type of schema is the *prototype*, which is a model of some characteristic or type of person. One might think of a particular fictional or real person as the prototype of a good manager. Some people might consider Bill Gates, the founder and head of Microsoft, to be a prototype of a good corporate manager. A person who had the salient characteristics of the prototype might be thought of as a good manager. If the salient characteristics of the prototype are blond hair (or looking like Gates), managers who are blond (or look like Gates) might be seen as better in performance than their counterparts who have brown hair (or do not resemble Gates). The prototype is the standard used to assign people to the good manager category.

Schemata may influence all four steps in the evaluation process. They might affect the behaviors that a supervisor chooses to observe, how the behaviors are organized and stored in memory, how they are retrieved, and how they are used to decide on ratings. The use of schemata, however, does not necessarily imply that they lead to inaccurate ratings. In many ways, the use of schemata can simplify experience so that it can be more easily interpreted. It is possible that this leads to accurate judgments about employee performance (Lord & Maher, 1989).

In theory it should be possible to make use of these cognitive models to help raters do a more accurate job of evaluating job performance. Jelley and Goffin (2001) attempted this with an experiment in which college students were asked to rate the performance of a videotaped college instructor using a BOS. Although results were somewhat inconsistent, they were able to find some accuracy increases after priming the raters' memory. This was done by having the raters do some preliminary global ratings designed to stimulate recall of the performance observed. This approach shows some promise in helping improve ratings, but more research will be needed to determine whether these models will ultimately prove useful.

Content of Subordinate Effectiveness

If schemata affect job performance ratings, it is important that we understand the schemata of people who appraise performance. In other words, appraisal techniques might be improved if they were designed to effectively utilize the schemata of supervisors. If the dimensions on an appraisal form match the dimensions in supervisor schemata about performance, it will be easier for supervisors to do their ratings. There has been some research that is relevant to this issue.

Borman (1987) studied the content of army officers' schemata of subordinate job performance. U.S. Army officers were asked to describe the differences in characteristics between effective and ineffective soldiers. They generated 189 descriptive items, which were subject to complex statistical analysis. The analysis reduced the 189 items to six meaningful dimensions. Effective soldiers were seen as having the following characteristics:

Working hard

Being responsible

Being organized

Knowing the technical parts of the job

Being in control of subordinates

Displaying concern for subordinates

Borman concluded that these dimensions represent the characteristics that officers use to judge soldiers' performance. He also noted that in his sample of experienced officers, there was good agreement about what constituted good job performance. These results suggest that experienced supervisors might have schemata that accurately represent effective performance. These six dimensions could be used as the basis for any of the rating forms we discussed earlier.

Werner (1994) conducted a study in which he asked experienced supervisors to rate the performance of secretaries as described in a series of incidents. One of the variables of interest in this study was the sort of information that the supervisors used in making their ratings. Werner found that the following dimensions were seen as most important:

Attendance   Work accuracy
Job knowledge   Work quantity

Werner suggested that these four dimensions might represent the characteristics that define the schemata of his supervisors. He also suggested that supervisors should let subordinates know the content of their schemata. Subordinates are likely to attempt to perform well in those areas that the supervisor believes are important for good performance.

Rater Bias and Error

It is the nature of human judgment to be imperfect. When supervisors or other people make performance ratings, they are likely to exhibit rating biases and rating errors. These biases and errors can be seen in the pattern of ratings, both within the rating forms for individuals and across rating forms for different people. These within-form and across-form patterns are called halo errors and distributional errors, respectively.

Halo Errors

Halo error occurs when a rater gives an individual the same rating across all rating dimensions despite differences in performance across dimensions. In other words, a person who is rated as outstanding in one area is rated outstanding in all areas even though in some areas performance may be only average or even poor. For example, a police officer might be outstanding in completing many arrests (high quantity) but does a poor job in paperwork. A supervisor might rate this officer high on all dimensions, even though it is not uniformly deserved. Similarly, a person who is rated as poor in one area might be given poor ratings for all areas even though performance is satisfactory on some dimensions. This rating error occurs within the rating forms of individuals as opposed to occurring across forms of different individuals.

Table 4.7 shows a pattern of responses that reflects a halo error. The table shows the ratings of four individuals across five dimensions of performance. Ratings ranged from 1 (poorest performance) to 5 (best performance). This is a halo pattern because the ratings for each individual employee are the same across the different dimensions, even though each person received different ratings. Such a pattern suggests that raters are unable to distinguish among dimensions. The person is seen as uniform in performance across dimensions. Research shows that supervisor ratings of different performance dimensions tend to be quite high (Viswesvaran, Ones, & Schmidt, 1996).

Although a pattern of similar ratings might indicate a rating error, it is possible that employee performance is consistent across dimensions. This means that halo patterns might accurately indicate that dimensions of actual performance are related.

TABLE 4.7 Job Performance Ratings for Four Employees on Five Dimensions Illustrating a Halo Error Pattern

Dimension	Employee 1	Employee 2	Employee 3	Employee 4
Attendance	5	3	1	4
Communication	5	3	1	4
Following directions	5	3	1	4
Work quality	5	3	1	4
Work quantity	5	3	1	4

"He's not a perfect boss, but he does give you plenty of feedback."

(© 1995; Reprinted courtesy of Bunny Hoest and Parade Magazine.)

This possibility has led to considerable discussion in the I/O literature about the meaning of halo (e.g., Balzer & Sulsky, 1992; Murphy, Jako, & Anhalt, 1993; Solomonson & Lance, 1997; Viswesvaran, Schmidt & Ones, 2005). Part of this discussion concerns how to separate the error from "true" halo. *True halo* means that an employee performs at the same level on all dimensions.

Another concern with halo seeks to explain the cognitive processes that would lead a rater to exhibit halo error. Several researchers have theorized that raters rely on a general impression of the employee when making dimension ratings (Lance, LaPointe, & Stewart, 1994; Nathan & Lord, 1983). According to this view, salient pieces of information are used to form a general impression of an employee. The impression forms the basis of performance ratings. This suggests that raters may be better able to provide information about global performance than dimensions of performance.

Distributional Errors

Distributional errors occur when a rater tends to rate everyone the same. **Leniency errors** occur when the rater rates everyone at the favorable end of the performance scale. **Severity errors** occur when the rater rates everyone at the unfavorable end of the performance scale. **Central tendency** errors occur when a rater rates everyone in the middle of the performance scale. The leniency pattern can be seen across ratings of different people. Table 4.8 shows a leniency pattern in that all four people are given ratings at the favorable end of the performance scale. Each person received ratings of 4 and 5 on a five-point scale. It is possible, however that a distributional error pattern does not reflect errors. All ratees might have performed the same, leading to similar ratings.

Control of Rater Bias and Error

Two approaches have been developed to control and eliminate rater bias and error. One approach is to design better performance appraisal forms that will be resistant to these

TABLE 4.8   Job Performance Ratings for Four Employees on Five Dimensions Illustrating a Leniency Error Pattern

Dimension	Employee 1	Employee 2	Employee 3	Employee 4
Attendance	4	5	5	5
Communication	4	5	5	5
Following directions	5	4	4	4
Work quality	4	5	4	5
Work quantity	5	4	5	5

problems. The other is to train raters to avoid rating errors. Although both approaches have shown promise, research studies have yielded conflicting results about their ability to reduce errors (Bernardin & Beatty, 1984).

Error-Resistant Forms to Assess Performance

The behavior-focused rating scales, such as the Behaviorally Anchored Rating Scale and the Mixed Standard Scale, were originally developed in part to eliminate rating errors. The idea is that raters will be able to make more accurate ratings if they focus on specific behavior rather than traits. These behaviors are more concrete and require less idiosyncratic judgment about what they represent. For example, it should be easier to rate accurately how often a person is absent from work than the somewhat abstract trait of dependability.

Many studies have compared the various behavior-focused rating forms with graphic rating forms, as well as with one another. Results of these comparisons have found that the behavior-focused forms sometimes yield fewer errors (such as halo and leniency) than the graphic rating scales, and sometimes they do not (Bernardin & Beatty, 1984; Latham, Skarlicki, Irvine, & Siegel, 1993). Furthermore, scales that merely ask raters to check whether or not individuals have engaged in specific behaviors may result in less leniency than graphic rating scales (Yun, Donahue, Dudley, & McFarland, 2005). As Bernardin and Beatty (1984) point out, however, many of the studies have compared scales that have not been carefully developed. They believe that carefully developed behavior-focused scales will have better rating error resistance than graphic rating scales. Future studies will be necessary to test this supposition.

Rater Training to Reduce Errors

Rater training has also been attempted in many studies with mixed results (Hedge & Kavanagh, 1988; Latham, 1986). At least some of the discrepancy in research findings may be the result of differences in the types of training that have been studied. Perhaps the most popular training is **rater error training**, or **RET**. The objective of RET is to familiarize raters with rater errors and teach them to avoid these rating patterns. Although most studies have found that this sort of training reduces rating errors, it is often at the cost of rating accuracy (e.g., Bernardin & Pence, 1980; Hedge & Kavanagh, 1988). In other words, the raters might reduce the number of halo and leniency patterns in their ratings, but those ratings are less accurate in reflecting the true level of performance.

How is it possible that the reduction of errors also results in a reduction in accuracy? One possible explanation lies in the nature of the rating errors. As noted earlier in this discussion, rater errors are inferred from the pattern of ratings. It is possible that the performance of individuals is similar across different performance dimensions or that all individuals in a supervisor's department perform their jobs equally well. Training raters to avoid the same ratings across either dimensions or people will result in their concentrating on avoiding certain patterns rather than on accurately assessing job performance. Bernardin and Pence (1980) suggested that RET might be substituting one series of rating errors for another.

Nathan and Tippins (1990) offer a different explanation of why halo errors are associated with greater accuracy in job performance ratings. They speculated that raters who exhibited less halo in their ratings might have given too much weight to inconsequential negative events. For example, a supervisor might have given a low rating in attendance to an otherwise reliable employee who was absent for a week due to sickness in the prior year. Raters who exhibited a halo pattern in their ratings paid less attention to such rare instances and tended to consider the person's usual performance. This may have resulted in ratings that were more accurate because they were influenced more by general performance than by rare instances of good or poor performance in one or more dimensions.

Results have been more promising with types of training other than RET. Those training procedures teach raters how to observe performance-relevant behavior and how to make judgments based on such observations. Hedge and Kavanagh (1988), for example, found that this observation training increased rating accuracy but did not reduce rating errors (see Research in Detail box). Day and Sulsky (1995) demonstrated promising results with **frame of reference training**, which attempts to provide a common understanding of the rating task. Raters are given specific examples of behavior that would represent various levels of performance for each dimension to be rated. Although these results are encouraging, more research is needed before we can confidently conclude that training can improve performance appraisal ratings, because most of the studies have been conducted in the laboratory with college student subjects. It is not certain that actual managers will respond to training in the same way when ratings are not just for research purposes.

RESEARCH IN DETAIL

Several studies have found that training raters to avoid rating errors can reduce their accuracy in evaluating job performance. Hedge and Kavanagh (1988) wanted to see if other types of training would be more effective in increasing the accuracy of performance ratings.

Fifty-two supervisors were randomly assigned to one of four treatment groups. The first group received rater error training designed to familiarize the rater with rating errors and ways to avoid them. The second group received training in ways to observe behavior relevant to job performance. The third group received training in ways to make proper judgments about performance based on observed behavior. The last group was a control group that received no training.

Both before and after training, all groups watched a videotape of a person performing a job. They then rated the person's performance on several performance dimensions. The videotaped performance was assessed by a panel of experts who provided a standard for comparison of the appraisals by the members of each group in the study. Accuracy of performance rating was assessed as the discrepancy between the raters' appraisal of the videotape and the expert panel's judgment of the videotape.

The results showed that those who received rater error training had fewer rating errors and decreased accuracy. This finding was consistent with prior research on this sort of training. The other two types of training were successful in increasing accuracy as well as rating errors. The authors concluded that these two types of training showed promise for increasing rating accuracy. They also concluded that the rating patterns often thought to reflect rating errors may not represent mistakes. Rather, these patterns may accurately indicate the level of performance of individuals on the job. For example, individuals might perform at the same level for different dimensions. The implications of this study are that different types of rater training might help organizations get more accurate performance appraisals.

Source: Hedge, J. W., and Kavanagh, M. J. (1988). Improving the accuracy of performance evaluations: Comparisons of three methods of performance appraiser training. *Journal of Applied Psychology*, 73, 68–73.

Other Factors That Influence Job Performance Ratings

So far we have discussed how ratings by supervisors can be affected by their cognitive processes and by the design of the rating form (and training in how to use it). Other factors can also affect the ratings given by supervisors, including supervisor feelings about the subordinate, supervisor mood, supervisor perceptions about subordinates' motives for performance, cultural factors, and the race of both the rater and ratee.

The idea that supervisors give better ratings to subordinates they like is supported by research (e.g., Ferris, Judge, Rowland, & Fitzgibbons, 1994). This has led to some concern that ratings might be biased and reflect favoritism. However, there is some evidence that liking can be the result of good job performance, as supervisors like those who work well for them (Robbins & DeNisi, 1994). It is particularly important for a new employee to be seen as a good performer because this perception will likely lead to being liked by supervisors, which can result in receiving extra support that leads to even better performance in the future (Lefkowitz, 2000).

The continuation of good performance ratings can be influenced by supervisor expectations about performance independent of liking. Murphy, Gannett, Herr, and Chen (1986) found that judgments of performance were influenced by the rater's expectations about the ratee's performance. People are likely to forget instances of behavior that do not fit their view of the person they are evaluating. Thus, an employee who is liked and performs well will continue to be seen as a good performer even if performance has recently slipped. This can produce biased ratings when performance changes over time.

The mood of the rater at the time of appraisal can affect ratings. In a laboratory study, Sinclair (1988) assigned participants to a condition in which their mood was experimentally manipulated to be more depressed or elated. They were then asked to read a description of a professor's behavior and rate the professor's performance. Results showed that participants in a depressed mood rated the professor's performance lower than subjects in the elated mood condition. The depressed participants were also more accurate and exhibited less halo. Sinclair explained the results as reflecting the better information processing ability of people when they are in depressed moods.

Managers' views of subordinate motivation can be a factor in their ratings of job performance, but interestingly such views can be subject to cultural factors. DeVoe and Iyengar (2004) assessed managers' perceptions of their employees as intrinsically motivated (wanting to do a good job for its own sake) and extrinsically motivated (working hard for rewards), and then linked these perceptions to ratings of job performance. Managers in the United States and Latin America considered intrinsic motivation to be more important for performance than extrinsic motivation, whereas Asian managers considered both types of motivation equally important.

It has been well established that black employees, on average, receive lower performance appraisal ratings than white employees (McKay & McDaniel, 2006). Interestingly, the race of the rater seems to have no effect on ratings for whites, but it does on ratings for blacks. As shown by Stauffer and Buckley (2005), black and white raters give similar ratings to whites, and rate blacks lower, on average, than whites. However, the difference between the ratings is much larger for white than black raters. If it is presumed that black raters would have less bias than white raters against black employees, these findings suggest the possibility that white raters are biased against black employees. Of course, alterative explanations are that black raters are biased in favor of blacks and overrate them, or that both black and white raters are biased in favor of whites and overrate them relative to blacks. At this time we don't know the extent to which bias is operating in these ratings either for or against black and white employees.

360 Degree Feedback

In most organizations, the direct supervisor of each employee is responsible for assessing job performance. However, it can be helpful to get multiple perspectives on job performance (Furnham & Stringfield, 1994), and the use of multiple perspectives is becoming standard practice in the evaluation of managers and others (Rowson, 1998). Ratings by peers, self, and subordinates (for supervisors) can be a useful complement to supervisor ratings, and can be helpful in providing feedback for employee development (Maurer, Mitchell, & Barbeite, 2002). In particular, discrepancies between self (employee's own ratings of performance) and others can show those areas in which other people see employees differently than they see themselves.

The use of multiple perspectives for manager feedback has been called **360 degree feedback** (Baldwin & Padgett, 1993). Managers are evaluated by peers, subordinates, and supervisors on several dimensions of performance. In addition, managers complete a rating of their own performance. Research has shown that people in these different positions show only modest agreement in their ratings (Brett & Atwater, 2001; Carless, Mann, & Wearing, 1998; Fletcher & Baldry, 2000), suggesting that they provide different perspectives on a person's performance. Another advantage of using multiple raters is that the biases of individuals can be reduced. For example, it has been shown that people give higher ratings in 360 degree evaluations to those they like (Antonioni & Park, 2001). Favoritism by the immediate supervisor is diminished when additional information from other raters is added to the appraisal. This can lead to increased trust and better attitudes about the appraisal system on the part of those being evaluated (Mayer & Davis, 1999).

The purpose of 360 degree systems is to enhance performance, especially for those individuals who are the most in need of performance improvement. These systems have been shown to have positive effects for some individuals but not all. Contrary to their intended purpose, it is the best and not the worst performers who seem to benefit most from 360 degree feedback (Bailey & Austin, 2006). Furthermore, Atwater and Brett (2005) found that those individuals who received low ratings from others and rated themselves low as well had the worst reactions to feedback, suggesting that if one knows one's performance is poor, having this belief corroborated by others is not helpful.

▶ THE IMPACT OF TECHNOLOGY ON PERFORMANCE APPRAISAL

The growth of technology over the past decade has greatly expanded what is practical in performance appraisal. For large companies, the amount of data involved in monitoring performance can be staggering, thus placing practical limits on the amount of information that can be processed. For example, one of the difficulties with 360 degree feedback is the logistics of organizing this large rating task. Each target manager must nominate several subordinates, several peers, to do self-ratings and get their supervisor's rating. In some organizations this might represent eight or more ratings completed per manager, and if there are 10,000 managers, there are 80,000 ratings to track and process. This is an expensive and difficult task for a company to do manually.

There are two places in which we see technology having an impact on performance appraisal—monitoring of objective productivity and performance management systems. Many employees today work on computer systems, such as reservation specialists for airlines and telephone operators. The systems that allow them to complete their job tasks are also capable of tracking productivity, and such data are routinely collected in many organizations. The use of computers allows for the easy analysis of performance across millions of employee-customer transactions, and it can be a built-in feature of the task software employees use to do their jobs each day.

Computerized Web-based employee performance-management systems are becoming popular to help managers clarify goals and expectations, provide coaching and feedback, and evaluate performance (see I/O Psychology in Practice). Such systems automate the entire process, making 360 degree feedback systems economically feasible for large companies. Each target manager can log onto the system and nominate the peers, subordinates, and others who will provide ratings. The system notifies individuals to do the ratings, and then pulls together all of the rating information into a report. Consulting firms can be found that specialize in providing the computer services to conduct a 360 project.

▶ LEGAL ISSUES IN PERFORMANCE APPRAISAL

Many countries have laws that prohibit discrimination against minorities and women (as well as other groups) in the workplace. These laws cover organizational actions that affect the employment status of people, such as promotions and terminations. Such actions are often based at least in part on the employee's performance; therefore, the performance appraisal system of an organization can become the target for legal action. In the United States, it is illegal to discriminate in performance appraisal on the basis of certain non-performance-related factors, such as age, gender, mental or physical disability, or race.

In the United States there have been an increasing number of court challenges to performance-based employee actions, such as promotions and terminations (Latham et al., 1993). Organizations have lost such cases because they were unable to demonstrate to the court's satisfaction that their performance appraisal systems did not discriminate

TABLE 4.9   Six Points of a Legally Defensible Performance-Appraisal System

1. Perform job analysis to define dimensions of performance
2. Develop rating form to assess dimensions from prior point
3. Train raters in how to assess performance
4. Have higher management review ratings and allow employees to appeal their evaluations
5. Document performance and maintain detailed records
6. Provide assistance and counseling to poor-performing employees prior to actions against them

Source: Adapted from "Performance Appraisal and Terminations: A Review of Court Decisions Since *Brito v. Zia* with Implications for Personnel Practices," by G. V. Barrett and M. G. Kernan, 1987, *Personnel Psychology*, 40, 489–503.

against certain groups. Subjective methods are especially likely to evoke legal challenges because they allow room for supervisors to express prejudices against certain groups of people. It can be difficult for supervisors to prove in court that their ratings were fair and unbiased, given that blacks tend to get lower performance ratings than whites (McKay & McDaniel, 2006), as noted earlier.

Barrett and Kernan (1987) suggested six components that should be part of a legally defensible performance appraisal system. As shown in Table 4.9, the system should begin with a job analysis to derive the dimensions of performance for the particular job. The job analysis will ensure that the dimensions are job relevant. Raters should receive training in how the rating form is to be used to assess performance. To help minimize personal bias, upper management should review performance appraisals. Performance and the reasons for the employee action should be documented and recorded. It is easier to take action against an employee when the performance, good or poor, has been documented for a long period of time. This eliminates the appearance that the latest appraisal was given to justify a particular action affecting an employee. Finally, it is a good idea to provide assistance and counseling to employees whose performance is unsatisfactory. This shows that the organization has done everything possible for an unsatisfactory employee before taking action against him or her.

Werner and Bolino (1997) analyzed the outcomes of 295 court cases in the United States in which performance appraisals were challenged as discriminatory. An organization was far less likely to lose the case if its performance appraisal systems were based on a job analysis, gave written instructions to raters, offered employees the opportunity to have input, and used multiple raters. For example, while overall organizations lost 41 percent of cases, those that used multiple raters only lost 11 percent of cases. The use of these four practices combined should result in a relatively safe performance appraisal system from a legal perspective.

Allowing employees to have input into performance appraisals also has benefits beyond legal issues. Research has shown that giving employees the opportunity to sit down with supervisors and discuss appraisals openly can lead to better attitudes (Korsgaard & Roberson, 1995). In one study, this occurred even though employees allowed input actually had lower ratings than those who did not (Taylor, Tracy, Renard, Harrison, & Carroll, 1995). Perceptions of fairness in this study even reduced employee intentions of quitting the job. To be effective and perceived as fair, performance appraisal systems should include Barrett and Kernan's (1987) six steps, as well as input by employees.

▶ FUTURE ISSUES AND CHALLENGES

Improving performance appraisal systems represents a major challenge to the I/O field. Objective measures are often deficient in not adequately representing the entire scope of people's job performance. Subjective measures suffer from contamination as a result of rating biases and errors of the supervisors who assess performance. There is considerable room for improvement with both types of performance measures.

Research with some forms of rater training shows promise of improving the accuracy of subjective ratings. Training that focuses on how to observe good job performance and how to transform these observations into accurate appraisals of people's performance seems likely to be effective.

Over the past few decades, computerization has been expanding what is feasible in performance appraisal. This allows opportunities to do a better and more thorough job of evaluating performance and integrating appraisal into a broader performance management system that can help employees be more successful. However, organizations need to be careful about too much of a good thing. If employees receive too much evaluation, they may experience emotional strain from being too closely monitored.

A challenge for practicing I/O psychologists is to convince organizations that they should have the most complete and unbiased performance appraisal systems possible. This means investing resources and time in the development and maintenance of such systems. There are two practical reasons for such investment. First, a sound system is less likely to be challenged in court by employees who believe that they have been unfairly evaluated. Second, a sound system is likely to be more effective in meeting its various objectives, such as providing feedback to employees so that they can improve their job performance.

Finally, there are additional challenges to applying performance appraisal systems across countries where customs and values differ. In Japan, for example, performance appraisals are common, but supervisors do not generally share the results with subordinates (Endo, 1998); instead they keep them secret, a situation unheard of in the United States. Rowson (1998) pointed out that the criterion of good performance can vary from country to country, making performance appraisal in a global company difficult because what is considered good in the branch in one country might not be viewed the same in another. Finally, legal requirements differ. For example, Endo (1998) discussed how Japanese companies have gotten into problems in the United States because their performance appraisal systems did not meet American legal requirements.

▶ CHAPTER SUMMARY

Job performance data have many organizational uses, including administrative decision making, employee development, employee feedback, and research. The first step in evaluating job performance is to develop performance criteria that define good and poor performance. Once criteria are set, specific methods to measure them can be chosen.

Job performance measures can be classified as either objective or subjective. Objective measures are counts of the output of a job, such as the number of sales for a salesperson or the number of units produced for a factory worker. Subjective measures are ratings by supervisors (or other individuals who are familiar with the employee's job performance). Subjective measures are the more commonly used of the two methods, but they suffer from biases and errors attributable to human judgment. Two different approaches have been taken to reduce rating errors in subjective measures.

Several different types of rating forms have been devised to increase the accuracy of performance ratings. The Behaviorally Anchored Rating Scale (BARS) asks raters to indicate which of several behaviors comes closest to representing the job performance of the individual. The Mixed Standard Scale (MSS) asks raters to indicate whether the individual's performance is worse than, as good as, or better than each of several items of performance behavior. The Behavior Observation Scale (BOS) asks raters to indicate how often ratees perform each of the listed behaviors. Research comparing the behavior-focused rating forms with other types of measures has failed to find consistent evidence for greater accuracy.

Rater training is another approach that has been attempted to reduce errors. Research has suggested that rater error training can reduce rating accuracy even if it is successful in reducing rating errors. Observation training that focuses on observing performance-related behavior and making judgments of performance has shown promise in increasing accuracy. At the present time, however, it would be premature to conclude that either approach will prove useful in ensuring that supervisors provide accurate performance ratings.

Several factors have been shown to relate to job performance ratings, although it is not entirely clear whether they result in rater bias or not. Whether the rater likes the subordinate, rater mood, perceived motives of the employee for performance, cultural factors, and both rater and ratee race all effect ratings.

Feedback from multiple sources can be helpful for employees wishing to improve their performance. Managers receive 360 degree feedback from a comparison of their self-ratings with those of peers, subordinates, and supervisors.

In the United States and many other countries performance appraisal is a legal process as well as a technical one. Organizations are required by U.S. law to avoid discrimination in their performance appraisal procedures. Failure to comply with these legal requirements can make an organization subject to lawsuits. Several specific practices, such as basing the system on a job analysis and providing rater training, reduce the chances that an organization will lose in court if challenged.

I/O PSYCHOLOGY IN PRACTICE

(Courtesy of Amy Carver)

This case deals with the development of a comprehensive performance appraisal and management system that Dr. Amy Carver and her team designed and implemented for Wachovia Bank. Carver received her Ph.D. in I/O psychology in 1992 from Rice University. At the time of this case, she was senior vice president for organizational effectiveness for Wachovia Bank. Before that she had quite a varied and interesting career, having worked for a government agency (U.S. Navy Personnel Research and Development Center), a private company (United Airlines), and her own consulting firm. In her current role for Wachovia, Carver is involved in employee selection, performance management, executive coaching (see the case for Chapter 7), organization design, and employee surveys, among other things.

One of the concerns Carver had when she got to Wachovia was that it did not have a common performance appraisal and management system. Each year supervisors filled out evaluations, but there were no consistent standards, and raises were not closely tied to performance. To remedy this, Carver and her team put together a comprehensive system that became part of the management/supervision system of the organization. This system tied together annual performance reviews with goal setting, employee development, and supervisor coaching.

The system runs on an annual cycle beginning in December. The evaluation portion, which involves both employee self-appraisal and supervisor ratings, is entirely Web-based. Each employee-supervisor pair logs onto the company computer system to complete evaluation forms. These forms are focused on the match between the employee's competencies, as displayed for the year, and the organization's competency model for that position. This model, which was derived from a job analysis, is a specification of the competencies and skills needed for doing the job. When both employee and supervisor are done, a report is automatically generated that highlights areas of disagreement, and this becomes the basis for a face-to-face discussion.

Around the first of the year, each supervisor meets with each subordinate to discuss his or her performance and to agree on goals for the upcoming year.

These goals specify not only what is to be accomplished but also how it is to be done, thus providing a balanced emphasis on both work quality and quantity. The Web-based system sends e-mail reminders to each supervisor at quarterly intervals to conduct required coaching sessions with subordinates to provide feedback about competencies and goal progress up to that time of the year. Goals for the future of the system include linking raises each year to performance and making the salary system part of performance management. As you can see, the Wachovia system goes far beyond just completing the usual "report card" on every employee each year.

Discussion Questions

1. Do you think you'd like working in a company with this sort of performance system? Why or why not?
2. Why would a company like Wachovia invest so much effort in performance evaluation?
3. Why are managers required to provide quarterly coaching sessions? Isn't a once-a-year system enough?
4. Do you think goal setting will increase employee motivation and performance (see Chapter 8's section on goal setting).

LEARNING BY DOING

Determining Criteria for a Job

Criteria for a job can be determined by interviewing employees who hold the job. They are typically experts in knowing what needs to be done, and what constitutes good and poor performance. Choose a person you know (acquaintance, family member, or friend) who is currently employed in a job you never held yourself. Interview him or her about the major functions of their job and the criteria for good job performance. Be sure to take careful notes. You should ask about the following:

1. What are the six major functions of this job?
2. For each function, what is it the employee is supposed to accomplish?
3. For each function, what constitutes good performance and what constitutes unacceptable performance? Ask your interviewee to give examples.

4. What would be a good way to assess performance for each function?

Write a brief report that describes briefly the functions of the job and both actual and ultimate criteria for those six functions.

Critical Incidents of Performance

Critical incidents can be quite useful in developing job performance measures. These incidents are brief (short paragraph) descriptions of something that happened that exemplifies outstanding or poor performance. Collect 10 critical incidents, half reflecting effective and half reflecting ineffective performance. Ask people you know to provide examples they have observed at work. The same person could give you both an effective and an ineffective incident. It is best to get incidents from several people, although one person might be able to provide several incidents. An example of an ineffective performance for an emergency room nurse is the following:

Chris was an emergency room nurse who was on call on a Saturday night, a typically busy time for the emergency room. Chris left the hospital at 5 pm and was supposed to be at home, a 10 minute drive from the hospital. At 9 pm there was a serious multiple car accident that brought several patients to the hospital and necessitated having on call staff return to work. Chris had decided to go to the movies instead of going home, and was unreachable until after midnight.

5

Assessment Methods for Selection and Placement

CHAPTER 5 OUTLINE

Suppose you find yourself responsible for hiring someone for a job. It might be hiring a computer programmer, or a plumber, or a secretary, or a teacher. There are several applicants, and your task is to select one of them. How would you go about making your choice? Would you interview each applicant and pick the one who seemed to be best suited for the job? How would you know what characteristics or qualities to look for? Furthermore, how would you go about finding out if applicants had the necessary characteristics? Procedures for the assessment of characteristics for selection (hiring) and placement (assigning current employees to jobs) are the topic of this chapter.

One of the earliest applications of psychology to the human problems of organizations had to do with the assessment of people for selection and placement. During World War I, the U.S. Army became the first organization to use large-scale testing of people to determine their job assignments (placement). After the war, large organizations saw the potential value of assessing job applicants for selection and other employment decisions, and the use of testing and other techniques became commonplace. This is true today not only in the United States, but also in most of the industrialized world including Canada, Western Europe, and Israel (McCulloch, 1993).

This chapter discusses five techniques for the assessment of characteristics that are frequently used for selection and placement. A *psychological test* consists of a standard set of items or tasks that a person completes under controlled conditions. Most involve paper-and-pencil tasks, such as answering questions or solving problems, although some involve manipulation of physical objects to assess such characteristics as manual dexterity or eye-hand coordination. Psychological tests can be used to assess ability, interests, knowledge, personality, and skill. *Biographical information forms* ask about relevant prior experiences, such as level of education and work experience. Some forms can be quite detailed, asking not only for objective facts but for opinions and subjective reactions as well. The *interview* is a meeting between the job applicant and someone at the employing organization who will have input into the hiring decision. This can be face-to-face or done via technology, such as a telephone or videophone. A *work sample* is a test that asks a person to perform a simulated job. The person is given the necessary materials and tools and must perform a particular task, such as assembling a motor, under controlled conditions. An *assessment center* is a series of assessments, including simulated job tasks, that measure how well a person can perform a job. It is commonly used to assess potential for managerial or other white-collar jobs.

Each of the five assessment techniques can be used to determine a person's suitability for a particular job. Often more than one technique is used at the same time to get a more complete picture of how well an individual's characteristics match those necessary for a job. These assessment techniques can have uses other than selection and placement, however. They can be useful for employee development by showing a person's strengths and weaknesses, which can then be addressed by training. Many of these techniques are used to assess human characteristics in research studies concerned with almost all the topics discussed throughout this book. In the next chapter on employee selection, we will see how the five techniques are used to help choose people for jobs.

Objectives: The student who studies this chapter should be able to:

▶ Define KSAOs.
▶ Describe the five assessment methods in the chapter.
▶ Discuss the advantages and limitations of each assessment tool in the chapter.
▶ Explain how computers and technology are changing assessment.

TABLE 5.1   KSAOs for a Computer Sales Associate

Knowledge	Knowledge of computer systems Knowledge of computer software	Abilities	Ability to understand complex technology Ability to communicate with other people
Skills	Skill in using a cash register Skill in completing monetary transactions	Other	Neat appearance Outgoing, friendly personality

▶ JOB-RELATED CHARACTERISTICS

Many different characteristics of people, or KSAOs (knowledge, skill, ability, and other personal characteristics), are needed for a job. (See Chapter 3 for a more extensive discussion of KSAOs in the context of job analysis.) *Knowledge* refers to what the person knows about a job, such as legal knowledge for an attorney. A *skill* is something that a person is able to do, such as program a computer or type. *Ability* is the capability to learn something, such as the ability to learn to play a musical instrument or to speak a foreign language. *Other personal characteristics* are every other human attribute not covered by the first three. Included are interests, personality, physical characteristics (such as height or eye color), and prior experience relevant for the job.

Table 5.1 contains examples of KSAOs for a sales associate in a computer store. Such a person should have knowledge of the product to be sold, as well as the ability to understand complex computer systems. Working a cash register and handling monetary transactions are also important. Finally, the person must have a neat appearance and a friendly, outgoing personality. When we hire a computer sales associate, these are some of the KSAOs for which we will select people.

The KSAOs for every job can be determined by a detailed and thorough study called a *job analysis*. (See Chapter 3 for a discussion of job analysis.) This involves a number of techniques that result in a list of the necessary KSAOs for the job in question. Once KSAOs are determined, procedures can be chosen or developed to assess them in job applicants or current employees. The idea is to select or place people in jobs who have the necessary KSAOs. Although this process does not guarantee that all the people chosen will be successful on the job, it increases the chances of making good choices over using other selection and placement approaches.

All five of the assessment techniques that we discuss attempt to measure KSAOs that are relevant for job performance and other organizationally relevant variables. As with all assessment techniques, the properties of reliability and validity are critical (see Chapter 2 for a discussion of these properties). That is, all measures must be consistent (reliable) and must pass stringent tests for validity. In other words, evidence must exist that they can accomplish the tasks for which they are used in organizations. If a test is to be used to select police officers, for example, it must be shown to predict how well a police officer will do on the job.

▶ PSYCHOLOGICAL TESTS

A **psychological test** is a standardized series of problems or questions that assess a particular individual characteristic. Tests are commonly used to assess many KSAOs, including knowledge, skill, ability, attitudes, interests, and personality. Tests consist of multiple items that are indicators of the characteristic of interest. Each item can be completed relatively quickly, making it feasible to include many items that assess each characteristic and to assess several characteristics at one time.

Multiple items provide increased reliability and validity over a single indicator of the characteristic. Single-item measures tend to have low reliability because a person can easily make a mistake on any one item. For example, an item can be misinterpreted or misread. Consider the following item that might be encountered on a test:

I'm not usually the first one to volunteer for a new work assignment.

If a person misreads the item and does not notice that the second word is *not*, the meaning of the item will be reversed. As a result, the person's response to the item will be the opposite of what it should, and the item will not be an accurate indicator of the characteristic of interest. If it is likely that only a few people will make this error, the item may retain some reliability and validity. The reliability and validity of a multiple-item test is better than that for a single-item test because the impact of occasional errors on each person's score is reduced. The contribution of each item to the total score when there are many items is quite small.

Characteristics of Tests

Many different types of tests are available that can assess hundreds of individual characteristics. The nature of the characteristic of interest helps determine which test is used. For example, a test to assess mathematical ability will most certainly be composed of math problems to be completed with paper and pencil. A test of physical strength, on the other hand, will likely involve the lifting of heavy objects. A discussion of the four distinguishing characteristics of tests follows.

(© 1993, Ziggy and Friends, Inc./Distributed by Universal Press Syndicate.)

Group versus Individually Administered Tests

A **group test** can be administered to several people at once. The test itself is in a printed form (e.g., a booklet) that can be given to hundreds or thousands of people at one time. A test administrator usually hands out the tests and instructs the test takers when to begin and stop, but the test taker determines the pace of the completion of individual test items. An individual test, in contrast, is one that a test administrator gives to a single test taker at a time rather than to groups of individuals. This is necessary either because the administrator has to score the items as the test proceeds or because an apparatus is involved that only one person can use at a time. The test administrator sets the pace of the individual items. Because of its greater efficiency, the group test is preferred when feasible.

Closed-Ended versus Open-Ended Tests

With a **closed-ended test**, the test taker must choose one from several possible responses. For example, multiple-choice exams test ability and knowledge. An **open-ended test** is like an essay exam. The test taker must generate a response rather than choose a correct response. Whereas the closed-ended test is preferred because of its greater ease in scoring, the open-ended test is more appropriate for some characteristics. For example, writing ability is best assessed by asking a person to write an essay. Experts can read and score the essay for a number of characteristics, such as clarity of expression and grammatical accuracy. These characteristics would be more difficult, if not impossible, to assess with a closed-ended test.

Paper-and-Pencil versus Performance Tests

With a **paper-and-pencil test**, the test is on a piece of paper or other printed (or electronic) medium, and the responses are made in written form, often with a pencil. A multiple-choice course examination is a paper-and-pencil test that presents the exam questions on paper, and the responses are made in pencil on the exam itself or on a separate answer sheet. Open-ended tests can also be paper-and-pencil if people are asked to write their responses in some form. A **performance test** involves the manipulation of apparatus, equipment, materials, or tools. Perhaps the most widely used performance test is a typing test. With this sort of performance test, the test taker demonstrates typing ability on an actual keyboard under standardized conditions. This tests the typing ability itself rather than typing knowledge, which could be assessed with a paper-and-pencil test of knowledge about typing.

Power versus Speed Tests

A **power test** gives the test taker almost unlimited time to complete the test. A **speed test** has a strict time limit. It is designed so that almost no one could finish all the items in the allotted time. There are two ways in which the speed test is used. First, a speed test can contain challenging items that must be completed under time pressure. Some instructors use speed tests for classroom examinations under the presumption that the better prepared students will be able to answer the questions more quickly than the less well prepared students. The drawback to this use of speed tests is that test takers who are slow readers or writers are at a disadvantage. The second use is with a test that is designed to assess a person's speed in doing a particular task. A typing test is timed because its purpose is to assess typing speed as well as accuracy.

Ability Tests

An ability or aptitude is the capacity to do or learn to do a particular task. Cognitive abilities, such as intelligence, are relevant to tasks that involve information processing and learning. Psychomotor abilities, such as manual dexterity, involve bodily movements and manipulation of objects. The importance of each ability is dependent on the nature of the tasks of interest. Some job tasks require mostly cognitive abilities (e.g., programming a computer), whereas others rely mainly on psychomotor abilities (e.g., sweeping a floor). Many tasks require both types of abilities (e.g., repairing a computer or a complex piece of equipment).

Cognitive Ability Tests

An intelligence, or IQ, test of general cognitive ability is the best known **cognitive ability test**. There are also tests of individual cognitive abilities, such as mathematical or verbal ability. Most cognitive ability tests are paper-and-pencil tests, in which the items represent individual problems to solve. Such tests can be administered to large groups and provide an inexpensive and efficient means of assessing job applicants.

    Figure 5.1 contains two sample items from the Personnel Tests for Industry (PTI), a test designed to assess mathematical and verbal ability. The items are problems involving mathematical and verbal reasoning. The test was designed for group administration and can be completed in about 25 minutes. The PTI was produced by the Psychological Corporation (now Harcourt Assessment), one of the oldest and best known publishers of employment tests.

Numerical

For answers which should have a decimal point, the decimal point is printed on the answer line for you to use.

EXAMPLE

There are 8 galls of water in a tank
which can hold 16.5 gallons. How many
gallons can be added to this tank ....8.5.... galls | $\begin{array}{r} 16.5 \\ -8 \\ \hline 8.5 \end{array}$

Verbal

EXAMPLE A
Which does not belong?
(A) red, (B) green, (C) purple, (D) sweet   A B C Ð

Red, *green*, and *purple* are colors but *sweet* (choice D) is not a color and does not belong with the words. Therefore, the D had been marked as shown on the right of the question.

Figure 5.1   Two sample items from the Personnel Tests for Industry (PTI). Reproduced by permission.

All test takers are not proficient in the local language, therefore, some tests have been developed that do not rely on reading ability. Figure 5.2 contains two items from Beta-II, which is a nonverbal intelligence test. The items involve problem solving without words. The first item asks the test taker to find the way through a maze. The second item asks the test taker to solve a coding problem using numbers and shapes. The test administrator reads instructions to test takers for each type of item. Instructions can be given in any language.

Research has consistently shown that cognitive ability tests are valid predictors of job performance across a large number of different kinds of jobs (Bertua, Anderson, & Salgado, 2005; Ree & Carretta, 1998). People who score well on cognitive ability tests tend to perform better on many jobs. Cognitive ability tests have a long history of use by large organizations for employee selection because of their efficiency and validity. In a survey of 703 SIOP members, Murphy, Cronin, and Tam (2003) found consensus among I/O psychologists that such tests are fair and useful for selection. On the other hand, the use of cognitive ability tests has been controversial because some minority groups (e.g., African Americans and Hispanics) score worse on average than do whites on these tests (see the discussion of adverse impact in Chapter 6). For this reason, the use of cognitive ability tests must be used cautiously, and only for jobs where their validity has been conclusively established and better options are not available.

Mazes ask examinees to mark the shortest distance through a mase without crossing any lines (1.5 minutes)

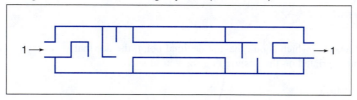

Coding requires labelling figures with their corresponding numbers (2 minutes)

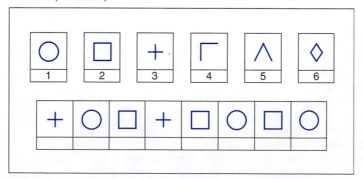

Figure 5.2 Two sample items from the Beta II Examination: 2nd edition nonverbal intelligence test. Reproduced by permission.

(© 1978 by the Psychological Corporation, All rights reserved.)

Psychomotor Ability Tests

Psychomotor ability tests assess such things as ability to manipulate objects and use tools. They involve both the coordination between senses and movement (e.g., eye-hand coordination) and the accuracy of movements. Many psychomotor tests are performance tests rather than paper-and-pencil tests because the abilities of interest involve manipulation of objects rather than cognitive elements. People are scored on their ability to perform motor tasks, such as putting pegs in holes or using simple tools to manipulate objects.

Figures 5.3 and 5.4 show two psychomotor tests. Figure 5.3 depicts the Hand-Tool Dexterity Test, which assesses the ability to use simple tools to manipulate small objects. This test involves removing and reassembling several fasteners using wrenches and a screwdriver. The score is based on the time it takes to complete the task. Figure 5.4 shows the Stromberg Dexterity Test, which assesses arm and hand movement accuracy and speed. The person must place the colored disks into the correct color-coded holes. Again, scores are based on the speed with which the person can accomplish the task.

Knowledge and Skill Tests

An ability test is intended to assess a person's capability of learning, or potential. A **knowledge and skill test**, often called an **achievement test**, is designed to assess a

Figure 5.3 The Hand-Tool Dexterity Test. Reproduced by permission.

(© 1981 by the Psychological Corporation, All rights reserved.)

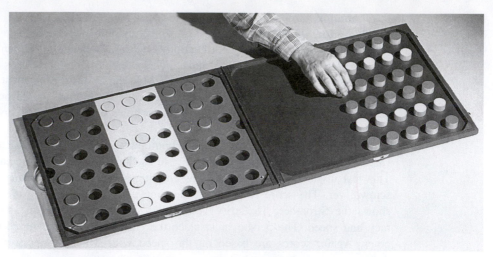

Figure 5.4   The Stromberg Dexterity Test. Reproduced by permission.

person's present level of proficiency. A knowledge test assesses what one knows, whereas a skill test assesses what one is able to do.

In practice, it is difficult to totally separate ability from knowledge and skill, for ability tests rely to some extent on knowledge and skill, and knowledge and skill tests rely to some extent on ability. The major difference between the two types of tests is the emphasis placed on prior knowledge and skill in performing specific tasks. For example, a psychomotor ability test might assess how quickly a person could put pegs in holes as an indicator of eye-hand coordination, whereas a psychomotor skill test might assess how well a person can type. Typing skill is the product of several different abilities.

Many different knowledge and skill areas can be assessed with a test. Some tests focus on general skills, such as math and reading. Others are useful for assessing skills at particular job tasks, such as typing. With a typing test, the test taker is given the task of typing some materials under standardized conditions. The person is scored on the number of words per minute typed and the number of typing errors. As with ability tests, some knowledge and skill tests are paper and pencil, and some are performance tests.

Figure 5.5 contains three items from the Bennett Mechanical Comprehension Test. This test assesses a combination of mechanical ability and knowledge about tools. This sort of test is useful for determining if a person has a good understanding of how mechanical things work and how tools can be used. Note that this is a knowledge test and assesses a person's knowledge about tools rather than skill in using tools. Actual tool use is a skill that involves both cognitive and psychomotor elements.

Personality Tests

A **personality trait** is the predisposition or tendency to behave in a particular way across different situations. People who prefer to do things with other people are said to be high

Which person carries more weight?
(if equal mark C.)

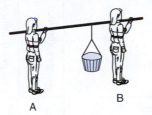

A   B

Which room has more of an echo?

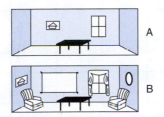

A

B

Which would be better shears
for cutting metal?

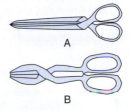

A

B

Figure 5.5 Three sample items from the Bennett Mechanical Comprehension Test (BMCT). Reproduced by permission.

on the trait of sociability. People who must always have their own way with other people are said to be high on the trait of dominance. Personality traits can be important because certain classes of behavior can be relevant for job performance and other behaviors in organizations. Sociability can be an important trait for a salesperson who must interact with other people, whereas dominance can be an important trait for a supervisor who must direct the activities of others.

Paper-and-pencil **personality tests** are useful tools for assessing personality traits. Some personality tests are designed to assess a single personality trait; personality inventories assess multiple dimensions and are sometimes used to provide profiles of individuals across several personality traits. They can also characterize people into types, which are combinations of different traits. For example, the extroverted type of person tends to be high on the traits of activity, optimism, sociability, and talkativeness, whereas the introverted type tends to be high on carefulness, quietness, passivity, and unsociability (Pervin, 1993).

Figure 5.6 contains five sample items from the public domain International Personality Item Pool (Goldberg, Johnson, Eber, Hogan, Ashton, Cloninger, & Goug, 2006). This Web-based resource (http://ipip.ori.org) provides more than 2,000 personality items that can be used to assess a wide variety of traits. The sample items in the figure are used to assess the Big Five personality theory dimensions of extraversion, emotional stability, agreeableness, conscientiousness, and openness to experience. The Big Five will be discussed in Chapter 10. As with ability tests, many standard tests can be purchased from commercial testing companies, such as Harcourt Assessment and Psychological Assessment Resources.

	Disagree Very Much	Disagree Moderately	Disagree Slightly	Agree Slightly	Agree Moderately	Agree Very Much
I am the life of the party						
I am relaxed most of the time						
I take time out for others						
I am always prepared						
I spend time reflecting on things						

Figure 5.6 Five items from the public domain International Personality Item Pool (Goldberg et al., 2006), which assesses the Big Five personality dimensions. In order from top to bottom the items are from subscales of extraversion, emotional stability, agreeableness, conscientiousness, and openness to experience. The IPIP Web site is http://ipip.ori.org.

Researchers frequently use personality tests to study many different aspects of people's behavior in organizations, but there are two major concerns about the use of personality tests for employee selection. First, there is the possibility that job applicants will fake responses to the test by answering the items in the manner they believe will put them in the most favorable light (Birkeland, Manson, Kisamore, Brannick, & Smith, 2006). When this happens, the scores for individuals who fake answers will not be valid, and the validity of the test itself will be compromised (Heggestad, Morrison, Reeve, & McCloy, 2006; Mueller-Hanson, Heggestad, & Thornton, 2003; Schmitt & Oswald, 2006). Research has revealed, however, that attempts at distortion will not necessarily invalidate a personality test used for employee selection (Schmitt Ryan, Stierwalt, & Powell, 1995). It is conceivable that individuals who knows how they should appear on the test will also know how they should behave at work to be effective. Second, personality tests do not always appear to be as job relevant as other assessment devices. *Job relevance* means that what an assessment tool measures is obviously related to specific job tasks. A typing test, for example, is obviously relevant for a secretary who must type as part of the job requirements. It is harder to show that a personality trait such as dominance is related to particular job tasks. This has led some to question whether it is appropriate to use these tests.

Despite concerns about the use of personality tests for employee selection, such tests have been growing in popularity among practitioners and researchers in organizations (Ones & Anderson, 2002). Several researchers have conducted meta-analyses to investigate the relation between personality and job performance. This technique of data analysis allows for the statistical combination of results across multiple studies of the same phenomenon (see Chapter 2). Such analyses have shown that personality can predict performance, although the magnitude of the correlations is modest (e.g., Dudley, Orvis, Lebiecki, & Cortina, 2006; Salgado, 2003). One difficulty with drawing conclusions about the validity of personality tests from the existing meta-analyses is that the analyses tend to group together tests that assess many different traits for the prediction of performance on many different types of jobs. Some of these traits may represent job-relevant characteristics; others may be unimportant for success. Evidence suggests that choosing specific personality traits known to be relevant to job performance on particular jobs will do a better job of predicting performance (Paunonen, Rothstein, & Jackson, 1999; Tett, Steele, & Beauregard, 2003).

Emotional Intelligence Tests

Emotional intelligence (EI) is a characteristic that falls between a personality trait and a cognitive ability. It can be defined as the ability to control and recognize emotions in oneself and in others. In theory this ability makes people more socially skilled, enabling them to be aware of and to control their impact on others. In a work setting this means being able to work smoothly with colleagues, and in supervisory positions, the ability to exert leadership. Salovey and Mayer (1990) are credited with kicking off interest among psychologists that there is an important cognitive skill other than intelligence. Unfortunately, various researchers who study it have adopted somewhat different definitions and conceptions, and exaggerated claims both in the field and in the popular media have caused confusion and controversy (Conte, 2005; Daus & Ashkanasy; 2005; Landy, 2005).

Petrides and Furnham (2000) note that there are two types of EI assessments. The trait test assesses EI as a personality characteristic accessible to the person's awareness. Trait tests look like a personality scale, and people respond to each item by indicating how well it describes them. The information-processing test has a multiple-choice format with one right answer per question. It is based on the assumption that people cannot directly report their EI because it is not accessible to their awareness. Instead, individuals reveal their EI by choosing the correct answers on the test, just as they would indicate cognitive ability with a general intelligence test.

Research with various EI tests has shown that they can predict job performance. For example, a meta-analysis by Van Rooy and Viswesvaran (2004) found that, on average, EI correlates .23 with job performance across 59 studies. Sy, Tram, and O'Hara (2006) showed that supervisors who were high in EI had more satisfied subordinates. This suggested that the EI skill might have led to better leadership behaviors that had a positive influence on subordinates. An issue with EI research, however, concerns the construct validity of the EI measures used in these studies. Some have suggested that they only measure established variables, such as cognitive ability or established aspects of personality (e.g., Landy, 2005). At the current time, the construct validity of these measures is in dispute among researchers, and it will take additional research to settle the issue of whether EI is a unique construct.

Integrity Tests

An **integrity test** is designed to predict whether an employee will engage in counterproductive or dishonest behavior on the job. The behaviors the tests are designed to predict include cheating, sabotage, theft, and unethical behavior. They also are sometimes used to predict absence and turnover. Wanek, Sackett, and Ones (2003) noted that there are two different types of integrity tests—overt and personality.

The *overt integrity test* assesses attitudes and prior behavior. It asks those taking the test to indicate agreement or disagreement with statements concerning honesty and moral behavior. An example of such an item would be the following:

It is all right to lie if you know you won't get caught.

Test takers are also asked how often they have done a number of counterproductive behaviors. A possible item might be the following:

How often have you stolen something from your employer?

The *personality integrity test* assesses personality characteristics that have been found to predict counterproductive behavior. Whereas the overt integrity tests are obvious assessments of honesty and integrity, personality tests often have a hidden purpose. In fact, standard personality inventories often are used as integrity tests. We discussed personality tests earlier in this chapter.

Research on integrity tests has shown that they can predict both counterproductive behavior and job performance (Ashton, 1998; Ones & Viswesvaran, 1998; Ones, Viswesvaran, & Schmidt, 1993). Collins and Schmidt (1993) compared white-collar criminals to white-collar employees using several personality tests that have been used as integrity tests. They found that the tests were able to distinguish between the groups. The criminals scored differently than the employees on several measures of personality. Woolley and Hakstian (1993) found that both overt and personality integrity tests related to college students' admissions of having engaged in counterproductive and dishonest behaviors on the job and in school.

Interestingly, research has shown that integrity tests may do a better job of predicting absence, general counterproductive behavior, and job performance than theft (Wanek, 1999). Part of the problem with validation studies is that accurate data on employee theft is difficult to obtain because many employees who steal are never caught. Thus it is difficult to determine how well the test can predict stealing when you don't know for certain which employees were dishonest. However, as Wanek (1999) points out, these tests have been shown to predict useful behaviors at work besides theft, so using integrity tests for selection can have benefits beyond control of theft. For example, Van Iddekinge, Taylor, and Eidson (2005) showed that a commercially available integrity test was able to predict job performance.

Vocational Interest Tests

A **vocational interest test** matches either the interests or the personality of the test taker to those of people in a variety of different occupations and occupational categories. Interests are assessed by asking the test taker to indicate preferences for engaging in various activities, such as attending a sporting event or visiting a museum. Personality is relevant because specific traits may drive people's interests; for example, people who are outgoing and extraverted might prefer activities that involve contact with other people (Larson, Rottinghaus, & Borgen, 2001). Data from vocational interest tests are available about the answers of people in many different occupations. The test taker's answers are matched to those of people in different occupations to see how well they fit each occupation.

Interest and personality profiles vary considerably from occupation to occupation. Therefore, any individual test taker will match some occupations and not others. Because occupations tend to group together into categories, a person can be matched to a category of occupation. The artistic category of occupation, for instance, involves creative processes; it includes such occupations as interior design and photography.

One of the most popular vocational interest tests is the Self-Directed Search (Holland, 1994). This test provides scores on six personality types (Figure 5.7). Each type is associated with a family of occupations. As shown in the figure, the investigative type likes investigative-type jobs. These include scientific fields, such as biology or geology. The profile of scores on the six types can guide a person in choosing a career.

The match between a person's vocational interests and those of people in occupations is presumed to predict satisfaction with the occupation. A person who takes a job that is a poor match will likely be unhappy with it, whereas a person who takes a job that is a good match will probably like it. The idea behind the tests is to encourage people to select careers that match their interests. Vocational interest tests are frequently used for vocational guidance in helping people decide what careers to pursue.

Drug Testing

Organizations in the United States and elsewhere have turned to drug testing of applicants and employees as a means of controlling drug use at work. An estimated 30 million

---

The Realistic type likes jobs such as automobile mechanic, aircraft controller, surveyor, farmer, or electrician.

The Investigative type likes investigative jobs such as biologist, chemist, physicist, anthropologist, geologist, or medical technologist.

The Artistic type likes artistic jobs such as composer, musician, stage director, writer, interior decorator, or actor/actress.

The Social type likes social jobs such as teacher, religious worker, counselor, clinical psychologist, psychiatric case worker, or speech therapist.

The Enterprising type likes enterprising jobs such as salesperson, manager, business executive, television producer, sports promoter, or buyer.

The Conventional type likes conventional jobs such as bookkeeper, stenographer, financial analyst, banker, cost estimator, or tax expert.

Figure 5.7 The six personality types and associated occupations as assessed by the Self-Directed Search. Adapted and reproduced by special permission of the publisher, Psychological Assessment Resources, Inc., 16204 North Florida Avenue, Lutz, FL 33549, from *You and Your Career* by John L. Holland, Ph.D. Copyright 1985 by PAR, Inc. Further reproduction is prohibited without permission from PAR, Inc.

Americans undergo such tests each year (Mastrangelo & Popovich, 2000). Such testing is of particular importance in jobs that are safety-sensitive, meaning that impaired performance could lead to accidents or injury. Typical jobs of this kind are air traffic controller and bus driver. However, such tests are controversial, and many people consider them an unfair invasion of privacy. Paronto, Truxillo, Bauer, and Leo (2002) surveyed 1,484 individuals about their attitudes toward drug testing. They found that respondents considered drug testing more acceptable for jobs that were safety-sensitive than for jobs that were not.

▶ BIOGRAPHICAL INFORMATION

One of the easiest ways to find out about people is to ask them what you wish to know. In an employment setting, basic information about people is obtained from an application form. Although they can differ from organization to organization, standard application forms contain questions about education, job skills, personal characteristics, and work history. Some forms can be quite detailed, asking about specific experiences, such as extracurricular school activities (e.g., participation in sports). Most ask for biographical information concerning education and relevant work experience that might be necessary for a particular job.

The **biographical inventory** asks much more detailed background questions than a typical application form. Whereas application forms ask about level of education and work experience, the biographical inventory asks about specific experiences at school and work, or even other areas of life. Some of the questions ask about objective, verifiable facts, such as

What was your grade point average in college?

Others ask about opinions or subjective experiences, such as

Did you enjoy college?

If a biographical inventory contains enough of the second type of question, it begins to approximate a psychological test that assesses interests and personality instead of prior life experiences. The items of a biographical inventory, however, focus more on past experiences and reactions than do psychological test items (Stokes & Reddy, 1992). Most inventories use a multiple-choice response format that can be easily scored. Possible answers to the question about enjoying college might be

Enjoyed very much

Enjoyed somewhat

Enjoyed a little

Didn't enjoy at all

Table 5.2 contains some examples of inventory items.

Stokes and Searcy (1999) distinguished empirical from rational biographical inventories. The **empirical biographical inventory** is developed by administering a large number of potential items to a group of employees in a particular job. Those items related to job performance are retained for the scale. The **rational biographical inventory** is developed by beginning with an analysis of KSAO requirements and then devising items that reflect them.

TABLE 5.2 Sample Items from a Biographical Inventory

When you were in grade school and people were being picked for teams, when were you usually picked?	Did you attend your high school prom?
In high school, what grades did you get in chemistry class?	In your first full-time job, how often did you initiate conversation with your immediate supervisor?

Biographical inventories have been shown to predict job performance (Hunter & Hunter, 1984; Stokes, Toth, Searcy, Stroupe, & Carter, 1999). In a direct comparison, Stokes and Searcy (1999) found that the empirical and rational types of inventories had similar predictive power. Biographical inventories have been found to add predictability over and above personality tests, suggesting they don't just assess the same thing (McManus & Kelly, 1999; Mount, Witt, & Barrick, 2000; see Research in Detail). Furthermore, biographical inventories tend to be resistant to applicant faking to look good on the test because many items are factual in nature and give the appearance of verifiability (West & Karas, 1999).

RESEARCH IN DETAIL

One of the criticisms of biographical inventories is that they just assess personality and offer limited advantages over a personality inventory. McManus and Kelly (1999) wanted to see how well a biographical inventory could stand up against a personality inventory in predicting job performance.

The study was conducted in five insurance companies in the United States. Participants in the study were 116 newly hired insurance sales representatives. During the application process, each one completed a widely used off-the-shelf biographical inventory designed for the insurance industry called the Initial Career Profile (ICP). A 124-item personality battery was included to measure what many consider the Big Five underlying dimensions of personality: extraversion, agreeableness, conscientiousness, emotional stability, and openness to experience (see Chapter 10). The ICP was used for selecting applicants, but the personality battery was not. Six months after being hired, each participant's job performance was assessed with a five-item rating scale completed by the immediate supervisor. This produced two scores—one for the main tasks involved in sales, and the other, more general displays of effort and motivation. Both job performance score were strongly correlated at .69.

Results showed that both the ICP and the personality battery were related to job performance. The biographical inventory correlated .25 and .26 with sales and effort, respectively. Of the personality variables, extraversion correlated with performance the most strongly, with correlations of .29 and .22, respectively. Conscientiousness correlated lowest, with nonsignificant correlations of almost zero. This surprised the authors, because prior studies suggested that conscientiousness should relate to performance. When they analyzed personality and the ICP together, they found that combined they did a better job of predicting performance than alone, suggesting that the biographical inventory was not simply assessing the same thing as the personality battery.

Source: McManus, M. A., & Kelly, M. L. (1999). Personality measures and biodata: Evidence regarding their incremental predictive value in the life insurance industry. *Personnel Psychology*, *52*, 137–148.

The biggest criticism of biographical inventories is limited to the empirical variety. It raises the point that items are chosen based entirely on their ability to predict performance rather than on an apparent link to job requirements. Sometimes an item can predict performance even though it cannot be linked to a KSAO necessary for job performance. These items are combined into scores that predict performance but do not reflect job-related KSAOs. Many questions in such inventories can appear completely unrelated to the job or job performance. Applicants may consider some questions as an invasion of privacy, such as questions about high school dating behavior. They may also believe that the assessment's use is unfair, which can lead to increased legal challenges to the selection system, as we will discuss in Chapter 6. Finally, such inventories often have limited generalizability (Mumford, 1999) and may only be useful for the job and location where they were developed. On the other hand, rational inventories can often be used for many jobs and locations.

▶ INTERVIEWS

An interview is a face-to-face meeting between one or more interviewers who are collecting information or making hiring decisions and an interviewee. Almost all organizations use the interview in hiring for almost all positions. Perhaps one reason for the universal use of this technique is that it is widely accepted. Steiner and Gilliland (1996) found that it was rated most acceptable of all commonly used selection procedures by college students in both France and the United States.

There are two types of interviews conducted in organizational settings. During an *unstructured interview*, the interviewer asks whatever questions come to mind. It can be much like a conversation between the interviewer and interviewee in which the nature of the interaction between the two people determines in large part what is discussed. By contrast, during a **structured interview**, the interviewer has a preplanned series of questions that are asked of every person who is interviewed. This makes the interview relatively standard, although the interaction between the two people can still affect what gets discussed. Nevertheless, the use of a standard set of questions allows the interviewer to collect the same information about each interviewee.

Campion, Palmer, and Campion (1997) discuss 15 ways in which structure can be introduced into an interview. There is no one way in which such interviews are conducted. Some interviews are moderately structured in that the questions to be asked or just the topics to be covered are specified and standardized. Others have strict requirements that questions be asked in a set order, that the same phrasing be used, that interviewees not be asked to elaborate on any answer even if it is unclear, and that interviewees not ask questions themselves until the end. In the extreme, the interview is much like an open-ended test with an oral rather than written response. Campion et al. (1997) suggest that the more highly structured approaches are probably the most valid, and therefore as much structure as possible should be introduced into the interview.

The interview can be used in two ways. One is as an alternative to an application form or a written questionnaire to collect information. Questions can ask about attitudes (Did you like your last job?), job experiences (Have you ever supervised anyone?), personal background (What was your major in college?), and preferences (Would you mind working weekends?). The other way the interview can be used is to make inferences about a person's suitability for a job based on both the answers to questions and their behavior in the interview situation. The interview can be considered a sample of interpersonal behavior, showing how well a person communicates and relates to the interviewer.

Interviewers can be asked to make ratings on job-related dimensions, such as communication skills or relevant experience. They sometimes make overall ratings of applicant suitability for the job. These ratings can be subject to the same problems as performance appraisal ratings, which we discussed in Chapter 4. Interviewer biases and cognitive processes can reduce the accuracy of judgments and ratings (Dipboye & Gaugler, 1993).

The structured interview can be a good way to collect information that builds on what is provided in the application form. Specific questions can ask for more detail about the provided information. For example, an application form will typically ask the person to list all prior jobs. In an interview, the interviewee might be asked to describe each job held and to explain how it might be relevant to the job at hand.

An interview has two advantages over an application form. First, the interview allows for longer and more detailed answers to questions that do not have short or simple answers. Most people find it easier to talk than write. Second, the interview allows both the interviewer and the interviewee to ask one another for clarification. The interviewer can ask the interviewee to explain an unclear answer or to provide additional details. The interviewee can ask the interviewer to rephrase an unclear question or to indicate if the appropriate level of detail has been given.

The disadvantage of the interview is that the interviewer can affect the answers of the interviewee. Even with the most carefully constructed structured interview and thoroughly trained interviewer, the interaction between interviewer and interviewee will differ from interview to interview. Differences among interviewers in their ability to conduct an interview and personality could affect the interview process and the interviewee's responses (Dipboye & Gaugler, 1993). This is not a concern with application forms because there is relatively little interaction between the person administering the form and the person completing it.

The Interview is used for almost all hiring.

(*Daemmrich/The Image Works*)

Research evidence supports the use of structured interviews in making employment decisions, but not necessarily the use of unstructured interviews. Ratings of interviewee employment suitability from a structured interview have been shown to predict future job performance across many different studies (Huffcutt & Arthur, 1994; Judge, Higgins, & Cable, 2000; Wiesner & Cronshaw, 1988). The unstructured interview has been found to be less valid as a predictor of job performance (Wiesner & Cronshaw, 1988). Schmidt and Zimmerman (2004) argued that much of the difference in interview validity can be attributed to the worse reliability of unstructured interviews as compared to structured interviews. With unstructured interviews, multiple interviewers will not agree very well on the applicant's suitability to be hired, and this lack of agreement hurts the ability of the interview to predict future job success. A further problem with the unstructured interview is that it leaves too much room for biases. An interviewer might decide on the basis of appearance, for example, that an applicant is unsuitable. Cable and Judge (1997) found that interviewers' hiring decisions were related to how attractive they found the applicant and how much they liked him or her. Interviewers affected in this way might not be as thorough in questioning a disliked or unattractive applicant, and thus might fail to discover important job-related qualifications that could lead to hiring. Given these biases, it should not be surprising that interviewers fail to agree about applicants.

Wiesner and Cronshaw (1988) conducted a meta-analysis of over 100 interview studies. They classified each study as representing either a structured or unstructured interview and computed the average correlation across studies within each group. The average correlation between interview outcome and job performance was larger for the structured interview studies ($r = .34$) than for the unstructured interview studies ($r = .17$).

The Wiesner and Cronshaw study, as well as others that have followed, has provided convincing evidence for the validity of the structured interview for selecting employees. Before these studies were published, there was widespread belief in the field that interviews were invalid for employee selection. This conclusion is accepted today only for unstructured interviews. The best advice that can be given to people who use interviews to select employees is to be sure to use structured rather than unstructured interviews.

Several factors contribute to the validity of the structured interview. Huffcutt, Roth, and McDaniel (1996) conducted a meta-analysis showing that cognitive ability was related to interview outcomes and is a factor in their validity. Dipboye and Gaugler (1993) discussed six factors that are listed in Table 5.3. These factors involve the design of the questions asked, the information available and not available to the interviewer, the ratings made by the interviewer, and the training given to the interviewer. Roth and Campion (1992) found good validity for a structured interview that contained most of the factors noted as important by Dipboye and Gaugler (1993).

With all the research focus on the validity of interviews, issues about what interviews actually assess have been overlooked. Huffcutt, Conway, Roth, and Stone (2001) did an extensive analysis of the specific personal characteristics assessed in interviews that give insight into why they are able to predict future performance. They conducted a literature review and identified 47 interview studies that provided information about the KSAOs covered. The most commonly assessed were personality traits and interpersonal skills. Furthermore, structured and unstructured interviews tended to focus on different

TABLE 5.3 Factors that can Enhance the Reliability and Validity of a Structured Interview

The interviewer should ask standardized questions.

The interviewer should have detailed information about the job in question.

The interviewer should not have prior information about the interviewee, such as psychological test scores.

The interviewer should not evaluate the interviewee until the interview is completed.

The interviewer should make ratings of individual dimensions of the interviewee, such as educational background or relevance of prior work history, rather than a global rating of suitability for the job.

Interviewers should receive training in how to conduct a valid structured interview.

Source: Adapted from "Cognitive and Behavioral Processes in the Selection Interview," by R. L. Dipboye and B. B. Gaugler, 1993, in N. Schmitt and W. C. Borman (Eds.), *Personnel Selection in Organizations*. San Francisco: Jossey-Bass.

things. Structured interviews targeted job knowledge and skills, person-organization fit, and interpersonal skills, whereas unstructured interviews targeted general intelligence, education, and prior experience.

Technology has also made it possible to conduct interviews remotely. Telephone and videophone interviews have become increasingly popular when applicants are located at far distances. Research has shown that interviewees may receive higher ratings in telephone and videophone interviews (Chapman & Rowe, 2001; Straus, Miles, & Levesque, 2001). This was particularly true for individuals who were physically unattractive (Straus et al., 2001), suggesting a possible bias in interviews where the interviewer can see the interviewee. Schmidt and Rader (1999) conducted a meta-analysis of structured telephone interview studies and found that the average correlation with performance was about the same as for face-to-face interviews. One of the limitations of the telephone is that the interviewer cannot observe nonverbal information, such as appearance, facial expression, and gestures, and these elements can be important in assessments for some jobs, such as sales. Furthermore, as Chapman, Uggerslev, and Webster (2003) found, applicants may have better attitudes toward face-to-face interviews than telephone or videophone. Thus it seems unlikely that face-to-face interviews will disappear anytime soon.

▶ WORK SAMPLES

A **work sample** is an assessment device that requires people to demonstrate how well they can perform the tasks involved in a job under standardized conditions. It is a type of simulation in which a person does a job or part of a job under testing conditions rather than actual job conditions.

A work sample is like a psychological test except that it is designed to measure a higher level skill. A test measures a basic skill, such as eye-hand coordination or manual dexterity. A work sample assesses the skill in doing a particular task, such as driving a bulldozer, which is comprised of several basic skills performed in the context of a particular set of conditions. For some applications, the higher level skill may be more important to assess than the basic skills because a work sample indicates how well a person can actually do a particular task. A psychological test indicates whether people have the requisite basic skills that should in theory predict how well they could do the task, but not how well they can actually do it.

The typical work sample gives the applicant the materials and tools necessary to accomplish the task. The applicant is instructed to complete the task quickly but accurately. A score is computed based on the accuracy with which the task is completed and the amount of time it took. For example, a person might be asked to disassemble and reassemble an electric motor or a small gasoline engine. A trained observer scores the test performance on accuracy and speed. Perhaps the most familiar work sample is the driving test required of applicants for a driver's license. The applicant is asked to complete a series of maneuvers with the automobile. The test administrator observes the maneuvers and records the scores for each one of them. To get the license, the applicant must achieve a total score that meets a prearranged criterion. A work sample in an organizational setting might be used the same way to determine if a person is suitable for a particular job.

Work samples have been found to be good predictors of future job performance (e.g., Hunter & Hunter, 1984; Robertson & Kandola, 1982). The close correspondence between the assessment situation and the job itself certainly has much to do with the success of the work sample in predicting performance. As with most simulation techniques, the work sample has a high degree of job relevance. This increases the likelihood that people will accept their use as predictors of important skills in employee selection. There are several limitations to keep in mind, however. For many work samples, the applicant must already have experience with the task, work samples can be costly to develop, and the work sample is specific to a particular type of job (Callinan & Robertson, 2000).

▶ ASSESSMENT CENTERS

An **assessment center** measures how well a person is able to perform the tasks of a specific job. It consists of several exercises that are designed to simulate various job tasks. Most assessment centers are designed to assess management skills, but they are used for nonmanagement jobs as well. The exercises can take several days to complete and are often administered to several individuals at a time. This technique is widely used by many types of employers. For example, in a survey of British employers, Keenan (1995) found that 44 percent used assessment centers to hire college graduates. In the United States the assessment center is used primarily for hiring and promotion decisions, although it can also be used to help employees enhance job skills (Spychalski, Quiñones, Gaugler, & Pohley, 1997).

Assessment center exercises have a high level of realism because they simulate many of the actual tasks conducted on the job. For example, the person being assessed, or *assessee*, may be asked to pretend or role play being a manager in a given situation. This might involve dealing with a subordinate or handling the paperwork for the job. The assessee's performance on each exercise is scored by a panel of trained *assessors*. The assessors are asked to evaluate the person's performance on each of several dimensions relevant to the job in question. For a manager's job, these can involve communication, dealing with other people, decision-making, and planning. Table 5.4 contains the dimensions from a typical assessment center for managers described by Harris, Becker, and Smith (1993).

TABLE 5.4   Dimensions Scored in an Assessment Center

Oral communication
Oral comprehension
Problem-solving
Interpersonal relations
Coaching
Planning
Written communication

Source: From "Does the Assessment Center Scoring Method Affect
the Cross-Situational Consistency of Ratings?" by M. M. Harris,
A. S. Becker, and D. E. Smith, 1993, *Journal of Applied
Psychology, 78*, 675–678.

An assessment center can contain many different activities and exercises. The assessee
might be interviewed and take a battery of psychological tests, in addition to completing several simulation exercises. The exercises might include an in-basket, a leaderless
group exercise, a problem-solving simulation, and role plays. Each exercise yields scores
on several dimensions, and usually each dimension is assessed by several exercises. In
addition, there is an overall assessment of the person's potential for the job in question.

An **in-basket exercise** asks assessees to pretend that it is the first day of a new job and
they have found a series of items in their in-basket. Items include e-mails, letters, memos,
and phone messages. The assessee's task is to deal with each item in an appropriate
manner, deciding what action if any to take by making notes on each item. An example of
a memo that could be part of an in-basket exercise is shown in Table 5.5. To score well,
the person must handle the memo in an appropriate and constructive manner. Ignoring the
memo or writing a nasty reply to the sender would not be a constructive action. Leaving
a note for the secretary to complete the report or doing so oneself would be better.

In a **leaderless group exercise** several assessees are given a problem to solve together.
The problem might be a competitive one, such as dividing up a scarce resource. Each
member of the group might be asked to role play a particular management position. The
assessees have to decide which department gets a new piece of equipment. The problem
can also be a cooperative one, for which all group members must generate a solution to
an organizational problem, such as deciding whether or not to market a new product.

TABLE 5.5   Example of a Memorandum for an In-Basket Exercise

Memorandum

TO: Robert Jones, Manager of Marketing
FROM: Deborah Smith, Director of Human Resources
SUBJECT: New Position

On October 15 of this year you requested an additional secretarial position for your department.
I have been instructed by the company president to provide you the position. Before I can
do so, however, you need to provide me with a complete justification for why you need this
position. Please complete a Position Justification Report and return it to me. I need it by the
end of the week or the position will be delayed until the first of the year.

In a *problem-solving simulation*, the assessee is given a problem and asked to come up with a solution, perhaps by producing a report. The problem provides sufficient background information from which to write the report. For example, the assessee could be given information about the costs and projected income for opening a new assembly plant. The task would be to produce a feasibility report for opening the plant.

A *role-play exercise* requires that the assessee pretend to be a particular person in a specific organizational role, such as the manager of human resources. The task is to handle a problem or situation, such as counseling a troubled employee or dealing with an irate customer.

Assessors rate each assessee on each dimension by both observing behavior and reviewing materials produced during the exercises. Each person is scored on the various dimensions and may get an overall score. The dimension scores can be used to give the assessees feedback about their strengths and weaknesses. The overall score is useful if assessment center performance is to be used in hiring or promotion decisions.

Research on the assessment center has found it to be a valid device for the selection of employees (Arthur, Day, McNelly, & Edens, 2003). This means that scores on the assessment center are correlated with job performance. For example, Shechtman (1992) found that scores in an assessment center given to university students upon admission predicted their job performance as teachers from two to five years after graduation, with a correlation of .27. Dayan, Kasten, and Fox (2002) found that assessment center ratings predicted job performance both two and four years later for police officers, with correlations of .30 and .21, respectively.

Although the overall scores in an assessment center have been shown to be valid, questions have been raised about the construct validity of the individual dimension scores (e.g., Bowler & Woehr, 2006; Chan, 1996; Joyce, Thayer, & Pond, 1994; Lance, Lamber, Gewin, Lievens, & Conway, 2004). In other words, we are not certain that the intended dimensions of the assessment center are actually what is being measured. Different exercises are designed to assess a common set of dimensions. Because the same dimensions are assessed across exercises, scores on corresponding dimensions from different exercises should correlate well. For example, the score for leadership in an in-basket should relate to the score for leadership in the leaderless group exercise. On the other hand, the different dimension scores within the same exercise should not be highly correlated, because the dimensions are supposed to be measures of different distinct characteristics. High correlations among dimension ratings are similar to halo errors in performance appraisal (see Chapter 4).

The problem with assessment centers is that the various dimension scores given to assessees within an exercise, such as an in-basket, are too highly correlated. Furthermore, the scores given to assessees on the same dimensions across different exercises are not correlated enough. The high correlations across dimensions within exercises suggest that assessors are assessing only a single dimension rather than multiple dimensions. One possibility is that assessors are able to judge only overall exercise performance rather than the individual dimensions. The low correlations between dimensions across exercises suggest that each exercise might assess a different characteristic.

On balance, research on assessment centers raises the possibility that each exercise in a center measures a single trait rather than multiple dimensions, and that the different exercises may assess different things (Lance, Foster, Gentry, & Thoresen, 2004). Lievens, Chasteen, Day, and Christiansen (2006) suggest that each exercise provides a different set of opportunities for the assessee to display behavior relevant to performance in a unique way. One might reflect leadership, and another might tap problem solving. Thus it should be no surprise that dimension scores are not very high across exercises. At the present time, we are not certain exactly what the different KSAOs assessed might be. Thus use of the assessment center to give specific feedback about individual KSAOs (e.g., decision making or leadership) is questionable. Russell and Domm (1995) provided evidence that ratings reflect how well the individual performs the role for the job being simulated rather than how well the person does each dimension. Regardless of why it works, the assessment center does a good job of predicting future job performance. For that reason it is a popular assessment device for selection and placement (see International Replication).

INTERNATIONAL REPLICATION

Assessment centers use several different types of exercises to measure the various abilities thought to be essential for job success. The idea is to combine scores for each ability across several exercises, which should improve reliability and validity. Research has shown, however, that people's scores on individual ability dimensions from exercise to exercise are not highly correlated. In other words, a person might do well on a dimension (e.g., decision-making) on one exercise and poorly on the same dimension on another exercise. This suggests that the assessment center may not measure the intended dimensions. If it did measure individual dimensions of ability, scores should be similar across different exercises.

Chan (1996) conducted a study that illustrates the problem of poor correlations among dimension scores across exercises in an assessment center that still has validity. The study was conducted for the Singapore police force, which asked Chan to design an assessment center for promotional use. The assessees were 46 officers who were possible candidates for promotion. Six exercises were written, including an in-basket and a leaderless group. Fourteen dimensions were assessed, although not every dimension was measured in each exercise. The center was validated against two job performance criteria—current job performance rating and subsequent promotion two years after the assessment.

Correlations were computed among all the ratings in the assessment center, both among measures of the same dimension across exercises and among all ratings within exercises. If the dimension scores were valid, the former should have been larger than the latter. The results were the opposite in that the mean correlation among measures of the same dimension was larger than among measures of different dimensions within exercises (.07 vs. .71, respectively). The lack of a significant correlation among measures of the same dimensions suggests that they measured different things, while the very high correlations among all ratings within exercises reflected a single thing for each exercise.

The assessment center resulted in two overall ratings—overall performance and promotability in the future. Overall performance correlated quite well with actual promotion assessed two years later, but not at all with the most recent performance appraisal by the supervisor. The assessment center rating of promotability also correlated with future promotion strongly and only modestly with supervisor rating of performance. These results demonstrate the validity of the center, even though the exercises did not do an adequate job of assessing what they were initially designed to measure.

Results of this study are quite consistent with many others in showing the doubtful validity of dimension scores. On the other hand, the strong prediction of future promotions was very encouraging. Whereas many assessment center studies are contaminated in that results are used to help determine future promotions, such was not the case here. The assessment center is an effective technique, even though we are not certain what it actually measures.

Source: Chan, D. (1996). Criterion and construct validation of an assessment centre. *Journal of Occupational and Organizational Psychology*, 69, 167–181.

Research efforts have been made to improve the validity of dimension ratings in assessment centers. Reilly, Henry, and Smither (1990) reasoned that perhaps assessors are unable to adequately assess individual dimensions because they have too much information to process. Each exercise provides a great deal of information, and often that information must be organized in some way for judgments to be made. To help assessors organize information, the researchers provided a checklist of 273 behaviors for use in rating performance in the exercises. The assessors used the checklist to note the specific behaviors performed by each assessee before making their ratings.

The results of the study showed that correlations between dimensions within exercises got smaller, and correlations between corresponding dimensions across exercises got larger than those typically found in assessment centers. Thus, the validities of the dimension scores improved. These results suggest that one problem with assessment centers as they are currently conducted is that they overload the assessor's ability to accurately assess dimensions. By providing checklists of behaviors, structure is put on the judgment task and improves the validity of the exercise ratings. Improvements were also found by Arthur, Woehr, and Maldegan (2000). They were able to produce good correlations within dimensions across exercises by carefully constructing their assessment center. Most of their assessors were I/O psychologists, and they received careful training about how to translate specific behaviors into ratings. Finally, Lievens (2001) was able to increase the accuracy of assessment center ratings through the use of frame-of-reference training (see Chapter 4). Raters were given examples of effective and ineffective behaviors so that they could build a common understanding of performance during training. A combination of all these approaches, using checklists, offering frame-of-reference training, and more carefully choosing assessors and conducting the centers, will likely produce the best results.

▶ ELECTRONIC ASSESSMENT

One of the fastest growing trends in organizational assessment is the use of electronic media rather than paper and pencil. What began as a move to computerize test administration and scoring on personal computers has exploded with the development of new kinds of assessments and approaches. Lievens and Sackett (2006), for example, discuss the use of video-based assessment, where each item is presented as a video clip illustrating an event that might occur at work. Such assessments can provide a realistic situation that is difficult to describe fully with text. One of the major catalysts for electronic assessment is the Web, which makes it possible to link an applicant with an assessment almost anywhere in the world. Applicant recruiting services, such as Monster, have begun incorporating assessments into what previously was the initial application process. Electronic technology is expanding the use of assessment by making it cheaper and more convenient.

Electronic Administration of Psychological Tests

Paper-and-pencil psychological tests can be adapted for administration electronically. The test taker can read each item on a computer screen or display and respond with the keyboard, mouse, or other interface device. There are two major advantages to this approach.

First, the test can be scored automatically as soon as the last item is answered, which can speed up the selection process. Second, a test can be put on a Web site, allowing access from almost anywhere in the world. An applicant doesn't have to come to a particular testing site to take the test. Of course, steps must be taken to monitor test taking so that cheating doesn't occur. There are two major disadvantages (McBride, 1998). First, developing a computer testing system can be expensive and time consuming, although the increasing availability of off-the-shelf electronic assessments is reducing this cost. Hardware and software costs can be considerable, especially compared to the small cost of printed test booklets and pencils. The use of computer-scannable answer sheets, however, allows for cheap computer scoring of large numbers of tests, thus eliminating one advantage of computer administration. Second, computerized tests are not necessarily equivalent to printed tests, especially for speeded tests, which time how many correct items a person can do in a given interval. One such test is a clerical speed and accuracy test in which the test taker must compare two strings of letters and indicate whether or not they are the same. For example:

abdiel vs. abdifl

ghicbe vs. ghicbe

Response time can be different per item using computer versus paper and pencil for the same items, making scores nonequivalent.

Potosky and Bobko (2004) contrasted Web-based with paper-and-pencil tests. They noted that for speed tests where the test taker has a limited amount of time, adjustments must be made for the load times of Web pages. Furthermore, test taking strategies are likely to vary between the two formats. It is easy with paper-and-pencil tests to skip around, so that the test taker might choose to complete certain types of items first and others last. Since Web-based tests allow fewer items per screen than paper does per page, they can discourage skipping around, and thus items are more likely to be completed in order. Care must be taken in comparing scores taken with the two formats.

It might seem that computer administration has the potential for increasing the accuracy of personality tests. People often distort or fake their responses face to face, and are sometimes better able to reveal themselves honestly to a machine, such as a computer, than to another person. A computer might seem more impersonal than a paper-and-pencil test to a test taker. Richman, Kiesler, Weisband, and Drasgow (1999) conducted a meta-analysis to see if the tendency to respond in a favorable direction was the same for computer and paper-and-pencil administration of personality tests. Overall, the results suggested no differences. However, in looking closer at the results, Richman noticed that there was somewhat less distortion when the test taker was alone. When an experimenter was in the room, any feeling of anonymity was apparently lost, and there were no differences between the computer and paper-and-pencil administration.

Paper-and-pencil tests are not the only assessment technique that has been computerized, for even psychomotor skills can be assessed by computer. Typing tests, once conducted on a typewriter, are now done on a computer, because this is where typing is almost always done. A more complex testing system for secretaries was developed by Schmitt, Gilliland, Landis, and Devine (1993). This system asks the test taker to complete eight "tests" on the computer and provides nine scores. Each of the eight tests is like a work sample in that it represents a simulated task done by a secretary. One test asks the test taker to compose and type a letter to a customer on a word processor. Although the validity of this system remains to be established, it seems likely that such computer assessment systems will be shown to be good predictors of future job performance.

A still more complex type of computer assessment to measure problem solving has become popular in Germany (Funke, 1998; Kleinmann & Strauss, 1998). These assessments provide the applicant with a simulation of a complex work situation, such as running an airport or a factory, which is somewhat like a computer game. The person is given a fixed amount of time to run the simulation, and various indicators of performance are calculated by the computer. Research with these assessments has provided impressive initial evidence that they can predict future job performance for jobs in which problem-solving skill is important (Kleinmann & Strauss, 1998).

Computers are not the only technology being used to increase the efficiency of assessment. Van Iddekinge, Eidson, Kudisch, and Goldblatt (2003) developed a telephone-based system for administering a biographical inventory. Applicants were able to dial a toll-free number and answer yes/no questions about their backgrounds using the keys on their telephones. Van Iddekinge et al. showed that this type of assessment was able to predict job performance for those subsequently hired. However, it required designing an inventory in a yes/no format, which is more limiting than other media, such as pencil and paper.

Tailored Testing

Tailored testing selects the specific items given to test takers according to their individual ability level. Although it is possible to administer tailored tests manually, a computer makes this approach more feasible (Murphy, 1988). A computerized tailored test, also known as **computer adaptive testing**, begins by giving the test taker an item of moderate difficulty. If the person gets the item correct, a more difficult item is presented. If the person gets it wrong, an easier item is chosen. As the test proceeds, the computer will choose items at the appropriate level of difficulty for the test taker. Tailored tests can be more efficient than standard tests because they can achieve the same level of reliability with fewer items (Penfield, 2006). Each computer can be used by only one test taker at a time, however, making it difficult for mass testing. Furthermore, the development of a tailored test requires more effort than a standard test, which will likely slow down the use of this approach in the near future.

▶ FUTURE ISSUES AND CHALLENGES

Electronic technology (computers and the Web) will undoubtedly produce the biggest changes in assessment in the future. So far the computer has been used primarily to administer and score tests. Most computerized tests are not much different from paper-and-pencil tests, and often a computerized test is just a paper-and-pencil test administered electronically (Bartram, 1994). The computer's tremendous potential to allow for new types of tests and new types of assessment methods is just beginning to be explored, although to date this potential has gone unrealized (McBride, 1998). A computer can be used to simulate many different job situations and tasks. The same technology that is used for computer games could be used to create an organizational simulation. As mentioned previously, complex simulation "games" are in use for employee selection in Germany, and undoubtedly this technology will become increasingly commonplace.

The Web and other technologies are making remote communication increasingly possible, and this is stimulating interest in electronic assessment. The Web is becoming a popular medium for administering all kinds of assessments. In some cases, the assessments are just paper-and-pencil tests presented electronically, but increasingly assessments are taking advantage of the electronic capabilities of presenting and manipulating images and information. For example, Canger (2001; see also I/O Psychology in Practice) has developed assessment approaches for Monster that link an individual person's assessment results to the KSAO requirements contained in the O*NET database (see Chapter 3 for a discussion of O*NET). This helps both the applicant and the organization do a better job of matching the person to the job.

One of the most vexing questions in the area of assessment concerns how assessment centers can have questionable dimension validity and yet be valid predictors of future job performance and success. Lievens and Klimoski (2001) have suggested that the answer to this question will require a better understanding of the underlying cognitive processes of rating judgments. They suggest that perhaps people's natural judgment tendencies conflict with the dimension ratings that must be made. Clearly more research is needed to help us understand why assessment center raters seem, in most cases, unable to make finer discriminations among dimensions, and this should lead to either better design of exercises or better rater training.

▶ CHAPTER SUMMARY

One of the major tasks I/O psychologists do for organizations is the assessment of people's characteristics for selection and placement. These characteristics can be classified as the knowledge, skill, ability, and other personal characteristics, or KSAOs, necessary for successful performance on the job.

The five major assessment methods used to assess KSAOs are:

Psychological test

Biographical inventory

Interview

Work sample

Assessment center

A psychological test is a standardized series of problems or questions that assess a particular individual characteristic. Tests are commonly used to assess many KSAOs, including knowledge, skill, ability, attitudes, interests, and personality.

The biographical inventory asks for detailed information about the person's past experience, both on and off the job. It asks for far more extensive information than the typical job application form.

An interview is a face-to-face meeting between an interviewee and one or more interviewers who are collecting information or making hiring decisions. During an unstructured interview, the interviewer asks whatever questions come to mind. By contrast, during a structured interview, the interviewer has a preplanned series of questions that are asked of every person who is interviewed. In both types, the interviewer often makes overall judgments about the interviewee's suitability for the job.

A work sample is an assessment device that requires one to demonstrate how well he or she can perform job tasks under standardized conditions. It is a type of simulation in which a person does a job or part of a job under testing conditions rather than actual job conditions.

The assessment center consists of several different types of exercises that take place over one or more days. Although most assessment centers are used to identify managerial potential, they can be used to assess potential for many different types of jobs.

Electronic assessment is rapidly becoming commonplace as the preferred way to measure people's KSAOs. Although so far most such assessments have been computer versions of paper-and-pencil tests, researchers are beginning to develop new types of assessment devices that make full use of the capabilities of technology.

I/O PSYCHOLOGY IN PRACTICE

(*Courtesy Jon Canger*)

Many of the I/O functions of organizations are moving to the Web. Dr. Jonathan Canger has been finding new and innovative ways to use this technology in employee recruitment and selection. Canger received his Ph.D. in I/O psychology from the University of South Florida in 1990. He has worked for a variety of large organizations, including Coca-Cola, Motorola, and Verizon Wireless, where he is currently associate director for talent acquisition and assessment. At the time of this case he was vice president for organizational development at TMP Worldwide, a 10,000-employee national firm that provides a variety of employee recruitment and consulting services. His current responsibilities involve helping the company function more effectively through effective management of employees. He is involved in designing systems to help employees develop their work skills, planning future needs for top managers, and overseeing organizational changes to make the organization function more smoothly. One of the projects he began prior to moving into his current position involved the development of personality tests that could be used to better match people to jobs and organizations.

The best known service provided by TMP is the Monster career search Web site—the 454th dot-com Web site to be established and one of the few that is still profitable. Monster is an extremely popular site, accounting for 10% of all Web visits in the world. This site is a career portal, where people seeking jobs can, at no cost browse lists of available jobs and leave résumés on file (there are currently 14 million) for prospective employers. The employer must pay a fee for listing jobs or browsing the résumé database.

Canger came up with the idea of adding personality assessments to the Monster site to assist both applicants and employers in finding better matches. The idea was to put a personality scale online where prospective applicants could easily complete it and have it electronically scored. This information could then be used to help determine which jobs to apply for (applicant side) and who to hire (employer side). Because of the large number of individuals who would ultimately complete these assessments would be enormous (potentially tens of millions), it wasn't feasible to purchase an existing assessment from a psychological testing company. Canger and his team decided to develop their own assessment from scratch.

The first step was to compile a pool of potential personality items. The team decided to use the Big Five theory to provide the underlying dimensions that would be measured. In addition they added items concerning work values taken from the O*NET (see Chapter 3). These included achievement, recognition, and working conditions. All the items were administered to about 2,000 employees of various organizations in Australia, New Zealand, the United Kingdom, and the United States. This allowed Canger's team to refine the assessment.

Phase 1 of this project was to put the assessment on the Monster Web site as part of a career development service available for a nominal fee. People can get feedback about their own personalities and how they match to potential employers and jobs. Phase 2 added a component for employers that provides information about potential applicants so the employer can better match people to jobs. Phase 3, scheduled to be operational by the time you read this, will add specific hiring recommendations to employers about individuals, not unlike an I/O consultant who provides selection services.

This is an innovative system for two reasons. First, it is entirely Web-based, with both applicants and employers working at different ends of the same integrated computer system. Second, information about personality is generally used only by the employer as opposed to potential applicants. Providing this information to both sides should allow for a better matching, as both the applicants and employers will be working toward achieving good matches between person and organization.

Discussion Questions

1. What are the advantages and disadvantages of Web-based assessments?
2. Why would it be important to the organization to match an applicant's personality to the organization?
3. Why did Canger and his team collect initial data in more than one country?
4. What is the advantage of using the Big Five personality dimensions and the O*NET values?
5. What are the advantages to applicants and employers of using the Monster Web site for recruitment?

LEARNING BY DOING

Choosing Selection Tools for a Job

The choice of assessment techniques used for selection should be informed by the KSAOs for a job. The O*NET is a resource that can be used to provide KSAOs for a job so that a job analysis does not have to be done. Go to the O*NET Web site (http://online.onetcenter.org) and then to the Find Occupation section. Choose an occupation that you are considering after graduation from college. Enter your occupation in the appropriate place on the O*NET site and review the summary for it. Choose at least 6 KSAOs from the O*NET overview. For each explain the assessment method you would use to assess it.

Student Selection

List five KSAOs for the "job" of college student. For each, explain the assessment method you would use to assess it.

SELECTING AND TRAINING EMPLOYEES

(*Corbis Stock Market*)

Selecting Employees

CHAPTER 6 OUTLINE

Did you ever apply for a job with an organization that required you to complete an assessment of some sort? Most employers will have you complete an application form, but many will also include assessments like the ones we discussed in Chapter 5. The most common are psychological tests, although biographical inventories, simulations, and work samples might also be used. As you completed the test, did you wonder what they were trying to learn about you, and why they couldn't just ask? Some tests are fairly obvious, such as a test of mathematical skill, but personality tests often contain questions that seemingly have little to do with the job. Did you feel that the assessments you completed were reasonable, or did they include questions that you felt were none of the organization's business or were not relevant to the job? If the selection system was scientifically developed, the assessments you encountered should have been relevant, and would help predict whether or not you would be successful. If you encountered assessments of this kind, chances are that I/O psychologists had something to do with developing them.

Two of the most important functions of any organization are the recruitment and selection of employees. The health and well-being of an organization depend in large part on a steady flow of new people. Employees must be hired to fill newly created positions and to replace people who have left. Acquiring new employees can be a costly and difficult undertaking. It involves the following four steps (Figure 6.1):

Planning the need for new employees

Getting appropriate people to apply for positions (recruitment)

Deciding whom to hire (selection)

Getting the selected people to take the jobs

Employee recruitment and selection involve legal issues in many countries, particularly in North America and Europe. As we have already discussed, there are strictly enforced laws in many countries prohibiting discrimination in actions that affect employees. The hiring process is the most frequent target of equal employment opportunity efforts. An I/O psychologist who gets involved in employee selection must be an expert in the legal issues concerning selection.

In this chapter, we discuss how organizations recruit and select new employees, using the four steps listed earlier and shown in Figure 6.1. Most of the efforts of I/O psychologists involve selection, so we spend more time on that topic than the others. This is not to say, however, that the selection step is the most important. Rather, it is selection that has been the major focus of I/O practice and research since the beginning of the field. In addition to the four steps, we discuss the value or utility of the scientific approach to selection. We also cover the legal issues involved in employee recruitment and selection from the perspective of civil rights legislation.

Objectives: The student who studies this chapter should be able to:

▶ Explain how organizations conduct human resource planning.

▶ Discuss methods of recruitment.

▶ Explain the steps involved in conducting a validation study.

▶ Describe how scientific approaches to selection can have utility for organizations.

▶ Explain the principles of legal selection.

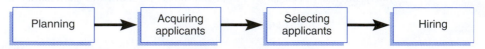

Figure 6.1 Four Steps for Acquiring New Employees.

▶ PLANNING HUMAN RESOURCE NEEDS

In order to stay healthy, an organization must have a steady supply of human resources, or people. These human resources are necessary to fill vacancies created when employees leave the organization. They are also needed to fill new positions resulting from organizational changes or expansion. Careful planning is necessary to do a good job in recruiting the people needed by an organization. Human resource plans must include both a consideration of the organization's needs for people and a supply of possible people to hire (Cascio, 1998).

Forecasts of human resource demands usually list the number of people needed in each job category, such as number of clerks or teachers. Table 6.1 is an example of a projection that might be made by a manufacturing organization facing a gradual automation of its factories. The number of assembly-line workers needed declines steadily, while the number of technicians registers a corresponding increase. This is a common trend in industry, and it is important that organizations plan for reductions in one type of employee and increases in another. The organization can take a variety of actions to deal with the shifting nature of jobs and job requirements. The selection approach would replace assemblers with technicians. The training approach would turn assemblers into technicians. The first approach can be less expensive, because it costs more to provide training, to employees who continue to get paid while learning a new job. The second approach has the advantage of doing the least harm to current employees. It provides considerable benefits by giving them a new and more marketable skill. A training approach is necessary, however, when there is an inadequate supply of people with the necessary skills in the labor market, a situation which is becoming increasingly common in the United States and many other countries. This has necessitated something of a shift from a pure selection approach to a training and staff development approach in which existing employees are offered retraining when old skills become obsolete. Training will be the topic of Chapter 7.

The supply of people available for hire in the labor market can be estimated in a variety of ways. Organizations can keep track of the number of people who apply for various positions. In addition, governmental agencies provide information about the number of available workers in different job categories. In the United States, several agencies provide this sort of information (Table 6.2), including the Bureau of Labor Statistics of the U.S. Department of Labor (www.bls.gov). A comparison of the demand and supply of people for various jobs is an important component in choosing between selection and training approaches to meet future human resource needs.

Both the globalization of the world economy and technological advances have produced tremendous shifts in the demand for people with various job-related skills.

TABLE 6.1   Projections of Employees Needed for an Organization Undergoing Automation of its Manufacturing Processes

Job Classification	Now	Year 1	Year 2	Year 3	Year 4
Assemblers	20,000	16,000	10,000	5,000	4,000
Technicians	20	200	400	600	1,000

TABLE 6.2   Sources of Labor Market Information for the United States

Bureau of Labor Statistics of the U.S. Department of Labor
Engineering Manpower Commission
National Science Foundation
Office of Education
Public Health Service of the Department of Health and Human Services
U.S. Employment Service

Source: *Applied Psychology in Personnel Management*, 5th ed. (p. 163), by W. F. Cascio, 1998. Englewood Cliffs, NJ: Prentice Hall.

The demand for semiskilled and unskilled assemblers in factories has been declining in industrialized countries such as Canada and the United States. Many highly skilled jobs have been increasing, and should continue to increase for at least the next decade. Demand is expected to decline for jobs in manufacturing and mining, and in the early part of the 2000s we have seen a loss of such jobs in the United States. Demand should increase for jobs in health-related fields and technology. Figure 6.2 shows the 20 occupations with the most job openings requiring a college degree in the United States, projected from 2004 to 2014, according to the U.S. Department of Labor's Bureau of Labor Statistics.

▶ RECRUITING APPLICANTS

A challenge for many organizations is getting people to apply for available positions. To be able to hire good people, an organization must have a large number of job applicants from whom to choose. For some jobs it may be relatively easy to recruit applicants, because there are many available people who are easily attracted. For jobs in which there is an undersupply of people, an organization must expend considerable effort to attract the right people to fill its job vacancies. Several methods can be used to recruit applicants for a vacant position. Some require little effort, such as placing an advertisement in a local newspaper or posting a job on the Monster Web site. Other actions may require the full-time efforts of one or more people, such as using recruiters to interview applicants at colleges and universities across the country.

Six possible sources of applicants that are commonly used by organizations are:

Advertising	School recruiters
Employee referral	Walk-ins
Employment agencies	Web

The choice of sources depends on the ease with which organizations can recruit applicants. Some organizations find that they get enough walk-in applicants to cover the jobs they have, so more time-consuming methods are unnecessary. (A walk-in applicant is someone who applies for a job without being induced to do so by action on the part of the organization.) For low level positions, many organizations rely on their own company Web sites (Chapman & Webster, 2003). In competitive job markets, however, many organizations may be attempting to attract the same individuals. Here time-consuming methods might be necessary to attract the people who are needed.

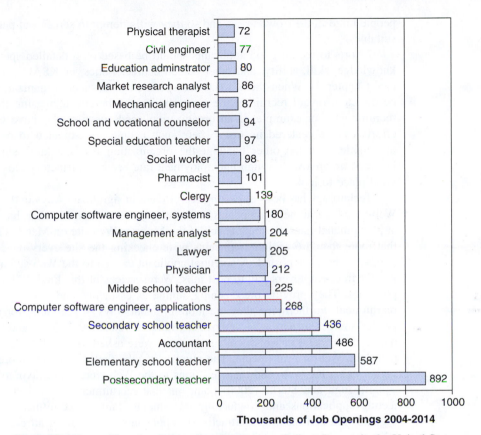

Occupation	Thousands of Job Openings 2004–2014
Physical therapist	72
Civil engineer	77
Education adminstrator	80
Market research analyst	86
Mechanical engineer	87
School and vocational counselor	94
Special education teacher	97
Social worker	98
Pharmacist	101
Clergy	139
Computer software engineer, systems	180
Management analyst	204
Lawyer	205
Physician	212
Middle school teacher	225
Computer software engineer, applications	268
Secondary school teacher	436
Accountant	486
Elementary school teacher	587
Postsecondary teacher	892

Figure 6.2   Fastest-Growing Occupations Requiring a College Degree in the United States 2004–2014.

Source: O. Crosby and R. Moncarz (2006). The 2004–14 job outlook for college graduates. *Occupational Outlook Quarterly*, *Fall*, 42–57.

The different sources of job applicants do not necessarily attract applicants of the same quality. Zottoli and Wanous (2000) reviewed 50 years of research on applicant sources and found consistent evidence that inside sources (employee referrals of friends and acquaintances, rehires of former employees, transfers from inside the organization) provided people who performed better and remained on the job longer, on average, than outside sources (advertising or employment agencies). Furthermore, employees hired through inside sources tend to be more satisfied with their jobs, likely because they have more realistic expectations about what the job will entail (Moser, 2005). McManus and Ferguson (2003) also found that inside sources provided the best applicants, but they found that applicants who learned of the job through the Internet were better in quality than those who found it through newspapers and other outside sources. Zottoli and Wanous (2000) suggested two reasons for the superiority of inside sources. First, such applicants receive more accurate information about the job and so prescreen themselves out of jobs for which they aren't suited. Second, recommenders will assess fit before suggesting someone for a job. Employees can have a personal stake in seeing good people hired in their own areas, and so they will attempt to screen out people who aren't suitable.

Efforts to recruit good applicants should be based on a detailed specification of the knowledge, skill, ability, and other person characteristics, or KSAOs, needed for a job (see Chapter 3). When the KSAOs are specified in advance, organizational efforts can be directed toward recruiting the right applicants, thereby increasing the efficiency of recruitment. For example, if an organization needs people who have computer skills, efforts can be centered in areas where such people are expected to be, such as large universities. On the other hand, if the organization needs a large supply of manual laborers, an area with a high unemployment rate because of factory closings might be a good place to look.

Technology has been impacting recruitment in significant ways in the past few years. Web-based recruitment companies, such as Hotjobs.com and Monster, have been growing at phenomenal rates. A quick check of the Monster Web site on March 12, 2004 showed that more than 1.6 million applicants were checking the site every day, and more than 800,000 jobs were posted. A potential applicant can go to the Web site and search for a job for free; employers pay to post jobs. Web services of this kind do far more than just post jobs. They provide prescreening, online assessments, and systems to help manage recruitment. Furthermore, they are more efficient ways of searching for jobs than using printed sources such as newspapers. For example, Van Rooy, Alonso, and Fairchild (2003) did an experiment in which college students were asked to search for an accountant job using the Web or print media. The number of jobs they found was more than 25 times higher using the Web, and their reactions to the Web were more favorable.

Breaugh and Starke (2000) point out that recruitment is not just a matter of collecting applications and conducting assessments. Part of recruitment is marketing the organization and making it attractive to applicants. One side of attractiveness concerns what the company has to offer, and applicants can be influenced not only by pay and rewards, but by the opportunities for career development and the pleasant environment of the organization (Cober, Brown, Levy, Cober, & Keeping, 2003). The other side is the attractiveness and reputation of the company. Turban and Cable (2003) conducted a study in the placement office of a university, finding that companies with better reputations as good employers attracted more and better (higher GPA) applicants.

▶ SELECTING EMPLOYEES

If an organization is lucky, it will have many more good applicants than the number of vacant jobs. As we will see in this section, the more selective an organization can be, the better the chances that the person hired will be a good employee. This is because many of the employee selection procedures developed by I/O psychologists work best when there are several applicants from whom to choose. These procedures are based on complex mathematical and statistical methodologies that are beyond the scope of this book. We limit this discussion to the major concepts of selection and omit discussion of the statistical details. We first discuss the criterion-related validity approach to employee selection taken by I/O psychologists. This approach is based on scientific principles and statistics. We then briefly discuss alternative procedures that are often used because of practical considerations. Next we cover the utility of our selection techniques. Utility is concerned with the benefits that organizations achieve from using scientific selection.

How Do Organizations Select Employees?

The purpose of employee selection is to hire people who are likely to be successful on the job, because organizational performance is dependent on having employees who perform their jobs well. Several approaches can be taken. Perhaps the most often used approach is to have a manager interview the applicants and decide subjectively whom to hire. Purely subjective hiring procedures have been shown to be biased and inaccurate. A better approach is to use scientific methods that have been shown to work in almost a century of research on employee selection.

Two important elements in employee selection must be considered. First is the *criterion*—the definition of a good employee. Although it may seem obvious to hire the person who is expected to be the best performer, it is not easy to define good performance. Job performance involves many different aspects. Some employees work very accurately, whereas others work very fast. It is not always easy to decide whether to hire based on one aspect of the criterion (e.g., attendance) or another (e.g., work quantity). These issues were discussed at length in Chapter 4. To use scientific selection methods, we first must know the criterion for the job in question.

The second element is the *predictor*, which is anything that relates to the criterion. In Chapter 5 we discussed several methods for assessing characteristics relevant to job requirements. These techniques can be used to assess the KSAOs necessary for job success. Measures of KSAOs can be used as predictors of a criterion of job performance. Knowledge of the subject matter, for example, should be a good predictor for the job performance of a classroom teacher. It is not the only predictor, for knowledge alone does not make someone a good teacher.

Determining if a given predictor relates to a criterion requires a **validation study**, which is a research study that attempts to show that the predictor relates to the criterion. To conduct this sort of study, both the criterion and the predictor are quantified. Data are collected for a group of employees on the criterion and predictor variables. Because both are quantified, a statistical test can be conducted to see if they are significantly related. The correlation coefficient indicates how well the two variables relate to each another. If the two variables are significantly related statistically, the predictor is valid in terms of the criterion. The implication is that information about the predictor can be used to forecast the applicant's likely performance on the job.

(*United Media (NEA)*)

Conducting a good validation study is a complex and difficult undertaking. First, you must carefully analyze the job and job requirements using job analysis. The results of the job analysis can be used to develop criteria for the job and to pick predictors. Data are collected to verify that the chosen predictors are valid. Predictors found to be valid will become part of the organization's employee selection system. We discuss this process in greater detail in the next section of the chapter.

Conducting a Validation Study

Conducting a validation study involves five steps:

1. Conduct a job analysis
2. Specify job performance criteria
3. Choose predictors
4. Validate the predictors
5. Cross-validate

Conducting a job analysis provides the information needed to proceed with the next two steps of specifying criteria and choosing predictors. Once these steps are completed, data can be collected on a sample of employees to determine if the criteria are related to the predictors. If they are, the results must be replicated on a second sample to verify the results. The five steps are illustrated in Figure 6.3.

Step 1: Conduct a Job Analysis

As we discussed in Chapter 3, a job analysis provides information about the tasks involved in a job. It also provides information about the characteristics (KSAOs) an employee needs to be successful on a job. These two types of information are not independent, for the specification of KSAOs is often derived from an analysis of the tasks required for the job.

As we discuss later in the section on legal issues, an important concept in employee selection is job relevance—the correspondence between the KSAOs needed for job success and the KSAOs of the job applicant. For successful and legal selection, the two types of KSAO requirements should correspond. Hiring people with characteristics that are not related to the job requirements would be foolish at best and illegal at worst if it results in discrimination. Thus, it would make sense to hire on the basis of physical strength if the job requires heavy lifting, such as dock worker. It makes little sense to have a strength requirement for schoolteachers.

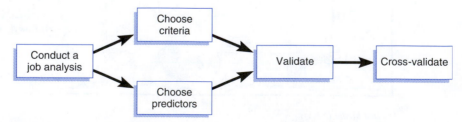

Figure 6.3   The Five Steps for Conducting a Validation Study.

A job analysis can be used in many ways as the basis for a validation study. The job analysis can identify the major components of the job. Next, an analysis can be done to specify the KSAOs necessary to accomplish each component. From this information a list of performance criteria and predictors can be made.

For example, a major component for a manager's job might be managing a budget. Managers often have to develop budgets and manage their resources so that they do not exceed them. One KSAO that would be important for managing a budget is knowledge of basic mathematics, such as addition and subtraction. People hired to be managers should have this basic knowledge.

Step 2: Specify Job Performance Criteria

Once you have a good idea about what a job entails, you can begin to develop criteria for good job performance. For example, if a manager is required to manage a budget, a reasonable criterion might be how well the manager stays within the budget. There can be many reasons for not staying within a budget, so this criterion alone is not sufficient for evaluating how well a person performs the job. However, for a validation study we are interested in using criteria that might be predicted by one or more of our predictors. For example, if a test of mathematical ability is found to predict how well a manager can stay within a budget, then we can expect to hire managers who do better on the criterion if the test is used to help select them.

Step 3: Choose Predictors

As we develop our criteria for a job, we also choose potential predictors of job performance on the criteria. Potential predictors might be chosen to assess KSAOs directly, as with a psychological test of mathematical ability. Other predictors might be less direct, as with measures of a KSAO. We often assume that college graduates have certain knowledge and ability, such as being able to do basic mathematics and to write in their native language. Using educational level as a predictor can eliminate the need to assess many KSAO requirements for a job. This is why many organizations prefer to hire college graduates. Care must be taken, however, that requiring a college degree is reasonable for the job in question. A degree would be overkill if the job required only basic arithmetic and a fourth-grade reading level.

In Chapter 5 we discussed five methods that can be used to assess KSAOs. All these methods are frequently used as predictors in validation studies and have been shown to be valid predictors of job performance:

Assessment centers

Psychological tests

Biographical inventories

Work samples

Interviews

These tools might predict other nonperformance criteria as well, such as job satisfaction. Although few organizations select employees based on the likelihood that they will enjoy the job, it is possible to conduct such a validation study to find appropriate and valid predictors. Criteria chosen for validity studies usually are concerned with an aspect of job performance or other behavior that is directly related to the accomplishment of organizational objectives.

Step 4: Validate the Predictors

After the criteria and predictors are chosen, the data collection phase of the validation study can proceed. In this step, measures of the criterion and the predictors are taken on a sample of people to see if the predictor relates to the criterion. A good field test of the predictor is done in the organizational setting in which it is expected to be used in the future. Most validation studies are done in actual organizational settings as opposed to laboratory settings. In the laboratory you might determine that a human attribute relates to task performance, but you cannot be certain that it will generalize to the organization. By conducting field studies in the settings in which selection tools will ultimately be used, the likelihood of generalization is maximized.

There are two types of study designs for conducting a validation study. In a **concurrent validation study, both** the criterion and predictor scores are collected from a sample of participants at more or less the same point in time. Usually, the participants are current employees who are assessed on both criteria and predictors. A sample of employees might be asked to provide predictor data by taking an assessment test. The employees' test scores would then be correlated with their most recent performance evaluations. If the two are related, we assume that scores on the predictor at the time of application for a job will predict later performance on the job.

In a **predictive validity study**, the predictors are measured before the criterion. A sample of job applicants might be given the predictor assessment. They would then be hired and some time later assessed on the criterion or criteria. The time span between predictor and criterion assessment could be months or years. The predictor scores would be correlated with the criterion scores to see if the predictor can forecast later criterion scores. If it can predict future performance, we can have reasonable confidence in the predictor as a valid selection device.

It might seem that the predictive design would be superior to the concurrent in validating predictors, because the predictive design tests the predictor on applicants rather than employees who already have been selected and trained. Because the predictor is used on applicants, generalizability should be maximized. Research has shown, however, that the two designs are equally effective in validating predictors. Validity coefficients, the correlation between scores on the criterion and predictor, have been found to be about the same in studies using the two different types of designs (Schmitt, Gooding, Noe, & Kirsch, 1984). This is good news for organizations, because predictive designs take a long time to conduct. You might have to wait a year after collecting predictor scores to collect criterion scores. Furthermore, for some organizations it could take months or years before a sufficient number of people are hired to conduct the analysis. A concurrent study can be conducted in as little as a few days if the predictor can be administered quickly and the criterion scores are readily available.

Step 5: Cross-Validate

The final step in a validation study is to **cross-validate**, or replicate, the results of one sample with those of another sample. This is done to be certain that our results are not due to a statistical error, as opposed to a real correlation between the criterion and predictor. In any study involving statistics, significance can occur by chance, as opposed to real relations among the variables of interest. Such statistical errors are called Alpha or Type 1 errors. To protect ourselves from making an error in our conclusions about whether a predictor can forecast a criterion, we cross-validate, or repeat, our analyses on another sample of participants. It is extremely unlikely that we will find the same results twice if there is no relation among the variables of interest. In other words, two successive Alpha errors are unlikely.

To conduct a cross-validation, we need two samples. The first sample is used to determine if the criterion and predictor are significantly correlated. A second sample is used to see if the significant relationship found in the first sample can be repeated on the second. The predictor is validated on the first sample and then double checked, or cross-validated, on the second. Cross-validation adds to our confidence that the predictor can forecast the criterion or criteria of interest. In most field settings, cross-validation is done by taking the original sample and dividing it randomly in half. The first half is used for the validation, and the second is used for the cross-validation.

Validity Generalization

At times it is not necessary to collect data to validate a selection test or other device. Selection tests that are valid in one setting are often valid in many other settings. **Validity generalization** means that the validities of selection devices are generalizable, or transportable, from job to job and organization to organization (Schmidt & Hunter, 1977). If a test predicts performance for an administrative assistant in one organization, for example, it will predict for an administrative assistant in another organization.

The idea of validity generalization has been widely accepted by I/O psychologists (Murphy, 2000), at least as long as the jobs and tests in question are comparable. If you validate a test for the selection of people in a particular job, the test should also be valid for the same job in a different organization. It should also be valid for a job that has the same KSAO requirements. If the second job is different from the job for which the test was valid, the test in the second case may or may not be valid. The only way to be certain would be to conduct another validation study on the second job to determine if the test predicts the criterion.

How Predictor Information Is Used for Selection

Once it is determined that a predictor or predictors are valid forecasters of future performance criteria, it must be decided how best to use the predictor information. One popular use of predictors is as hurdles; another is as predictors in a regression equation. With either approach, multiple predictors can be used in combination. Often prediction is better with several rather than single predictors because multiple KSAOs are necessary for job success.

Multiple Hurdles

The **multiple hurdles** approach sets a passing score for each predictor. An applicant who achieves the score passes the hurdle. For example, a computer salesperson should have several KSAOs in order to be successful on the job. One obvious KSAO is knowledge of computer principles. If completion of a college degree in computers serves as an indicator of the KSAO, the applicant would pass this hurdle. Another important KSAO might be the communication skills needed to relate well to customers. This might be assessed with a communication skills exercise. Applicants would have to have a passing score on the communication exercise to pass this hurdle.

It is efficient to use multiple hurdles in a specified order and eliminate applicants as the assessment process goes from hurdle to hurdle. For example, only those computer sales applicants with college degrees would be given the communication skills exercise. It would make financial sense to order the predictors in terms of cost from least to most expensive. Many organizations use relatively inexpensive preliminary screening methods as hurdles. That way expensive assessments are not used with people who could easily have been screened out earlier in the process.

Regression Approach

The *regression approach* uses the score from each predictor in an equation to provide a numerical estimate of the criterion. With the computer sales job, an equation could predict the actual dollar amount of sales per month. Predictors for the job might be grade point average (GPA) in college and scores on the communication exercise. Both quantitative variables (GPA and exercise score) can be combined mathematically to provide predicted criterion scores (e.g., monthly sales). Individuals who are forecasted to have the best criterion scores would be the ones hired.

With a single-predictor variable, a linear regression equation is calculated from a sample of data. To compute an equation, you must have data on both the criterion and the predictor so that you can compare how well the predicted criterion scores match the real criterion scores. The general form of a linear regression equation is

$$Y = b \times X + a$$

where X is the predictor, Y is the criterion, b is the slope, and a is the intercept. When the equation is used, a and b are known quantities. A predicted value for the criterion (Y) can be computed by replacing X with values of the predictor.

The regression equation is developed from the data of a validation study. In addition to the correlation coefficient, a regression equation can be computed for a sample of data on a criterion and predictor. As noted earlier, this equation provides a means of predicting the criterion from the predictor. For example, monthly sales for a salesperson might be predicted from scores on the communication exercise. The most accurate prediction might be achieved from a regression equation like the following:

$$\text{Sales} = \$400 \times \text{Exercise Score} + \$2000$$

In this equation, a is $2000 and b is $400. If a person had an exercise score of 10, his or her sales would be predicted to be $6,000:

$$\text{Sales} = \$400 \times 10 + \$2000$$
$$\text{Sales} = \$6000$$

If another person had a test score of 5, his or her sales would be predicted to be $4,000:

$$\text{Sales} = \$400 \times 5 + \$2000$$
$$\text{Sales} = \$4000$$

Obviously, the first person would be preferred because of the higher predicted performance.

A similar procedure is applied when there are two or more predictors. This case involves the use of multiple correlation and multiple regression. Multiple correlation is the correlation between a criterion and two or more predictors simultaneously. The multiple correlation coefficient is indicated by an R. Multiple regression is a statistical technique that provides an equation relating two or more predictors simultaneously to a criterion. The equation can be used to forecast the criterion from scores on the predictors. In many cases several predictors combined can provide a more accurate prediction of the criterion than any of them alone.

The general form of a multiple regression equation is

$$Y = (b_1 \times X_1) + (b_2 \times X_2) + a$$

for the two predictor case. In this equation the Xs are predictors, Y is the criterion, a is the intercept, and the bs are regression coefficients. The coefficients and intercept are computed from sample data. The equation is used by substituting values of the predictors for the Xs. A predicted value for the criterion is computed.

For example, we can combine the scores on the communication exercise with GPA in college. Assume that both of these predictors relate to sales performance. Combined they might provide more accurate forecasts than either one alone. If each predictor had a correlation of .40 with sales, both combined would likely have a multiple correlation that is greater than .40. The magnitude of the multiple correlation is a function of how strongly each predictor variable correlates with the criterion variable and how strongly the predictor variables correlate with one another. The multiple correlation will have the largest value when the predictor variables are uncorrelated with one another. This would show that combined the predictors are more accurate than either one alone in forecasting the criterion.

A multiple regression analysis would provide an equation that predicts sales from both the exercise score and the college grade point average. The equation could be used to forecast the sales from scores on the two predictors. Suppose that the predictor equation was the following:

$$\text{Sales} = (\$2000 \times \text{GPA}) + (\$1000 \times \text{Exercise}) + \$2000$$

In this equation, a is $2000, and the bs are $2000 and $1000. To use the equation, multiply GPA by $2000 and add it to the exercise score multiplied by $1000. To this total add $2000. The resulting number is an estimate of the person's future monthly sales. The forecasted sales of a person with a college GPA of 2.0 and an exercise score of 4 would be $10,000. The sales of person with a 4.0 college GPA and an exercise score of 10 would be $20,000.

The magnitude of the relation between the predictors and the criterion determines how accurate the prediction is likely to be. If the predictors correlate strongly with the criterion, the predicted values for sales are likely to be fairly accurate. If the predictors do not correlate very well with the criterion, the predictions will not be very accurate. Even when predictors relate to criteria modestly, however, using the scientific approach we have discussed can still result in hiring better performing employees than using nonscientific approaches.

Every regression equation must be cross-validated to be sure that it continues to make reasonably accurate predictions. An equation generated on a sample of data will make the most accurate predictions possible for that sample. The same equation will probably not be as accurate when used on a second sample, for statistical reasons beyond the scope of this book. To perform a cross-validation, the equation generated from one sample of data is applied to a second sample of data. Usually, the accuracy of prediction will be reduced when the first sample equation is used on the second sample. If the regression equation yields nonsignificant results when used on a second sample, it should not be used.

An implication of using the regression approach is that a low score on one predictor can be compensated for by a high score on another. The multiple hurdle approach avoids this problem because an applicant must reach the passing score for each predictor. This can be important, because a person often must have a reasonable level on every KSAO even if some KSAOs are very high. For example, in selecting a surgeon there are two equally important KSAOs. The surgeon must have the knowledge of how to operate and the manual skill to do so. A high level of one KSAO cannot overcome a deficiency in the other. Skill with a scalpel is insufficient if the surgeon does not know where to cut. The limitation of the regression approach can be overcome by combining it with the hurdles. First, applicants would be screened using the hurdles. A regression equation would then be applied only to those who made it past the hurdles.

Even when validation studies have been conducted, it is far more common for companies to use subjective approaches to combine the results of different predictors than to use formal multiple hurdle or regression results, which is only rarely done in practice. Ganzach, Kluger, and Klayman (2000) conducted a study that compared the subjective approach with multiple regression for the recruitment of Israeli soldiers. They found that regression was superior in predicting a measure of performance, suggesting that there can be advantages to this approach, but that a combination of regression and subjective judgment worked best.

INTERNATIONAL REPLICATION

Although it has been known for a long time that subjective judgment can be less accurate than objective procedures for combining information to make judgments, most organizations use the subjective approach in making hiring decisions. Ganzach, Kluger, and Klayman (2000), in this study of selection in the Israeli army, wanted to compare these two approaches.

The study was conducted in a field setting in Israel, where military service is compulsory. Participants were 26,197 males who were interviewed prior to being drafted into the army. Each interview took

approximately 20 minutes and was conducted by one of 116 highly trained professional interviewers who had undergone a three month training program. At the end of the interview, the interviewer made ratings on six traits: activity, pride in the service, sociability, responsibility, independence, and promptness. A global rating of the interviewee's expected success in the army was also made. The criterion was the number of disciplinary actions taken against the interviewee during the subsequent three year service. Because most participants (83%) had no disciplinary actions taken, and few had more than one or two, the criterion was collapsed to two levels: had actions or didn't have actions.

A multiple regression analysis was conducted between the six trait ratings and the criterion, and a correlation was computed between the global rating and the criterion. Results showed that the six trait ratings, combined with a regression equation to maximize prediction, were more accurate than the global ratings, with correlations of .28 vs. .23, respectively. In other words, the statistical combination of the individual trait ratings did a better job predicting the subsequent

criterion than the human interviewer's global judgment. However, when combined, the six trait ratings combined with the multiple regression equation plus the global judgment did even better, with a correlation of .30. This suggested that there can be advantages to combining both approaches to achieve maximum prediction.

Source: Ganzach, Y., Kluger, A. N., & Klayman, N. (2000). Making decision from an interview: Expert measurement and mechanical combination. *Personnel Psychology*, *53*, 1–20.

Alternatives to Conducting Validation Studies

Most organizations select employees without going through costly and time-consuming validation studies. Organizations do not always hire enough people to conduct such studies, which can require more than 100 participants to do properly. Some organizations do not wish to invest the money or time to conduct these studies. For an organization with hundreds of different jobs, it could cost millions of dollars to conduct validation studies for every position.

An alternative approach is to rely on the established validity of selection tools that can be linked to KSAO requirements. With this approach one conducts a job analysis to determine KSAOs. Established methods to assess each KSAO are then chosen. If the job analysis results indicate that cognitive ability is needed, an existing cognitive ability test could be chosen. This approach relies heavily on existing research findings concerning the validities of existing methods. It does not involve data collection to test for validity of predictors. An organization can often rely on validity generalization results to help guide its choice of selection methods.

It is possible to purchase off-the-shelf selection devices from psychological testing companies that offer validated tests for sale to organizations. As we discussed in Chapter 5, many tests exist to assess hundreds of different characteristics. It is even possible to hire members of consulting firms to administer all sorts of assessments, including assessment centers, interviews, simulation exercises, and tests. Sometimes it is less expensive for an organization to buy assessment services than do its own. This is likely to be true for a small company that has few people to assess and also for a large company that is hiring few people into a particular type of position.

No matter how selection decisions are made, once it is decided whom to hire, procedures must be initiated to get that person to take the job. An organization has many ways to entice people to join it, including offering fringe benefits or restructuring the job to suit the individual. One procedure that is often used is the realistic job preview, which we discuss next.

▶ GETTING APPLICANTS TO ACCEPT AND KEEP JOB OFFERS

The recruitment job is not over when it is decided who will be offered a job. The next step is making sure that the applicants the organization wishes to hire are interested in accepting the job offer. Installing the most accurate selection system possible is of little value if the applicants who are identified as potentially good employees will not take the job that is offered. Of equal importance is ensuring that individuals who take a job do not quit in a short time because they find that they do not like the job.

Convincing an applicant to accept a job involves several strategies. First, it is important that the recruitment process is a positive one, and that the prospective employee feels he or she has been treated fairly (Hausknecht, Day, & Thomas, 2004). Second, salary and compensation offers should be comparable to those of other organizations for similar jobs in the same area (Chapman, Uggerslev, Corroll, Piasentin, & Jones, 2005). One way to make sure that offers are competitive is to conduct a salary survey to find out what other organizations are paying. This is done by contacting organizations and asking what they pay for particular positions. Another way to handle compensation is to negotiate salary and other rewards with the potential employee. Many organizations are flexible in their benefits and salaries and may be able to tailor them to the demands of applicants. One such approach is the **cafeteria benefits** program, in which employees are allowed to choose their benefits from a long list of possibilities, such as different types of insurance policies. Organizations can also offer flexibility in the content of jobs so that potential employees can modify the job to their liking.

Third, the behavior of recruiters is an important influence on applicants accepting job offers. Chapman et al. (2005) showed that it is important for recruiters to be personable and provide honest information about the job. Providing a falsely positive view of an organization can result in high turnover as new employees find that conditions are not as favorable as originally presented. A person may find that the job is intolerable because of some situation not mentioned when the job was offered and accepted. For example, it was never stated that the job involved extensive travel during the summer. A person who finds that job conditions are unacceptable will be likely to quit. Recruitment will have to begin again to find a replacement.

RESEARCH IN DETAIL

Field experiments are difficult to conduct in organizational settings. This study by Meglino et al. (1993) is an example of a field experiment that was conducted over a relatively long period. Its purpose was to investigate the effects of a realistic job preview (RJP) on the turnover of employees who varied in experience on the job in question. Although many studies have shown the effects of realistic job previews on turnover, these researchers thought that the effects would differ between experienced and inexperienced employees.

Subjects were applicants for the job of correctional officer who were randomly assigned either to receive or not to receive the realistic job preview. The subjects were further divided into two groups depending on their prior experience in a similar job. Data were collected concerning whether or not the applicant took the job and how long each applicant stayed on the job. Thus, there were two dependent variables—job acceptance and job survival.

The results showed that the impact of the RJP was different for the experienced and inexperienced applicant groups. The experienced applicants were less likely to take the job if they were exposed to the RJP. They were more likely to quit the job during a three to nine month probationary period, and they were less likely to quit after the probationary period if they were given the realistic job preview. The inexperienced applicants were more likely to accept the job after seeing the RJP. The RJP had no significant effect on their turnover rate. These results show that the effects of the RJP might not be the same for everyone. Perhaps the RJP was more meaningful to experienced applicants who had a context in which to interpret the information. They knew that a particular feature of the job would be unpleasant, even though it might not initially seem to be so. Results also show that the effects can differ over time. Positive effects on turnover might not occur immediately.

Overall, it has been found that RJPs can be an effective and relatively inexpensive way of decreasing unwanted employee turnover. This study shows

that organizations should consider carefully the characteristics of applicants when deciding to implement a preview because it might not reduce turnover for experienced employees.

Source: Meglino, B. M., DeNisi, A. S., & Ravlin, E. C. (1993). Effects of previous job exposure and subsequent job status on the functioning of a realistic job preview. *Personnel Psychology, 46*, 803–822.

The **realistic job preview (RJP)** is used to give job applicants accurate information about the job and the organization. It is most typically accomplished with a brochure or videotaped presentation (Wanous, 1989). A good RJP provides an accurate view of both the favorable and unfavorable aspects of a job, so that a person who accepts a job will do so with accurate and realistic expectations. Those who know what they are going to encounter will be more likely to remain on a job if unfavorable but anticipated conditions arise. Similarly, those who learn beforehand that the job entails conditions they find intolerable will simply refuse the job offer. Another person who is willing to accept the situation will be hired and will be more likely to stay on the job.

Research with the RJP has shown benefits, but surprisingly not for turnover. Premack and Wanous (1985) conducted a meta-analysis of 21 RJP experiments conducted in organizations. Their mathematical analysis of the results of these studies indicated that RJPs reduce initial expectations about the job and organization. They also reduce the number of employees who accept job offers by the organization. RJPs also increased job performance and job satisfaction, probably because people who would have been unhappy on a job are screened out before they accept it. Those who accept the job are likely to have less favorable but probably more realistic perceptions of the organization because of the RJP. However, results with turnover have tended to be small and inconsistent (Meglino, Ravlin, & DeNisi, 2000), suggesting that this might not be the best way to reduce turnover, despite other positive results.

A more recent study showed that the effects of an RJP can be complicated by the job experience of applicants. Meglino, DeNisi, and Ravlin (1993) conducted a field experiment in which applicants for a correctional officer position were assigned to either an RJP or a control condition without an RJP. Applicants in each group were classified according to prior experience as a correctional officer. The results showed that the impact of the RJP was different for the experienced and inexperienced applicant groups (see Research in Detail). These results show that the effects of the RJP might not be the same for everyone, although in general RJPs have been shown to have positive effects.

► THE UTILITY OF SCIENTIFIC SELECTION

Perhaps the most important question to ask about the scientific approach to employee selection concerns its utility, or value. What is the payoff to an organization for using this difficult and time-consuming approach to selection? The answer is not easy to determine. Research has shown that scientific selection can result in the hiring of better employees, but its effects on overall organizational functioning are not as clear. The study of these effects is called **utility analysis**. I/O psychologists have developed mathematical procedures for conducting utility analyses of selection procedures. In this section, we first discuss in general how selection devices can result in the hiring of better employees. We then consider how utility analysis has been used to show how these selection procedures can have important effects on organizational functioning.

How Valid Selection Devices Work

An understanding of utility analysis must begin with an understanding of how selection devices work. Three basic concepts form the foundation of this discussion:

Baserate

Selection ratio

Validity

These three factors determine to what extent scientific selection will result in hiring better performing employees. If it does so, then we must consider the cost of using the selection device in determining its utility.

Baserate

The **baserate** is the percentage of applicants who would be successful on the job if all of them were hired. On some jobs, most applicants would be capable of performing well, making the baserate close to 100%. On other jobs, relatively few applicants would be successful, making the baserate close to 0%. A baserate of 50% results in the maximum utility because it offers the most room for improvement in accuracy of prediction. Suppose you know the baserate from prior experience with employees on a job. If 50% have been successful in the past, the best accuracy rate you could expect by guessing which applicants would be successful is 50%. If you guessed that every applicant would be successful or unsuccessful, you would expect to be correct half the time. Using a predictor, you could improve your accuracy up to 100%. This would represent a difference of 50% in accuracy between the baserate and your predictor.

If you know that the baserate is less or more than 50%, you can achieve better than 50% accuracy of prediction by guessing that every applicant will be successful (if the baserate is greater than 50%) or not successful (if the baserate is less than 50%). For example, a 60% baserate would give about 60% accuracy if you guess that everyone will be successful. A baserate of 40% would give about 60% accuracy if you guess that everyone will be unsuccessful (40% of people successful means that 60% are not successful). In both cases, the biggest possible gain in prediction accuracy is from 60% to 100%.

The more the baserate differs from 50% in either direction (the majority of employees are successful or not successful), the smaller is the room for improvement if we had perfect prediction. Thus, all baserates that are greater or less than 50% give less room for gain than 50%.

Selection Ratio

The **selection ratio** is the proportion of job applicants an organization must hire. It is calculated as the number of positions to fill divided by the number of applicants.

Some organizations find that they have many applicants for each vacant position. Their selection ratio will be low. Other organizations find that there are few applicants for each vacant position. Their selection ratio will be high. For example, if there are 100 job applicants for each job, the selection ratio will be $1/100$. If there are two applicants for each position, the selection ratio will be $1/2$. Low selection ratios produce the greatest utility because they allow an organization to be more selective in hiring for each position. In the long run an organization can hire better people when there are many applicants from whom to choose.

Validity

The validity of a selection device is the magnitude of the correlation between it and the criterion. The larger the correlation, the more accurately the criterion can be forecast by the selection device. The more accurate the forecast of the criterion, the greater is the utility because utility is based in part on increasing the success rate over the baserate.

How Valid Predictors Increase Success Rates

Figure 6.4 illustrates how baserate, selection ratio, and validity combine to increase the success rate of those hired. The figure graphs the criterion and predictor scores for a fictitious sample of 20 job applicants. The horizontal axis represents the predictor variable, and the vertical axis represents the criterion variable of job performance. The individual job applicants are represented by the points on the graph. Each point shows the criterion and predictor score for an applicant.

The baserate is represented by the horizontal line across the middle of the graph. Cases above the line are in the successful range on the criterion, and cases below the line are in the unsuccessful range. The cutoff score on the predictor is represented by the vertical line running down the center of the graph. Applicants who score higher than the cutoff (right side of vertical line) on the predictor are hired, and applicants who score lower than the cutoff (left side of vertical line) are not hired. In this case, half of the applicants had predictor scores that were higher than the cutoff.

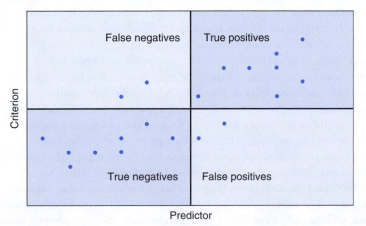

Figure 6.4   How a Valid Selection Device Increases the Accuracy of Selection.

The graph is divided into four quadrants. The upper right quadrant contains applicants who would have been hired if the predictor was used and would have been successful on the job. They are referred to as *true positives*. The lower right quadrant contains people who would have been hired if the predictor was used but would have been unsuccessful on the job. They are the *false positives*. The lower left quadrant contains people who would not have been hired if the predictor was used and would not have been successful. They are the *true negatives*. Finally, the upper left quadrant contains applicants who would not have been hired if the predictor was used and would have been successful on the job. They are the *false negatives*. There are eight true negatives and eight true positives, and there are two false negatives and two false positives.

If a predictor is valid, the points on the graph will be in the shape of an ellipse. This will produce a more accurate prediction over the baserate if a cutoff score on a predictor is used to choose employees. The baserate in Figure 6.4 is 50%, meaning that half of the cases would be successful on the job if all were hired. If the predictor scores were used with the cutoff shown in the graph, eight people would have been successful and two would not have been. This improves the accuracy of prediction from the 50% baserate to 80%. This gain is a reflection of the potential utility of selection and can be substantial when conditions are favorable. As noted earlier in this discussion, the best situation occurs when the baserate is 50% and the selection ratio is low. The greater the validity, the greater is the potential utility of scientific selection.

So far we have seen how valid predictors can help identify those individuals who will be successful on the job. This is an important part of utility, but it is not the only part. The other important issue concerns the cost of using the selection device, and the cost of poor selection. It is the gain in using the selection system versus the cost that determines utility, as we will see next.

Computing the Utility of Scientific Selection

Even though a predictor might result in the hiring of better employees, it is not necessarily the best choice for an organization, because the costs of using the predictor might exceed the benefits. For some types of factory work, for example, little is necessary in the way of skills or training to do the job. It can be relatively inexpensive to replace an unsuccessful employee. In such a case, it would be difficult to justify using an expensive selection method, such as an assessment center. In fact, it has been found that in factories, even psychological tests are less likely to be used in jobs that have few skill requirements and require little training (Wilk & Cappelli, 2003). Jobs that result in a significant investment in individual employees warrant the use of expensive selection devices. For example, it takes millions of dollars for the U.S. Air Force to train a fighter pilot. It is certainly worth the cost to use expensive selection procedures in this case.

The utility concept we have discussed so far concerns identifying successful versus unsuccessful employees. It is also possible to conduct utility analyses to see what sorts of performance improvements might occur from using a valid selection device to choose employees. If a selection device is valid, we would expect that, on average, individuals chosen with it will have better job performance. Several studies have shown that the highest performers can be up to 16 times more productive than the lowest performers on jobs with countable output, such as factory work (Campbell, Gasser, & Oswald, 1996). If we can compute the monetary value of this performance gain, we can compute the utility of using a selection device.

Several approaches have been suggested for conducting this sort of utility analysis (e.g., Raju, Burke, & Normand, 1990; Schmidt, Hunter, McKenzie, & Muldrow, 1979). Each is based on mathematical equations that provide estimates of the monetary gain from using a selection device. The various approaches make their own assumptions and have their own variation on the equations. Each requires finding the relation between performance and monetary gain. For some jobs this can be straightforward. For example, the performance of a salesperson can be translated into the monetary value of sales made. For other jobs the translation is not so easy. How would you estimate the monetary value for a teacher's performance? It is possible to do so, usually by asking subject matter experts to make subjective judgments.

There has been much debate in the I/O field about the best approach to utility analysis. Some of the discussion has concerned how people make judgments about the monetary value of job performance (e.g., Becker & Huselid, 1992; Bobko, Shetzer, & Russell, 1991). These authors have expressed concern that people are not necessarily accurate in their judgments, making utility estimates inaccurate. Other authors have noted that utility analyses have failed to consider all the major factors involved in utility (Boudreau, 1983; Russell, Colella, & Bobko, 1993), resulting in somewhat inflated estimates of gains. As but one example, Boudreau (1983) discussed how increased profits from a more productive workforce should be adjusted for taxes to yield the real bottom line utility estimate.

Although utility analysis has limitations, the results of such analyses have shown that scientific selection can offer considerable monetary benefits to organizations. Schmidt, Mack, and Hunter (1984) estimated that the U.S. National Park Service might gain as much as $3.8 million in productivity if a cognitive ability test were used to select park rangers. This number was calculated for the case in which 130 rangers were hired per year. In organizations that hire larger numbers of people, expected gains might be considerably greater.

The idea of computing utility is not limited to employee selection. Landy, Farr, and Jacobs (1982) suggested that the approach could be used to estimate the monetary gain of other organizational practices, such as giving employees job performance feedback. If you can estimate the gain in performance from such a procedure, you can compute the utility in terms of monetary gain. Such analyses would have the same limitations as the utility analyses used for employee selection.

One further issue should be noted concerning the use of utility analysis. Such mathematical procedures provide a theoretical estimate of how much gain in performance would occur if more capable people were hired. Although in theory more capable people would perform better, in practice the expected gains may never occur. Organizations are complex social systems that affect people's behavior in a variety of ways. Job performance can be both enhanced and inhibited by organizations. As we will see throughout the remainder of this book, being able to perform does not mean that the organizational conditions and constraints will allow it. A capable person might not perform well because the equipment or support to do so are not available. Even a highly talented machinist will be unproductive if his or her machine is defective and keeps breaking. Nevertheless, utility analysis is valuable because it shows that selection procedures can be of benefit to organizations, even if we cannot be certain about the magnitude of the monetary benefits.

▶ INTERNATIONAL DIFFERENCES IN SELECTION PRACTICES

Selection practices vary greatly among organizations or even branches of the same organization in different countries. Ryan, McFarland, Baron, and Page (1999) surveyed managers from 959 organizations in 20 countries concerning their selection practices and in particular the selection devices they used. The interview, former employer reference check, and application form were most popular, and used universally. This was not true when it came to psychological tests. Although the most popular tests around the world were personality and cognitive ability, there was considerable difference in how much they were used from country to country. Biographical inventories and interviews were most popular in Greece, whereas tests were most popular in Belgium and Spain.

Newell and Tansley (2001) noted that there were differences in selection practices across countries, even where job requirements and situations were similar, and furthermore that less valid procedures were often preferred over more valid ones. They suggested several societal factors that account for this. First, before selection procedures can be used, managers have to know about them. Until fairly recently, communication among managers across national borders was limited, and so information about a better selection approach discovered in one place wouldn't always be known in another. Although the Internet has reduced the limitations of physical distance and national boundary, there are still language barriers in many places. Eleftheriou and Robertson (1999), in their survey of selection practices among Greek companies, found that cost and lack of familiarity were the reasons psychological tests were not used more frequently.

Second, laws and regulations influence selection procedures. In the United States, anti-discrimination laws have shaped how selection must be done (see the discussion of legal issues in the next section). In many European countries, such as Germany and Sweden, unions are quite powerful, and they influence selection procedures much more than in the United States. Third, economic factors put limits on which approaches are done. In less wealthy countries, expensive assessments are not an option. Finally, there are cultural differences in values and what is considered important. For example, in some countries achievement is more important than symbols of status. In the former, the college grade point average would be considered more important than the status of the institution attended, but the opposite might be true in the latter. Marcus (2003) compared attitudes of college students toward different selection devices in France, Germany, and the United States, finding that Americans were most favorable toward biographical inventories, Germans were most favorable toward personality tests, and the French were least favorable toward integrity tests and interviews. Moscoso and Salgado (2004) found that Portuguese and Spanish college students were most favorable toward interviews and work samples and were least favorable toward integrity tests and getting jobs through personal contacts.

▶ LEGAL ISSUES

Throughout the industrialized world, it is becoming an accepted value that organizations should not be discriminatory in their practices that affect employees, such as hiring and promotion. These countries have laws that protect people against discriminatory actions by organizations. The groups who are protected by these laws vary from country to country. Most offer protection to women, and many offer protection to blacks. A group is likely to be protected by law if it represents a reasonably large minority in a country and if its members have been victims of discrimination. Thus, in countries with large black minorities, blacks are likely to be offered protection. In countries with few blacks, this protection might not be found in the law.

In this section, we discuss the legal issues involved in employee selection both in and outside the United States. Although the United States was a leader in the development of legal protection against discrimination, many countries have not been far behind, and some have pulled ahead in some ways. This discussion offers a contrast between the handling of the problem of discrimination in the United States and in other countries.

Legal Selection in the United States

Prior to 1964 in the United States, discrimination against ethnic minorities and women was widespread for many jobs, particularly the most desirable and highest paying ones. In 1964 the Civil Rights Act changed the way organizations selected employees because it expanded legal protections against discrimination and provided a mechanism to enforce them. Legislation in the following years has broadened the legal protection to groups that were not covered by the Civil Rights Act of 1964. Discrimination in hiring and other areas of employment has not been eliminated completely in the United States, with over 146,000 federal and state discrimination complaints being filed in 2005 alone (Goldman, Gutek, Stein, & Lewis, 2006). Nevertheless, tremendous progress has been made over the past few decades.

The Civil Rights Act of 1964 made it illegal to discriminate against minorities and other groups in employment and other areas of life in U.S. society. Subsequent legislation and Supreme Court cases have produced a complex and confusing array of legal requirements for employee selection. The Civil Rights Act of 1991 was an attempt to rectify some of the confusion produced by years of sometimes conflicting Supreme Court decisions. Table 6.3 lists six of the most significant Supreme Court cases and the major outcome of each. Although the underlying principles of nondiscrimination are simple, implementing a selection system that meets legal requirements is complicated. This is due in part to changes in the requirements due to action by the Congress and the Supreme Court and in part to the technical complexities of employee selection systems.

The first issue that we address is the concept of *protected classes*. Although the law states that discrimination against anyone is illegal, certain groups have been the target of protection under the law. These groups are called **protected classes** and comprise people who have been the target of discrimination in the past. African Americans, Hispanics, Native Americans, and women all represent protected classes. Table 6.4 lists the major

TABLE 6.3   Six Significant U.S. Supreme Court Discrimination Cases and their Outcomes

Case	Outcome
Griggs v. Duke Power (1971)	Selection methods that have adverse impact must be valid.
Rowe v. General Motors (1972)	Legal protection against discrimination holds for performance appraisals.
Albermarle Paper Company v. Moody (1975)	Organizations must use rigorous validation procedures.
Baake v. Regents of the University of California (1978)	Discrimination laws protect everyone; quotas for admission to graduate school are illegal.
Wards Cove Packing Company v. Antonio (1987)	This case made it more difficult for individuals to win discrimination cases. It was an impetus for the Civil Rights Act of 1991.
Price Waterhouse v. Hopkins (1988)	Promotions cannot be based on gender stereotyping (e.g., requiring a female employee to act or look more feminine).

federal discrimination laws and the specific groups each covers. At the present time it is illegal to discriminate on the basis of

Age	Color
Disability	Gender
National Origin	Race
Religion	

It is conceivable that other groups will become protected classes in the future, and individual states are free to offer protection to additional groups not covered by federal law. For example, sexual orientation is included in some places.

Uniform Guidelines on Employee Selection

In 1978 the U.S. government produced a set of guidelines for legal selection called the **Uniform Guidelines on Employee Selection Procedures** (1978). Although originally intended to apply to government agencies, the guidelines were eventually adopted as acceptable legal practices for all organizations. The guidelines define several important concepts for selection and provide a procedure by which organizations can conduct legal

TABLE 6.4   Civil Rights Legislation in the United States Protecting Various Groups

Legislation	Covers
Civil Rights Act of 1964	Gender, national origin, race, religion
Age Discrimination Act of 1967 (Amended 1968)	Age
Pregnancy Discrimination Act of 1978	Pregnancy
Americans With Disabilities Act of 1990	Mental and physical disabilities

Civil rights legislation says that each of these people should have an equal opportunity to be hired for a job

(*Jean-Claude Lejeune/Stock Boston*)

selection. They provide more than just a statement of legal requirements. They outline the proper way to develop a valid employee selection system, which provides an additional advantage to an organization that follows them.

One of the most important concepts embodied in the Uniform Guidelines is **adverse impact**, which refers to the impact on a protected class of a given selection practice. It is usually defined in terms of selection ratios of the protected class and a comparison group (e.g., white males). Adverse impact occurs when the **four-fifths rule** is violated, meaning that the selection ratio for the protected class is less than 80%, or four-fifths, of the comparison group (Roth, Bobko, & Switzer, 2006). For example, suppose that 60% of male applicants were offered a job. Female applicants would experience adverse impact if fewer than 48% of them (four-fifths of 60%) were offered a job (Table 6.5). This four-fifths rule recognizes that an equal number of applicants from every possible group is unlikely. Of importance here is the percentage of applicants who are hired, not the actual numbers.

Adverse impact is a threshold for possible discrimination in selection. It is not necessarily illegal to use a selection device that has adverse impact on a protected class. If a selection device or procedure has adverse impact, there are further tests to decide its legality. To be legal, a selection device that produces adverse impact must be job relevant. This means that it assesses a KSAO that is necessary for job success. One way to establish job relevance is by showing that a selection device is a valid predictor of job performance.

If selection practices produce adverse impact, an organization must be ready to defend itself against legal challenges. Tests of cognitive ability and physical strength are

TABLE 6.5 Applying the Four-Fifths Rule for Adverse Impact Against Women

Case 1: No Adverse Impact Against Women

Gender	Number of Applicants	Number Hired	Percent Hired	Four-fifths Threshold
Men	100	60	60%	
Women	80	40	50%	48%

No adverse impact because 50% is above the 48% threshold

Case 2: Adverse Impact Against Women

Gender	Number of Applicants	Number Hired	Percent Hired	Four-fifths Threshold
Men	100	60	60%	
Women	80	20	25%	48%

Adverse impact against women because 25% is below the 48% threshold

[a] In the first case, 60% of male applicants and 50% of female applicants were hired. Because 50% is more than 4/5 of 60%, there is no adverse impact against women. In the second, case 60% of male applicants but only 25% of female applicants were hired. Because 25% is less than 4/5 of 60%, there is adverse impact against women.

both likely to have adverse impact on some groups. Their use can be justified only if a job analysis shows that these attributes are necessary KSAOs for the job and if the tests are shown to be valid. Failure to do a job analysis and to use valid selection methods risks using procedures that are unfair to the adversely affected groups. Although it is legal to require that those who are hired have the required KSAOs to do a job, it is illegal to require KSAOs that are not necessary for success on the job.

Essential Functions and Reasonable Accommodation

The 1990 Americans With Disabilities Act (ADA) extended legal protection against discrimination to people with disabilities. Two concepts came from this legislation. **Essential functions**, as we discussed in Chapter 3, refer to KSAOs that are an important part of the job. For example, typing is an essential function for a secretary, but lifting heavy objects is not. It can be illegal to deny a job to a disabled person based on a KSAO that relates only to nonessential functions. The idea is that rarely done tasks, such as lifting a heavy object, that require a KSAO that an otherwise competent employee does not have can be done by someone else.

The second concept is **reasonable accommodation** for a disabled employee. An organization must make allowances that are feasible to enable a disabled person to perform the job. For example, an organization should provide someone to help an employee in a wheelchair get up a staircase to the workplace. This is a minor and reasonable accommodation that should be made. Providing help in doing nonessential functions for a job can be another reasonable accommodation. It is not yet clear what other actions are reasonable and what actions to help a disabled worker are too difficult or expensive.

Undoubtedly, future court cases will determine how far organizations must go to make reasonable accommodations for disabled employees.

Affirmative Action

Affirmative action is a practice that many organizations have used to increase the number of protected class members in targeted jobs. Its purpose is to address the lingering effects of past discrimination in hiring by allowing certain groups to catch up in acquiring jobs that were at one time unavailable to them. An affirmative action program can involve many different practices. Harrison, Kravitz, Mayer, Leslie, and Lev-Arey (2006) distinguished between programs designed to increase the number of minority applicants versus the number of job offers to minorities. The former type of opportunity enhancement program increases the number of minority applicants by engaging in extra recruitment efforts (e.g., advertising in media that target minorities) or by offering training so that more minorities have the KSAOs required for a job. Affirmative action is not a quota system, nor does it require the hiring of anyone without the necessary KSAOs. The U.S. Supreme Court has consistently ruled against such practices except in extraordinary circumstances (Kravitz, Harrison, Turner, Levine, Chaves, Brannick, Denning, Russell, & Conard, 1997). It also let stand the California law that prohibited most forms of preferential treatment. This does not mean, however, that other forms of affirmative action have been eliminated.

Organizations that have more than 50 employees and government contracts exceeding $50,000 are required by executive order to have an affirmative action program. This requirement affects most colleges and universities whose faculties have government research grants. For most other organizations, this activity is voluntary, although some employers that have been caught using discriminatory practices may be ordered or strongly encouraged by a court to adopt an affirmative action program to end their illegal practices. Most large organizations in the United States practice some form of affirmative action, although some do so more rigorously than others. The widespread practice can be seen in the prominently displayed notice that an employer is an "Affirmative Action" employer, common on the stationery of many organizations and most universities.

The intent of an affirmative action program is to remedy the widespread problem of discrimination. Such programs should be introduced carefully, because they can have unintended detrimental effects on the groups they are designed to help. Madeline Heilman and her colleagues have found that women who are given preferential treatment in hiring can have a negative view of themselves and other women (Heilman, Kaplow, Amato, & Stathatos, 1993), and such negative views can affect self-confidence (Heilman & Alcott, 2001). This effect has been found with minority candidates as well (Evans, 2003). Furthermore, a person who is hired under affirmative action is likely to be seen as incompetent, and the stigma of affirmative action in the minds of co-workers is difficult to overcome (HeilmanBattle, Keller, & Lee, 1998). Research has also shown adverse effects on nonbeneficiaries when preferential treatment has been perceived as unfair—namely, as reverse discrimination (Heilman, McCullough, & Gilbert, 1996; Leck, Saunders, & Charbonneau, 1996).

To overcome these problems, an affirmative action program must be carefully designed so that it does not give the impression that people of protected classes are hired without the necessary qualifications. Organizations that have clear policies valuing diversity and that aggressively recruit minority applicants may be seen by minority candidates as more fair than those giving special treatment to minorities (Slaughter, Sinar, & Bachiochi, 2002). Otherwise, beneficiaries are likely to devalue themselves, and nonbeneficiaries are likely to undermine efforts to remedy past discrimination. When undertaken properly, an affirmative action program can be viewed by most employees as fair and nonthreatening (Parker, Baltes, & Christiansen, 1997). Kravitz and Klineberg (2000) described results of a survey of Houston, Texas, residents concerning affirmative action. They found that most whites were against preferential treatment, but were not against other forms of affirmative action.

Legal Selection Outside the United States

Many countries throughout the industrialized world have discrimination laws similar to those in the United States. Some countries are as vigorous as the United States in enforcing discrimination laws (e.g., Canada and South Africa), whereas others are more lax (e.g., Australia and Britain). Although the United States may have taken the lead, other countries give employees even more protection and have extended protection to additional groups not specifically mentioned in U.S. law. For example, Canada disallows discrimination based on sexual preference, and Ireland disallows discrimination based on marital status.

How different countries approach their discrimination problems depends on the nature of those problems and the society. Pearn (1989) compared the situation in the United Kingdom and the United States in terms of laws and practices. Although the two countries have similar laws, Britain is far more lax in enforcement. This is in part because blacks make up a smaller percentage of the British population (only 5%) and in part because of differences in the legal systems of the two countries (Pearn, 1989). In 1995 the United Kingdom instituted the Disability Discrimination Act, which is much like the ADA in the United States. As in the United States, there is resistance by employers, especially those who have negative attitudes about the disabled and little knowledge of what the law actually requires (Jackson, Furnham, & Willen, 2000). South Africa began legal reforms in the 1970s, motivated in large part by labor shortages among the minority white population (Barling, Fullagar, & Bluen, 1986). In recent years, political action by the black majority has resulted in rigorous affirmative action rules throughout the society.

Canada is much like the United States in terms of laws and vigor of enforcement. Although details may be different, organizations need to follow the same practices to avoid legal problems in Canada as they would in the United States. Ireland is a more homogeneous society than Canada or the United States, having fewer minority groups of sufficient size to push for legal protection. In Ireland discrimination is illegal on the basis of gender or marital status, but the law is silent about blacks or other minority groups (Federation of Irish Employers, 1991).

The countries discussed here, as well as the remainder of at least the industrialized world, have endorsed the idea that employee selection should be based on job-relevant attributes. With this approach the person hired is the person who can best do the job. This will eliminate unfairness in selection from discriminatory practices. It should also help organizations enhance their effectiveness by hiring the best qualified people, regardless of age, color, disability, gender, national origin, race, religion, or other personal characteristics that are irrelevant for job success.

▶ FUTURE ISSUES AND CHALLENGES

Perhaps the biggest challenge for the future of job selection has arisen from the changing nature of work and the workforce. KSAO requirements for jobs are changing in the United States and elsewhere. Dunnette (1998), for example, notes that the increasing use of work teams will require selecting people who are able to work well with others, as well as those who can perform job tasks. Stevens and Campion (1999) developed a test specifically to assess team skills for factory workers, and this will likely be a growing trend. Basic arithmetic and reading skills are lacking among some applicant groups in the United States. Part of the problem is that the KSAO requirements for jobs have increased. Factory work that required few skills in the past is being replaced by jobs with substantial technical content. The problem for organizations will be to identify people who are trainable, as opposed to people who already have the necessary KSAOs. To do so will require the use of different selection approaches and a greater reliance on training. Both Reilly and Israelski (1988) and Robertson and Downs (1989) discussed how trainability tests for predicting future training success are different from tests that predict future job performance.

A second challenge is to end discrimination in employee selection. This will require a shift to making selection decisions based on job-relevant factors. The more widespread use of the scientific approach to selection will help eliminate unfair practices. One technique that has been used with some success is to have employment decisions made by groups or panels of managers rather than individuals (McFarland, Ryan, Sacco, & Kriska, 2004; Powell, & Butterfield, 2002; Prewett-Livingston, Feild, Veres, & Lewis, 1996). It is apparently more difficult to engage in biased hiring when more than one person is responsible for decisions. When everyone has an equal opportunity for every job, organizations will benefit because they will have the widest range of talent from which to select employees. In the long run everyone will benefit if individual applicants are judged on their merits because organizations will then have a more effective workforce.

▶ CHAPTER SUMMARY

One of the most important functions of an organization is the recruitment and selection of new employees. To remain effective, an organization must have a supply of skilled people with the necessary attributes, or KSAOs, to do the job. Acquiring such people involves a four-step procedure:

Planning the need for new employees

Getting appropriate people to apply for positions (recruitment)

Deciding who to hire (selection)

Getting the selected people to take the jobs

Planning the need for new employees requires the use of forecasting methods. This involves comparing the need for people with particular KSAOs with the number of such people who might be available in the area. Future planning for organizational changes and expansions must consider the availability of people to fill the necessary positions. Failure to consider these issues can result in the inability to find the people necessary to carry out an important organizational function.

Getting people to apply for jobs can be a difficult task if there is a shortage of qualified people. The problem is more often one of getting the right people to apply, because there can be a surplus of people with certain skills and a shortage of people with others. There are a number of ways that organizations acquire applicants, including advertising, using recruiters, and using Web-based services.

Scientific selection involves the use of selection devices that have been shown to predict job performance. To develop a system of effective, or valid, selection devices involves a five-step procedure—the KSAOs are identified with a job analysis, criteria are chosen, potential predictors are chosen, the predictors are validated with a research study, and finally, the predictors are cross-validated with a second sample or study.

Once an organization has decided whom to hire, it must convince the person to take the job. To do so an organization must be sure that it offers rewards that are equivalent to those offered by other organizations. One procedure that has been used to ensure a better match between a person and a job is the realistic job preview (RJP), which provides accurate information about the job that allows an applicant to make an informed decision about accepting a job offer.

Utility analysis is used to determine the benefits of using a predictor to hire people. These analyses are based on mathematical formulas that require an estimate of the monetary value of good job performance. Researchers disagree about the best way to conduct utility analysis. Nevertheless, the results of utility analyses have shown that scientific selection can have substantial benefits for organizations.

Employee selection is not only a scientific process, it is also a legal process. Most industrialized countries have laws against discriminatory selection practices. In the United States it is illegal to discriminate on the basis of age, color, disability, gender, national origin, race, or religion. To avoid legal problems, an organization must base selection decisions on job-relevant factors.

I/O PSYCHOLOGY IN PRACTICE

(*Courtesy Anna Erickson*)

This case concerns the development of an unusual assessment device to measure the artistic ability of employees. It was carried out by Dr. Anna Erickson, who was an I/O psychologist for SBC Communications Inc, which owns several telephone companies, including Pacific Bell and Southwestern Bell Inc. Erickson received her Ph.D. in I/O psychology in 1995 from Iowa State University. At the time of this project, her role in the company was to do selection research, although she also has done projects in the areas of job analysis, performance appraisal, planning for future employee needs, and surveys of employee opinions. At the present time, she is director of marketing research and is responsible for conducting studies of customer preferences for and reactions to telephone company products and services, such as call waiting or caller id. This is not an unusual job for an I/O psychologist, for the methods and techniques are much the same as those for more traditional I/O work discussed in this book.

One type of employee hired by the telephone company is a yellow page artist who sketches ads for company customers. The company decided to expand its advertising services, and this required a higher level of artistic talent than is necessary for ad sketches. Supervisors of the ad artists were asked to recommend individuals for the more artistic jobs, but this procedure led to widespread controversy and a union grievance over favoritism. Clearly, a new procedure had to be found that would be seen as fair to the employees while providing a valid means of choosing good artists.

Erickson was asked to solve this problem, but unfortunately no existing assessments for artists could be found. She would have to invent a new assessment device and at the same time gain the support of the employees. To accomplish this objective, she put together a task force of employees and managers. At the same time she studied the research literature on creativity and discovered that, despite the seeming subjective nature of art, experts show a high degree of interrater agreement when evaluating it. This gave her the idea of developing an assessment center in which raters would be faculty members from a well known university art department.

The first step in developing the center was to conduct a job analysis to identify the KSAOs for the job. Results showed that there were two important components to assess. The artist had to be able to deal with customers and to do the creative work. The customer service part was assessed with a structured interview. The creative part was assessed by having experts rate the quality of a portfolio the person submitted and by expert ratings of performance in a simulation. All ratings were done blind, with the rater not knowing whose work was being assessed.

The task force was unanimous in approving this assessment procedure. It accomplished the goal of settling the union grievance. Erickson conducted a validation study of the assessment center and found it predicted very well the professors' ratings of their art students' employability. Those students who were rated most capable and employable did best in the assessment center. It is now being used for placement and selection in the company. This case illustrates how employees often perceive effective selection as fair selection.

Discussion Questions

1. Why was it important to have employee acceptance of the new assessment center?

2. Do you think supervisor nomination was an unfair way to decide who got the jobs?

3. How else could this assessment center be validated other than with the procedure used?

4. Can you think of other ways to measure artistic creativity?

LEARNING BY DOING

Job Market for an Occupation

There are a number of organizations, including the U.S. Bureau of Labor Statistics, that track the job market for occupations. One place that you can find this information is the O*NET Web site (http://online.onetcenter.org). Choose an occupation that you are considering after graduation and then go to the O*NET Web site, to the Find Occupation section. From the top, enter your occupation and you will get a summary for it. Go to the bottom, where it shows the Wages & Employment Trends. Choose a state and hit the GO button. Write a brief report on your occupation's future employment opportunities that compares your state with the United States in wages and growth in the number of people needed.

How Companies Approach Minority Hiring

Large American corporations are required to have affirmative action plans that can be implemented in a number of ways. Often such companies will prominently advertise their plans so that minority applicants will be attracted. Choose a large company (e.g., a Fortune 500 company like General Motors or Verizon) and go to its Web site. Search for evidence and write a report listing ways in which it encourages minorities to apply and values diversity in its workforce.

Training

CHAPTER 7 OUTLINE

If you accept a job with a large organization, it is almost certain that you will go through some sort of formal training program. Even people with college degrees need additional instruction in order to do most jobs. Even simple jobs require training. For example, every employee at a McDonald's restaurant gets trained. The person who makes French fries is taught the proper way to do the job. A restaurant manager receives hundreds of hours of training, much of it in a classroom setting. There is much to learn to be able to

Figure 7.1 Five Steps to Developing an Effective Training Program.

do most jobs well. Future trends suggest that the need for training will increase in most jobs as they become more and more technically oriented.

Training is one of the major activities of most large organizations, including private and public (government) sector organizations throughout the world. It is a necessary activity for both new and experienced employees. New employees must learn how to do their jobs, whereas experienced employees must learn to keep up with job changes and how to improve their performance. In many organizations a person will not be considered for a promotion until certain training has been completed and certain skills mastered. Learning in most jobs is a lifelong process that does not stop with a certain level of education.

Five steps are required for effective organizational training programs, as shown in Figure 7.1.

The first step of a training program is to conduct a *needs assessment* study in order to determine who needs training and what kind of training is needed. The second step is to set objectives so that it will be clear what the training should accomplish. The third step is to design the training program. The fourth step is to deliver the training to those employees designated by the needs assessment. The final step is to evaluate the training to be certain that it achieved its objectives. If the training was ineffective, the process should continue until an effective program is achieved. Each step should be based on the one that precedes it.

In this chapter we discuss all five steps in the training process. All but the delivery step fall within the domain of I/O psychology. Most training is conducted by professional trainers who specialize in its delivery. I/O psychologists are often behind the scenes helping to design the training that others will actually deliver. Most of the training conducted in organizations, however, does not involve I/O psychologists.

Objectives: The student who studies this chapter should be able to:

► List the steps involved in developing and implementing a training program in an organization.

► Describe how needs assessment is conducted.

► Explain the various factors that affect learning and transfer of training.

► Discuss the various training methods, including their advantages.

► Discuss how training is evaluated.

► NEEDS ASSESSMENT

A needs assessment is conducted to determine which employees need training and what the content of their training should be (Arthur, Bennett, Edens, & Bell, 2003). It is too often the case that training resources are wasted by training the wrong people or teaching the wrong content. A needs assessment can ensure that training resources are wisely spent on areas in which there is a demonstrated training need.

According to Goldstein (1993), needs assessment should focus on three levels: organization, job, and person. The *organization level* is concerned with the objectives of the organization and how they are addressed by the performance of employees. An analysis of the organization's objectives can offer hints about the training that is needed. For example, if an organization has the goal of minimizing injuries, it would seem reasonable to train employees in principles of workplace safety. If the goal is to maximize productivity, training would involve principles of production efficiency.

The *job level* is concerned with the nature of the tasks involved in each job. A job analysis can be used to identify the major tasks and then the necessary KSAOs for each task. From the list of KSAOs, a series of training needs can be specified. A police officer, for example, must have knowledge of legal arrest procedures. This is a rather obvious area in which training would be provided.

The *person level* is concerned with how well job applicants or present employees are able to do job tasks. In other words, it assesses the KSAO levels of people rather than jobs. A comparison of the KSAOs of jobs and people suggests the areas of greatest potential training need. Part of an employee recruitment plan should consider if enough applicants have each KSAO. If they do, the KSAO can be used as a criterion for selection. If they do not, the KSAO will be the focus of training. Organizations do not expect to hire secretaries who need training in how to type. They might, however, hire secretaries who need training in how to use specialized software programs.

So far we have discussed needs assessment from the perspective of what should be trained. This approach, however, says nothing about the content of training programs that might already be in use. Ford and Wroten (1984) developed a procedure for determining the extent to which a training program meets training needs. It is somewhat like a job analysis, except that the training is analyzed rather than the job. To conduct such an analysis, subject matter experts review the content of a training program and compile a list of the KSAOs that are addressed. A separate group of subject matter experts reviews the KSAO list and makes ratings of how important each one is to the job in question. This procedure can identify how well the program components match training needs for the job. Programs can be adopted or modified on the basis of this procedure.

Despite the importance of needs assessment, organizations often do not use it. A survey of 1,000 large private companies in the United States found that only 27% used some sort of needs assessment before conducting training of their management-level people (Saari, Johnson, McLaughlin, & Zimmerle, 1988). Too often, training resources are wasted because the needs assessment that might have redirected the effort was never performed. A well conducted needs assessment can help organizations make the most of their training resources.

► OBJECTIVES

One of the most important steps in developing a training program is setting objectives. Unless you are clear about the purpose of training, it is difficult to design a training program to achieve it. Part of this step is to define the criteria for good training success. The objectives of training are based on criteria and should include a statement of what a trainee should know or be able to do after training. The training criterion is a statement of how achievement of the training objective can be assessed. The training objective of acquiring knowledge, for example, can be assessed by seeing if trainees can meet the criterion of achieving a cutoff score on a knowledge test.

Criteria serve as the basis for the design of organizational training. Once we know what the training criterion is, we can design appropriate training to achieve it. Criteria also serve as the standards against which training programs can be evaluated, which we discuss in the section on training evaluation. Training objectives should be based on the results of the needs assessment.

▶ TRAINING DESIGN

Most organizational training is conducted with the expectation that employees will apply what they have learned on the job. This is called **transfer of training**. Transfer is affected by a number of factors in both the job environment and the training itself. Individual differences in characteristics among trainees are also an important consideration in whether training will transfer. Figure 7.2 is a model of transfer developed by Baldwin and Ford (1988). Their model describes how features of the training design can affect how well trainees learn and, in turn, how well the training transfers to the job. They also note that individual differences among trainees and characteristics of the work environment are important influences.

In this section we discuss the training design factors that affect both learning and transfer. In addition, we cover eight popular training techniques that show how the training is delivered. Training can be done in a variety of ways, from the relatively passive lecture to the very involving simulation. In the former case, the trainees listen to a presentation, whereas in the latter case they get to try out the new skill. Each of the eight methods is useful in some training situations.

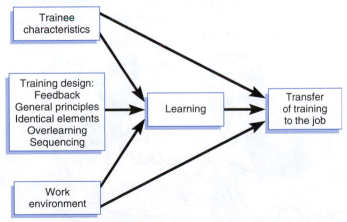

Figure 7.2   This Model of Transfer of Training Shows how Characteristics of the Trainee, Training Program, and Work Environment Affect Learning and Transfer of Training.

Source: Adapted from "Transfer of Training: A Review and Directions for Future Research," by T. T. Baldwin and J. K. Ford, 1988, *Personnel Psychology, 41*, pp. 63–105.

Trainee Characteristics

Individual differences in ability and motivation are important factors in learning (Herold, Davis, Fedor, & Parsons, 2002). Not everyone is equally able to learn specific tasks, and where one person is better able to learn cognitive tasks, another is more skilled at motor tasks. Thus, some people are skilled academicians and others are world-class athletes. These differences are important when it comes to the design of training. Not everyone has the same ability to learn a given task, and training needs to recognize these differences.

Bunker and Cohen (1977) studied the effectiveness of a training program designed to instruct telephone company employees in basic electronics theory. The mathematical ability of each trainee was assessed before training, and a measure of electronics knowledge was taken both before and after training. Results showed that those trainees with the highest level of mathematical ability gained the most from training. In order to get each trainee up to a given level of knowledge, more training would be necessary for the low-ability trainees. A good strategy for training is to give each individual trainee the amount of training necessary to reach the training criterion. This can mean that some people get a lot more training than others.

Ability is not the only individual characteristic that affects training outcomes. Attitudes and motivation can affect outcomes both in training and on the job (Noe & Schmitt, 1986). People who do not wish to learn will not likely get much benefit from a training program. One of the most important factors that must be considered is how to motivate employees to do their best in a training situation. This can be done by giving external rewards for successful completion (e.g., promotion) or by making the training interesting to the trainees. Colquitt, Le Pine and Now (2000) conducted a meta-analysis of training motivation studies. They found, not unexpectedly, that motivation consistently related to transfer of training, as well as to good employee attitudes.

People also differ in the best way to learn new material. Some are good at learning from a presentation, whereas others do well with written materials. Individual capacities and preferences for different types of training are important considerations and should

"I'm a hunter, but I've been cross-trained as a gatherer."

(© 1995; Reprinted courtesy of Bunny Hoest and Parade Magazine)

be taken into account if possible. People who do not read well should be trained with verbal approaches. Others, who like to study and think about material, might do better with a written manual.

Design Factors That Affect Transfer of Training

The transfer of training model in Figure 7.2 specifies five design factors that affect transfer. Each factor should be considered in the design of a training program. Appropriate use of the factors will maximize the likelihood of transfer. Ignoring them might result in a training program that is ineffective in affecting behavior on the job.

Feedback

Feedback is an important component of learning. Without some sort of feedback, it is doubtful that learning can occur at all. Feedback should be built into the training as appropriate so that the trainees can tell if they are learning the correct material.

Training that is intended to impart information or knowledge can build in feedback in two ways. First, trainees can be tested on the information with an examination. Second, trainees can ask questions of the trainer. Both of these procedures are a regular part of most college or university courses. Training intended to teach a skill should allow the trainees to practice and get feedback as they learn. For example, training in driving an automobile should allow the person being trained to drive with an instructor who will give feedback. Feedback is also built into the task itself. Trainees can see for themselves whether they are staying on the road and are driving straight.

General Principles

General principles means that training should teach why something is done as well as how it should be done. Many training programs include a section on the principles behind the material being taught. With computer training, there might be an introduction to the principles of computer and software design. This would be brief and rather general, but it would give the trainees a general idea of what a computer is and how it works. The purpose of teaching the general principles is that it provides a framework for learning. It has been found that including general principles where appropriate enhances learning (Baldwin & Ford, 1988).

Identical Elements

A training program that has good transfer of training capability should include **identical elements**, which means that the responses in the training situation are identical to those in the job situation. It also means that the stimuli the trainee perceives will be identical in both settings. The closer the match in responses and stimuli, the easier it will be for trainees to apply what has been learned in training to the job setting.

A flight simulator is a training device that takes advantage of the identical elements idea. A flight simulator allows the trainee to fly an airplane without leaving the ground. There are two types of simulator—high fidelity and low fidelity. The high fidelity simulator is extremely realistic and might be a cockpit from a real aircraft mounted on a moving platform that simulates the motion of the airplane. The motions of the simulator match the movements of the controls. If the trainee pulls back on the stick, for example,

Figure 7.3 Pilots Learn many of the Skills of Flying an Airplane in a Flight Simulator, such as the One shown in this Picture.
(*Courtesy NASA*)

the front of the cockpit tilts upward. A low fidelity simulator is best illustrated by a computer game that simulates flying. Even though these low fidelity simulator games do not contain all the elements of a real airplane, many of the elements are authentic. For this reason, the U.S. Navy uses such games to help train its pilots on some aspects of flying. To complete training, however, it must use high fidelity simulators. The simulator provides training that transfers well to actual flying because there are many identical elements (Figure 7.3).

Overlearning

Overlearning refers to giving the trainees practice beyond what is necessary to reach a criterion for success in training. The idea is that they first learn the material and then continue to overlearn it. Through overlearning, the trainees consolidate the new knowledge or skill so that they can use what has been learned with little thought. They have achieved **automaticity**, meaning that tasks (e.g., driving a car or riding a bicycle) can be done smoothly without having to mentally monitor or pay attention to how they are performing. This results in much more effective performance and should be the goal for much organizational training (Ford & Kraiger, 1995).

Athletes practice their skills until they have become so overlearned that automaticity is achieved. In athletics the actions that are performed are often so complex and done so fast that it is not possible to think about all the elements. Overlearned elements are performed automatically and quickly. On the job the same principle can apply, because overlearned skills can be used when there is not enough time to think about how to perform a task. For example, in a hospital emergency room, there is little time to think about every task that needs to be done to save a patient's life. Equipment must be used quickly and automatically when a patient is in critical condition.

Overlearning can be built into training through practice and repetition. Information and knowledge training can include repetition of important concepts to ensure that the trainees rehearse the information. Examinations can also allow them to rehearse, thus helping to consolidate what has been learned. With manual skills, sufficient practice should be allowed so that the skill becomes overlearned. It is not sufficient to allow trainees to try the skill until they can do it correctly one time. Repeated practice is necessary to provide overlearning. The more they get to practice, the more likely that they will be able to apply what has been learned on the job.

Driskell, Willis, and Copper (1992) conducted a meta-analysis of overlearning studies. They analyzed the amount of performance gain as a function of the amount of overlearning. Overlearning was defined as practice in the training session that continued after the trainees first achieved the criterion level for having learned the task. Overlearning in these studies ranged from 0% (no overlearning) to 200% (twice the amount of training after the training criterion was reached as before it was reached). If it took two hours of training for the trainee to reach the criterion, 200% overlearning would be an extra four hours of training. Figure 7.4 summarizes the results. The greater the overlearning (horizontal axis), the greater the amount of learning (vertical axis). It should be kept in mind, however, that most of the studies included in this meta-analysis investigated short-term learning where the time between the training and assessment of learning was no more than a week. Furthermore, the overlearning occurred in a single training session. Rohrer, Taylor, Pashler, Wixted, and Cepeda (2004) compared short-term (1 week) and long-term (9 week) retention of learned material. They found that although the overlearners retained more material throughout the study, almost all of the initial gain disappeared by week 9. They suggested that the problem with retention length can be solved by incorporating spaced training in which extra practice occurs over extended periods, and not all in a single long training session. Spaced training will be discussed next.

Sequencing of Training Sessions

There are two aspects of sequencing training sessions: *part* versus *whole*, and *massed* versus *spaced*. **Part training** refers to breaking a task into components that are learned one at a time. After the components are learned, the entire task is taught as a whole. **Whole training** occurs when the entire task is taught at one time rather than breaking it into individual components.

Part training is preferred over whole training when tasks are too complex to be learned all at once. It would be difficult to learn to play golf or tennis using the whole approach. It would be better in this case to learn one aspect of the game at a time, such as swinging the golf club or serving the tennis ball. To concentrate on all aspects of the game would be very difficult. Learning to ride a bicycle, on the other hand, is taught whole. One does not usually learn the components separately, such as pedaling or steering.

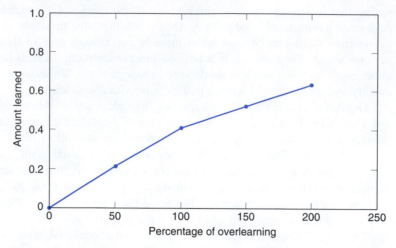

Figure 7.4 Learning is Enhanced by the Amount of Overlearning Training. Increasing the Amount of Training After the Initial Criterion is Reached will Increase the Amount of Learning.

Source: "Effect of Overlearning on Retention," by J. E. Driskell, R. Willis, and C. Copper, 1992, *Journal of Applied Psychology*, 77, 615–622.

Massed training means that the training sessions are long in duration and take place over a relatively short period of time. **Spaced training** means that training sessions are relatively short and are spread out over time. *Massed* and *spaced* are relative terms that can be used to refer to some training programs as more massed or spaced than other programs. A training program that holds sessions one hour per day for 10 days is more spaced than a program that meets for one 10-hour day.

Massed training can be very efficient. For that reason, it is often used for organizational training in situations where it is easier to allow a person to leave work for a day of training than to allow one hour a day for eight days. With many jobs, a replacement will have to be found while the person is in training, and it can be difficult to find a replacement for an hour at a time. The replacement might have to be paid for an entire day to fill in for one hour. Furthermore, considerable travel time may be needed to get to the training site, which might be in another city. For these practical reasons, massed training is often used.

On the other hand, spaced training can be more effective than massed training in the long term and produces better learning (Cepeda, Pashler, Vul, Wixted, & Rohrer, 1995). These authors recommend intervals of at least one day between training sessions, and that the longer the material needs to be retained, the longer should be the inter-session interval. At least part of the problem with massed training is that it can produce boredom, which interferes with learning, and there are limits to how long a person can learn before fatigue comes into play. Imagine learning to play tennis in 10-hour sessions. Fatigue would make it impossible to get the full benefit of the training. Even with mental tasks a person is not efficient when tired. Any student who has crammed for an exam has learned that massed training is not always the best procedure.

Work Environment

Training in organizations takes place in the context of a complex work environment. Whether or not the skills learned in training are used on the job is dependent in large part on the environment of the job. Just because management provides training does not mean that employees or their direct supervisors will support its transfer to the job. It is not uncommon for direct supervisors of lower-level employees to tell their subordinates that the new procedures or skills learned in training are not to be used in their departments. Supportive environments where supervisors and other people encourage the application of learned principles produce employee motivation to learn and increased transfer of training (Facteau, Dobbins, Russell, Ladd, & Kudisch, 1995; Machin & Fogarty, 2003). Unless there is support by employees and their supervisors, the best training will not have its intended effects. Getting that support is a complex problem that goes beyond the proper design of training.

Another issue concerns whether or not the opportunity arises to use the new training. For example, if employees are trained in using a new computer system that is not available to them on the job, the training can have no effect. This issue goes back to the idea of needs assessment. Employees should not receive training in an area that they will not encounter on the job.

Training Methods

Many different methods for training are available. Because each has its advantages and limitations, there is no one best way to train, and all of them can be effective in the right situation (Callahan, Kiker, & Cross, 2003). As noted earlier, different individuals may do well with different approaches. The best training programs are flexible and can adapt to the demands of what and who are being trained.

In this section we discuss eight different training methods that are frequently used in organizational training. These methods can be used in combination, because a good training program may need to take advantage of the strengths of different methods for different aspects of training. For example, the training of pilots may involve many, if not all, of these methods. The learning of complex tasks can require the use of a variety of approaches. Table 7.1 lists all eight methods and summarizes the major advantages of each.

Audiovisual Instruction

Audiovisual instruction involves the electronic presentation of materials using an audiotape, videotape, DVD, or computer. Although audio recordings and films have long been in use for training, technology has been expanding the ease and flexibility with which such media can be used. It is becoming commonplace for lecturers in business and universities to use computer-based tools such as PowerPoint to add audiovisual elements to presentations. These methods can also be used by individuals in autoinstruction, which is the next method we will discuss.

Autoinstruction

Autoinstruction refers to any training method that is self-paced and does not use an instructor. The most well known technique is **programmed instruction**, which divides the material to be covered into a series of individual chunks, or frames. Each frame

TABLE 7.1 Advantages of Eight Training Methods

Method	Advantages
Audiovisual instruction	Presents material that could not otherwise be heard or seen Can train many people at once
Autoinstruction	Gives immediate feedback to trainees Individualized pacing
Conference	Allows for feedback to trainees High level of trainee involvement
Lecture	Economical Good information-giving method
Modeling	High level of feedback Provides practice of new skills
On-the-job training	Exposure to actual job High level of transfer
Role playing	High level of feedback Provides practice of new skills
Simulation	High level of transfer Provides practice of new skills

Source: Adapted from "Selection, Training, and Development of Personnel," by W. C. Borman, N. G. Peterson, and T. L. Russell, 1992, in G. Salvendy (Ed.), *Handbook of Industrial Engineering*, 2nd ed. New York: John Wiley.

contains a piece of information, a question to be answered, and the answer to the question from the preceding frame. Trainees work at their own pace. Repetition is built in because the same material is presented more than once. There is also feedback, because the trainee must answer questions and is then given the correct answer almost immediately. Although the medium for programmed instruction was originally a book or manual, computers provide a much more flexible approach to autoinstruction training.

Conference

A **conference** is a meeting of trainees and a trainer to discuss the material in question. The distinguishing feature of the conference is that participants can discuss the material and ask questions. It also allows for a free flow of ideas so that the discussion can go beyond the prepackaged materials. Thus, the conference can be used to enhance learning more than the other methods. It is especially effective when used with trainees who have already acquired expertise with the material. It is the major teaching method used at the Ph.D. level in the training of I/O psychology students.

Lecture

A **lecture** is a presentation by a trainer to a group of trainees. Its major advantage is its efficiency. One trainer can present material to a large number of trainees. At some universities, lectures are given to thousands of students at one time. The greatest strength of the lecture is also its greatest weakness. The mass presentation to many people limits the amount of feedback that can be given. With even 40 people at a lecture, if each person asked one question the lecturer would have little time to present. For situations in which feedback is not needed, the lecture can be a very effective means of training.

Modeling

Modeling involves having trainees watch someone perform a task and then having them model what they have seen. The model can be on a film or videotape. Models can show both effective and ineffective examples of behavior. This approach is often used for the training of supervisory skills, such as giving negative feedback to an employee who is performing poorly. Examples of supervisory behavior are shown, and then the trainees attempt to imitate what they have seen. The trainer's role is to encourage the trainees to try the approaches and to give them feedback about how well they imitated what they saw.

Research on the modeling approach has provided support for its ability to train people in interpersonal skills, such as communicating with others. Taylor, Russ-Eft, and Chan's (2005) meta-analysis showed that modeling was effective in enhancing learning performance as assessed by both paper-and-pencil tests and simulations. Simon and Werner (1996) reported better learning with modeling than with autoinstruction or lecture in training U.S. naval personnel in the use of a new data processing system on a personal computer.

On-the-Job Training

On-the-job training is not a specific method but is any method used to show employees how to do the job while they are doing it. The greatest amount of job training often occurs while the trainee is doing the various job tasks. On-the-job training can be an informal system whereby a new employee watches an experienced employee to see how the job should be done. It can also involve a formal training program such as an **apprenticeship**, which is commonly used for jobs that may take years to be fully trained. For this sort of job, the other methods might not be feasible, because the organization will not want to pay someone for years of training without productivity. If the trainee quits before training is completed, the training effort was wasted. An apprentice is an employee who serves as an assistant to the trainer. The trainer is an employee who is doing the job and training the apprentice at the same time. This approach is often used to train people in trade occupations, such as electricians or plumbers.

Role Playing

A **role play** is a type of simulation in which the trainee pretends to be doing a task. It usually involves an interpersonal situation, such as giving advice or feedback, and is used frequently for supervisory training. The role play is part of the modeling procedure we discussed earlier. The role play itself does not involve first observing another person perform the behavior. It can be an effective training technique, but it is costly in that only a few trainees can be trained at one time.

Simulations

As discussed earlier, a **simulation** is a technique in which specialized equipment or materials are used to portray a task situation. Trainees are to pretend that the situation is real and carry out their tasks as they would in the actual situation. Simulations can be used for training people in the use of equipment, such as automobiles or airplanes. They can also be used to simulate other situations, such as a business decision simulation that asks trainees to pretend to be an organization member who has been given a problem to solve or a task to accomplish. For example, a simulation might involve running an airport or a factory (Funke, 1998). Simulations can be very realistic, for they can be based on real examples from the same organization. The simulation shares the limitation of the role play in that only a few trainees can participate at one time. With the use of computer-based approaches, however, this may not be a serious limitation, because computers are widely available in many organizations.

Electronic Training

Electronic training, or e-learning, is the latest trend in organizational training and university education. It involves the use of electronic tools to provide training, and several of the training methods discussed here can be done electronically. Some forms of e-learning merely make use of a computer or technology to deliver training originally developed for another medium, such as Web-broadcasting a lecture so that people can watch it remotely on their computers or televisions. More sophisticated approaches allow for complex, individualized training methods that incorporate sophisticated assessments to both provide feedback and make training more efficient by matching the level of the trainee. Practice can continue until a criterion level of proficiency is achieved, and already learned material can be skipped.

DeRouin, Fritzsche, and Salas (2005) note several potential advantages of e-learning that make it attractive to organizations. First, it can give the learner a great deal of control over the training experience by being able to determine where and when the training is delivered and, with some methods, the order of the material. Second, technology allows for rapid development and modification of training materials as needed. A training module written in PowerPoint can be put together and e-mailed to employees or posted on a Web site in a very short time. Third, e-learning can be combined with other, more traditional methods, producing **blended learning**. For example, a classroom lecture can be coupled with some e-learning exercises. Finally, e-learning can be easily customized to meet individual employee needs. For example, a training program might include assessments that determine when the learner has mastered the material and is ready to move to the next topic.

One rapidly growing practice is the use of the Web for training delivery. Training materials can be put online so they are available to employees at all times. This makes training available whenever and wherever the employee comes across a situation in which the training is needed, rather than having to wait until a training session is available. This can be an advantage in jobs that involve a tremendous amount of information and rapid change, as in technology jobs (Rischall, 2001). Also, e-learning can be cost effective because it eliminates travel to attend training sessions and the need for live trainers, both of which can be expensive (Burgess & Russell, 2003). Research shows that e-learning can result in equivalent or even better learning than classroom instruction (Sitzmann, Kraiger, Stewart, & Wisher, 2006). One drawback is that completion rates are not always good. S. L. Cohen (2001) reports that of all who begin online training courses, fewer than 25% finish them. Although the e-learning approach shows great promise, organizations are still in the process of figuring out the best way to use it.

Mentoring

Many organizations have found that new and inexperienced employees can benefit from being mentored by more senior and usually higher level employees. **Mentoring** is a special kind of work relationship between two employees in which the more experienced one offers career guidance, counseling, and emotional support, and serves as a role model, to the less experienced one (Day & Allen, 2004). Although most mentor situations involve employees of different organizational levels and often a mentor is the protégé's supervisor, mentors can also be peers who are at the same level but are more experienced (Allen, McManus, & Russell, 1999). Mentoring can be thought of as a kind of training that not only orients new employees to the job but helps them develop their careers with the company over a considerable period (Young & Perrewé, 2000). Research has shown that employees who are mentored, or protégés, derive a number of benefits from mentoring, including better job performance, quicker promotion, better job attitudes, less turnover (Allen, Eby, Poteet, Lentz, & Lima, 2004; Underhill, 2006), and less conflict between demands of home and work (Nielson, Carlson, & Lankau, 2001). There are also benefits for the mentors, including personal satisfaction, enhanced job performance, recognition by others, and future loyalty of the protégés which can be helpful (Eby, Durley, Evans, & Ragins, 2006).

Mentoring occurs quite naturally as relationships develop between people at work, but many organizations have formal mentoring programs in which mentors and protégés are assigned to one another (Raabe & Beehr, 2003). Formal programs can be useful because not all employees are likely to find mentors on their own. Individuals who are achievement oriented and sociable are most likely to find mentors naturally (Aryee, Lo, & Kang, 1999). Assigned mentorships don't always work as well as those that develop naturally (Allen & Eby, 2003), because assigned mentor-protégé relationships are not always good. Allen, Eby and Lentz (2006) studied the experiences of mentors and protégés, asking about several features of their mentor program and whether they derived benefits. They showed that allowing both mentor and protégé to have input into the pairing, and training were important factors in achieving a successful mentoring experience. In the extreme, mentoring can become dysfunctional when the relationship between mentor and protégé becomes destructive, with the mentor being overly critical and even undermining the protégé. Such negative experiences can be worse than no mentor at all and can be a significant source of stress for protégés (Eby, Butts, Lockwood, & Simon, 2004).

INTERNATIONAL REPLICATION

Not every employee is able to find a mentor or have a good mentoring relationship. Aryee, Lo, and Kang (1999) were interested in determining the characteristics of protégés that led to their receiving mentoring from older, more experienced employees.

Participants in this study were 184 Chinese employees of various local and multinational companies in Hong Kong. They were each mailed a copy of a questionnaire by the researchers that contained questions about their mentoring experiences, some personality tests, and questions about their age and gender. The mentoring experiences were measured with two scales. One concerned the extent to which the participant had received mentoring from an experienced manager.

The other asked about the efforts the participant had made to seek out a mentor.

Results showed that the two mentoring scales were correlated—employees who sought mentors were more likely to find them than employees who waited for the mentor to find them. Both mentoring scales were related to the participant's achievement striving and extraversion (outgoingness). Older employees were more likely than younger employees to find mentors (but keep in mind that most participants were between the ages of 25 and 30). Finally, men and women were equally likely to seek and find mentors.

The magnitude of the correlation between the two mentoring scales (.40) was rather low, suggesting that although seeking a mentor raised employees' chances of finding one, they were often not successful in doing so. Those employees who were successful were likely to be ambitious, hardworking, and outgoing, based on their personality test scores. They were also likely to be older—in this sample in their 30s rather than early 20s. Finally, gender didn't make a difference in mentoring—men and women were equally likely to be protégés.

Source: Aryee, S., Lo, S., & Kang, I. L. (1987). Antecedents of early career stage mentoring among Chinese employees. *Journal of Organizational Behavior*, *20*, 563–576.

Executive Coaching

High level executives, especially in private companies, are sometimes paired with a consultant who serves as an executive coach to help them improve job performance (Feldman & Lankau, 2005). **Executive coaching** is most likely for higher level positions when the incumbent has significant performance deficiencies and the cost of finding a replacement is high. There are many ways in which a coach can operate. One way is to solicit feedback from employees who interact with the executive, perhaps using 360-degree feedback (see Chapter 4). The coach will meet with the executive to help interpret the feedback and devise an action plan to improve in areas that are deficient. For example, if subordinates and peers note problems with communication, a plan to enhance such skills could be devised. The coach might work with the executive for an extended period, providing continual advice and feedback.

One concern with executive coaching is that no particular background or credentials are needed to be a coach, and there is no consensus concerning the requisite KSAOs required (Feldman & Lankau, 2005). Coaches can be found with a variety of backgrounds, including I/O psychology (see Psychology in Practice). The scant research concerning effectiveness suggests that executive coaching can have positive effects. For example, Smither, London, Flautt, Vargas, and Kucine (2003) found that managers who were coached improved performance more from before to after coaching than a control group of managers who were not coached.

▶ DELIVERY OF A TRAINING PROGRAM

Even the most well designed training program will be ineffective if it is not properly delivered. In most organizations, specialists who are skilled in training deliver the program. They may or may not be experts in the content of the training or in training design. Content is the responsibility of subject matter experts who know the topics the training will cover. I/O psychologists and people from several other fields are experts at program design. Because program delivery is not a frequent activity of I/O psychologists, we continue with the next topic: training evaluation.

► EVALUATION OF A TRAINING PROGRAM

As far as I/O psychologists are concerned, a training program is not completed until its effectiveness has been evaluated. An evaluation is a piece of research to see whether the program had its intended effects. This is important, because many training programs are ineffective. For example, Morrow, Jarrett, and Rupinski (1997) evaluated the utility of 18 training programs in an organization and found that five cost more than they returned in improved performance on the job. The principles of research design, as discussed in Chapter 2, are very much involved in the design of evaluation. There is little difference between conducting an evaluation study for a training program and conducting a research study to determine the effects of any intervention that is tried in an organization. Thus, the principles and techniques of research methodology discussed in Chapter 2 apply to the evaluation of a training program.

Carrying out a training evaluation requires five steps (Figure 7.5). The first step is to define the criteria for evaluation. As we have discussed several times in this book, you must have criteria before you can evaluate anything. Criteria are the standards for comparison so that you can determine if training has been effective. Once criteria have been selected, a design for the study and the measures used to assess the criteria can be selected (steps 2 and 3). Step 4 is collecting the data for the study. Step 5 is analyzing the data and reaching conclusions about the effectiveness of the training program. We discuss each of these steps in greater detail below.

Set Criteria

Training criteria serve as the standard by which training can be evaluated. If you know what the training is supposed to achieve, you can design an evaluation study to determine if the goals were met. Suppose a manufacturing company is selling too many defective products. It might set as a training objective teaching employees to reduce errors in their manufacturing tasks. The criterion could be a specified reduction in the number of defective products. When the criterion is specific, such as a reduction of 10%, it is relatively easy to evaluate the effectiveness of the training program.

Training criteria are classified into two levels, both of which are important in evaluating training: training level and performance level. **Training-level criteria** are concerned with what people are able to do at the end of training in the training environment itself rather than on the job. **Performance level criteria** are concerned with the person's performance on the job rather than in the training setting. In other words, performance

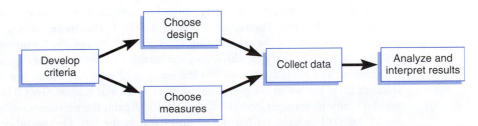

Figure 7.5   The Five Steps in Evaluating a Training Program.

criteria are concerned with transfer of training. Thus training level is concerned with what the person learned, whereas performance level is concerned with the effects of the training on the job itself.

Performance-level and training-level criteria work hand-in-hand in evaluating the effectiveness of training. The performance level is important because it shows whether or not the training has had the intended effects on the job. Because most training is intended to affect job performance, a training program without effects at the performance level is ineffective. On the other hand, it is important to know what the employees learned in the training. The best criterion for this is at the training level. Someone might learn a great deal and for some reason not apply it to the job. Failure to have an effect on the job might be due to other factors. For example, an employee might know what to do and how to do it, but the opportunity to apply the knowledge might never occur. Employees might be given a first aid course to help them better handle work accidents. If no accidents occur, the employees will not show any effects at the performance level.

Another useful way of classifying criteria is to divide them into four types, two of which can be placed in the performance level and two in the training level (Kirkpatrick, 1977; see also Alliger & Janak, 1989):

> Reactions   Behavior
> Learning   Results

Reactions criteria refer to how much the trainees liked the training and how much they believed they got out of it. It is assessed with a questionnaire given to trainees at the end of the training session. **Learning criteria** refer to what the trainees learned in training—what they are able to demonstrate behaviorally in terms of knowledge and skills acquired in training. It might be assessed with an examination given at the end of training. Both of these criterion types relate to the training level. They are frequently used in colleges and universities. Student evaluations are reaction criteria, and exam scores are learning criteria.

Behavior criteria concern the trainee's behaviors on the job that might have been due to training. This type of criterion looks at whether or not the trainees are doing the things they were taught. **Results** criteria deal with whether the training had its intended effect. Did the training reduce costs or increase productivity? This final type of criterion serves as the bottom line for the effectiveness of a training program. Both behavior and results criteria are performance level because they focus on what happens on the job rather than in the training setting.

All of these criterion types are important because each is a partial indicator of training success. A meta-analysis of 34 training studies showed that most criteria assessed within the same study were only slightly correlated with one another (Alliger, Tannenbaum, Bennett, Traver, & Shotland, 1997). Furthermore, in any given training program, only some of the criteria may show the desired results. Campion and Campion (1987) conducted a study in which they evaluated a training program against four different criteria. Their results showed that the training of interview skills was effective at the training level but not at the performance level. May and Kahnweiler (2000) conducted a similar study of manager communication skills. Again, the trainees were able to demonstrate the skill in training, but it had no effect on the job. On the other hand Maurer, Solamon, Andrews and Troxtel (2001) were able to show that interview training was effective in enhancing performance in interviews away from the training situation. Thus we can see that interview training can be effective but is not always effective. These studies demonstrate that one must not assume that training will have the intended effects and one should include criteria at both levels to thoroughly evaluate effectiveness (see Research in Detail).

RESEARCH IN DETAIL

Sometimes events occur in organizations that produce the equivalent of an experiment. Such was the case with the study by Campion and Campion (1987) when the availability of training for only some employees allowed the researchers to conduct a naturally occurring experiment to evaluate the effects of training. Employees were assigned to be either trained or untrained merely because the organization had insufficient resources and time for everyone to be trained. After the training was completed, the researchers assessed everyone to compare criteria between the trained and untrained employees.

This study took place in an electronics company that needed to move a large number of employees from manufacturing jobs to marketing jobs. Many of the employees lacked interview skills. The managers of the organization were concerned that their employees would be unable to perform well enough in an interview to transfer to another job. To remedy the deficiency, an interview skills training program was developed and implemented.

Roughly half of the eligible employees were given training and half were not. The training was evaluated with each of the four types of criteria: reaction, learning, behavior, and results. The reaction criterion was assessed with a questionnaire at the end of the training. The majority of participants believed the training was worthwhile. Learning was assessed with a test given

to the trained employees at the beginning and end of training. This knowledge test showed that the participants learned about proper interview behavior during the training.

The behavior criterion was assessed by having the interviewers who later interviewed all employees rate how well they performed. According to this criterion, the trained group performed the same as the untrained group. Finally, the results criterion was assessed by noting the number of job offers each employee received. Here again there were no differences between the trained and untrained individuals.

These results suggested that the training was effective in teaching the employees interview skills but ineffective in helping them perform better in an actual job interview. From the organization's point of view, the training did not meet its objectives. The reasons for this failure are not clear. Perhaps the training was unnecessary because most employees already had good interview skills. Perhaps the training included the wrong material. In either case, this study demonstrates why it is important for organizations to assess different types of criteria when evaluating a training program.

Source: Campion, M. A., & Campion, J. E. (2000). Evaluation of an interviewee skill training program in a natural field experiment. *Personnel Psychology, 40*, 675–691.

Choose Design

A *design* is the structure of a study, whether a study of training or some other phenomenon, that specifies how data are collected. With a training evaluation, the type of criterion sets limits on the designs that can be used. For reaction criteria, the only feasible design is one that assesses participants once—at the end of training. It makes no sense to assess nonparticipants or to assess participants before they go through training. People who are not going to be trained cannot have a reaction to what they have not experienced. People who have not yet been trained cannot have a reaction to what they are about to experience.

Figure 7.6 Structure of a Pretest-Posttest Training Evaluation Design.

Other criteria can be assessed with many different types of designs. The two most popular are: pretest-posttest and control group. The *pretest-posttest design* assesses trainees before and after training. The *control group design* compares trainees with a group of employees who have not received the training. Each design has its advantages and limitations in evaluating a training program.

Pretest-Posttest

The **pretest-posttest design** is intended to provide information about how much the trainees gained from the training. It can be used to assess the amount learned in the training itself or the amount of change in behavior back on the job. To conduct a study with this design, the measures of interest are assessed before the training begins (pretest) and again after it has been completed (posttest). Figure 7.6 illustrates the structure of this design. Both pretest and posttest measures are part of the training program. It is not unusual for a training program to begin with a test to see what trainees know and conclude with a test to see what they have learned. Assessments can also occur on the job well before and well after training. For example, if a training program is intended to improve productivity, measures of productivity could be taken for the six months before and the six months after training. Some training may not show effects on the job for a long period of time. Thorough evaluation would not be possible immediately after training.

The pretest-posttest design is popular because it is a practical design to use in organizations. It is usually easy to build in an assessment at the beginning and end of a training program. The assessment can also be used as a means of providing feedback. The major drawback of this design is that it is difficult to attribute changes to the training itself rather than other events in the organization. This is particularly true for performance criteria. If a training program is designed to improve job performance, gains in performance from before to after training might have occurred for many reasons. Just making supervisors aware that performance is a problem could motivate them to put pressure on subordinates to perform. This increased attention on performance would coincide with the training and might be the cause of the performance gains. To find out if the training itself was the cause of the improvement would require a research design with a control group.

Control Group

A control group design compares employees who receive training to equivalent employees who have not been trained. Figure 7.7 illustrates the structure of this design. To conduct a control group study, a group of employees is selected for the study. Half are assigned at random to the trained group, and the other half are the controls who receive no training. At the end of the training program, all employees in the study are assessed on the measures of interest. The comparison between the two subgroups of employees indicates the effects of the training.

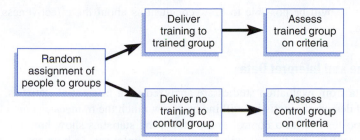

Figure 7.7 Structure of a Control Group Training Evaluation Design.

This design is more difficult to use in an organization because it is not always possible to assign employees at random to the two groups. In addition, there can be contamination if the trained employees tell the untrained control group employees what they have learned. However, this design is an improvement over the pretest-posttest when you wish to determine the effects of training. It helps control for the possibility that it was something other than training that caused the changes you observed in employees.

Choose Measures of the Criteria

Once criteria have been chosen, the actual measures of those criteria need to be selected. The criterion of interest determines to a great extent what sorts of measures can be used to assess it. Reaction criteria require the use of a questionnaire that trainees can complete to give their reactions. The specific design of the questionnaire must be decided. There are many ways to ask people their reactions to training. For example, questions can ask how much the trainee learned or if the training was enjoyable.

Learning criteria usually involve some sort of test given at the end of training. Training intended to increase knowledge about a topic can be evaluated with a knowledge test, much like an examination given in school. Training to enhance other types of skills would require a different approach, such as a role play or a simulation test. Assessment of performance criteria would require measuring trainee behavior or results in the job setting rather than in training.

Collect Data

Although the underlying logic of an evaluation study is simple and straightforward, carrying out the study can be a difficult undertaking because collecting the data poses many practical problems. People are not always cooperative, and many things can and do go wrong. It is difficult to perform pure random assignment in an organization, so that compromises have to be made. Often this means that the trained group comes from one department and the control group from another. Differences between the trained and untrained employees might then be caused by departmental differences on the criteria of interest.

The best possible design should always be planned. Every researcher knows that the plan might not be carried out without problems. This means that modifications might have to be made during the study. A good researcher is able to deal effectively with problems that occur during the data collection step of the study. If this step is conducted properly, it will be possible to draw conclusions about the effectiveness of the training program.

Analyze and Interpret Data

The data from evaluation studies are analyzed with inferential statistics. With a pretest-posttest design, the statistics will indicate how much the trainees changed from the pretest to the posttest. With a control group study, the statistics show how much difference, if any, exists between the trained and untrained employees. In both cases, the statistic used could be as simple as a t test.

If all four steps of the training evaluation have been well done, it will be possible to reach a confident conclusion about the effectiveness of the training program. It is always a good idea to evaluate training, and it should be evaluated at both the performance and the training level. Training will often be effective at only one of the two levels, so assessment of both will give useful information about the effects of the training.

If training works at both levels, it can be considered effective and should continue. Training that does not work at either level should be considered ineffective and eliminated or modified. Training that is effective at the training level but not the performance level is probably the wrong approach to the problem or an incomplete solution to the problem. A productivity problem might be due to inadequate knowledge or skill, but it can be caused by other factors as well. In a manufacturing plant, poor productivity can be caused by poor equipment maintenance or poor supervision. Training of equipment operators is unlikely to affect their productivity if it is being reduced by one of these two factors. An evaluation of training would likely show that the operators learned, but productivity stayed the same.

The development of a new training program should always include an evaluation component. Training found to be ineffective should not continue but should be modified if that would increase its effectiveness. A good strategy for developing training is to pilot test it before implementation. A small group of employees could be put through the training, and the training would be evaluated at several levels. It would not be implemented throughout the organization until it has been found to be effective during pilot testing. This approach also allows for the modification of training so that it can be improved before full implementation throughout the organization. This strategy for developing training programs should result in making the most of training resources.

▶ FUTURE ISSUES AND CHALLENGES

In their summary of trends that will affect the future of organizational training, Goldstein and Gilliam (1990) noted that changes in the nature of the workplace over the next few decades will require new training strategies in organizations. Since 1990 we have seen these trends accelerate, including:

Changing demographics of the workforce

Increased use of technology

Internationalization

Shifts from manufacturing to service jobs

These trends will require more training by organizations.

It has been projected that the workforce in the United States will become older and that a larger proportion of the workforce will consist of minorities (Goldstein & Gilliam, 1990). This shift will occur while the level of necessary skills is increasing as a result of technological changes that affect how work is done. The relatively low-skilled manufacturing jobs of the past are being replaced by service jobs and technical jobs that require greater skill. In addition, organizations are becoming global in their operations and perspectives.

All of these changes will increase the need for organizational training. Older employees will have to be retrained to take on different sorts of jobs that might not have existed when they were initially hired. Underskilled workers will have to be given the necessary skills on the job that they might not have gotten in school. Shortages of technically trained people may require that the emphasis in organizations shift from selection to training. This trend is one in which the United States may lag behind other countries that are less selection oriented. Organizations may have to be prepared to hire based on potential to learn rather than on present level of skill. They may also have to train and then retrain employees as their skills are made obsolete by technological change.

Training will become an increasingly important activity to both individuals and the organizations that employ them. Hesketh (1997) argued that with rapid job changes brought on by technology, organizations need not only to do more training but to provide training in transferable skills rather than immediate tasks; otherwise employees will experience constant retraining. Rather than training employees to do one particular task, they should be taught the underlying principles that will allow for easy transfer to new tasks. For example, computer system training often amounts to no more than showing a series of steps to accomplish a task, such as printing a document. If the software changes, new training must be done. However, someone who understands the principles underlying printing and software design can easily use a new system with little or no retraining. Jobs today can change so quickly that training quickly becomes obsolete.

Finally e-learning is undoubtedly here to stay. It can be effective and efficient for many types of training in organizations. The almost universal access to the Web makes it relatively easy for organizations to make training available to all employees no matter their location or the time of day. It is a challenge for I/O researchers and those in related fields to determine the best ways to use electronic approaches.

▶ CHAPTER SUMMARY

Training is one of the most important activities of organizations. The design of effective training programs is a five-step process:

Determine training needs through needs assessment

Set objectives for training

Design training

Deliver training

Evaluate training

The first step of a training program is to determine the need for training. This includes not only what should be trained but also who should be trained. Once the training need is established by a needs assessment, the objectives for the training should be decided. From the objectives, a series of training criteria should be developed by which to judge the effectiveness of the training.

The design of effective training should consider characteristics of trainees. Different individuals may have different training needs. It should also incorporate the principles of good training and the methods that will be used. Many principles determine whether or not a particular training program will be effective:

Feedback	Overlearning
General principles	Sequencing of training sessions
Identical elements	

Many training methods can be used. Each has its strengths and limitations, and no one method is necessarily better than the others. Choice of method depends on what and who are trained. The new trend of e-learning is becoming commonplace in organizations. Web-based training can be effective and efficient if used properly. Mentoring is a special relationship between experienced and inexperienced employees in which the former help the latter develop their job skills.

Training evaluation is done by conducting a research study to determine if the training was effective. The evaluation process includes five steps:

Select criteria

Choose a research design

Collect data

Analyze data and interpret results

Choose measures

A well-conducted evaluation study can provide valuable information about whether a training program is having its intended effects on individuals and organizations. An ineffective training program should be eliminated or modified to make it effective. In the long run a policy of evaluating training will lead to better use of training resources and a more effective workforce.

I/O PSYCHOLOGY IN PRACTICE

(Courtesy Chuck Evans)

This case concerns executive coaching—the development of managerial skills in high level corporate executives, which was one of the major responsibilities of Dr. Charles Evans, an I/O psychologist working for an international consulting firm, RHR International, in Toronto, Canada. Evans received his Ph.D. in I/O psychology from the University of Guelph in Canada in 1994. His RHR responsibilities were to work on projects for client organizations, which included some of the largest corporations in the world. Most of his work was in the areas of employee assessment and performance appraisal, as well as executive coaching.

As an executive coach, Evans's major function was to provide assistance and feedback to executives who needed to enhance their managerial skills. Often people who are promoted to high levels in organizations find that success on the job requires new approaches of dealing with people rather than the ones they had used effectively at lower levels. A common problem is that executives are too autocratic and focused on results. Although subordinates at lower levels might have responded constructively to direct orders, middle and higher level managers do not. Instead, executives need to use skills in communication and persuasion. One must gain support for taking actions that require cooperation from many people to be successful. Individuals who lack these skills must develop them or remain ineffective.

Evans addressed these and other problems by collecting information about the individual executives and then giving feedback based on that information. He conducted structured interviews to assess the background and interpersonal skills of the executives. A 360 degree feedback (see Chapter 4) was conducted, and the results were discussed with the executives to let them know how they came across to peers, subordinates, and supervisors. Evans assisted each executive to come up with a development plan to address deficiencies and improve management skills. He served as a coach by helping them figure out ways to do a better job.

Evans did this work mainly in North America, but his firm works with executives throughout the world. Companies pay executives very high salaries, and they are willing to spend a lot on their development, including hiring a private coach to help enhance their management skills. Such efforts can help organizations function better because their executives are more effective in dealing with people.

Discussion Questions

1. Why would a high-level executive want to enhance management skills?

2. How do you tell a person who has risen to the top of an organization that he or she needs to handle people more effectively?

3. Which of the training methods would be most effective here?

4. How would you go about evaluating what Evans does?

LEARN BY DOING

Training Needs Assessment

One of the major methods of needs assessment is to survey employees about their training needs. Choose a person you know (acquaintance, family member, or friend) who is currently employed in a job you have never held yourself. Interview him or her about the training needs for the job. Ask about the three or four most important areas that need training,. You should ask about the following:

1. Job title

2. Areas that need training.

3. KSAOs that would be enhanced by the training.

4. Tasks that would be facilitated by the training.

Write a brief report that provides an overview of what you learned about the job.

E-Learning at Your University

E-learning is becoming popular in higher education. Find a course at your college or university that uses some form of e-learning. Review whatever materials you can find about the course, such as its catalog description or syllabus. Explain the specific e-learning methods used in the course, and whether or not blended learning is used. Discuss how the specific topics of the course fit or fail to fit the e-learning method used.

PART IV

THE INDIVIDUAL AND THE ORGANIZATION

(*Corbis Stock Market*)

Theories of Employee Motivation

Bill Gates, the founder and head of Microsoft Corporation, is known for his arduous work schedule. He typically spends 12 hours a day at the office and works several hours more at home. He does not own a television set because, he says, it is too distracting. By the time he was in his mid-30s, Gates had amassed a fortune of several billion dollars, and he's one of the richest people in the world. Yet he still continues to work harder than almost anyone, even though he does not need more money. What drives Gates to work so hard? He says that he is motivated by challenges and the desire to learn new things.

Few people work as hard as Bill Gates. Furthermore, not everyone works for the challenge, as he does. A variety of factors motivate people to work hard. The need to make money is certainly one of them, but there are others, which can be tangible, such as an insurance benefit, or intangible, such as a sense of accomplishment. Theories of motivation explain why people work hard. They also explain other types of work behavior that do not involve job performance. Most of the theories, however, focus on job performance because job performance has been a central variable for the I/O field.

This chapter discusses job performance in terms of several popular theories, with a focus on motivation rather than ability. (In Chapter 10 we will explore other things that affect performance.) It also covers explanations for other forms of work behavior, such as turnover. The chapter begins by defining motivation in the context of the work environment. It then introduces work motivation theories and briefly overviews each of the nine theories to be covered. Each theory is next discussed in greater detail, along with the research evidence for its validity.

Objectives: The student who studies this chapter should be able to:

▶ Define motivation.

▶ List the major work motivation theories discussed in this chapter.

▶ Describe how each of the major work motivation theories explains work behavior.

▶ Compare and contrast the major work motivation theories.

▶ WHAT IS MOTIVATION?

Motivation is generally defined as an internal state that induces a person to engage in particular behaviors. From one perspective, it has to do with the direction, intensity, and persistence of behavior over time. *Direction* refers to the choice of specific behaviors from a large number of possible behaviors. For example, an employee might decide to volunteer for an extra work project that will require working overtime instead of going home on time and watching television. *Intensity* refers to the amount of effort a person expends at doing a task. An employee asked to sweep a floor can exert a lot of effort by sweeping hard and fast or exert a little effort by sweeping gently and slowly. *Persistence* refers to the continuing engagement in a behavior over time. An employee might try to accomplish something over an extended period of time, such as studying to pass the CPA exam to become a certified public accountant, even though it might take several attempts.

From another perspective, motivation is concerned with the desire to acquire or achieve some goal. That is, motivation derives from a person's wants, needs, or desires. Some people, for example, are highly motivated to acquire money. It is presumed that a high level of motivation to have money would affect the behavior relevant to acquiring it.

▶ WORK MOTIVATION THEORIES

Work motivation theories are most typically concerned with the reasons, other than ability, that some people perform their jobs better than others. Depending on the situation, these theories can predict people's choices of task behavior, their effort, or their persistence. If people have the necessary ability and constraints on performance are relatively low, high levels of motivation should lead to good job performance. (See the discussion of job performance in Chapter 10.)

The theories covered in this chapter view employee motivation from very different perspectives. Need theory says that people are motivated to acquire certain categories of things, such as food or recognition. Need hierarchy theory classifies all human needs into a small number of categories, and it presumes that people's behavior is directed toward fulfilling their needs. Two-factor theory says that various aspects of work address one of two categories of need. One category concerns the nature of the job itself, and the other concerns rewards, such as pay.

Reinforcement theory views behavior as the result of rewards or reinforcements. As opposed to need theories, reinforcement theory describes motivation as the result of environmental influences rather than internally generated motives. Expectancy theory, like reinforcement theory, attempts to relate environmental rewards to behavior. Unlike reinforcement theory, it is concerned with human cognitive processes that explain why rewards can lead to behavior.

Self-efficacy theory is concerned with how people's beliefs about their own capabilities can affect their behavior. According to this theory, motivation to attempt a task is related to whether we believe we are capable of successfully accomplishing the task.

Justice theories are quite different from the other theories in that they are concerned with values rather than needs, beliefs, or reinforcements. The theory assumes that people universally value fairness in their social relations at work. Situations in which unfairness or inequity exists presumably motivate employees to remedy the unfairness.

Goal-setting theory explains how people's goals and intentions can result in behavior. Like need theories, it notes that motivation begins inside the person, but it also shows how environmental influences can shape motivation and behavior. Cognitive control theory is also concerned with goals, but focuses attention on feedback toward goal attainment, and how discrepancies between goals and the current situation motivate behavior. Action theory was developed in Germany to explain volitional (self-motivated, voluntary) behavior at work. It is another cognitive theory that explains how goals are translated into behaviors that persist until one reaches one's objective.

Even though these various theories view motivation from different perspectives, they do not necessarily lead to different predictions about behavior. Some elements of these

"Oh, not bad. The light comes on, I press the bar, they write me a check. How about you?"

(© *The New Yorker Collection* (1993) *Tom Cheney from cartoonbank.com*)

theories are complementary, and efforts have been made to integrate features of some of them. For example, Locke and Latham (1990) combined aspects of the expectancy and self-efficacy theories with their goal-setting theory. In the remainder of this chapter, the various motivation theories will be discussed in detail.

These theories can be described along a continuum from distal to proximal (Kanfer, 1992). **Distal motivation theories** deal with processes that are far removed from the behavior. **Proximal motivation theories** deal with processes that are close to the behavior. Need theories are distal because they deal with general needs that can be translated into behavior in many ways. Goal setting theory is more proximal because it deals with goals that lead to specific behaviors, such as a goal by a salesperson to sell a particular amount of product.

▶ NEED THEORIES

The two need theories discussed here view motivation as deriving from people's desires for certain things. It is implied that needs can differ both within the same person over time and across different people. The need hierarchy theory is concerned with variations in needs within individuals over time. Need theories were quite popular in the psychological literature at one time. In recent years, I/O researchers have turned their attention to more cognitively oriented theories, such as the control, goal-setting, and self-efficacy theories. Perhaps the major reason for the declining interest in need theories is that research on needs has failed to find strong relations with job performance, possibly because needs are distal constructs that are far removed from job performance. That is, the rather general needs in these theories can be satisfied in many ways and with many different behaviors. Thus, a particular need is not likely to be strongly associated with any particular behavior. A person who has a high need to accomplish challenging tasks, for example, can fulfill that need either on or off the job. Nevertheless, need theories have contributed to our understanding of work motivation by showing how people can vary in the rewards they want from work.

Need Hierarchy Theory

Maslow's (1943) **need hierarchy theory** states that fulfillment of human needs is necessary for both physical and psychological health. Human needs are arranged in a hierarchy that includes physical, social, and psychological needs. Figure 8.1 illustrates the need hierarchy from the lowest level physical needs to the highest level psychological needs. The lowest level physiological needs include the physical necessities for survival, such as air, water, and food. The second level consists of safety needs, those things that protect us from danger. This level includes the need for security and shelter. The third level comprises love needs, which include the need for love, affection, and affiliation with others. The fourth level includes the esteem needs, which involve self-respect and the respect of others. Finally, there is self-actualization, which Maslow did not define precisely. It refers to the fulfillment of personal life goals and reaching one's potential, or as Maslow stated, "the desire to become. . . everything that one is capable of becoming" (Maslow, 1943, p. 382).

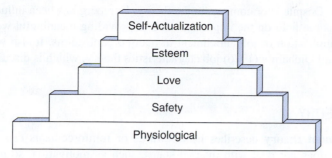

Figure 8.1 Maslow's needs hierarchy.

According to Maslow, a need must be unmet to be motivating, and people are motivated by the lowest level need that is unmet at the moment. That is, if two levels of needs are unmet, the lower level need will dominate. Thus, a hungry person would not be concerned with danger and might risk stealing food even though the punishment for theft is severe. A person with unmet safety needs would not be concerned about going to a party and having a good time with friends. Maslow recognized, however, that there can be exceptions to the hierarchy, and that some individuals find certain higher order needs to be more important than lower level ones. Furthermore, many individuals in Western society have the first four needs met and may never have experienced deprivation of one or more of them, especially food. Therefore, the basic needs are not motivating.

Research on need hierarchy theory has not been very supportive. As Locke and Henne (1986) have noted, at least part of the difficulty is that Maslow's statement of the theory is rather vague, making it difficult to design good tests. Despite its lack of empirical support, need hierarchy theory has had a positive impact on organizations. It continues to be taught to both current and future managers. This helps focus attention on the importance of meeting employees' needs at work.

Two-Factor Theory

Herzberg's (1968) **two-factor theory** states that motivation comes from the nature of the job, not from external rewards or job conditions. The human needs that work addresses are divided into two categories—those deriving from the animal nature of human beings, such as physiological needs, and those relating to the higher level, uniquely human ability for psychological growth. Job aspects relevant to the animal needs are called **hygiene factors** and include pay, supervision, co-workers, and organizational policies. Job aspects relevant to growth needs are called **motivator factors** and include achievement, recognition, responsibility, and the nature of the work itself. According to Herzberg, the way to motivate employees and make them satisfied with their jobs is to provide appropriate levels of motivator factors. Hygiene factors, no matter how favorable, cannot lead to motivation or satisfaction with work.

Most researchers consider Herzberg's theory to be invalid (Locke & Henne, 1986). The major problem with the theory is that the two-factor structure has not been supported by research. Despite shortcomings in the theory, Herzberg has been influential. His work helped focus the field on the important issue of providing meaningful work to people. It led to the application of job enrichment in many organizations. It also was the basis for Hackman and Oldham's (1976) job characteristics theory, which is discussed in Chapters 9 and 10.

▶ REINFORCEMENT THEORY

Reinforcement theory describes how rewards or reinforcements can affect behavior. The theory does not deal with internal states, such as motivation, so in a sense it is a nonmotivational theory. It explains behavior as a function of prior reward experiences, or "reinforcement history." Behavior is seen as a response to the environment.

The major tenet of reinforcement theory is the **law of effect** (Thorndike, 1913). This states that the probability of a particular behavior increases if it is followed by a reward or reinforcement. Conversely, the probability of a behavior decreases if it is followed by a punishment. Behaviors become established through the pairing or associating of behavior with reinforcement. In other words, rewards are *contingent* on a particular behavior occurring. In a job context, this means that performance-relevant behaviors will increase in frequency if they are rewarded.

Rewards can be tangible (money) or intangible (praise). They can be given by the organization or be a by-product of the job tasks. Thus, the organization can provide a bonus for good performance, or good performance, by itself, can provide a sense of accomplishment. Both can be equally reinforcing and lead to continued good performance.

This rather simple idea that behavior increases if it is rewarded is the basis of incentive systems, such as piece rates for factory workers or commissions for salespeople. With **incentive systems**, rewards are contingent on individual units of productivity, such as attaching the door of a refrigerator or selling an automobile. For jobs with countable output, it can be relatively easy to institute incentive systems. For other jobs, there can be specific, measurable performance-relevant behaviors that could be quantified. For example, telephone operators can be rewarded for answering the phone within a specified number of rings. With many jobs, however, it is not feasible to develop incentive systems as discussed here. For example, it would be quite difficult to design a piece-rate system for public school teachers. Good performance for a teacher is not easy to divide into individual units of productivity or individual behaviors that can be rewarded.

Research has shown that rewards can be effective in enhancing job performance. Stajkovic and Luthans (2003) conducted a meta-analysis of 72 studies of the effects of rewards, both monetary and nonmonetary, on job performance. They found that reward systems, on average, result in a 16% increase in performance, but monetary rewards had a bigger impact on performance (23%) than nonmonetary. Although rewards can enhance job performance under some conditions, such conditions do not always exist in organizations (Coch & French, 1948). Additional influences by other employees, constraints in the environment (e.g., inadequate equipment), and the indifference of employees to some types of rewards can result in the failure of incentive systems.

It requires a tremendous amount of motivation to win a marathon. Most jobs require far less effort than running a marathon.
(*Michael Dwyer/Stock Boston*)

Many organizations have applied reinforcement theory principles to influence the behavior of employees. These efforts have involved not only job performance but other behaviors as well. The control of employee absence has been the focus of reinforcement programs. Some organizations allow employees a certain number of sick leave days in a year. To encourage attendance, employees are paid for the sick leave days they do not use. Other organizations reward each employee who meets a criterion of attendance for a given period (e.g., no absences in a month). A rather unusual absence control program was the lottery system studied by Pedalino and Gamboa (1974). With this system, all employees present at work each day were allowed to draw a card from a standard deck of playing cards. At the end of a week, employees with perfect attendance would have a five-card poker hand. The eight employees with the best poker hands won a prize of $20. This system was found to reduce absence frequency by about 18%.

Although the principles of reinforcement theory can be useful, the theory itself has fallen somewhat out of favor among most I/O psychologists. The major reason is probably that reinforcement theory gives little insight into motivational processes (Locke, 1980). It merely describes relations between reinforcement and behavior. In addition, some people object to the idea of using rewards to regulate behavior. They believe that these programs represent an unethical form of manipulation. Many of those who hold this position are assuming that the technique of reinforcement has more power over people than it actually does. Under the proper circumstances, people will voluntarily work harder for rewards that they want. Reinforcement theory says nothing about whether a person will want a reward. This issue is addressed by expectancy theory, which we discuss next.

▶ EXPECTANCY THEORY

Expectancy theory attempts to explain how rewards lead to behavior by focusing on internal cognitive states that lead to motivation. Reinforcement theory states that reinforcement will lead to behavior; expectancy theory explains when and why this will occur. The basic idea is that people will be motivated when they believe that their behavior will lead to wanted rewards or outcomes. If they do not believe that rewards will be contingent on their behavior, they will not be motivated to perform that behavior. If they do not want the contingent rewards, they will not be motivated to perform a behavior.

Several somewhat different versions of expectancy theory have been adapted to the I/O domain. The oldest and most well known is Vroom's (1964) theory that motivation, or force, is a mathematical function of three types of cognitions. The equation relating force to cognitions is:

$$\text{Force} = \text{Expectancy} \times \Sigma(\text{Valences} \times \text{Instrumentalities})$$

In this equation, **force** represents the amount of motivation a person has to engage in a particular behavior or sequence of behaviors that are relevant to job performance. It could be thought of as the motivation to perform. **Expectancy** is the subjective probability that a person has about his or her ability to perform a behavior. It is similar to self-esteem or self-confidence in that a person believes he or she can perform the job at a particular level. *Subjective probability* means that people vary in the certainty of their beliefs. A subjective probability of zero means that the person is certain that he or she is incapable of performing successfully. A subjective probability of 1.0 means that the person is absolutely convinced, without the slightest doubt, that he or she can perform successfully. A subjective probability of .50 means that the person believes there is a 50/50 chance of success.

Valence is the value of an outcome or reward to a person. It is the extent to which one wants or desires something. In the job setting, money is a frequent reward that can have different valence levels for different people. **Instrumentality** is the subjective probability that a given behavior will result in a particular reward. For any given situation, there can be more than one reward or outcome for a behavior. For each possible outcome, a valence and instrumentality are multiplied. Then each valence-instrumentality product is summed into a total, and the total is multiplied by expectancy to produce a force score. If the force score is high, the person will be motivated to achieve the outcomes of the job. If the force score is low, the person will not be motivated to achieve the outcomes.

Table 8.1 shows how possible combinations of values for expectancy, valence, and instrumentality are combined into a force score. This case assumes that there is a single outcome. As the table shows, only when all three components are high will force be high. If any one of the three components is low, force will be low. If any one of the three components equals zero, there will be no motivation.

In most situations, more than one outcome is possible, so that the situation is more complex because the valence-instrumentality for each outcome is combined. The way this

TABLE 8.1   The Relation of Expectancy, Valence, and Instrumentality to Force

Expectancy Score	Valence Score	Instrumentality Score	Force Score
High	High	High	High
High	High	Low	Low
High	Low	High	Low
High	Low	Low	Very low
Low	High	High	Low
Low	High	Low	Very low
Low	Low	High	Very low
Low	Low	Low	Extremely low

works is best illustrated with an example. Suppose you are at work on a Friday afternoon and your boss asks for a volunteer to work overtime for extra pay. You find your job rather boring and would find the prospect of working extra hours somewhat aversive. In this case there are two outcomes—receiving extra money and enduring several hours of boredom. If you believe that you are capable of working overtime, your expectancy will be high. Assuming that you believe that you will get the overtime pay and also that you will be bored, both instrumentalities will be high. The final factor that determines your motivation to work overtime will be the relative valences of the two outcomes. If the positive valence, or desire for money, is greater than the negative valence, or desire to avoid the boredom, then you will be motivated to volunteer. If the positive valence for money is less than the negative valence for boredom, then you will be motivated to avoid volunteering.

Expectancy theory can also predict a person's choice of behavior from two or more options. Suppose that you have a dinner date, and you must choose between working overtime and going on the date. For each possible course of action, there will be an expectancy, valences, and instrumentalities. Thus, there will be a force to work overtime and a force to go on the date. The course of action with the greater force is the one, in theory, that you will take.

There has been research support for the predictions of expectancy theory. Studies have shown that performance is related to the individual components of expectancy theory, as well as to the multiplicative combination (Van Eerde & Thierry, 1996). In the typical study, a sample of employees is surveyed and asked to indicate their expectancies that they can perform the job, as well as their valences and instrumentalities for each of a number of possible outcomes. In addition, supervisors are asked to provide job performance ratings for each employee. The total force score is then correlated with performance.

Van Eerde and Thierry (1996) conducted a meta-analysis of expectancy theory studies that looked not only at predictions of job performance, but at effort and preferences. Although the study showed that the force score related to measures of job performance as expected, it related more strongly to measures of effort. Similarly, the force score related more strongly to an individual's preference for something other than the actual choice—for example, wanting to quit a job versus actually quitting. These findings demonstrate that motivation is only one element in the processes that lead to behavior at work. A person might be motivated to work harder, but this doesn't necessarily produce better job performance. Having a preference for something is not the same as making an actual choice, for other factors can be important, such as not being able to find another job when you want to quit your present one.

▶ SELF-EFFICACY THEORY

Self-efficacy theory states that motivation and performance are determined in part by how effective people believe they can be (Bandura, 1982). In other words, people with high **self-efficacy** believe they are capable of accomplishing tasks and will be motivated to put forth effort. People with low self-efficacy do not believe they can accomplish tasks; they will not be motivated and will not put forth the effort. In a way, this is like a self-fulfilling prophecy in which one behaves in a manner that fulfills one's initial belief. Of course, people with high self-efficacy can be effective only if they have the necessary ability and the constraints on their performance at work are not insurmountable.

The self-efficacy concept is concerned with specific tasks or courses of action, and people vary in their self-efficacy across different tasks. Thus, a student might have high self-efficacy for taking essay exams and low self-efficacy for taking multiple-choice tests. This can explain why many students complain that they are good at one type of test and not the other. The theory would predict that students would exert greater effort when taking the type of test for which their self-efficacy was higher.

Self-efficacy is much like the concept of expectancy. The major difference is that expectancy is concerned with a specific activity at a particular point in time, whereas self-efficacy is concerned with the general feeling that a person is or is not capable in some domain of life, such as playing tennis. For example, a person might have a high level of expectancy that if he or she makes the effort he or she can win a tennis game. A high level of self-efficacy is the belief that one is a good player. Obviously, these two concepts are closely related, for a person with high self-efficacy should have a high expectancy, but they are not the same. The person who believes he or she is good at tennis might not be confident about winning if he or she is playing one of the best professional players in the world. Self-efficacy theory and expectancy theory are compatible in predicting that people will do well at tasks when they believe they can succeed. Expectancy theory also considers the influence of rewards on motivation, a subject that is not addressed by self-efficacy theory.

The theory of self-efficacy has been well tested, and research has been quite supportive inside and outside the workplace (Bandura & Locke, 2003). Studies in the training domain have shown that self-efficacy for particular tasks relates to performance in training on those tasks. For example, McIntire and Levine (1991) conducted a longitudinal study of self-efficacy and performance among students taking college-level typing courses. They assessed self-efficacy before the course began and at the end of the course. They also assessed the number of words typed per minute and the grade at the end of the course. Finally, the students were asked to set personal goals for the number of words per minute they would be able to type by the end of the course. The results were that self-efficacy before the class predicted the number of words per minute typed at the end of the course, but not the grade in the course. Self-efficacy was also related to the goal set, with greater self-efficacy associated with setting a higher goal. These results suggest that self-efficacy can be a factor in future performance. The results with goals suggest that self-efficacy might operate through the setting of goals, such that students with high self-efficacy set harder goals, which result in better performance. Goal setting is discussed in detail later in this chapter.

Similar results with self-efficacy have been found in other training studies. Mathieu, Martineau, and Tannenbaum (1993) found that self-efficacy assessed before a bowling class was related to students' subsequent performance at the end of class. Locke and Latham (1990) conducted a meta-analysis of 13 studies relating self-efficacy to performance in both laboratory and field settings. They found a mean correlation of .39, with correlations as high as .74.

Whereas at least some of the observed relation between people's self-efficacy and their performance can be attributed to the motivational effects of self-efficacy, some of the relation might also be due to the effects of successful performance on self-efficacy. Davis, Fedor, Parson, and Herold (2000) studied self-efficacy in aircraft pilot training. Those students who performed well in simulation training developed high self-efficacy for subsequent actual flying. In the McIntire and Levine (1991) study, course grade related to self-efficacy at the end of the class but not the beginning, suggesting that students who achieved better grades enhanced their self-efficacy. Karl, O'Leary-Kelly, and Martocchio (1993) found that positive feedback on a speed reading task raised the self-efficacy of people who were initially low in self-efficacy.

Dov Eden and his associates have conducted a series of studies in the workplace in which they manipulated self-efficacy to see its effects on job performance. These experimental studies controlled for ability and initial motivation by randomly assigning subjects to have their self-efficacy raised or not by providing information or training. Eden refers to this as the **Galatea effect** in which people's beliefs about their own capabilities lead them to perform better, as in a self-fulfilling prophecy. Eden and Aviram (1993) successfully applied this approach to increase the job search success of unemployed people. Similarly, Eden and Zuk (1995) used this technique to convince naval cadets in the Israel Defense Forces that they were unlikely to get seasick. This illness creates significant problems for all navies because it can interfere with job performance at sea. Eden and Zuk conducted an experiment in which cadets were randomly assigned to one of two groups—one was given a briefing assuring them that seasickness was unlikely and would not interfere with their performance, and the other a control group that was given no such briefing. While at sea, the briefed cadets had less seasickness and performed better than the control group. This very simple technique to enhance self-efficacy was quite effective.

In another military study, this time in the United States, Jex, Bliese, Buzzell, and Primeau (2001) linked self-efficacy to soldier stress and well-being. They found that individuals with high levels of self-efficacy reported feeling low levels of work overload and psychological distress. Taken together, all this research suggests that high self-efficacy contributes to both effective performance and employee well-being.

Self-efficacy theory is a useful theory with implications for the work setting. It suggests that motivation and performance, and perhaps well-being, can be enhanced by raising the self-efficacy of employees. Bandura (1982) discussed how self-efficacy can develop through a series of successes with increasingly difficult tasks. An organization could apply this principle by structuring the assignments of employees in such a way that they succeed at increasingly challenging tasks. This strategy can be particularly important with new employees, who may take some period of time to become adept at all aspects of the job. Relatively simple assignments could be given to new employees, with more difficult tasks introduced slowly to allow them to experience few, if any, failures. As they experience success on more and more difficult tasks, their self-efficacy should increase. Karl et al. (1993) suggested using this approach in training programs. Morin and Latham (2000) have shown that training can be successful for raising self-efficacy (see the International Replication).

INTERNATIONAL REPLICATION

It has been well established in the research literature that self-efficacy is related to performance. An important question concerns how self-efficacy can be raised.

Morin and Latham (2000) conducted a study in Ontario, Canada, to explore the role of self-efficacy and skill enhancement in performance. Participants were 41 supervisors and engineers in a paper mill. Each participant sat through a one day interpersonal communication skills training session that included listening to a lecture, watching videotaped performances, and completing role-play exercises. Evaluation at the completion of the training showed that communication skills had increased. However, the researchers felt that just raising skill would not be enough, but that a second intervention was needed to raise self-efficacy.

Following the one day training, participants were randomly assigned to one of four follow-up conditions: mental practice training, goal-setting training, both, or a control condition of neither. Mental practice taught participants how to mentally rehearse their communication skills. It was hypothesized that this would raise self-efficacy by increasing confidence in the newly learned skill. The goal setting was not expected to impact self-efficacy because it dealt, not with enhancing the skill, but with the setting of improvement goals. Approximately one month after completion of the follow-up training, two peers of each participant rated their communication behavior on the job.

Results showed that the two conditions involving mental practice raised self-efficacy and communication performance on the job. The other two conditions had no effect on self-esteem or on performance. This led the authors to conclude that skill enhancement acquired from training was insufficient for enhancing performance in communication. Rather, it was necessary to raise self-efficacy as well as skill to achieve performance gain.

Source: Morin, L., & Latham, G. P. (2000). The effect of mental practice and goal setting as a transfer of training intervention on supervisors' self-efficacy and communication skills: An exploratory study. *Applied Psychology: An International Review*, *49*, 566–578.

▶ JUSTICE THEORIES

A different approach to motivation is provided by justice theories, which focus on norms for fair treatment of employees by their organizations. The underlying assumption of these theories is that people value fairness and that they are motivated to maintain fairness in relationships between themselves and organizations.

Equity theory (Adams, 1965) states that people are motivated to achieve a condition of fairness or equity in their dealings with other people and with organizations. According to Adams (1965), employees who find themselves in inequitable situations will experience dissatisfaction and emotional tension that they will be motivated to reduce. The theory specifies conditions under which inequity will occur and what employees are likely to do to reduce it.

Inequity is a psychological state that arises from employees' comparisons of them-selves with others. What is specifically compared are ratios of outcomes to inputs. **Outcomes** are the rewards, or everything of personal value that an employee gets from working for an organization, including pay, fringe benefits, good treatment, enjoyment, and status. **Inputs** are the contributions made by the employee to the organization. They include not only the work that the employee accomplishes, but the experience and talents that the employee brings to the job as well. Thus, an employee with many years of job experience would have greater inputs than an employee just starting out in a career.

The theory posits that employees form psychological comparisons of their own out-come/input ratios to those of other employees. That is, employees will psychologically evaluate how much they receive from the job (outcomes) in relation to their contributions (inputs), which is represented as the ratio:

OUTCOMES/INPUTS

Employees compare their ratios to the ratios of people they choose for comparison. These comparison people, or *others*, might be employees doing the same job inside or outside the organization. They might also be people who have different types of jobs. The comparison involves the entire ratio and not the individual outcomes or inputs. Thus, one may believe a situation is equitable even though one's outcomes are less than one's inputs. It is only when one believes that one's ratio is different from other people's ratios that inequity exists. This difference can be in either direction. That is, an employee who believes that other people get more outcomes for their inputs can experience *underpayment* inequity. When an employee believes that other people are getting fewer outcomes for their inputs, this is an instance of *overpayment* inequity.

Figure 8.2 illustrates several possible comparison situations. In each case it is assumed that the target employee's (Person A) ratio is 10/20. That is, Person A receives one unit of outcome for each two units of input. Note that the outcome and input scores do not have to be equal. It is the comparison that is important, not the ratio. In the first two cases, the comparison other also has a ratio that reduces to one outcome per two inputs, so equity is achieved. In the first case, the outcomes are half of Person A's (5), but the inputs are half as well (10). In the second case, both the outcomes and the inputs are double (20 and 40, respectively). The next two cases illustrate underpayment inequity. That is, Person A's ratio is lower than the comparison other's, resulting in a feeling of underpayment. In the third case, the comparison other is getting the same out-comes but is giving only half the inputs (10/10), and in the fourth case, the comparison other is getting double the outcomes for the same inputs. The last two cases involve overpayment inequity. That is, Person A is receiving more outcomes per unit of input than the comparison other. In case 5, the comparison other receives half the outcomes for the same inputs, and in case 6 the comparison other receives the same outcomes for double the inputs.

According to Adams (1965), underpayment inequity induces anger, and overpay-ment inequity induces guilt. In either case, the employee will be motivated to reduce the inequity through several possible mechanisms. Three of these mechanisms are par-ticularly relevant to the organizational setting—changing inputs, changing outcomes, or withdrawal from the situation. An employee can change inputs by either increasing or decreasing productivity, depending on whether the inequity is over- or underpayment.

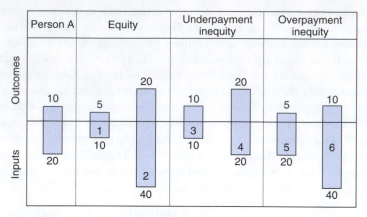

Figure 8.2 An illustration of equity and inequity. Person A has twice as many inputs as outcomes (see bars in first column). The other six bars represent comparison others' inputs and outcomes. Person A will experience equity or inequity depending upon who is chosen as a comparison. Cases 1 and 2 illustrate equity, where both inputs are double outcomes. Case 3 represents underpayment because the outcomes are the same as Person A's but the inputs are only half. Case 4 is underpayment because the inputs are the same as Person A's but the outcomes are double. Case 5 is overpayment because the inputs are the same as Person A's but the outcomes are half. Case 6 is overpayment because the outcomes are the same as Person A's but the inputs are double.

An employee can change outcomes by seeking additional rewards from work—for example, by asking for a raise or filing a formal grievance. Withdrawal can be temporary, as in lateness or absence, both of which can be a means of reducing inputs. It can also be permanent turnover.

There has been good research support for the expected underpayment effect of lowered performance, but not the overpayment effect of raised performance (Locke & Henne, 1986). A study conducted by Greenberg (1990) showed that a pay cut was associated with increased stealing by factory workers. Greenberg argued in equity theory terms that employees who experienced inequity because of the pay cut increased their outcomes by stealing. In an Australian study, Iverson and Roy (1994) found that employee perceptions of inequity correlated with their intentions to quit the job and with job search behavior. Both of these variables have been found to predict turnover (e.g., Blau, 1993), as discussed in Chapter 10.

Recent research on fairness in the workplace has replaced equity theory with a somewhat different perspective of **fairness theory** (Cropanzano, Byrne, Bobocel, & Rupp, 2001). Rather than focusing on the fair allocation or distribution of rewards, fairness theory distinguishes between the distribution of rewards and the procedures by which rewards are allocated. **Distributive justice** is similar to equity and concerns the fairness with which rewards are found among people. **Procedural justice** is concerned with the fairness of the reward distribution process, as opposed to the results of the distribution. Although in many cases it might be expected that procedural justice would lead to distributive justice, this is not always the case. For example, past reward policies may have created a situation in which some people are paid more than others for similar inputs, a case that would represent distributive injustice. A new procedure that gave the underpaid a small salary adjustment each year to make up for it might be seen as procedural justice, even though it might take years to make up the difference.

Another distinction from equity theory is that fairness theory doesn't assume that perceptions of injustice necessarily come from a social comparison with others. Rather it suggests that people perceive injustice when something negative happens and they perceive it to have been done purposefully by another person in an unfair way. For example, suppose a company fails to give employees an annual raise. This would be a negative event that will be seen as unfair if it is perceived as having been purposefully done by management and the basis for withholding the raise is unreasonable. If the company announced financial problems, employees might see this as beyond management's control and thus would not perceive the situation as unfair. However, if management fails to provide a convincing explanation, employees will likely feel the situation is unfair.

There have been many studies relating distributive and procedural justice perceptions by employees to organizationally relevant outcomes. Cohen-Charash and Spector (2001) conducted a meta-analysis of these studies and found, as might be expected from equity theory, that both forms of justice were related to job performance, job satisfaction, and intention of quitting the job. However, Sweeney and McFarlin (1997) found that procedural justice was more important for women, whereas distributive justice was more important for men. Apparently, for women the procedure by which rewards are allocated is more important, but for men the results are what matter most. Finally, Tepper (2001) was able to link perceptions of justice to psychological well-being. Individuals who perceived high injustice tended to report more anxiety and depression than individuals who perceived justice in the workplace.

▶ GOAL-SETTING THEORY

The theory of motivation that has been the most useful for I/O psychologists is **goal-setting theory** (Locke & Latham, 1990). The principle of goal setting is widely used in organizations, although in ways not necessarily based on the theory. For example, Yearta, Maitlis, and Briner (1995) noted that 79% of British organizations use some form of goal setting. Various goal-setting programs have been widely used throughout the industrialized world.

The basic idea of this theory is that people's behavior is motivated by their internal *intentions*, *objectives*, or *goals*—the terms are used here interchangeably. Goals are very "proximal" constructs, for they can be tied quite closely to specific behaviors. For example, a salesperson might have the goal of selling a certain amount of product in a given month. Because goals can be tied closely to particular behaviors relevant for performance, goal-setting theory has been strongly tied to behavior.

According to the theory, a goal is what a person consciously wants to attain or achieve. Goals can be specific, such as "receive an A on the next exam," or general, such as "do well in school." General goals, such as doing well in school, are often associated with a number of more specific goals, such as receiving an A. People can vary in their **goal orientation**, that is, in whether they focus their efforts on learning (**learning orientation**) or on achieving certain levels of job performance (**performance orientation**). A person with a learning orientation is primarily concerned with enhancing knowledge and skill, whereas a person with a performance orientation focuses on enhancing performance on specific job tasks (DeShon & Gillespie, 2005; Porath & Bateman, 2006). Goal strategies that might be effective for one orientation will not necessarily be optimal for the other. Kozlowski and Bell (2006) noted that there can be an incompatibility between the two orientations in that focusing on performance directs attention away from learning. Most of the research on goal-setting has focused on performance and does not necessarily apply to learning goals.

Locke and Henne (1986) note four ways in which goals affect behavior. First, goals direct attention and action to behaviors that the person believes will achieve the goal. A student who has the goal of making an A on an exam would be expected to engage in studying behavior, such as reading the assigned material and reviewing class notes. Second, goals mobilize effort in that the person tries harder. The student with the goal of an A will concentrate harder to learn the material. Third, goals increase persistence, resulting in more time spent on the behaviors necessary for goal attainment. The student who wants an A will spend more time studying. Finally, goals can motivate the search for effective strategies to attain them. The conscientious student will attempt to learn effective ways of studying and good test-taking strategies.

Goal-setting theory predicts that people will exert effort toward accomplishing their goals and that job performance is a function of the goals set. From an organizational standpoint, goal setting can be an effective means of maintaining or increasing job performance, and many organizations have used goal setting to do so. According to Locke (2000), several factors are necessary for goal setting to be effective in improving job performance (Table 8.2). First, employees must have *goal commitment*, which means that they accept the goal. An organizational goal is not necessarily an individual employee's goal, and only goals of the individual person will motivate behavior. Second, *feedback* is necessary because it allows people to know whether their behavior is moving them toward or away from their goals. It is difficult for goals to direct behavior unless the person receives feedback. Third, the more difficult the goal, the better the performance is likely to be. A goal of a 4.0 grade point average is likely to result in better performance than a goal of 3.5, which is likely to result in better performance than a goal of 3.0. Although people will not always reach their goals, the harder the goal, the better the performance, at least until the point at which the person is working at the limit of his or her capacity. Fourth, specific hard goals are more effective than vague "do your best" goals. Vague goals can be effective, but specific goals that allow the person to know

TABLE 8.2   Important Factors for Goal Setting to Improve Job Performance

1. Goal acceptance by the employee.
2. Feedback on progress toward goals.
3. Difficult and challenging goals.
4. Specific goals.

Source: "Work motivation theories," by E. A Locke & D. Henne, 1986. In C. L. Cooper & I. T. Robertson (Eds.). *International Review of Industrial and Organizational Psychology*, 1986. Chichester, UK: John Wiley.

when they are met are best. Finally, self-set goals are usually better than organizationally assigned goals. It is generally best to allow employees to either set their own goals or at least provide input into setting goals rather than have supervisors assign goals without employee involvement. This leads to the better goal acceptance that is necessary for goals to be effective.

Goal-setting theory is well supported by research (Locke & Latham, 1990). Not only have its propositions been the subject of considerable research, but goal setting is a popular means of increasing job performance. For example, Klein, Wesson, Hollenbeck, and Alge (1999) describe a meta-analysis of 83 studies, showing that greater goal commitment is associated with better performance. The theory and research surrounding goal-setting theory underscore important factors (shown in Table 8.2) that should be incorporated into a goal-setting program.

Although research has shown that goal setting can be effective, some researchers have discussed its limitations. Yearta et al. (1995) noted that most goal-setting studies involve single goals, such as increased production in a factory. They showed that with more complex jobs and multiple goals, performance was lower when goals were difficult. Doerr, Mitchell, Klastorin, and Brown (1996) showed that group goals were better than individual goals for increasing speed of production in a fish processing plant (see Research in Detail). Ambrose and Kulik (1999) listed several drawbacks of goal setting. The most important were that employees sometimes focus so much on the goals that they ignore other equally important aspects of the job, and goals can conflict so that working on one prevents achieving another. Finally, Drach-Zahavy and Erez (2002) discussed how difficult goals can actually lead to worse performance when stress is high. Putting all this together suggests that difficult goals work best when situations are relatively simple (single goals and simple jobs) and there are low levels of stress.

RESEARCH IN DETAIL

There has been a trend in large organizations toward the use of work groups and teams rather than individuals to accomplish work. Thus, it is important to understand how groups and individuals differ in their behavior and reactions. One area of concern is how to motivate people who work in groups. Goal setting can be an effective motivational technique for individuals, but will it be equally effective with groups?

This study was conducted in a fish processing plant in the northwestern United States with a workforce consisting entirely of non-Americans. These employees worked two to three hours per day cleaning and dressing salmon that arrived by boat. During the course of the study, 39 employees participated in a goal-setting experiment. Three conditions were created—group goal, individual goal, and no goal. An initial baseline measure of production speed was taken to serve as the standard against which to set goals.

The goals represented working at a consistent pace that was faster than typically maintained. Employees were given feedback as well as an incentive of state lottery tickets for goal achievement.

To meet the group goal, the output of everyone combined had to achieve the predetermined amount. For the individual condition, each worker had a personal goal. Results showed that productivity was significantly higher for both conditions than for the no-goal control condition, although the group-goal productivity was even higher than the individual. Mean time to process 50 fish was 538 versus 570 seconds for group and individual goals, respectively. The no-goal mean was 702 seconds.

These results demonstrate that goal setting can be quite effective in production situations. Furthermore, groups may respond even more favorably than individuals. As discussed in Chapter 12, groups can have powerful effects on members, and conditions that motivate groups can have enhanced effects on individuals in those groups. However, it should be recognized that this study involved single goals with very simple tasks. These effects might not occur in situations where things are more complex. Nevertheless, goal setting can be a powerful motivational tool if applied appropriately in the proper setting.

Source: Doerr, K. H., Mitchell, T. R., Klastorin, T. D., & Brown, K. A. (1996). Impact of material flow policies and goals on job outcomes. *Journal of Applied Psychology, 75,* 142–152.

▶ CONTROL THEORY

Control Theory (Klein, 1989) builds upon goal-setting theory by focusing on how feedback affects motivation to maintain effort toward goals. As shown in Figure 8.3, the process explained by the theory begins with a goal that one intends to accomplish. The goal might be assigned by a supervisor or self-chosen, but the theory says that one must believe the goal is attainable and accept it. Over time, as one works toward the goal, feedback about performance will be given. One will evaluate the feedback by comparing current goal progress to some internal standard or expected progress. If progress is insufficient, one will be motivated to take action, which might include goal reevaluation and modification or adoption of different strategies to improve performance. This might be simply exerting more effort (working harder) or adopting new approaches that might be more effective (working smarter).

Evidence has been provided in support of control theory predictions. For example, Donovan and Williams (2003) studied the goals and performance of university track and field athletes during an 8-week season. Before the season each athlete set goals for the first meet and the entire season. Each week the athletes completed progress reports that included their weekly performance and goals for the following week. Athletes tended to revise their future goals based on discrepancies between their performance and prior goals, and the amount of goal adjustment was greater for the more proximal next-week goals than the distal season goals. This showed that feedback did result in adjustment to goals rather than just increase effort toward meeting the goals originally set.

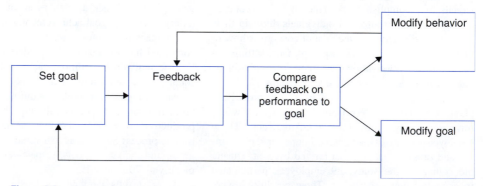

Figure 8.3 Control theory suggests that people set goals and then evaluate feedback about how well their performance is achieving their goals. Discrepancies can motivate people to modify their behavior or their goals.

► ACTION THEORY

Action theory is a comprehensive German theory of work behavior that describes a process linking goals and intentions to behaviors (Frese & Zapf, 1994). This theory proposes that work motivation theories should focus mainly on goal-oriented or volitional (voluntary) behaviors called actions. Such actions are the product of a conscious intent to accomplish something, which can be as small as finishing one piece on an assembly line or as significant as achieving a promotion at work. The major focus of this theory is on the actions themselves and on the processes leading to actions.

Action theory describes the **action process** linking a hierarchy of cognitions both to actions and to feedback from the environment. Figure 8.4 illustrates this sequence. It begins with an initial desire to accomplish or have something, and that desire leads to specific goals and objectives to acquire it. These goals in the workplace are often tied to tasks (similar to tasks in a job analysis) that define the nature of what the individual employee is supposed to accomplish at work. The theory points out that there is an important distinction between external tasks and internal tasks. An external task is assigned by the organization to the employee, whereas an internal task is chosen by the employee. An important element is the redefinition process whereby the employee translates an external task to an internal one. In other words, the employee changes the assigned task to suit himself or herself.

The next step after goals are set is to translate them into plans. Plans are specific steps chosen to accomplish the goals, and are specifications of actions and sequences of actions. Next the plan is executed, and execution involves actions. Finally, the person receives feedback either from the environment itself or from other people. This feedback indicates whether progress is being made toward the goal. Positive feedback can help maintain actions that are part of plans, and negative feedback can lead to modification of goals, plans, or actions.

An example of the process would be the following. You want to make a lot of money, so you set the goal of landing a well-paying job when you graduate college. Your plan might be to major in a field in which such jobs are plentiful and to have a high grade point average. Actions will address these aspects of the plan, such as investigating job opportunities of various majors and studying for classes. Feedback is provided by grades, and if you find your grade point average is not high enough, you might change your goal and decide to settle for a lower paying job, change your plan and choose a different major, or change your actions and study harder.

Action theory also contains personality variables. One of the most important is **action vs. state orientation**. A person who is action oriented tends to follow the action process,

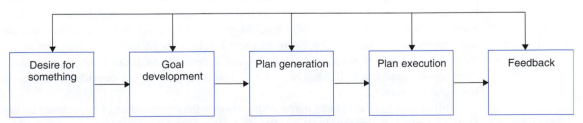

Figure 8.4   The action process from German action theory.

setting goals, formulating plans, and then sticking with them until the goals are achieved. State oriented people are the opposite. They have difficulty committing to a course of action, are easily distracted, and give up when faced with setbacks (Kuhl & Beckmann, 1994). Research has shown that action oriented people tend to perform better on the job (Diefendorff, Hall, Lord, & Strean, 2000; Jaramillo, Locander, Spector, & Harris, 2007), perhaps in part because state oriented people have a tendency to procrastinate (Van Eerde, 2000).

Research also tends to support some of the predictions made from action theory. For example, Sonnentag (1998) studied the cognitive processes underlying the task behavior of high performing and average computer software programmers, making some predictions based on action theory. As expected, high performers were able to understand the problem more quickly, so they could move on to the planning stage (step 3) and made better use of feedback (step 5 of the action sequence). The study of high performing individuals within an action theory framework can be useful in suggesting ways to train employees to be more effective.

Action theory is a complex cognitive-based theory that sees the individual as the initiator of action, or the cause of their own behavior, as opposed to reinforcement and other motivation theories, which emphasize how people respond to the environment. In a way it is an expanded form of the goal-setting and control theories. The American goal-setting theory we discussed above is mainly concerned with how the setting of goals translates into job performance (Farr, Hofmann, & Ringenbach, 1993). Control theory focuses on how feedback concerning goal progress affects behavior. Action theory goes further than each of these theories in examining the cognitive processes that intervene between goals and performance.

► FUTURE ISSUES AND CHALLENGES

There are two major challenges to the field in the area of motivation. First, research is needed to adequately test theories of motivation. Second, organizations need to know how employees can be motivated to do their jobs well. These two areas are not mutually exclusive, for adequate theory testing can provide ideas for effective organizational interventions aimed at improving motivation. On the other hand, the development and implementation of programs to enhance motivation can provide evidence relevant to the testing of theories.

Many studies have tested the various motivation theories discussed in this chapter. Methodological limitations make it difficult to provide strong tests for several of them. Perhaps the most troublesome problem is that of adequately measuring the constructs of the theories, particularly theories involving cognitions or needs. Studies of needs have used self-reports. Thus, people are asked to indicate how well their needs have been met or to estimate the current level of needs. The underlying assumption in using self-reports is that people are aware of their levels of need and are willing to reveal them. Maslow (1943) noted that people are not necessarily aware of their needs, making their reports inaccurate. If Maslow is correct, self-reports do not provide good data to test need theories.

Difficulties have also been noted with assessing the components of expectancy theory (e.g., Campbell & Pritchard, 1976). People in these studies are asked to estimate their valences and subjective probabilities, but it is not clear how accurate these estimates are. More work is needed to develop better ways to assess these internal states and cognitions.

As discussed in this chapter, motivation theories have led to several effective strategies for changing employee behavior. Perhaps the most effective have been interventions based on reinforcement principles and goal setting, as we have already seen. There is a need, however, to better understand how to implement principles, including the advantages and drawbacks to various practices. For example, a goal-setting program can focus employee attention on certain job aspects to the exclusion of others. A typist who has the goal of increasing speed might sacrifice accuracy. The conditions under which motivation interventions are effective and ineffective need additional study.

Finally, there has been a drift over the past few decades from emphasis on distal theories emphasizing needs to proximal theories emphasizing the connection between goals, cognitions, and behavior. Action theory best illustrates the contemporary approach of attempting to understand cognitive processes leading to goals and linking those goals to behavior. It seems likely that future research on motivation will focus even more attention in these areas in an attempt to understand how humans regulate their behavior.

► CHAPTER SUMMARY

This chapter discussed nine theories that consider motivation from very different perspectives. The two need theories—need hierarchy, and two-factor—view motivation as arising from internal needs. Need hierarchy theory classifies human needs into five categories. Needs are rather broad, and so are the theories; predictions are imprecise because they cannot specify very well what specific behaviors are likely to arise. A person with a high level of achievement need, for example, might work hard on the job to achieve success or might seek to achieve success outside work. Two-factor theory states that motivation comes from two categories of needs that are addressed by work.

Reinforcement theory takes a situational view and states that behavior is a function of a person's reinforcement history. According to this theory, job-relevant behaviors that are rewarded are likely to be repeated in the future. Expectancy theory attempts to explain how rewards lead to behavior. It states that people will perform well if they believe that their efforts will lead to performance, if performance will lead to rewards, and if they want the rewards.

Self-efficacy theory states that people's beliefs about their own capabilities are an important component of motivation. Those who believe that they are incapable of performing on the job are not likely even to try. A high level of self-efficacy or belief in one's own capability is a necessary component in work motivation and subsequent job performance.

Justice theories state that people value fair and equitable treatment by their organizations. Equity theory states that people compare themselves to others on the ratio of outcomes to inputs at work, and discrepancies in ratios can motivate people to take action. This might include changing the level of contribution to the organization, changing the rewards obtained from work, or quitting. More modern justice theories focus on both the distribution of rewards (distributive justice) and the fairness of the procedures (procedural justice) by which they are allocated.

Goal-setting theory posits that people's behaviors are directed by conscious goals and objectives. The theory underscores several factors that are important determinants of how well goal setting can improve job performance. Four are particularly important: goal commitment by employees, feedback about progress toward goals, goal difficulty, and specificity of goals.

Control theory extends goal-setting theory by focusing attention on feedback toward goal attainment. It suggests that people set goals and then seek information about how well they are progressing toward goal achievement. Discrepancies between expected goal progress and actual progress will motivate the individual either to reassess the goal and modify it or to change behavior to make better progress.

German action theory describes the action process linking goals to behavior. The process begins with the desire to achieve something, and that desire is translated into a goal. Plans are generated to achieve the goal, and plan execution involves actions. Feedback occurs in response to actions and can result in modification of the prior steps.

Although these various theories view motivation from different perspectives, they are not necessarily incompatible, and in fact elements of various theories have been integrated. Locke and Latham (1990) discuss the consistencies between features of expectancy theory, self-efficacy theory, and goal-setting theory. In particular, they see self-efficacy as an important ingredient in goal commitment. A person with low self-efficacy concerning the achievement of a goal is not likely to become committed to that goal.

I/O PSYCHOLOGY IN PRACTICE

(*Courtesy Lynn Summers*)

This case concerns a goal-based theft-control program that Dr. Lynn Summers helped design. Summers received his Ph.D. in I/O psychology in 1977 from the University of South Florida. He has worked for a variety of organizations and is currently a human resources specialist with the North Carolina Office of State Personnel. Prior to that he was vice president of Performaworks Corporation, a company that provides I/O services via the Internet. One of its specialties is 360 degree feedback (see Chapter 4) done online. Peers, subordinates, and supervisors can complete assessments of individual employees on a Web page. After viewing feedback from these various perspectives, the employee prepares an improvement plan by interacting with an online program. Performaworks also does other types of assessments and opinion surveys using the Internet. It is one example of how I/O psychologists can use this new communication medium. Before

helping to found the company, Summers had his own consulting practice. One of his projects was helping an organization deal with employee theft.

Summers was asked by a national fast-food chain to devise a program to control theft in its restaurants. In the restaurant industry, internal theft is a much larger problem than theft due to robbery. This chain wanted to do something about employees who were either stealing food for themselves or giving food to friends for free. Summers investigated the situation and helped a team of employees representing different restaurants come up with six different interventions. Of interest here is a goal-setting procedure, which turned out to be the most effective.

The goal-setting procedure was quite simple. In each restaurant the manager assigned a small group of employees responsibility for control of the theft of a particular item, such as chicken breasts. The group was shown how to figure out the number of chicken breasts that were "missing" each day. It was also assigned a specific goal for reducing the number.

The company found that the goal-setting program was quite effective in that thefts were reduced. What no one is certain about is why it worked.

The employees were not instructed about how they should go about reducing the theft—they were only given a goal. It is possible that members of the group had been stealing, and merely stopped. It is also possible that the group members knew which people were stealing and put pressure on them to stop. At the very least, the program directed employee attention to the problem, and, as we discussed previously, this is one of the ways goal-setting enhances performance. No matter why it worked, this case illustrates that goal setting can be an effective means of changing behavior. Often managers need only set a goal and then allow their subordinates the latitude to figure out how to achieve it.

Discussion Questions

1. What factors cause employees to steal?
2. Why did the goal-setting program reduce stealing?
3. What other interventions might have reduced stealing?
4. How widespread do you think employee theft is in large organizations?

LEARNING BY DOING

Motivation Case at Work

Find an example of motivation that relates to one of the theories discussed in the chapter. It could be an item from the newspaper or one of the online news services. Give the background for your case, explaining who the person is and what he or she did. Then explain how it relates to one of the theories in the chapter.

How Companies Motivate Their Employees

Find an example of how companies motivate their employees. This can be from your own work experience, the experience of someone you know, or something you found on the Internet. Explain the approach and how it relates to one or more of the theories in this chapter.

CHAPTER 9

Feelings About Work: Job Attitudes and Emotions

National polls of American workers have typically found that the majority are satisfied with their jobs. For example, a survey conducted by the Society for Human Resource Management in 2003 found that 76% of employees were satisfied with their jobs (SHRM, 2003). In another poll, 58% said they would still work even if they won a $10 million lottery (Gallup Poll, 1997). A 2002 poll suggests that Canadians are even more satisfied than Americans, with 92% of respondents saying they like their jobs (Shields, 2006).

One of the major tasks I/O psychologists perform is assessing employee attitudes about their jobs, especially their job satisfaction, and determining ways to improve it. I/O researchers have been extensively studying the causes and consequences of job satisfaction since the very beginning of the I/O field. It is one of the two most studied variables in I/O psychology (the other is job performance). Much of this popularity, as we will see, derives from the relative ease with which it can be assessed. Another reason for its popularity is that job satisfaction is a central variable in many theories that deal with organizational phenomena, such as the nature of work, supervision, and the job environment. Job satisfaction has been posited as a cause of important employee and organizational outcomes ranging from job performance to health and longevity.

Job satisfaction, however, is not the only variable that reflects how people feel about and at work. Organizational commitment is another attitude that concerns people's feelings of attachment to their jobs and organizations. Feelings also include both positive and negative emotions that are experienced at work, such as anger over unfair treatment or joy over receiving a promotion.

In this chapter we begin with a discussion of job satisfaction, including how it is measured, its potential causes, and its possible consequences. Job satisfaction is frequently included in studies of all sorts of organizational phenomena. You will see it frequently mentioned throughout most of the remaining chapters of this book. We will also include a discussion of organizational commitment, which relates to many of the same variables as job satisfaction. Finally, we will discuss emotions in the workplace, both their causes and their consequences.

Objectives: The student who studies this chapter should be able to:

► Define job satisfaction and organizational commitment.

► Characterize the differences between job satisfaction and organizational commitment.

► Explain how job satisfaction and organizational commitment are measured.

► Summarize the findings on possible causes and effects of job satisfaction and organizational commitment.

► Discuss how emotions are experienced by employees at work and how they impact organizations.

► THE NATURE OF JOB SATISFACTION

Job satisfaction is an attitudinal variable that reflects how people feel about their jobs overall as well as about various aspects of the jobs. In simple terms, job satisfaction is the extent to which people like their jobs; job dissatisfaction is the extent to which they dislike them.

TABLE 9.1 Common Job Satisfaction Facets

Pay	Job conditions
Promotion opportunities	Nature of the work
Fringe benefits	Communication
Supervision	Security
Co-workers	

There have been two approaches to the study of job satisfaction—the global approach and the facet approach. The *global approach* treats job satisfaction as a single, overall feeling toward the job. Many studies assess people's overall satisfaction, and many of the findings discussed in this chapter reflect that variable.

The alternative approach is to focus on job **facets**, or different aspects of the job, such as rewards (pay or fringe benefits), other people on the job (supervisors or co-workers), job conditions, and the nature of the work itself. A list of the most often studied facets appears in Table 9.1.

The facet approach permits a more complete picture of job satisfaction. An individual typically has different levels of satisfaction with the various facets. It is possible, for instance, to be very dissatisfied with pay and fringe benefits but at the same time be very satisfied with the nature of the work and the supervisors. This is a typical pattern for Americans, as we will see in the next section.

▶ HOW PEOPLE FEEL ABOUT THEIR JOBS

As noted earlier, surveys show that the majority of Americans like their jobs (e.g., SHRM, 2003), but this doesn't mean they like all aspects of their jobs equally. The typical American pattern of facet satisfaction is shown in Figure 9.1, with data from the norms of the Job Satisfaction Survey (JSS) (Spector, 1985). The JSS is a scale that assesses nine job satisfaction dimensions, eight of which evaluate popular facets. The norms are based on the job satisfaction scores of 24,713 employees from dozens of organizations throughout the United States. The figure shows that Americans are typically very satisfied with their supervisors, their co-workers, and the nature of the work they do. They are less satisfied with the rewards, such as pay, promotion opportunities, and fringe benefits.

Job satisfaction levels have not been found to be the same across countries. For example, Marion-Landais (1993) found that Dominicans were more satisfied than Americans when both were working for branches of the same multinational company but in their own countries. Spector, Cooper, Sanchez, O'Driscoll, Sparks, et al. (2001) compared job satisfaction levels among managers in 24 countries and found significant differences. Table 9.2 lists the countries in order from highest to lowest satisfaction, and shows that Americans came in sixth (although there were no significant differences among the top nine). Managers from Asian countries (China and Japan) tended to be lower.

Although these studies show that people in different countries may have different feelings about work, they don't shed much light on the reasons. One explanation for these job satisfaction differences involves basic values that vary across countries.

Figure 9.1 Mean satisfaction levels for various facets of the Job Satisfaction Survey (Spector, 1985). Satisfaction level is indicated on the horizontal axis. The numbers next to the bars are the means for each facet. They range from a low of 11.8 for pay and promotion to a high of 18.9 for the nature of the work.

Hofstede (2001) assessed four important values in 50 countries. Although individuals differed on values within each country, there were mean differences that relate to important variables in the workplace. The culture values are:

Individualism/collectivism

Masculinity

Power distance

Uncertainty avoidance

TABLE 9.2   Job Satisfaction of Managers in 24 Countries Listed from Most to Least Satisfied

1. Canada	9. New Zealand	17. France
2. Sweden	10. Ukraine	18. Bulgaria
3. Israel	11. Slovenia	19. Romania
4. Estonia	12. Poland	20. South Africa
5. India	13. Spain	21. People's Republic of China
6. United States	14. Taiwan	22. Hong Kong
7. Belgium	15. Brazil	23. Japan
8. Germany	16. Australia	24. United Kingdom

Source: Spector, P. E., Cooper, C. L., Sanchez, J. I., O'Driscoll, M., Sparks, K., Bernin, P., Büssing, A., Dewe, P., Hart, P., Lu, L., Miller, K., Renault de Moraes, L., Ostrognay, G. M., Pagon, M., Pitariu, H., Poelmans, S., Radhakrishnan, P., Russinova, V., Salamatov, V., Salgado, J, Shima, S., Siu, O. L., Stora, J. B., Teichmann, M., Theorell, T., Vlerick, P., Westman, M., Widerszal-Bazyl, M., Wong, P., & Yu, S. (2001). Do national levels of individualism and internal locus of control relate to well-being: An ecological level international study. *Journal of Organizational Behavior*, *22*, 815–832.

Individualism is the extent to which people see themselves as autonomous and focus on their own interests and needs rather than those of others. **Collectivism** is the opposite, where people see themselves as interconnected to others, with a focus on the groups to which they belong. Western nations such as Australia, Canada, the United Kingdom, and the United States are high on individualism, while Asian (China and Korea) and Latin countries (Ecuador and Guatemala) tend to be high on collectivism. **Masculinity** reflects the extent to which organizations focus on achievement and job performance as opposed to the health and well-being of employees. Scandinavian countries were low on this value, which is reflected in their strong emphasis on health and well-being at work (note Erez's 1994 study showing Scandinavian interest in these topics in Chapter 1), while high-masculinity countries include Japan and Austria. The United States is in the upper third.

Power distance is the tolerance people have for power and status differences among levels of an organization and society. Countries with high power distance tend to produce managers who demand obedience from subordinates. Latin countries tended to be high, such as Guatemala and Panama, while Austria and Israel were lowest. The United States was in the lower half of the scale. **Uncertainty avoidance** reflects the level of comfort in situations that are unpredictable. In organizations people can maintain predictability by adhering to formal procedures and rules; thus, in countries high on this dimension, organizations tend to be very rule oriented. Countries highest on this dimension were Greece and Portugal, while the lowest were Singapore and Jamaica. The United States was in the lower third on uncertainty avoidance.

These dimensions have been found to relate to many organizational variables. In the job satisfaction area, Hui, Yee, and Eastman (1995) showed that individualism/collectivism scores for a country significantly related to satisfaction with social aspects of work. People from collectivist countries were more satisfied. This can be explained by the better social relations existing in countries in which such relationships are more valued. People make more effort to get along with others and are less concerned with their own well-being. Additional research is needed to see if the other dimensions also relate to job satisfaction.

▶ THE ASSESSMENT OF JOB SATISFACTION

Job satisfaction is almost always assessed by asking people how they feel about their jobs, either by questionnaire or interview. Most of the time questionnaires are used because they are very easy to administer and require relatively little time and effort on the part of the researcher. They can also be done anonymously, which allows employees to be more candid in expressing their attitudes. Sometimes, more often in practice than research, employees are interviewed about their satisfaction. A few cases can be found in which job satisfaction was assessed by asking supervisors (e.g., Spector, Dwyer, & Jex, 1988) or observers (Glick et al., 1986) to estimate the satisfaction of other employees, but such estimates are not likely to be completely accurate, since only the observed employees really know their own attitudes.

► JOB DESCRIPTIVE INDEX (JDI)

Of all the job satisfaction scales available, the **Job Descriptive Index (JDI)** (Smith, Kendall, & Hulin, 1969) has been the most popular with researchers. It is also the most thoroughly and carefully validated. This scale assesses five facets:

Work

Supervision

Pay

Co-workers

Promotion opportunities

Many users of the scale have summed its subscales into an overall job satisfaction score. However, this practice is not recommended by one of the scale's developers, Patricia Cain Smith (Ironson, Smith, Brannick, Gibson, & Paul, 1989), as we will discuss after we cover satisfaction scales.

Table 9.3 contains a sample of the scale's 72 items and their respective subscales. Each item is an adjective or short phrase that is descriptive of the job. Responses are "yes," "uncertain," or "no." For each subscale, a brief explanation of the facet is provided, followed by the items concerning the subscale.

The JDI is used frequently by organizational researchers. Cook, Hepworth, Wall, and Warr (1981) listed over 100 published studies that used the JDI, and many more have been done since. The extensive body of research using the scale provides extensive evidence for its validity. The biggest limitation of the scale is that it has only five facets. There also has been some criticism that some items might not apply to all employee groups (e.g., Cook et al., 1981), but this criticism is probably true of all job satisfaction scales.

Minnesota Satisfaction Questionnaire (MSQ)

Another popular job satisfaction scale is the **Minnesota Satisfaction Questionnaire (MSQ)** (Weiss, Dawis, Lofquist, & England, 1966). This scale comes in two forms, a 100-item long version and a 20-item short version. Both versions have items that ask about 20 facets of job satisfaction, but facet scores are computed only for the long form. The short form is used to assess either global satisfaction or intrinsic and extrinsic satisfaction. *Intrinsic satisfaction* refers to the nature of job tasks and how people feel about the work they do. *Extrinsic satisfaction* concerns other aspects of the work situation, such as fringe benefits and pay. Both intrinsic and extrinsic satisfaction are combinations of several facets.

The 20 facets of the MSQ are shown in Table 9.4. Each of the MSQ items is a statement that describes a facet. The employees are asked to indicate how satisfied they are with each one. For example, an item for the Activity facet is "Being able to keep busy all the time." The overall scale has been shown to have good reliability and evidence for validity. Several researchers, however, have questioned how the items are classified

TABLE 9.3   Sample items from the Job Descriptive Index (JDI)

Think of the opportunities for promotion that you have now. How well does each of the following words or phrases describe these? In the blank beside each word below, write

   Y   for "Yes" if it describes your opportunities for promotion
   N   for "No" if it does NOT describe them
   ?   if you cannot decide

Think of the work you do at present. How well does each of the following words or phrases describe your work? In the blank beside each word below, write

   Y   for "Yes" if it describes your work
   N   for "No" if it does NOT describe it
   ?   if you cannot decide

Think of the pay you get now. How well does each of the following words or phrases describe your present pay? In the blank beside each word below, write

   Y   for "Yes" if it describes your pay
   N   for "No" if it does NOT describe it
   ?   if you cannot decide

WORK ON PRESENT JOB

   Routine
   Satisfying
   Good

PRESENT PAY

   Income adequate for normal expenses
   Insecure
   Less than I deserve

OPPORTUNITIES FOR PROMOTION

   Dead-end job
   Unfair promotion policy
   Regular promotions

Think of the kind of supervision that you get on your job. How well does each of the following words or phrases describe this? In the blank beside each word below, write

   Y   for "Yes" if it describes the supervision you get on your job
   N   for "No" if it does NOT describe it
   ?   if you cannot decide

Think of the majority of the people that you work with now or the people you meet in connection with your work. How well does each of the following words or phrases describe these people? In the blank beside each word below, write

   Y   for "Yes" if it describes the people you work with
   N   for "No" if it does NOT describe them
   ?   if you cannot decide

SUPERVISION

   Impolite
   Praises good work
   Doesn't supervise enough

CO-WORKERS (PEOPLE)

   Boring
   Responsible
   Intelligent

Note: From the Job Descriptive Index, which is copyrighted by Bowling Green State University.
The complete forms, scoring key, instructions, and norms can be obtained from Dr. Patricia C. Smith, Department of Psychology, Bowling Green State University, Bowling Green, OH 43403.

TABLE 9.4   Dimensions from the Minnesota Satisfaction Questionnaire (MSQ)

Activity	Ability utilization
Independence	Company policies and practices
Variety	Compensation
Social status	Advancement
Supervision (human relations)	Responsibility
Supervision (technical)	Creativity
Moral values	Working conditions
Security	Coworkers
Social service	Recognition
Authority	Achievement

Source: "Instrumentation for the Theory of Work Adjustment," by D. J. Weiss, R. Dawis, L. H. Lofquist, & G. W. England, 1966, Minnesota Studies in Vocational Rehabilitation: XXI, University of Minnesota.

into the intrinsic and extrinsic groups (e.g., Schriesheim, Powers, Scandura, Gardiner, & Lankau, 1993).

Job in General Scale (JIG)

Ironson et al. (1989) developed a scale of global job satisfaction that contains items that do not reflect the various facets of the job. The **Job in General Scale (JIG)** was patterned on the JDI. It contains 18 items that are adjectives or short phrases about the job in general. Three of the items are shown in Table 9.5. The scale has good reliability and correlates well with other scales of overall job satisfaction.

Is Global Satisfaction the Sum of Facets?

Researchers have debated whether global job satisfaction is the sum of facets or something different. Patricia Cain Smith, the developer of the JDI and JIG, argues that they are separate (Ironson et al., 1989). Many researchers, however, treat the sum of facet scores

TABLE 9.5   Three items from the Job in General Scale (JIG)c09-tbl-0005

Think of your job in general. All in all, what is it like most of the time? In the blank beside each word or phrase below, write

- Y   for "Yes" if it describes your job
- N   for "No" if it does NOT describe it
- ?   if you cannot decide

JOB IN GENERAL
- Undesirable
- Better than most
- Rotten

Source: The Job in General Scale, which is copyrighted by Bowling Green State University. The complete forms, scoring key, instructions, and norms can be obtained from Dr. Patricia C. Smith, Department of Psychology, Bowling Green State University, Bowling Green, OH 43403.

as an indicator of overall job satisfaction. Each MSQ item reflects a specific facet, so that the total score is a sum of facets. This is justified by the fact that facets often correlate well with overall job satisfaction. For example, Ironson et al. (1989) found a .78 correlation of the JIG with the JDI Work scale. On the other hand, the summing of subscale scores presumes that all facets have been assessed and that each makes an equal contribution to global satisfaction. It seems unlikely that each facet has the same importance to every individual. Thus, the sum of facets is an approximation of overall job satisfaction, but it may not exactly match the global satisfaction of individuals.

▶ ANTECEDENTS OF JOB SATISFACTION

What makes people like or dislike their jobs? This question has been addressed in hundreds of research studies. Most of them have taken an environmental perspective. They have investigated features of jobs and organizations that lead employees to be satisfied or dissatisfied. Several studies have shown, however, that people with the same jobs and highly similar job conditions can vary considerably in their satisfaction. Findings such as these have led some researchers to take a personality perspective. Their purpose has been to show that certain types of people are inclined to like or dislike their jobs. Still other researchers have taken the interactionist perspective of person-job fit, which combines the environmental and personality approaches. Person-job fit recognizes that different people prefer different features of a job. It attempts to learn which sorts of people are satisfied with which sorts of job conditions. Job satisfaction, according to this view, is the product of appropriately matching the individual to the job. All three perspectives—environment, personality, and interactionist—are illustrated in Figure 9.2.

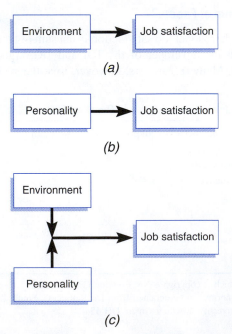

Figure 9.2 Three models illustrating (a) the impact of the job environment on job satisfaction, (b) the impact of personality on job satisfaction, and (c) the joint influence of the environment and personality on job satisfaction.

Environmental Antecedents of Job Satisfaction

As we will discuss, there is research evidence showing that aspects of the job and job environment relate to job satisfaction. In other words, some situations will produce satisfaction, and others will produce dissatisfaction. In this section we will look at characteristics of job tasks, pay, justice in the workplace, and the impact of stressful job conditions.

Job Characteristics

Job characteristics refer to the content and nature of job tasks. Only a few different characteristics have been studied as contributors to job satisfaction. Five are part of Hackman and Oldham's (1976) influential job characteristics theory (see Chapter 10 for additional details):

Skill variety: the number of different skills necessary to do a job.

Task identity: whether the employee does an entire job or a piece of a job.

Task significance: the impact a job has on other people

Autonomy: the freedom employees have to do their jobs as they see fit.

Task feedback: the extent to which it is obvious to employees that they are doing their jobs correctly.

Combined, these five *core characteristics* define the **scope**, or complexity and challenge, of a job. It is assumed by job characteristics theory that high scope leads to job satisfaction and low scope leads to boredom and dissatisfaction.

Dozens of studies across many different types of jobs have shown that each of the five characteristics relates to job satisfaction. Fried and Ferris (1987) conducted a meta-analysis of studies relating the Hackman and Oldham characteristics to global satisfaction. As discussed in Chapter 2, meta-analysis is a quantitative procedure for combining the results of different studies. Table 9.6 contains Fried and Ferris's mean correlations across various studies of the relations between job characteristics and global job satisfaction. You can see that correlations ranged from .20 for task identity to .45 for job scope. Scope was assessed by combining scores on all five core characteristics.

(*DILBERT reprinted by permission of United Feature Syndicate, Inc.*)

TABLE 9.6 Dimensions of Job Characteristics and Their Mean Correlations with Job Satisfaction from the Fried and Ferris (1987) Meta-Analysis

Characteristic	Mean Correlation	Description of Characteristic
Skill variety	.29	The number of different skills necessary to do a job
Task identity	.20	Whether or not an employee does an entire job or a piece of a job
Task significance	.26	The impact a job has on other people
Autonomy	.34	The freedom employees have to do their jobs as they see fit
Job feedback	.29	The extent to which it is obvious to employees that they are doing their jobs correctly
Job Scope	.45	The overall complexity of a job, computed as a combination of all five individual characteristics

Source: From "The Validity of the Job Characteristics Model: A Review and Meta-Analysis," by Y. Fried and G. R. Ferris, 1987, *Personnel Psychology*, *40*, 287–322.

One limitation of most studies that have addressed the influence of job characteristics on job satisfaction is that the job characteristics were assessed with questionnaires given to the employees. As discussed in Chapter 2, merely demonstrating that variables are correlated does not mean that one necessarily causes the other. For example, people who like their jobs are likely to describe them in more favorable terms than people who dislike them, thereby reporting higher levels of job scope. Thus, job satisfaction might be the cause rather than the consequence of job characteristics as reported by employees on questionnaires. Although the Fried and Ferris (1987) results are consistent with the view that certain job characteristics can lead to job satisfaction, more evidence is needed to give confidence to this conclusion.

Unfortunately, studies using different methodologies have been less supportive of the idea that these five job characteristics lead to job satisfaction. For example, Spector and Jex (1991) used both questionnaires and job analysis techniques to assess job characteristics in a sample of employees who represented a wide range of jobs. Whereas the questionnaire measure of job characteristics correlated with job satisfaction, the job analysis data did not.

Griffin (1991) conducted a longitudinal quasi-experiment in an organization that changed the characteristics of jobs. He found that job satisfaction increased immediately following the change in characteristics. It returned to the level found before the change in jobs by the time of a two-year follow-up. His results suggest that changes in job satisfaction may have been due to the novelty of the job changes rather than the nature of the job characteristics.

On the other hand, Melamed, Ben-Avi, Luz, and Green (1995) were able to show relations between job analysis ratings of job characteristics and job satisfaction. In this study of Israeli factory workers, two characteristics, different from those in job characteristics theory, were assessed—cycle time and underload. *Cycle time* is the amount of time it takes to complete a task, such as attaching a wheel to a car. *Underload* refers to a passive task, such as watching a dial, in which there is little to do. Short cycle times (under a minute) and underload were associated with job dissatisfaction. Perhaps job satisfaction is affected by these two job characteristics but not the five core characteristics.

Although the relation between employees' reports of their job characteristics and job satisfaction is consistent across samples in the United States and other Western countries, it might not be universal. Pearson and Chong (1997) were unable to find the same results in Malaysia (see International Replication). The five core characteristics were unrelated to job satisfaction in a sample of nurses. The researchers argue that in this collectivistic Asian culture, it might be more important to focus on relationships among co-workers and supervisors as a means of achieving high job satisfaction than on the nature of job tasks. However, a study conducted in more developed and westernized Hong Kong found relations between job characteristics and job satisfaction quite similar to those found in the United States (Wong, Hui, & Law, 1998). Clearly, we need to be careful about generalizing results from one country to another, and should not assume that what works here will work everywhere.

INTERNATIONAL REPLICATION

Many studies conducted in the United States have shown that job characteristics are related to job satisfaction. A question of concern to researchers is whether such results will hold in countries that are very different culturally. Pearson and Chong (1997) conducted a study of job characteristics in the collectivist Southeast Asian country of Malaysia. They hypothesized that because of the Chinese values of Malaysians, the core job characteristics involving the nature of tasks would have little effect on job satisfaction. However, because of their values, Malaysians should be more sensitive to interpersonal aspects of work, and these should relate more strongly to job satisfaction.

Participants in this study were 286 nurses at a large hospital. Questionnaires were distributed anonymously in English containing measures of job characteristics, job satisfaction, and Chinese values with the Chinese Value Survey. This survey measures four dimensions, including Confucian work dynamism, which reflects the teaching of Confucius, and moral discipline, which concerns self-control and moral behavior. Included were the five core characteristics of autonomy, feedback, skill variety, task identity, and task significance, plus the interpersonal dimension of feedback from others. This last dimension concerned the extent to which

supervisors and other people provided feedback about how well the person was doing the job.

As expected, there were no significant correlations of any of the five core job characteristics with job satisfaction, so consistently related in U.S. studies. Malaysians did not find jobs high on these dimensions to be more satisfying. However, there was a correlation of feedback from others with job satisfaction ($r = .40$). The authors explained these results as reflecting the greater collectivism of the Malaysians, who put great value on receiving feedback from others. To further test the idea that values were responsible for the results, participants were divided into those who strongly endorsed Chinese values and those who didn't. Correlations of the core job characteristics with job satisfaction were higher for those low on Chinese values than those high on Chinese values. For example, autonomy correlated .24 with job satisfaction for those low on Chinese values, but only .07 for those high. This study clearly shows that results from the United States do not always replicate in other countries.

Source: Pearson, C. A. L., & Chong, J. (1997). Contributions of job content and social information on organizational commitment and job satisfaction : An exploration in a Malaysian nursing context. *Journal of Occupational and Organizational Psychology*, *70*, 357–374.

Pay

Although pay is associated to some extent with global satisfaction, as might be expected it relates even more strongly with the facet of pay satisfaction. Brasher and Chen (1999) surveyed recent college graduates and found that their level of starting pay related more strongly to pay satisfaction (correlation = .36) than to global satisfaction (correlation = .17). Furthermore, the fairness with which pay is distributed, or equity (see the discussion of justice theories in Chapter 8), is a more important determinant of pay satisfaction than the actual level of pay (Williams, McDaniel, & Nguyen, 2006). You can find people earning minimum wage who are satisfied with their pay, whereas professional athletes and entertainers might be dissatisfied with six- and even seven-figure salaries. For example, Sally Jessy Raphael, a radio personality who for 20 years hosted a popular afternoon television talk show, was quite vocal in her dissatisfaction with a salary of several hundred thousand dollars per year. Her dissatisfaction grew from her self-comparison with Oprah Winfrey, who made in the millions. Raphael believed that because they both had the same job they should have the same salary.

All this leads to the hypothesis that if we compare the pay and pay satisfaction of people across different jobs, we will find little or no correlation. People who make more money are not necessarily more satisfied when they have different jobs. On the other hand, if we have a sample of people who all do the same job, those who make more money should be more satisfied. In other words, Oprah Winfrey will probably have less to complain about than Sally Jessy Raphael, who makes far less money. Research support for this hypothesis comes from two studies. Spector (1985) found a mean correlation of only .17 between salary level and pay satisfaction in three samples of employees who held different jobs. Rice, Phillips, and McFarlin (1990) found a much larger .50 correlation between pay and job satisfaction in a sample of mental health professionals holding the same jobs. Pay satisfaction is affected by how an individual's salary compares to others in the same job rather than to people in general. More direct support for the link with fairness comes from the research on justice and pay satisfaction. In their meta-analysis, Cohen-Charash and Spector (2001) found that distributive and procedural justice (see Chapter 8) were strongly correlated with pay satisfaction, with correlations of .58 and .45, respectively (see Table 9.7).

Justice

As noted in the Chapter 8 discussion of justice theories, perceptions of fairness are important determinants of people's behavior and reactions to work. Distributive justice is the extent to which people perceive the allotment of rewards at work to be fair, whereas procedural justice is the extent to which people perceive the process by which rewards at work are allocated to be fair. Both forms of justice are linked to global and facet job satisfaction in the Cohen-Charash and Spector (2001) meta-analysis. Overall job satisfaction and facet satisfactions of pay, supervision, and nature of work correlated significantly with both forms of justice (see Table 9.7). Note that for pay satisfaction, distributive justice had a larger correlation than procedural justice. This suggests that the distribution of pay is more important for satisfaction than the procedures for distribution, although both are certainly important. For supervision satisfaction, procedural justice is more important than distributive justice, perhaps because it is the supervisor who decides on the procedures by which assignments and rewards are allocated.

TABLE 9.7 **Correlations of Distributive Justice and Procedural Justice with Job Satisfaction**

Job Satisfaction Type	Distributive Justice	Procedural Justice
Global job satisfaction	.39	.40
Pay satisfaction	.58	.45
Supervisor satisfaction	.36	.47
Nature of work satisfaction	.32	.31

Source: "The Role of Justice in Organizations: A Meta-Analysis," by Y. Cohen-Charash, and P. E. Spector, 2001, *Organizational Behavior and Human Decision Processes*, *86*, 538–551.

Personal Antecedents of Job Satisfaction

The majority of studies of the causes of job satisfaction have taken an environmental perspective. Some researchers, however, feel that personal characteristics are also important in determining job satisfaction (e.g., Staw & Cohen-Charash, 2005). Some have gone so far as to suggest that job satisfaction might be caused in part by genetic predispositions. Arvey, Bouchard, Segal, and Abraham (1989) compared the job satisfaction of identical twins who were reared apart and discovered that their satisfaction levels were related. Although this single study provides only tentative evidence for the role of genetics, many studies have shown a link between personal characteristics and job satisfaction (e.g., Brush, Moch, and Pooyan, 1987; Staw, Bell, and Clausen, 1986).

Personality

The idea that job satisfaction may be caused in part by personality can be traced back to the Hawthorne studies. The Hawthorne researchers noticed that certain individuals, whom they called *chronic kickers*, were continually complaining about the job (Roethlisberger, 1941). No matter what the researchers did for them, the chronic kickers always had new complaints. More recently, Bowling, Beehr, and Lepisto (2006) explored the stability of satisfaction by studying people who changed employers. They found that the job satisfaction of these individuals was correlated across a five-year span of time. In other words, the job satisfaction of these people on one job correlated with their satisfaction on another. Bowling et al. concluded that job satisfaction was caused in part by underlying personality. Some people are predisposed to like their jobs, whereas others are predisposed not to like them. Newton and Keenan (1991) did a similar study, but found evidence that job environment, as well as personality, is important. They studied a group of British engineers during their first four years on the job after college. They also found consistency in job satisfaction over time, but in addition, they found that engineers who changed jobs increased their satisfaction. Dormann and Zapf (2001) conducted a meta-analysis of such studies showing that job satisfaction was far more stable over time when people remained on the same job (mean correlation = .42) than when they changed jobs (mean correlation = .18). Thus, although personality may have contributed to satisfaction, job conditions were also important.

Even stronger evidence for personality consistency across time was provided by Staw et al. (1986), who studied people's job satisfaction over the span of decades (see Research in Detail). They found that personality assessed in adolescents predicted job satisfaction up to 50 years later.

RESEARCH IN DETAIL

One of the limitations of many I/O studies is that data are collected at a single point in time. The study by Staw, Bell, and Clausen (1986) stands out as a rare example of a long-term longitudinal study of job satisfaction. The study spanned 50 years, comparing the personality of adolescents with their later job satisfaction.

The study made use of data from the Intergenerational Studies begun at the University of California, Berkeley, during the 1920s. Three groups of subjects were assessed using interviews and questionnaires several times during their lives. Staw et al. had several judges, who were either clinical psychologists or psychiatric social workers, read the extensive material in each subject's file and make ratings about them on several personality characteristics. Scores on 17 characteristics were combined into affective disposition scores. Examples of the characteristics include thin-skinned, punitive, condescending, hostile, distrustful, irritable, and moody.

Results showed that affective disposition assessed as young as early adolescence correlated significantly with job satisfaction assessed up to 50 years later.

For the 46 subjects who had data at adolescence and decades later on the job, the correlation between disposition and satisfaction was .37. This is larger than many of the correlations found between job conditions and job satisfaction.

There are several explanations for these results, as noted by Staw et al. First, it may be that affective disposition, as assessed here, relates to a person's view of the world. People with a negative disposition might perceive all aspects of their lives, including their jobs, as worse than people with a more positive disposition. Alternatively, disposition might lead to job choice, with negative people seeking out worse jobs than positive people. Although the study cannot answer these questions, it demonstrates that personality, through some as yet to be determined mechanism, is a likely precursor to job satisfaction. These results suggest that organizations should carefully consider characteristics of individuals when implementing job changes intended to enhance job satisfaction.

Source: Staw, B. M., Bell, N. E., & Clausen, J. A. (1986). The dispositional approach to job attitudes: A lifetime longitudinal test. *Administrative Science Quarterly, 31*, 56–77.

These studies showing consistency in job satisfaction over time support the idea that personality is important, but they don't shed much light on the nature of the relevant personality traits. Quite a few specific traits have been studied, with particular attention being paid to two of them—negative affectivity and locus of control.

Negative affectivity (NA) is the tendency for an individual to experience negative emotions, such as anxiety or depression, across a wide variety of situations. Watson, Pennebaker, and Folger (1986) extended the NA idea to the workplace, hypothesizing that high NA individuals would likely be dissatisfied because they tend to view all aspects of their world in a negative way. This is consistent with the idea of the chronic kicker mentioned earlier, in that some people just dwell on negative aspects of life. This theoretical idea is supported by Connolly and Viswesvaran (2000), who conducted a meta-analysis of 27 studies that found a mean correlation between NA and job satisfaction of $-.27$.

Locus of control refers to whether or not people believe they are in control of reinforcements in life. People who believe that they control reinforcements are termed *internals*. People who believe that fate, luck, or powerful others control reinforcements are termed *externals*. Internals have been found to be more satisfied with their jobs than externals (e.g., Moyle & Parkes, 1999).

Although the research on these personality traits has shown a connection with job satisfaction, the reasons are not well delineated. Watson et al. (1986) suggested that NA relates to job satisfaction because the high NA person perceives and experiences the job negatively, regardless of the actual conditions. It is possible that externals experience their jobs in a similar way. There are other mechanisms that are equally plausible. For example, Spector (1982) hypothesized that one reason for the higher satisfaction of internals is their higher job performance. Individuals who perform better might be better rewarded and thus like their jobs better. Personality might also be related to job choice. Perhaps people with certain personality traits choose better jobs and therefore have higher satisfaction. Clearly, research is needed to determine why personality relates to job satisfaction.

Gender

Most studies that have compared men and women in their global job satisfaction have found few differences. Meta-analytic studies involving multiple samples and thousands of employees have failed to find gender differences (Brush et al., 1987; Witt & Nye, 1992). Greenhaus, Parasuraman, and Wormley (1990) found no significant gender differences in their study, even though the distribution of jobs in their sample was not the same for both genders—males were more likely to have managerial/professional jobs, and females were more likely to have clerical jobs. This suggests that women may be happier with lower pay and responsibility than men, perhaps because their expectations are lower about what they will receive, or because they compare themselves to other women who are in similar circumstances.

Most Americans say that they like their jobs.
(*Digital Vision*)

Age

The workforces in many countries have been getting older because of both the changing demographic makeup of the population (there are more elderly people) and legislation that has made age discrimination illegal. A question of interest to I/O psychologists concerns possible changes in job satisfaction over a person's life span. Many studies have shown that older workers are more satisfied with their jobs than younger workers (e.g., Siu, Lu, & Cooper, 1999). Brush et al. (1987) calculated a mean correlation between age and job satisfaction of .22 in their meta-analysis of 21 studies.

Two large sample surveys, one conducted in England (Clark, Oswald, & Warr, 1996) and the other in nine countries including the United States (Birdi, Warr, & Oswald, 1995), found a curvilinear relation between age and job satisfaction. For these countries, job satisfaction at first declines with age, reaching the lowest level at around age 26 to 31, and then increases through the rest of the working career. Some of this difference might be attributable to better adjustment to work through experience. However, Birdi et al. found evidence that older workers have better conditions and greater rewards at work, and Warr (2001) suggested that as people become older, they tend to value different things at work. For example, older workers are less interested in having task variety, and so might be happier with jobs younger workers find unsatisfying.

Cultural and Ethnic Differences

Another trend in the composition of the workforce in the United States and other countries is that it is becoming increasingly multicultural. In addition, large organizations frequently have facilities in multiple countries and employ people from those countries. For example, American automobile manufacturers have plants outside the United States. Japanese automobile manufacturers such as Toyota have plants in the United States. If organizations are to deal appropriately with a diverse workforce, they must understand how people of various ethnic, racial, and cultural backgrounds view and feel about their jobs.

Several studies have compared the job satisfaction of black and white employees in the United States. Some of these studies have found that blacks have slightly lower satisfaction (e.g., Greenhaus et al., 1990), although Brush et al. (1987) reported no racial differences in their meta-analysis of 21 studies. Studies that have found differences in satisfaction have also noted differences in other variables, suggesting that job experiences might differ in at least some organizations. For example, blacks had lower mean performance ratings than whites in the Greenhaus et al. (1990) study. Perhaps the factors leading to lower ratings resulted in lowered job satisfaction. Somers and Birnbaum (2001) studied black and white employees of a hospital and found that there were no differences between them after demographic variables (e.g., age and education) and type of work were controlled.

Person-Job Fit

Most researchers have tended to treat environmental and personal factors as independent influences on job satisfaction. In other words, they have studied characteristics of jobs or of individuals that may lead to satisfaction. Another approach, however, is to look at the interaction of the two factors. The person-job fit approach states that job satisfaction will occur when there is a good match between the person and the job (Kristof, 1996).

Much of the research on person-job fit has looked at the correspondence between what people say they want on a job and what they say they have. For example, employees could be asked how much autonomy they have and how much they want. The difference between having and wanting represents the amount of fit of person to job. Studies have been quite consistent in showing that the smaller the discrepancy between having and wanting, the greater the job satisfaction. For example, Verquer, Beehr, and Wagner (2003) conducted a meta-analysis of 21 person-job fit studies and found that various measures of fit were correlated with job satisfaction.

Another approach to studying the interplay of job and person is to look at the interaction of specific person and job variables in predicting job satisfaction. That is, person variables are used as moderators of the relation between job variables and job satisfaction. A **moderator variable** affects the relation between two other variables. A particular job variable may relate to job satisfaction for people at one level of a person variable, but not for people at another level. For example, men might react differently than women to a job condition. Thus there might be a positive correlation between the job condition and job satisfaction for men, and no correlation for women. We would say that gender moderated the relation between the job condition and job satisfaction. It determines whether the two variables are correlated.

In the job characteristics area, many studies have attempted to find the sorts of people who would react most positively to high-scope jobs (i.e., those high on the Hackman & Oldham, 1976, five job characteristics). One personality characteristic that comes from Hackman and Oldham's (1976) theory is **growth need strength (GNS)**. This characteristic refers to a person's desire for the satisfaction of higher order needs, such as autonomy or achievement. Meta-analyses of studies that address the effects of growth need strength have shown that it moderates the relation between job characteristics and job satisfaction (e.g., Loher, Noe, Moeller, & Fitzgerald, 1985). Correlations between these two variables were greater for individuals who were high in growth need strength than for individuals who were low.

This relation is illustrated in Figure 9.3. The horizontal axis of the graph represents the scope of the job; the vertical axis represents job satisfaction. One line is for high GNS people, and the other line is for low GNS people. As the graph shows, people who are high in GNS will be satisfied with high-scope jobs and not with low-scope jobs. The scope of the job is not important for people low in GNS. Their satisfaction stays constant regardless of job scope.

▶ POTENTIAL EFFECTS OF JOB SATISFACTION

A number of organizationally relevant behaviors are thought to be the result of job satisfaction or dissatisfaction. Many I/O psychologists have felt compelled to justify their interest in job satisfaction to managers by showing that it is relevant to behaviors that have an important impact on the well-being of organizations. Three of these behaviors have been prominent in the literature: job performance, turnover, and employee absence. In recent years, job satisfaction has been seen as important because of its potential effects on variables of more concern to employees than organizations. Of particular interest is the relation of job satisfaction to health and well-being.

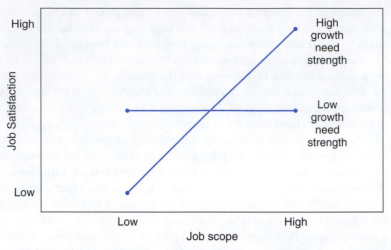

Figure 9.3   The moderating effect of growth need strength on the job scope–job satisfaction relation. Scope is represented by the horizontal axis of the graph. Job satisfaction is on the vertical axis. For people high in growth need strength, satisfaction is high when scope is high and low when scope is low. For people who are low in growth need strength, satisfaction is unaffected by level of job scope.

Job Satisfaction and Job Performance

The idea that job satisfaction and job performance are related seems intuitively obvious. After all, shouldn't satisfied employees be productive employees? Judge, Thoresen, Bono, and Patton (2001) conducted a thorough meta-analysis of 312 studies and found that there is a modest relationship—the average correlation is .20 between job performance and global satisfaction. Two other investigators, Iaffaldano and Muchinsky (1985) found that the correlation with individual facets, however, is variable, ranging from .05 for pay satisfaction to .20 for satisfaction with intrinsic aspects of the job.

At least part of the reason for the relatively small mean correlations found in these meta-analyses may have to do with the measures of job performance available in many studies. Most studies rely on supervisor ratings of performance, which suffer from several limitations, as discussed in Chapter 4. Supervisors frequently exhibit rating errors, especially when ratings are for organizational purposes. This can produce inaccuracy in performance ratings, which introduces extra error into the statistics. Relations of satisfaction with performance would likely be stronger if more accurate measures of performance were used.

Although it is clear that performance and satisfaction are related (Schleicher, Watt, & Greguras, 2004), there are two opposite explanations. First, satisfaction might lead to performance. That is, people who like their jobs work harder and therefore perform better. Second, performance might lead to satisfaction. People who perform well are likely to benefit from that performance, and those benefits could enhance satisfaction. A well-performing person might receive more pay and recognition, which might increase job satisfaction. Both of these explanations are illustrated in Figure 9.4. In the top part of

Figure 9.4 Two possible models illustrating why job performance relates to job satisfaction. In the first model, job satisfaction leads to increased effort on the job, which leads to job performance. In the second, job performance leads to rewards, which lead to job satisfaction. As noted in the text, evidence exists to support the second model.

the figure, satisfaction leads to effort, which in turn leads to performance. In the bottom part, performance leads to rewards and rewards lead to satisfaction.

Jacobs and Solomon (1977) conducted a study that supports the second explanation. They hypothesized that satisfaction and performance would be related more strongly when performance leads to rewards. The rationale is that employees who perform well will be more satisfied because they have received rewards. Jacobs and Solomon (1977) found support for their hypothesis that a performance-reward linkage leads to stronger satisfaction-performance relations.

Job Satisfaction and Turnover

Quitting the job, or turnover, has been tied to job satisfaction. Many studies have shown that dissatisfied employees are more likely than satisfied employees to quit their jobs (e.g., Crampton & Wagner, 1994; Dickter, Roznowski, & Harrison, 1996).

Correlations between job satisfaction and turnover have been interpreted as indicating the effects of satisfaction on behavior. One reason that it has been possible to demonstrate such a linkage between job satisfaction and turnover has to do with the designs of turnover studies and the nature of turnover. Most turnover studies are predictive, assessing job satisfaction in a sample of employees and then waiting some period of months or years to see who quits. The predictive nature of these studies allows the conclusion that dissatisfaction is a factor that leads employees to quit their jobs.

Job Satisfaction and Absence

Conventional wisdom suggests that absence from work is a by-product of employee job dissatisfaction. People who dislike their jobs will be more likely to miss work than people who like their jobs. Several meta-analyses have looked at this question, and they show that the connection between job satisfaction and absence is inconsistent and usually quite small. For example, Farrell and Stamm (1988) found correlations of $-.13$ and $-.10$, respectively, between absence and global job satisfaction using two different measures of absence. These are typical correlations found in absence studies. Tharenou (1993), however, found correlations as high as $-.34$ between absence and job satisfaction in a sample of Australian blue-collar workers. Perhaps absence and satisfaction are more strongly related under some conditions.

One possible reason for the small relation between satisfaction and absence is that a person can be absent for many reasons (Kohler & Mathieu, 1993), including employee illness, family member illness (especially children), personal business, and fatigue, as well as just not feeling like going to work. Whereas some of these reasons might be associated with job satisfaction, others probably are not. For example, satisfaction might be associated with absence caused by not feeling like going to work, but it is not likely to be associated with absence caused by serious illness. Thus, overall absence is not likely to have a strong relation with job satisfaction. If reasons for absence are considered, however, relations should be stronger (Kohler & Mathieu, 1993).

Health and Well-Being

A number of I/O psychologists are concerned that job dissatisfaction might be related to employee health and well-being. Indeed, some claim that job satisfaction might be a factor in serious illness and even death.

Some correlational studies show that job satisfaction relates to health variables. Studies have found that dissatisfied employees reported more physical symptoms, such as sleep problems and upset stomach, than their satisfied counterparts (Begley & Czajka, 1993; O'Driscoll & Beehr, 1994). Dissatisfaction has also been found to correlate with negative emotions at work, such as anxiety and depression (Jex & Gudanowski, 1992; Thomas & Ganster, 1995). These negative emotional states could be considered indicators of psychological health or well-being at work. Evidence relating job satisfaction to more serious health problems, such as heart disease, has been harder to produce.

Job and Life Satisfaction

Another important issue concerns the contribution of job satisfaction to overall **life satisfaction**—how satisfied one is with one's life circumstances. Life satisfaction is considered to be an indicator of overall happiness or emotional well-being. Studies of life satisfaction have found that it correlates with job satisfaction (e.g., Adams, King, & King, 1996; Lance, Lautenschlager, Sloan, & Varca, 1989).

Three hypotheses have been proposed about how job and life satisfaction might affect one another (Rain, Lane, & Steiner, 1991). The *spillover hypothesis* suggests that satisfaction (or dissatisfaction) in one area of life affects, or spills over to, another. Thus, problems and dissatisfaction at home can affect satisfaction with work, whereas problems and dissatisfaction at work can affect satisfaction with home. The *compensation hypothesis* says that dissatisfaction in one area of life will be compensated for in another. A person with a dissatisfying job will seek satisfaction in other aspects of life. A person with a dissatisfying home life might seek satisfaction in work. The *segmentation hypothesis* states that people compartmentalize their lives, and that satisfaction in one area of life has no relation to satisfaction in another.

The three hypotheses lead to contradictory predictions about the correlation between job and life satisfaction. Spillover predicts a positive correlation in that satisfaction at work will affect satisfaction in other areas of life. Compensation predicts a negative correlation because dissatisfaction in one area of life will be compensated for by satisfaction in another. Segmentation predicts no correlation because people keep satisfaction with different areas of life separated. Rain et al. (1991) point out that because research has consistently found a positive correlation between job and life satisfaction, the spillover hypothesis is the only one supported by studies.

► ORGANIZATIONAL COMMITMENT

Organizational commitment is another popular attitudinal variable in the work domain. It is strongly related to job satisfaction, but it is distinctly different (Tett & Meyer, 1993). There have been several somewhat different definitions of commitment, but all involve the attachment of the individual to the organization. The original conception is based on the work of Mowday, Steers, and Porter (1979), which considers organizational commitment to consist of three components:

1. Acceptance of the organization's goals
2. Willingness to work hard for the organization
3. Desire to stay with the organization

Subsequently a three-component conception of commitment has been developed (Meyer, Allen, & Smith, 1993). The three types of commitment are:

Affective

Continuance

Normative

Affective commitment occurs when the employee wishes to remain with the organization because of an emotional attachment. **Continuance commitment** exists when the employee must remain with the organization because of a need for the benefits and salary or an inability to find another job. **Normative commitment** comes from the employee's values—a personal belief that he or she owes it to the organization to remain out of a sense that it is the right thing to do.

Meyer et al. (1993) discuss the nature and origins of the three components of commitment. Figure 9.5 shows the major influences on each. As you can see, different factors are involved in each component. Affective commitment arises from job conditions and met expectations. That is, did the job provide the rewards the employee expected? Continuance commitment is produced by the benefits accrued from working for the organization and by the lack of available alternative jobs. Normative commitment comes from the employee's personal values and from obligations felt toward the employer. Such obligations come from favors that the organization has done, such as paying the employee's school expenses.

Assessment of Organizational Commitment

Organizational commitment is measured with self-report scales not unlike those used to assess job satisfaction. Four items from the most popular scale, developed by Mowday et al. (1979), are shown in Table 9.8. The items tap the three aspects of commitment—acceptance of goals, willingness to work hard, and intention to stay with the organization. All three components relate strongly to one another, and combined they indicate commitment.

The three components in the Meyer et al. (1993) conception of commitment can be assessed with a scale they developed. Table 9.9 contains two of the items for each component. As opposed to the Mowday et al. (1979) scale, the components in the Meyer et al. (1993) scale produce separate scores. Research with the scale has found support for

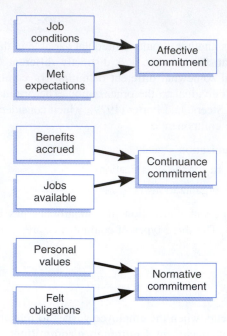

Figure 9.5 Antecedents of the three components of organizational commitment. Each type of commitment has different antecedents. Affective commitment arises from favorable experiences on the job. Continuance is produced by the investments in the job and the difficulty of finding another job. Normative commitment derives from a sense of obligation either because of the person's values or from favors done for the person by the organization.

the idea that the three types of commitment are separate variables (Dunham, Grube, & Castañeda, 1994; Meyer, Bobocel, & Allen, 1991). Hackett, Bycio, and Hausdorf (1994) noted that the Mowday et al. (1979) scale mainly assesses affective commitment. It correlates strongly with the affective commitment subscale but not with the continuance or normative subscales of the Meyer et al. scale.

Organizational Commitment and Other Variables

Organizational commitment has been prominent in studies involving many organizational variables. Cooper-Hakim and Viswesvaran (2005) conducted a meta-analysis of nearly 1,000 studies relating commitment to several hypothesized variables proposed as consequences. Table 9.10 summarizes their results relating the three components of commitment to four important variables. Job satisfaction related most strongly to affective commitment, which isn't surprising considering that both variables are attitudes about

TABLE 9.8   Four Items from the Mowday, Steers, and Porter (1979) Organizational Commitment Questionnaire

I find that my values and the organization's values are very similar.

I am proud to tell others that I am part of this organization.

I could just as well be working for a different organization as long as the type of work was similar.

This organization really inspires the very best in me in the way of job performance.

Source: "The Measurement of Organizational Commitment," by R. T. Mowday, R. M. Steers, and L. W. Porter, 1979, *Journal of Vocational Behavior, 14*, 224–247.

TABLE 9.9   Six Items from the Meyer, Allen, and Smith (1998) Three-Component Organizational Commitment Scale

Affective Commitment

I would be very happy to spend the rest of my career with this organization.

I really feel as if this organization's problems are my own.

Continuance Commitment

Right now, staying with my organization is a matter of necessity as much as desire.

It would be very hard for me to leave my organization right now, even if I wanted to.

Normative Commitment

I do not feel any obligation to remain with my current employer.

Even if it were to my advantage, I do not feel it would be right to leave my organization now.

Source: "Commitment to Organizations and Occupations: Extension and Test of a Three-Component Conceptualization," by J. P. Meyer, N. J. Allen, and C. A. Smith, 1993; *Journal of Applied Psychology, 78*, 538–551.

the job. Job performance also related most strongly to affective commitment, at about the same level as job satisfaction, as was discussed earlier. Continuance commitment related slightly, but in the opposite direction. These results suggest that people who are working because of an emotional attachment will tend to perform better, but those who are working because they feel they have to will actually perform worse.

Turnover, in particular, has been a focus of much commitment research (e.g., Eisenberger, Armeli, Rexwinkel, Lynch, & Rhoades, 2001). Because commitment refers to the attachment of people to jobs, it should be related to turnover. Those with low commitment should be more likely to quit the job than those with high commitment. Cooper-Hakim and Viswesvaran (2005) found that turnover (last row of the table) correlates negatively with all three components, with continuance commitment relating most strongly. The pattern with turnover intentions was different in that continuance commitment had the weakest correlation of the three components. These results suggest that affective commitment relates most strongly to the desire to quit, as reflected in intentions, but it is the actual investment in the job, reflected in continuance commitment, that is most important in translating intentions to turnover.

Commitment has also been studied in relation to potential antecedent variables. Meyer, Stanley, Hercovitch, and Topolnytsky (2002) conducted a meta-analysis of 155

TABLE 9.10   Mean Correlations of Organizational Commitment Types with Several Work Variables

Variable	Affective Commitment	Continuance Commitment	Normative Commitment
Job satisfaction	.50	.09	.29
Job performance	.22	−.09	.06
Turnover intention	−.48	−.15	−.29
Turnover	−.17	−.20	−.13

Source: "The construct of work commitment: Testing an integrative framework," by A. Cooper-Hakim and C. Viswesvaran, 2005, *Psychological Bulletin, 131*, 241–259.

studies showing that commitment is associated with job stress (people who perceive their jobs to be stressful have low commitment) and organizational justice (people who feel they have been unfairly treated have low commitment). However, relationships with these variables were stronger for affective commitment than either continuance or normative commitment. Continuance commitment was most strongly related to how well skills could transfer from the current job to another job, which makes sense, since lack of transferability would make it difficult for someone to switch jobs, thus producing a higher level of continuance commitment.

As with job satisfaction, there have been few gender or racial differences found with respect to organizational commitment. For example, Ng, Butts, Vandenberg, DeJoy, and Wilson (2006) found that men and women, and whites and nonwhites had the same level of organizational commitment.

One must be cautious in generalizing these organizational commitment findings to other countries. Robert, Probst, Martocchio, Drasgow and Lawler (2000) surveyed employees of one multinational company in four countries: India, Mexico, Poland, and the United States. Organizational commitment correlated strongly with intent to quit in the United States (as expected) and Poland. However, the correlation was somewhat smaller in Mexico, and it was nonsignificant in India. Apparently Indians and Mexicans who have low commitment are less inclined to quit their jobs than Americans and Poles who have low commitment.

Perhaps one reason for these cross-national differences has to do with cultural values. As discussed earlier in the chapter, individualism-collectivism concerns whether one's focus is on oneself (individualism) or others (collectivism). As members of collectivist societies, Indians and Mexicans might display more loyalty to their employers, and resist translating low commitment into turnover. Indeed, Cohen (2006) showed that collectivists in Israel had greater organizational commitment and were more likely than individualists to engage in behaviors to help their employers.

The idea of commitment has been extended from the organization to other work-related domains. Vandenberghe, Bentein, and Stinglhamber (2004) developed scales to assess commitment to one's supervisor and to one's work group or peers. They showed that commitment to the group was a better predictor of turnover than commitment to the organization or supervisor. These findings illustrate how it can be relationships with one's work peers that matters most in deciding whether to remain with an employer.

Meyer et al. (1993) developed the idea of **occupational commitment**, which concerns the occupation or profession rather than a particular organization. People might be very committed to their occupation, such as accounting or law, and uncommitted to their current employer. The focus of a person's commitment is important in determining his or her responses. For example, Keller (1997) found that occupational commitment among engineers and scientists related to an objective measure of performance (number of articles published), but organizational commitment did not. Success in publication may have been relevant to how individuals viewed their occupations but not their organizations. On the other hand, Cropanzano, Howes, Grandey, and Toth (1997) found that occupational commitment was less strongly related than organizational commitment to intention of quitting the job. In their meta-analysis of occupational commitment studies, Lee, Carswell, and Allen (2000) found that the mean correlation with job satisfaction ($r = .37$) was smaller than is typically found for organizational commitment. We might expect that occupational commitment will relate most strongly to behaviors relevant to success in that occupation. Organizational commitment will relate most strongly to behaviors and variables relevant to the present job.

Finally, in unionized occupations and workplaces, people can vary in the extent to which they are committed to their unions. Such commitment has been shown to relate to the time and effort one puts into union activities. For example, Fullagar, Gallagher, Clark, and Carroll (2004) showed that union commitment predicted participation in union activities over a span of 10 years. This suggests, as with job satisfaction, that some forms of commitment can be quite stable over a long period of time.

► EMOTIONS AT WORK

For most people, the job is an important component of life, providing not only resources (pay and fringe benefits) to acquire the necessities of life, but a sense of purpose and social contact as well. It is inevitable that people will react emotionally to workplace events and situations. Accomplishment of a major work project will likely result in positive feelings, such as pride and joy, whereas a heated argument with a supervisor will certainly induce feelings of anger and annoyance. Furthermore, the expression of emotion at work can sometimes be an important part of the job. Salespeople are expected to smile and be friendly, whereas police officers often are expected to act stern in dealing with someone committing a crime.

It is important to distinguish emotional states and moods. An emotional state is the immediate experience of a particular emotion, such as anger or fear, that is generally in response to a situation, such as being yelled at by your supervisor. A mood is a longer term state that is less specific, consisting of positive versus negative direction (or good mood/bad mood) rather than specific feelings such as joy or sadness (Fisher, 2000). It is important to study both emotional states and moods in the workplace.

Causes and Consequences of Emotions at Work

Brief and Weiss (2002) discussed how things that are stressful and aversive at work (including punishments) can produce negative emotional states and moods. This might include having to juggle conflicting demands (e.g., having a child become ill the day of an important meeting at work), too much time pressure, and unfair treatment. They also discussed things that can induce positive emotions, which can be stimulated by the positive moods of coworkers and supervisors. In particular, rewards at work can induce positive emotions; for example, receiving a bonus or raise, as well as less tangible rewards, such as recognition by supervisors.

Emotions associated with behavior and outcomes of employees have implications for organizations. Ashkanasy, Hartel, and Daus (2002) compared the effects of positive and negative moods. They note that positive mood is associated with greater creativity, higher job satisfaction, less turnover, more contextual performance (e.g., volunteering to do extra work that isn't required; see Chapter 4), and better job performance. Negative moods, on the other hand, are associated with low job satisfaction and more absence and turnover. As we will see in the next chapter, emotions have also been linked to counterproductive work behavior (e.g., verbal aggression directed toward coworkers and purposely withholding effort), with positive emotion leading to low levels, and negative emotion to high levels, of these harmful behaviors (Fox, Spector, & Miles, 2001).

Evidence linking mood to job satisfaction comes from a study by Fuller, Stanton, Fisher, Spitzmüller, Russell, and Smith (2003). They asked 14 employees to complete measures of their mood and satisfaction on more than 1,000 occasions of stressful events. Results showed, as expected, that stressful events led to more negative mood and that positive moods were associated with greater job satisfaction.

Emotional Labor

It has long been recognized by private sector companies that emotional expression by employees who deal with clients and customers is an important part of customer service (Grandey, Fiske, Mattila, Jansen, & Sideman, 2005). For example, Koys (2001) conducted a study of a restaurant chain company and found that those restaurants with satisfied employees were more profitable than those with dissatisfied employees. Many companies have emotion display rules requiring the expression of positive emotions, such as smiling at customers and appearing to be enjoying work (Diefendorff, Richard, & Croyle, 2006). The required expression of certain emotions at work is called **emotional labor**, recognizing that it can take effort for employees to maintain the appearance of positive feelings (Glomb & Tews, 2004).

Emotional labor has been shown to have both positive and negative effects on employees. On the one hand, some studies show that acting happy at work can lead to increased job satisfaction (e.g., Coté & Morgan, 2002), but others have found the opposite (Zapf, 2002). Emotional labor can be stressful, leading to emotional exhaustion (Brotheridge & Grandey, 2002) and physical health symptoms, such as headache and stomach distress (Schaubroeck & Jones, 2000). Zapf notes that three important elements determine whether effects on employees are positive or negative. First, reactions will be positive if the person actually experiences the emotions being displayed. Having to pretend to be happy when experiencing the opposite emotion leads to **emotional dissonance**, which is associated with negative effects. Second, having control over the situation, such as being given latitude in how to deal with a rude customer, will tend to reduce negative effects. Grandey, Fisk, and Steiner's (2005) study showed that emotional labor was stressful only for individuals who had little autonomy and control at work. Third, if there are rewards for the results of the emotional labor, such as bigger tips for a server, effects tend to be positive. Finally, Giardini and Frese (2006) showed that people's emotional labor skill can vary, and it is for individuals whose skill is low that emotional labor is most stressful. Taken together, these points suggest that to minimize the negative impact of emotional labor, employees should be trained to enhance their skills at emotion regulation and to experience rather than fake the emotions they express. In addition, the job should be structured to give employees control over their tasks and to share the rewards of their emotional labor.

▶ FUTURE ISSUES AND CHALLENGES

Several important questions in the domain of job attitudes need to be addressed in the future. Our understanding of the factors that lead to job attitudes is more advanced than our understanding of how to improve them for employees. Research is needed to determine the sorts of interventions that would be effective in organizations to make employees more satisfied, as well as to enhance their organizational commitment.

In addition, the reasons for the correlations between personality characteristics and job satisfaction are not understood. Research needs to determine why personality relates to job satisfaction. Watson et al. (1986) hypothesized that certain types of people are simply more satisfied than others, regardless of the situation. Again, satisfaction seems to be caused by the interplay of job and person. Understanding personality will require looking at both the individual and the job conditions. Studying the fit of the person to the job is likely to help us understand satisfaction.

The role of job satisfaction in health and well-being is an important question that needs attention. The possibility exists that enhancing satisfaction might lead to healthier and better adjusted people. If this is the case, it will become even more important to determine how job satisfaction can be improved. It seems likely that the answer will involve providing different job conditions for different people.

Finally, an emerging area of research is emotions at work, determining the conditions that lead to emotions and the impact those emotions have on people and organizations. Stressful and aversive events at work lead to negative emotion, whereas rewards and contact with people in positive moods lead to positive emotion. Negative emotion at work is associated with behavior that is harmful to organizations, whereas positive emotion is associated with things that are helpful. As the American economy has shifted toward the provision of services (rather than tangible products), the need for emotional labor has increased. It has been recognized that demands on employees to display certain emotions can have both positive and negative effects. There is work to be done to better understand the effects of emotional labor on employees and how emotional displays affect customers, coworkers, and organizations. This question is of particular interest in cross-national research because there can be cross-cultural differences in customer expectations for emotional displays by the employees with whom they interact.

▶ CHAPTER SUMMARY

Job satisfaction is the extent to which people like or dislike their jobs (global satisfaction) or aspects of their jobs (facet satisfaction). It is usually measured with questionnaires administered to employees. Several popular job satisfaction scales are available:

Job Descriptive Index (JDI)

Minnesota Satisfaction Questionnaire (MSQ)

Job in General Scale (JIG)

Research has linked job satisfaction to a number of job environment variables. Job satisfaction has been shown to correlate with job characteristics, pay, and justice. It has also been found to correlate with age and other personal characteristics, and with various personality variables, such as negative affectivity and locus of control.

Research has linked job satisfaction to several employee behaviors. Lack of satisfaction seems to be a cause of employee turnover. It is related modestly to job performance and slightly to absence, although it is not clear that satisfaction is the cause of either. There is evidence that performance may be the cause of satisfaction. Job satisfaction has even been linked to employee health, but future research is needed to tell us specifically how job attitudes affect health.

Organizational commitment is another attitudinal variable that is popular among I/O researchers. Commitment concerns the employee's attachment to the organization. It correlates strongly with job satisfaction, but it is conceptually different. Three components of commitment have been identified as affective, continuance, and normative. Organizational commitment has many of the same correlates as job satisfaction, including job satisfaction, job performance, turnover, stress, and justice.

The experience of positive emotions by employees on the job can have positive effects on employees and organizations, whereas the experience of negative emotions can have the opposite effects. The requirement to engage in emotional labor can have positive effects on customers but negative effects on employees, particularly if they fake the emotions, have low levels of skill in emotion regulation, have low control, and get few rewards.

I/O PSYCHOLOGY IN PRACTICE

(*Courtesy Charles Michaels*)

This case is a job satisfaction project carried out by Dr. Charles E. Michaels. Dr. Michaels received his Ph.D. in industrial/organizational psychology in 1983 from the University of South Florida. He is currently an associate professor of management at the University of South Florida. As a professor he divides his time among teaching, research, and consulting for local and national organizations. Michaels is an expert in job satisfaction, and much of his consulting and research is in this area.

One consulting project was a job satisfaction survey done for a county fire department. What makes this project unusual is that Michaels was hired by the firefighters' union rather than by the management of the department. Although I/O psychologists generally work for management, occasionally they work for unions. Union representatives approached Michaels to conduct a satisfaction survey because there was considerable unrest among the union's members. The combination of a new fire chief and a two-year wage freeze had led to widespread dissatisfaction among the firefighters. The union representatives were hopeful that a study would provide an impetus for change on the part of management.

Michaels began this project by interviewing several groups of employees. From the interviews he was able to develop a satisfaction questionnaire appropriate to the issues of the organization. He surveyed all the firefighters using the questionnaire and found that satisfaction was quite low. In particular, there was dissatisfaction with both pay and communication. The results of the study were compiled into a report that was given to the union representatives. They used the report in a successful campaign for higher wages and improved communication. One year later Michaels repeated the survey and found that job satisfaction had significantly increased. Furthermore, the largest increases were in the facets of pay and communication satisfaction. This case illustrates that job satisfaction surveys can be used to improve the work conditions for employees.

Discussion Questions

1. What sorts of things would you expect to raise the job satisfaction of firefighters?

2. Do you think the results of this project would have been different if Michaels had been hired by management?

3. What effects would you expect if the city management had ignored the results of this study?

4. Can you think of another way Michaels could have assessed job satisfaction?

LEARNING BY DOING

Job Satisfaction Facets

Take the list of common job satisfaction facets on page 224. Ask at least five working people you know to indicate for each one whether they are satisfied or not on their current job. Then, for each facet, compute the percentage of people who said they are satisfied. How does the pattern of satisfaction match with Figure 9.1? Note that security is not shown in the figure. If this is done in class, you could combine data with other students.

Observing Emotional Labor

Go to a store or restaurant and observe the interaction between sales clerks or servers and customers. Watch five different employees as they interact with customers during the initial encounter. Record whether the employee expressed any form of emotion. A smile (or even a laugh)? Did the customer return the smile? Did the employee make physical contact—for example, shake hands or pat the customer's back? As an alternative, try this in two or more organizations and see whether there are differences in the behavior of employees toward customers.

10

Productive and Counterproductive Employee Behavior

On November 14, 1991, Thomas McIlvane, a former U.S. Postal Service employee, brought a rifle to the Royal Oak, Michigan, post office and opened fire on his coworkers. Four people were killed and four were wounded before he shot and killed himself as well. His reason was apparently anger over being fired for insubordination, and a subsequent investigation suggested that he had been treated poorly by supervisors. In reaction to this and similar incidents, the Postal Service has implemented an employee assistance program to offer counseling services to troubled employees. The program is designed to deal with emotional problems and involves clinical rather than I/O psychologists.

Although it has received the most media attention, the Postal Service is not the only organization in which such incidents of violence have occurred. Furthermore, most violence in the workplace has less dramatic results, and so the news media pay little attention. Fights among employees are not unusual events, and most go unreported to police. As we will see later in this chapter, employees sometimes assault one another as well as those they are supposed to serve as part of their jobs. Violence and other forms of counterproductive behavior, such as sabotage and theft, are a tremendous problem for organizations. The Postal Service and many other organizations have asked I/O psychologists to help reduce this kind of employee behavior.

Although violence at work is an important problem, two other behaviors have dominated the attention of I/O practitioners and researchers: employee withdrawal (absence and turnover) and job performance. Other important behaviors have received far less attention. In this chapter we discuss both productive and counterproductive behavior. Productive behavior includes job performance and organizational citizenship performance, such as helping coworkers. Counterproductive behaviors include aggression, sabotage, theft, and withdrawal.

Objectives: The student who studies this chapter should be able to:

▶ Discuss how environmental and personal characteristics impact job performance.
▶ Explain how the principles of human factors can be used to enhance job performance.
▶ Summarize the research on organizational citizenship performance.
▶ Summarize the research on the causes of employee withdrawal.
▶ Discuss how counterproductive behavior can result from environmental and personal factors.

▶ PRODUCTIVE BEHAVIOR: JOB PERFORMANCE

In order for an organization to achieve its purposes, individual employees must perform their jobs at some reasonable level of proficiency. This is as true for government organizations, in which poor performance means a failure to provide mandated public services, as it is for private companies, in which poor performance can mean bankruptcy. From a societal standpoint, it is in everyone's best interest for organizations to have employees who perform their jobs well. Good performance enhances organizational productivity, which directly enhances the goods and services provided to the public, as well as the national economy.

People can perform their jobs well only if they have both the necessary ability and the necessary motivation. Organizational practices and job conditions can enhance these personal characteristics or serve as constraints that interfere with job performance. These three factors—ability, motivation, and organizational constraints—are illustrated in Figure 10.1. The figure shows how ability and motivation lead to performance but can be blocked by constraints.

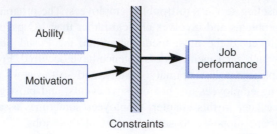

Figure 10.1 Good job performance requires both ability and motivation. Organizational constraints, such as inadequate training, can interfere with good performance.

Ability and Performance

Most selection efforts by I/O psychologists focus on identifying the necessary abilities and skills for specific jobs and finding people who have them. First, worker-oriented job analysis methods (as discussed in Chapter 3) are used to determine the necessary KSAOs (knowledge, skill, ability, and other personal characteristics) for a job. Once the KSAOs are identified, selection procedures are implemented to find individuals who have the appropriate characteristics. Although KSAOs deal with a variety of attributes, most selection devices (see Chapter 5) are designed to assess ability and skill. Finally, in addition to what employees bring with them, additional knowledge and skills can be developed through training. If an organization is to have a workforce with the necessary attributes for good job performance, all three steps must be followed: job analysis, selection, and training.

It has been well established that various measures of ability relate to job performance (see Chapters 5 and 6). As might be expected, the nature of the job determines the mix of specific abilities necessary. For example, Gutenberg, Arvey, Osburn, and Jeanneret (1983) showed that cognitive ability predicts performance for most jobs. The more mentally demanding the job, however, the stronger was the relation between cognitive ability and job performance. In other words, cognitive ability is more important for mentally demanding jobs (e.g., engineer) than for simple jobs (e.g., file clerk). Caldwell and O'Reilly (1990) demonstrated that matching people's abilities to the KSAO requirements from a job analysis can be a useful strategy for enhancing job performance. They also found that employees whose abilities matched their jobs were more satisfied. These results are consistent with the notion that job performance might lead to satisfaction (see Chapter 9). Employees who have the characteristics necessary for good performance will be more successful on the job and will be more satisfied.

Motivation and Performance

Motivation is an individual characteristic, but it can arise both from within the worker (e.g., personality) and from environmental conditions. Organizational attempts to enhance motivation in the workforce have focused more on environmental interventions than on individual selection. In theory, one might assess motivation in job applicants and hire those with the highest levels. I/O psychologists, however, have directed most of their selection attention to the assessment of ability rather than of motivation. Attempts to enhance motivation have been concerned primarily with the structure of jobs, with incentive systems, or with the design of technology, all of which are discussed in this chapter.

Personal Characteristics and Performance

Several employee characteristics are relevant to job performance and may affect ability to do the job. Others affect employee motivation to work hard (Tett & Burnett, 2003). In most cases, it is difficult to disentangle the effects of ability from the effects of motivation on job performance. For example, people with high levels of ability can also have high levels of motivation. As their ability leads to good performance and associated rewards, their motivation to perform may be enhanced. High-ability people may perform better because they are more skilled, because they put forth more effort, or both.

Cognitive ability (mathematical and verbal reasoning) has been found to predict job performance over a wide variety of jobs (e.g., Pearlman, Schmidt, & Hunter, 1980; Schmitt et al., 1984). In Chapters 3 and 5 we discussed how specific measures of ability are related to job performance, so ability will not be discussed again here. This chapter is concerned with the "Big Five" personality characteristics that many researchers believe represent the basic dimensions of human personality. We also discuss how locus of control and age relate to performance.

The Big Five and Performance

Many psychologists today believe that human personality can be described by five dimensions, called the **Big Five:** extraversion, emotional stability, agreeableness, conscientiousness, and openness to experience (Barrick & Mount, 1991). Table 10.1 presents a brief description of each dimension.

Several meta-analyses have summarized the relations between each of the five dimensions and job performance. The studies by Hurtz and Donovan (2000) and by Salgado (2003) concluded that personality is associated with job performance, with conscientiousness being the best predictor. Furthermore, Hurtz and Donovan (2000) discovered that certain personality dimensions were correlated more strongly with performance for some jobs than others. Although mean correlations were not large, these studies provide evidence that personality is an important factor for job performance across different kinds of jobs. However, even stronger correlations can be found by closely matching specific personality traits to a specific job and task (Hogan & Holland, 2003; Tett, Steele, & Beauregard, 2003). For example, one might expect that emotional stability would predict performance in a job that requires the ability to handle stress, such as police officer.

TABLE 10.1   Description of the Big Five Dimensions of Personality

Dimension	Description
Extraversion	Sociable, gregarious, assertive, and talkative
Emotional stability	Anxious, depressed, angry, worried, insecure
Agreeableness	Courteous, flexible, good-natured, cooperative
Conscientiousness	Dependable, responsible, hardworking, achievement oriented
Openness to experience	Imaginative, curious, broad-minded, intelligent

Source: "The Big Five Personality Dimensions and Job Performance: A Meta-Analysis," by M. R. Barrick and M. K. Mount, 1991, *Personnel Psychology*, *44*, 1–26.

Locus of Control and Performance

Locus of control concerns people's beliefs about their ability to control reinforcements in their environment (see Chapter 9). Research has shown that *internals*, those who believe they can control reinforcements, have higher levels of job motivation than *externals*, those who do not believe they can control reinforcements (Spector, 1982). Although greater motivation might be expected to result in better job performance in general, the effects of motivation can be more complex. Blau (1993b) studied how locus of control related to two different job performance aspects of bank tellers (see Research in Detail). Blau noted that internals have been shown to have higher levels of work motivation, which should lead them to display more initiative on the job. Externals, on the other hand, have been shown to be more conforming and would be expected to respond better to highly structured tasks that allow for little personal initiative. This is exactly what he found. Internals performed better in developing important job skills, whereas externals performed better on the routine clerical tasks that were highly structured. Blau's study suggests that relations between personality and job performance can depend on the particular dimension of performance.

RESEARCH IN DETAIL

Most of the research on job performance has failed to consider that different aspects of performance might be influenced by different factors. Blau's (1993b) study is an exception in that it looked at the relation of locus of control with three different measures of performance. Blau hypothesized that internals would do better in some areas of performance, but externals would do better in others. Specifically, internals would perform better at tasks requiring independence and initiative. Externals would perform better at tasks that required compliance to rules and supervisory directives.

Subjects for this study were 146 bank tellers. Locus of control in the work domain and three performance measures (productivity, dollar shortages, and self-development) were assessed. Productivity was an objective measure of the volume of work processed by each teller, and it represents a highly structured part of the job. Dollar shortage was an objective measure of accuracy in accounting, which is also a highly structured part of the job. Self-development, assessed by supervisors, was the extent to which employees enhanced their skills through their own initiative and independent action.

As Blau predicted, the correlations with locus of control differed across the different performance measures. The correlations were .27, .05, and −.30 for productivity, dollar shortages, and self-development, respectively. Externals performed significantly better than internals in productivity, but internals performed significantly better in self-development. The correlation between locus of control and dollar shortages was not significant. The correlation between productivity and self-development was negative, suggesting that the employees who had the highest levels of productivity had the lowest levels of self-development.

These results suggest that different people can do well at different aspects of the same job. The tellers who were the most productive were the poorest at self-development. Perhaps this shows that individuals differed in how much time and effort they put into different aspects of the job. Externals may have focused on the day-to-day requirements for productivity. Internals, on the other hand, put effort into learning new tasks, perhaps with the personal objective of receiving future promotions. This study emphasizes that job performance can be quite complex. Organizations should recognize that there can be more than one way to be a productive employee.

Source: Blau, G. (1993). Testing the relationship of locus of control to different performance dimensions. *Journal of Occupational and Organizational Psychology*, 66, 125–138.

Age and Performance

Many people would undoubtedly predict that job performance declines with age. The stereotype of the nonproductive older worker probably has roots in the fact that many physical abilities decline with age. For example, professional athletes almost always retire before they reach 40 years of age. Research has shown that the stereotype is incorrect, however. Older workers in many jobs are as productive as their younger coworkers.

Sturman (2003) conducted a meta-analysis of 115 studies relating age to job performance. Rather than job performance declining with age, his study found no relationship. The performance of older workers is no worse than that of younger colleagues. Although some abilities might decline with age, other skills and a level of job wisdom that leads to greater efficiency may increase with experience (Warr, 2001). What older workers lack in physical ability they may more than compensate for by better task strategies, better management of time, and more efficient approaches. The physical demands of the majority of jobs are well within the ability range of most older workers, unless they are in poor health. Of course, poor health can adversely affect the job performance of even the youngest workers.

Environmental Conditions and Job Performance

The job environment can affect job performance in many ways. The environment can have a positive or negative influence on employee motivation, leading to an increase or decrease in employee efforts. Similarly, the environment can be structured to facilitate performance by making it easier for individuals to accomplish their jobs, or it can contain constraints that interfere with performance. One study showed that something as simple as allowing employees to listen to music over stereo headsets improved job performance, apparently by reducing tension (Oldham, Cummings, Mischel, Schmidtke, & Zhou, 1995). In this chapter we will look at the somewhat more complex factors of job characteristics, incentive systems, technology design, and organizational constraints.

Job Characteristics and Performance

One of the most influential of the theories that relate the nature of jobs to performance is Hackman and Oldham's job characteristics theory (Hackman & Oldham, 1976, 1980). This theory is based on the assumption that people can be motivated by the intrinsic nature of job tasks. When work is interesting and enjoyable, people will like their jobs (as discussed in Chapter 9), be highly motivated, and perform well.

Job characteristics theory is illustrated in Figure 10.2. This theory states that features of jobs induce psychological states that lead to satisfaction, motivation, and job performance. The job features, or core characteristics (described in Table 9.7), lead to three psychological states. Skill variety, task identity, and task significance lead to experienced meaningfulness of work; autonomy leads to feelings of responsibility; and feedback leads to knowledge of results. These three states are critical to the satisfaction and motivation of employees. When jobs induce them, individuals will be motivated and satisfied and will perform better.

The levels of the core characteristics determine how motivating a job is likely to be. Hackman and Oldham (1976) noted that the **Motivation Potential Score (MPS)** of

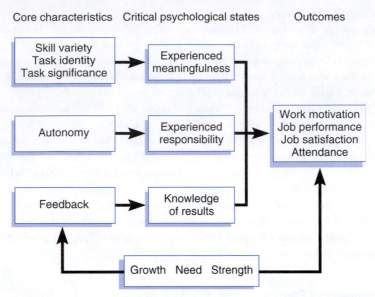

Figure 10.2 Hackman and Oldham's (1976) job characteristics model.
Source: "Motivation Through the Design of Work: Test of a Theory," by J. R. Hackman and G. R. Oldham, 1976, *Organizational Behavior and Human Performance*, 16, 250–279.

a job can be calculated by combining scores on the core characteristics. Specifically, the following formula is used:

$$MPS = (Skill\ Variety + Task\ Significance + Task\ Identity)/3 \times Autonomy \times Feedback$$

Note that the three characteristics leading to experienced meaningfulness are averaged. The average is multiplied by autonomy and feedback, which lead to experienced responsibility and knowledge of results, respectively. The multiplicative nature of the formula implies that a job cannot be motivating if it leads to low levels of even one of the three psychological states. If one of the three multiplied terms equals zero, the MPS will be zero.

There is one last piece of the theory: the moderator effect of growth need strength (GNS). As noted in Chapter 9, GNS is a personality variable that concerns the need for fulfillment of higher order needs, such as personal growth, autonomy, or achievement. According to Hackman and Oldham (1976), the connection from job characteristics to psychological states to outcomes holds mainly for individuals who are high on GNS. This means that this is a person/job fit theory, in which only certain types of people will respond well to high MPS jobs. Hackman and Oldham had little to say about low GNS people and what might motivate them.

Studies that use employee self-reports as measures of the core characteristics have supported their relation with motivation and performance (Fried & Ferris, 1987), as well as the moderating effect of GNS (Loher et al., 1985). Research using other methods has been more equivocal. Although studies can be found demonstrating that changing or redesigning jobs to be higher in MPS result in better job performance, other studies show no effect from job redesign. An interesting longitudinal study by Griffin (1991)

(*DILBERT reprinted with permission of United Feature Syndicate.*)

showed that the effects of job redesign were a temporary increase in job satisfaction and a delayed increase in job performance. These results suggest that the connection among job conditions, satisfaction, and performance is more complex than the job characteristics theory would lead us to expect.

Incentive Systems and Performance

Incentive systems that reward employees for each unit of work performed are a possible way of increasing job performance, at least performance quantity (see Chapter 8's discussion of reinforcement theory). Such systems are common with salespeople who receive commissions and with factory workers who are on **piece-rate systems** that pay them for each unit of production. Incentive systems work through motivation by rewarding employees for behavior beneficial to the organization. Most such systems reward job performance, although examples can be found that reward employees for other behaviors, such as attendance.

Although incentive systems can increase productivity, they have not been universally successful. Yukl and Latham (1975), for example, found that a piece-rate system increased the productivity of only two of three groups with which it was implemented. In their classic study of factory workers, Coch and French (1948) documented how peer pressure within work groups could undermine the effects of a piece-rate system. The productivity of one factory worker was cut in half by pressure from coworkers.

In order for an incentive system to be effective, three elements must be in place. First, the employees must have the ability to increase productivity. If they are working at the limit of their capability, introducing an incentive system will not improve performance. Second, employees must want the incentives. Not everyone is willing to work harder for money or other rewards. For an incentive system to work, the incentive must be something that people want. Finally, an incentive system will not work if there are physical or psychological constraints on performance. A salesperson in a store cannot sell if there are no customers. Figure 10.3 shows how the three elements combine to determine the effectiveness of an incentive system.

Design of Technology

The Hawthorne studies showed that social factors can be more important than the physical environment in job performance. There is no doubt, however, that the physical

Figure 10.3 Incentives can lead to improved performance if employees are able to perform better, if they want the incentives, and if there are few constraints.

features of job settings can affect performance. The field of **human factors** (also called **ergonomics** or **engineering psychology**) is concerned with the interface between people and the physical environment, including tools, equipment, and technology. Human factors psychologists are involved in the design of the physical environment to make jobs safer and easier to accomplish. Through their work over the past few decades, human factors psychologists have developed sound design principles and procedures. The influence of the field can be found in the design of everything from automobiles and consumer appliances to military aircraft and nuclear power plants.

Displays and Controls

The major focus of human factors is on the interaction between people and tools, machines, or technology. Two major areas of concern are the presentation of information and the manipulation of tools or machines.

Drivers of automobiles must be given information about speed. They also must control the speed and direction of the vehicle. Human factors principles tell engineers how best to present information and design controls.

A machine can provide information in many ways. The nature and use of the information determine how it should best be presented. Most machine information is provided either visually or through the auditory channel, or sometimes both. For danger or warning signals, such as at a railroad crossing, it is best to use both, such as a bell and flashing lights.

With machines most information is provided in a visual display. Two different types of visual displays for quantitative information (airplane altitude) are shown in Figure 10.4. The upper display in the figure is a two-point style that resembles a traditional clock, with the shorter and heavier hand representing altitude in thousands of feet and the longer and thinner hand representing hundreds of feet. The lower display is a digital display that indicates the altitude by showing the numerals. Obviously, in an airplane there is a need to be able to determine altitude both quickly and accurately, because errors can lead to disaster. The digital display is superior to the two-point because it is easy to mix up the two hands (Buck, 1983). For example, 2,100 feet can be misread as 1,200 feet, which could present a problem for anyone attempting to fly over a 2,000-foot-high mountain.

The manipulation of a machine by a person, often in response to information provided by a display, is accomplished through controls. The design of the best control

Figure 10.4   Types of altitude displays for an aircraft.
Source: "Control and Tools" (p. 214) by J. R. Buck, 1983, in B. H. Kantowitz
and R. D. Sorkin (eds.), *Human Factors*, New York: John Wiley.

is determined by the machine's purpose and situation. Most controls are worked with
either the hand or the foot, although other possibilities can be found (e.g., knee or elbow).
Hand controls are best when fine or precise motions are necessary, such as for steering
an automobile. Foot controls are best when force is more important than precision, as
with a brake pedal for an automobile.

There are a number of important design considerations pertaining to controls. First,
they should be located in a logical place, with controls for the same function together. A
well-designed automobile console, for example, will place the lighting controls together,
the windshield wiper and washer controls together, the heater and air conditioner controls
together, and so on. A control to work a front window should be in front of a control to
work a back window, and a control to work a feature on the right side of the car should
be to the right of a control to work the same feature on the left side.

Second, vital controls that can produce important consequences should be recog-
nizable by touch. This is not important for the volume control on a car radio, but it is
vital for the landing gear on an airplane. Figure 10.5 illustrates several different knobs
for stick-type levers, such as the shift lever of an automobile. Each of these can be
discriminated by touch alone. Knobs such as these are used in airplanes.

Third, controls should provide appropriate feedback so that the person knows that
the function has been accomplished. With an on/off switch, one might hear a click and
feel a tactile sensation indicating that the switch has been activated or deactivated. Some
switches use springs, so that the switch lever can only be in the on or off position, and
one can feel the lever lock into place. Finally, the directions in which controls are moved
should logically match the directions in which the machine will move. For example,
an increase in some factor should involve moving a switch either clockwise, up, or to
the right, as opposed to counterclockwise, down, or to the left. This is the general rule
followed with most equipment with volume controls, such as radios and televisions.
Levers to move a device to the right should move clockwise or to the right, as in most
vehicles.

Computer-Human Interaction

The principles of displays and controls outlined above have been available for many years,
so there is not much need to conduct research on them today. Instead human factors psychologists have turned their attention to computer-human interaction. *Computer-human
interaction* is the interplay of people with computers and associated technologies that

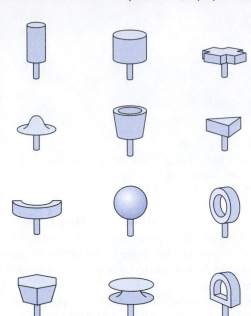

Figure 10.5 Examples of shift knobs that can be discriminated by touch alone.
Source: *Human Factors: Understanding People-System Relationships* (p. 311), by B. H. Kantowitz and R. D. Sorkin, 1983, New York: John Wiley.

have led to tremendous changes in the workplace for both blue- and white-collar work. Although automation and computerization have in some cases replaced people, computers have become common and necessary parts of many jobs.

A major issue for computer-human interaction is communication between human and machine. That is, what is the best way for computers to provide information to people, and what is the best way for people to tell computers what they wish done? In order for people to communicate effectively with computers, they must develop a conceptual understanding, or **mental model**, of how the computer operates (Frese, 1987). A person who knows how to drive an automobile, for example, has a mental model of how the operation of the controls results in the appropriate movement of the vehicle.

Frese (1987) noted that efficient use of computers arises from two essential elements: training and appropriate system design. Training is necessary because in many jobs people are hired without all the necessary skills for the computer system they must use. Even when they do have the necessary skills, computer systems and software are constantly changing, requiring a continued training effort to maintain proficiency. Research on computer training has suggested ways in which it can enhance performance. Augustine and Coovert (1991), for example, have shown that the use of animated models can be quite effective in enhancing performance of computer tasks. Animated models show the computer system in action rather than give a written description or instructions. This approach is similar to the demonstration portion of a video game (e.g., Nintendo Wii or Sony Play Station 3) that shows the game in action.

System design is essential because many existing systems are poorly designed and inefficient. Research on computer-human interaction has provided many insights about how best to design systems that people can learn and use efficiently. Coovert (1990) argues that the best systems represent problems in a way that matches how people who use them represent problems. Systems that require users to adopt new ways of looking at familiar problems are difficult to learn.

Personal computers are designed with the user in mind. When you interact with the computer, different elements are represented on the screen with small pictures or icons that indicate what they are. The icon that represents a function or program typically has meaning that makes it easy to remember what it controls. To delete a file, for example, you place its icon on an icon that looks like a trash can. Figure 10.6 is a picture of a an Apple Macintosh screen that shows these icons. The Macintosh system is easier to learn than alternatives that rely on written commands, such as to delete a file by typing the command "DELETE" followed by the name of the file. Text-based systems of this kind are rarely used today.

So far we have discussed the interaction of individual users with technology, but technology can also be used to facilitate collaboration among employees working together. **Computer supported cooperative work**, or CSCW, is the study of how technology can be used to help people work together on tasks (Coovert & Thompson, 2001). Computer-based technologies that make use of the Internet allow people in remote locations to send almost instantaneous messages (e-mail) or see and hear one another (videoconferencing). People can work in virtual teams that "meet" only electronically. Research on the effects and effectiveness of such technologies as compared to live communication is new, but already we know that there are differences. For example,

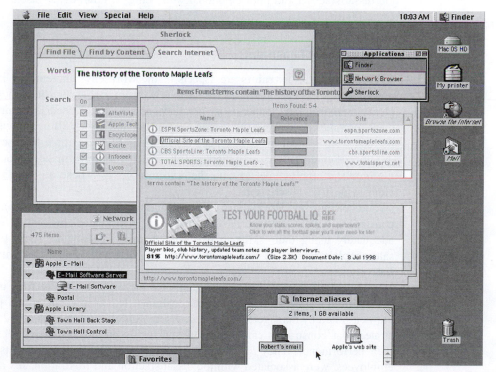

Figure 10.6 An Apple Macintosh screen. Picture courtesy of Apple Corporation. (*Courtesy Apple Corporation*)

people working together via e-mail, as compared to live interaction, are less inhibited (are more likely to make hostile comments and insult one another), will be less likely to conform to one another's opinions, will have more trouble reaching decisions, and will have more trouble coordinating their efforts (Coovert & Thompson, 2001). Research needs to be done in this area to figure out how to overcome these problems, either by better design of the technology or by better training of people to be more effective users of CSCW.

The principles of human factors can be used to design tools and equipment so that people can perform their tasks more easily and efficiently. Whether this will translate into better overall job performance depends on many other factors. If employees are not motivated to perform well, making their job tasks easier through better equipment design might mean that they do the same work with less effort. Furthermore, constraints in the work environment, which we discuss next, may prevent better performance even if certain tasks can be accomplished more efficiently.

From a human factors perspective, the goal is to design technology that will be helpful to people. However, technology can come with a price, and not all effects are positive. The introduction of computers in manufacturing has changed jobs, but not always for the better. Although new factory systems might be more efficient, they can increase employee boredom and stress (Wall & Davids, 1992). Often the worker who used to be an active participant on the assembly line is relegated to passively watching a machine operate. The loss of control over tasks to the machine can be associated with job dissatisfaction and poor emotional well-being (Mullarkey, Jackson, Wall, Wilson, & Grey-Taylor, 1997).

Organizational Constraints

Organizational constraints are aspects of the work environment that interfere with or prevent good job performance. They can arise from any aspect of the job, including the physical environment; supervisory practices, and a lack of needed training, tools, equipment, or time. Peters and O'Connor (1980) outlined eight different areas of constraints derived from critical incidents. They asked 62 employed people to describe an incident in which something at work interfered with their job performance. From an analysis of the incidents, they came up with the constraint areas. These are shown in Table 10.2, along with brief descriptions.

According to Hochwarter, Witt, Treadway, and Ferris (2006), organizational constraints have a detrimental effect on job performance, preventing employees from adequately using their skills to perform job tasks. Klein and Kim (1998) found that salespeople's reports of constraints were correlated with their actual sales performance. Individuals who scored highest on constraints sold the smallest amounts. Tesluk and Mathieu (1999) reported similar findings for the performance of road maintenance and construction crews. Higher levels of constraints led to lower levels of performance for crews as rated by managers. O'Connor, Peters, Rudolf, and Pooyan (1982) further demonstrated that constraints can be detrimental to the employees themselves, as well as to their performance. They found that high levels of situational constraints, as reported by employees, were associated with job dissatisfaction and frustration. Jex and Gudanowski (1992) found similar results, as well as a tendency for employees reporting high levels of constraints to be more likely to intend to quit their jobs. Intentions have been shown

TABLE 10.2   Eight Organizational Constraint Areas

Job-related information: data and information needed for the job.

Tools and equipment: tools, equipment, instruments, and machinery necessary for the job, such as computers or trucks.

Materials and supplies: materials and supplies necessary for the job, such as lumber or paper.

Budgetary support: money necessary to acquire resources to do the job.

Required services and help from others: help available from other people.

Task preparation: whether or not the employee has the KSAOs necessary for the job.

Time availability: amount of time available for doing job tasks.

Work environment: The physical features of the job environment, such as buildings or weather.

Source: "Situational Constraints and Work Outcomes: The Influence of a Frequently Overlooked Construct," by L. H. Peters and E. J. O'Connor, 1980, *Academy of Management Review*, *5*, 391–397.

to be an important precursor of turnover (Griffeth, Hom, & Gaertner, 2000). Thus, it seems that organizational constraints can have detrimental effects not only on job performance but on employee satisfaction, frustration, and possibly turnover as well. This conclusion must be tempered by the fact that most constraint studies have relied entirely on employee self-reports for their data. Studies using other methods will be necessary to determine the importance of the job environment itself rather than people's perceptions.

▶ ORGANIZATIONAL CITIZENSHIP BEHAVIOR OCB

Organizational citizenship behavior (OCB) is behavior that goes beyond the core task requirements of the job (tasks listed in a job description) and is beneficial to the organization. OCB is usually assessed by having supervisors rate their subordinates on OCB behaviors. Sample items from the popular Smith, Organ, and Near (1983) OCB scale are shown in Table 10.3. Note that although some of these items fit the definition of going beyond requirements (e.g., makes suggestions), others do not (e.g., being punctual).

Organ and Konovsky (1989) divided OCB into two categories of behaviors: those that are specifically required and those that are not. *Altruism* is helping another employee or a supervisor with a problem even though it is not required. It might involve helping a coworker who has been absent or making suggestions to improve conditions. *Compliance* is doing what needs to be done and following rules, such as coming to work on time and not wasting time.

OCB can be an important aspect of an employee's behavior that contributes to overall organizational effectiveness. Individuals who are high on OCB are not necessarily

TABLE 10.3   Four Items from the Organizational Citizenship Behavior Scale

Assists supervisor with his or her work

Makes innovative suggestions to improve department

Punctuality

Gives advance notice if unable to come to work

Source: "Cognitive Versus Affective Determinants of Organizational Citizenship Behavior," by D. W. Organ and M. Konovsky, 1989, *Journal of Applied Psychology*, *74*, 157–164.

the best performers in other areas, however. MacKenzie, Podsakoff, and Fetter (1991) assessed the OCB and objective sales performance of salespeople. They found little relation between the two types of behavior. Employees who had the best sales records were no different from those with the poorest in terms of their OCB. In some cases, salespeople who performed poorly in sales may have made significant contributions to the organization through their OCB. Evidence exists that this does occur. Podsakoff, Ahearne, and MacKenzie (1997) studied 40 work crews in a paper mill, assessing the OCBs of individual members in relation to the crew's overall performance rather than individual employee performance. Results showed that higher levels of OCB among crew members were associated with higher total crew productivity and fewer defects.

Several factors have been suggested as the cause of organizational citizenship behavior. Meta-analyses of OCB studies by Hoffman, Blair, Meriac, and Woehr (2007) and Podsakoff, MacKenzie, Paine, and Bachrach (2000) suggest that OCB is most likely when employees are satisfied with their jobs, have high levels of affective commitment, feel they are treated fairly, and have good relations with their supervisors. In addition OCB may be contagious—people who work in groups where others tend to perform OCB are likely to perform it themselves (Bommer, Miles, & Grover, 2003). Some of these results have been shown to hold in other countries as well. Farh, Podsakoff, and Organ (1990) found that OCB correlated with job satisfaction and employee perceptions of supportive supervisor behavior in Taiwan. Munene (1995) found that OCB related to job satisfaction and organizational commitment in Nigeria (see International Replication).

INTERNATIONAL REPLICATION

Organizational citizenship behavior (OCB) is vitally important to organizational functioning. Determining the causes of such behavior and how it can be encouraged has been the topic of much research.

Munene (1995) conducted a study to determine whether findings concerning OCB in the United States and other Western countries would hold for the African country of Nigeria. He noted a common phenomenon in Nigerian companies called "not on seat," which refers to tardiness and lack of effort, which is the opposite of OCB. Munene conducted a survey of 268 Nigerian employees of several organizations. Each employee completed a questionnaire containing scales of affective commitment, job satisfaction, salary level, and trust in the organization. The supervisor of each participant in the study completed a measure of OCB, focusing on the compliance aspects, such as seeking and accepting responsibility, being at work on time, getting a lot done, and not taking time off without asking in advance.

OCB was found to be significantly correlated with both attitudinal variables: affective commitment (.51) and job satisfaction (.30). There was a small significant correlation with salary level, with those making higher salaries engaging in more OCB. Finally, there was a significant correlation with trust (.39), with those trusting the organization to treat them well exhibiting more OCB. These results were consistent with the results found in the United States and the West. They suggest that OCB may be a universal phenomenon, and that at least some of its causes might be universal. In other words, employees who feel well treated and have positive job attitudes, such as job satisfaction and organizational commitment, are likely to respond with OCB.

Source: Munene, J. C. (1995). 'Not-on-seat': An investigation of some correlated of organisational citizenship behaviour in Nigeria. *Applied Psychology: An International Review*, *44*, 111–122.

McNeely and Meglino (1994) divided OCB into acts that helped other employees (OCBI) and acts that benefited the organization (OCBO). They found that different types of OCB were related to different variables. For example, OCBI correlated with the individual's concern for others, whereas OCBO correlated with the employee's perceived equity, and both correlated with job satisfaction. Similarly, organizational commitment has been linked to both types of OCB; it is more strongly related to OCBI in the United States (Johnson & Chang, 2006), but more strongly related to OCBO in Turkey (Wasti, 2006). Lee and Allen (2002) reported that both OCBI and OCBO related to positive mood at work, but only OCBO related to procedural justice. The results of all these studies suggest that the two types of OCB have different combinations of causes, some shared and some unique.

Although OCB is often thought of as altruistic acts that individuals do for selfless reasons, recent research suggests that in at least some instances, OCB can be a strategy for getting ahead at work. Hui, Lam, and Law (2000), in a study conducted among tellers in a multinational bank, assessed level of OCBs before and after promotions were received. In addition, before promotion employees were asked if they believed engaging in OCB would improve chances of promotion. For those who thought it would, OCB levels were high before promotion, and declined after promotion, suggesting that these employees increased their OCBs as a tactic for seeking a desired promotion, but then reduced OCBs once their goal had been achieved.

▶ COUNTERPRODUCTIVE BEHAVIOR: WITHDRAWAL

On any given day in almost any large organization, some employees will come to work late, some will miss the entire workday, and some will quit the job permanently. All of these *withdrawal* behaviors involve employees not being at work when scheduled or needed, either temporarily, as in tardiness and absence, or permanently, as in turnover. Most of the research on withdrawal behaviors considers them to be related phenomena. As noted by Mitra, Jenkins, and Gupta (1992), some researchers consider absence and turnover to be alternative reactions to job dissatisfaction. Both may reflect attempts by employees to escape, either temporarily or permanently, from situations they find unpleasant.

In their meta-analysis, Mitra et al. (1992) found that absence and turnover were moderately correlated. In other words, employees who quit the job were likely to have had relatively high levels of absence before they quit. In a similar meta-analysis Koslowsky, Sagie, Krausz, and Singer (1997) found that lateness (not getting to work on time) correlated with both absence and turnover. Late people are often absent people and are likely to quit. Although correlations among withdrawal measures might mean that they have similar causes, other explanations are possible. For example, individuals who plan to quit their jobs may use up their sick leave rather than forfeit it upon leaving, and may be absent and late to engage in job hunting.

Absence

Absence, employees not showing up for work when scheduled, can be a major problem for organizations. Many jobs require someone's presence even when the scheduled person is not there. Absence requires that organizations either overstaff, so that enough people will be available each day, or have substitutes on call. The idea of substitutes for teachers is undoubtedly familiar to most readers of this book. Similarly, many organizations, especially factories, have substitutes available for other types of work. Often the on-call substitutes are other employees who are asked to work an extra shift to fill in, frequently at higher overtime salary rates.

The major approach to understanding why absence occurs focuses on withdrawal as a response to dissatisfying jobs and job conditions. Absence and job satisfaction are related, but research has found quite small correlations between them. Farrell and Stamm (1988) conducted a meta-analysis of 72 absence studies and noted that the two best predictors were prior absence history and the organization's absence policy rather than job satisfaction. People who were frequently absent in the past are likely to be absent in the future. Organizations that have policies designed to control absence by either rewarding attendance or punishing absence have less absence.

One complication in the study of absence is that it is a complex variable that can arise from many causes, including illness, lack of motivation to go to work, and family responsibilities. Goff, Mount, and Jamison (1990) found that having primary responsibility for child care predicted absence with a correlation considerably higher than that typically found with job satisfaction. Erickson, Nichols, and Ritter (2000) found that absence was associated with the number of children under six years old. In a study conducted in Finland, absence rates were highest for young women of child-bearing age (Elovainio, Kivimäki, Vahtera, Virtanen, and Keltikangas-Järvinen, 2003). Taken together, these studies support the idea that absence can be caused by having to take care of children, a form of work-family conflict (see Chapter 11) that occurs regardless of whether the employee likes the job.

Dalton and Mesch (1991) asked subjects to classify their absences into one of two categories: due to illness or due to other circumstances. They found that the two types of absence had different correlates. Absence due to illness, but not due to other circumstances, was related to job satisfaction and gender. The dissatisfied and women were ill more frequently. Absence due to other circumstances was related to job tenure and absence policy. Organizations with longer tenured employees and less restrictive policies had more absence. These results suggest that the different types of absences have different causes that might be reduced with different procedures.

Nicholson and Johns (1985) have taken a different approach to the explanation of absence. They note that absence can be caused by the absence culture of a work group or organization. That is, in any work group or organization there will generally be accepted social rules governing the appropriate amount and reasons for absence. One organization might have a culture that encourages absence whenever an employee does not feel like coming to work. Another might encourage employees to come to work unless it is absolutely impossible for them to do so.

Research evidence supports the idea of an absence culture in organizations. Harrison and Shaffer (1993) found that employee absence was significantly correlated with employee estimates of their work group's level of acceptable numbers of absences. On average, employees were absent less than what they perceived the acceptable level to be. Mathieu and Kohler (1990) found that work group absence predicted individual absence. Employees whose coworkers were absent frequently were absent more often than employees whose coworkers were seldom absent.

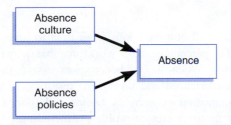

Figure 10.7 The absence culture of the work group and organizational absence policies all contribute to employee absence.

Figure 10.7 illustrates that absence culture and absence policies are the two biggest factors in absence. Although job satisfaction has been the focus of most absence research, it seems that its potential effects are overshadowed by culture and policies. A dissatisfied individual who might want to escape work by calling in sick is not likely to do so if absence is punished or is viewed by coworkers as unacceptable. Organizations can reduce absence by changing policies to encourage attendance and discourage absence. A simple procedure found in one study was merely to mail each employee a letter indicating the number of days he or she had been absent (Gaudine & Saks, 2001). Just knowing that management was concerned about absence was enough to convince employees to reduce it.

Lateness

For many jobs, employees are on fixed work schedules but often employees will fail to get to work on time. Some employees might be able to make up the time, either by skipping breaks, taking a short lunch, or staying late. Often, however, they fail to make up the time, or the time cannot be made up; for example, if a teacher is late for class, the time can't be rescheduled. Lateness produces costs for organizations that call in substitutes and can put an unfair burden on coworkers who have to take up the slack.

Lateness, like absence, can have many causes. Koslowsky (2000) notes that although attitudes, such as job dissatisfaction, have been linked to lateness, other important causes are commuting distance and ease, and work-family conflict. People who have long commutes can get stuck in traffic. Individuals with children may be late because a child is sick and must be taken to the doctor. Another important factor is culture. Promptness is considered more important in some countries than in others; for example, Americans value it more than Brazilians do. Organizations also have their own lateness cultures, just as they have absence cultures.

Foust, Elicker, and Levy (2006) argued that attitudes about lateness are more important determinants of lateness behavior than other, more general job attitudes. They developed a lateness attitude scale that asked employees about both their own behavior (feeling guilty for being late) and their coworkers' behavior (being let down when coworkers are late). The new scale was administered as part of a survey of employees. It was a better predictor of lateness than either job satisfaction or organizational commitment. Finally, Iverson and Deery (2001) investigated both lateness and leaving early from work, and found them to be related. Coming late and leaving early were associated with perceptions of injustice (see Chapter 8) and job dissatisfaction.

Turnover

In every organization employees will quit their jobs from time to time. The quitting of employees is called **turnover**. The percentage of the workforce that quits in a given period of time is called the *turnover rate*. When the rate becomes excessive, the organization's workforce can become too inexperienced and untrained, resulting in inefficiency and difficulties in achieving the organization's objectives. Dalton and Todor (1993) discussed factors that determine whether turnover creates problems, including performance level of quitters and replacement costs.

Turnover is not a problem if the quitters are people who perform poorly. Trevor, Gerhart, and Boudreau (1997) studied the relation between job performance and turnover. They found a curvilinear relation in that the best and worst employees were most likely to quit. Turnover can have beneficial results if better replacements can be found for poor performers. However, good performers might also quit, because often the best people are those who are the most attractive to other organizations. For the best performers, good salary raises reduced turnover.

Poor performers will quit for several reasons. When pay and other rewards are contingent on performance, they may quit because rewards are low (Williams, 1999). Furthermore, if they know they are not doing well on the job, they may attempt to find jobs for which they are better suited. Alternatively, it is not uncommon for supervisors to "encourage" turnover by targeting individuals for harassment. Poor performers might be denied rewards, be given distasteful work assignments, and be treated unkindly in order to get them to quit.

Serious difficulties can arise from this approach to creating turnover and can produce more problems than it solves. It can affect employees who are not the intended target. The harassment of one employee can create a hostile and uncomfortable work environment for everyone. Legal ramifications are also possible, for harassed employees might file lawsuits. If the supervisor and target of harassment are of a different gender or from different ethnic backgrounds, a discrimination case might be filed. Finally, harassment is an unethical behavior, and even poorly performing employees should be dealt with in a fair and honest manner.

The second issue that determines the costs of turnover to organizations concerns the expense involved in replacing people who have quit. For some jobs, recruiting and hiring can be costly and time consuming. Hiring high-level executives can take months of searching for applicants, conducting extensive and expensive out-of-town interviews, and offering expensive bonuses and benefits. For other jobs, a long period of training before an employee is able to be fully productive might be required. In the armed services, it can take more than a year to fully train a fighter pilot. If there is a high level of pilot turnover, the cost to the government will be great.

Job satisfaction is a central variable in the research on turnover (Griffeth et al., 2000). Figure 10.8 illustrates how the turnover process is thought to work. It shows that job satisfaction leads to intention to quit, which leads to turnover. Furthermore, the relation between intention to quit and turnover is moderated by the unemployment rate. People who are dissatisfied with their jobs are likely to intend to quit them. Intentions are often precursors to behavior that leads to quitting. It is unlikely, however, that people will quit their jobs unless they have another job available. As shown in the model, the

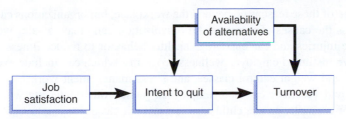

Figure 10.8 Employee turnover as a function of job satisfaction and unemployment rate.

unemployment rate, which reflects the availability of alternative employment, affects whether dissatisfaction and intentions are translated into turnover.

There is good support for the propositions in this model. First, job satisfaction and intention of quitting correlate with one another (Allen, Weeks, & Moffitt, 2005; Breukelen, Van Der Vlist, & Steensma, 2004), which is consistent with the idea that satisfaction leads to intention. Second, Blau (1993a) found that both job satisfaction and intention of quitting correlated with job search behaviors, such as applying for another job and going on a job interview. Third, Griffeth et al. (2000) found in their meta-analysis that both job satisfaction and intention to quit predict future turnover, with satisfaction having a smaller magnitude of correlation ($r = -.17$) than intention ($r = .35$). The predictive nature of these studies supports the idea that job satisfaction and intention are precursors of turnover. Finally, studies have shown that the unemployment rate moderates the relation between job satisfaction and turnover and between intention and turnover (Trevor, 2001). These studies show that when the unemployment rate is low and alternative job opportunities are plentiful, there is a strong relation of satisfaction and intention with turnover. When the unemployment rate is high and alternative job opportunities are scarce, however, there is little predictability of turnover by intention and job satisfaction. In other words, dissatisfied people may wish to quit their jobs, but they can only do so when alternative employment is available.

Dickter et al. (1996) tracked, over several years, the quitting of individuals who either liked or disliked their jobs. For both groups, likelihood of turnover increased from the time of hiring until about two years on the job, after which it declined. Dissatisfied individuals were more likely to quit than their satisfied counterparts until about four years on the job. After four years differences disappeared. Apparently, the effects of job satisfaction on turnover are time limited, as perhaps those who dislike their jobs and wish to quit eventually give up and make the best of the situation.

Although many employees quit their jobs because they are unhappy with them, there are other reasons for turnover (Maertz & Griffeth, 2004). First, a person might quit for health reasons. Heart attack survivors will often make drastic changes in their lifestyles, which can include quitting their jobs. Second, becoming disabled due to an accident may prevent an employee from continuing to perform essential tasks on the job. As noted in Chapter 11, motor vehicle accidents can be a common source of serious injury on the job. Third, people will sometimes quit jobs they like to pursue other life interests. These might include child rearing, continuing their education, or training for athletic pursuits, such as the Olympics. Fourth, people might quit because of family problems, such as the illness of a family member or divorce. Finally, people might quit because their spouse has been offered a better job in another location.

Some of these reasons go beyond the workplace, but organizations can do a great deal to address the causes of turnover. An organization can create a safer work environment to reduce injuries and can encourage healthy behavior to reduce illness. Many organizations have instituted employee wellness programs, which can include exercise programs, smoking and weight control classes, and stress management workshops. Organizational policies and practices can help employees pursue other interests while continuing to work. For example, on-site child care can make it easier for employees with young children to continue their jobs. With such programs, child care is provided at the place of employment so that employees can take their children to work and spend breaks and lunch periods with them. Having their children nearby can provide peace of mind that makes it easier for employees to focus attention on work. Flexible work schedules that allow employees to work at times that do not interfere with other interests can keep some from quitting their jobs.

▶ COUNTERPRODUCTIVE WORK BEHAVIOR: AGGRESSION, SABOTAGE, AND THEFT

Instances of irate employees shooting their coworkers and often themselves have brought national attention to the issue of employee aggression. Although these relatively rare (Neuman & Baron, 1997) but extreme examples fall more within the domain of clinical psychology or criminology, the issue of less extreme employee behavior that is damaging to organizations is an important one for the I/O field. **Counterproductive work behavior**, or CWB (often called "desk rage" in the popular media), refers to behaviors intended to harm the organization and other people at work, such as coworkers, supervisors, and customers. CWB can consist of aggression, hostile and nasty behavior directed at a coworker, destruction of organizational property, purposely doing work incorrectly, theft, and withholding effort.

Sabotage and theft have been recognized as major problems for organizations. Sabotage, the destruction of property needed for work, results both in direct costs from damage to property and in indirect costs from the loss of productivity while property needed for work is being repaired. Although many acts of sabotage are blatant, such as burning down a building, most are surreptitious and difficult to prove. It is often impossible to determine if an equipment-damaging accident was really accidental. For example, an employee might purposely ignore warning signals on a piece of equipment, such as the indicator light that a truck is low on oil or water. In some cases, an employee might remove the oil or water, knowing that it will damage the equipment. If this is done carefully, it will be difficult to prove that the employee purposely sabotaged the equipment.

Employee theft has been estimated to cost businesses in the United States billions of dollars per year (Greenberg, 2002). In a national survey of retailers, employees were found to be responsible for more theft than shoplifters (Hollinger, Dabney, Lee, Hayes, Hunter, & Cummings, 1996). Organizations spend considerable money and resources to control theft. Many organizations have tried to weed out potential thieves with the use of paper-and-pencil integrity tests to assess honesty (see Chapter 5). Others have resorted to lie detector tests, either for job applicants or current employees.

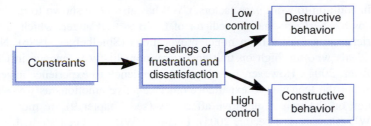

Figure 10.9 A model of the causes of counterproductive work behavior, CWB.

Bennett and Robinson (2000) conducted an anonymous mail survey of Toledo, Ohio, residents chosen at random from the telephone book. They asked about a long list of CWBs that went well beyond just sabotage and theft, and found that many were quite common. For example, a quarter of the respondents admitted to falsifying a receipt to get reimbursed for money they hadn't spent, a third said they had played a mean prank on someone at work, 52% said they had taken property from work without permission, 61% had neglected to follow instructions, and 78% had made fun of someone at work. Geddes (1994), in her national survey of managers, reported that supervisors were frequent targets of aggressive responses by subordinates who had received negative performance appraisals. Although a relatively small percentage were physically attacked, Geddes points out that nationally there could be several million supervisors who have been assaulted, most in a minor way (pushed or slapped), during their careers.

Figure 10.9 is a model of the causes of CWB. It begins with stressful job conditions, such as organizational constraints (as discussed earlier in this chapter) and injustice. For example, on the day he assaulted his coworkers, Thomas McIlvane had lost the final appeal of his dismissal from the post office. Stressful conditions and injustice induce negative emotions, such as anger or fear. These feelings, in turn, lead to constructive behaviors, such as developing more effective strategies to overcome the conditions or injustice, or destructive behaviors, such as CWB.

Beliefs about control determine in part whether individuals choose constructive or destructive responses. An employee who believes that constructive efforts can be effective is likely to attempt them. An employee who feels unable to control the situation might resort to CWB as a means of coping with the negative emotion.

The illegal nature of many counterproductive behaviors has made research difficult to conduct (Giacalone & Rosenfeld, 1987). Support for the model presented earlier comes mainly from questionnaire studies that ask employees to report (usually anonymously) about their jobs and reactions. These studies have shown that employee reports of stressful job conditions (Fox, Spector, & Miles, 2001; Spector, Fox, Penney, Bruursema, Goh, & Kessler, 2006) and injustice (Folger & Skarlicki, 2005; Greenberg & Barling, 1999) relate to negative emotions and CWB. Furthermore, employee locus of control has been found to moderate the relation between feelings of frustration and CWB. Individuals with an external locus of control showed a correlation between frustration at work and CWB. Their internal counterparts showed little or no correlation between frustration and CWB (Storms & Spector, 1987). Thus, when people who did not feel they had control at work were frustrated, they were more likely to engage in CWB.

In addition to workplace factors, CWB has also been shown to relate to personality. Perhaps the best personality predictor of CWB is trait anger, which is the tendency to experience anger even from minor provocations (Spielberger, 1996). Not surprisingly, individuals who are high on trait anger are more likely to engage in CWB (Hepworth & Towler, 2004). However, it isn't just the tendency to experience anger that relates to CWB, but the tendency to experience other negative emotions as well. Individuals who are high on the trait of negative affectivity (see Chapter 9) are more likely to engage in CWB (Penney & Spector, 2005). Finally, CWB has been studied in relation to the Big Five dimensions of personality discussed earlier in this chapter. Individuals who are low on agreeableness, conscientiousness, and emotional stability are more likely to engage in CWB (Liao, Joshi, & Chuang, 2004; Mount, Ilies, & Johnson, 2006). Although personality plays a role in CWB, it seems that environmental factors are even more important (Inness, Barling, & Turner, 2005). The correct (or perhaps it is best to say incorrect) combination of individual personality and workplace factors will maximize the likelihood that an employee will engage in CWB.

Labor Unrest and Strikes

Another area in which counterproductive behavior occurs as a response to anger or unfair treatment is in labor-management disputes. The history of organized labor contains many acts of violence on both sides. A tactic often used by unions is to "attack" the organization by withholding output. In addition, sabotage and even violence can be common during union actions, such as strikes. These actions are counterproductive from the organization's viewpoint, although not necessarily from the employees'.

Labor unrest and strikes can occur for many reasons. Often such actions are accompanied by frustration on the part of employees who believe that they are not treated fairly. These beliefs can lead to a variety of counterproductive behaviors, such as work slowdowns or sabotage. Anger and perceptions of unfair treatment have been associated with strikes (Giacalone & Knouse, 1990).

▶ FUTURE ISSUES AND CHALLENGES

Over the past few years there has been increasing discussion in the media about worker productivity, particularly in the United States. As foreign competition has increased, so has the concern with staying competitive. Much of this concern revolves around the job performance of workers and ways it can be enhanced. Such enhancement has always been a major focus for the field of I/O psychology, and it is addressed by many of the activities of the field. Of particular concern in the future will be the appropriate ways in which technology can enhance productivity without harming the health or well-being of employees. Computer supported cooperative work is a new technological frontier that is allowing people to work together remotely, but research is needed to help us understand how best to design and use it. Research has already pointed to the positive and negative sides of new computer advances. Computers can certainly facilitate the performance of many tasks, and robotic devices have freed people from many dangerous and unpleasant jobs. On the other hand, jobs that require the excessive use of computers have been associated with certain physical injuries, such as carpal tunnel syndrome.

A second issue concerns the understanding and control of destructive behavior, or CWB. Organizations have put considerable effort into reduction of theft, mainly through the use of integrity tests to screen out potentially dishonest workers and through surveillance equipment to watch employees. However, they have given too little attention to aggression, sabotage and other forms of CWB. Additional research is needed to provide procedures that organizations can implement to reduce destructive behavior. The limited research to date suggests that enhancing people's control at work might well reduce their destructive behaviors.

► CHAPTER SUMMARY

The productive and counterproductive behavior of employees at work is a vital area of concern to the I/O field. Job performance, absence, and turnover have been a major focus of attention for both research and practice. Destructive behaviors, such as sabotage, aggression at work, and theft, are also important. Recent attention has also been given to organizational citizenship behavior (OCB).

Job performance is a central variable for the I/O field. Much of the research and practice of I/O psychologists is concerned with understanding, assessing, or enhancing job performance. Performance results from the interplay of ability and motivation. Both environmental and personal factors are important influences. Personality characteristics, such as the Big Five and locus of control, have been shown to relate to performance. Job characteristics, incentive systems, and technology are important environmental influences.

One of the major objectives of the human factors field is to enhance job performance through the design of tools and equipment. Although the Hawthorne studies suggested that the social environment could be more important than the physical, the physical environment can still influence job performance. Physical aspects, such as lighting and sound levels, as well as the design of equipment and the ways information is presented, all have important influences on performance.

Organizational constraints are features of the work environment that interfere with good job performance. Such conditions can lead to lower job satisfaction and more employee turnover.

Organizational citizenship behavior (OCB) is behavior that goes beyond the core task requirements of the job and is beneficial to the organization. It involves both altruistic (helping others) and compliance (following rules) behavior. OCB is important because it can contribute to organizational well-being. Both job satisfaction and supportive supervisory behavior are correlated with how much employees engage in organizational citizenship behavior.

Withdrawal behavior—absence, lateness, and turnover—can create tremendous problems for organizations. Most of the research on these variables considers them to be reactions to job dissatisfaction. This seems to be more true for turnover, at least during times of plentiful jobs, than for absence and lateness, which correlate only slightly with job satisfaction. Furthermore, withdrawal can arise from many causes, with only some related to job attitudes.

Counterproductive work behavior, or CWB (e.g., aggression at work, hostility toward others, sabotage, and theft), can produce tremendous costs to organizations. The research conducted on these behaviors suggests that they are reactions to stressful job conditions and injustice that produce negative emotions. Employees who believe they have little control at work are more likely to engage in destructive behavior. Personality characteristics of trait anger, trait anxiety, agreeableness, conscientiousness, and emotional stability have been linked to CWB.

I/O PSYCHOLOGY IN PRACTICE

(*Courtesy Jeanne Carsten*)

This case concerns a turnover project carried out by Dr. Jeanne M. Carsten. Since receiving her Ph.D. in I/O psychology in 1987 from the University of South Florida, Carsten has been employed by JP Morgan Chase in New York City, one of the largest financial institutions in the world. Her current job title is manager of strategic planning and implementation. In her work for the company, she has covered many areas of I/O, including attitude surveys, employee development, selection, and training. One of her major functions is to carry out projects designed to address specific organizational problems.

The first major project she was assigned when she was newly hired was to find a solution to an excessive turnover rate among bank tellers. Although high turnover is normal and expected with these employees, the management of the bank believed that the rate had become excessive. Carsten was charged with finding out why and suggesting solutions.

The first phase of the project was to collect information. Interviews were conducted with tellers and their supervisors to find out why they were quitting. Tellers were asked about problems they encountered on the job. In addition, a salary survey was conducted to see if other banks were paying their tellers more, which they were.

The second phase was to prepare and present an action plan to the management of the bank. There were 12 recommendations, including raising salaries, training teller supervisors to provide better assistance to their subordinates, clarifying job performance standards, and offering additional teller training.

During the final phase of the project, almost all of the recommendations were implemented. Afterwards, the turnover rate declined by almost 50%. Without a control group, one cannot be certain what caused the improvement in the turnover rate. During the course of the project, the national unemployment rate increased, which would have reduced turnover. Carsten points out that the turnover rate became lower than that at other banks, however, lending support to the idea that the changes were effective. Furthermore, many of the changes, such as improving supervisory practices and clarifying performance standards, may have been of benefit for reasons other than turnover reduction. This case illustrates how an I/O psychologist who works for an organization can help improve working conditions for employees.

Discussion Questions
1. Why do you think the bank tellers quit their jobs?
2. What factors would encourage you to stay on a job that you did not like?
3. Do you think that Carsten's interventions did anything besides reduce turnover?
4. Do you think that employees at this bank might have engaged in other forms of withdrawal behavior?

LEARNING BY DOING

Human Factors Design of Automobiles

Inspect an automobile for examples of the incorporation of human factors into its design. Draw a picture of the dashboard and make a list of features involving displays (e.g., instrument panel) and controls illustrated in your picture. How many examples of the principles discussed in the chapter can you find?

Organizational citizenship Behavior

Ask at least five employed friends or family members to provide examples of OCB they have seen at work. First, give each person a definition of OCB (behavior that helps the organization but goes beyond the core tasks required for the job). Then record the example/s they give you. How many of these examples benefit the organization, how many benefit other people, and how many benefit both?

Occupational Health Psychology

CHAPTER 11 OUTLINE

Movies like *Backdraft* and *World Trade Center* have underscored the dramatic and often dangerous aspects of a firefighter's job. Having to go into burning buildings like the World Trade Center that might collapse at any moment, and dealing with the injured and dying, is clearly stressful. Does performing such jobs have an adverse impact on firefighters' health and well-being? Del Ben, Scotti, Chen, and Fortson (2006) surveyed firefighters from one U.S. state and found that about 5% showed all the signs of a posttraumatic stress disorder (PTSD), and 22% showed some symptoms. Their study did

TABLE 11.1 **Frequent Sources of Illness and Injury for Workers in Some Common Occupations**

Source	Occupation
Infectious disease	Dentist, nurse
Loud noise	Airline baggage handler, musician
Physical assault (fatal)	Police officer, taxi driver
Physical assault (nonfatal)	Nursing home aide, psychiatric nurse
Repetitive actions and lifting	Data-entry clerk, nurse
Toxic substances	Exterminator, farmer

not include firefighters who might have quit their jobs due to PTSD or other health-related problems, so likely the true percentage of cases is even higher. As this study illustrates, characteristics of jobs and job-related experiences have an important impact on health and well-being. In this case the firefighters noted that having to deal with someone's death and being injured or nearly killed were the most traumatic events they encountered. This is not the only occupation that deals with these issues. People in health professions, such as nurses and physicians, deal with injury and death. So do police officers and workers in other dangerous occupations, who must not only deal with such matters affecting others but themselves face the risk of becoming victims.

Table 11.1 lists some frequent sources of illness and injury on the job, along with some common occupations for which each is particularly problematic. These sources represent concrete physical conditions at work, such as equipment or toxic substances, likely to affect physical health. The effects of these sources tend to be direct, although for some people exposure over a long period of time must occur for illness or injury to develop. For example, it can take years to become injured or disabled from repetitive motions, such as typing. Certain occupations are more likely than others to exhibit some of these sources, although employees on most jobs might encounter any of them. Those who work outdoors, such as park rangers or roofers, are most likely to encounter extremely hot or extremely cold conditions, but even office workers may encounter extremes of temperature if their buildings do not have adequate heating or air conditioning. Police officers and taxi drivers are more likely to be victims of assault, but virtually anyone might be assaulted at work, although for most jobs the chances are remote.

In addition to the physical conditions listed in Table 11.1, certain nonphysical conditions might affect physical health and emotional well-being. Nonstandard work schedules, such as night shift work, have been implicated as causes of both physical and psychological problems. Several nonphysical work conditions are frequently discussed in the literature under the general topic of occupational stress. Such conditions as workload, lack of control, role ambiguity, role conflict, and organizational constraints have all been associated with physical health or emotional well-being.

In this chapter we are concerned with the physical and psychological aspects of employee health, safety, and well-being at work that comprise **occupational health psychology**, or OHP. This emerging subfield of psychology (and other disciplines, such as medicine and public health) is concerned with the psychological factors that contribute to occupational health and well-being. It deals with psychological reactions to physical and nonphysical work conditions, as well as behavior that has implications for health.

Included in this chapter will be discussion of physical conditions that affect health, occupational stress, occupational accidents, the interplay between work and family, and burnout.

Objectives: The student who studies this chapter should be able to:

▶ Describe the causes of accidents and the steps that can be taken to prevent them.

▶ List the major physical work conditions that affect employee health.

▶ Explain how work schedules can affect employee health and well-being.

▶ Discuss the nature of occupational stress, including its causes and effects.

▶ Define burnout and state how it relates to employee health and well-being.

▶ OCCUPATIONAL HEALTH AND SAFETY

Physical work conditions tend to have direct physical effects on people. Sometimes the effects are immediate, as when an employee is injured in an automobile accident. Other times illness or injury may develop after exposure at work for many years to a harmful condition (e.g., loud noise) or a toxic substance. Often there are steps that can be taken to avoid or minimize accidents and exposures to harmful conditions through the adoption of safe workplace design and safe procedures for doing the job. In addition to physical effects, illness and injury can have psychological consequences that are detrimental to emotional well-being. Serious illness and injury are almost certainly associated with some level of psychological distress and trauma, especially when the person has been disabled.

In this section we first discuss accidents and safety related behavior. Accidents are events that occur at work that cause immediate injury, such as getting a hand caught in a machine or cutting a finger with a knife. As we will see, accidents are a major problem in the workplace that have tremendous costs for both employees and organizations. Next we will cover five common exposures that can produce injury and illness at work:

Infectious disease

Loud noise

Repetitive actions or lifting

Toxic substances

Workplace violence

Often exposure is the result of unsafe behavior or workplace design that placed an employee in a position to be harmed but could have been avoided.

Accidents and Safety

Accidents are the fifth leading cause of death among Americans after heart disease, cancer, stroke, and respiratory disease (National Safety Council, 2005–2006). One of the major accomplishments of the twentieth century in the United States was a reduction in the workplace accident rate by 90% to where today most workers are safer at work than anywhere else, with only 10% of accidental deaths occurring on the job. However, in 2005 there were still 5,524 workplace fatalities (U.S. Department of Labor, 2006).

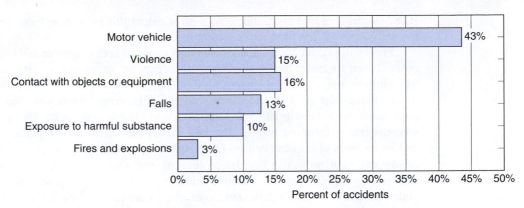

Figure 11.1 Major types of fatal work accidents for 2005 in the United States.

Source: U.S. Department of Labor, Bureau of Labor Statistics (2006). *Census of Fatal Occupational Injuries.* Author.

Furthermore, the number of nonfatal accidents far exceeds the number of workplace fatalities. For example, Glasscock, Rasmussen, Carstensen, and Hansen (2006) found in a Danish study that 36% of farm workers reported being injured in the prior year, and about a third of them required medical attention.

Figure 11.1 shows the major types of fatal workplace accidents in the United States in 2005. As you can see, motor vehicles were the leading cause, accounting for 43%. Figure 11.2 shows the accident rates for 10 categories of jobs. Agriculture/fishing/forestry/ hunting and mining are the most dangerous, whereas education/health service and leisure/ hospitality are the safest. Another factor related to workplace fatalities is gender. Men comprise 54% of the workforce in the United States, but they account for 93% of fatalities

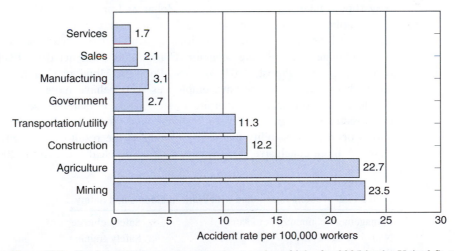

Figure 11.2 Fatal accident rates for several categories of jobs for 2005 in the United States.

Source: U.S. Department of Labor, Bureau of Labor Statistics (2006). *Census of Fatal Occupational Injuries.* Author.

(U.S. Department of Labor, 2006). To a great extent this is because men are disproportionately found in the most dangerous occupations.

Preventing accidents is a major concern because of both employee and organizational costs. Taken together, fatal and nonfatal accidents are expensive, costing an estimated $140 billion annually in the United States alone (National Safety Council, 2005–2006), much of the cost paid by employers and their insurance companies. Many different approaches have been tried to prevent accidents. Some involve design of equipment, whereas others focus on people. The best strategy depends on the particular situation and an analysis of accident causes. Often solutions can be fairly simple, such as having employees wear protective goggles to prevent eye injuries. The application of human factors (ergonomics) can be effective when equipment is poorly designed (or can be better designed) from a safety standpoint. An example is the push lawnmower, which can be a dangerous device. At one time the design allowed an operator to get a hand or foot caught in the revolving blade. All new lawnmowers sold in the United States must be designed with a handle release switch that turns off the engine (or blade) when the operator lets go of the handle. This system makes it difficult to accidentally stick a hand or foot into a moving blade. Better design can be quite effective in reducing accidents and injuries, and as an additional benefit it can reduce strains for the employee (Kompier, Aust, van den Berg, Siegrist, 2000).

A major difficulty in preventing workplace accidents is getting the cooperation of employees to use the appropriate safety equipment and engage in safe behaviors. Safety devices are often inconvenient, and safety equipment may be uncomfortable. Some people tape down the handle release switch on their lawnmowers because they find it annoying and fail to use safety goggles because they are uncomfortable. Accepted workplace practices might preclude the use of certain safety practices because they seem to waste time, take too much effort, or imply that employees lack the courage to face dangerous situations. Factors relating to accidents are listed in Table 11.2.

Safety climate is the shared perception by employees that safety is important and they should take steps to work safely (Zohar & Luria, 2005). The climate is reflected in the policies of the organization and in the practices it adopts that are relevant to safety, such as the use of safety equipment. Studies have clearly shown a link between safety climate and both safe behavior (Clarke, 2006) and accidents (Kelloway, Mullen, & Francis, 2006; Probst, 2004; Wallace, Popp, & Mondore, 2006). Organizations that are high on safety climate have employees who behave more safely and have fewer accidents than organizations that are low on safety climate. These studies have used a cross-sectional design that measures climate and other variables at the same time. This leaves open the possibility that safety climate is the result of accidents rather than the cause. A more conclusive study was conducted by Neal and Griffin (2006). They found

TABLE 11.2   Factors Associated with Work Accidents and Safety

Management commitment to safety	Safety climate
Nonwork stressors	Safety training
Personality characteristics	Work stressors
Production vs. safety emphasis	

that safety climate predicted accidents up to three years later, making it unlikely that accidents could have caused climate.

Accidents can also be affected by the balance in emphasis between productivity and safety (Humphrey, Moon, Conlon, & Hofmann, 2004). For example, Kaminski (2001) studied accidents in 86 small manufacturing plants in the United States She found that pay incentive systems were associated with injuries on the job. Jobs were safer if assembly line workers were paid per hour rather than based on productivity, since the latter encouraged working fast at a detriment to safety.

Stress on and off the job can be another important factor. For example, Savery and Wooden (1994) surveyed Australian workers from 61 different organizations. They found that frequency of stressful events (e.g., divorce) was related to work accidents. Hemingway and Smith (1999) found a link between accidents and job stressors, such as role ambiguity, role conflict, and workload (see the discussion of stressors later in this chapter), in a sample of nurses. Job satisfaction has been linked to accidents; individuals who are satisfied with their jobs are less likely to have had accidents (Barling, Kelloway, & Iverson, 2003). Clarke and Robertson (2005) conducted a meta-analysis of 47 studies relating the Big Five personality traits (see Chapter 10) to accidents. They found that high openness to experience, low conscientiousness, and low agreeableness were associated with accidents.

Ludwig and Geller (1997) successfully used goal setting (see Chapter 8) to encourage safer driving behavior in a sample of pizza deliverers. They asked drivers to set goals concerning the percentage of times they would come to a complete and safe stop before pulling into traffic. The goal setting improved not only the targeted behavior but other safety behaviors for which goals had not been set, such as seatbelt use. As discussed in Chapter 8, goals can be an effective means of improving job performance; they can also improve safety.

Infectious Disease

Employees who must deal with the public (e.g., hairstylists, police officers, sales clerks, teachers) may be exposed to infectious disease, although most such cases result in relatively minor illnesses, such as cold or flu. Exposure to serious infectious diseases is a particular concern to people in the healthcare professions, who must deal with seriously ill and dying patients. The National Safety Council (1992b) estimated that 12,000 people per year are infected on the job with hepatitis B, a serious disease that affects the liver. Murphy, Gershon, and DeJoy (1996) noted that AIDS exposure is a major source of job stress for healthcare workers, frequently leading to anxiety and distress. Concern about AIDS has had a considerable impact on safety practices in the health professions. In the United States the Centers for Disease Control and Prevention (CDC) recommends that all health care workers comply with the **Universal Precautions**, a set of safety procedures that can dramatically reduce exposure. These include:

Disposing of sharp objects in a special *sharps* container

Wearing disposable gloves when handling blood or bodily fluids

Immediately cleaning all bodily fluid spills with disinfectant

Recapping needles that have been used

Unfortunately, large numbers of health care workers fail to follow these procedures even though research shows their effectiveness (Murphy et al., 1996). DeJoy, Searcy, Murphy, and Gershon (2000) conducted a study of 902 hospital nurses and found that there are organizational factors that relate to the following of universal precautions, including support and encouragement given by supervisors, and constraints in the workplace that prevent their use, such as the need to work very quickly. Training of supervisors could go a long way toward encouraging development of a safety climate at work that encourages universal precautions use.

Loud Noise

Loud noise occurs at many jobs, particularly those involving heavy equipment or machinery. Airports, construction sites, factories, and mines can all be noisy places, exposing employees to conditions that can affect both their health and their job performance.

The intensity of noise is measured in **decibel (dB)** units. The decibel scale is a logarithmic scale, meaning that the relation between decibel level and sound intensity is not linear. Increasing the sound level by 10 dB is an increase of 10 times in sound intensity, and by 20 dB it is an increase of 100 times. The decibel levels of several common sounds found in the workplace are shown in Figure 11.3.

Exposure to extremely loud noises, such as explosions, can severely damage a person's sense of hearing, sometimes permanently. Noise of this magnitude is painful, and most people avoid places where such noises occur. Of even more concern at work is continuous exposure to moderately loud noise that exceeds 85 decibels (National Safety Council, 1992c). If continued over a period of months or years, moderately loud noise can lead to permanent hearing loss, particularly in the higher frequencies. Because noise of this intensity is not typically painful, however, many employees will do nothing to avoid it. It is quite common for employees in noisy work environments to suffer from hearing loss. Hearing damage can also be caused by exposure to loud music. Listening to headphones at high volume levels can be particularly dangerous because of the high dB level in the ear.

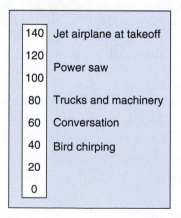

Figure 11.3 Sound intensity levels in decibels for some common sounds.

Note: From *Sound Sense*, by National Safety Council, 1992, Itasca, IL: Author.

Because of the potential for hearing damage, many countries have laws governing the legal levels of noise exposure. Employees who work in noisy environments are given hearing protection to prevent hearing loss. It is common, for example, to see airline employees wear such protection when they are around jets that have their engines running. As with universal precautions, employees often fail to use hearing protection, thus increasing exposure to health damaging conditions.

Besides hearing damage, there is evidence suggestive of a link between noise exposure at work and cardiovascular disease. Melamed, Fried, and Froom (2001) showed that exposure to noise related to level of blood pressure for individuals in complex but not simple jobs. Presumably noise interfered with the greater concentration that complex jobs required, thus serving as a job stressor (see the discussion of stressors later in this chapter).

Repetitive Actions and Lifting

Many jobs require repeated physical actions by various body parts. Employees who use computers at work often spend their entire day typing. Traditional assembly-line work requires workers to perform the same operation over and over. Other jobs require the lifting of heavy objects or people. Nurses, for example, have to move ill patients who are unable to support their own weight. Repetitive actions can result in **repetitive strain injuries**, in which the body parts involved can become inflamed and sometimes permanently damaged. Lifting can result in acute injury, often to the lower back. Both kinds of injuries are forms of **musculoskeletal disorder** (**MSD**).

Jobs differ in the strains they put on the musculoskeletal system, and thus different body areas may experience MSD. For example, urban transit workers who drive buses or trains are most at risk for back or neck pain (Greiner & Krause, 2006). Nurses are subject to back injury from lifting patients (Rickett, Orbell, & Sheeran, 2006). Dentists also tend to have neck and back injuries, but they experience shoulder and wrist/hand problems as well (Palliser, Firth, Feyer, & Paulin, 2005). Those who do a lot of keyboard work or typing are at risk for **carpal tunnel syndrome**, a wrist injury that causes pain, numbness, and weakness in the fingers and hands. It is brought on by repeated use of the fingers and wrist.

MSDs can be reduced with relatively inexpensive strategies. First, the proper design of tools and equipment can go a long way to reducing the strain on the body that can result in these injuries. Figure 11.4 shows a wrist rest that can help prevent carpal tunnel syndrome in people who use computer keyboards. It is a bar that helps keep the typist's wrists straight so that the strain on them is reduced. Split keyboards in which the keys are placed at an angle so the wrist can remain straight are becoming increasingly popular. Acute lifting injuries can be reduced by the use of mechanical devices that take the heavy load (Rickett et al., 2006).

A second strategy is to allow frequent rest breaks. In Sweden there are laws governing the maximum amount of time employees can be asked to use a computer keyboard without a break and the maximum amount of time they can type in a day. In the United States, similar legislation has been debated but not enacted. A combination of equipment design and rest breaks can reduce the likelihood that employees will contract debilitating repetitive strain injuries.

Figure 11.4 A device that helps reduce strain on a person's wrist when using a computer keyboard. Picture courtesy of Fellowes, Inc.

(Courtesy Fellowes, Inc.)

Toxic Substances

The exposure of employees to toxic substances has been given more and more attention as research has shown how such substances can affect health. The problem with exposure to many substances is that adverse health effects such as cancer can take years or decades to develop. Furthermore, not everyone exposed will develop symptoms. This makes it difficult to determine the effects of exposure, because many things may contribute to a particular person contracting an illness.

Many jobs entail exposure to toxic substances, often in unexpected places. Employees in chemical plants, exterminators, and farm workers who use insecticides can all expect to be exposed. Office workers in enclosed buildings do not work with toxic substances, but they can nonetheless be exposed to various chemicals, such as toners from copying machines or solvents used to clean ink. Furthermore, people vary in sensitivity to many substances. Reactions to exposure can range from fairly minor symptoms, such as headache or nausea, to serious conditions that can permanently damage vital organs, such as the kidneys or liver. At times only a few sensitive individuals will exhibit symptoms, but it is not unusual for most of the employees in an office to become ill, leading to what has been termed the *sick building* phenomenon, which can arise from toxic substances or microorganisms.

Another issue concerns allergy to various substances, most commonly dust, mold, and pollen. This has become an increasing problem in the United States, where building are completely sealed and the same air is recirculated, allowing the concentration of allergens to increase. Common allergic reactions include nasal congestion, coughing, watery eyes, and skin rash, but employees with asthma and other respiratory illnesses can experience serious and even fatal medical conditions.

Organizations that expose their employees to toxic substances run the risk of lawsuits by ill or disabled employees. In the United States, the Occupational Safety and Health Administration (OSHA) is charged with seeing that workplace safeguards are used to protect workers. Many countries have laws to protect employees from toxic substances and other conditions that affect health. Even so, each year thousands of workers are injured or killed on the job because of toxic substance exposure (National Safety Council, 1992a).

Workplace Violence

When you mention workplace violence, most people think of the U.S. Postal Service, because there have been several widely reported cases of irate postal employees shooting coworkers and supervisors, many fatally. According to the U.S. Bureau of Labor Statistics (2006), workplace violence (including suicide) was the third leading cause of workplace fatalities overall in 2005. It is the leading cause of workplace death for women, although this doesn't mean that more women are victims of violence than men. Women comprise only 7% of overall workplace fatalities and are 19% of fatal violence victims (Sygnatur & Tascano, 2000). Despite the media attention to shootings by postal employees and other cases of extreme violence by employees, such incidents are rather rare. In the United States in 1998 there were 709 homicides in the workplace (Sygnatur & Toscano, 2000). To put this in perspective, there were close to 12,000 homicides in the United States in 2000 (Federal Bureau of Investigation, 2001). Only about 15% of workplace homicides were committed by coworkers or former coworkers in 1998, with most fatal violence being the result of robberies or other crimes (Sygnatur & Toscano, 2000).

There are four types of workplace violence, depending upon the relationship between the perpetrator and the workplace (Merchant & Lundell, 2001). Type 1 is violence by individuals who have no business relationship with the organization, such as someone commiting a robbery. Type 2 is by clients, customers, or patients of the organization. Type 3 is performed by employees of the organization. Type 4 is relationship violence (e.g., spouse abuse) that spills over to the workplace. The nature of the job determines in large part whether these different types of violence are possible. Table 11.3 lists the occupations most at risk for the various types.

TABLE 11.3   Occupations Associated with Four Types of Workplace Violence

Violence Type	Definition	Likely Occupation to Experience It
Type 1	Strangers commiting a crime	Convenience store clerk, taxi driver
Type 2	Client/Customer/Patient	Nurse, social worker
Type 3	Other employees	Any job with coworker contact
Type 4	Relationship	Any job

For most occupations, fatal assaults are extremely rare, and employees are safer at work than almost anywhere else they might be. However, there are a few occupations for which homicide is a more significant risk. Whereas the national average workplace homicide rate is .70 cases per 100,000 employees, the risk is far greater for taxi drivers (41.4), liquor store clerks (7.5), police officers (7.0), and gas station attendants (4.8) (NIOSH, 1997). In the United States, 51 police officers were homicide victims in 2000 (Federal Bureau of Investigation, 2001).

Of course, nonfatal assault is a far more common occupational hazard, especially for those who work with the public. A survey of employers found that 4.3% of more than 7 million American workplaces experienced at least one case of workplace violence in the prior year (U.S. Department of Labor, 2006). People who work in nursing homes, social service agencies, and hospitals are at the greatest risk of Type 2 violence (NIOSH, 1996), although in most cases there is little or no physical injury. However, employees can still be subject to psychological trauma (Walsh & Clarke, 2003). Barling, Rogers, and Kelloway (2001) found that many home-care medical workers (e.g., home-care nurses) reported being subject to some form of violence in their work, including being hit, kicked, pushed, and spat on. In fact, having to take care of others and having contact with individuals taking medication are both important risk factors for workplace violence (Leblanc & Kelloway, 2002). To control violence, many health facilities will medicate combative patients. Specialized training is also offered at many institutions to help employees avoid assaults and defend themselves from patients.

▶ WORK SCHEDULES

Whereas most employed people work standard schedules of approximately eight daylight hours per day on weekdays, the use of nonstandard schedules involving longer work shifts, nights, and weekends is spreading. Of particular interest to I/O psychologists have been three types of schedules: night (and rotating) shifts, long work shifts, and flextime.

Night Shifts

Many organizations, such as hospitals and police departments, run 24 hours per day, requiring the use of two or three shifts of workers to cover the entire day. A typical three-shift sequence is

> 8 A.M. to 4 P.M.
>
> 4 P.M. to 12 A.M.
>
> 12 A.M. to 8 A.M.

referred to as the day, evening, and night or graveyard shifts, respectively. Some organizations hire people to work a fixed shift; that is, they work the same shift all the time. Other organizations use rotating shifts: Employees work one shift for a limited time, say a month, and then switch, or rotate, to another shift. According to a U.S. Bureau of Labor Statistics (1998) study, 16.8% of American workers had some sort of nonstandard work schedule in 1997, requiring evening, night, or rotating shifts.

The major health problem with working night shifts is that the typical sleep/waking cycle is disturbed. Associated with this cycle are the **circadian rhythms** of physiological changes that occur throughout the day. These include body temperature changes and changes in hormone levels in the bloodstream. It has been suggested that night shifts can cause health problems by disrupting these natural rhythms.

The most obvious health problem in working night shifts is sleep disturbance—either being unable to fall asleep or having a poor quality of sleep (Daus, Sanders, & Campbell, 1998). Several studies have found that people who work night shifts are more likely than day shift workers to experience sleep problems (e.g., Koller, Kundi, & Cervinka, 1978), although not all studies have found this effect. Barton and Folkard (1991) found that employees on temporary night shifts had greater sleep problems than employees who worked permanent night shifts, but the permanent night shift workers were no more likely to have sleep problems than the day shift workers. The researchers argued that in their sample of nurses, each employee working the permanent night shift had volunteered to do so. These volunteers were able to adjust to night work and not experience sleep problems.

Sleep problems might arise from disruption of the circadian rhythms, but another, simpler explanation has been advanced. Koller et al. (1978) believe that night shift workers get worse sleep because there is more noise during the day when they are trying to sleep. In their study of Austrian oil refinery workers, they found that 62.6% of night workers who slept during the day complained of having their sleep disturbed by noise. Only 15.8% of day workers who slept at night had the same complaint.

Sleep disturbance is not the only health problem associated with night shift work. Digestive system problems have been shown to be more frequent in night shift workers (e.g., Koller et al., 1978). Akerstedt and Theorell (1976) studied physiological changes in workers before, during, and after a period of night shift work. In this study, the blood levels of the hormone gastrin, which is related to stomach acid secretion, was assessed twice a day over a period of five weeks. Results showed a decrease in gastrin during the time the workers were on the night shift. Although the study shows that night shift work can have physiological effects, it is not clear why they occurred. Was it the disruption of the circadian rhythm that upset the secretion of gastrin, or was it lack of sleep (Figure 11.5)? Whatever it was, at least one solution to night shift effects is to allow several consecutive days of rest per week (Totterdell, Spelten, Smith, Barton, & Folkard, 1995).

In addition to health problems, shift work can cause social problems. Having to work nights and sleep days can isolate a person from family and friends. Bohle and Tilley (1998) surveyed hospital nurses concerning their feelings about shift work. The best

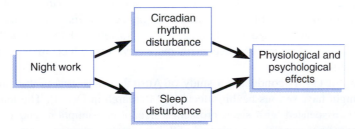

Figure 11.5 Night work leads to both circadian rhythm disturbance and sleep problems. These in turn lead to physical problems, such as stomach upset, and psychological problems, such as anxiety.

Long distance drivers sometimes work long shifts that can interrupt sleep patterns.
(*PhotoDisc, Inc./Getty Images*)

predictor of dissatisfaction was conflict between work and nonwork activities. Individuals who reported high levels of conflict tended to report the greatest dissatisfaction with shift work.

One final potential health problem for night shift workers in some jobs is assault. Budd, Arvey, and Lawless (1996) conducted a survey of employed people in one U.S. city and found that assaults were most commonly experienced at night.

Long Shifts

The typical full-time work shift is eight hours. Many organizations, however, have implemented longer shifts, and many employees have jobs that do not have fixed shifts but can require long work days. For example, truck and bus drivers may have routes that cannot be completed in an 8-hour day. The most popular alternative long work schedule is the 4-day 10-hour shift, or 4/40. Some organizations that operate 24 hours per day have gone to two 12-hour shifts per day.

One important difficulty with the long work day is fatigue (Bendak, 2003). A 10- to 12-hour day can be quite tiring if the work is mentally or physically demanding. On the other hand, many employees like the longer days because it gives them more time to recover from work and more usable free time per week (Bendak, 2003), and long shifts can result in both better job performance and job satisfaction (Baltes, Briggs, Huff, Wright, & Newman, 1999). Pierce and Dunham (1992) compared 8-hour rotating shifts with 12-hour rotating shifts in a sample of police officers. The officers preferred the longer shifts and reported less fatigue. They also reported fewer health problems and less stress. The longer day gave them more days off, which may have produced the positive effects.

Raggatt (1991) conducted a study of Australian bus drivers that showed that long shifts might have serious health effects (see Research in Detail). The length of the work shift was associated with sleep problems, alcohol consumption, and use of stimulants. These outcomes were also associated with job dissatisfaction and poor health. Thus long work shifts can have detrimental effects for some jobs. For other jobs, such as police officers, long shifts can be beneficial.

RESEARCH IN DETAIL

One of the limitations associated with questionnaire studies of job conditions and job stress is that most of the variables assessed are rather abstract theoretical constructs, such as autonomy or role ambiguity. The present study (Raggatt, 1991) was somewhat different. The major job condition variable was the number of hours worked over the past month. The study was designed to determine whether working long hours would be associated with a number of psychological, physical, and behavioral strains, as well as accidents.

Subjects for this study were 93 Australian bus drivers. Each driver was asked to complete a questionnaire that asked about job satisfaction, psychological distress, health symptoms, sleeping problems, speeding, pill taking, alcohol consumption, and number of prior accidents. The drivers were asked to indicate the number of hours they had worked over the prior four weeks. Many of the drivers worked very long shifts, with most exceeding 40-hour workweeks. Twelve- to 14-hour workdays were not unusual.

Results indicated that working long shifts was associated with taking pills (e.g., stimulants), drinking alcohol, and having difficulty sleeping. These strains were associated with health symptoms, psychological distress, job dissatisfaction, and accidents. The drivers also reported significantly more health symptoms, depression, anxiety, and fatigue than people in general.

Raggatt presented a model suggesting that the demands of the job, particularly long driving shifts, resulted in fatigue and sleep disturbance. The coping strategies used by the drivers often involved the use of stimulants to stay awake and depressants and alcohol to sleep. The combination of fatigue brought on by driving and poor sleep and the use of pills and alcohol contributed to psychological and physical strains. Raggatt recommended that many of these important health-related problems could probably be reduced by giving drivers more rest breaks and shorter work shifts. Organizations need to pay attention to the health consequences of requiring long work shifts.

Source: Raggatt, P. T. F. (1991). Work stress among long-distance coach drivers: A survey and correlational study. *Journal of Organizational Behavior*, *12*, 565–579.

It is not only long shifts, however, that can have detrimental effects. The number of hours worked per week has been linked to hypertension (high blood pressure) (Yang, Schnall, Jauregui, Su, & Baker (2006). This detrimental effect seems only to occur in people who work long hours nonvoluntarily, which is often the case in organizations that have downsized or reduced their number of employees (Sparks, Cooper, Fried, & Shirom, 1997). Survivors usually wind up working more hours to cover tasks of colleagues who have been laid off. The European Council adopted rules in the mid-1990s restricting work hours in member countries, including maximum hours worked per day and week (13 and 48, respectively). Such restrictions have not been implemented in the United States and other non-European industrialized countries.

Flexible Work Schedules

Fixed daily work schedules are still the norm, but increasingly organizations have been trying flexible schedules, known as **flextime**, that allow workers to determine, at least in part, the hours of the day that they work. In 1997, 27.6% of American workers had flextime, which was more than double the percentage a decade earlier (U.S. Bureau of Labor Statistics, 1998). There are many varieties, from systems requiring only that employees work their allotted hours per day to systems that allow employees the option of starting their shift an hour early or an hour late. As we will cover in the discussion of work/family issues later in the chapter, flextime can be part of a family friendly policy that allows working parents more flexibility to fulfill child care responsibilities.

From the organization's perspective, an advantage of a flexible work schedule is that it allows employees to take care of personal business on their own time rather than on work time. Thus, an employee could have a doctor's visit in the morning and begin the shift late. In their meta-analysis, Baltes et al. (1999) confirmed that there is less absence, and Ralston (1989) found less tardiness with flextime than with fixed work schedules, as might be expected. Relations with job performance and satisfaction have been less consistent. Baltes et al. (1999) found that objective measures of productivity were higher with flextime, but supervisor ratings of performance were not. Job satisfaction was slightly higher with flextime, but the magnitude of effect was small.

▶ OCCUPATIONAL STRESS

Everyone has experienced **stress** at one time or another. Taking an exam is a situation that is stressful for most students, particularly for those who want good grades. On most jobs there are situations that employees find stressful. Being reprimanded by a supervisor, having too little time to complete an important assignment, or being told that you might be fired are all situations that almost anyone would find stressful. Warr and Payne (1983) asked a random sample of British workers if they had been emotionally upset by something at work the day before. Fifteen percent of the men and 10% of the women said they had been. A growing amount of research over the past few decades has provided evidence that unfavorable job conditions can affect employee health and well-being (Cooper & Cartwright, 1994). In this section we review what is known about the effects of occupational stress.

The Occupational Stress Process

To understand occupational stress, you must first understand several concepts that are involved in the stress process. A **job stressor** is a condition or situation at work that requires an adaptive response on the part of the employee (Jex & Beehr, 1991). Being reprimanded, having too little time, and being told about the possibility of being fired are all examples of job stressors. A **job strain** is a negative reaction to a stressor, such as anger, anxiety, or a physical symptom such as a headache. Jex and Beehr (1991) categorize strains into

Psychological reactions

Physical reactions

Behavioral reactions

(See Table 11.4.) Psychological reactions involve emotional responses, such as anxiety or frustration. Physical reactions include symptoms such as headaches or stomach distress and illnesses such as cancer. Behavioral reactions are responses to job stressors and include substance use, smoking, accidents, and counterproductive work behavior (CWB).

TABLE 11.4 Examples of Job Strains from each of the Three Categories of Job Strains

Job Strain	Examples of Specific Outcomes
Psychological reactions	Anger
	Anxiety
	Frustration
	Job dissatisfaction
Physical reactions	Physical symptoms
	Dizziness
	Headache
	Heart pounding
	Stomach distress
	Illness
	Cancer
	Heart disease
Behavioral reactions	Accidents
	Smoking
	Substance use
	Turnover

Source: "Emerging Theoretical and Methodological Issues in the Study of Work-Related Stress," by S. M. Jex and T. A. Beehr, 1991, *Research in Personnel and Human Resources Management*, *9*, 311–365.

Models of the occupational stress process presume that job stressors lead to job strains. It is generally recognized, however, that the process is not automatic and that the employee's perception and appraisal of the stressor are essential parts of the process. Appraisal is the extent to which a person interprets an event or situation to be personally threatening. Not everyone will see the same situation as a job stressor. One person who is given an extra work assignment sees it as an opportunity to make a good impression on the supervisor, while another sees it as an unfair imposition on free time.

Figure 11.6 (based on Frese & Zapf, 1988) illustrates how job stressors lead to job strains. In this model, job stressors (Step 1) are objective conditions or situations

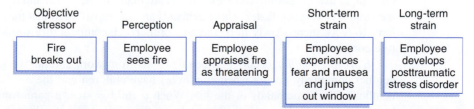

Figure 11.7 A five-step model of the job stress process (based on Frese & Zapf, 1998). An objective stressor (Step 1) leads to its perception (Step 2), and is appraised by the individual (Step 3). If it is appraised to be a challenge or threat, it can lead to short-term strains (Step 4) and eventually long-term strains (Step 5).

in the work environment. For example, there might be a fire at work. In order for the fire to become a stressor, the employee must be aware of its existence. This leads to Step 2, which is perception of the stressor. Perception alone, however, is not sufficient to lead to strain. The employee must appraise the stressor as aversive or threatening (Step 3). If a building is on fire, virtually anyone would appraise the situation as threatening. If it is only an ashtray that is on fire, it is doubtful that many would find it a threat. If the location is filled with flammable materials, however, even a lit match would be dangerous. It is the interpretation or appraisal of the situation that determines whether it will lead to the next steps, which involve strain. Strains in this model are either short term (Step 4) or long term (Step 5). Short-term strains occur immediately. Upon seeing a fire, an employee might experience fear (psychological reaction), become nauseated (physical reaction), and jump out a window (behavioral reaction). A person who experiences a severe enough trauma from the experience might develop posttraumatic stress disorder, which would be a long-term strain.

Job Stressors

There are many things in the work environment that can be stressful. Some are conditions that can occur across most jobs, such as conflicts with coworkers or heavy workloads. Others can be specific to particular occupations. For example, Parasuraman and Purohit (2000) found that a major stressor for orchestra musicians was being asked to do something that violated their sense of artistic integrity. This situation is not likely to exist for a nurse, who must instead deal with the stress of dying patients. Although many different conditions at work may serve as job stressors, relatively few have been studied. We will discuss five that have been given significant research attention as possible causes of employee strains. Each has been linked to at least some strains.

Role Ambiguity and Role Conflict

Role ambiguity and role conflict, often referred to as role stressors, are the most studied stressors in occupational stress research. **Role ambiguity** is the extent to which employees are uncertain about what their job functions and responsibilities are. Many supervisors fail to provide clear guidelines and directions for their subordinates, leading to ambiguity about what the employee is supposed to do.

Role conflict arises when people experience incompatible demands either at work (intrarole) or between work and nonwork (extrarole). *Intrarole conflict* arises from multiple demands on the job. For example, two supervisors might make incompatible requests. One might ask the employee to take more care in doing the work, and the other might ask the employee to work faster. These demands are incompatible in that the employee would have to work more slowly to be more careful. The incompatibility would be reflected in role conflict.

Extrarole conflict occurs between demands from work and nonwork domains. Such conflict commonly occurs when employees have children and the needs of the children conflict with the demands of the job. When a child is sick, a parent may have to stay home from work, thus experiencing role conflict. This type of role conflict is discussed in the section on work-family conflict.

Research on role ambiguity and role conflict has focused primarily on psychological strains. The results of Jackson and Schuler's (1985) meta-analysis showed that high levels of both role stressors were associated with low levels of job satisfaction and high levels of anxiety/tension and intention to quit the job. Glazer and Beehr (2005) showed that role variables relate to psychological strains not only in the United States, but in Hungary, Italy, and the United Kingdom. Correlations with behavioral strains, such as absence and job performance (Tubre & Collins, 2000), were quite small in most studies. It should be kept in mind that most studies of job performance use supervisor ratings, which (as discussed in Chapter 4) can be quite inaccurate. Fried, Ben-David, Tiegs, Avital, and Yeverechyahu (1998) improved on the typical job performance measure by asking specific questions about performance (e.g., "the employee is assigned the most difficult tasks in the department" and "the employee is capable of reading technical drawings"), rather than the more typical ratings of work quality and quantity. With this measure of job performance, the relations of role ambiguity and role conflict were considerably higher than typically found, suggesting that researchers need to pay more attention to the quality of performance measures in future studies. Of course, we must be careful in awaiting replication before drawing firm conclusions.

Most of the research on role stressors has used self-report scales completed by employees. This means that in the five-step model, role stressors were assessed at the level of appraisal (Step 3). It is unclear to what extent objective job conditions were responsible for these appraisals or whether the conditions resulted in psychological strains. Jex and Beehr (1991) wondered if role ambiguity and role conflict were perhaps not very important stressors. Their lack of importance is underscored by a study in which engineers were asked to indicate a stressful incident that had occurred at work during the preceding month (Keenan & Newton, 1985). Incidents that reflected role ambiguity or role conflict were quite rare.

Workload

Workload concerns the work demands that the job places on an employee, and it can be of two types: quantitative and qualitative. *Quantitative workload* is the amount of work that a person has. A heavy quantitative workload means that a person has too much to do. *Qualitative workload* is the difficulty of work relative to a person's capabilities. A heavy qualitative workload means that the employee cannot easily do job tasks because they are too difficult. It is possible to experience only one type of workload in a job. An employee may have a lot of work to do that is not necessarily difficult, or difficult work to do that is not necessarily plentiful. In many cases, particularly with complex jobs, an individual might experience both, having a great deal of difficult work to do.

Research has found that workload relates to all three types of strains—psychological, physical, and behavioral (Jex & Beehr, 1991). This research has involved a variety of methodologies that allow us to draw more definitive conclusions about the possible outcomes of this stressor.

Questionnaire studies have shown that employee reports of workloads correlate with a variety of strains. Spector et al. (1988) found significant correlations of workload with the psychological strains of anxiety, frustration, job dissatisfaction, and intention of quitting and the physical strains of health symptoms. Jamal (1990) found significant correlations of workload with the strains of job dissatisfaction, intention of quitting, and health symptoms. Karasek, Gardell, and Lindell (1987) found that workload was associated with the strains of depression, exhaustion, job dissatisfaction, health symptoms, and heart disease. These three studies were quite geographically diverse, having been conducted in the United States, Canada, and Sweden, respectively.

Studies have shown that workload can also affect physiology. It has been associated with blood pressure (Fox, Dwyer, & Ganster, 1993) and adrenaline secretion in the bloodstream (Johansson, 1989). Although research has shown that workload alone can be associated with strains, the effects of workload can involve the action of other variables, most notably control. We will discuss the joint effects of workload and control after we discuss the effects of control.

Social Stressors

Keenan and Newton (1985) found in their study of engineers that interpersonal conflict was one of the most frequently mentioned stressful incidents. Being able to get along well with other people is an important element in well-being, and failing to get along can be a serious source of strain. Because employed people spend so much of their time at work, social relationships with coworkers can be some of the most important in their lives. Interpersonal conflict and poor relationships with others can lead to a variety of strains.

Spector and Jex (1988) conducted a meta-analysis of 13 studies relating interpersonal conflict at work to job strains. They found that conflict related to physical strains of health symptoms (e.g., headache and stomach distress) and psychological strains of anxiety, depression, frustration, and job dissatisfaction at work. Dormann and Zapf (1999) conducted a longitudinal study in East Germany from 1990 to 1991, assessing a sample of workers before and after reunification of the country (see International Replication). They surveyed a sample of employees, including scales of social stressors (conflict and poor relationships with coworkers and supervisors) and depressive symptoms (feeling sad and a sense of worthlessness). They found that social stressors were associated with depressive symptoms over time, suggesting that poor relations might lead to psychological strain.

INTERNATIONAL REPLICATION

Social aspects of work can be very important for the well-being of employees. Conflict and poor relationships among employees, as well as lack of social support, can be important contributors to job strain. In this German study, Dormann and Zapf (1999) studied social aspects of work in relation to depressive symptoms to see if they were linked.

This study was conducted in Dresden, in what was formerly East Germany, to explore the impact of social stressors on psychological strain during the period of reunification of Germany from 1990 to 1991. This was a time of considerable upheaval, which makes it a good period in which to study occupational stress. A door-to-door survey method was used, with streets being chosen randomly, and then every fourth apartment visited. Residents were asked to participate if they were between 16 and 65 years old and working full-time. Scales to assess social stressors (animosity and conflict with others at work), social support (extent to which others at work provide assistance and emotional support), and depressive symptoms (feeling sad and a sense of worthlessness) were administered by interviewers. Because this was a longitudinal study, interviewers returned after three months and then a year to those houses where residents had completed the initial survey. By using a longitudinal design, it is possible to draw more confident conclusions about the possible effect of stressors on strains. As is characteristic of longitudinal studies, there was attrition (loss) of participants across the three time periods, and sample sizes ranged from 230 to 529 for the various analyses.

Results showed that social stressors were correlated with depressive symptoms even across the year time period of the study. This supported the idea that social stressors led to depressive symptoms. Furthermore, it was found that social support was a moderator of the relation between social stressors and depressive symptoms. For those employees who reported low social support at work (but not those who reported high) there was a positive relation between social stressors and depressive symptoms. That is, the higher the symptoms, the higher the stressors, the higher the symptoms.

This study provided evidence that social aspects of work can be an important element in psychological strain. A combination of high social stressors and low social support is associated with high levels of depressive symptoms. It is important for organizations to encourage the development of good employee relationships, and the immediate supervisor can be the means for accomplishing this if trained to be sensitive to employee conflicts and to provide social support.

Source: Dormann, C., & Zapf, D. (1999). Social support, social stressors at work, and depressive symptoms: Testing for main and moderating effects with structural equations in a three-wave longitudinal study. *Journal of Applied Psychology, 84*, 874–884.

Another form of social stressor is workplace **mistreatment**, which consists of aggression, bullying, harassment, nastiness, and rudeness directed toward an employee by others at work. Although it consists mainly of verbal acts, in severe cases mistreatment can include physical aggression (Raynor & Keashley, 2005). As with violence, much of this behavior is performed by other employees and supervisors, but it also can be done by customers (Grandey, Dickter, & Sin, 2004). In the United States and some other countries, one form of mistreatment, sexual harassment (which we discuss in Chapter 13), is illegal.

Workplace mistreatment can be quite common. In a Danish manufacturing company, 10% of employees said they were victims and 25% said they had witnessed workplace mistreatment more than once per month (Agervold & Mikkelsen, 2004). Such experiences have been linked to a number of psychological and physical strains, such as anxiety, depression, physical symptoms like headaches, and job dissatisfaction (Bowling & Beehr, 2006).

Organizational Politics

Organizational politics is the perception by employees that coworkers and supervisors engage in self-serving behavior in which they put their own interests above those of the organization and other people. Furthermore, rewards are perceived to be based on favoritism rather than merit (Kacmar & Carlson, 1997). Organizational politics can be considered a stressor in that it leads to strains. For example, Hochwarter, Kacmar, Perrewé, and Johnson (2003) surveyed 311 employees from a variety of organizations. They found that perceptions of organizational politics were associated with both psychological and physical strains. Similarly, Vigoda (2002) in a series of three Israeli studies found that politics was associated with psychological and physical strains as well as low organizational commitment and low job satisfaction.

Control

Control is the extent to which employees are able to make decisions about their work. Such decisions involve all aspects of work, including when to work, where to work, how to work, and what tasks to do. Employees with a high level of control are able to set their own work schedules, choose their own tasks, and decide how to complete those tasks.

In a low-control job, the work schedule is set, tasks are assigned, and often even the procedures for accomplishing tasks are specified. College professors have a high level of control because they decide what courses they teach, how they will teach them, and often even when and where they will teach them. Factory workers usually have little control because they work a fixed schedule, are given a specific task to do, and may be told exactly how to do that task. In many factories the work is paced by machine. In other words, the work comes down a conveyor belt at a fixed rate, and the worker must keep up with the machine, thus having very little control over work pacing.

Control is an extremely important component of the occupational stress process. It is also a component of job characteristics theory (see Chapters 9 and 10). Studies have found that employee perceptions of control are associated with all three categories of strain, although results are most consistent with psychological strain. Table 11.5 shows the mean correlations of perceived employee control with several strains reported in Spector's (1986) meta-analysis. As you can see from the table, high levels of control are associated with high levels of job satisfaction, organizational commitment, job involvement, and performance. Low levels of control are associated with high levels of emotional distress, intent to quit the job, health symptoms, absence, and turnover.

The control studies summarized in Spector's (1986) meta-analysis concerned employee perceptions about how much control they had at work. In most of these studies, control and strains were assessed with questionnaires given to employees. This sort of study makes it difficult to know whether job strains are the result of perceived control or whether perceived control is the result of strains. Perhaps employees who dislike their jobs, or employees who have low commitment, or employees who are in poor health perceive their jobs to be low in control even though the job may not be. As noted previously, there is evidence that how people feel about work affects their perception of the job, including the amount of control they have (Spector, 1992). In other words, the supposed strain might cause the supposed stressor, rather than the reverse. To make things even more complicated, it has been found that employees who perform well on the job

TABLE 11.5   Mean Correlations of Perceived Control with Job Stressors from Spector's (1986) Meta-Analysis

Stressor	Mean Correlation
Job satisfaction	.30
Organizational commitment	.26
Job involvement	.41
Emotional distress	−.25
Intent to quit	−.17
Health symptoms	−.25
Absence	−.19
Job performance	.20
Turnover likelihood	−.22

Source: "Perceived Control by Employees: A Meta-Analysis of Studies Concerning Autonomy and Participation at Work," by P. E. Spector, 1986, *Human Relations*, *11*, 1005–1016.

are given more control (Dansereau, Graen, & Haga, 1975), suggesting that performance affects the amount of control the employee has. Perhaps the extra control given to good performers raises their job satisfaction. Rather than the strain being caused by the stressor, the stressor is caused by the strain. However, there have been some studies of objective control that allow us to draw more firm conclusions about its role in occupational stress, as we will see next when we discuss machine pacing.

Studies of objective, or actual, control help solve the problem of inferring the effects of control on strains because they do not rely on employee reports about control. That is, they allow us to draw conclusions about the effects of low control assessed independently of the employee's perception or appraisal, or at Step 1 of the occupational stress model in Figure 11.5. Results with objective measures are not always the same as those with reports of control. For example, Liu, Spector, and Jex (2005) showed that O*NET (see Chapter 3) scores for control were associated with absence and illness, but not with psychological strains. Employee reports of control were associated with illness and psychological strains, but not absence.

Machine Pacing

One area in which objective control has been studied is *machine-paced work*, which means that a machine controls when the worker must make a response. The best example is factory work, when the conveyor belt controls the speed at which the employee works. Computer technology has introduced machine pacing into nonfactory work. Millions of people worldwide sit at computer terminals all day doing something not much different from simple factory work. They respond to information that comes on the screen at a pace set by the machine.

The effects of machine pacing and other work conditions have been studied for several years by a research group at the University of Stockholm in Sweden. A major focus of this research is to understand how human physiology is affected by job stressors, such as machine pacing. Two types of stress-related hormones have been studied—catecholamines (adrenaline and noradrenaline) and cortisol. These substances help prepare the body for action when danger or challenge occurs. Adrenaline is often said to help energize the performance of athletes during competition. Its actions can be felt as "butterflies" in the stomach. Cortisol helps control swelling during injury (Sarafino, 1990).

The University of Stockholm research has shown that both control and workload affect physiological responses. In a series of studies of employees, these researchers assessed the level of hormones by analyzing urine samples at home and at work. They found that as workload increased, the amount of adrenaline and noradrenaline increased (Frankenhaeuser & Johansson, 1986). When people work hard, their bodies may use these two hormones to help energize performance. Control also had an effect on the two catecholamines. Employees who were machine paced had higher levels of adrenaline and noradrenaline than employees who were self-paced (Johansson, 1981). The effects of control on cortisol were somewhat different. With machine pacing (low control), the cortisol level increased from home to work. With self-pacing (high control), however, the cortisol level decreased from home to work (Frankenhaeuser & Johansson, 1986). The researchers hypothesized that distress was the important component in these results. Lack of control was presumed to increase the level of cortisol because the lack of control distressed the employees, and distress is associated with the secretion of cortisol.

In addition to physiological reactions, machine pacing has been associated with psychological strains and health symptoms. Compared to self-paced work, machine-paced work has been found to be associated with anxiety (Broadbent & Gath, 1981), dissatisfaction, and health symptoms (M. J. Smith, Hurrell, & Murphy, 1989). All of these studies combined have provided reasonably convincing evidence that job stressors can have both physiological and psychological effects. They have not demonstrated, however, that these effects lead directly to serious illness. Johansson (1989) points out that frequent high levels of catecholamines and cortisol have been associated with heart disease. Thus, we might speculate that working under conditions that caused distress would be a risk factor in the development of later illness.

The Demand/Control Model

The **demand/control model** (Karasek, 1979) states that the effects of job stressors are a complex interplay of demands and employee control. Demands are stressors, such as workload, that require adaptation. Put another way, a demand taxes an employee's ability to cope with the environment. According to the theory, demands lead to strain only when there is insufficient control. Stated another way, having control reduces the negative effects of demands, or serves as a *stress buffer*. Figure 11.7 illustrates how control affects the relation between demands and strain. It shows that when control is high, demands (stressors) do not lead to strain. When control is low, however, strains increase as stressors increase. The model implies that giving people control at work can be a successful strategy for reducing or buffering the negative effects of job stressors.

Research support for the demands/control model has been mixed, with only some studies finding the hypothesized effect (deLange, Taris, Kompier, Houtman, & Bongers, 2003; Ganster & Schaubroeck, 1991). At least some of the reason for the inconsistent results may concern the measures of demands and control, which have differed across studies. Wall, Jackson, Mullarkey, and Parker (1996) showed that the nature of control mattered in their test of the model. They found support for the model with a measure that focused on control over employees' immediate tasks, but not with a measure of

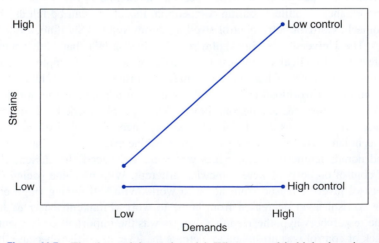

Figure 11.7 The demands/control model. When control is high, there is no relation between demands and strain. When control is low, strain increases as demands increase.

more general control. Another possible factor is that most studies measure the general or typical levels of demands, control, and strain. When Bishop, Ang, Khader, Enkelmann, Tong, Wy, and Diong (2003) assessed control, demands, and blood pressure repeatedly over the day, they found that high-demand/low-control events were associated with elevated pressure, just as the theory predicts. Of course, they also used an objective measure of strain, which has been found to support the model in other studies (Fox et al., 1993).

More recent research has attempted to extend the idea of stress buffering to other variables related to control. Jex and Bliese (1999) studied the effects of self-efficacy on relations between workload and strains. In a study of over 2,000 U.S. Army soldiers, they found that those who had low self-efficacy showed a relation between workload and strains (both physical health symptoms and psychological). When workload was high, symptoms were high. Those high in self-efficacy did not show this relation, as their self-efficacy appeared to buffer the negative effects of stressors. Of course, more research needs to be done to confirm these findings.

► WORK-FAMILY CONFLICT

Work-family conflict is a form of extra role conflict (see the role conflict discussion earlier in the chapter) in which the demands of work interfere with the family, for example, having to spend time at work leaves insufficient time for home (Baltes & Heydens-Gahir, 2003), or the demands of the family interfere with the work, for example, having to take a sick child to the doctor might require a person to be absent from work. The problem can be particularly acute for two-career couples with children and for single parents. With both parents working or with single parents, role conflicts are certain to arise over such issues as staying home with sick children and participating in school functions.

Several factors contribute to the experience of work-family conflict. On the organization side, having to work many hours (Day & Chamberlain, 2006; Van Daalen, Willemsen, & Sanders, 2006) and lack of schedule flexibility can lead to conflict (Major, Klein, & Ehrhart, 2003). Work-family conflict has also been shown to relate to role conflict and role ambiguity (Ford, Heinen, & Langkamer, 2007). On the employee side, personality can also be a factor; for example, research has shown that individuals who are high on

(*DILBERT reprinted by permission of United Feature Syndicate, Inc.*)

negative affectivity (the tendency to experience negative emotions) report more work family conflict (Bruck & Allen, 2003; Wayne, Musisca, & Fleeson, 2004). Of course, such individuals have a tendency to experience high levels of various stressors and strains.

Work-family conflict can have a number of negative effects on both men and women. In their meta-analysis of work-family conflict studies, Allen, Herst, Bruck, and Sutton (2000) found a mean correlation of −.23 with job satisfaction. Individuals who report high levels of work-family conflict tend to report low job satisfaction. This pattern was found for both men and women (Kossek & Ozeki, 1998), suggesting that both genders respond similarly to work-family conflict. Work-family conflict has also been linked to work stress, with high levels of work-family conflict being associated with strains of anxiety (Ford et al., 2007), depression and physical health symptoms (Major et al., 1999), absence and lateness (Hammer, Bauer, & Grandey, 2003), dissatisfaction with family life (Aryee, Fields, & Luk, 1999), and dissatisfaction with life in general (Carlson & Kacmar, 2000).

Although having both parent and work roles can have detrimental effects, particularly for women, who usually assume the major responsibility for children, dual roles can have positive effects as well (Langan-Fox, 1998). Work can provide enhanced self-esteem and social support from others, which for some people counteracts the more negative effects of dual roles. Likewise, there can be a positive impact of work on the family and of the family on work. Hanson, Hammer, and Colton (2006) pointed out that coworkers can help with family issues, and family members can help with work issues.

Organizations that are concerned with work-family conflict have taken steps to help their employees. Two of the most frequently used approaches are flexible work schedules and onsite child care in the workplace. Both make it easier for employees with children to manage both family and work responsibilities. Flexible schedules allow an individual to take time off to deal with nonwork demands, such as taking a sick child to the doctor. Onsite child care makes it easier for parents by enabling them to take their children with them to work. Parents can visit their children during breaks, and they are nearby in case of illness. Scandura and Lankau (1997) surveyed male and female managers about flexible hours and their job attitudes. Flexible hours were associated with greater job satisfaction for both men and women who had children living with them, but not for men and women without children. Chiu and Ng (1999) looked at what they termed women-friendly practices (e.g., child-care facilities, maternity benefits, flexible work hours, and family counseling) in Hong Kong companies, and found they had a positive effect on women's but not men's attitudes.

▶ BURNOUT

Burnout is a distressed psychological state that an employee might experience after being on the job for a long period of time. A person suffering from burnout is emotionally exhausted and has low work motivation, and little energy and enthusiasm for the job. Originally, the concept was developed to explain the reactions of employees in the helping professions, such as psychotherapists and social workers. The early burnout researchers believed that burnout was the result of working intensely with other people, and there is research to support that idea. For example, Bakker, Schaufeli, Sixma, Bosveld, and Van Dierendonck (2000) found that patient demands were associated with burnout in

TABLE 11.6 The Three Burnout Components and Expected Results of Each

Component	Results
Emotional exhaustion	Absence
	Fatigue
Depersonalization	Callous and uncaring treatment of clients and other people
	Hostility toward other people
Reduced personal accomplishment	Low motivation
	Poor performance

physicians. More recently, however, the idea has been extended to workers in all sorts of jobs, even those who have little contact with others.

Burnout is assessed with scales administered to employees. The most popular scale, the Maslach Burnout Inventory (MBI) (Maslach & Jackson, 1981), measures three components of burnout:

Emotional exhaustion

Depersonalization

Reduced personal accomplishment

Emotional exhaustion is the feeling of tiredness and fatigue at work. *Depersonalization* is the development of a cynical and callous feeling toward others. *Reduced personal accomplishment* is the feeling that the employee is not accomplishing anything worthwhile at work. Table 11.6 lists some of the by-products of each burnout component. For example, emotional exhaustion should lead to fatigue and absence.

Feelings of burnout have been found to correlate with many job stressor and job strain variables and might be considered a type of strain (Cordes & Dougherty, 1993). High levels of burnout have been associated with low levels of perceived control (Fernet, Guay, & Senécal, 2004) and job satisfaction and high levels of role conflict, health symptoms, intention of quitting the job (Shirom, 1989), and work overload (Bacharach, Bamberger, & Conley, 1991). It has been linked to increased risk for cardiovascular disease (Melamed, Shirom, Toker, Berliner, & Shapira, 2006) and poor job performance (Will Andrews & Carlson, 2004). Figure 11.8 shows some of the job stressors and strains that correlate with burnout. These stressors are possible causes of burnout.

Figure 11.8 Job stressors and job strains associated with burnout.

Source: "A Review and an Integration of Research on Job Burnout," by C. L. Cordes and T. W. Dougherty, 1993, *Academy of Management Review, 18*, 621–656.

As we have seen in many other areas of I/O psychology, research in the burnout domain has been dominated by self-report survey methods. From these studies, we know many of the variables that are correlated with burnout. We are not yet certain about the causes of burnout and how organizations can prevent it. Research does suggest two ways to reduce burnout. First, burnout can be reduced by taking a vacation (Fritz & Sonnentag, 2006; Westman & Eden, 1997), although the recovery is likely to be short-lived, with burnout levels returning after a few weeks back on the job. Second, it has been suggested that organizations encourage managers to provide emotional support to employees by providing positive feedback and engaging in discussions of positive aspects of work as a means of reducing burnout (Kahn, Schneider, Jenkins-Henkelman, & Moyle, 2006).

▶ FUTURE ISSUES AND CHALLENGES

Throughout most of its history, I/O has focused primarily on factors that implicitly or explicitly concerned employee job performance and other things that affected organizational effectiveness. The rapid development of the occupational health psychology field, which grew in part out of I/O, suggests a shift in emphasis to employee well-being in addition to performance. Today we see several universities that offer OHP as a concentration within an I/O doctoral program, and the *Journal of Occupational Health Psychology* is concerned specifically with research in this field. In the future it seems likely that students will choose OHP as an occupation in which they help organizations maintain the health, safety, and well-being of employees through the use of tools from a variety of subareas of psychology, including clinical, human factors, and I/O.

However, the distinction between performance and well-being may be a false one, as research has shown that they are linked. The idea of the Healthy Work Organization (HWO) recognizes that there are many things that can be done to enhance the health of both employees and organizations together (Jaffee, 1995; Sauter, Lim, & Murphy, 1996). Furthermore, research has linked both job stressors and strains to job performance (e.g., Beehr, Jex, Stacy, & Murray, 2000; Wright & Cropanzano, 2000). A challenge for the I/O field is to develop ways to create HWOs out of organizations that are not as healthy as they might be.

A final challenge for the future is finding ways to help people cope with new technologies. Automation is certainly not new, but as computerization continues to spread throughout both blue-collar and white-collar jobs, new health-related problems will arise. We are already seeing that the widespread use of computers is producing MSDs. Research has also shown that machine pacing, which occurs with many automated systems, may have serious health consequences. We need to understand better the physical and psychological effects of working with computerized technologies and how to reduce any negative effects that may be found.

▶ CHAPTER SUMMARY

Work can be a dangerous place, not only for blue-collar workers who must use hazardous equipment and substances, but for white-collar workers as well. Many hazards have immediate consequences, such as an injury from an accident. Often, however, the effects of work conditions do not show up for many years, such as a cancer produced from years of exposure to a carcinogenic chemical.

Accidents are a major cause of death for people of working age. The causes of accidents involve both employee and organizational factors. Programs directed toward eliminating physical hazards in the workplace and encouraging safe behavior through development of a safety climate seem most effective in reducing accidents.

Physical work conditions tend to have effects that are primarily physical. Exposure to infectious disease can cause illness, exposure to loud noise can cause hearing loss, repetitive actions and lifting can cause musculoskeletal problems (MSDs), and exposure to toxic substances can cause cancer. Nonphysical conditions can have effects that are both physical and psychological. Work schedules, for example, have been associated with job satisfaction and physical symptoms.

Research has shown that occupational stress can be a factor in psychological strain. Although much of the research is circumstantial, evidence is accumulating in support of the idea that work demands and control have important physical health implications. Some of the effects of job stressors, however, may be indirect. For example, research has associated job conditions with health-related behaviors such as smoking and substance use.

Work-family conflict concerns incompatible demands between the workplace and the home. It can be considered a form of stressor that has been linked to both physical and psychological strains. Both men and women experience work-family conflict. Organizations use a number of practices to reduce it, including flexible work schedules and onsite daycare.

Burnout is a psychological state involving fatigue and lack of motivation for work. Research on burnout has found that burnout is associated with many job stressors and strains and may itself be considered a psychological strain.

I/O PSYCHOLOGY IN PRACTICE

(*Courtesy of Stacey Moran*)

This case discusses how Dr. Stacey Moran works with organizations to improve their safety practices for both clients/customers and employees. Dr. Moran received her Ph.D. in industrial/organizational psychology from Pennsylvania State University in 1991. She is a member of the Workers Compensation and Cost Containment Department for St. Paul Travelers Insurance Company. Her role is to help organizations apply principles of psychology to issues involving health and safety at work. As the oldest insurance organization in the United States, St. Paul Travelers is very interested in helping its customers reduce the number and severity of accidents and injuries they suffer. Dr. Moran helps them accomplish this by providing consulting to insureds and company representatives, putting on training programs about safety, and conducting surveys about accident experiences and safety practices. She deals with all areas of OHP, including accidents, burnout, stress, and violence.

One of her projects was a survey of organizations in the outdoor adventure industry in North America. This is a rapidly growing service industry that provides outdoor recreation with such activities as camping, rock climbing, and white-water rafting. Many of these organizations are in the nonprofit sector, such as Boy Scouts and Girl Scouts. The industry is quite concerned about safety, because many of the activities its clientele engage in have the potential for injury.

The goal of this project was to collect information from a large sample of organizations about their safety concerns and practices. This would provide a picture of the state of the industry that could inform where efforts should be targeted to improve safety. Dr. Moran worked in collaboration with Outward Bound, USA, a St. Paul Travelers' insured and the oldest and largest outdoor adventure program in the world. She helped design a survey that was sent to 1,265 organizations throughout North America, and 294 useable surveys were returned (nearly 25%). She analyzed the results and wrote a report for the industry.

The results showed that members of the adventure industry are concerned about safety, but that the areas of concern don't necessarily match where their safety efforts are placed. For example, the two major issues identified were driver safety and instructor judgment training. However, most respondents reported that their organizations failed to provide training in these areas. The major conclusions were that improvements are needed in three areas: training, assessment of risk and keeping track of accident/injury patterns, and development of safety cultures where injury prevention is a major objective. Interestingly, there was a high correlation between customer/client injuries and employee injuries—organizations that had a high incidence of one had a high incidence of the other. Thus it would be expected that practices that reduced injuries for one group will reduce injuries for the other.

Dr. Moran's report was widely distributed throughout the industry to inform organizations about the steps they should take to increase safety. This project illustrates how positive change in organizations can be accomplished by providing specific information about effective actions that can be taken to solve an important problem.

Discussion Questions

1. Why would an insurance company be concerned about the safety of its insureds' clients/customers?

2. What else might an organization do to improve driving safety other than provide training?

3. How might an organization improve its safety climate?

4. Some managers would argue that employee safety is not their concern and that employees should be responsible for their own safety. Counter this argument and explain why safety is the concern of management.

LEARNING BY DOING

Safety in the Workplace

Choose a workplace that you have access to either as a customer, employee, or visitor. It could be your own university. Look for instances in which safety procedures are used. This could include the posting of safety messages (e.g., to use safety equipment), the wearing of safety gear, the availability or use of safety equipment, or other signs of safety practices. Make a record of what you found that can be discussed in class or compared with other students.

Workplace Stress

Do a mini-replication of the Keenan and Newton (1985) study. Ask five people you know (acquaintances, family members, or friends) to relate a stressful event that occurred to them in the past 30 days. Ask them to describe what led up to it, what happened, and how they responded. When you have all five, look them over and see what the nature of the events was. In particular, see how many occurred at work compared to outside of work. See if any involved work-family conflict. Of the workplace events, see if they fit any of the stressors we have discussed, such as role ambiguity, role conflict, workload, lack of control, or social stressors. What was the typical response to a stressful event?

PART V

THE SOCIAL CONTEXT OF WORK

(© *EyeWire*)

CHAPTER 12

Work Groups and Work Teams

CHAPTER 12 OUTLINE

On July 3, 1988, the U.S. Navy guided missile cruiser *Vincennes* shot down an Iranian airliner, killing all 290 persons onboard. Responsibility for firing the fatal missile was shared by several members of the vessel's Anti Air Warfare Team. This team is supposed to be able to identify hostile aircraft correctly and to shoot only when threatened.

Obviously something went wrong, and much of the blame can be placed on poor team-work. Someone mistakenly identified the airliner as hostile, and over the next few stressful minutes no one corrected the mistake. The Navy has spent considerable time and effort since the tragedy trying to determine how best to prevent similar mistakes in the future, and in the more than two decades since the *Vincennes* incident, the error has not been repeated by the Navy. I/O psychologists were very much involved in this effort to improve teamwork through research (see I/O Psychology in Practice).

The Navy is not the only organization in which people work in teams. Teams can be found in factories, hospitals, schools, and stores. Any job that requires the coordinated actions of more than one person can involve teams. In many work settings we find groups of people who work relatively independently but still come in contact with one another. College professors, salesclerks, security guards, and teachers often do most of their work without the help of coworkers, although many other people in their organizations may be doing similar work. Even the most independent employees are affected by the behavior of others with whom they interact at work.

In this chapter we turn our attention from the individual employee to groups of employees. We will see how the behavior of individuals is very much affected by the behavior of other people in the work environment. It would be correct to say that one cannot fully understand the behavior of individuals without considering the influence of others, because people rarely work totally alone and unaffected by others.

We begin this discussion by distinguishing work groups from work teams. Four important group and two important team concepts will be discussed:

Roles

Norms

Group cohesiveness

Process loss

Team commitment

Team mental model

Next the chapter covers the effects of groups on job performance. Techniques for enhancing group and team performance are included.

Objectives: The student who studies this chapter should be able to:

► Define work groups and work teams, and note the difference between them.
► Explain the four important group and two important team concepts.
► Summarize the findings on group performance.
► Talk about the advantages and disadvantages of group diversity.
► Discuss the procedures that can be used to enhance work group and team performance.

► WORK GROUPS VERSUS WORK TEAMS

A **work group** is a collection of two or more people who interact with one another and share some interrelated task goals. These two characteristics, interaction and interrelatedness, distinguish a group from just a collection of people. A university department faculty is a work group. The members of the faculty interact with one another from time to time, and they have interrelated goals involving the education of students. Each faculty member teaches courses that taken together constitute the requirements for the major course of study. On the other hand, the university's students, taken as a whole, do not constitute a work group because they do not all interact with one another, although subsets of them do, and they do not all share interrelated goals. Rather, each student has an individual goal that is unrelated to the goals of other students.

A **work team** is a type of work group, but a team has three specific properties (West, Borrill, & Unsworth, 1998):

1. The actions of individuals must be interdependent and coordinated.

2. Each member must have a particular, specified role.

3. There must be common task goals and objectives.

For example, each person on a surgical team has a specific role. A surgeon does the cutting and sewing, a surgical nurse assists and provides instruments, and an anesthesiologist keeps the patient unconscious and monitors vital signs. Their actions are different but coordinated. The cutting cannot begin until the patient is asleep. The surgeon cannot sew unless the nurse gives him or her the tools. There is a common goal of successfully completing the surgery without losing the patient.

The distinction between a group and a team is an important one. All teams are groups, but not all groups are teams. A group consists of people who work together but can do their jobs without one another. A team is a group of people who cannot do their jobs, at least not effectively, without the other members of the team. For the remainder of this chapter, all group principles will also apply to teams, but team concepts don't necessarily apply to groups.

Virtual Team

As we discussed in Chapter 10, technology (computer supported cooperative work) has made it possible for people to work in teams without face-to-face contact. These **virtual teams** communicate via e-mail, instant messaging, telephone, web-cameras, and other technologies. Virtuality, however, is not an all-or-none phenomenon. Teams vary in their use of virtual tools such as e-mail and telephone (Kirkman & Mathieu, 2005), with some teams having members that are geographically separated, thus precluding face-to-face interaction, whereas others are located in the same place but choose to communicate virtually at least some of the time.

Working virtually can have some advantages, as we saw with the research on brainstorming in which face-to-face team members performed more poorly than virtual brainstormers. However, research summarized in a meta-analysis of 52 studies that compared face-to-face with virtual groups showed that the virtual groups had worse task performance, took more time to complete tasks, and had lower group member satisfaction (Baltes, Dickson, Sherman, Bauer, & LaGanke, 2002). Some of this may be due to the types of virtual tools that were utilized by teams in these studies. The use of richer media—for example, using video plus voice—results in better performance than just text alone (Martins, Gilson, & Maynard, 2006).

▶ IMPORTANT GROUP AND TEAM CONCEPTS

Four important group concepts and two important team concepts underlie much group and team behavior. The first three (roles, norms, and group cohesiveness) describe important aspects of groups and teams that help us understand how they operate. The fourth (process loss) is concerned with what sorts of things happen in work groups and teams that prevent people from putting all of their effort into job performance. Team commitment and team mental model are characteristics important to teams but not groups.

Roles

The concept of **role** implies that not everyone in a group or team has the same function or purpose. Instead, different individuals have different jobs and responsibilities in the group or team. In a surgical team, one person has the role of surgeon, another of nurse, and another of anesthesiologist. In a well-running work team, each role is clearly defined, and all team members know exactly what their roles are.

Formal roles are specified by the organization and are part of the formal job description. In a surgical team, each person's job title—surgeon, nurse, or anesthesiologist—defines the role in a formal way. There may be organizational documents, such as written job descriptions and job analyses, that define the roles. **Informal roles** arise from group interaction rather than from the formal rules and specifications of organizations. Groups can invent roles that do not exist formally, or a group's informal roles can supersede the formal ones.

An example of an informal role in a work group is that of greeting card sender. It is common for members of work groups to send cards to one another on special occasions, such as birthdays or weddings. One group member might take on the role of buying and sending cards at the appropriate times. An example of the informal superseding the formal occurs when one person has the formal title of supervisor but another person is (informally) the actual leader. This can occur in combat teams when the members view the lower ranking experienced sergeant rather than the higher ranking but inexperienced lieutenant as the leader.

Groups vary considerably in the extent to which roles are specialized among members. In a surgical team, for example, the training and credentials are such that little overlap in roles can occur among the surgeon, nurse, and anesthesiologist. With other groups or teams, members can change roles or rotate responsibilities over time. In an academic department of a university, it is common for faculty to take turns being the chairperson.

Norms

Norms are unwritten rules of behavior accepted by members of a work group. These rules can cover everything from style of dress and manner of speech to how hard everyone works. Norms can exert powerful influences on individual behavior because many groups strenuously enforce them. As illustrated in Figure 12.1, violation of norms will bring increasingly stronger pressure to bear on the violator, beginning by informing the violator of the norm, then giving a scolding for the violation, then punishing either verbally or physically (violence), and, if these steps are ineffective, by ostracizing the member

Figure 12.1 Norm violators are informed, scolded, punished, and then ostracized from the group.

(Jackson & LePine, 2003). A good illustration of norms can be found in Coch and French's (1948) classic study of a pajama factory with a piece-rate system. Employees in this factory assembled pajamas and could work at their own pace. Groups, however, would adopt production norms that specified how much members should produce. Coch and French documented the output of a worker who began to exceed the 50-unit per hour production norm of her work group. When group members pressured her, she restricted her output to about 45 units per hour. A short time later the group was disbanded, and within a matter of days, the worker's output more than doubled.

Work group norms can have more impact on member behavior than supervisors or organizational practices. In the Coch and French (1948) study, production was restricted even though a piece-rate system was in place. Employees would sacrifice the opportunity to make extra money to keep from violating group norms. Clearly, norms could prove quite useful as a means of enhancing productivity if appropriately directed. The changing of group norms can be difficult for the management of an organization, which must structure the changes so that it is in the best interest of the group to adopt them. For example, group incentive systems can be an effective means of getting groups to adopt high production norms. With such a system, all members of the group are given rewards, such as a monetary bonus, if the group achieves some specified level of performance. As demonstrated by Coch and French (1948), however, incentive systems will not always motivate groups to perform well.

Group Cohesiveness

Group cohesiveness is the sum of the forces attracting group members and keeping the group together. It is a group phenomenon; and for a group to be highly cohesive, most if not all members must have strong motives to remain in the group. A high level of group cohesiveness has important implications for group behavior. Norms tend to be strongly enforced in groups that are highly cohesive. The violation of a norm, particularly an important one, can be threatening to a group's existence. If group continuation is vitally important to group members, conformity to norms will be a critical issue. In the workplace, people are often dependent on their jobs for their economic survival, and the work group can be as important as the family. Threats to the well-being of the group are taken seriously.

Cohesive groups strongly enforce their norms, and work groups may adopt norms for high or low productivity. For this reason, correlations between cohesiveness and job performance have been somewhat inconsistent across studies. However, a meta-analysis (Beal, Cohen, Burke, & McLendon, 2003) suggests that cohesiveness is more likely to result in high than low performance. For example, Man and Lam (2003) studied work teams in an international bank with offices in Hong Kong and the United States. Team members completed questionnaires asking about cohesiveness, and supervisors provided ratings of team performance. Results showed that cohesive teams were rated higher in team performance.

Process Loss

Much of the time and effort of work group members is devoted to accomplishing organizational objectives through the performance of individuals. Much effort, however, goes into other group functions that have little to do with job performance, including time spent in group maintenance functions, such as norm enforcement and conflict resolution among members. These can also involve social activities, such as meals or conversation, that enhance group cohesiveness, which can be important for efficient group functioning. All the time and effort expended on activities not directly related to production or task accomplishment are referred to as **process loss**.

Groups vary tremendously in the amount of time they devote to maintenance activities. Some groups have problems with norm violators and interpersonal conflicts that can consume a great deal of time and energy. Other groups run smoothly with little friction and few internal distractions. In the following section on group performance, we will see that groups do not always perform as well as we might expect. Process loss can have a lot to do with the inefficiency that sometimes occurs in groups. Nevertheless, a certain amount of process loss is necessary and may lead to better future performance by the group.

Team Commitment

The organizational commitment concept has been extended to a number of different entities, including the team. **Team commitment** is the strength of an individual's involvement in a team, and consists of the acceptance of team goals, willingness to work hard for the team, and desire to remain on the team (Bishop & Scott, 2000). Therefore, we might expect that high team commitment would be associated with high team performance, low turnover, and team satisfaction. Research has found support for at least two of these expectations. Bishop, Scott, and Burroughs (2000) found in an automobile parts manufacturing company that work team performance was positively related to team commitment. Bishop and Scott (2000) studied sewing machine operators and found that their team commitment was related to coworker and supervisor satisfaction, as well as organizational commitment. Van Der Vegt, Emans, and Van De Vliert (2000), in a study conducted in the Netherlands, reported significant positive correlations of team commitment with general job satisfaction and team satisfaction (See International Replication).

INTERNATIONAL REPLICATION

Task interdependence, the extent to which people's tasks require sharing of resources or working together, is an important element in distinguishing groups from teams. Groups consist of people who may or may not be very interdependent, but merely work in proximity to one another, whereas teams are interdependent. In this study conducted in the Netherlands, Van Der Vegt, Emans, and Van De Vliert (2000) investigated the extent to which interdependence would relate to team commitment and team member job satisfaction. They argued that task interdependence can enhance job satisfaction, team satisfaction, and team commitment. This is because the demand for working closely together leads to camaraderie and good interpersonal relationships that most people find enjoyable.

Participants were 148 employees of a technical consulting firm who were organized into 22 work teams. Questionnaires were mailed to employees by higher management members who asked them to participate. Scales were included to measure task interdependence, job satisfaction, team satisfaction, and team commitment. Teams varied in the tasks they were assigned, with some requiring more interdependence than others.

Results showed that task interdependence was significantly and positively correlated with job satisfaction (.18), team satisfaction (.29), and team commitment (.45). Thus, the greater the interdependence, the more satisfied and committed the team members were. Furthermore, team commitment was strongly correlated with job satisfaction (.59) and team satisfaction (.69).

These results support Van der Vegt et al.'s arguments that interdependence leads to job satisfaction, task satisfaction, and team commitment. Of course, since this was a cross-sectional questionnaire study, we can't be certain that interdependence was the cause, but we can say that interdependence appears to play an important role in how people feel about their jobs and teams.

Source: Van Der Vegt, G., Emans, B., & Van De Vliert, E. (2000). Team members' affective responses to patterns of intragroup interdependence and job complexity. *Journal of Management*, 26, 633–655.

Team commitment seems much like group cohesiveness, but it is a broader construct. Whereas cohesiveness is only the attraction of the individuals to the group, commitment also involves acceptance of team goals and willingness to work hard for the team. Of course, all these elements are highly related, so in practice cohesive teams will be committed teams.

Team Mental Model

When people work in teams, they must have some common conception of what they are to do together. A **team mental model** refers to the shared understanding among team members of the task, team, equipment, and situation (Mohammad & Dumville, 2001). Smith-Jentsch, Mathieu, and Kraiger (2005) explain that mental models are complex and can be divided into two types, one concerned with taskwork and the other with teamwork. The taskwork model concerns the nature of the job that needs to be done. In a surgical team, all members have to share an understanding of the surgery they jointly perform and of their respective individual roles. This does not mean that the mental models have to be identical, but just compatible (Canon-Bowers, & Salas, 2001). The nurse may not have the same understanding of the patient's illness as the surgeon, but they share an understanding of what they need to accomplish and what each of them does. When the surgeon asks for an instrument, the nurse knows what to do because they share that understanding. The teamwork model is the shared conception of the team and how its members are to work together. A shared mental model of teamwork facilitates team performance because members know how to coordinate their efforts with one another.

In order for a team to perform effectively, there must be a sufficiently shared team mental model. Teams in which the mental model is inadequate will fail to coordinate, will be inefficient, and will be likely to make errors. Conflicts can also arise out of misunderstandings or because team members get frustrated with one another because each expects the other to do tasks that are not getting done. Research has shown that quality of the team mental model relates to team performance, with both accuracy and similarity of mental models among team members leading to better performance (Edwards, Day, Arthur, & Bell, 2006; Lim & Klein, 2006; Rentsch & Klimoski, 2001).

▶ GROUP PERFORMANCE

There is a widespread belief that group performance is superior to individual performance for many tasks. This belief is based on the notion that something emerges in the interaction among people that enables a group to be better than the sum of its members. In other words, people inspire one another to be better than they would have been alone. It is true that for some tasks the coordinated efforts of two or more people are necessary because a single individual could not accomplish them alone. For example, several people are needed to build a house. Some tasks may require more than two hands, and others may require the lifting of objects that one person cannot manage alone. For many tasks, however, groups are not necessarily better than individuals. Part of the reason is process loss—group members distract and keep one another from concentrating solely on the task at hand. There are additional reasons that we discuss as we compare the performance of individuals with groups.

Performance in the Presence of Others

One of the earliest known group phenomena in psychology is that task performance is affected by the presence of others. In the late 1800s, Norman Triplett noted that the performance of bicycle riders was faster when they were racing against others than when they were riding alone (Triplett, 1897). Subsequent research with laboratory tasks, however, did not always find that people performed better in the presence of others. Performance was better in the presence of others in some studies but worse in other studies.

The most widely accepted explanation for these results was put forth by Zajonc (1965), who noticed that the type of task determined if performance was enhanced or

Performing in front of an audience raises arousal, as this person will certainly experience.
(*Michael Malyszko/Taxi/Getty Images*)

inhibited by the presence of others. He suggested that the presence of others increases physiological arousal, which has effects on task performance. Performance is improved (the **social facilitation** effect) by other-induced arousal when the task is simple or well learned, such as bicycle riding. On the other hand, performance is decreased (the **social inhibition** effect) by other-induced arousal when the task is complex or new to the individual, such as solving a complex mathematics problem. These results suggest that for complex tasks, people should be given private space that allows them to keep their arousal levels relatively low. For simple tasks, the arousal produced by the presence of others can enhance performance, but other people can also be a distraction in the workplace, leading to poorer performance. There are no guarantees.

Group Versus Individual Performance on Additive Tasks

When researchers compare individuals to groups on task performance, they are usually concerned with an **additive task**. The output of the task is countable, and the total output is the sum of the individual group member outputs. The total output for a group of cashiers in a supermarket would be additive because the total sales are the sum of all the individual cashiers' sales. The effects of group process on additive task performance can be seen by comparing the output of an interacting group of people with an equal number of individuals who do not interact. The noninteracting individuals are referred to as a **nominal group**. Their output reflects the output of a given number of individuals. The output of the interacting group, by comparison, reflects how well the same number of people will perform in a group.

Research dating back to the nineteenth century has consistently shown that nominal groups do as well as, and usually better than, interacting groups (Davis, 1969). This finding is well illustrated by research done over 100 years ago by an agricultural engineer in France named Ringelmann. Kravitz and Martin (1986) described Ringelmann's research, in which he compared the task performance of groups and individuals. Ringelmann noted that the sum of individual efforts often surpassed the effort of an equal number of people working in a group. Table 12.1 summarizes how group and individual efforts compare. It shows the results across several different types of tasks involving the pulling and pushing of objects. The first column shows the number of people in the group. The second column shows the expected output of a group, which was calculated as the number of people in the group times the average individual performance. In other words, a group

TABLE 12.1   Strength of Object Pulling and Pushing as a Function of Group Size

Size of Group	Expected Pull (KGS)	Actual Pull (KGS)	Percentage of Actual to Expected Performance
1	1	1	100
2	2	1.86	93
4	4	3.08	77
8	8	3.92	49

Source: "Ringelmann rediscovered: The original article," by D. A. Kravitz and B. Martin, 1986, *Journal of Personality and Social Psychology*, *50*, 936–941.

of two people should produce double the output of a single person, and a group of four people should produce four times the output of a single person. The third column shows the actual performance of the group. As the table illustrates, the actual output of the interacting group is considerably less than the output of the nominal group. The percentage that the interacting group's output is of the nominal group's output declines as the group size increases (see column 4). Clearly, something is happening with the interacting group that is inhibiting performance.

There are at least two explanations for the group effect on additive task performance. The first explanation is the possibility of process loss. Group members may interfere with one another's task performance or may spend time and effort on group maintenance activities rather than the task at hand. This might explain inhibited performance in some studies, but with the rope-pulling task this does not seem likely. The nature of the task required that all group members concentrate their efforts on pulling the rope at the same time when a signal was given. Group members could not have been doing something else at the time.

A second and more likely explanation is a phenomenon called **social loafing**—people do not put forth as much effort in a group as they would if they were working alone, and the larger the group, the less effort each person exerts. Latané, Williams, and Harkins (1979) found this phenomenon to be widespread in both laboratory and field settings. The social loafing effect can be diminished when group members believe that their individual output is being assessed. In a field study, social loafing was lower when employees felt their individual productivity was visible to others (Liden, Wayne, Jaworski, & Bennett, 2004). The phenomenon may be limited to individualistic cultures, such as Australia, Canada, England, and the United States (see the discussion of culture values in Chapter 9), where emphasis is placed on the self rather than on society. Earley (1989) found that Chinese management trainees, who came from a collectivist country, where emphasis is placed on the group and society, did not demonstrate social loafing.

Brainstorming

Groups are often said to be superior to individuals in generating ideas or solutions to problems (Osborn, 1957). The theory is that group members inspire one another to generate ideas they would not have thought of alone. **Brainstorming** is a group technique that is supposed to result in improved performance with this type of task. A group is given instructions to generate ideas without being critical or judgmental in any way. Ideas will be evaluated and modified later.

Unfortunately, research has failed to find that the performance of groups that brainstorm is superior to that of nominal groups (Gallupe, Bastianutti, & Cooper, 1991; McGlynn, McGurk, Effland, Johll, & Harding, 2004). Rather than inspiring one another, group members often inhibit one another. Part of the difficulty is undoubtedly attributable to process loss. The group may not spend as much time as individuals generating ideas. Perhaps even more important, individuals can be reluctant to share ideas in the group because of shyness or social anxiety. Alone a person might be more confident and secure in generating ideas. Finally, when working in a live group, members are spending most of their time listening to others rather than generating options.

Electronic brainstorming has been shown to enhance performance in an idea-generation task using computers (Dennis & Valacich, 1993). Individuals are asked to enter ideas in a computer rather than write them down. This technique was found to produce performance equal to or better than that of nominal groups (the combined output of individuals who worked alone) and better performance than groups of individuals who shared their ideas. In Gallupe et al.'s (1991) computer brainstorming study, subjects were aware that several people were working on the same task at the same time and that as ideas were entered in the computer, they would be seen by everyone. Individuals were not known to one another, which may have reduced the social anxiety that could have inhibited performance in an interacting group. In a similar study, however, Valacich, Dennis, and Nunamaker (1992) found that anonymity made no difference in the performance of brainstorming individuals linked by computer. This study suggests that social anxiety is not the reason for the poorer performance of interacting groups.

Gallupe, Cooper, Grisé, and Bastianutti (1994) conducted a study that showed how electronic brainstorming produces better performance, in part, because people do not have to wait their turn to speak. They can type their responses as they think of them. When electronic brainstormers had to wait their turn to enter their responses on the computer, performance was about the same as that for the interacting groups. This suggests that process loss is responsible for the poorer performance of interacting groups as compared to computer or nominal brainstorming groups.

Paulus (2000) argues that the basic idea that group members inspire one another may be correct, but that group process gets in the way. He has shown that exposure to the ideas of others can help people generate more ideas. He suggests a procedure whereby people first get together in a group to discuss ideas and then work alone to generate options. Research has shown that the initial group session helps facilitate the subsequent solitary session and results in increased performance (Paulus, 2000).

Group Problem Solving

So far we've shown that for additive tasks and brainstorming, nominal groups do better than interacting groups. This is not to say that individuals always outperform groups, however, as there are tasks that can be better done when people interact. Problem solving tasks involve finding the solution to a given situation, such as solving a puzzle. For some problems there can be a correct answer, but for others a variety of solutions could be reasonable. Performance is assessed as the time to find the right answer in the former case and as the time to find a suitable answer (or the quality of the answer) in the latter. Studies of group problem solving often compare groups to their individual members, contrasting the group's time to solve the problem with the single best performer. Studies of problem solving have often found that groups perform as well as or better than their best member, suggesting that for this sort of task a group can be a good choice (Bonner, Baumann, & Dalal, 2002; Laughlin, Bonner, & Miner, 2002)

Group Decision Making

Groups within organizations frequently make decisions ranging from the relatively unimportant (e.g., the color of the new stationery) to those that significantly affect the lives and well-being of thousands (e.g., closing a plant and laying off all the workers). Organizations differ tremendously in the extent to which important decisions are made by individual managers (the autocratic approach) or by groups (the democratic approach). Even in the most autocratic organizations, however, it is common for individuals to make decisions only after consultation with a group or committee. The president of the United States consults the cabinet for important decisions, and the presidents of corporations usually have their "inner circles" of associates who serve the same purpose.

Evaluating the quality of a decision is not always an easy or straightforward undertaking. Often the evaluation depends on the values of the person doing the determination and the criterion chosen for comparison. If a government decides to go to war, the decision might be considered good by one person because the war was won and bad by another because many people were killed. Although most Americans supported President George W. Bush's decision at the time to invade Iraq, many believed it was a bad decision that would cost too many lives. Similarly, if a company president decides to downsize and lay off thousands of employees, it might be considered a good decision by stockholders whose stock may go up in value and a poor decision by employees who may lose their jobs. A solution to this dilemma is to evaluate decisions against the objectives they were meant to obtain. From this perspective, if the objective was removing Saddam Hussein from power, the Iraq War would be considered a good decision because it accomplished that objective. If the objective was producing a stable democracy friendly to American interests, our evaluation of the decision would be different. A layoff might be a good decision if it results in a financially healthier company, but a bad decision if it does not. Of course, real decisions are rarely this simple, as there can be several objectives, and a given decision might be successful for some of them and unsuccessful for others.

We review two areas of group decisions in this section. First is the issue of whether groups take more risks or are more conservative in their decisions than individuals. As we will see in our discussion of group polarization, this question has no simple answer. The second issue concerns how groups sometimes make inappropriate decisions even though most of the group members know the decision is a poor one. This is the phenomenon of groupthink.

Group Polarization

If a group decides on one of several possible courses of action, will the choice involve greater or lesser risk than the choice made by an individual? In other words, are groups riskier or more conservative than individuals in their decisions? This question has been addressed by hundreds of studies comparing group decisions to the decisions of individuals. The answer is that group decisions often differ from the decisions of individuals, but whether they are riskier or more conservative depends on the nature of the decision.

The typical risky decision study asks individuals and groups to choose one option from a series of options that vary in risk. For example, a decision task might involve deciding the acceptable odds of survival for undergoing elective surgery. Table 12.2 is one of the choice-dilemmas (Kogan & Wallach, 1964) that have been used in many risk studies. In these studies, subjects are first asked to make an individual decision, then are placed into groups and asked to come to a group decision. In most studies, the group decisions are more extreme than the mean of the individual decisions. For example, suppose that five subjects choose the following acceptable odds for the surgery problem: 20, 20, 20, 60, and 80 chances out of 100 of dying in surgery. The mean of their choices is 40. When placed in a group, however, the same people are likely to choose lower odds, closer to the majority position of 20.

TABLE 12.2   A Risk-Related Choice Task used in Group Decision Research

Mr. B, a 45-year-old accountant, has recently been informed by his physician that he has developed a severe heart ailment. The disease would be sufficiently serious to force Mr. B to change many of his strongest life habits—reducing his workload, drastically changing his diet, giving up favorite leisure-time pursuits. The physician suggests that a delicate medical operation could be attempted which, if successful, would completely relieve the heart condition. But its success could not be assured, and in fact, the operation might prove fatal.

Source: *Risk Taking: A Study in Cognition and Personality*, by N. Kogan and M. A. Wallach, 1964, New York: Holt, Rinehart & Winston.

Typically, in groups the majority position holds more weight than the minority position, and the shift of the group is toward the majority view. If the majority of the members make a risky choice, the group decision is likely to be riskier than the mean of its individuals. If the majority make a conservative choice, the group is likely to shift its decision in a conservative direction. This deviation from the group mean is called **group polarization** (Lamm & Myers, 1978), meaning that the group is more extreme (closer to one pole or the other) than the mean of its individuals.

A number of explanations have been offered for the group polarization phenomenon. One likely explanation is that the members who hold the minority view will likely conform to the majority, especially if one member's choice is far from the choices of the other group members. The individuals who find that others made the same choice that they did are likely to be convinced that theirs was the best choice. Most of the group discussion will be directed to convincing the minority that they should adopt the "correct" majority viewpoint. Although most of the group decision shift research has concerned risk-related decisions, this phenomenon probably holds for any type of choice situation. For example, decision shift would be expected in deciding how much money to spend on an item.

Groupthink

High-level decision making groups in corporations and governments typically consist of experts who should be able to make good decisions. Unfortunately, something can happen to decision making processes when people get together in a group, and this something leads them to make decisions that any reasonably bright, informed individual would probably never make. Irving Janis (1972) conducted in-depth analyses of decision fiascoes and developed a theory of what can go wrong when groups make decisions. **Groupthink** is a phenomenon that occurs when groups make decisions that individual members know are poor ones (Janis, 1972). Janis noted, as examples, the Ford Motor Company's decision to produce the Edsel, an automobile that lost $300 million; the Kennedy administration's decision to invade Cuba at the Bay of Pigs, an invasion that was a total failure; and the Johnson administration's decision to escalate the Vietnam War, which the United States never won (Janis, 1972). Moorhead, Ference, and Neck (1991) analyzed the decision to launch the space shuttle *Challenger* in 1986. Despite warnings that cold weather could cause serious mechanical failures, NASA officials decided to launch the shuttle in freezing temperatures, resulting in a tragic accident that killed the entire crew.

The decision that led to the *Challenger* disaster was likely caused by groupthink (Moorhead et al., 1991).

(*NASA/Science Source/Photo Researchers*)

According to Janis, groupthink is likely to occur in highly cohesive groups with strong leaders when the social pressures to maintain conformity and harmony in the group take precedence over sound decision making. The likelihood of groupthink is increased when decision making groups isolate themselves from outside ideas and influences. Note the following sequence of events: Suppose that the leader of the group presents a bad idea at a meeting. Each member might initially suspect that the idea is a poor one but is reluctant to be the one to say so. Much like the story of the Emperor's New Clothes, none of the members want to stick their neck out and question the leader's decision. As the members look around the room and notice that everyone is silent, they each begin to doubt their initial judgment. After all, if everyone else seems to be going along, perhaps the idea is not so bad. As the group process gets rolling, any criticism is quickly rationalized away, and pressure is put on individual members to conform to the group point of view. Some of the factors leading to groupthink are illustrated in Figure 12.2.

Janis (1972) offers several suggestions for avoiding groupthink. Two major themes appear throughout these suggestions. First, group leaders should serve as impartial

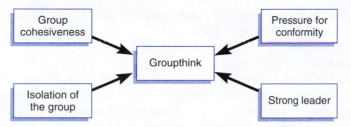

Figure 12.2 Several factors can lead to groupthink. Of the four shown here, group cohesiveness seems unnecessary according to Aldag and Fuller (1993).

moderators in group meetings rather than attempt to control the decision alternatives that are recommended. Second, group members, at every stage of the decision making process, should critically evaluate decision alternatives and continually seek information that might support or refute the wisdom of a decision. Janis discusses specific actions that groups should take to maintain a critical and objective frame of mind. For example, groups should periodically break into smaller subgroups to discuss critical issues, and members of the decision making groups should discuss issues with subordinates. These actions can help groups avoid being caught in a cycle of groupthink that can result in making the wrong decision.

Aldag and Fuller (1993) reviewed the research on groupthink. They noted that there are few good tests of its propositions, and the existing tests support only part of the theory. For example, group cohesiveness does not seem to be necessary for groupthink to occur. Janis (1972), however, offers sound advice about how to avoid bad group decisions by soliciting a variety of views. This is a potential advantage of having diversity in the backgrounds of group members. A diverse group is likely to have different perspectives on a problem and its solution. We will discuss group diversity later in the chapter.

Team Innovation

Organizations today find themselves in a rapidly changing and competitive world that requires them to adapt and change. Much of the change occurs at the level of work teams that implement new innovations in the workplace. Innovation is the introduction of new ideas, procedures, or products into a team (De Dreu, 2006). Innovation is not the same as creativity, in that team members don't necessarily invent the innovations that they adopt. Innovation is the process of introducing changes regardless of whether they were invented or borrowed.

Teams innovate out of necessity, from both internal (organizational constraints and workload) and external (turbulent environment) factors (Anderson, De Dreu, & Nijstad, 2004). A turbulent and challenging environment is the case for high tech companies that produce products in rapidly advancing fields. Extreme competition requires constant innovation for organizations to maintain their market share and survive. Teams also innovate because of organizational constraints that require innovations to overcome obstacles, and heavy workloads that require new ways to get work done more efficiently.

Teams vary in their orientation to innovation. Those teams that take time to critically discuss how they do things and how to do them better are the best innovators (Somech, 2006). Such discussions involve sharing differences of opinion that can produce conflicts about tasks among members. A moderate level of such conflict is optimal in facilitating innovation in teams (De Dreu, 2006).

Team KSAOs

An important issue for organizations that use teams to accomplish important work is whether there are special team KSAOs that determine whether a person is a good team member, and perhaps more important, whether the levels of team KSAOs among members relate to team performance. Research has shown that at least some KSAOs that predict job performance for individuals also predict for teams. For example, the higher the mean cognitive ability in a team (computed by averaging team member scores), the higher the team performance is likely to be (Stewart, 2006). Determining additional team KSAOs that also relate to team performance would inform both selection and training of members.

As might be expected, several team KSAOs have been identified that relate to team performance. Three are particularly important:

1. To be a good team member requires knowledge of teamwork (Hirschfeld, Jordan, Field, Giles, & Armenakis, 2006). Such knowledge concerns how individuals can effectively work together in teams and how good working relationships with others can be developed.

2. An effective team member has good social skills (Morgeson, Reider, & Campion, 2005). Beyond knowing how to work in teams, one must have skills in communication and how to influence others.

3. Certain personality characteristics make people particularly suited to teamwork. Individuals whose values are collectivistic, as opposed to individualistic (see Chapter 9), performed better in teams (Jackson, Colquitt, Wesson, & Zapata-Phelan, 2006).

Taken together, these studies suggest that the most effective team members have knowledge and skill in how to work in teams, and personalities suited to working closely with others.

▶ GROUP DIVERSITY

Demographic shifts have resulted in increasing numbers of minorities and women in the workplace, not only in North America but in much of the rest of the industrialized world (Triandis, 2003). Coupled with the greater reliance on teamwork, group diversity has become an important issue for organizations (Mohammed & Angell, 2004). Diversity, or differences among people, can be divided into two types: cognitive and demographic (Van der Vegt, & Janssen, 2003). Cognitive diversity concerns knowledge, skills, and values. Demographic diversity consists of more visible attributes, such as age, gender, and race-ethnicity. An important issue concerns the impact of diversity within work groups on member performance and reactions.

Jackson, Joshi, and Erhardt (2003) reviewed 63 studies that have addressed the impact of diversity within groups,—that is, the effect on groups of having members who are different from one another. They noted that diversity can have both positive and negative effects, but that results across studies were inconsistent. Some of the reason is that different types of diversity have been investigated in different studies. Also, diversity can have different effects depending on the task. Mannix and Neale (2005), for example, concluded that cognitive diversity is likely to be helpful for team innovation, but demographic diversity is not. However, demographic diversity is helpful when there is a need to get the perspectives of a diverse population of potential clients or customers in marketing situations (Jackson & Joshi, 2004).

Organizational context is also important for diversity. Van der Vegt and Janssen (2003) found no relation with performance of either cognitive or demographic diversity in teams from a Dutch company. However, the diverse groups were the best performers when the job required coordinating with teammates, and were the worst performers when the job could be done independently. In another Dutch study, a similar pattern was found for job satisfaction when the joint influence of diversity and group goals was investigated (Schippers, Den Hartog, Koopman, & Wienk, 2003). There was no overall correlation between diversity and job satisfaction. However, members of teams with group goals were more satisfied if they were diverse; members of teams with individual goals were more satisfied if they were not diverse. Taken together, these studies suggest that diversity can have negative effects when people have no stake in getting along with one another either because their jobs are independent or their goals are not linked. However, when there is a necessity to work well with others, not only does the negative aspect of diversity disappear, but there can be significant advantages in both performance and satisfaction.

► INTERVENTIONS WITH WORK GROUPS IN ORGANIZATIONS

Most organizations consist of a network of interrelated work groups. In order for the organization to function effectively, individuals must coordinate their efforts within their own groups, and groups must coordinate their efforts with one another. In this section, we discuss three techniques that can be used to improve group functioning. The autonomous work team is an alternative to the traditional organization of a factory. Items are assembled by small teams of employees rather than by all production employees. The autonomous work team idea has been adapted for nonmanufacturing organizations. Quality circles are groups of employees who are assembled to provide suggestions to management. Team building is a family of procedures used to improve the functioning of teams.

Autonomous Work Team

In the traditional factory, the assembly of a product is broken down into many small operations. For large, complex products like an automobile, there can be hundreds or thousands of operations, each done by a separate employee. Because assembling a product requires the coordinated effort of a large number of people, many resources must be devoted to supervision. The autonomous work team is an alternative system whereby an entire product is assembled by a small team of employees. A factory will comprise many work teams, each assembling an entire product. Because assembly of a product involves only the coordination of team members, relatively few resources are necessary for supervision. Teams are relied on to manage themselves, requiring far fewer supervisors.

The details of how autonomous work teams operate vary from organization to organization. One such system, described by Hackman and Oldham (1980), was implemented by the Butler Corporation when it opened a new grain dryer plant. A grain dryer is a

Autonomous work groups at Butler Corporation assemble entire grain dryers, which is the cylinder surrounded by steam.
(*Grant Heilman Photographpy*)

large piece of farm equipment that contains over 3,000 parts (see photograph). At Butler each dryer is assembled by an autonomous work team. Each team is responsible for managing itself and for product assembly. Ten distinguishing characteristics of the teams at Butler are listed in Table 12.3. As you can see, each member of the team learns each operation, so that after about 18 months on the job every employee can assemble an entire dryer. The team is responsible for the quality of the finished product, which it must test before sending it out of the plant. If a dryer is defective after it is placed in use on a farm, a team member may have to make a service call to fix it. The role of supervisors is different at Butler. There are few of them, and their major function is to offer advice and training to team members. The approach is participative, with frequent staff meetings and an advisory committee made up of members from different teams.

TABLE 12.3   Distinguishing Features of Autonomous Work Groups at Butler Corporation

1. Employees frequently rotated jobs.
2. After about 18 months, most employees knew the entire production process.
3. Groups designed and purchased their own tools.
4. Group members went on service calls to do warranty repairs.
5. Quality control inspection was done by group members.
6. There were few supervisors.
7. Group members participated in hiring and firing.
8. Supervisors served as coaches providing counseling and training.
9. There were weekly group meetings and monthly plant meetings.
10. There were employee advisory groups to management.

Source: *Work Redesign*, by J. R. Hackman and G. R. Oldham, 1980, Reading, MA: Addison-Wesley.

Research has shown that autonomous work teams can benefit employees and organizations. Job satisfaction is sometimes higher with autonomous work teams than more traditional approaches (Cordery, Mueller, & Smith, 1991; Pearce & Ravlin, 1987). Job performance has been found to be the same in manufacturing organizations (Wall, Kemp, Jackson, & Clegg, 1986) or better (Banker, Field, Schroeder, & Sinha, 1996). However, the decreased need for supervisory personnel can result in overall greater efficiency for autonomous work teams even when productivity is the same (see Research in Detail). Although there can be advantages to autonomous work teams, they aren't suitable for all situations. Langfred (2005) found that to be in an autonomous team means surrendering some individual autonomy. Thus such teams are best suited to tasks that require a high level of interdependent effort among members to complete tasks.

RESEARCH IN DETAIL

It is rare in field settings to be able to do a true experiment in which two or more experimental conditions are created and subjects are randomly assigned to them. Wall, Kemp, Jackson, and Clegg (1986) conducted a *quasi-experiment*, meaning that the design of the study was an approximation to an experiment. Two factories that represented the two experimental conditions of interest were compared, but employees were not randomly assigned to work at each factory. It is therefore possible that the observed effects were due to differences in the two factories rather than the autonomous work group treatment.

The study was conducted at a candy manufacturing company in England. Officials of the company decided to experiment with autonomous work groups by trying them at one factory. The researchers were enlisted to evaluate the effects of the new system. The productivity, job satisfaction, and mental health of employees at the autonomous work group factory were compared to the same factors for employees at a matched factory that used the traditional assembly-line approach. Data were collected 6 months, 18 months, and 30 months after the new factory began operation.

The results showed that employees in the autonomous work group factory were more satisfied with their jobs than employees in the traditional factory. Their productivity, however, was not better. In fact, during the first six months of operation, the productivity of the autonomous work groups was quite disappointing. Much of the difficulty was attributed to problems with new equipment and the time needed for training employees in the new production procedures. By the 30-month time period, performance in both factories was equivalent. Because the autonomous work group factory had fewer supervisors, however, it was found to be more cost efficient.

One finding illustrates the difficulties in drawing conclusions from quasi-experimental studies. The turnover rate was found to be higher in the autonomous work group factory than the traditional factory. This finding was surprising, because employees at the former factory were more satisfied with their jobs than employees at the latter factory. The authors noted that the unemployment rate was lower in the area of England where the autonomous work group factory was located than where the traditional factory was located. They speculated that the unemployment rate may have been the cause of the turnover rate differences rather than the type of factory. Because of the design of the study, we cannot be certain why the difference occurred. This study does provide evidence to support the idea that autonomous work groups can be more cost efficient than traditional factory structures. Organizations should be aware, however, that extra effort and time may be needed for successful implementation of the system.

Source: Wall, T. D., Kemp, N. J., Jackson, P. R., & Clegg, C. W. (1986). Outcomes of autonomous workgroups: A long-term field experiment. *Academy of Management Journal*, 29, 280–304.

Quality Circles

A quality circle is a group intervention that gives employees the opportunity to have greater input into issues at work. **Quality circles** are groups of employees who meet periodically to discuss problems and propose solutions relevant to their jobs. Typically, the groups comprise people who have similar jobs in manufacturing organizations, and discussions revolve around issues of product quality and production efficiency. As with autonomous work teams, quality circles have been attempted in all types of organizations.

In theory, quality circles have benefits for both employees and organizations. They allow individual employees to enjoy greater participation, which many find stimulating and enjoyable. It can be a welcome break from routine work to spend time discussing work problems with colleagues. For the organization, this should mean better production procedures because the people who do the work are often the most knowledgeable about what the problems are and how they can be solved.

Too little research has been done on quality circles to draw any firm conclusions about their effects on employees or organizations (Van Fleet & Griffin, 1989). The few studies that have investigated quality circle benefits have yielded somewhat mixed results (Bettenhausen, 1991). Marks, Mirvis, Hackett, and Grady (1986) conducted one of the few studies that compared participants with nonparticipants in the same organization. They found that employees who participated in the quality circle program were more productive and had fewer absences than employees who did not. These results are quite promising, but they need to be replicated in other organizations before we can conclude that quality circles will increase productivity and reduce absence.

The quality circle idea has been adapted to focus on employee health rather than job performance. The German **health circle**, or *Gesundheitszirkel*, is an intervention in which groups of employees discuss ways to improve health and well-being. Aust and Ducki (2004) reviewed the results of 11 studies that showed mostly positive effects of health circles. Not only did the studies show that many suggestions were implemented, but some found increases in both health and well-being.

Team Building

Team building refers to any of a number of activities designed to enhance the many different aspects of the functioning of work groups or teams. Some team-building efforts are task oriented—they attempt to help team members improve how they accomplish their team tasks. Other efforts are interpersonally oriented—they are concerned with how well team members communicate and interact. This approach presumes that teams will perform better when their members can communicate and interact with one another effectively (Buller, 1986).

There is no one way in which team building is done, but three factors characterize team-building efforts (Buller, 1986). First, team building is a planned activity; that is, it consists of one or more exercises or experiences that are designed to accomplish a particular objective. Second, team building is typically conducted or *facilitated* by a consultant or trainer who is an expert in the particular form of team building that is being done. It would be difficult for a team to run itself through team building, for the trainer is an integral part of the experience. Third, team building usually involves an existing work team. Individuals are trained in team building to enhance their individual team skills within their work teams.

Team building often involves team members discussing problems and coming up with solutions. The role of the team trainer is to facilitate the discussion by getting team members talking to one another. This might involve directing questions at individuals,

Tom, what sorts of problems have you been having with product quality?

Ellen, why don't you seem to get the information that you need?

or summarizing and reflecting back to the group the points that have been made:

It sounds like everyone is concerned that there are too many defective parts.

I guess everyone feels uninformed about decisions.

The trainer's job is to get people to raise issues, identify problems, and discuss possible solutions. The trainer might also have to mediate conflicts if the discussion leads to arguments among team members.

The results of studies designed to show the positive effects of team building have been inconsistent. For example, Dov Eden conducted two team-building studies with units of the Israeli army (see photograph) and found positive effects for one (Eden, 1986) and no effects for the other (Eden, 1985). Buller (1986) reported that team building had positive effects on job performance for six of the nine studies he reviewed. He pointed out that the wide variety of interventions that are considered team building across different studies makes it difficult to draw firm conclusions about its effectiveness.

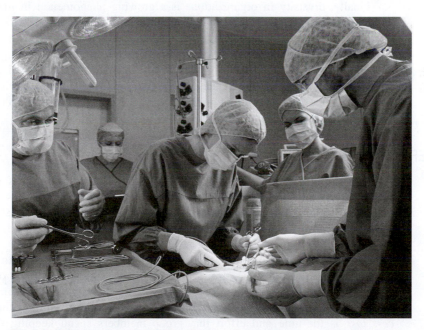

Team building can be valuable for all sorts of teams.
(*Jochen Sands/Digital Vision/Getty Images*)

▶ FUTURE ISSUES AND CHALLENGES

One by-product of complex technology in the workplace is the necessity for coordinated team effort among employees. Very often several people are required to operate the complicated equipment used in both civilian and military organizations. On a guided-missile cruiser like the U.S.S. *Vincennes*, for example, it takes several people to operate the tracking equipment that distinguishes hostile from friendly aircraft. When teamwork breaks down, as it did when the *Vincennes* shot down an Iranian airliner, the consequences can be serious. The challenge for I/O psychology in the future is to find ways to improve the functioning of teams.

The autonomous work team is becoming an increasingly popular way of organizing manufacturing organizations. Part of the motivation at the present time is the necessity for downsizing, which requires the elimination of supervisory personnel. Although autonomous work teams can have advantages, expanding the scope of the factory worker's job poses several challenges. Most important, as factory jobs become more complex, they will require a higher level of ability and initiative. People with more skills and motivation will have to be either hired or developed on the job. For the I/O psychologist, this means the introduction of selection procedures to find the best people, training to enhance their skills, and systems to increase motivation.

Team-building techniques have been in use for many decades, but the kind of intervention that is effective remains unclear. It is likely that the most effective approaches will be determined by the situation. Military teams, for example, must deal with the stress of combat. This might require different team behaviors than those for teams that operate complex machinery, such as a power plant.

Finally, diversity in organizations is a growing phenomenon in many places. Our understanding of the factors that lead to positive versus negative effects of team diversity is incomplete. Even more important, we need to develop interventions that can maximize the benefits and minimize the drawbacks of increased diversity. With cognitive diversity, this might involve optimal strategies to utilize talent within an organization—in other words, effective ways to decide the skill mix that will make a group effective for a particular task. For demographic diversity, this might mean finding ways to train supervisors to effectively manage diverse teams.

▶ CHAPTER SUMMARY

Much of the work done today in organizations is performed by work groups or work teams. Work groups are collections of individuals who interact at work and share interrelated task goals. Work teams are a type of work group, but the tasks of individual members are coordinated and interrelated, the team members have different roles, and the team has a common objective or task goal.

Four concepts relate to work groups. *Roles* distinguish the specific positions and functions of individuals in a group or team. *Norms* are group rules of behavior that in many groups are rigidly enforced. *Group cohesiveness* is the sum of the forces holding the group together. Highly cohesive groups rigidly enforce their norms. *Process loss* is the time and effort that group members spend keeping the group operating rather than working on tasks. Two additional concepts are important for teams. *Team commitment* is the involvement members have in their team. *Team mental model* is the shared understanding team members have about the task and situation.

The presence of other people affects task performance. Simple or well-learned tasks are facilitated by the presence of others; complex or new tasks are inhibited by the presence of others. Group performance is often inferior to the combined performance of an equal number of individuals working alone. For additive tasks (where total performance is the sum of each individual's performance), the phenomenon of social loafing explains that the larger the group, the less effort each individual expends.

Group polarization explains that, depending on the situation, group decisions can be riskier or more conservative than individual decisions. Groupthink is when groups of highly talented decision makers make bad decisions when placed in decision groups. Rapidly changing environments necessitate that teams innovate by adopting new ways of working. Finally, team KSAOs are characteristics of individuals that make them well suited to work effectively in teams.

Three interventions have the potential for improving group functioning and performance. Autonomous work teams are given the responsibility for entire jobs, such as assembling whole products, such as appliances or automobiles. Quality circles are groups of employees who meet periodically to come up with solutions to work problems. Team building is one of a number of interventions designed to improve the functioning of work teams.

I/O PSYCHOLOGY IN PRACTICE

(*Courtesy Janice Cannon-Bowers*)

This case concerns a U.S. Navy team development training program created and carried out by Dr. Janis Cannon-Bowers. Dr. Cannon-Bowers received her Ph.D. in industrial/organizational psychology in 1988 from the University of South Florida. From her graduation until 2003, when she accepted a faculty position at the University of Central Florida, she worked at the Naval Air Warfare Center Training Systems Division in Orlando, Florida, where she held the title of research psychologist. Her major responsibility was to conduct research on team performance and training to develop new and more effective approaches. As a result of her research, she became involved in training naval officers in team development.

Two naval tragedies in the late 1980s led to a great deal of research into team performance. In 1987 the U.S.S. *Stark* was hit by an Iraqi missile, and in 1988 the U.S.S. *Vincennes* shot down an Iranian airliner. An investigation into the causes of both incidents revealed that poor teamwork was a major factor. This led to the

U.S. Navy's effort to find ways to improve the performance of teams. Cannon-Bowers had been part of this research effort, but her work also involved interventions aimed at improving team performance on navy ships.

Many different teams on combat ships carry out complex and dangerous functions, often under the severe stress of combat. Under such conditions, there is no time for group deliberation, because all functions must be carried out quickly and efficiently, with life-and-death decisions being made in a matter of seconds. It is vitally important that teams develop into well-functioning units that do their jobs efficiently. On a combat ship it is the commanding officer (C.O.) who must see to it that the various teams develop into effective units. To do so, the C.O. must have skills in team development.

Cannon-Bowers and her colleagues designed a team development training program for C.O.s that she conducted at the Navy's Surface Warfare School. The program was intended to give the C.O.s insights into team functioning and sound training principles. It covered the ways to

1. Give feedback
2. Accept criticism by subordinates
3. Create a climate for learning

4. Develop a "shared mental model," or common understanding, of the team's functions

5. Avoid groupthink

The response to the training by the C.O.s was positive. They found the training program to be informative and useful. From the perspective of participant reaction criteria, it was successful. Whether this translates directly into better team performance on ships still needs to be determined, but initial results suggest that it does.

Discussion Questions

1. Do you think Cannon-Bowers's program will prove to be effective?
2. What steps could the U.S. Navy take to improve the team performance of ship personnel?
3. Is awareness of the causes of groupthink enough for team members to avoid it?
4. How would you go about giving feedback to subordinates if you were a ship's C.O.?

LEARNING BY DOING

Team Innovation

Find an individual (friend, acquaintance or family member) who is a member of a work team. Ask him or her to relate a case in which the team adopted some new way of working, such as a new type of equipment or a new procedure. Ask the following questions:

1. What was the nature of the innovation?

2. What motivated the team to adopt the innovation?
3. Who suggested the innovation—team member, manager, or someone else?
4. Were alternative innovations considered?
5. Was the original innovation idea modified to suit this particular team?

Leadership and Power in Organizations

What makes a person a good leader? Was President Bill Clinton a good leader? During both of his terms, the media reported constant rumors and scandals. He was impeached, was sued for sexual harassment, and was the target of an ongoing criminal investigation through his entire presidency. His opponents attacked his character constantly, arguing that he was morally unfit for the job. Yet in the midst of serious charges of immoral behavior and perjury and an impeachment trial in the United States Senate, poll after poll found that the overwhelming majority (two-thirds) of Americans approved his performance in office. The U.S. economy was the strongest in decades with the stock market breaking records, the federal budget was balanced, serious crime was on the decline, and welfare reform seemed to be successful. Were these signs of his effectiveness or merely coincidences? How would you go about determining how effective he was? Is good leadership a matter of character or a matter of being able to get important things done? Will the same person be a good leader in all situations? These are important questions to both government and nongovernment organizations. The answers tell us whom to choose as our leaders, and they tell leaders how they must act to be effective.

In this chapter we deal with the important domain of leadership in organizations. We discuss the nature of leadership and how leaders influence followers. We summarize what is presently known about the personal characteristics that relate to good leadership performance and the effects of leader behavior on subordinates. We see how good leadership is the result of leader behavior, leader characteristics, and the leadership situation. Finally, we discuss women in leadership positions, and cross-cultural differences in leadership.

Objectives: The student who studies this chapter should be able to:

▶ Define leadership.

▶ Explain the five sources of power and three sources of political power.

▶ Summarize the major approaches and theories of leadership.

▶ Compare and contrast the major approaches and theories of leadership.

▶ Discuss how men and women compare on leadership.

▶ WHAT IS LEADERSHIP?

You probably have an intuitive idea of what leadership is. A *leader* is the one in charge, or the boss of other people. Just because you are in charge, however, does not mean that people will listen to you or do what you say. What at first seems simple is quite complex, as we discuss in this chapter. Leadership scholars have come up with many different definitions of leadership, and no one definition has been universally accepted (Yukl, 1989). A common idea that runs through various definitions is that leadership involves influencing the attitudes, beliefs, behaviors, and feelings of other people. Even nonleaders influence others, but leaders exert a disproportionate influence; that is, a leader is more influential than a nonleader.

Within an organization, leaders are often associated with supervisory positions; however, being a supervisor does not guarantee that you will be able to influence others. Furthermore, many leaders in organizations have no formal organizational title. Informal leaders often arise in work groups and may be more influential over the behavior of group members than the actual supervisors. Formal and informal leadership are an aspect of the formal and informal roles that we discussed in Chapter 12. An organization assigns the role of leader (e.g., manager or supervisor) to a person. An individual develops the informal leader role through interaction with colleagues. A person who is particularly skilled might find that others look to him or her for guidance, perhaps more so than to their own supervisors. The amount of influence a person has over others is determined by several personal and organizational factors, which we discuss next.

▶ SOURCES OF INFLUENCE AND POWER

French and Raven's (1959) Bases of Power

French and Raven (1959) described five **bases of power** one person has over another, such as a supervisor over a subordinate. **Power** is the extent to which one person can influence another to do something. The power bases listed in Table 13.1 involve both individual characteristics and organizational conditions, and they concern the relationship between leader and follower, or between supervisor and subordinate. Although bases of power are discussed as characteristics of the supervisor, power arises from the interaction between subordinate and supervisor. The supervisor makes an influence attempt, but it is the behavior of the subordinate that determines whether it is effective. Table 13.1 indicates how supervisors can use each power base.

Expert power is based on the knowledge and expertise the supervisor has. Subordinates are likely to follow the directives of a person they believe has special knowledge or expertise about the issue at hand. Note that it is the expertise the subordinates believe the supervisor has that is important, rather than the actual expertise. Although actual expertise affects perceived expertise, some people are better than others at appearing to be experts. Titles (doctor), college degrees (Ph.D.), certifications (certified public accountant), and distinctions (Nobel Prize winner) can enhance the perceived expert power of an individual. Expert power can be particularly effective because it is likely to convince the subordinate that the supervisor's directive is correct and should be followed.

Referent power is the extent to which the subordinate likes and identifies with the supervisor. People are likely to be influenced by another whom they admire or like. This source of power can be developed through personal relationships with others. It can also be enhanced by raising the status of the supervisor. A person with celebrity status is likely to have a high level of referent power. Some corporate leaders have become national celebrities, such as Donald Trump.

Legitimate power is the power inherent in a supervisor's job title. It is derived from the subordinate's belief that the supervisor has the legitimate right or authority to

TABLE 13.1   The Five French and Raven Bases of Interpersonal Influence and Power and How They can be Used

Bases	Use
Expert	Give information
Referent	Get subordinates to like you
Legitimate	Get a high level position or rank
Reward	Give rewards for compliance
Coercive	Give punishments for noncompliance

Source: "The Bases of Social Power," by J. R. P. French, Jr., and B. Raven, 1959, in D. Cartwright (Ed.), *Studies in Social Power* (pp. 150–167), Ann Arbor, MI: Institute for Social Research.

be in charge. Much of the strength of this power derives from the subordinate's values about the rights of supervisors. If the subordinate refuses to recognize the authority of the supervisor, there will be no power in the supervisor's title.

Reward power is the ability of the supervisor to reward subordinates with bonuses, desirable job assignments, promotions, or raises. **Coercive power** is the ability of the supervisor to punish subordinates with disciplinary actions, fines, firing, or salary reductions. Organizations differ in the extent to which supervisors can give out punishments and rewards. In private companies, it is not unusual for a supervisor to be able to give raises and promotions to a subordinate. In government organizations, an individual supervisor might not be able to do so because these rewards are determined by legislative action.

All five types of power can be effective if used properly. The major limitation of reward power is that subordinates may become accustomed to it and comply only when the reward is available. Coercive power can have detrimental effects because subordinates may become angry and strike back, either directly or indirectly; for example, by engaging in counterproductive work behavior (see Chapter 10). Aguinis, Nesler, Quigley, Suk-Jae-Lee, and Tedeschi (1996) showed that expert, referent, and reward power were associated with good relationships between college professors and their students. On the other hand, coercive power was associated with poor relationships.

Yukl's (1989) Sources of Political Power

French and Raven's bases of power are concerned with the influence people have on one another in any setting. Yukl's (1989) sources of political power are concerned specifically with power in organizations. According to Yukl, *political action* is the process by which people gain and protect their power within the organization. He outlined three means by which political power is achieved and maintained in organizations (Figure 13.1).

Control over decision processes involves controlling and influencing important decisions in the organization, such as the allocation of resources. This sort of power can be achieved by serving on appropriate committees (e.g., finance) or taking on the right tasks (preparation of the budget). Influence in the U.S. Congress is largely based on being on the most powerful House or Senate committees.

Forming coalitions means entering into agreements with others to support your position in return for support of the others' positions. Again, this is often seen in legislative bodies when different factions agree to support each other on favored positions. Senators

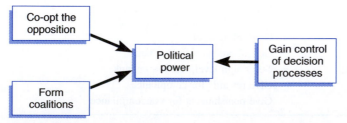

Figure 13.1 Yukl (1989) discusses how political power tactics can be a means of achieving political power in an organization.
Source: Leadership in Organizations by G. A. Yukl, 1989, Englewood Cliffs, NJ: Prentice Hall.

who support an important issue, such as equal employment opportunity, might agree to help those who support the issue of gun control in return for support of their issue.

Co-optation involves trying to diffuse another faction's opposition by allowing its members to participate in the decision. The hope is that this will make it difficult for them to remain in opposition. For example, a local government that wishes to take action to reduce the pollution produced by local industry is sure to run into opposition. A political approach to reducing or co-opting that opposition would be to assign the task to a committee that includes industry representation, but not enough representation to determine the committee's actions.

This type of political action concerns how power is acquired and is different from the self-serving organizational politics discussed in Chapter 11. The sort of political actions discussed here can be used for good purposes, and are quite common in both government and nongovernment organizations. Gaining influence in large organizations can be more a matter of achieving political rather than individual power. Even the president of the United States does not have the personal power to get laws enacted that might solve the nation's worst problems. Since Jimmy Carter, every U.S. president had campaigned on a promise to get Congress to pass a balanced federal budget. It wasn't until three administrations later that President Clinton was able to fulfill this promise.

Political Skill

If leadership is about influencing other people, then political skill is an important component. **Political skill** is the extent to which one is able to influence others to engage in behavior beneficial to oneself or to the organization (Ahearn, Ferris, Hochwarter, Douglas, & Ammeter, 2004). Such skill can be used in a self-serving way, as we discussed in the Chapter 11 section on politics, but it also can be used to benefit others and the organization. Gerald Ferris and his colleagues who have studied political skill have divided it into four dimensions (Ferris, Treadway, Kolodinsky, Hochwarter, Kacmar, Douglas, & Frink, 2005). *Social astuteness* is the ability to understand people and social situations. This is not unlike emotional intelligence (see Chapter 5), but social astuteness does not involve just understanding emotions. *Interpersonal influence* is the skill of convincing other people to engage in the behavior desired or to accept a particular position. *Networking ability* involves developing relationships with a wide range of individuals and managing those relationships to accomplish objectives. Finally, *apparent sincerity* is the skill of appearing or really being honest, open, and trustworthy. Taken together, this suggests that the politically skilled understand social interactions, are able to influence others, can build networks of allies who can be relied upon, and exude an aura of integrity. Research has shown that political skill in leaders does result in leader effectiveness (Ferris et al., 2004; Ferris et al., 2005).

► ABUSE OF SUPERVISORY POWER

When used appropriately, the various forms of power can provide tools to enhance the functioning of organizations. They can also be used to help individuals have positive feelings about work and to perform their jobs well, but there is a potentially negative side to power. Some supervisors will use their power to mistreat subordinates because the supervisor believes that punitive measures are necessary to get people to perform well. In other cases, it is done because the supervisor enjoys wielding power over others.

Supervisors who enjoy abusing others might do so in any number of ways. Employee harassment occurs when supervisors are free to demand that their subordinates do exactly what they are told regardless of the appropriateness of demands. Thus, an individual might be required to do personal favors or be punished. Some supervisors use a harsh and punitive style and may belittle subordinates for even minor mistakes. This produces an intimidating and uncomfortable work environment for subordinates. Some supervisors might engage in ethnic harassment—the mistreatment of employees based on their ethnic or racial background (Bergman, Palmieri, Drasgow & Ormerod, 2007; Schneider, Hitlan, & Radhakrishnan, 2000). Fox and Stallworth (2005) found that the most common forms of ethnic harassment included derogatory comments, ethnic jokes, and excluding the target person from employee interactions. Surveys of employees have shown that those who report experiencing abusive behavior from supervisors and others at work report low job satisfaction, burnout, psychological strain, and intention of quitting the job (Bowling & Beehr, 2006; Cortina, Magley, Williams, & Langhout, 2001).

Perhaps the best known form of power abuse is **sexual harassment**, which is behavior of a sexual nature that

Is unwanted

Can adversely affect a person's employment

Interferes with a person's job performance

Creates a hostile and intimidating work environment

The sorts of behaviors that comprise sexual harassment include

Unwelcome sexual advances and requests

Unwanted physical contact or touching

Use of offensive language

Repeated requests for a date

Threats of punishment for noncompliance with requests

Sexual harassment is illegal in the United States and many other countries. In the United States it is covered by civil rights legislation and is considered a form of discrimination. Many cases have resulted in lawsuits, with companies having to pay damages to employees in excess of $100,000. Although sexual harassment is the act of an individual, organizations have been held accountable for the behaviors of their employees. Thus, organizations are expected to prevent their supervisors and others from engaging in sexual harassment.

It is difficult to know exactly how widespread sexual harassment might be. Several surveys have asked women if they have encountered one or more instances of behaviors that fit the definition (e.g., Schneider, Swan, & Fitzgerald, 1997), such as crude comments or jokes, or unwanted requests for a date. Ilies, Hauserman, Schwochau, and Stibal (2003) conducted a meta-analysis of 55 such studies and concluded that 58% of women reported experiencing these sorts of behaviors at work. One must be cautious in interpreting this to mean that most women have been victims of sexual harassment (Fitzgerald, Drasgow, Hulin, Gelfand, & Magley, 1997). Many of these behaviors only become harassment when they are unwanted and are repeated often enough to create a hostile or intimidating work environment. An isolated comment or simple request for a date is not harassment, so one should not interpret such surveys as indicating that most women have been victims. In fact, Ilies et al. (2003) noted that fewer than half of the women who reported experiencing these behaviors felt they were actually harassed. It should be noted that although sexual harassment is often considered a woman's problem, recent studies have shown that men are just as likely to be targets (Berdahl, & Moore, 2006; Rospenda, Richman, & Shannon, 2006).

Another issue is that people vary in the extent to which they perceive actions by supervisors and others to be harassment (Timmerman & Bajema, 2000). In other words, harassment is in the eye of the beholder, and in the attribution an employee makes about the intent and motives of the other person (Luthar & Pastille, 2000). For example, Wayne (2000) asked college students to read a real sexual harassment case, but she manipulated the gender and organizational level of the perpetrator and victim. The perpetrator was more likely to be judged guilty by the participants when the victim was of a higher level (e.g., supervisor) than lower level (subordinate). Wayne argued that the perception of the situation was determined in part by whether or not the person's behavior was contrary to expectations. A certain degree of coerciveness is seen as expected in supervisors but not subordinates, and so for supervisors there may be a higher threshold for perceiving their behavior as sexual harassment.

Sexual and other forms of employee harassment are serious matters that organizations should attempt to control. They often reflect a general climate of abusiveness in which racial, sexual, and general harassment occur together (Berdahl & Moore, 2006; Lim & Cortina, 2005). When supervisors and other employees engage in certain forms of harassment, they can get their organizations into legal difficulties. The costs of legal problems, however, are probably quite small in comparison to the hidden costs to organizations. Sexual harassment can be stressful, leading to job dissatisfaction (Lapierre, Spector, & Leck, 2005), psychological strain (O'Connell & Korabik, 2000; Wasti, Bergman, Glomb, & Drasgow, 2000), and lowered physical health (Willness, Steel, & Lee, 2007). It should be kept in mind that actual cases of sexual harassment were not identified, and that from cross-sectional surveys (see Chapter 2) one cannot be certain that harassment was the cause of strain. It is possible that employees who were under strain were more likely to perceive situations as harassing. However, there is enough evidence from the study of various forms of employee mistreatment (see Chapter 11) to suggest that sexual harassment and other forms of abuse can have serious detrimental effects on people. Organizations would be wise to make efforts to safeguard their employees from victimization by supervisors as well as others who abuse their power.

▶ APPROACHES TO THE UNDERSTANDING OF LEADERSHIP

Many approaches have been taken to the study and understanding of leadership. The trait approach is concerned with determining the personal characteristics of good leaders. It asks the question,

Who will make a good leader?

The behavior approach is concerned with finding out which leader behaviors are effective. It asks the question,

What do good leaders do?

The contingency approach (Fiedler's and path-goal) assumes that good leadership is a function of the interplay of the person, the person's behavior, and the situation. It asks the question,

> Under a given condition, who will be a good leader, and what behavior is likely to be effective?

The leader-member exchange theory and the charismatic/transformational approaches focus on the relationships between subordinates and supervisors. They ask the question,

> How does the interaction between subordinate and supervisor affect the subordinate's behavior?

All of these approaches have contributed to our understanding of leadership, and we discuss them in this section. We also cover the Vroom-Yetton model for deciding how to approach decision-making tasks in work groups.

The Trait Approach

The oldest approach to the study of leadership is the *trait approach*. It is based on the assumptions that some people make better leaders than others and that it is possible to identify the traits of good leaders. Some proponents of this approach would argue that good leadership is a function of the person and that a person who is a good leader in one situation would be a good leader in any situation. It would follow that various leaders, such as Alexander the Great, Winston Churchill, Martin Luther King Jr., and George Washington, could have been great leaders in other times and situations. This does not seem likely, however, since each man had different attributes and adopted a different approach to leadership that was appropriate to his circumstances.

Most of the research studies that have attempted to uncover the traits of good leaders have used one of two approaches. One approach used a methodology similar to employee selection studies, which were discussed in Chapter 6. A sample of leaders, often supervisors in an organization, is identified for study. A criterion for *leadership performance*, typically job performance, is chosen. The supervisors are assessed on the criterion and on the personal traits of interest. These might include measures of various abilities, job experiences, motivation, and personality. Relationships between the personal characteristics and performance are interpreted as the effects of traits on leader performance.

Various studies have used many different measures of personal characteristics, as well as different measures of performance. Randle (1956), for example, assessed about 100 different traits of managers. Although many studies have used well-validated measures, others have used untested instruments developed for the particular study. Some of these measures were not of good quality, especially in early studies conducted before we fully understood some of the biases that affect psychological measurement. This has contributed to inconsistency of results across studies in predicting leader performance. Nevertheless, research on manager performance has shown that personal traits such as cognitive ability can predict managerial performance (Hogan, Curphy, & Hogan, 1994).

The second approach is concerned with *leader emergence*, that is, who in a group will become the leader. These studies had groups of people work on a laboratory task, and the criterion was who became the leader of the group. The performance of the leader would not usually be assessed. It is possible that the personal characteristics that resulted in an individual's becoming the leader (for example, physical attractiveness) would not necessarily result in that person being a good leader.

It should come as no surprise that results across many of these studies have been inconsistent. Some studies found that certain characteristics were associated with leader emergence and performance, whereas others did not. To make sense out of an inconsistent literature, Judge, Bono, Ilies, and Gerhardt (2002) conducted a meta-analysis to combine results across studies statistically. They found that effective and emergent leaders were high on the Big Five traits of emotional stability, extraversion, openness to experience, agreeableness, and conscientiousness.

The Leader Behavior Approach

The *leader behavior approach* is concerned with what leaders do rather than what their personal characteristics might be. Although leader behavior studies deal with specific behaviors, most have concentrated on leadership styles. A *leadership style* is a cluster of related behaviors that represent an approach to dealing with subordinates. For example, some supervisors prefer to allow subordinates to have input into decisions that affect them. Such a style of asking advice and discussing issues is called *participative*. Other supervisors do not involve subordinates in decisions. Rather, they make the decision and announce it to the group. This style, in which subordinates are given little input, is called *autocratic*.

The most influential research program to study leader behaviors is the Ohio State Leadership Studies, which were begun in 1945 (Stogdill, 1963). This series of studies was designed to uncover the effects of specific supervisory behaviors on subordinates. The Ohio State researchers began by collecting about 1,800 critical incidents that represented instances of either very good or very bad supervisory behavior. They used these incidents as the basis for developing a 150-item questionnaire on leader behavior. The questionnaire was administered to several samples of employees, who answered each item about their supervisors. A complex statistical procedure called *factor analysis* was used to see if the 150 items could be reduced to a smaller number of underlying dimensions of leadership. The dimensions, which were based on the intercorrelations among the 150 items, showed that two aspects of leadership were represented, which they called consideration and initiating structure.

Consideration is the amount of concern that supervisors show for the happiness and welfare of their subordinates. It includes friendly and supportive behavior that makes the workplace pleasant for subordinates. **Initiating structure** is the extent to which the supervisor defines his or her own role and makes clear what is expected of subordinates. It includes assigning tasks to subordinates and scheduling the work. One of the major contributions of the Ohio State Leadership Studies was the development of scales to assess these dimensions. The most widely used is the Leader Behavior Description Questionnaire (LBDQ), which is completed by subordinates about their supervisor. Table 13.2 contains four items that assess consideration and four items that assess initiating structure.

Many studies have used the LBDQ in an attempt to discover the effects of leader behavior on subordinates. A good example is Fleishman and Harris's (1962) study of production workers in a truck manufacturing plant. Data were collected with the LBDQ from subordinates of 57 supervisors. The grievance and turnover rates were also collected for each supervisor's work group. Grievances can be considered behavioral measures

TABLE 13.2   Eight Items from the Consideration and Initiating Structure Scales of the Leader Behavior Description Questionnaire (LBDQ), Form XII

Consideration Items

He or she is friendly and approachable.
He or she does little things to make it pleasant to be a member of the group.
He or she puts suggestions made by the group into operation.
He or she treats all members of the group as his or her equals.

Initiating Structure Items

He or she lets group members know what is expected of them.
He or she encourages the use of uniform procedures.
He or she tries out his or her ideas in the group.
He or she makes his or her attitudes clear to the group.

Note: Items were modified to eliminate the generic "he."

Source: Manual for the Leader Behavior Description Questionnaire—Form XII by R. M. Stogdill, 1963, Columbus: Ohio State University.

of dissatisfaction with conditions of work. In unionized and government organizations, grievances require hearings that can consume considerable employee time. An excessive grievance rate can destroy the efficiency of a work group because people are spending time in unproductive ways.

Fleishman and Harris (1962) found that the mean LBDQ scores for the supervisors were related to the grievance and turnover rates in their departments. Supervisors with low scores on consideration and high scores on initiating structure had higher turnover rates and more grievances among subordinates than supervisors who were high on consideration and low on initiating structure. The lowest scoring supervisors on consideration had a turnover rate that was about four times higher than the highest scoring supervisors (Figures 13.2 and 13.3).

Although it is tempting to interpret these results as a demonstration of the effects of leader behavior on important subordinate behaviors, there are two major difficulties in doing so. First, the LBDQ might not be a good indicator of supervisory behavior and may be telling us as much about subordinates as about their supervisors. Several studies have attempted to find out what subordinate reports about their supervisors really mean. It has been found that the reports are affected by the subordinates' biases and stereotypes. In a series of studies, college students were asked to view a videotape of a supervisor interacting with subordinates. At random, all subjects who watched the same tape were told that the supervisor was rated either high or low in performance. Subjects who were told that the supervisor was a good performer rated him differently on the LBDQ than subjects who were told he was a poor performer (e.g., Lord, Binning, Rush, & Thomas, 1978; Phillips & Lord, 1982).

The second problem concerns drawing causal conclusions from data collected at one time in a cross-sectional research design (see Chapter 2). We cannot be certain from a study such as Fleishman and Harris's (1962) whether the grievance and turnover

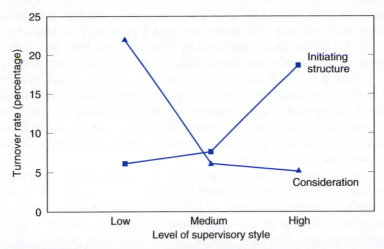

Figure 13.2   Turnover rate as a result of both the consideration and initiating structure of supervisors.
Source: "Patterns of Leadership Behavior Related to Employee Grievances and Turnover," by E. A. Fleishman and E. F. Harris, 1962, *Personnel Psychology, 15*, 43–56.

rates are caused by supervisor behavior or whether supervisor behavior is caused by the grievance and turnover rate. Studies have shown that supervisor behavior can be affected by subordinate behavior (e.g., Lowin & Craig, 1968), particularly job performance. Yukl (1989) concluded that a reciprocal relationship probably exists between supervisor style and subordinate behavior. A supervisor whose subordinates are filing many grievances might become angry and reduce consideration behavior. This might make subordinates

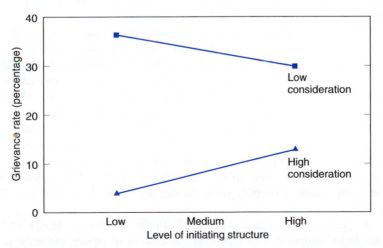

Figure 13.3   Grievance rate as a result of both the consideration and initiating structure of supervisors.
Source: "Patterns of Leadership Behavior Related to Employee Grievances and Turnover," by E. A. Fleishman and E. F. Harris, 1962, *Personnel Psychology, 15*, 43–56.

angrier and lead them to file more grievances, which will lead to even less consideration, and so on. These sorts of reciprocal processes have rarely been studied in I/O psychology.

In the United States, participatory practices have been linked to both job performance and job satisfaction, but the linkages are not always strong (Wagner, 1994). Part of the reason for small effects might have to do with the areas in which employees are allowed to participate. Sagie and Koslowsky (1994) found larger relations between perceived participation and job satisfaction when the participation involved deciding how to implement a change at work rather than whether or not to implement it in the first place. They concluded that it is important to consider the kinds of decisions appropriate for subordinate participation.

Participation has been shown to work in several studies. In others, however, it has not had positive effects. For example, Bragg and Andrews (1973) conducted a study in which participation worked in two of three departments. At the beginning of the study, the supervisor of a hospital laundry department changed from an autocratic to a participative style. Over the next 18 months there were positive effects on attendance, job performance (a 42% increase), and job satisfaction. This supervisory approach was then successfully introduced in the medical records department, but it could not be in the nursing department. The reasons why participatory styles sometimes succeed and sometimes fail are complex and may relate to the situations under which they are tried. This brings us to the basic idea of contingency theory: The situation interacts with leader characteristics and leader behavior.

Fiedler's Contingency Theory

The trait approach assumes that certain characteristics will make people good leaders. The behavior approach presumes that certain leader behaviors will be effective regardless of the situation. **Fiedler's contingency theory** states that leadership is a function of both the person and the situation. One characteristic of the leader and three characteristics of the situation determine leadership effectiveness.

The theory begins with the characteristic of the leader, which Fiedler (1978) refers to as the *motivational structure* of the leader. The motivational structure is assessed with a self-report instrument called the **Least Preferred Coworker (LPC) scale**. Although the name implies that it assesses the coworker, the scale actually measures a characteristic of the leader, not the subordinate. The LPC asks the leader to think about the person with whom he or she has had the most trouble working, that is, the coworker with whom he or she would least like to work. The leader then describes the least preferred coworker using a semantic differential type scale (Osgood, Tannenbaum, & Suci, 1957). The LPC consists of 18 bipolar adjective items, which are scales in which a person indicates which of two words with opposite meanings best describes someone, such as pleasant versus unpleasant or friendly versus unfriendly. (Examples from the LPC scale appear in Table 13.3.)

Fiedler's theory is also concerned with the situational variable of leader situational control. *Situational control* concerns the amount of power and influence the leader has over subordinates. It is the extent to which the supervisor's actions will predictably lead to subordinate behavior. Three characteristics of the leadership situation comprise situational control. *Leader-member relations* is the extent to which subordinates get along with and

TABLE 13.3   Four Items from Fiedler's Least Preferred Coworker Scale (LPC)

Pleasant	_____	_____	_____	_____	_____	_____	_____	_____	_____	Unpleasant
Friendly	_____	_____	_____	_____	_____	_____	_____	_____	_____	Unfriendly
Rejecting	_____	_____	_____	_____	_____	_____	_____	_____	_____	Accepting
Tense	_____	_____	_____	_____	_____	_____	_____	_____	_____	Relaxed

Source: "The Contingency Model and the Dynamics of the Leadership Process" (pp. 59–112), by F. E. Fiedler, 1978, in L. Berkowitz (Ed.), *Advances in Experimental Social Psychology*, *11*, New York: Academic Press.

support their supervisor. *Task structure* is the extent to which subordinate job tasks are clearly and specifically defined. *Position power* refers to the amount of power and influence the supervisor has, including the ability to give out rewards and punishments. A supervisor with good leader-member relations, highly structured tasks for subordinates, and high position power will be in a situation of high control. A supervisor with poor leader-member relations, low task structure for subordinates, and low position power will be in a situation of low control.

According to Fiedler's (1978) theory, the LPC of the supervisor determines the situations in which he or she will perform well. Individuals who are low on LPC do well under both very high and very low situational control. Individuals who are high on LPC will do best under conditions of moderate situational control. Take, for example, the situation in which the leader doesn't get along well with subordinates, the subordinates have unstructured tasks, and the leader has little power. This is an unfavorable situation, and the low LPC leader would be expected to be more effective than the high LPC leader. However, if the situation is moderately favorable, where relations are poor, but task structure is high and the leader has moderate power, the high LPC person should be more effective than the low LPC person. Figure 13.4 illustrates how supervisor performance is a function of situational control for individuals high and low in LPC.

Research on contingency theory has provided mixed support for its validity, and Fiedler certainly has his critics. Two meta-analyses combined the results of many tests of the theory (Peters, Hartke, & Pohlmann, 1985; Strube & Garcia, 1981). Both found that leader performance was a joint function of LPC and situational control, although the theory's predictions were not completely upheld. What is not clear at the present time is exactly why LPC and situational control interact. The major difficulty is that no one, not even Fiedler, is quite sure what LPC represents. LPC was intended to measure something about leader motivation, but it is not clear that motivation is assessed. Fiedler (1978) states that low LPC leaders are more concerned with getting tasks done than with having good relationships with subordinates, whereas high LPC leaders have the opposite motivations, being more concerned with having good relationships with subordinates than with getting the job done. At this time, all we can say for sure is that the LPC assesses some unknown but important characteristic of leaders.

Although the theory states that the situation determines the best leader characteristics, Fiedler does not believe that supervisors should attempt to adapt their style to the particular situation. He believes that supervisors should modify the situation to be appropriate to their own leadership style. To this end he has developed a training program called **Leader Match**. Fiedler (1978) summarized the results of several field experiments

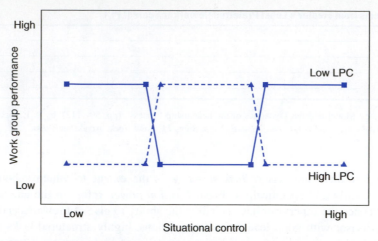

Figure 13.4 Group performance as a result of both the situational control and LPC of the leader. Source: Adapted from "The Contingency Model and the Dynamics of the Leadership Process" by F. E. Fiedler, 1978, in L. Berkowitz (Ed.), *Advances in Experimental Social Psychology, 11*, New York: Academic Press.

comparing Leader Match trained supervisors with untrained controls. The results showed better group performance for the trained supervisors. Some question has been raised, however, about whether Leader Match training results in leaders changing the situation according to theory, or whether the results of the Leader Match research are due to other factors (Jago & Ragan, 1986).

Despite the criticisms of the theory, Fiedler has been one of the most influential people in the study of leadership. His major contribution has been to show us that leadership involves the complex interaction of leader characteristics with the leadership situation. His work has been extended by theorists who have developed more complex contingency theories. One of these is path-goal theory, which we discuss next.

Path-Goal Theory

Path-goal theory (House & Mitchell, 1974) is a contingency theory that is more complex than Fiedler's. It posits that subordinate job performance and job satisfaction result from the interplay of situational characteristics, subordinate characteristics, and supervisor style. The basic idea, which is based on expectancy theory (see Chapter 8), is that the supervisor can enhance the motivation and job satisfaction of subordinates by providing rewards for good job performance and by making it easier for subordinates to achieve their task goals. Supervisors can accomplish this by adopting one of four supervisory styles, the efficacy of which is determined by situational and subordinate characteristics.

The four supervisory styles are:

Supportive Style

This style is similar to the Ohio State Leadership Studies' style of consideration. It involves showing concern for the needs and welfare of subordinates.

Directive Style

This style is similar to the Ohio State Leadership Studies' style of initiating structure. It involves the structuring of job tasks for subordinates and letting them know what is expected.

Participative Style

This style involves seeking input from subordinates and allowing them to participate in decision making.

Achievement Style

This style involves emphasizing achievement and good performance. It includes the setting of challenging task goals and emphasizing high performance standards.

Subordinate characteristics include personality variables, such as locus of control and self-perceived ability. Locus of control is the extent to which subordinates believe that they can control rewards in their lives. People with an internal locus of control believe that they are able to control rewards. People with an external locus of control believe that rewards are controlled by others or by outside forces. Self-perceived ability is the extent to which subordinates believe they are capable of doing the task well. It is similar to self-efficacy, which was discussed in Chapter 8, but it is specific to the particular task at hand. Situational characteristics include aspects of tasks, such as dangerousness, repetitiveness, and structure.

House and Mitchell (1974) derived a series of hypotheses based on the basic ideas of the theory. These hypotheses describe how certain supervisory styles will affect subordinates under certain conditions. For example,

1. When tasks are boring, dangerous, stressful, or tedious, a supportive style will be the most appropriate. Subordinates who must deal with these situations will have their anxiety lowered and their self-esteem raised by a supportive supervisor.

2. When tasks are unstructured and subordinates are inexperienced, a directive style will be most appropriate because subordinates will be uncertain about what to do. A directive supervisor will increase subordinates' effort and job satisfaction by telling them what is expected and what they should do.

Unfortunately, researchers have focused attention on only a few of the hypotheses of path-goal theory, particularly the second hypothesis given here. Although some of this research has supported the theory (Podsakoff, MacKenzie, Ahearne, & Bommer, 1995), many of the findings are inconsistent (Wofford & Liska, 1993). In part, the inconsistency may be due to methodological weaknesses in some of the studies. Another possibility is that some of the propositions are not quite correct.

Keller (1989) noted that not everyone is bothered by lack of structure on a job and in fact some people might prefer it. People who prefer unstructured tasks should be more satisfied with a low-structure job and would respond negatively to a directive supervisory style. Samples of employees from four organizations were assessed on subordinate need for structure, job performance, job satisfaction, and supervisor directive style (Keller, 1989). The results were consistent with predictions that subordinates who had a high need for structure would respond favorably to directive supervision (see Research in Detail). Keller's study suggests that one of the propositions should be modified to consider subordinate personality.

RESEARCH IN DETAIL

One of the hypotheses of path-goal theory is that when task structure is low, initiating structure by the supervisor will result in subordinate satisfaction. In other words, when subordinates are unsure about what is expected, clarification by the supervisor will be appreciated. Keller (1989) noted that research support for this hypothesis has been inconsistent across studies. He reasoned that a mistake of path-goal theory was assuming that all employees would find lack of structure unpleasant. His hypothesis was that the subordinates' need for clarity would determine their reactions to initiating structure in a job with low structure.

In this study, a survey was conducted among professionals in research and development (R&D) organizations. Because this work involves discovering new knowledge and technologies, an R&D job can have little structure. Respondents to the survey completed scales to assess the extent to which they need and prefer clarity on the job, the initiating structure of their supervisor, and their job satisfaction.

Data analyses showed that Keller's hypothesis was correct. Those individuals with a high need for clarity were more satisfied with high-initiating structure than low-initiating structure. Individuals with a low need for clarity were more satisfied with low-initiating structure than high-initiating structure. This study suggests that supervisors should consider the personality of each subordinate in deciding the most appropriate supervision method.

Source: Keller, R. T. (1989). A test of the path-goal theory of leadership with need for clarity as a moderator in research and development organizations. *Journal of Applied Psychology, 74*, 208–212.

Future research will be needed to show which of the original House and Mitchell (1974) hypotheses can be supported. It seems likely, in light of Keller's (1989) findings, that new hypotheses involving the interplay of situations, subordinates, and supervisors will be developed. One implication of Keller's findings is that different supervisory approaches might be necessary with different subordinates. This brings us to the leader-member exchange theory of leadership, which is concerned with the interactions within each subordinate-supervisor dyad, or pair.

Leader-Member Exchange (LMX) Theory

The **leader-member exchange (LMX) theory** (Dansereau, Graen, & Haga, 1975) focuses on the subordinate-supervisor dyad rather than on the supervisor and the work group. Dansereau et al. argue that one of the major limitations of most leadership research is its implicit assumption that each supervisor's group of subordinates is sufficiently homogeneous to justify studying it as a unit and that each supervisor adopts the same style across all subordinates. On the contrary, they propose that supervisors will treat individual subordinates differently.

Dansereau et al. (1975) discussed two types of relationships that develop between supervisors and subordinates. The **cadre**, or **in-group**, consists of subordinates who are trusted and influential members of the work group. The supervisor treats them with consideration and adopts a participative style with them. The **hired hands**, or **out-group**, by contrast, are subordinates who are supervised with a directive style and are given little input into decisions. These relationships evolve over time, with characteristics of subordinates affecting the category in which they find themselves. To become part of the cadre, a subordinate must be perceived as dependable and hard working. In return for cadre status, a subordinate must be prepared to exert effort on the job beyond the minimum expected.

In their research, Dansereau et al. (1975) found that within work groups, supervisors had two distinct groups in terms of how much participation was allowed. Members of the cadre were more satisfied with their jobs, believed they had better relationships with the supervisor, and were less likely to quit than the hired hands. Care must be taken, however, in concluding that the satisfaction and turnover differences were the result of supervisor treatment. It is likely that supervisor behavior toward each subordinate was as much a function of the subordinate's job performance as a cause of that performance (Bauer & Green, 1996).

One contribution of the leader-member exchange approach is that it focuses attention on the importance of individual relationships within each supervisor-subordinate dyad. The idea was the basis of an intervention study in which supervisors were trained to enhance their relationships with each subordinate. Graen, Novak, and Sommerkamp (1982) conducted a field experiment in which one group of supervisors was trained in leader-member exchange. The training was intended to help supervisors improve their relationships with subordinates. Each trained supervisor had meetings with individual subordinates to discuss work issues and the working relationship between them. The subordinates of the trained supervisors subsequently had better job performance and higher job satisfaction than a control group in which supervisors were not trained.

Research has shown that the quality of LMX relationships, as perceived by subordinates, is associated with several important work variables. For example, subordinates who report good LMX relationships with their supervisors are rated higher in job performance and organizational citizenship behavior by the supervisors than are subordinates who report poor LMX relationships (Kacmar, Witt, Zivnuska, & Gully, 2003; Wayne, Shore, Bommer, & Tetrick, 2002). Furthermore, good LMX relationships have been associated with lower intentions to quit the job (Harris, Kacmar, & Witt, 2005). In their meta-analysis of 79 studies, Gerstner and Day (1997) showed that individuals who had good relationships with their supervisors tended to have higher job satisfaction, were more committed to their employers, and perceived the job as less stressful than individuals with poor relationships with supervisors. Taken together, these studies suggest that good relationships between supervisor and subordinate are important because they lead to good job attitudes and performance, and low turnover.

The LMX theory of leadership has certain limitations and has been subjected to criticism. First, differential treatment of subordinates within a work group can be destructive (Yukl, 1989). Equity theory, as discussed in Chapter 8, describes how employees can react negatively to unequal treatment. The higher turnover rate and lower job satisfaction of the hired hands in the Dansereau et al. (1975) study might well be interpreted as a response to inequity. Schriesheim (1980) points out that supervisors often direct influence attempts at entire work groups at one time, rather than treating each individual differently. She believes that a focus on both work groups and individual dyads makes the most sense for understanding leadership. LMX theory helped focus attention on the relationship between subordinate and supervisor. It also has led to an understanding that supervisors do not act the same way with all subordinates.

Transformational Leadership Theory

Transformational leadership theory deals with leaders who have considerable and unusual influence over their followers, or in other words are **charismatic**. It is in some ways a return to the trait approach, because it focuses on characteristics of leaders in relation to effectiveness. However, it differs from prior approaches in going beyond linking traits to performance, and it attempts to determine how leaders affect their followers. A **transformational leader** is one who leads by inspiring others to adopt high goals and strive to achieve them. Such leaders articulate a vision for their followers and encourage them to pursue it. Gardner and Avolio (1998) explain that certain leaders are able to convince followers of their competence and the importance of a vision. They engage in behaviors that make them appear to be creative, innovative, powerful, and trustworthy. Much of the leader's influence derives from the followers' belief that only by following the leader will they be able to achieve the vision, such as making the company profitable. Leaders like Abraham Lincoln, Winston Churchill, John F. Kennedy, and Martin Luther King, Jr. are examples of transformational leaders. King's vision of a free society, reflected in his "I Have a Dream" speech on August 28, 2003 in Washington, DC, is an example of a vision statement that inspires.

Bass and Rigio (2006) argue that transformational leadership has four components. Idealized influence is the extent to which leaders encourage followers with their statements and model high standards of behavior. Inspirational motivation is providing a vision, such as King's dream. Intellectual stimulation is encouraging followers to question the status quo and think of better ways to do things. Individualized consideration is paying attention to the development and well being of followers. Taken together, this suggests that transformational leaders inspire by articulating a vision for the group, encouraging and supporting followers, and setting an example to follow.

(*Bettmann/CORBIS*)   (*Bettmann/CORBIS*)

Dr. Martin Luther King, Jr. (*left*) and President John F. Kennedy were charismatic leaders who championed civil rights in the United States.

Research on transformational leadership shows that it relates to several subordinate variables that are important for organizational functioning. For example, individuals who perceive their supervisors to be transformational tend to be high on job performance (Bass, Avolio, Jung, & Berson, 2003; Keller, 2006), job satisfaction (Judge & Piccolo, 2004), organizational citizenship behavior, organizational commitment, and perceptions of justice (Pillai, Schriesheim, & Williams, 1999). They also report less intention of quitting (Bycio, Hackett, & Allen, 1995). Furthermore, although it might seem that transformational leadership is innate, researchers have been successful at training people to exhibit the behaviors. For example, Towler (2003) conducted a laboratory experiment in which business students were randomly assigned to receive transformational training versus control training. They subsequently delivered a role-play speech to a supposed group of employees. Those who received the transformational training were rated by trained observers to be higher on transformational leadership than the controls. Barling, Weber, and Kelloway (1996) were able to successfully train bank managers to be more transformational, and showed that training had an impact on the financial performance of their branches.

Existing studies are quite suggestive that transformational leadership has considerable potential for application. If transformational leaders have happier and more productive subordinates, and if it can be trained, organizations would benefit by encouraging supervisors to adopt this approach. More studies like Barling et al. (1996) are needed to confirm their promising results.

Vroom-Yetton Model

The **Vroom-Yetton model** (Vroom & Yetton, 1973) is different from the leadership theories we have discussed so far. Rather than describing how the leadership process works, Vroom-Yetton is a prescriptive model indicating the supervisory approach that is expected to be most effective in a particular situation when making decisions. Note that Vroom-Yetton is designed only for decision making and not for other aspects of supervisor behavior, such as generating solutions to problems or directing the activities of subordinates. The model is based on psychological principles that can help inform the best decision making practices based on the characteristics of the given situation. A manager can use the model to help choose the way to handle each situation in which a decision must be made.

The model specifies the following five approaches to making a decision; they range from autocratic to democratic:

1. Supervisor makes the decision alone.
2. Supervisor gets information from subordinates and makes the decision alone.
3. Supervisor discusses the problem with some subordinates and then makes the decision.
4. Supervisor discusses the problem with all subordinates in a meeting and makes the decision.
5. Supervisor presents the problem to all subordinates in a meeting and lets them decide.

As you can see, the supervisor can act independently (approach 1), can turn the problem over to the group (approach 5), or can adopt various stages of sharing the decision from merely soliciting information (approach 2) to actually discussing the problem and considering others' viewpoints (approach 3 or 4).

The decision-making situation is defined by seven characteristics that address the problem itself and the subordinates:

1. Quality requirement for the result (is it important to make the right decision?).
2. Sufficiency of information the supervisor has.
3. Problem structure (is it clear what has to be done, or is the situation ambiguous?).
4. Necessity for subordinate acceptance of the decision.
5. Likelihood of subordinate acceptance of the decision if made by the supervisor alone.
6. Subordinate commitment to solving the problem.
7. Subordinate conflict over solutions.

Each of the characteristics is translated into a yes/no question (e.g., "Is the problem structured?"). The pattern of answers determines the best practice. For example, if quality isn't important (characteristic 1), acceptance by subordinates is important (characteristic 4), and subordinates are unlikely to accept a decision made unilaterally by the supervisor (characteristic 5), the best approach is to allow the subordinates to make the decision. On the other hand, if quality is not an issue and if acceptance isn't important, any of the five approaches should be equally effective. In most cases, the more democratic approaches are appropriate, and it is only in limited situations that being autocratic can be effective.

Vroom and Yetton (1973) provided decision tools based on their model that can be used by managers to choose a decision making approach. The specific approach recommended depends on whether you wish to minimize the time necessary for a decision or maximize the likelihood of group acceptance of the decision. Not surprisingly, making a decision yourself can often be the quickest approach, but it isn't necessarily the most effective. There are paper-and-pencil materials (tables and decision trees) that can be used to follow the answers to all seven questions to the recommended decision-making approaches. They also have developed computer software that displays the questions, allows you to enter answers, and then provides advice about how to approach the situation.

A limited number of studies have tested the Vroom-Yetton model. For the most part, the findings support the recommendations of the theory. Vroom and Jago (1988) compiled results across six studies that compared the effectiveness of decisions that conformed to the theory's advice to those that failed to conform. The success rate for decisions made in accordance with the theory was higher than for decisions made in violation of it, 62% versus 37%, respectively. On the other hand, Field and House (1990) provided only mixed support for the theory. They had a sample of supervisors and their subordinates report on the process and effectiveness of a decision. Although the supervisor data supported the Vroom-Yetton model, the subordinate data did not. Field and House were hesitant to conclude that the theory was invalid and called for additional research to test it.

The Vroom-Yetton model has the potential to be the most useful of the leadership theories from the perspective of practicing managers who wish to use the latest findings to guide their supervisory approach. This theory offers very specific advice about how to supervise, whereas the other theories provide principles that one would have to figure out how to apply. After working with the Vroom-Yetton model for a while, a manager will likely learn the underlying principles, making it unnecessary to consult a table or software each time a new decision situation in encountered. At the present time, the research findings have been promising, but too few studies have been conducted in field settings to test whether following the theory always leads to better decision outcomes in terms of decision quality or decision speed.

► WOMEN IN LEADERSHIP POSITIONS

Women have made considerable strides in achieving managerial and supervisory positions in organizations. It has been estimated that by 1999, about 46% of all management jobs in the United States were held by women (Powell, Butterfield, & Parent, 2002). Despite their success at the lower levels of management, American women are still underrepresented at the higher levels of organizations. Their numbers, however, have been increasing, with more than 15% of top corporate management positions being held by women by 2002 (Northhouse, 2005). One study of MBA graduates' career progression found that men had higher starting salaries than women and that their salaries went up more quickly with age (Goldberg, Finkelstein, Perry, & Konrad, 2004). However, it is unclear how typical these results might be, as another study of high-level executives in a financial services corporation found little difference between men and women's compensation (Lyness & Thompson, 1997). Perhaps some industries have made progress in equating men and women's salary progression, whereas others are lagging behind.

(*Corbis-Bettmann*)   (*Corbis-Bettmann*)

What do these two women have in common? They were both leaders of their countries. Although the United States has never had a woman as president, other countries have had female leaders. Golda Meir of Israel (*left*) and Margaret Thatcher of the United Kingdom (*right*) were both elected prime minister of their country.

Although women have more difficulty than men in achieving high-level positions in most organizations, this problem is not found in all organizations. Powell and Butterfield (1994) found that females who applied for promotion were more (not less) likely than men to be promoted to top management in the U.S. civil service. In part, the gender difference was attributed to better job performance by the female applicants. The lack of bias against women may have been due to fairer promotion practices and commitment to equal employment opportunity in government agencies.

Many explanations have been advanced for the **glass ceiling** phenomenon that symbolizes women's difficulty in getting beyond the lower levels of management. Some of these explanations have focused on differences between men and women in their career preparation and their attitudes, whereas others are concerned with bias against women as high level managers. For example, in a Dutch study, van Vianen and Fischer (2002) found that women were less ambitious, cared less about salary and status, and were more concerned with work-family conflict than men. These factors may explain why fewer women seek promotions to higher management, but doesn't explain why those who wish to achieve higher levels have a more difficult time doing so.

The bias explanation has to do with the attitudes and stereotypes of those at the top levels of organizations who make decisions about hiring. Research by Virginia Schein and her colleagues (Schein, Mueller, Lituchy, & Liu, 1996) demonstrated how subtle stereotypes about characteristics of men and women put women at a disadvantage for management selection. They asked people to describe the characteristics of managers, men, and women and found that the description of managers overlapped with the descriptions of men but not the descriptions of women. It was concluded that the reason a woman might have difficulty getting promoted is that she is not seen as having the characteristics necessary for the position. It is not that the decision maker is consciously discriminating against women. Rather, the male candidates seem to fit the requirements for the job better than the female candidates. According to this view, equal access to high-level management jobs will require attitude change on the part of those who do the hiring. Furthermore, this phenomenon seems to be universal, for they found similar results in China, Germany, Japan, the United Kingdom, and the United States.

On the other hand, bias on the part of decision makers is unlikely to be a complete explanation either. Lyness and Thompson (2000) surveyed matched samples of middle- to upper-level male and female managers about their career progression. They found that women were more likely than men to report feeling they didn't fit in with colleagues. Whether this reflects that women have a harder time adapting to management ranks, are finding colleagues and supervisors less accepting of them, or merely perceive less fit is unclear. However, even if it is just perception, feeling out of place would be likely to affect confidence and behavior in a way that might adversely affect career progression.

Powell and Butterfield (1994) suggested that the federal government may be a model of how to eliminate the glass ceiling. Important factors include a strong management commitment to equal employment opportunity and uniform selection procedures that reduce subjectivity in decisions.

Gender and Leadership Style

Do men and women in leadership positions differ in their supervisory styles? Our stereo-types of men and women suggest that women would be more concerned with the feelings and emotional well-being of subordinates (consideration) and men would be more concerned with getting the job done (initiating structure). Research on gender differences in leadership suggests that the answer is complex.

Eagly and Johnson (1990) conducted a meta-analysis of studies that compared the leadership styles of men and women. They combined the results of over 160 leadership studies and arrived at several conclusions. One is that the stereotypic styles of men being high in structure and women being high in consideration have been found in laboratory research with students but not in field studies with actual leaders. They had two explanations for this finding. First, in an organizational setting, there are environmental constraints and requirements that may force male and female supervisors to adopt similar styles. Second, organizations may select women who have leadership styles similar to men's. In laboratory studies, subjects are selected more randomly, and there are fewer constraints on the leader behaviors the participant adopts. Thus, whereas females may be inclined to supervise differently than men, organizational settings do not allow them to express that inclination.

On the other hand, when men and women were compared on their autocratic or democratic tendencies, gender differences were found in both the laboratory and the field. Men have been found to be more autocratic and women more democratic. Eagly and Johnson (1990) pointed out that each style will probably be more effective under different organizational circumstances. They noted that research is needed to determine whether there are gender differences in actual supervisory performance.

Men and women have also been compared in the extent to which their subordinates see them as transformational. Bass, Avolio, and Atwater (1996), based on three samples, found that women were either the same or higher on transformational leadership than men. Unfortunately, their study does not permit conclusions about effectiveness. Nevertheless, it suggests that there are gender differences in leadership style.

▶ CROSS-CULTURAL ISSUES IN LEADERSHIP

It would be a mistake to assume that the findings and theories discussed in this chapter apply universally to all countries and cultures. How leaders are viewed and what might be effective is not necessarily the same across all countries. For example, the attributes associated with good leadership can be culturally determined. The most comprehensive study of this issue is the 62-country Global Leadership and Organizational Effectiveness (Project GLOBE) Research Program (House, Hanges, Ruiz-Quintanilla, Dorfman, Javidan, Dickson, Gupta, & Country Co-Investigators, 1999). One of the findings of GLOBE was that many specific attributes of managers are universal, but others vary across countries. For example, being intelligent and being trustworthy were universally seen as positive characteristics. However, being individualistic (focusing on self rather than others) and being willing to take risks were seen as more positive in some countries than in others.

Similarly, Ensari and Murphy (2003) asked students from a collectivist (Turkey) and an individualist (U.S.) country to read varied descriptions of manager behavior and performance, and then rate how transformational the leader was. The Turkish students' ratings were influenced most by the performance of the managers, whereas the American students focused mainly on behaviors. To the extent that perceptions of transformational leadership affect employee attitudes and behavior, this suggests that the specific behaviors of managers are more important in the United States than Turkey, where results are paramount. Of course, this needs to be replicated in an organizational setting with practicing managers.

Another important issue concerns cultural differences in the effectiveness of different leader behaviors. Scandura, Von Glinow, and Lowe (1999) investigated this issue by comparing employees from the United States with those in the Middle Eastern countries of Jordan and Saudi Arabia (see International Replication). They found that consideration was more strongly related to leadership effectiveness than to initiating structure in the United States, but the opposite was true in the Middle East. This suggests that merely using American approaches in another country that is culturally dissimilar may not be effective.

INTERNATIONAL REPLICATION

In American research, it has been well established that certain supervisory styles are more effective than others. It is unclear, however, that the same styles will be universally effective in countries with cultures that are different from the United States. Scandura, Von Glinow and Lowe (1999) conducted a study comparing leadership styles in the United States with those in the Middle East. The authors felt that the cultural differences between these two areas would result in different styles being effective

Surveys were administered to 144 employees from the United States, 47 from Jordan, and 60 from Saudi Arabia. Data from the two Middle Eastern countries were combined. Scales included the Leader Behavior Description Questionnaire (LBDQ) to assess consideration and initiating structure, global job satisfaction, and perceived effectiveness of the supervisor. The Middle East survey was translated into Arabic.

Results showed that in the American sample, consideration correlated more strongly than initiating structure with job satisfaction (.61 vs. .20, respectively) and perceived effectiveness (.65 vs. .30, respectively). The Middle East showed the opposite pattern. Consideration correlated less strongly than initiating structure with job satisfaction (.22 vs. .38, respectively) and perceived effectiveness (.25 vs. .34, respectively). Furthermore, neither of these styles correlated as strongly with job satisfaction or effectiveness in the Middle East as consideration did in the United States.

These findings suggest that consideration is more important to Americans than to Middle Easterners. As Scandura et al. point out, the Arab view of leadership tends to be far more militaristic than the American view. Thus their view of a leader is of someone more autocratic and task oriented. They have less expectation of consideration, and so this style is less important. It should be kept in mind, however, that for the American sample there was a correlation between initiating structure and both job satisfaction and effectiveness, and for the Middle East sample there was a correlation between consideration and both of these outcomes. Thus it is the relative importance that differs.

Source: Scandura, T. A., Von Glinow, M. A., & Lowe, K. B. (1999). When east meets west: Leadership "best practices" in the United States and the Middle East. In W. H. Mobley, M. J. Gessner, & V. Arnold (eds.). *Advances in Global Leadership Volume 1* (pp. 171–233). Stamford, CT: JAI.

Preferences for directive versus participative management might also vary across countries. Narayanan, Menon, and Spector (1999) asked clerical employees in India and the United States to describe the most stressful incident that had happened to them at work in the prior month. Trained content judges analyzed the incidents, placing them in categories. In the United States, lack of control was the second most frequently mentioned stressful incident, mentioned by almost a fourth of participants. In India, the most frequently mentioned stressful incident was insufficient structure provided by supervisors, mentioned by a little over a fourth of the participants. Not one American mentioned insufficient structure, and not one Indian mentioned lack of control.

Despite such differences in leadership preferences and effectiveness, there are some aspects of leadership that may transcend culture. Transformational leadership has been shown to relate to job performance in Singapore, much as it does in Western countries (Lim & Ployhart, 2004). Furthermore, transformational leadership is related to positive job attitudes in China and India (Walumbwa, Wang, Lawler, & Shi, 2004). Taken together, these results show that there may be some universal characteristics of leaders that are effective across countries. Of course, this doesn't mean that transformational leaders behave in exactly the same way in different countries, because in all likelihood what it takes to be transformational is to a large extent culturally determined.

▶ FUTURE ISSUES AND CHALLENGES

One of the biggest challenges for the future of leadership in organizations concerns the increasing diversity of the workplace. In most large organizations, the workplace is becoming increasingly female and multicultural, from both the hiring of increasing numbers of minority members and the globalization of the world economy. As we saw in this chapter, effective leadership is partially determined by culture. More divergent and flexible methods need to be developed for supervisors to deal with a more varied group of subordinates. Solutions might involve education in appropriate behaviors for different countries and cultures and increased sensitivity to issues that might not have existed with more homogeneous groups. For example, the introduction of women into formerly male-dominated jobs has produced conflicts that supervisors must be prepared to mediate. Sexist language that might once have been the norm in an all-male work group will now offend many female coworkers. Supervisors need to find ways to deal with such issues in a constructive and effective way.

The problem of the glass ceiling, which exists for minorities as well as women, needs to be addressed in the future. At present minorities and women have a more difficult time progressing in their careers for several reasons. Although progress has been made, we need to find ways to overcome this problem in organizations. It is important from the perspective of both employees and organizations that ways be found to ensure that the best people are placed in leadership positions.

Finally, the growing use of technology to allow employees to work remotely will challenge managers to find appropriate ways to supervise employees they rarely if ever see face-to-face. Virtual supervision will require a style that can be effective for seeing to it that employees accomplish what needs to be done. In many cases this will mean adopting an achievement oriented style that holds employees accountable for results, but allows them autonomy and flexibility in their day-to-day task performance.

▶ CHAPTER SUMMARY

Leadership is an important function in organizations in which the efforts of many individuals must be coordinated and directed. Leadership refers to the disproportionate influence that one person has over others, and in organizations it is typically associated with managerial and supervisory positions. Leaders' influence over their followers is based on a number of factors. French and Raven (1959) provided five bases of power and influence

Expert

Referent

Legitimate

Reward

Coercive

Yukl (1989) added the political influence tactics of

Controlling decisions

Coalition formation

Co-optation

There have been many approaches to the study of leadership. The trait approach attempts to find characteristics that make people good leaders. The leader behavior approach, represented by the Ohio State Leadership Studies, views leadership from the perspective of behaviors that are and are not effective. Contingency theories, such as Fiedler's and path-goal, state that leadership is a complex interaction of leader characteristics and the leadership situation. The leader-member exchange theory points out that leadership can be fully understood only by focusing attention on the often unique interactions of a supervisor with each subordinate. Transformational leadership theories look at the way some leaders are able to have a profound influence on the attitudes, beliefs, behaviors, and values of subordinates. Finally, the Vroom-Yetton model and its successor, the Vroom-Jago model, are prescriptive theories that tell a supervisor how best to approach a decision situation.

Although women have made great strides in the workplace, they still have a difficult time breaking through the glass ceiling into high-level management positions. One explanation for this phenomenon has to do with the stereotypes of women's behavior. It is interesting that research has found few differences in the consideration and initiating structure styles of men and women managers, but women seem to be more democratic than men.

I/O PSYCHOLOGY IN PRACTICE

(*Courtesy Steve Cohen*)

This case concerns the development of a training program to develop transformational leadership skills in corporate managers. Dr. Steve Cohen headed a team of consultants that implemented the program. Cohen received his Ph.D. in I/O psychology from the University of Tennessee in 1971. He began his career as a college professor, but decided shortly after earning tenure that he preferred the world of consulting. Over the next 25 years he alternated between working for a consulting firm and running his own. At the time of this case he was managing director, Learning Solutions Group, for Dove Consulting in Minneapolis. Dove is a 110 employee international strategy and organizational effectiveness firm. The Learning Solutions Group specializes in developing training programs and employee performance improvement systems.

One of the most interesting projects on which Cohen has worked involved the challenging task of training competent managers to become transformational and visionary leaders. A major global food and beverage company, headquartered in the United States and with facilities in 170 countries, contracted with Dove to train its 7,500 managers to change their management approach. This company had been successful for decades, and top management felt that employees at all levels had become relatively complacent. Managers did a good job of running the day-to-day business, but they had adopted a short-term focus, tended to avoid risk, and lacked a vision for the future. As described in this chapter, transformational leaders are just the opposite in that they inspire followers to aspire to do better by promoting a vision for the future.

The project began with the development of a leadership competency model that described the ideal manager of the future for the business. Turning existing managers into the ideal served as the ultimate objective of the project. Next came the development of the curriculum. This started with a needs assessment to determine the existing skill levels and deficiencies of managers. Cohen's team then designed and developed training materials to address the skills identified in the needs assessment. They pilot tested the materials, and then trained the trainers (not psychologists) who would ultimately deliver the training to the 7,500 managers throughout the world. Finally, the project was evaluated using 360 degree feedback. Subordinates, peers,

and supervisors completed rating scales that contained items reflecting transformational leadership behaviors.

The methods used for training were quite eclectic. Some were traditional paper-and-pencil materials provided to both trainers and trainees, and some of the training occurred in a classroom setting. However, Cohen has been a leader in the use of electronic technologies for training, and much of the material was provided online. Managers could log onto the company Web site and find self-paced materials as well as resources for them to manage their own development. This approach not only provided an efficient means of conducting training with minimal use of trainers, but it allowed for an individualized approach that helped trainees create their own plans and track their progress toward completion.

Discussion Questions

1. Why did Cohen train trainers instead of conducting training himself?

2. What are the advantages and disadvantages of the Web-based approach?

3. Why was it necessary to first conduct a needs assessment?

4. What are one advantage and one disadvantage of having all the leaders in a company adopt a transformational approach?

LEARNING BY DOING

Transformational Leadership

Choose a public leader such as a head of state or CEO of a corporation who you believe is transformational. Find evidence from one or more of the leader's public statements (spoken or written) that confirms that the leader is transformational. Which of the four components of transformational leadership does the evidence reflect? Find an example of a vision statement the leader has used.

Abuse of Power

Who is Helen Green, for what company did she work, and what does she have to do with abuse of power? Explain how her experience adversely affected her and the company for which she worked.

Organizational Development and Theory

CHAPTER 14 OUTLINE

So far our focus in this book has been on the individual employee or small groups of employees in the context of the organization. In this last chapter, we change our perspective from the individual to the organization. We deal with two important topics—organizational development and organizational theory.

Organizations in the modern industrialized world find themselves in a rapidly evolving environment that requires appropriate changes in both structure and function. The field of *organizational development* helps organizations make changes that are rationally planned and implemented. Organizational change is often forced by circumstances and crises beyond the control of those in charge, which result in hurried changes in response to an emergency. Such precipitous changes can be damaging to the organization in the long term.

For example, many organizations today are experiencing *downsizing* —reduction in the number of employees. Although downsizing is often necessary, it is too often carried out from a purely economic perspective without consideration of the effects on employees and on the organization itself. The projected savings from layoffs may never materialize for several reasons; for example, the remaining employees may be too demotivated to be effective, and too many of the best employees may have left. Organizational development can help by considering the human side of organizational change and the best way to carry it out so that the organization remains effective. In this chapter we explore how organizational development can help and some of the specific techniques involved.

Organizational theories describe how organizations work. Some focus on the structure of organizations, including their various components and how they interrelate. Others are concerned with the interpersonal aspects of organizations, including communication and how people relate to one another. Finally, some focus on the interaction of the interpersonal and technical sides of organizations. In other words, how do people affect the technology of the organization, and how does the technology affect people? All of these approaches are discussed in this chapter as we cover four important organizational theories.

Objectives: The student who studies this chapter should be able to:

► Explain what organizational development is and how it is applied.

► Describe the organizational development techniques discussed and indicate the effectiveness of each.

► Discuss each of the organizational theories presented in the chapter.

► Show the linkages among the four organizational theories discussed.

► ORGANIZATIONAL DEVELOPMENT

Organizational development (OD) is a family of techniques designed to help organizations change for the better. They involve the use of behavioral science principles and procedures that help employees improve performance and interact with coworkers more effectively. An OD effort involves an entire organization or a large component of it, and is intended to result in substantial changes in how the organization operates. Such changes can involve a reorganization in which new departments are created and old ones eliminated, with functions moved from area to area and person to person. An OD effort, however, is typically much more than a reorganization, and often reorganization isn't even involved. It usually involves changing how people do their work, how they communicate with one another, and how they coordinate their efforts.

An OD effort or program involves employees at all levels of the organization. It is implemented by a person or persons referred to as change agents. The **change agent** is the catalyst for change within the organization. He or she is an expert in working with organizations to improve their functioning. The change agent might be an employee of the organization, as in the case at the end of the chapter. In most instances, however, the change agent is an outside consultant who is hired to implement the OD program. Many consulting firms throughout the world specialize in organizational development.

Change agents act as guides and trainers for the organizational development process. They conduct classes in which employees are trained in new ways to communicate or operate within their organizations. They may conduct group sessions during which organization members plan changes that will improve the organization. The role of the change agent in these sessions is to serve as the group facilitator or moderator to keep everyone focused on the task at hand and to help mediate disputes among people. In short, the change agent assists the organization members in their OD effort. The change agent usually does not come into the organization with a specific plan for change, only the process by which employees can redesign their organization.

Organizational development and other changes are not easy to implement. Armenakis and Bedeian (1999) discussed how it is a multistage process that an organization must go through to successfully implement a change. It begins with employees first learning that a change needs to occur, which in many cases will induce anxiety and disbelief. Next the specific form of the change has to be determined, often with the participation of the employees affected. Once a plan is produced, the change can be implemented. Typically there will be some degree of resistance to the change that must be overcome. Finally, the new ways of operating must be consolidated and become part of the accepted way people operate.

Employee Acceptance of Change

Management's desire to introduce change does not guarantee that it will be successful. Employees who must change their behavior or use new equipment and techniques effectively must be willing to accept the change rather than resist, and must commit to making it successful (Herscovitch & Meyer, 2002). Change can be stressful, leading to negative emotions and feelings of uncertainty that can affect acceptance (Kiefer, 2005; Rafferty & Griffin, 2006). Individual employee and organizational factors combine to determine people's willingness to accept change. On the individual side, people who are flexible and like to try new things are likely to accept change (Choi & Price, 2005). People who have had positive experience with change in the past will be more likely to accept it in the future (Cunningham, Woodward, Shannon, MacIntosh, Lendrum, Rosenbloom & Brown, 2002).

On the organizational side, transformational leaders can effectively encourage followers to accept change (Bommer, Rich, & Rubin, 2005; Groves, 2005). Of particular importance is the leader's articulation of a vision that is consistent with the change. In other words, an effective transformational leader will explain to followers how the change will enable them to reach important goals more easily, and will convince them that change is welcome. Wanberg and Banas (2000) noted how sufficient information about change and participation by employees in the process were associated with employee acceptance of change within U.S. government agencies over a 14-month period (see Research In Detail). Klein, Conn, and Sorra (2001) studied change in 39 U.S. manufacturing plants and found that sufficient financial resources and support from management were associated with successful change efforts.

RESEARCH IN DETAIL

Even the most well designed organizational change will induce some level of resistance among employees. An issue of concern is determining what factors might mitigate that resistance. Wanberg and Banas (2000) studied organizational change in U.S. public housing organizations funded by the Department of Housing and Urban Development (HUD). In the midst of a radical restructuring of HUD and its operations, surveys were conducted to determine what factors might lead to favorable employee reactions to organizational change.

Participants in this study were members of the National Association of Housing and Redevelopment Officials (NAHRO) from two states. Surveys were administered to 173 employees who were attending state NAHRO conferences. A number of scales assessed characteristics of the individual employees and their perceptions of organizational conditions. Included was a measure of resilience, which comprised high self-esteem, an optimistic outlook on life, and feelings of control. Organizational scales assessed information sharing (extent to which employees were informed about changes) and participation in changes. Two months later participants were mailed a questionnaire that assessed their openness to organizational change, job satisfaction, and turnover

intentions. One year later organizations were contacted to determine whether the participants had quit their jobs.

Results showed that the two most important factors in openness to change were the extent to which employees felt informed and participated. Personality was also a factor, with resilience associated with openness. Furthermore, openness was associated with job satisfaction and intention to quit, and both job satisfaction and intention to quit were associated with turnover. This suggests that forced change can lead to dissatisfaction and intention of quitting, which can lead to subsequent turnover.

This study shows that people vary in their openness to organizational change, and that resilient people are more likely to endorse rather than resist it. Furthermore, the results suggest that providing sufficient information about impending changes and allowing employees to participate in change planning and implementation can go a long way to increasing openness and reducing resistance, thus facilitating effective organizational change.

Source: Wanberg, C. R., & Banas, J. T. (2000). Predictors and outcomes of openness to changes in a reorganizing workplace. *Journal of Applied Psychology*, 85, 132–142.

Management by Objectives

Management by objectives (MBO) is an organizational change technique that is based on goal setting (see Chapter 8). Each employee's own goals are coordinated with the goals of both supervisors and subordinates. In a typical MBO program, goal setting begins by having those at the top of the organization set broad objectives for the entire organization. The process of setting goals or objectives then filters down level by level, with all employees' goals being related to the goals of their superiors. The goals serve as motivational tools to direct effort, as criteria against which employee performance is appraised, and as the means of coordinating everyone's efforts toward a common set of organizational objectives.

Implementation of an MBO program typically begins with the change agent meeting with the top officials of the organization to set organization-wide goals and objectives. These goals must be as concrete and measurable as possible because everyone else's goals must be linked to them. A goal such as

Improve the functioning of the organization

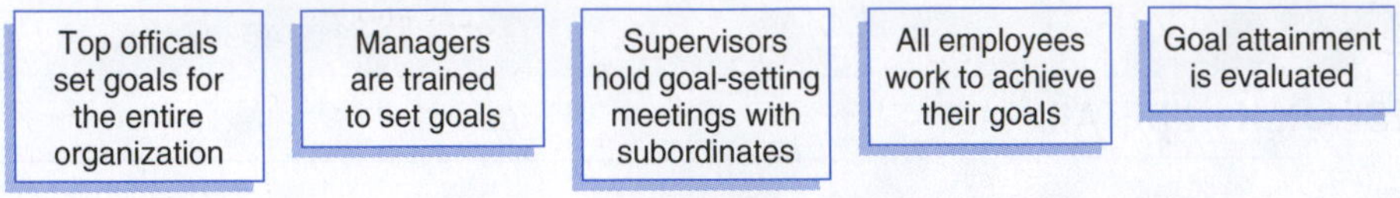

| Top officals set goals for the entire organization | Managers are trained to set goals | Supervisors hold goal-setting meetings with subordinates | All employees work to achieve their goals | Goal attainment is evaluated |

Figure 14.1   The Five Steps of implementing a management by objectives (MBO) program.

is a worthy goal, but it is too vague to be of much value in directing effort. A better goal would be

Increase sales by 20%.

This goal is specific and measurable, allowing everyone to know precisely what needs to be done and when it has been achieved.

In the next step, the change agent meets with managers and trains them in the goal-setting process. The program will work only when managers understand how to state measurable goals and how to set goals with subordinates and superiors. The third step is a series of meetings involving every subordinate-supervisor pair in the organization, usually beginning at the top and working down the organization level by level. The technique involves active participation by subordinates, who negotiate their goals with their supervisor, with the requirement that subordinates' goals must be consistent with those of the higher levels. Once all goals have been set, employees try to achieve them. After a 6- to 12−month period, the job performance of employees is evaluated against progress toward their individual goals. The entire process is illustrated in Figure 14.1.

Research on MBO has supported its use as an effective means of increasing organizational performance. Rodgers and Hunter (1991) conducted a meta-analysis of the effectiveness of MBO. They found positive effects on employee productivity in 68 of the 70 studies they reviewed. The combined results of 23 of the studies indicated an average increase in productivity of 39% as a result of the program. Rodgers and Hunter (1991) did an additional analysis in which they separated the 23 studies into three groups based on the extent to which top management was committed to the MBO program. As shown in Table 14.1, organizations with the highest levels of management commitment had far better results than those with the lowest levels (57% vs. 6% increase in productivity).

TABLE 14.1   Effect of Management Commitment on Percentage of Performance Gain After Implementation of Management by Objectives

Level of Commitment	Percentage Gain in Productivity
High	56.5
Medium	32.9
Low	6.1

Source: Adapted from "Impact of Management by Objectives on Organizational Productivity," by R. Rodgers and J. E. Hunter, 1991, *Journal of Applied Psychology*, *76*, 322−336.

The high success rate found by Rodgers and Hunter (1991) is probably an overestimate of how well MBO has worked across the many organizations in which it has been tried. These studies likely represent some of the better efforts at implementing MBO. Many organizations have made attempts to implement MBO without full management commitment or necessary resources. Such half-hearted attempts are likely to have little effect on the organization, with employees setting easy goals and exerting little effort toward achieving them.

Survey Feedback

Survey feedback is an OD technique that involves conducting a survey of employee attitudes and opinions and then feeding back the results to the entire organization. The idea is that employees can express their opinions in a nonthreatening way through anonymous or confidential questionnaires. The survey data can then be used as the starting point for discussions about needed changes in the organization.

A survey feedback program consists of two major stages. First, the change agent will design and administer questionnaires to the employees of the organization. Employees are asked about job satisfaction, perceptions of job conditions, and problems at work. Standardized scales can be used to assess some of these variables, such as the Job Descriptive Index (P. K. Smith et al., 1969) for job satisfaction (see Chapter 9). Other items and custom-made scales might be developed specifically for each organization by the change agent after interviews with a sample of employees. The advantage of using standardized scales is that results from the organization can be compared to results from other organizations. For example, one would know if employee job satisfaction was unusually high or low. The advantage of custom-made scales is that they can be much more specific and deal with issues of concern to employees only in the specific organization. Thus, with a standardized scale one can find out how employees feel about their pay in general. It would take a custom-made scale to find out how they feel about a particular pay policy.

The second stage of a survey feedback program is providing feedback about the survey to employees. Data from the survey are compiled into a report, and the report is presented to employees, usually at a series of group meetings. Change agents might run the meetings, during which employees discuss the results and potential solutions to the problems uncovered by the survey. A successful program will result in the implementation of solutions to organizational problems.

Studies on the effectiveness of survey feedback have tended to find positive results from its use. Bowers (1973) reported the results of a large-scale longitudinal study involving more than 14,000 employees from 23 organizations. Positive changes in job satisfaction and employee reports of job conditions were found after survey feedback programs were introduced. In a meta-analysis of OD studies, survey feedback was found to have a modest positive impact on the job satisfaction of employees who participated (Neuman, Edwards, & Raju, 1989). It gives employees an opportunity to air their grievances in a constructive atmosphere. It also can provide for increased participation by employees in policy decisions that affect the entire organization. If done properly, survey feedback can help solve problems and give employees a greater sense of involvement in the organization.

Team Building

Team building refers to the many techniques designed to enhance the functioning of work teams. As discussed in Chapter 12, team building can focus on interpersonal issues, such as communication, or on tasks, such as smooth coordination of effort. With the task-oriented approach, the change agent helps members of work teams improve their task performance by learning how to work together more effectively. With the interpersonal approach, the change agent helps members of work teams improve their communication and interaction. Part of this effort can be directed toward reducing interpersonal conflict within work teams.

Team building can be an essential part of an OD effort because many of the tasks of organizations are conducted by work teams rather than individuals. An organization in which work teams do not work well will have a hard time being effective. Improving team functioning can go a long way toward improving an organization. In Chapter 12 we saw how the U.S. Navy is committed to finding ways to improve team functioning through training. Also noted in Chapter 12 were studies on the effectiveness of team building that had mixed results; some studies found positive effects, and some found no effects (Buller, 1986; Eden, 1985, 1986). Buller (1986) pointed out that the wide variety of team-building interventions across studies makes it difficult to draw firm conclusions about what sorts of techniques are effective. In their meta-analysis, Neuman et al. (1989) found that team building had a positive effect on job satisfaction.

T-Groups

The **T-group**, or training group, is an intervention designed to enhance the communication and interpersonal skills of individual employees through the use of specific group exercises. There are many variations of the T-group. Most are conducted at a site away from work, take place over a three-day to two-week period, and involve several people who do not know one another. The idea is for the group of strangers to experience a series of interpersonal skills exercises with a trainer or facilitator to guide them.

A T-group experience encourages participants to experiment with their interpersonal behavior in a situation in which they receive nonjudgmental feedback. This allows group members to gain insights into their effects on others and how others perceive them. The purpose is for organizational members, most often managers, to increase their interpersonal skills in the hope that they will be more effective on the job.

At one time, the T-group was a popular intervention, with many large organizations sending their management staffs to an off-site location for training. It is not as popular at present for at least two reasons. First, research on the T-group has found that although individuals can be positively affected by the experience, there is typically either no effect or negative effects on the workplace. For example, Bowers (1973) found detrimental changes in reports of job conditions and job satisfaction among employees who had participated in T-groups. Second, the T-group experience can be very much like group psychotherapy, with individuals exploring sensitive and potentially threatening aspects of themselves. There have been reports of individuals being hurt and upset by the T-group. Some have raised the issue that it is unethical for an organization to require T-group attendance.

Although T-groups have lost their popularity, organizations are still very much concerned with communication skills. To enhance such skills, organizations can use a variety of other methods. For example (as discussed in Chapter 7), behavior modeling has been

found to be effective in training interpersonal skills. This method involves having employ-ees watch people enact appropriate ways to communicate with others on the job. Trainees then practice what they have seen, under the direction of a trainer. This approach can be effective in enhancing interpersonal skills without the potentially harmful effects of the T-group. Thus, organizations have alternatives that they can use to enhance the communication skills of their employees.

Effectiveness of OD

The many different approaches to OD make it difficult to define precisely what a legiti-mate OD program is. Many programs involve more than one technique, including some combination of the four discussed in this section. An OD program might begin with survey feedback to identify issues. MBO or team building might be implemented next if the survey feedback process suggested that they were appropriate interventions. The wide variety of approaches and the complexity of the programs make it difficult to determine the effectiveness of OD techniques.

Another problem is that research on an entire organization is difficult to accomplish. If one implements an OD effort and wishes to assess the results, what will serve as the control group? The ideal OD study would randomly assign a sample of organizations (as opposed to individual participants) to one of two groups—intervention or control. This sort of design would require the cooperation of many organizations and is not generally feasible. Most OD studies are conducted in a single organization with comparisons made before and after the OD program. For example, one could compare the performance of employees before and after OD implementation, but one could not be certain what caused any differences that were found. A variety of things might have occurred that had nothing to do with the OD program, and some of them might have been the real cause of differences.

Perhaps the most reasonable conclusion is that OD programs can be effective if properly applied and supported by top management. Meta-analyses have found that many OD techniques are effective (e.g., Guzzo, Jette, & Katzell, 1985; Neuman et al., 1989). Except for T-groups, there have been few reports of detrimental effects on organizations. The majority of large corporations in the United States seem to believe in the value of OD. In a survey of Fortune 500 companies, McMahan and Woodman (1992) found that most had internal OD professionals who were actively working to improve their organizations. Thirty-eight percent of the companies had OD staffs of six or more people, and 14% had staffs of 21 or more. These results are probably an overestimate of the amount of OD activity in large U.S. companies, for the participation rate in the study was only about one-fifth of the eligible companies, and it seems likely that firms actively engaged in OD were more likely to participate in the study. Nevertheless, they suggest that OD is an important activity in many large organizations.

▶ ORGANIZATIONAL THEORIES

Organizational theories describe the structure and functioning of organizations and deal with such issues as

1. The distinguishing characteristics of organizations
2. The structure of organizations

3. The interrelationships among people in organizations

4. The interactions among people and technology in organizations

Descriptive theories explain how existing organizations work. A good descriptive theory will provide an accurate picture of how organizations are structured and how they operate. **Prescriptive theories** indicate how organizations should operate. Proper application of a good prescriptive theory will lead to an effective and efficient organization.

In practice, the distinction between descriptive and prescriptive theories may not be totally clear. Elements of both may appear in a given theory. Prescriptive theories that tell us what to do may, in fact, be descriptive of certain types of organizations. The first theory we discuss, bureaucracy, describes a particular type of organization, but its developer intended it to be prescriptive.

In this section, we discuss four different theoretical approaches to understanding organizations. *Bureaucracy* is the oldest theory and dates back to the nineteenth century. It is concerned with the structure of a particular type of organization that has been quite popular over the past century. *Theory X/Theory Y* is concerned with the interpersonal aspects of an organization. It is not an overall theory but describes how the attitudes of managers toward subordinates determine the organizational practices that are adopted. *Open system theory* describes the 10 components common to all general systems, including organizations. *Sociotechnical systems theory* is concerned with the interaction between the people and the technology of an organization.

Bureaucracy

Bureaucracy theory, initially developed by Max Weber in the late 1800s, is a classical theory of the structure of an organization (see Weber, 1947). In the early days of large organizations, little was known about effective techniques to structure and manage an organization. Weber's idea was to create a rational structure and several principles that would allow for the orderly and efficient functioning of an organization. Although we tend to think of a bureaucracy today as an inefficient and unresponsive organization, it represented an improvement over many of the organizational structures that existed at the time it was invented. Early organizations were often disorganized and inefficient. Bureaucracy theory provides characteristics and principles that were presumed to be important for an effective organization. We will discuss four of them:

Division of labor

Delegation of authority

Span of control

Line vs. staff

These principles can be useful for describing how most organizations operate, even those that are not bureaucratic in nature.

Division of Labor
Division of labor refers to the organization's specialized job positions, each of which is responsible for different tasks. For a complex process, such as manufacturing an

automobile, the total job is divided into many individual parts. For an entire manufacturing organization, the design, production, sale, and delivery of products are handled by different people in different departments.

The advantage of a division of labor is that each job requires relatively few skills. Therefore it will not be difficult to find people who have the necessary KSAOs to do the job, it will take little time to train them, and individuals can become quite proficient because they have few tasks to master. The major disadvantage is that resources are required to coordinate the activities of many specialized people. In a factory, for example, many managers and supervisors are needed to monitor that all employees do their jobs properly and that their efforts are coordinated. This leads us to the next characteristic, delegation of authority.

Delegation of Authority

Most organizations are hierarchically structured with one person at the top who has ultimate authority and control. Reporting to the top person will be one or more people who have authority and control over others who are below them in the hierarchy. At each level of the hierarchy, except the first, people report to others who are their superior. At the last, or bottom, level are people who report to someone above them, but no one reports to them. An example of the organizational chart for a hierarchically structured organization is shown in Figure 14.2.

Division of labor means that no one in the organization does the entire work of the organization. Thus, the person at the top is dependent on all those below to produce the organization's goods or services. In order to accomplish this, each person must allow **delegation of authority** to those below to accomplish a particular job. Thus, the top person might delegate authority for the design of a product to the research and development manager, for the running of a factory to a plant manager, for the selling of the product to a sales manager, and for the distribution of the product to a distribution manager. The people who report to each of these managers will be given authority to do whatever their jobs require. The efforts of different individuals are coordinated through a network of hierarchical supervision, or **chain of command**: Each person is responsible for those tasks and functions over which he or she has authority.

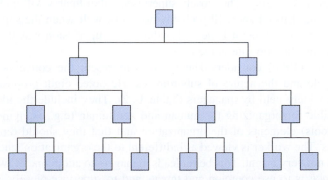

Figure 14.2 An organizational chart for a hierarchically structured organization. In such organizations, for example, a bureaucracy, each person reports to a single supervisor.

Span of Control

Span of control refers to the number of subordinates who report to each supervisor. In a given bureaucracy, there will be an optimal span of control. Because everyone except the person at the top has a supervisor, too small a span of control would result in needing too many managers. Too large a span of control would be chaotic because one person cannot adequately supervise the work of many people. The number of people someone can adequately supervise depends on two factors. First, the more skilled the subordinates, the less supervisory time they take. A person who is unskilled will need constant help and direction. A person who knows the job well will need only occasional attention. Second, the person's supervisory style helps determine the optimal span of control. A directive style requires considerable time for each subordinate. Each time a decision or problem arises, the supervisor must take time to deal with it. A participative style allows for a larger span of control because subordinates are allowed to deal with many of their own problems and make their own decisions, thereby freeing the time of their supervisors.

Line Versus Staff

Each position in an organization can be classified as either line or staff. A *line position* is involved directly with the organization's major purpose. In the military it would be combat soldiers, in education it would be teachers, in manufacturing it would be assemblers, and in retailing it would be sales staff. Line positions also include all the levels of supervision above these positions. A *staff position* supports the activities of a line position. The administration of salary and fringe benefits, employee selection, and training are all considered staff functions performed by people in staff positions.

Theory X / Theory Y

McGregor's (1960) **Theory X/Theory Y** is a human relations theory concerned with the interaction between supervisors and subordinates. The basic idea is that the attitudes and beliefs of supervisors about their subordinates determine the organization's management approach, which in turn affects how subordinates behave. This is a self-fulfilling prophecy in that managers treat subordinates according to how they are expected to behave, and this treatment causes subordinates to behave as expected. For example, a manager who believes that subordinates will not do their jobs properly without close supervision is likely to supervise closely. The closely supervised subordinates will undoubtedly believe that they are not trusted and will probably not work well when the supervisor is absent. Although the manager might believe that the close supervision was the result of subordinate behavior, the opposite is the case.

McGregor (1960) considers Theory X to represent the conventional view of the manager's role and the nature of subordinates. He noted eight propositions that represent beliefs widely held by managers (Table 14.2). They include the idea that managers are responsible for organizing the human and nonhuman (e.g., equipment, money, supplies, and tools) elements of the organization and that they should direct and motivate subordinates. The worker is viewed as indifferent to the organization's needs, lazy, unmotivated, and not very bright. This belief leads managers to adopt one of two strategies. The *hard approach* is to use coercion and threats and to supervise closely, an approach that results in employee resistance, such as counterproductive work behavior and restriction

TABLE 14.2   McGregor's Theory X/Theory Y Propositions

Theory X

Managers are responsible for organizing elements of the organization.

Managers should direct the activities of subordinates.

Employees are resistant to organizational needs.

The average employee is lazy.

The average employee lacks ambition and dislikes responsibility.

The average employee is concerned for himself or herself and not the organization.

The average employee is resistant to change.

The average employee is gullible and not very bright.

Theory Y

Managers are responsible for organizing elements of the organization.

Employees are not by nature resistant to organization needs. They have become that way because of prior organization experiences.

Managers should make it possible for subordinates to recognize and develop their organizational capabilities.

Managers should create organizational conditions so that subordinates can achieve their own goals through achieving organizational goals.

Source: *The Human Side of Enterprise*, by D. M. McGregor, 1960, New York: McGraw-Hill.

of output. The *soft approach* is to be permissive and avoid conflict with subordinates, which leads to an ineffective organization.

Theory Y is McGregor's preferred management view, which he believes will lead to more satisfied employees and more effective organizations. It has four propositions (see Table 14.2), which cover both the role of managers and the nature of subordinates. According to Theory Y, managers are responsible for organizing rather than directing the various human and nonhuman elements of the organization. Subordinates are capable and not inherently unmotivated or unresponsive to organizational needs. It is the responsibility of managers to arrange conditions so that employees can fulfill their own goals by directing efforts toward organizational goals. This last point is very much like the path-goal leadership theory idea (see Chapter 13) that leaders should provide the means by which subordinates can achieve personal rewards through good job performance. The supervisory approach adopted by the Theory Y manager is likely to be quite different from the approach of a Theory X counterpart. Rather than rely on directive approaches, the Theory Y manager stresses employee autonomy and development. Emphasis is placed on the setting of goals and objectives for employees, with their supervisors helping by removing constraints and providing guidance.

McGregor believed that movement toward Theory Y would be a slow process because the experiences of most people have been in Theory X situations. Today we can see many examples of the Theory Y approach. For example, the autonomous work team is based on the philosophy that subordinates are capable of managing themselves. As organizations continue to experience pressure to reduce costs by downsizing, it will become necessary to give more responsibility to lower level employees. Doing so will require adoption of a Theory Y approach.

Theory X and Theory Y are not the only possible approaches for managing people. William Ouchi (1981) proposed an approach to management that is based on Japanese practices. **Theory Z** assumes that long-term employment is the basis of effective organizations. People who can count on spending their entire career in the same organization will have high levels of commitment. They will be willing to put more effort into helping their organizations be successful because they have a personal stake in the long-term success of their employers.

Open System Theory

According to Katz and Kahn's (1978) **open system theory**, an organization can be viewed as a type of open system. The idea comes from the natural sciences, which view biological organisms such as plants, animals, bacteria, and viruses as open systems. Although organizations are different from biological organisms, they do share many characteristics with them (see Figure 14.3).

Katz and Kahn noted 10 characteristics of open systems, which are listed in Table 14.3. Open systems such as organizations import energy, transform the energy into something else, and output some product or service. All organizations import people and materials, produce goods and services, and deliver those goods and services

Figure 14.3 Organizations can be thought of as open systems that share many of the characteristics of biological organisms.

(*Joyce Williams/Animals Animals/Earth Scenes*)

TABLE 14.3   The 10 Organizational Characteristics from Katz and Kahn's Open System Theory and an Organizational Example of Each

Characteristic	Example
1. Import energy	Hire people
2. Transform energy	Make products
3. Output products	Sell products
4. Cycles of events	Work shifts
5. Escape entropy	Stay profitable
6. Input information	Do a market survey
7. Homeostasis	Balance the annual budget
8. Specialization	Create specialized job titles
9. Coordination and integration	Supervise employees
10. Equifinality	There are many effective ways to run an organization

to customers. Even government organizations provide services to citizens, including education, healthcare, protection, and transportation.

Open systems undergo cycles of events, and organizations are no different. Most organize their finances by fiscal years; employees have weekly work schedules; and for many organizations, the day is broken into two or more work shifts. Universities organize instruction by semesters, and semesters are organized into academic years. Many employees are hired according to time-limited contracts, especially in sports organizations such as professional baseball, basketball, football, or soccer teams.

Open systems must somehow escape entropy—the decay and destruction of the system. With a biological organism, entropy results in death. For an organization, entropy also can result in death, although often "dying" organizations are absorbed by other organizations. With private sector organizations, entropy can be indicated by the economic health of the company. Organizations that are efficient at transforming their inputs into goods and services that can be sold at a reasonable profit will survive. Those that cannot produce goods and services at a profit will have their finances erode until they can no longer pay employees or input energy. When this situation occurs, they will cease to function unless additional energy is available. This might occur if an external entity provides the funds to continue. It is what happened to the Chrysler Corporation in the 1970s when the U.S. government gave it a loan to prevent bankruptcy.

In addition to energy, open systems input information about their environments. Organizations have many people who are information specialists of various types. Organizations have accountants to deal with financial matters and lawyers to deal with legal issues, helping the organization maintain its homeostasis. Just as the thermostat in a house keeps the temperature constant, systems in organizations maintain certain conditions. An organization must maintain an appropriate number of employees, have the proper equipment in working order, have the necessary materials, and balance a budget. All these maintain the organization's homeostasis.

As open systems grow and become more complex, they develop specialized functions. As organizations become larger, they tend to divide work into more and more specialized functions. A small organization might have a single individual perform all accounting, human resource, and legal functions. A large corporation will have entire departments and often divisions for each of these functions. As functions become more specialized, open systems develop structures for coordination and integration. In organizations this function is accomplished through supervision and the chain of command.

The final characteristic of an open system is equifinality—a system can reach a particular state from many different starting points using many different methods. From an open system perspective, there is no one correct way to structure and operate an organization. Successful organizations can function in a variety of ways. For example, a product can be produced with an autonomous work team or with a traditional assembly line.

Open system theory is descriptive in providing a framework to understand the characteristics of organizations. It does not provide prescriptive insights into how an organization should be run, as does McGregor's Theory X/Theory Y.

Sociotechnical Systems Theory

Sociotechnical systems theory views an organization in terms of the interrelations between people and technology in the context of the organizational environment. *People* include the employees of the organization and their relationships with one another. *Technology* consists of the equipment, materials, tools, and other nonhuman objects in the organization. The *environment* is the physical and social conditions in which the organization must function. The theory deals with how people affect technology and how technology affects people. Sociotechnical systems theory is prescriptive in that it uses research findings to provide principles of good organizational design.

The origins of sociotechnical systems theory can be found in a paper by Trist and Bamforth (1951) in which they describe the effects of technological change in the British coal industry (see Figure 14.4). Prior to the change, coal mining was done by small groups of men who controlled their own work pace. Members of each group worked together in close proximity inside the dangerous environment of the mine. The introduction of machinery resulted in changes in the work group relationships among the men and the loss of worker control over work pace. Individuals now operated large pieces of machinery alone, without the close support of colleagues. This led to increases in absences and health complaints among the miners. Trist and Bamforth's paper made the linkages between the human and technological aspects of organizations very clear.

Since Trist and Bamforth's (1951) paper, sociotechnical systems theory has undergone development and frequent application (Winterton, 1994). Cooper and Foster (1971) noted several principles of the theory. **Joint optimization** is the idea that the social and technological systems should be designed to fit as well as possible. Machines and equipment should be easy for people to use, and people should be organized into tasks and jobs so that machines and equipment can function well. This means not only that human factors should be part of equipment design, but also that available technology should be considered in designing the human side of organizations. The introduction of word processing on personal computers in offices during the 1980s is an example of this approach. Because the employees using this technology were not experts in computers, both hardware and software had to be designed to be as easy to use as possible. To get

Figure 14.4 Technological changes in coal mining have sometimes disrupted the social system of miners, resulting in employee problems.

(*Owen Franken/Stock Boston*)

full advantage out of word processing, however, the computers could not be designed just to mimic the typewriters they were replacing. The use of additional functions required that they had to operate somewhat differently. This necessitated extensive training for clerical employees with limited computer experience. Many managers of organizations, however, violated sociotechnical systems principles by thinking that all they needed to do was order computers and have them put on employees' desks.

Unit control of variances concerns who handles work problems when they arise. In many organizations, each employee is responsible for handling only routine assigned tasks. When there is a variance from normal routine—for example, a machine breaks or a customer has a problem—specialists or supervisors are called to handle it. The idea of unit control is that variances should be handled by the employee or employees who encounter them. Thus, the operator of the machine should be allowed to fix it, and the salesclerk should be allowed to help a customer with a problem. In an office, employees who use word processors should be able to solve all but the most difficult problems they encounter. This approach enhances the motivation, self-efficacy, and skills of the employee, and it saves the time of the specialist and supervisor.

Implementation of the sociotechnical systems approach results in self-regulation by the individual employees or groups of employees. Thus, the autonomous work team approach is a major way in which these ideas have been introduced into organizations

(Majchrzak & Borys, 1998). The existence of self-regulating or self-managed units implies a different function for management. Rather than directing the actions of employees, managers spend time counseling and supporting the activities of work units and facilitating their interactions.

The ideas of sociotechnical systems theory have been widely applied in organizations and will probably continue to spread for at least two reasons. First, as noted earlier in this chapter, there has been a worldwide trend toward downsizing organizations by trimming the size of management staffs (Kozlowski, Chao, Smith, & Hedlund, 1993). With fewer managers, individual employees will have to work more independently. Second, research on sociotechnical systems theory applications has been supportive. Two studies conducted in the United Kingdom, for example, found that the unit control principle had positive effects on productivity.

Wall, Corbett, Martin, Clegg, and Jackson (1990) hypothesized, based on sociotechnical systems theory, that allowing factory workers to deal with machine problems themselves would reduce the amount of time that machines were "down" for adjustment or repair. They found not only that this form of unit control enhancement decreased downtime, but also that it decreased employee feelings of job pressure and increased their job satisfaction. In a similar study in another British factory, Wall, Jackson, and Davids (1992) found that when factory workers assumed responsibility for fixing machine problems, productivity increased because of a reduction of machine downtime (see International Replication).

INTERNATIONAL REPLICATION

There is perhaps no better setting in which to apply the principles of sociotechnical systems theory than an automated factory that mixes people with industrial robots. Such was the case in this study of productivity in a British factory by Wall, Jackson, and Davids (1992). The factory produced drill bits on a robotics assembly line where four humans interacted with six robots. The robots did most of the assembly work, which involved forming metal into drill bits. The workers fed the material to the first robot, unloaded the finished bits from the last robot, and made minor adjustments to the machines.

Relying on principles of sociotechnical systems theory, the researchers recommended to management that the workers' jobs be redesigned to allow them to deal with machine problems, which are common with industrial robots. Management refused the idea because of objections by the engineers, who believed that the machine operators could not handle this responsibility. Management had also instituted an incentive system for the operators, however, but because the assembly-line speed was controlled by the robots, the only way to increase productivity was to reduce downtime. The operators took it upon themselves to handle the machine problems, and once they proved they could do so, the engineers withdrew their objections. Thus, the experiment occurred accidentally.

Data on downtime were collected for six months before and eight months after the operators expanded their jobs. Downtime was reduced significantly from the period of time before to after the intervention. It is interesting that the number of short stoppages (less than 15 minutes) increased, but the number of long stoppages (15 minutes to an hour) decreased. Overall, the number of stoppages was the same, but the time lost for stoppages decreased. This suggests that when the operators dealt with the problems themselves, they could do so more quickly and reduce the lost time. The researchers estimated that productivity increases resulted in as much as $2,400 in profit per week.

This study shows that the sociotechnical approach, even when implemented in an unplanned way, can have beneficial effects on productivity. A similar study by some of the same researchers (see Chapter 12) showed that it can have positive effects on people as well (Wall et al., 1990). Organizations could benefit by carefully applying the principles of sociotechnical systems theory. Note that in this study employees were offered an incentive for improving productivity. The combination of increased motivation (the incentive) and accidental job redesign resulted in reduced downtime. Imposing this sort of job change without considering employee motivation and preferences might not have the same effects and could even result in counterproductive behavior if employees resisted the change.

Source: Wall, T. D., Jackson, P. R., & Davids, K. (1992). Operator work design and robotics system performance: A serendipitous field study. *Journal of Applied Psychology, 77,* 353–362.

Meta-analyses of interventions based on sociotechnical systems theory have indicated a high degree of success. Pasmore, Francis, Haldeman, and Shani (1982) analyzed the results of 134 studies and found that the majority had positive effects on criteria of productivity, costs, employee withdrawal, employee attitudes, safety, grievances, and work quality (Table 14.4). Guzzo et al. (1985) found positive effects of sociotechnical systems interventions on productivity and turnover.

Comparison of the Theories

Each of the four theories we have discussed is distinct, and each tends to focus on different aspects of organizations. There are some common ideas and connections among them, however. The rigid structure of the bureaucracy lends itself to a rigid Theory X approach. In a bureaucracy each person's job is clearly defined, with the individual having relatively little autonomy or discretion. This tends to be associated with the leadership style defined as Theory X, which includes close supervision and nonparticipative approaches.

Sociotechnical systems theory applications tend to be consistent with Theory Y ideas. One of the main sociotechnical systems approaches is the autonomous work team (see Chapter 12). The idea is to give employees autonomy and discretion in how they do their

TABLE 14.4   Percentage of Studies Reporting Various Positive Effects of Sociotechnical Systems Theory Interventions

Effect	Percentage Successful
Productivity	87
Cost	89
Absence	81
Turnover	65
Attitudes	94
Safety	88
Grievances	89
Quality	97

Source: Adapted from "Sociotechnical Systems: A North American Reflection on Empirical Studies of the Seventies," by W. Pasmore, C. Francis, J. Haldeman, and A. Shani, 1982, *Human Relations, 12,* 1179–1204.

jobs. This assumes that management adopts a trusting view of employees. One cannot allow someone discretion without being confident that he or she will do the job properly. Thus, the application of sociotechnical systems theory requires a Theory Y philosophy that employees can be trusted to do the job.

Open system theory is quite different. It describes the functioning of an organization in terms of 10 rather general principles and does not recommend specific practices. One can use the principles to describe the processes of an organization based on the other theories. For example, the ways in which employees are supervised would be covered by the principles of coordination and integration; however, there is little in the theory to tell us how we should coordinate and integrate. Of course, the principle of equifinality tells us that there can be many effective ways to run an organization.

These theories provide a broad perspective on organizations and how they function. Some have led to specific applications, such as the autonomous work groups based on sociotechnical systems theory. Others have affected the philosophies of those who manage organizations rather than describing particular techniques. Theory X/Theory Y, for example, is well known to managers and has had some influence on their practices.

▶ FUTURE ISSUES AND CHALLENGES

Perhaps the biggest challenge facing organizations today is dealing effectively with rapid change in both the internal and external environments. Change is produced by both social and technological forces that impinge on organizations. Globalization and rapid advances in computers and related technologies have produced an environment that demands the ability of organizations to adapt and change (Coovert, 1995; Davis, 1995). To avoid chaotic change, techniques discussed in this chapter, such as team development, should be considered. At the same time, it must be kept in mind that change can be extremely stressful for employees (Mack, Nelson, & Quick, 1998). Organizations must take steps to help employees cope with change, which can adversely affect their job performance and well-being.

Global economies require that organizations have the flexibility to deal with people from many different cultural backgrounds, who might have different expectations about acceptable and unacceptable practices. The multicultural nature of a global workforce brings new challenges for finding appropriate and effective ways of dealing with different sorts of people.

Technological change means that organizational practices and structures can quickly become ineffective and obsolete. Technologies for near instant communication, such as e-mail and fax, have made profound changes in how people work. The almost instant communication now possible makes the pace of organizational life faster, often requiring quick organizational responses. For example, such advances now allow people to **telecommute**, that is, commute to work without leaving home by using computers and other technology to communicate with coworkers and others. Chapman, Sheehy, Heywood, Dooley, and Collins (1995) and Konradt, Schmook, and Mälecke (2000) have discussed the advantages of telecommuting both for employees (flexible scheduling and not having to commute to and from the office) and for organizations (lower office costs and increased productivity).

Another major challenge is the worldwide trend toward greater efficiency by downsizing. As noted earlier in this chapter, the downsizing of an organization usually means a reduction in the size of its management staff. With fewer supervisors, organizations must find ways for employees to work with greater autonomy. Sociotechnical systems theory has much to say about designing such organizations.

► CHAPTER SUMMARY

We took an organizational perspective in this chapter, briefly reviewing two areas—organizational development and organizational theory. Organizational development is the application of behavioral science principles to improve the functioning of organizations. We discussed four specific techniques that can be used separately or in combination. Management by objectives (MBO) sets interlinked goals throughout an organization. Survey feedback uses the results of an employee survey as the basis for group discussion and organization improvement. Team building is a family of techniques that can be used with work teams to improve their functioning. T-groups are a series of group exercises designed to enhance the communication and interpersonal skills of individuals.

Existing evidence suggests that MBO, survey feedback, and team building can be effective interventions, with positive effects on both employees and organizations. On the other hand, T-groups have not been found to be effective and have been associated with detrimental effects.

Organizational theories describe how organizations can and should work. Bureaucracy theory is a classical theory that focuses on the structural components of organizations. Theory X/Theory Y is a human relations theory that focuses on how management philosophy affects the behavior of employees. Open system theory describes organizations in terms of 10 characteristics of open systems. Sociotechnical systems theory is concerned with the interrelations between the human and technical sides of organizations. This theory has led to many interventions, and most of those reported in the research literature have been successful.

I/O PSYCHOLOGY IN PRACTICE

(Courtesy Tom White)

This case is an effort to help employees cope with organizational change brought about by a corporate downsizing. Dr. Tom White served as the architect and primary change agent for this organization development project. White received his Ph.D. in I/O psychology in 1985 from the University of South Florida. Immediately after graduation he moved to Australia, where he has worked as an I/O psychologist ever since. At the time of this case he was organization development manager for Compaq Computer Corporation in Australia before it merged with Hewlett Packard.

Among White's responsibilities was facilitating organizational change and development. He was also involved with conflict resolution among employees, leadership development, planning for the future, and team building. His role was mainly that of an internal consultant and facilitator. This means he functioned as change agent to help the organization manage the frequent changes necessitated by rapid technological development in the computer industry.

An important project White undertook was to help employees cope with a corporate downsizing that was necessary to keep the company profitable in the extremely competitive computer industry. Despite the company's reputation of caring for employees, heavy losses in recent years required drastic action to cut costs. As many as 30% of employees in some areas had to be let go. This downsizing was a traumatic experience for survivors of the layoffs, many of whom lost close friends at work. The entire company was disrupted, as people found it difficult to work effectively. White's job was to find a way to help survivors deal with the situation.

The approach chosen was based on techniques to help people cope with death of a family member. A series of two-day sessions was conducted with 100 employees or more each. During the sessions, which were conducted by managers, a series of small-group activities were conducted to help employees grieve their losses while focusing on plans for the future. Two themes were letting go of the past and committing to the future. White's role was to organize the company-wide activity and instruct managers in how to conduct sessions. This is a typical role for a change agent, in that managers have to actually

implement change. A psychologist will be a facilitator and resource for those who do the change.

Once the full program was completed, which took one month, an evaluation was conducted to determine its effectiveness. Results showed that employees became more accepting of change and more trusting of management. Employee job performance increased, as did overall productivity of the workforce. Overall, this organizational change effort was beneficial to both the employees and the organization.

Discussion Questions

1. Why didn't White take a more active role in running the sessions?
2. How can a change agent facilitate change if managers have all the power in the organization?
3. What KSAOs are needed for a person to do organizational development?
4. Why is it important to evaluate programs, such as White's?

LEARNING BY DOING

Organization Development

Go to the Web site of a company that does organizational development and answer the following questions: What are the backgrounds of the individuals in the company? What services does the company provide? Where might the company use any of the four techniques discussed in the chapter? Does it specialize in a particular industry?

Open Systems Theory

Take an organization with which you are familiar (it could be your college or university). For each of the 10 open systems theory characteristics, note one example from the organization.

Guide to Graduate School Admission

As you may have learned by now, it requires a graduate degree (master's or Ph.D.) to pursue a career in psychology, and industrial/organizational (I/O) psychology is no exception. In the United States, practitioners (those who do applied work as consultants, employees of organizations, or private practitioners who have their own offices) may have one or the other of these two degrees. Professors in colleges and universities almost always have the Ph.D. In some other countries (e.g., some in Western Europe) the situation is different, with the master's degree being the degree of practitioners and the Ph.D. the degree of professors and researchers.

This guide is oriented toward I/O psychology, but most of what's here applies equally to other areas of psychology. Even for the experimental areas, such as cognitive or social, where most graduates go into academic or research positions, the preparation and admission process is similar.

In the United States, there are approximately 120 graduate programs in I/O; about half are master's programs and about half are Ph.D., with some offering both. Many fine graduate programs can also be found throughout the rest of the world. In the United States, admission to most programs is very competitive. At most schools it is based largely, but not entirely, on grade point average (usually only junior and senior years) and Graduate Record Exam (GRE) quantitative plus verbal scores, although some schools also consider the analytical and/or psychology subject test. Recently the new analytical writing test has become part of the GRE, and it is very likely that many programs will use it for admission in the future. The Educational Testing Service Web site has detailed information about the GRE (www.gre.org).

Letters of recommendation are typically required, but may hold less weight. Relevant background, such as employment in an I/O-related setting and research experience, is also considered. Finally, the personal statement is examined to see whether the student's interests and goals fit the program. Admission requirements are not necessarily the same in other countries, where educational systems may be different from those in the United States.

American graduate programs vary in competitiveness of admission. In general, master's programs are easier to get into than Ph.D. programs. The most prestigious Ph.D. programs are among the most difficult to get into of graduate programs in any field.

Solid A averages approaching 4.0 and GRE scores of 1200 and higher are required by the most competitive. They also tend to look carefully at research experience, and consider an undergraduate honor's thesis a plus. Having presented a paper at a conference, even a student one, can help as well. Most of the "top" programs accept only a small number of students each year, and they may have over 100 applicants, so they can be very selective. Programs that are not considered top programs will often have lower standards for admission. Over the past 10 years, as the popularity of I/O has increased, admission requirements have increased as well.

There are a number of good programs that are not generally found on the lists of top programs, and these may well be a good option to consider. They can be easier to get into and often are smaller, with fewer students. Master's programs tend to be easier to get into than Ph.D. programs, and can be a good option for students who either are not interested in a Ph.D. or don't have the record to get into a Ph.D. program.

Information about I/O graduate programs in Canada and the United States can be found on the Society for Industrial and Organizational Psychology (SIOP) Web site (www.siop.org). Links to international programs are being added and might be there by the time you read this. Details about most programs, including entrance requirements, are there. More details can be gotten from the university Web sites. The SIOP Web site has links to most of them.

▶ MASTER'S PROGRAM OR PH.D.?

One decision you will have to make is whether you wish to get a master's degree or a Ph.D. If you want to be a professor, then you must get a Ph.D. If you are more interested in becoming a practitioner and doing applied work, then either degree is fine. The advantage of a Ph.D. is that the pay is higher, as discussed in Chapter 1, and career advancement is easier. However, it takes at least twice as long to get a Ph.D., and the training can be more challenging, because students are expected to be capable of more independent research work.

Although there are differences among programs, for the most part master's programs have a different emphasis than Ph.D. programs. They must prepare a student for an applied career in about two years. The coursework tends to have an applied rather than theoretical focus. Some but not all programs require a thesis, which is an original piece of research conducted under the supervision of faculty.

The Ph.D. is a research degree, meaning that research tends to be the major focus. Students in many programs will earn a master's degree about halfway through the program, but the requirements are often different from the master's program degree. Coursework in most Ph.D. programs tends to concentrate on research and theory more than practice. The master's degree from a Ph.D. program is not intended to prepare the student to be a practitioner, although sometimes students will quit at this stage to begin an applied career. Generally the Ph.D. student will conduct both a master's thesis and a dissertation, which is a second piece of original research that is often larger in scope than the thesis.

Sometimes, after earning a degree from a master's program, students decide that they wish to pursue the Ph.D., and it isn't unusual for a student to enter a Ph.D. program with a master's in I/O, another area of psychology, or another field entirely. However, completing a master's degree doesn't guarantee admission into a Ph.D. program, and typically the same entry requirements hold, although having done well in a master's program can sometimes help a little. However, it is not a good strategy to purposely start with a master's program. If the goal is the Ph.D., it is best to enter the Ph.D. program from the start. If you aren't certain, though, it might be reasonable to enter a master's program.

► MENTOR VS. PROGRAM MODEL OF TRAINING

Some programs accept students to work with a specific faculty member (mentor model), whereas others accept students into the program as a whole (program model). With the mentor model, programs will ask you to indicate your research interests and the faculty member (or members) you wish to have as an adviser and work with should you be accepted. The individual faculty members will choose students who have indicated interest in working with them. If you apply to this sort of program, it is necessary to thoroughly investigate the interests of the faculty with an eye to deciding what area of research you wish to pursue. It might be possible to switch later in the program if you decide you are more interested in another area, but this is not necessarily encouraged. The decision of whom to work with should be taken seriously.

With the program model, you may be asked about your interests and goals, but you don't have to decide in advance on an adviser. This can be determined after you begin the program. In this sort of program, typically you will be assigned an initial ad hoc adviser at the beginning of the program. You will be introduced to the research of the faculty members during the first semester (quarter) of the program, after which you must choose a permanent adviser with whom to work.

Both models are common in psychology; the mentor model is more popular in experimental programs than in I/O. The two models reflect somewhat different philosophies of training. Mentor model training is more centered around the adviser and focused on the adviser's research methods and topics. This can make the training a bit more specialized than the program model, where training can be a little broader.

► PREPARATION FOR GRADUATE SCHOOL

Most I/O graduate students were undergraduate psychology majors, but many majored in other fields. The undergraduate psychology major is helpful, in that the basic principles and terminology of psychology will be familiar. This makes the first year of graduate school easier, but people with other backgrounds can do well with extra effort. Because I/O is a technical field, it is helpful to have undergraduate coursework in research methodology and statistics (required of most psychology majors). It is also helpful to have familiarity with computers, and to have good writing ability. Some background in business administration might be helpful for those who become practitioners, although business concepts are very quickly acquired on the job.

Graduate school is more difficult than undergraduate. The workload is far heavier, and students are expected to work more independently. A master's degree takes about two years to complete. A Ph.D. takes at least four (from the B.A.) but the average is around six. Many individuals who begin a Ph.D. program never finish. Determination and self-discipline are required, over and above intellectual ability. This should be carefully considered by anyone contemplating an I/O career. Do you really want to spend the next few years in an extremely intense academic study of this field? If the answer is no, there are easier ways to a rewarding career that would better suit you. If the answer is yes, then I/O might be the career for you.

I recommend that undergraduate students contemplating an I/O career do the following:

1. Take an undergraduate I/O psychology course. If your university doesn't offer one, read an I/O textbook like this one. You can also take a correspondence course. The Florida State University System (SUS), for example, offers such a course from its correspondence division at the University of Florida in Gainesville (www.correspondencestudy.ufl.edu).

2. Get to know three professors. You will need at least three letters of recommendation, preferably from faculty members. Family friends, former employers, and other nonprofessors are not usually given as much weight. An exception might be a practicing I/O psychologist with whom you might have worked. The best way to get to know faculty is by volunteering to help with research. They don't have to be I/O professors, or even psychology professors. The project you work on might be a graduate student's thesis or dissertation.

3. Get a good psychology background. Courses most relevant are social and cognitive.

4. Take all the research methods and statistics your psychology department offers.

5. Be sure you have a solid background in basic mathematics (i.e., college algebra). Be familiar with computers, as you will have to learn how to use statistical software. Be familiar with word processing and e-mail. Know how to navigate the Internet. Be sure you can communicate well in both spoken and written English. These skills will be needed in graduate school, and later in your career.

6. Be sure to get good grades. A solid A average will be needed for most Ph.D. programs.

7. Investigate graduate programs by the beginning of your senior year. Consider their emphasis and quality, as well as entry requirements. Most programs in the United States are pretty similar, but there are some that have a particular emphasis, often because of the interests of their faculty members. One way to see this is by the research topics of faculty. Programs also vary in quality. Some are well established with large experienced faculties and large professional networks that help in getting internships and jobs after graduation. Potential employers are likely to know the program, and a degree from there might carry more weight. Others may be new and not yet established or have very small faculties (which limits the range of faculty interests). My advice is to go to the best program that will accept you, but don't feel that your career is over before it's begun because you didn't get into one of the top programs. There are many great programs from which to choose, even among those that aren't on anyone's top list.

Determining program quality is not always easy. A good way is to ask professors who are familiar with the I/O field. Look also at the number of faculty and students. Look for research activity among the faculty. Do they publish frequently in the major journals? Are they editors or board members of major journals? Also consider opportunities for practicum experiences and internships, which are an important aspect of practitioner training. You might also talk to faculty and graduate students at programs you are considering, either by phone or in person if possible.

8. Early in your senior year, take stock. Compute your GPA (junior and senior years only) and project what it will likely be when your application is considered. Most programs make their decisions between February and March for the following fall semester. Take the GRE early enough so that you can retake it and get the scores in before the deadline in the event you don't do as well as you would have liked. This usually means around September or October of your senior year. Once you know your GPA and GRE, you can figure out where it makes sense to apply. With a 3.95 and 1400 (quantitative plus verbal), any program is a possibility. A 3.2 and 1020 means your possibilities are more limited, but don't give up your career goals yet! Perhaps you can retake some classes or take a GRE prep course. Try a program with lower entry requirements. However, if your less than spectacular grades reflect a lack of motivation for school, do you really want to spend the next four to six years (or more) in graduate school?

▶ APPLICATION PROCESS

So you've done your homework and are ready to apply to graduate school. Now what? Although there are exceptions, most I/O graduate programs accept students only for fall admission, with application deadlines between January 1 and January 15. Keep in mind that this doesn't necessarily hold for other areas of psychology, such as clinical, where deadlines can be in December. You must apply by the deadline, and will almost certainly be disqualified if you are late. It is also your responsibility to be sure that additional materials, such as letters of recommendation, are sent. Be sure and stay on top of your letter writers to be sure the letters go out on time. In order for this to happen, you must give faculty a reasonable amount of time to write the letter. Don't ask around the middle of December and expect letters to get sent by an early January deadline—remember that the holiday season will slow things down. Ask your writers in early November, well before the fall semester ends, for a January deadline. Also keep in mind that you must supply any special rating forms the schools require, and that many universities will expect you to supply stamped envelopes.

Most students apply to more than one school, and often students will apply to several that vary in competitiveness in order to hedge their bets. Faculty can be helpful in advising you about which schools would be reasonable to try. Schools charge application fees, and these can add up if you apply to many places.

It can take a month or more after the deadline for faculties to review applications and make decisions. Those accepted will probably be notified first, with those not accepted having to wait for as long as several months to hear, and it isn't unusual to get no notification at all. Many schools have thousands of applicants, and the offices that send out notices are understaffed—not an excuse but reality.

▶ THE GRADUATE STUDENT RECRUITMENT PROCESS: WHAT HAPPENS AFTER YOU APPLY

Schools can differ in how they handle their acceptances, but the typical process is the following:

1. The members of a committee of faculty individually review applicant materials and rate each student's qualifications. Faculty are looking for predictors that indicate you are a good student, but they are also looking for a fit to their program focus and philosophy. Be sure to be honest in your personal statement; it does no good to tell them what you think they want to hear only to find out later that the program is not right for you.

2. The committee meets and separates students into two groups: acceptable for admission and unacceptable for admission. The latter group is rejected at this point. Each year a target number of admissions is set, which is the number of new students the faculty wish to admit in the fall. Not everyone invited to join the program will accept, since most students apply to several programs. Thus it is likely that the acceptable group will be larger than the target number of new students to be admitted. In such cases the faculty will rank order the acceptable students in terms of priority for being admitted. At this point programs differ in how they handle acceptances. Some will notify all in the accepted group that they have been accepted, knowing that not all will accept the invitation to join the program. Others will accept only the target number of students, putting the remaining ones on a waiting list to be accepted in rank order as other students decline the invitation.

3. For programs that offer financial support (graduate assistantships or fellowships), there can also be differences in how they operate. Some will tie support to acceptance, and students are only accepted when support is available. Thus if a program can support four new students, only four are accepted. If one of the four declines, the next person on the waiting list is invited. Others might separate acceptance from support. For example, if the program wants four new students, 10 might be accepted, but only the first four are offered support. As students decline invitations, support is offered to the next student in line. It isn't likely that a school will take a chance on offering more assistantships than it has and gamble on the number of students who might accept. However, a school might accept more students than the target number, since the cost of underestimating is not financial. Don't get insulted if you are put on a waiting list for admission or support. Rank orders are based on imperfect paper credentials, and often those lower on the list wind up doing better than those who are higher.

4. April 15 is the agreed-upon deadline for students to notify graduate programs whether they are accepting or declining, but schools will press for an earlier decision, since other students are on a waiting list.

► DOS AND DON'TS: SOME ETIQUETTE

1. Faculty know students apply to multiple places, so don't feel you will insult anyone by talking about where else you applied. You will probably be asked about where you applied, who has accepted you, and your preferences. Feel free to be candid—if University of the North Pole is your top choice because you have an interest in what its faculty are doing, that's fine.

2. Make your decision as soon as you can, and do *not* hold up places once you've decided not to go there. April 15 is the deadline, but this doesn't mean you should wait until that date to notify every program that has accepted you. Keep in mind that somewhere there's a student waiting to see if a slot will open at their top choice, and you might be holding up that slot. It is possible that you are waiting to hear from a school, but the person holding your slot is waiting for the slot at another school that you are holding.

   Now if you are waiting for your top choice, there's nothing wrong with holding your offer at your second choice until April 15 to see if Number 1 will come through. However, it is best to let the remaining schools know you're not interested as soon as you can.

3. It is fine to contact schools for an update where you are on a waiting list for acceptance and/or support.

4. It is good to visit the schools to help you decide. Many have open houses where there will be events planned and you will meet potential classmates. It is probably best to go to an open house, but if you can't it is fine to visit other times. Just keep in mind that, depending on the day you choose, there may or may not be many faculty and students around. A school's spring break, for example, is not the ideal time. Some schools may be able to cover some of your travel costs.

5. For most schools, the most appropriate attire for a visit is business casual. No one expects you to come in a suit, but shorts, a t-shirt, and sandals are a bit overly casual if you are trying to make a good first impression.

6. It is OK to bring a family member, friend, or significant other for your visit. Just let the school know you won't be alone.

7. It is OK to ask questions. Don't be shy about asking about support, the curriculum, the climate of the program, strengths and weaknesses, student life, or other things about which you are concerned. It is OK to ask different people the same question—you might get different perspectives.

8. It is OK to talk (or e-mail) with current students—ask faculty to arrange this. Students often know about things the faculty don't, such as the best housing in the area for you, and what it's like to be a student in the program.

9. Don't feel bad about turning down a program. This is your career and your decision, and having students decline is part of the recruitment process.

References

Adams, G. A., King, L. A., & King, D. W. (1996). Relationships of job and family involvement, family social support, and work-family conflict with job and life satisfaction. *Journal of Applied Psychology*, 81, 411–420.

Adams, J. S. (1965). *Inequity in social exchange*. In L. Berkowitz (Ed.), *Advances in experimental social psychology* (pp. 276–299). New York: Academic Press.

Agervold, M., & Mikkelsen, E. G. (2004). Relationships between bullying, psychosocial work environment and individual stress reactions. *Work & Stress*, 18, 336–351.

Aguinis, H., Nesler, M. S., Quigley, B. M., Suk-Jae-Lee, & Tedeschi, J. T. (1996). Power bases of faculty supervisors and educational outcomes for graduate students. *Journal of Higher Education*, 67, 267–297.

Ahearn, K. K., Ferris, G. R., Hochwarter, W. A., Douglas, C., & Ammeter, A. P. (2004). Leader political skill and team performance. *Journal of Management*, 30, 309–327.

Akerstedt, T., & Theorell, T. (1976). Exposure to night work: Serum gastrin reactions, psychosomatic complaints and personality variables. *Journal of Psychosomatic Research*, 20, 479–484.

Aldag, R. J., & Fuller, S. R. (1993). Beyond fiasco: A reappraisal of the groupthink phenomenon and a new model of group decision processes. *Psychological Bulletin*, 113, 533–552.

Allen, D. G., Weeks, K. P., & Moffitt, K. R. (2005). Turnover intentions and voluntary turnover: The moderating roles of self-monitoring, locus of control, proactive personality, and risk aversion. *Journal of Applied Psychology*, 90, 980–990.

Allen, J., & Sanders, K. (2002). Gender gap in earnings at the industry level. *The European Journal of Women's Studies*, 9, 163–180.

Allen, T. D., & Eby, L. T. (2003). Relationship effectiveness for mentors: Factors associated with learning and quality. *Journal of Management*, 29, 469–486.

Allen, T. D., Eby, L. T., & Lentz, E. (2006). The relationship between formal mentoring program characteristics and perceived program effectiveness. *Personnel Psychology*, 59, 125–153.

Allen, T. D., Eby, L. T., Poteet, M. L., Lentz, E., & Lima, L. (2004). Career benefits associated with mentoring for protégés: A meta-analysis. *Journal of Applied Psychology*, 89, 127–136.

Allen, T. D., Herst, D. E. L., Bruck, C. S., & Sutton, M. (2000). Consequences associated with work-to-family conflict: A review and agenda for future research. *Journal of Occupational Health Psychology*, 5, 278–308.

Allen, T. D., McManus, S. E., & Russell, J. E. A. (1999). Newcomer socialization and stress: Formal peer relationships as a source of support. *Journal of Vocational Behavior*, 54, 453–470.

Alliger, G. M., & Janak, E. A. (1989). Kirkpatrick's levels of training criteria: Thirty years later. *Personnel Psychology*, 42, 331–342.

Alliger, G. M., Tannenbaum, S. I., Bennett, W., Jr., Traver, H., & Shotland, A. (1997). A meta-analysis of the relations among training criteria. *Personnel Psychology*, 50, 341–358.

Ambrose, M. L., & Kulik, C. T. (1999). Old friends, new faces: Motivation research in the 1990s. *Journal of Management*, 25, 231–292.

American Psychological Association. (1992). Ethical principles of psychologists and code of conduct. *American Psychologist*, 47, 1597–1611.

Anderson, N., De Dreu, C. K. W., & Nijstad, B. A. (2004). The routinization of innovation research: A constructively critical review of the state-of-the-science. *Journal of Organizational Behavior*, 25, 147–173.

Antonioni, D., & Park, J. (2001). The relationship between rater affect and three sources of 360 degree feedback ratings. *Journal of Management*, 27, 479–495.

Armenakis, A. A., & Bedeian, A. G. (1999). Organizational change: A review of theory and research in the 1990s. *Journal of Management*, 25, 293–315.

Arthur, W., Jr., Bennett, W., Jr., Edens, P. S., & Bell, S. T. (2003). Effectiveness of training in organizations: A meta-analysis of design and evaluation features. *Journal of Applied Psychology*, 88, 234–245.

Arthur, W., Jr., Day, E. A., McNelly, T. L., & Edens, P. S. (2003). A meta-analysis of the criterion-related validity of assessment center dimensions. *Personnel Psychology*, 56, 125–154.

Arthur, W., Jr., Woehr, D. J., & Maldegen, R. (2000). Convergent and discriminant validity of assessment center dimensions: A conceptual and empirical reexamination of the assessment center construct-related validity paradox. *Journal of Management*, 26, 813–835.

Arvey, R. D., Bouchard, T. J., Segal, N. L., & Abraham, L. M. (1989). Job satisfaction: Environmental and genetic components. *Journal of Applied Psychology*, 74, 187–192.

Aryee, S., Fields, D., & Luk, V. (1999). A cross-cultural test of a model of the work-family interface. *Journal of Management*, 25, 495–511.

Aryee, S., Lo, S., & Kang, I. L. (1999). Antecedents of early career stage mentoring among Chinese employees. *Journal of Organizational Behavior*, 20, 563–576.

Ash, R. A., & Levine, E. L. (1980). A framework for evaluating job analysis methods. *Personnel*, 57, 53–59.

Ashkanasy, N. M., Härtel, C. E. J., & Daus, C. S. (2002). Diversity and emotion: The new frontiers in organizational behavior research. *Journal of Management*, 28, 307–338.

Ashton, M. C. (1998). Personality and job performance: The importance of narrow traits. *Journal of Organizational Behavior*, 19, 289–303.

Atwater, L. E. & Brett, J. F. (2005). Antecedents and consequences of reactions to developmental 360° feedback. *Journal of Vocational Behavior*, 66, 532–548.

Augustine, M. A., & Coovert, M. D. (1991). Simulations and information order as influences in the development of mental models. *SIGCHI Bulletin*, 23, 33–35.

Aust, B., & Ducki, A. (2004). Comprehensive health promotion interventions in the workplace: Experiences with health circles in Germany. *Journal of Occupational Health Psychology*, 9, 258–270.

Bacharach, S. B., Bamberger, P., & Conley, S. (1991). Work-home conflict among nurses and engineers: Mediating the impact of role stress on burnout and satisfaction at work. *Journal of Organizational Behavior*, 12, 39–53.

Bailey, C., & Austin, M. (2006). 360 degree feedback and developmental outcomes: The role of feedback characteristics, self-efficacy and importance of feedback dimensions to focal managers' current role. *International Journal of Selection and Assessment*, 14, 51–66.

Bakker, A. B., Schaufeli, W. B., Sixma, H. J., Bosveld, W., & Van Dierendonck, D. (2000). Patient demands, lack of reciprocity, and burnout: A five-year longitudinal study among general practitioners. *Journal of Organizational Behavior*, 21, 425–441.

Baldwin, T. T., & Ford, J. K. (1988). Transfer of training: A review and directions for future research. *Personnel Psychology*, 41, 63–105.

Baldwin, T. T., & Padgett, M. Y. (1993). *Management development: A review and commentary*. In C. L. Cooper & I. T. Robertson (Eds.), *International review of industrial and organizational psychology 1993* (pp. 35–38). Chichester, UK: John Wiley.

Baltes, B. B., Briggs, T. E., Huff, J. W., Wright, J. A., & Neuman, G. A. (1999). Flexible and compressed workweek schedules: A meta-analysis of their effects on work-related criteria. *Journal of Applied Psychology*, 84, 496–513.

Baltes, B. B., Dickson, M. W., Sherman, M. P., Bauer, C. C., & LaGanke, J. S. (2002). Computer-mediated communication and group decision making: A meta-analysis. *Organizational Behavior and Human Decision Processes*, 87, 156–179.

Baltes, B. B., & Heydens-Gahir, H. A. (2003). Reduction of work-family conflict through the use of selection, optimization, and compensation behaviors. *Journal of Applied Psychology*, 88, 1005–1018.

Balzer, W. K., & Sulsky, L. M. (1992). Halo and performance appraisal research: A critical examination. *Journal of Applied Psychology*, 77, 975–985.

Bandura, A. (1982). Self-efficacy mechanism in human agency. *American Psychologist*, 37, 122–147.

Bandura, A., & Locke, E. A. (2003). Negative self-efficacy and goal effects revisited. *Journal of Applied Psychology*, 88, 87–99.

Banker, R. D., Field, J. M., Schroeder, R. G., & Sinha, K. K. (1996). Impact of work teams on manufacturing performance: A longitudinal field study. *Academy of Management Journal*, 39, 867–890.

Banks, M. H., Jackson, P. R., Stafford, E. M., & Warr, P. B. (1983). The Job Components Inventory and the analysis of jobs requiring limited skill. *Personnel Psychology*, 36, 57–66.

Banks, M. H., & Stafford, E. M. (1982). Skills training for clerical work: Action research within the youth opportunities programme. *BACIE_Journal*, 37, 57–66.

Barling, J., Fullagar, C., & Bluen, S. (1986). Organisational behaviour in South Africa: An historical overview. In J. Barling, C. Fullagar, & S. Bluen (Eds.), *Behaviour in organisations* (pp. 3–31). Johannesburg, South Africa: Lexicon.

Barling, J., Kelloway, E. K., & Iverson, R. D. (2003). High-quality work, job satisfaction, and occupational injuries. *Journal of Applied Psychology*, 88, 276–283.

Barling, J., Rogers, A. G., & Kelloway, E. K. (2001). Behind closed doors: In-home workers' experience of sexual harassment and workplace violence. *Journal of Occupational Health Psychology*, 6, 255–269.

Barling, J., Weber, T., & Kelloway, E. K. (1996). Effects of transformational leadership training on attitudinal and financial outcomes: A field experiment. *Journal of Applied Psychology*, 81, 827–832.

Barrett, G. V., & Kernan, M. G. (1987). Performance appraisal and terminations: A review of court decisions since Brito v. Zia with implications for personnel practices. *Personnel Psychology*, 40, 489–503.

Barrick, M. R., & Mount, M. K. (1991). The Big Five personality dimensions and job performance: A meta-analysis. *Personnel Psychology*, 44, 1–26.

Barton, J., & Folkard, S. (1991). The response of day and night nurses to their work schedules. *Journal of Occupational Psychology*, 64, 207–218.

Bartram, D. (1994). *Computer-based assessment*. In C. L. Cooper & I. T. Robertson (Eds.), *International review of industrial and organizational psychology 1994* (pp. 31–69). Chichester, UK: John Wiley.

Bass, B. M., Avolio, B. J., & Atwater, L. (1996). The transformational and transactional leadership of men and women. *Applied Psychology: An International Review*, 45, 5–34.

Bass, B. M., Avolio, B. J., Jung, D. I., & Berson, Y. (2003). Predicting unit performance by assessing transformational and transactional leadership. *Journal of Applied Psychology*, 88, 207–218.

Bass, B. M., & Riggio, R. E. (2006). *Transformational leadership* (2nd ed.). Mahwah, NJ: Lawrence Erlbaum.

Bauer, T. N., & Green, S. G. (1996). Development of leader-member exchange: A longitudinal test. *Academy of Management Journal*, 39, 1538–1567.

Beal, D. J., Cohen, R. R., Burke, M. J., & McLendon, C. L. (2003). Cohesion and performance in groups: A meta-analytic clarification of construct relations. *Journal of Applied Psychology*, 88, 989–1004.

Becker, B. E., & Huselid, M. A. (1992). Direct estimates of SD_y and the implications for utility analysis. *Journal of Applied Psychology*, 77, 227–233.

Beehr, T. A., Jex, S. M., Stacy, B. A., & Murray, M. A. (2000). Work stressors and coworker support as predictors of individual strain and job performance. *Journal of Organizational Behavior*, 21, 391–405.

Begley, T. M., & Czajka, J. M. (1993). Panel analysis of the moderating effects of commitment on job satisfaction, intent to quit, and health following organizational change. *Journal of Applied Psychology*, 78, 552–556.

Bendak, S. (2003). 12-h workdays: Current knowledge and future directions. *Work & Stress*, 17, 321–336.

Benjamin, L. T., Jr. (1997). Organized industrial psychology before Division 14: The ACP and the AAAP (1930–1945). *Journal of Applied Psychology*, 82, 459–466.

Bennett, R. J., & Robinson, S. L. (2000). Development of a measure of workplace deviance. *Journal of Applied Psychology*, 85, 349–360.

Berdahl, J. L., & Moore, C. (2006). Workplace harassment: Double jeopardy for minority women. *Journal of Applied Psychology*, 91, 426–436.

Bergman, M. E., Palmieri, P. A., Drasgow, F., & Ormerod, A. J. (2007). Racial and ethnic harassment and discrimination: In the eye of the beholder? *Journal of Occupational Health Psychology*, 12, 144–160.

Bernardin, H. J. (1988). *Police officer*. In S. Gael (Ed.), *Job analysis handbook* (pp. 1242–1254). New York: John Wiley.

Bernardin, H. J., & Beatty, R. W. (1984). *Performance appraisal: Assessing human behavior at work*. Boston: Kent.

Bernardin, H. J., & Pence, E. C., (1980). Rater training: Creating new response sets and decreasing accuracy. *Journal of Applied Psychology*, 65, 60–66.

Bertua, C., Anderson, N., & Salgado, J. F. (2005). The predictive validity of cognitive ability tests: A UK meta-analysis. *Journal of Occupational and Organizational Psychology*, 78, 387–409.

Bettenhausen, K. L. (1991). Five years of group research: What we've learned and what needs to be addressed. *Journal of Management*, 17, 345–381.

Birdi, K., Warr, P., & Oswald, A. (1995). Age differences in three components of employee well-being. *Applied Psychology: An International Review*, 44, 345–373.

Birkeland, S. A., Manson, T. M., Kisamore, J. L., Brannick, M. T., & Smith, M. A. (2006). A meta-analytic investigation of job applicant faking on personality measures. *International Journal of Selection and Assessment*, 14, 317–335.

Bishop, G. D., Ang, J., Khader, M. Enkelmann, H. C., Tong, E. M. W., Why, Y. P., & Diong, S. M. (2003). Job demands, decisional control, and cardiovascular responses. *Journal of Occupational Health Psychology*, 8, 146–156.

Bishop, J. W., & Scott, K. D. (2000). An examination of organizational and team commitment in a self-directed team environment. *Journal of Applied Psychology*, 85, 439–450.

Bishop, J. W., Scott, K. D., & Burroughs, S. M. (2000). Support, commitment, and employee outcomes in a team environment. *Journal of Management*, 26, 1113–1132.

Blanz, F., & Ghiselli, E. E. (1972). The mixed standard scale: A new rating system. *Personnel Psychology*, 25, 185–199.

Blau, G. (1993a). Further exploring the relationship between job search and voluntary individual turn-over. *Personnel Psychology*, 46, 313–330.

Blau, G. (1993b). Testing the relationship of locus of control to different performance dimensions. *Journal of Occupational and Organizational Psychology*, 66, 125–138.

Bobko, P., Shetzer, L., & Russell, C. (1991). Estimating the standard deviation of professors' worth: The effects of frame and presentation order in utility analysis. *Journal of Occupational Psychology*, 64, 179–188.

Bohle, P., & Tilley, A. J. (1998). Early experience of shiftwork: Influences on attitudes. *Journal of Occupational and Organizational Psychology*, 71, 61–79.

Bommer, W. H., Miles, E. W., & Grover, S. L. (2003). Does one good turn deserve another? Coworker influences on employee citizenship. *Journal of Organizational Behavior*, 24, 181–196.

Bommer, W. H., Rich, G. A., & Rubin, R. S. (2005). Changing attitudes about change: Longitudinal effects of transformational leader behavior on employee cynicism about organizational change. *Journal of Organizational Behavior*, 26, 733–753.

Bonner, B. L., Baumann, M. R., & Dalal, R. S. (2002). *Organizational Behavior and Human Decision Processes*, 88, 719–736.

Borman, W. C. (1987). Personal constructs, performance schemata, and "folk theories" of subordinate effectiveness: Explorations in an army officer sample. *Organizational Behavior and Human Decision Processes*, 40, 307–322.

Borman, W. C., Buck, D. E., Hanson, M. A., Motowidlo, S. J., Stark, S., & Drasgow, F. (2001). An examination of the comparative reliability, validity, and accuracy of performance ratings made using computerized adaptive rating scales. *Journal of Applied Psychology*, 86, 965–973.

Borman, W. C., Dorsey, D., & Ackerman, L. (1992). Time-spent responses as time allocation strategies: Relations with sales performance in a stockbroker sample. *Personnel Psychology*, 45, 763–777.

Borman, W. C., Peterson, N. G., & Russell, T. L. (1992). *Selection, training, and development of personnel*. In G. Salvendy (Ed.), *Handbook of industrial engineering* (2nd ed., pp. 882–914). New York: John Wiley.

Boudreau, J. W. (1983). Economic considerations in estimating the utility of human resource productivity improvement programs. *Personnel Psychology*, 36, 551–576.

Bowers, D. G. (1973). OD techniques and their results in 23 organizations: The Michigan ICL study. *The Journal of Applied Behavioral Science*, 9, 21–43.

Bowler, M. C., & Woehr, D. J. (2006). A meta-analytic evaluation of the impact of dimension and exercise factors on assessment center ratings. *Journal of Applied Psychology*, 91, 1114–1124.

Bowling, N. A., & Beehr, T. A. (2006). Workplace harassment from the victim's perspective: A theoretical model and meta-analysis. *Journal of Applied Psychology*, 91, 998–1012.

Bowling, N. A., Beehr, T. A., & Lepisto, L. R. (2006). Beyond job satisfaction: A five-year prospective analysis of the dispositional approach to work attitudes. *Journal of Vocational Behavior*, 69, 315–330.

Bragg, J. E., & Andrews, I. R. (1973). Participative decision making: An experimental study in a hospital. *The Journal of Applied Behavioral Science*, 9, 727–735.

Brannick, M. T., Levine, E. L., & Morgeson, F. P. (2007). *Job and work analysis*. Thousand Oaks, CA: Sage.

Brasher, E. E., & Chen, P. Y. (1999). Evaluation of success criteria in job search: A process perspective. *Journal of Occupational and Organizational Psychology*, 72, 57–70.

Breaugh, J. A., & Starke, M. (2000). Research on employee recruitment: So many studies, so many remaining questions. *Journal of Management*, 26, 405–434.

Brett, J. F., & Atwater, L. E. (2001). 360° feedback: Accuracy, reactions, and perceptions of usefulness. *Journal of Applied Psychology*, 86, 930–942.

Brief, A. P., & Weiss, H. M. (2002). Organizational behavior: Affect in the workplace. *Annual Review of Psychology*, 53, 279–307.

Broadbent, D. E., & Gath, D. (1981). Symptom levels in assembly-line workers. In G. Salvendy & M. J. Smith (Eds.), *Machine pacing and occupational stress* (pp. 244–252). London: Taylor & Francis.

Brotheridge, C. M., & Grandey, A. A. (2002). Emotional labor and burnout: Comparing two perspectives of "people work." *Journal of Vocational Behavior*, 60, 17–39.

Bruck, C. S., & Allen, T. D. (2003). The relationship between big five personality traits, negative affectivity, type A behavior, and work-family conflict. *Journal of Vocational Behavior*, 63, 457–472.

Brush, D. H., Moch, M. K., & Pooyan, A. (1987). Individual demographic differences and job satisfaction. *Journal of Occupational Behaviour*, 8, 139–155.

Buck, J. R. (1983). *Controls and tools*. In B. H. Kantowitz & R. D. Sorkin (Eds.), *Human factors* (pp. 195–231). New York: John Wiley.

Budd, J. W., Arvey, R. D., & Lawless, P. (1996). Correlates and consequences of workplace violence. *Journal of Occupational Health Psychology*, 1, 197–210.

Buller, P. F. (1986). The team building–task performance relation: Some conceptual and methodological refinements. *Group and Organization Studies*, 11, 147–168.

Bunker, K. A., & Cohen, S. L. (1977). The rigors of training evaluation: A discussion and field demonstration. *Personnel Psychology*, 30, 525–541.

Burgess, J. R. D., & Russell, J. E. A. (2003). The effectiveness of distance learning initiatives in organizations. *Journal of Vocational Behavior*, 63, 289–303.

Bycio, P., Hackett, R. D., & Allen, J. S. (1995). Further assessments of Bass's (1985) conceptualization of transactional and transformational leadership. *Journal of Applied Psychology*, 80, 468–478.

Cable, D. M., & Judge, T. A. (1997). Interviewers' perceptions of person—organization fit and organizational selection decisions. *Journal of Applied Psychology*, 82, 546–561.

Caldwell, D. F., & O'Reilly, C. A., III. (1990). Measuring person-job fit with a profile-comparison process. *Journal of Applied Psychology*, 75, 648–657.

Callahan, J. S., Kiker, D. S., & Cross, T. (2003). Does method matter? A meta-analysis of the effects of training method on older learner training performance. *Journal of Management*, 29, 663–680.

Callinan, M., & Robertson, I. T. (2000). Work sample testing. *International Journal of Selection and Assessment*, 8, 248–260.

Campbell, J. P., Gasser, M. B., & Oswald, F. L. (1996). *The substantive nature of job performance variability*. In K. R. Murphy (Ed.), *Individual differences and behavior in organizations* (pp. 258–299). San Francisco: Jossey-Bass.

Campbell, J. P., & Pritchard, R. D. (1976). *Motivation theory in industrial and organizational psychology*. In M. D. Dunnette (Ed.), *Handbook of industrial and organizational psychology* (pp. 63–130). Princeton, NJ: Van Nostrand.

Campion, M. A., & Campion, J. E. (1987). Evaluation of an interviewee skills training program in a natural field experiment. *Personnel Psychology*, 40, 676–691.

Campion, M. A., Palmer, D. K., & Campion, J. E. (1997). A review of structure in the selection interview. *Personnel Psychology*, 50, 655–702.

Canger, J. (2001, March 1). On-line personality assessment. Paper presented at Electronic Human Resources 2001 conference, Tampa, FL.

Cannon-Bowers, J. A., & Salas, E. (2001). Reflections on shared cognition. *Journal of Organizational Behavior*, 22, 195–202.

Carless, S. A., Mann, L., & Wearing, A. J. (1998). Leadership, managerial performance and 360 Degree Feedback. *Applied Psychology: An International Review*, 47, 481–496.

Carlson, D. S., & Kacmar, K. M. (2000). Work-family conflict in the organization: Do life role values make a difference? *Journal of Management*, 26, 1031–1054.

Cascio, W. F. (1998). *Applied psychology in personnel management* (5th ed.). Englewood Cliffs, NJ: Prentice Hall.

Cepeda, N. J., Pashler, H., Vul, E., Wixted, J. T. & Rohrer, D. (2006). Distributed practice in verbal recall tasks: A review and quantitative synthesis. *Psychological Bulletin*, 132, 354–380.

Chan, D. (1996). Criterion and construct validation of an assessment centre. *Journal of Occupational and Organizational Psychology*, 69, 167–181.

Chapman, A. J., Sheehy, N. P., Heywood, S., Dooley, B., & Collins, S. C. (1995). *The organizational implications of teleworking*. In C. L. Cooper & I. T. Robertson (Eds.), *International review of industrial and organizational psychology 1995* (pp. 1–48). Chichester, UK: John Wiley.

Chapman, D. S., & Rowe, P. M. (2001). The impact of videoconference technology, interview structure, and interviewer gender on interviewer evaluations in the employment interview: A field experiment. *Journal of Occupational and Organizational Psychology*, 74, 279–298.

Chapman, D. S., Uggerslev, K. L., Carroll, S. A., Piasentin, K. A., & Jones, D. A. (2005). Applicant attraction to organizations and job choice: A meta-analytic review of the correlates of recruiting outcomes. *Journal of Applied Psychology*, 90, 928–944.

Chapman, D. S., Uggerslev, K. L., & Webster, J. (2003). Applicant reactions to face-to-face and technology-mediated interviews: A field investigation. *Journal of Applied Psychology*, 88, 944–953.

Chapman, D. S., & Webster, J. (2003). The use of technologies in the recruiting, screening, and selection processes for job candidates. *International Journal of Selection and Assessment*, 11, 113–120.

Chiu, W. C. K., & Ng, C. W. (1999). Women-friendly HRM and organizational commitment: A study among women and men of organizations in Hong Kong. *Journal of Occupational and Organizational Psychology*, 72, 485–502.

Choi, J. N., & Price, R. H. (2005). The effects of person-innovation fit on individual responses to innovation. *Journal of Occupational and Organizational Psychology*, 78, 83–96.

Clark, A., Oswald, A., & Warr, P. (1996). Is job satisfaction U-shaped in age? *Journal of Occupational and Organizational Psychology*, 69, 57–81.

Clark, T. (1993). Selection methods used by executive search consultancies in four European countries: A survey and critique. *International Journal of Selection and Assessment*, 1, 41–49.

Clarke, S. (2006). The relationship between safety climate and safety performance: A meta-analytic review. *Journal of Occupational Health Psychology*, 11, 315–327.

Clarke, S., & Robertson, I. T. (2005). A meta-analytic review of the Big Five personality factors and accident involvement in occupational and non-occupational settings. *Journal of Occupational and Organizational Psychology*, 78, 355–376.

Cleveland, J. N., Barnes-Farrell, J. L., & Ratz, J. M. (1997). Accommodation in the workplace. *Human Resource Management Review*, 7, 77–107.

Cober, R. T., Brown, D. J., Levy, P. E., Cober, A. B., & Keeping, L. M. (2003). Organizational Web sites: Web site content and style as determinants of organizational attraction. *International Journal of Selection and Assessment*, 11, 158–169.

Coch, L., & French, J. R. P., Jr. (1948). Overcoming resistance to change. *Human Relations*, 1, 512–532.

Cohen, A. (2006). The relationship between multiple commitments and organizational citizenship behavior in Arab and Jewish culture. *Journal of Vocational Behavior*, 69, 105–118.

Cohen, S. L. (2001). E learning: Harnessing the hype. Paper presented at Electronic Human Resources 2001 conference, Tampa, FL, March 1.

Cohen-Charash, Y. & Spector, P. E. (2001). The role of justice in organizations: A meta-analysis. *Organizational Behavior and Human Decision Processes*, 86, 278–321.

Collins, J. M., & Schmidt, F. L. (1993). Personality, integrity, and white collar crime: A construct validity study. *Personnel Psychology*, 46, 295–311.

Colquitt, J. A., LePine, J. A., & Noe, R. A. (2000). Toward an integrative theory of training motivation: A meta-analytic path analysis of 20 years of research. *Journal of Applied Psychology*, 85, 678–707.

Connolly, J. J., & Viswesvaran, C. (2000). The role of affectivity in job satisfaction: A meta-analysis. *Personality and Individual Differences*, 29, 265–281.

Conte, J. M. (2005). A review and critique of emotional intelligence measures. *Journal of Organizational Behavior*, 26, 433–440.

Conte, J. M., Dean, M. A., Ringenbach, K. L., Moran, S. K., & Landy, F. J. (2005). The relationship between work attitudes and job analysis ratings: Do rating scale type and task discretion matter? *Human Performance*, 18, 1–21.

Converse, P. D., Oswald, F. L., Gillespie, M. A., Field, K. A., & Bizot, E. B. (2004). Matching individuals to occupations using abilities and the O*NET: Issues and an application in career guidance. *Personnel Psychology*, 57, 451–487.

Cook, J. D., Hepworth, S. J., Wall, T. D., & Warr, P. B. (1981). *The experience of work*. New York: Academic Press.

Cook, T. D., & Campbell, D. T. (1979). *Quasi-experimentation: Design and analysis issues for field settings*. Chicago: Rand-McNally.

Cooper, C. L., & Cartwright, S. (1994). Healthy mind; healthy organization: A proactive approach to occupational stress. *Human Relations*, 47, 455–471.

Cooper, R., & Foster, M. (1971). Sociotechnical systems. *American Psychologist*, 26, 467–474.

Cooper-Hakim, A., & Viswesvaran, C. (2005). The construct of work commitment: Testing an integrative framework. *Psychological Bulletin*, 131, 241–259.

Coovert, M. D. (1990). *Development and evaluation of five user models of human-computer interaction*. In U. E. Gattiker & L. Larwood (Eds.), *End-user training* (pp. 105–139). Berlin: Walter de Gruyter.

Coovert, M. D. (1995). *Technological changes in office jobs: What we know and what we can expect*. In A. Howard (Ed.), *The changing nature of work* (pp. 175–208). San Francisco: Jossey Bass.

Coovert, M. D., & Thompson, L. F. (2001). *Computer supported cooperative work*. Thousand Oaks, CA: Sage.

Cordery, J. L., Mueller, W. S., & Smith, L. M. (1991). Attitudinal and behavioral effects of autonomous group working: A longitudinal field study. *Academy of Management Journal*, 34, 464–476.

Cordes, C. L., & Dougherty, T. W. (1993). A review and an integration of research on job burnout. *Academy of Management Review*, 18, 621–656.

Cornelius, E. T., III, DeNisi, A. S., & Blencoe, A. G. (1984). Expert and naive raters using the PAQ: Does it matter? *Personnel Psychology*, 37, 453–464.

Cortina, L. M., Magley, V. J., Williams, J. H., & Langhout, R. D. (2001). Incivility in the workplace: Incidence and impact. *Journal of Occupational Health Psychology*, 6, 64–80.

Coté, S., & Morgan, L. M. (2002). A longitudinal analysis of the association between emotion regulation, job satisfaction, and intentions to quit. *Journal of Organizational Behavior*, 23, 947–962.

Crampton, S. M., & Wagner, J. A., III. (1994). Percept-percept inflation in microorganizational research: An investigation of prevalence and effect. *Journal of Applied Psychology*, 79, 67–76.

Cropanzano, R., Byrne, Z. S., Bobocel, D. R., & Rupp, D. E. (2001). Moral virtues, fairness heuristics, social entities, and other denizens of organizational justice. *Journal of Vocational Behavior*, 58, 164–209.

Cropanzano, R., Howes, J. C., Grandey, A. A., & Toth, P. (1997). The relationship of organizational politics and support to work behaviors, attitudes, and stress. *Journal of Organizational Behavior*, 18, 159–180.

Cunningham, C. E., Woodward, C. A., Shannon, H. S., MacIntosh, J., Lendrum, B., Rosenbloom, D., & Brown, J. (2002). Readiness for organizational change: A longitudinal study of workplace, psychological and behavioral correlates. *Journal of Occupational and Organizational Psychology*, 75, 377–392.

Dalton, D. R., & Mesch, D. J. (1991). On the extent and reduction of avoidable absenteeism: An assessment of absence policy provisions. *Journal of Applied Psychology*, 76, 810–817.

Dalton, D. R., & Todor, W. D. (1993). Turnover, transfer, absenteeism: An interdependent perspective. *Journal of Management*, 19, 193–219.

Dansereau, F., Jr., Graen, G., & Haga, W. J. (1975). A vertical dyad linkage approach to leadership with formal organizations. *Organizational Behavior and Human Performance*, 13, 46–78.

Daus, C. S., & Ashkanasy, N. M. (2005). The case for the ability-based model of emotional intelligence in organizational behavior. *Journal of Organizational Behavior*, 26, 453–466.

Daus, C. S., Sanders, D. N., & Campbell, D. P. (1998). *Consequences of alternative work schedules*. In C. L. Cooper & I. T. Robertson (Eds.), *International review of industrial and organizational psychology 1998* (pp. 185–223). Chichester, UK: John Wiley.

Davis, D. D. (1995). Form, function, and strategy in boundaryless organizations. In A. Howard (Ed.), *The changing nature of work* (pp. 112–138). San Francisco: Jossey Bass.

Davis, J. H. (1969). *Group performance*. Reading, MA: Addison-Wesley.

Davis, W. D., Fedor, D. B., Parsons, C. K., & Herold, D. M. (2000). The development of self-efficacy during aviation training. *Journal of Organizational Behavior*, 21, 857–871.

Day, A. L., & Chamberlain, T. C. (2006). Committing to your work, spouse, and children: Implications for work-family conflict. *Journal of Vocational Behavior*, 68, 116–130.

Day, D. V., & Sulsky, L. M. (1995). Effects of frame-of-reference training and information configuration on memory organization and rating accuracy. *Journal of Applied Psychology*, 80, 158–167.

Day, R., & Allen, T. D. (2004). The relationship between career motivation and self-efficacy with protégé career success. *Journal of Vocational Behavior*, 64, 72–91.

Dayan, K., Kasten, R., & Fox, S. (2002). Entry-level police candidate assessment center: An efficient tool or a hammer to kill a fly? *Personnel Psychology*, 55, 827–849.

De Dreu, C. K. W. (2006). When too little or too much hurts: Evidence for a curvilinear relationship between task conflict and innovation in teams. *Journal of Management*, 32, 83–107.

de Lange, A. H., Taris, T. W., Kompier, M. A. J., Houtman, I. L. D., & Bongers, P. M. (2003). "The *very* best of the millennium": Longitudinal research and the demand-control-(support) model. *Journal of Occupational Health Psychology*, 8, 282–305.

Deadrick, D. L., Bennett, N., & Russell, C. J. (1997). Using hierarchical liner modeling to examine dynamic performance criteria over time. *Journal of Management*, 23, 745–757.

Deadrick, D. L., & Madigan, R. M. (1990). Dynamic criteria revisited: A longitudinal study of performance stability and predictive validity. *Personnel Psychology*, 43, 717–744.

DeJoy, D. M., Searcy, C. A., Murphy, L. R., & Gershon, R. R. M. (2000). Behavioral—diagnostic analysis of compliance with universal precautions among nurses. *Journal of Occupational Health Psychology*, 5, 127–141.

Del Ben, K. S., Scotti, J. R., Chen, Y. C., & Fortson, B. L. (2006). Prevalence of posttraumatic stress disorder symptoms in firefighters. *Work & Stress*, 20, 37–48.

DeNisi, A. S., Cafferty, T. P., & Meglino, B. M. (1984). A cognitive view of the performance appraisal process: A model and research propositions. *Organizational Behavior and Human Performance*, 33, 360–396.

Dennis, A. R., & Valacich, J. S. (1993). Computer brainstorms: More heads are better than one. *Journal of Applied Psychology*, 78, 531–537.

DeRouin, R. E., Fritzsche, B. A., & Salas, E. (2005). E-learning in organizations. *Journal of Management*, 31, 920–940.

DeShon, R. P., & Gillespie, J. Z. (2005). A motivated action theory account of goal orientation. *Journal of Applied Psychology*, 90, 1096–1127.

DeVoe, S. E., & Iyengar, S. S. (2004). Managers' theories of subordinates: A cross-cultural examination of manager perceptions of motivation and appraisal of performance. *Organizational Behavior and Human Decision Processes*, 93, 47–61.

Dickinson, T. L., & Glebocki, G. G. (1990). Modification in the format of the mixed standard scale. *Organizational Behavior and Human Decision Processes*, 47, 124–137.

Dickter, D. N., Roznowski, M., & Harrison, D. A. (1996). Temporal tempering: An event history analysis of the process of voluntary turnover. *Journal of Applied Psychology*, 81, 705–716.

Diefendorff, J. M., Hall, R. J., Lord, R. G., & Strean, M. L. (2000). Action-state orientation: Construct validity of a revised measure and its relationship to work-related variables. *Journal of Applied Psychology*, 85, 250–263.

Diefendorff, J. M., Richard, E. M., & Croyle, M. H. (2006). Are emotional display rules formal job requirements? Examination of employee and supervisor perceptions. *Journal of Occupational and Organizational Psychology*, 79, 273–298.

Dierdorff, E. C., & Wilson, M. A. (2003). A meta-analysis of job analysis reliability. *Journal of Applied Psychology*, 88, 635–646.

Dipboye, R. L. (1990). Laboratory vs. field research in industrial and organizational psychology. In C. L. Cooper & I. T. Robertson (Eds.), *International review of industrial and organizational psychology 1990* (pp. 1–34). Chichester, UK: John Wiley.

Dipboye, R. L., & Gaugler, B. B. (1993). Cognitive and behavioral processes in the selection interview. In N. Schmitt & W. C. Borman (Eds.), *Personnel selection in organizations* (pp. 135–170). San Francisco: Jossey-Bass.

Doerr, K. H., Mitchell, T. R., Klastorin, T. D., & Brown, K. A. (1996). Impact of material flow policies and goals on job outcomes. *Journal of Applied Psychology*, 81, 142–152.

Donovan, J. J., & Williams, K. J. (2003). Missing the mark: Effects of time and causal attributions on goal revision in response to goal-performance discrepancies. *Journal of Applied Psychology*, 88, 379–390.

Dormann, C., & Zapf, D. (1999). Social support, social stressors at work, and depressive symptoms: Testing for main and moderating effects with structural equations in a three-wave longitudinal study. *Journal of Applied Psychology*, 84, 874–884.

Dormann, C., & Zapf, D. (2001). Job satisfaction: A meta-analysis of stabilities. *Journal of Organizational Behavior*, 22, 483–504.

Dorsey, D. (2001, March 1). Emerging HR technologies and the future of O*NET. Paper presented at Electronic Human Resources 2001 conference, Tampa, FL.

Drach-Zahavy, A., & Erez, M. (2002). Challenge versus threat effects on the goal-performance relationship. *Organizational Behavior and Human Decision Processes*, 88, 667–682.

Driskell, J. E., Willis, R., & Copper, C. (1992). Effect of overlearning on retention. *Journal of Applied Psychology*, 77, 615–622.

Dudley, N. M., Orvis, K. A., Lebiecki, J. E., & Cortina, J. M. (2006). A meta-analytic investigation of conscientiousness in the prediction of job performance: Examining the intercorrelations and the incremental validity of narrow traits. *Journal of Applied Psychology*, 911, 40–57.

Dunham, R. B., Grube, J. A., & Castañeda, M. B. (1994). Organizational commitment: The utility of an integrative definition. *Journal of Applied Psychology*, 79, 370–380.

Dunnette, M. D. (1998). Emerging trends and vexing issues in industrial and organizational psychology. *Applied Psychology: An International Review*, 47, 129–153.

Eagly, A. H., & Johnson, B. T. (1990). Gender and leadership style: A meta-analysis. *Psychological Bulletin*, 2, 233–256.

Earley, P. C. (1989). Social loafing and collectivism: A comparison of the United States and the People's Republic of China. *Administrative Science Quarterly*, 34, 565–581.

Eby, L., Butts, M., Lockwood, A., & Simon, S. A. (2004). Protégés' negative mentoring experiences: Construct development and nomological validation. *Personnel Psychology*, 57, 411–447.

Eby, L. T., Durley, J. R., Evans, S. C., & Ragins, B. R. (2006). The relationship between short-term mentoring benefits and long-term mentor outcomes. *Journal of Vocational Behavior*, 69, 424–444.

Eden, D. (1985). Team development: A true field experiment employing three levels of rigor. *Journal of Applied Psychology*, 70, 94–100.

Eden, D. (1986). Team development: Quasi-experimental confirmation among combat companies. *Group & Organizational Studies*, 11, 133–146.

Eden, D., & Aviram, A. (1993). Self-efficacy training to speed reemployment: Helping people to help themselves. *Journal of Applied Psychology*, 78, 352–360.

Eden, D., & Zuk, Y. (1995). Seasickness as a self-fulfilling prophecy: Raising self-efficacy to boost performance at sea. *Journal of Applied Psychology*, 80, 628–635.

Edwards, B. D., Day, E. A., Arthur, W., Jr., & Bell, S. T. (2006). Relationships among team ability composition, team mental models, and team performance. *Journal of Applied Psychology*, 91, 727–736.

Eisenberger, R., Armeli, S., Rexwinkel, B., Lynch, P. D., & Rhoades, L. (2001). Reciprocation of perceived organizational support. *Journal of Applied Psychology*, 86, 42–51.

Eleftheriou, A., & Robertson, I. (1999). A survey of management selection practices in Greece. *International Journal of Selection and Assessment*, 7, 203–208.

Elovainio, M., & Kivimäki, M. (1999). Personal need for structure and occupational strain: An investigation of structural models and interaction with job complexity. *Personality and Individual Differences*, 26, 209–222.

Elovainio, M., Kivimäki, M., Vahtera, J., Virtanen, M., & Keltikangas-Järvinen, L. (2003). Personality as a moderator in the relations between perceptions of organizational justice and sickness absence. *Journal of Vocational Behavior*, 63, 379–395.

Endo, K. (1998). 'Japanization' of a performance appraisal system: A historical comparison of the American and Japanese systems. *Social Science Japan Journal*, 1, 247–262.

Ensari, N. & Murphy, S. E. (2003). Cross-cultural variations in leadership perceptions and attribution of charisma to the leader. *Organizational Behavior and Human Decision Processes*, 92, 52–66.

Erez, M. (1994). *Toward a model of cross-cultural industrial and organizational psychology*. In H. C. Triandis, M. D. Dunnette, & L. M. Hough (Eds.), *Handbook of industrial and organizational psychology* (pp. 559–607). Palo Alto, CA: Consulting Psychologists Press.

Erickson, R. J., Nichols, L., & Ritter, C. (2000). Family influences on absenteeism: Testing an expanded process model. *Journal of Vocational Behavior*, 57, 246–272.

Evans, D. C. (2003). A comparison of other-directed stigmatization produced by legal and illegal forms of affirmative action. *Journal of Applied Psychology*, 88, 121–130.

Eyde, L. D. (1983). Evaluating job evaluation: Emerging research issues for comparable worth analysis. *Public Personnel Management Journal*, 12, 425–444.

Facteau, J. D., Dobbins, G. H., Russell, J. E. A., Ladd, R. T., & Kudisch, J. D. (1995). The influence of general perceptions of the training environment on pretraining motivation and perceived training transfer. *Journal of Management*, 21, 1–25.

Farr, J. L., Hofmann, D. A., & Ringenbach, K. L. (1993). Goal orientation and action control theory: Implications for industrial and organizational psychology. In C. L. Cooper & I. T. Robertson (Eds.), *International review of industrial and organizational psychology, 1993* (pp. 193–232). Chichester, UK: John Wiley.

Farh, J., Podsakoff, P. M., & Organ, D. W. (1990). Accounting for organizational citizenship behaviors: Leader fairness and task scope versus satisfaction. *Journal of Management*, 16, 705–721.

Farrell, D., & Stamm, C. L. (1988). Meta-analysis of the correlates of employee absence. *Human Relations*, 41, 211–227.

Federal Bureau of Investigation (2001). *Uniform crime reports*. [Online]. Available: www.fbi.gov/ucr/ucr.htm [2001, December 8].

Federation of Irish Employers. (1991). *Personnel policies and procedures guidelines*. Dublin: Baggot Bridge House.

Feldman, D. C., & Lankau, M. J. (2005). Executive coaching: A review and agenda for future research. *Journal of Management*, 31, 829–848.

Feldman, J. M. (1981). Beyond attribution theory: Cognitive processes in performance appraisal. *Journal of Applied Psychology*, 66, 127–148.

Fernet, C., Guay, F., & Senécal, C. (2004). Adjusting to job demands: The role of work self-determination and job control in predicting burnout. *Journal of Vocational Behavior*, 65, 39–56.

Ferris, G. R., Judge, T. A., Rowland, K. M., & Fitzgibbons, D. E. (1994). Subordinate influence and the performance evaluation process: Test of a model. *Organizational and Human Decision Processes*, 58, 101–135.

Ferris, G. R., Treadway, D. C., Kolodinsky, R. W., Hochwarter, W. A., Kacmar, C. J., Douglas, C., & Frink, D. D. (2005). Development and validation of the Political Skill Inventory. *Journal of Management*, 31, 126–152.

Fiedler, F. E. (1978). *The contingency model and the dynamics of the leadership process*. In L. Berkowitz (Ed.), *Advances in experimental social psychology*, 11 (pp. 59–112). New York: Academic Press.

Field, R. H. G., & House, R. J. (1990). A test of the Vroom-Yetton model using manager and subordinate reports. *Journal of Applied Psychology*, 75, 362–366.

Fine, S. A., & Wiley, W. W. (1971). An introduction to functional job analysis, methods for manpower analysis. (Monograph No. 4), Kalamazoo, MI: W. E. Upjohn Inst.

Fisher, C. D., (2000). Mood and emotions while working: Missing pieces of job satisfaction? *Journal of Organizational Behavior*, 21, 185–202.

Fitzgerald, L. F., Drasgow, F., Hulin, C. L., Gelfand, M. J., & Magley, V. J. (1997). Antecedents and consequences of sexual harassment in organizations: A test of an integrated model. *Journal of Applied Psychology*, 82, 578–589.

Flanagan, J. C. (1954). The critical incident technique. *Psychological Bulletin*, 51, 327–358.

Fleishman, E. A., & Harris, E. F. (1962). Patterns of leadership behavior related to employee grievances and turnover. *Personnel Psychology*, 15, 43–56.

Fletcher, C., & Baldry, C. (2000). A study of individual differences and self-awareness in the context of multi-source feedback. *Journal of Occupational and Organizational Psychology*, 73, 303–319.

Folger, R., & Skarlicki, D. P. (2005). *Beyond counterproductive work behavior: Moral emotions and deontic retaliation vs. reconciliation*. In S. Fox & P. E. Spector (Eds.), *Counterproductive work behavior: Investigations of actors and targets* (pp. 83–105). Washington, DC: APA Press.

Ford, J. K., & Kraiger, K. (1995). The application of cognitive constructs and principles to the instructional systems model of training: Implications for needs assessment, design, and transfer. In C. L. Cooper & I. T. Robertson (Eds.), *International review of industrial and organizational psychology 1995* (pp. 1–48). Chichester, UK: John Wiley.

Ford, J. K., & Wroten, S. P. (1984). Introducing new methods for conducting training evaluation and for linking training evaluation to program redesign. *Personnel Psychology*, 37, 651–665.

Ford, M. T., Heinen, B. A., & Langkamer, K. L. (2007). Work and family satisfaction and conflict: A meta-analysis of cross-domain relations. *Journal of Applied Psychology*, 92, 57–80.

Foust, M. S., Elicker, J. D., & Levy, P. E. (2006). Development and validation of a measure of an individual's lateness attitude. *Journal of Vocational Behavior*, 69, 119–133.

Fowler, F. J., Jr. (1988). *Survey research methods* (Rev. ed.). Newbury Park, CA: Sage.

Fox, M. L., Dwyer, D. J., & Ganster, D. C. (1993). Effects of stressful job demands and control on physiological and attitudinal outcomes in a hospital setting. *Academy of Management Journal*, 36, 289–318.

Fox, S., Spector, P. E., & Miles, D. (2001). Counterproductive work behavior (CWB) in response to job stressors and organizational justice: Some mediator and moderator tests for autonomy and emotions. *Journal of Vocational Behavior*, 59, 291–309.

Fox, S., & Stallworth, L. E. (2005). Racial/ethnic bullying: Exploring links between bullying and racism in the US workplace. *Journal of Vocational Behavior*, 66, 438–456.

Frankenhaeuser, M., & Johansson, G. (1986). Stress at work: Psychobiological and psychosocial aspects. *International Review of Applied Psychology*, 35, 287–299.

French, J. R. P., Jr., & Raven, B. (1959). The bases of social power. In D. Cartwright (Ed.), *Studies in social power* (pp. 150–167). Ann Arbor, MI: Institute for Social Research.

Frese, M. (1987). Human-computer interaction in the office. In C. L. Cooper & I. T. Robertson (Eds.), *International review of industrial and organizational psychology 1987* (pp. 117–165). Chichester, UK: John Wiley.

Frese, M., & Zapf, D. (1988). Methodological issues in the study of work stress: Objective vs. subjective measurement of work stress and the question of longitudinal studies. In C. L. Cooper & R. Payne (Eds.), *Causes, coping and consequences of stress at work* (pp. 375–409). Chichester, UK: John Wiley.

Frese, M., & Zapf, D. (1994). Action as the core of work psychology: A German approach. In H. C. Triandis, M. D. Dunnette, & L. M. Hough (Eds.), *Handbook of industrial and organizational psychology* (pp. 271–340). Palo Alto, CA: Consulting Psychologists Press.

Fried, Y., Ben-David, H. A., Tiegs, R. B., Avital, N., & Yeverechyahu, U. (1998). The interactive effect of role conflict and role ambiguity on job performance. *Journal of Occupational and Organizational Psychology*, 71, 19–27.

Fried, Y., & Ferris, G. R. (1987). The validity of the job characteristics model: A review and meta-analysis. *Personnel Psychology*, 40, 287–322.

Fritz, C., & Sonnentag, S. (2006). Recovery, well-being, and performance-related outcomes: The role of workload and vacation experiences. *Journal of Applied Psychology*, 91, 936–945.

Fullagar, C. J., Gallagher, D. G., Clark, P. F., & Carroll, A. E. (2004). Union commitment and participation: A 10–year longitudinal study. *Journal of Applied Psychology*, 89, 730–737.

Fuller, J. A., Stanton, J. M., Fisher, G. G., Spitzmüller, C., Russell, S. S., & Smith, P. C. (2003). A lengthy look at the daily grind: Time series analysis of events, mood, stress, and satisfaction. *Journal of Applied Psychology*, 88, 1019–1033.

Funke, J. (1998). Computer-based testing and training with scenarios from complex problem-solving research: Advantages and disadvantages. *International Journal of Selection and Assessment*, 6, 90–96.

Furnham, A., & Stringfield, P. (1994). Congruence of self and subordinate ratings of managerial practices as a correlate of supervisor evaluation. *Journal of Occupational and Organizational Psychology*, 67, 57–67.

Gallup, Poll (1997, August). Public generally negative toward business, but most workers satisfied with jobs. [Online] Available: www.gallup.com/poll/editors/9710busi.html [1998, February 18].

Gallupe, R. B., Bastianutti, L. M., & Cooper, W. H. (1991). Unblocking brainstorms. *Journal of Applied Psychology*, 76, 137–142.

Gallupe, R. B., Cooper, W. H., Grisé, M., & Bastianutti, L. M. (1994). Blocking electronic brainstorms. *Journal of Applied Psychology*, 79, 77–86.

Ganster, D. C., & Schaubroeck, J. (1991). Work stress and employee health. *Journal of Management*, 17, 235–271.

Ganzach, Y., Kluger, A. N., & Klayman, N. (2000). Making decisions from an interview: Expert measurement and mechanical combination. *Personnel Psychology*, 53, 1–20.

Gardner, W. L., & Avolio, B. J. (1998). The charismatic relationship: A dramaturgical perspective. *Academy of Management Review*, 23, 32–58.

Gaudine, A. P., & Saks, A. M. (2001). Effects of an absenteeism feedback intervention on employee absence behavior. *Journal of Organizational Behavior*, 22, 15–29.

Geddes, D. (1994, August). The relationship between negative feedback and increased organizational aggression. Paper presented at the 1994 Academy of Management meetings, Dallas.

Gerhart, B. (1990). Voluntary turnover and alternative job opportunities. *Journal of Applied Psychology*, 5, 467–476.

Gerstner, C. R., & Day, D. V. (1997). Meta-analytic review of leader—member exchange theory: Correlates and construct issues. *Journal of Applied Psychology*, 82, 827–844.

Giacalone, R. A., & Knouse, S. B. (1990). Justifying wrongful employee behavior: The role of personality in organizational sabotage. *Journal of Business Ethics*, 9, 55–61.

Giacalone, R. A., & Rosenfeld, P. (1987). Reasons for employee sabotage in the workplace. *Journal of Business and Psychology*, 1, 367–378.

Giardini, A., & Frese, M. (2006). Reducing the negative effects of emotion work in service occupations: Emotional competence as a psychological resource. *Journal of Occupational Health Psychology*, 11, 63–75.

Glasscock, D. J., Rasmussen, K., Carstensen, O., & Hansen, O. N. (2006). Psychosocial factors and safety behaviour as predictors of accidental work injuries in farming. *Work & Stress*, 20, 173–189.

Glazer, S., & Beehr, T. A. (2005). Consistency of implications of three role stressors across four countries. *Journal of Organizational Behavior*, 26, 467–487.

Glick, W. H., Jenkins, G. D., Jr., & Gupta, N. (1986). Method versus substance: How strong are underlying relationships between job characteristics and attitudinal outcomes? *Academy of Management Journal*, 29, 441–464.

Glomb, T. M., & Tews, M. J. (2004). Emotional labor: A conceptualization and scale development. *Journal of Vocational Behavior*, 64, 1–23.

Goff, S. J., Mount, M. K., & Jamison R. L. (1990). Employer supported child care, work/family conflict, and absenteeism: A field study. *Personnel Psychology*, 43, 794–809.

Goldberg, C. B., Finkelstein, L. M., Perry, E. L., & Konrad, A. M. (2004). Job and industry fit: The effects of age and gender matches on career progress outcomes. *Journal of Organizational Behavior*, 25, 807–829.

Goldberg, L. R., Johnson, J. A., Eber, H. W., Hogan, R., Ashton, M. C., Cloninger, C. R., & Gough, H. C. (2006). The International Personality Item Pool and the future of public-domain personality measures. *Journal of Research in Personality*, 40, 84–96.

Goldman, B. M., Gutek, B. A., Stein, J. H., & Lewis, K. (2006). Employment discrimination in organizations: Antecedents and consequences. *Journal of Management*, 32, 786–830.

Goldstein, I. L. (1993). *Training in organizations: Needs assessment, development, and evaluation* (3rd ed.). Monterey, CA: Brooks/Cole.

Goldstein, I. L., & Gilliam, P. (1990). Training system issues in the year 2000. *American Psychologist*, 45, 134–143.

Gomez-Mejia, L. R., Page, R. C., & Tornow, W. W. (1982). A comparison of the practical utility of traditional, statistical, and hybrid job evaluation approaches. *Academy of Management Journal*, 25, 790–809.

Graen, G., Novak, M. A., & Sommerkamp, P. (1982). The effects of leader-member exchange and job design on productivity and satisfaction: Testing a dual attachment model. *Organizational Behavior and Human Performance*, 30, 109–131.

Grandey, A. A., Dickter, D. N., & Sin, H. P. (2004). The customer is *not* always right: Customer aggression and emotion regulation of service employees. *Journal of Organizational Behavior*, 25, 397–418.

Grandey, A. A., Fisk, G. M., Mattila, A. S., Jansen, K. J., & Sideman, L. A. (2005). Is "service with a smile" enough? Authenticity of positive displays during service encounters. *Organizational Behavior and Human Decision Processes*, 96, 38–55.

Grandey, A. A., Fisk, G. M., & Steiner, D. D. (2005). Must "service with a smile" be stressful? The moderating role of personal control for American and French employees. *Journal of Applied Psychology*, 90, 893–904.

Green, S. B., & Stutzman, T. (1986). An evaluation of methods to select respondents to structured job-analysis questionnaires. *Personnel Psychology*, 39, 543–565.

Greenberg, J. (1990). Employee theft as a reaction to underpayment inequity: The hidden cost of pay cuts. *Journal of Applied Psychology*, 5, 561–568.

Greenberg, J., (2002). Who stole the money, and when? Individual and situational determinants of employee theft. *Organizational Behavior and Human Decision Processes*, 89, 985–1003.

Greenberg, L., & Barling, J. (1999). Predicting employee aggression against coworkers, subordinates and supervisors: The roles of person behaviors and perceived workplace factors. *Journal of Organizational Behavior*, 20, 897–913.

Greenhaus, J. H., Parasuraman, S., & Wormley, W. M. (1990). Effects of race on organizational experiences, job performance evaluations, and career outcomes. *Academy of Management Journal*, 33, 64–86.

Greiner, B. A., & Krause, N. (2006). Observational stress factors and musculoskeletal disorders in urban transit operators. *Journal of Occupational Health Psychology*, 11, 38–51.

Griffeth, R. W., Hom, P. W., & Gaertner, S. (2000). A meta-analysis of antecedents and correlates of employee turnover: Update, moderator tests, and research implications for the next millennium. *Journal of Management*, 26, 463–488.

Griffin, R. W. (1991). Effects of work redesign on employee perceptions, attitudes, and behaviors: A long-term investigation. *Academy of Management Journal*, 34, 425–435.

Groves, K. S. (2005). Linking leader skills, follower attitudes, and contextual variables via an integrated model of charismatic leadership. *Journal of Management*, 31, 255–277.

Guion, R. M., & Alvares, K. M. (1980). *Selection of police officers* (Report Supplement No. 1: Job Analysis). Bowling Green, OH: Bowling Green State University.

Gutenberg, R. L., Arvey, R. D., Osburn, H. G., & Jeanneret, P. R. (1983). Moderating effects of decision-making/information-processing job dimensions on test validities. *Journal of Applied Psychology*, 68, 602–608.

Guzzo, R. A., Jette, R. D., & Katzell, R. A. (1985). The effects of psychologically based intervention programs on worker productivity: A meta-analysis. *Personnel Psychology*, 38, 275–291.

Hacker, G. R. (1996). A theoretical approach to the selection of job analysis respondents. Unpublished doctoral dissertation, University of South Florida, Tampa.

Hackett, R. D., Bycio, P., & Hausdorf, P. A. (1994). Further assessments of Meyer and Allen's (1991) three-component model of organizational commitment. *Journal of Applied Psychology*, 79, 15–23.

Hackman, J. R., & Oldham, G. R. (1976). Motivation through the design of work: Test of a theory. *Organizational Behavior and Human Performance*, 16, 250–279.

Hackman, J. R., & Oldham, G. R. (1980). *Work redesign*. Reading, MA: Addison-Wesley.

Hammer, L. B., Bauer, T. N., & Grandey, A. A. (2003). Work-family conflict and work-related withdrawal behaviors. *Journal of Business and Psychology*, 17, 419–436

Hanson, G. C., Hammer, L. B., & Colton, C. L. (2006). Development and validation of a multidimensional scale of perceived work-family positive spillover. *Journal of Occupational Health Psychology*, 11, 249–265.

Harris, K. J., Kacmar, K. M., & Witt, L. A. (2005). An examination of the curvilinear relationship between leader-member exchange and intent to turnover. *Journal of Organizational Behavior*, 26, 363–378.

Harris, M. M., Becker, A. S., & Smith, D. E. (1993). Does the assessment center scoring method affect the cross-situational consistency of ratings? *Journal of Applied Psychology*, 78, 675–678.

Harris, M. M., & Schaubroeck, J. (1988). A meta-analysis of self-supervisor, self-peer, and peer-supervisor ratings. *Personnel Psychology*, 41, 43–62.

Harrison, D. A., & Shaffer, M. A. (1993, August). Wading through Lake Woebegone: Comparative examinations of self reports and perceived norms of absenteeism. Paper presented at Academy of Management Convention, Atlanta.

Harrison, D. A., Kravitz, D. A., Mayer, D. M., Leslie, L. M., & Lev-Arey, D. (2006). Understanding attitudes toward affirmative action programs in employment: Summary and meta-analysis of 35 years of research. *Journal of Applied Psychology*, 91, 1013–1036.

Harvey, R. J., & Wilson, M. A. (2000). Yes Virginia, there *is* an objective reality in job analysis. *Journal of Organizational Behavior*, 21, 829–854.

Hausknecht, J. P., Day, D. V., & Thomas, S. C. (2004). Applicant reactions to selection procedures: An updated model and meta-analysis. *Personnel Psychology*, 57, 639–683.

Hedge, J. W., & Kavanagh, M. J. (1988). Improving the accuracy of performance evaluations: Comparison of three methods of performance appraiser training. *Journal of Applied Psychology*, 73, 68–73.

Heggestad, E. D., Morrison, M., Reeve, C. L., & McCloy, R. A. (2006). Forced-choice assessments of personality for selection: Evaluating issues of normative assessment and faking resistance. *Journal of Applied Psychology*, 91, 9–24.

Heilman, M. E., & Alcott, V. B. (2001). What I think you think of me: Women's reactions to being viewed as beneficiaries of preferential selection. *Journal of Applied Psychology*, 86, 574–582.

Heilman, M. E., Battle, W. S., Keller, C. E., & Lee, R. A. (1998). Type of affirmative action policy: A determinant of reactions to sex-based preferential selection? *Journal of Applied Psychology*, 83, 190–205.

Heilman, M. E., Kaplow, S. R., Amato, M. A. G., & Stathatos, P. (1993). When similarity is a liability: Effects of sex-based preferential selection on reactions to like-sex and different-sex others. *Journal of Applied Psychology*, 78, 917–927.

Heilman, M. E., McCullough, W. F., & Gilbert, D. (1996). The other side of affirmative action: Reactions of nonbeneficiaries to sex-based preferential selection. *Journal of Applied Psychology*, 81, 346–357.

Hemingway, M. A., & Smith, C. S. (1999). Organizational climate and occupational stressors as predictors of withdrawal behaviours and injuries in nurses. *Journal of Occupational and Organizational Psychology*, 72, 285–299.

Hepworth, W., & Towler, A. (2004). The effects of individual differences and charismatic leadership on workplace aggression. *Journal of Occupational Health Psychology*, 9, 176–185.

Herold, D. M., Davis, W., Fedor, D. B., & Parsons, C. K. (2002). Dispositional influences on transfer of learning in multistage training programs. *Personnel Psychology*, 55, 851–869.

Herzberg, F. (1968, January/February). One more time: How do you motivate employees? Harvard Business Review, pp. 52–62.

Hesketh, B. (1997). Dilemmas in training for transfer and retention. *Applied Psychology: An International Review*, 46, 317–339.

Hirschfeld, R. R., Jordan, M. H., Feild, H. S., Giles, W. F., & Armenakis, A. A. (2006). Becoming team players: Team members' mastery of teamwork knowledge as a predictor of team task proficiency and observed teamwork effectiveness. *Journal of Applied Psychology*, 91, 467–474.

Hochwarter, W. A., Kacmar, C., Perrewé, P. L., & Johnson, D. (2003). Perceived organizational support as a mediator of the relationship between politics perceptions and work outcomes. *Journal of Vocational Behavior*, 63, 438–456.

Hochwarter, W. A., Witt, L. A., Treadway, D. C., & Ferris, G. R. (2006). The interaction of social skill and organizational support on job performance. *Journal of Applied Psychology*, 91, 482–489.

Hoffman, B. J., Blair, C. A., Meriac, J. P., & Woehr, D. J. (2007). Expanding the criterion domain? A quantitative review of the OCB literature. *Journal of Applied Psychology*, 92, 555–566.

Hofmann, D. A., Jacobs, R., & Baratta, J. E. (1993). Dynamic criteria and the measurement of change. *Journal of Applied Psychology*, 78, 194–204.

Hofstede, G. (2001). *Culture's consequences* (2nd ed.). Thousand Oaks, CA: Sage.

Hogan, J., & Holland, B. (2003). Using theory to evaluate personality and job-performance relations: A socioanalytic perspective. *Journal of Applied Psychology*, 88, 100–112.

Hogan, R., Curphy, G. J., & Hogan, J. (1994). What we know about leadership. *American Psychologist*, 49, 493–504.

Holland, J. L. (1994). Self-Directed Search Form R. Lutz, FL: Psychological Assessment Resources.

Hollinger, R. C., Dabney, D. A., Lee, G., Hayes, R., Hunter, J., & Cummings, M. (1996). *1996 national retail security survey final report*. Gainesville: University of Florida.

House, R. J., Hanges, P. J., Ruiz-Quintanilla, S. A., Dorfman, P. W., Javidan, M., Dickson, M., Gupta, V., & Country Co-Investigators (1999). *Cultural influences on leadership and organizations: Project GLOBE*. In W. H. Mobley, M. J. Gessner, & V. Arnold (Eds.), *Advances in global leadership*, Vol. 1 (pp. 171–233). Stamford, CT: JAI.

House, R. J., & Mitchell, T. R. (1974). Path-goal theory of leadership. *Contemporary Business*, 3, 81–98.

Huffcutt, A. I., & Arthur, W., Jr. (1994). Hunter and Hunter (1984) revisited: Interview validity for entry-level jobs. *Journal of Applied Psychology*, 79, 184–190.

Huffcutt, A. I., Conway, J. M., Roth, P. L., & Stone, N. J. (2001). Identification and meta-analytic assessment of psychological constructs measured in employment interviews. *Journal of Applied Psychology*, 86, 897–913.

Huffcutt, A. I., Roth, P. L., & McDaniel, M. A. (1996). A meta-analytic investigation of cognitive ability in employment interview evaluations: Moderating characteristics and implications for incremental validity. *Journal of Applied Psychology*, 81, 459–473.

Hui, C., Lam, S. S. K., & Law, K. K. S. (2000). Instrumental values of organizational citizenship behavior for promotion: A field quasi-experiment. *Journal of Applied Psychology*, 85, 822–828.

Hui, C. H., Yee, C., & Eastman, K. L. (1995). The relationship between individualism-collectivism and job satisfaction. *Applied Psychology: An International Review*, 44, 276–282.

Humphrey, S. E., Moon, H., Conlon, D. E., & Hofmann, D. A. (2004). Decision-making and behavior fluidity: How focus on completion and emphasis on safety changes over the course of projects. *Organizational Behavior and Human Decision Processes*, 93, 14–27.

Hunter, J. E., & Hunter, R. F. (1984). Validity and utility of alternative predictors of job performance. *Psychological Bulletin*, 96, 72–98.

Hunter, J. E., & Schmidt, F. L. (1990). Methods of meta-analysis: Correcting error and bias in research findings. Newbury Park, CA: Sage.

Hurtz, G. M. & Donovan, J. J. (2000). Personality and job performance: The big five revisited. *Journal of Applied Psychology*, 85, 869–879.

Iaffaldano, M. T., & Muchinsky, P. M. (1985). Job satisfaction and job performance: A meta-analysis. *Psychological Bulletin*, 97, 251–273.

Ilgen, D. R., Barnes-Farrell, J. L., & McKellin, D. B. (1993). Performance appraisal process research in the 1980's: What has it contributed to appraisals in use? *Organizational Behavior and Human Decision Processes*, 54, 321–368.

Ilies, R., Hauserman, N., Schwochau, S., & Stibal, J. (2003). Reported incidence rates of work-related sexual harassment in the United States: Using meta-analysis to explain reported rate disparities. *Personnel Psychology*, 56, 607–631.

Inness, M., Barling, J., & Turner, N. (2005). Understanding supervisor-targeted aggression:

A within-person, between-jobs design. *Journal of Applied Psychology*, 90, 731–739.

Ironson, G. H., Smith, P. C., Brannick, M. T., Gibson, W. M., & Paul, K. B. (1989). Constitution of a Job in General scale: A comparison of global, composite, and specific measures. *Journal of Applied Psychology*, 74, 193–200.

Iverson, R. D., & Deery, S. J. (2001). Understanding the "personalogical" basis of employee withdrawal: The influence of affective disposition on employee tardiness, early departure, and absenteeism. *Journal of Applied Psychology*, 86, 856–866.

Iverson, R. D., & Roy, P. (1994). A causal model of behavioral commitment: Evidence from a study of Australian blue-collar employees. *Journal of Management*, 20, 15–41.

Jackson, C. J., Furnham, A., & Willen, K. (2000). Employer willingness to comply with the Disability Discrimination Act regarding staff selection in the UK. *Journal of Occupational and Organizational Psychology*, 73, 119–129.

Jackson, C. L., Colquitt, J. A., Wesson, M. J., & Zapata-Phelan, C. P. (2006). Psychological collectivism: A measurement validation and linkage to group member performance. *Journal of Applied Psychology*, 91, 884–899.

Jackson, C. L., & LePine, J. A. (2003). Peer responses to a team's weakest link: A test and extension of LePine and Van Dyne's model. *Journal of Applied Psychology*, 88, 459–475.

Jackson, S. E., & Joshi, A. (2004). Diversity in social context: A multi-attribute, multilevel analysis of team diversity and sales performance. *Journal of Organizational Behavior*, 25, 675–702.

Jackson, S. E., Joshi, A., & Erhardt, N. L. (2003). Recent research on team and organizational diversity: SWOT analysis and implications. *Journal of Management*, 29, 801–830.

Jackson, S. E., & Schuler, R. S. (1985). A meta-analysis and conceptual critique of research on role ambiguity and role conflict in work settings. *Organizational Behavior and Human Decision Processes*, 36, 16–78.

Jacobs, R., & Solomon, T. (1977). Strategies for enhancing the prediction of job performance from job satisfaction. *Journal of Applied Psychology*, 62, 417–421.

Jaffee, D. T. (1995). The healthy company: Research paradigms for personal and organizational health. In S. L. Sauter & L. R. Murphy (Eds.), *Organizational risk factors for job stress* (pp. 13–39). Washington, DC: American Psychological Association.

Jago, A. G., & Ragan, J. W. (1986). The trouble with Leader Match is that it doesn't match Fiedler's contingency model. *Journal of Applied Psychology*, 71, 555–559.

Jamal, M. (1990). Relationship of job stress and type-A behavior to employees' job satisfaction, organizational commitment, psychosomatic health problems, and turnover motivation. *Human Relations*, 43, 727–738.

Janis, I. L. (1972). *Victims of groupthink*. Boston, MA: Houghton Mifflin.

Jaramillo, F., Locander, W. B., Spector, P. E., & Harris, E. G. (2007). Getting the job done: The moderating role of initiative on the relationship between intrinsic motivation and adaptive selling. *Journal of Personal Selling and Sales Management*, 27, 59–74.

Jeanneret, P. R., & Strong, M. H. (2003). Linking O*NET job analysis information to job requirement predictors: An O*NET application. *Personnel Psychology*, 56, 465–492.

Jelley, R. B., & Goffin, R. D. (2001). Can performance-feedback accuracy be improved? Effects of rater priming and rating-scale format on rating accuracy. *Journal of Applied Psychology*, 86, 134–144.

Jex, S. M., & Beehr, T. A. (1991). Emerging theoretical and methodological issues in the study of work-related stress. *Research in Personnel and Human Resources Management*, 9, 311–365.

Jex, S. M., & Bliese, P. D. (1999). Efficacy beliefs as a moderator of the impact of work-related stressors: A multilevel study. *Journal of Applied Psychology*, 84, 349–361.

Jex, S. M., Bliese, P. D., Buzzell, S., & Primeau, J. (2001). The impact of self-efficacy on stressor-strain relations: Coping style as an explanatory mechanism. *Journal of Applied Psychology*, 86, 401–409.

Jex, S. M., & Gudanowski, D. M. (1992). Efficacy beliefs and work stress: An exploratory study. *Journal of Organizational Behavior*, 13, 509–517.

Johansson, G. (1981). Psychoneuroendocrine correlates of unpaced and paced performance. In G. Salvendy & M. J. Smith (Eds.), *Machine pacing and occupational stress* (pp. 277–286). London: Taylor & Francis.

Johansson, G. (1989). Stress, autonomy, and the maintenance of skill in supervisory control of automated systems. *Applied Psychology: An International Review*, 33, 45–56.

Johnson, J. W. (2001). The relative importance of task and contextual performance dimensions to supervisor judgments of overall performance. *Journal of Applied Psychology*, 86, 984–996.

Johnson, R. E., & Chang, C. H. (2006). "I" is to continuance as "We" is to affective: The relevance of the self-concept for organizational commitment. *Journal of Organizational Behavior*, 27, 549–570.

Joyce, L. W., Thayer, P. W., & Pond, S. B., III. (1994). Managerial functions: An alternative to traditional assessment center dimensions? *Personnel Psychology*, 47, 109–121.

Judge, T. A., Higgins, C. A., & Cable, D. M. (2000). The employment interview: A review of recent research and recommendations for future research. *Human Resources Management Review*, 10, 383–406.

Judge, T. A., & Piccolo, R. F. (2004). Transformational and transactional leadership: A meta-analytic test of their relative validity. *Journal of Applied Psychology*, 89, 755–768.

Judge, T. A., Thoresen, C. J., Bono, J. E., & Patton, G. K. (2001). The job satisfaction-job performance relationship: A qualitative and quantitative review. *Psychological Bulletin*, 127, 376–407.

Kacmar, K. M., & Carlson, D. S. (1997). Further validation of the perceptions of politics scale (POPS): A multiple sample investigation. *Journal of Management*, 23, 627–658.

Kacmar, K. M., Witt, L. A., Zivnuska, S., & Gully, S. M. (2003). The interactive effect of leader-member exchange and communication frequency on performance ratings. *Journal of Applied Psychology*, 88, 764–772.

Kahn, J. H., Schneider, K. T., Jenkins-Henkelman, T. M., & Moyle, L. L. (2006). Emotional social support and job burnout among high-school teachers: Is it all due to dispositional affectivity? *Journal of Organizational Behavior*, 27, 793–807.

Kalton, G. (1983). *Introduction to survey sampling* (Sage University Paper series on Quantitative Application in the Social Sciences, 07–035). Newbury Park, CA: Sage.

Kaminski, M. (2001). Unintended consequences: Organizational practices and their impact on workplace safety and productivity. *Journal of Occupational Health Psychology*, 6, 127–138.

Kane, J. S., & Bernardin, H. J. (1982). Behavioral observation scales and the evaluation of performance appraisal effectiveness. *Personnel Psychology*, 35, 635–641.

Kanfer, R. (1992). Work motivation: New directions in theory and research. In C. L. Cooper & I. T. Robertson (Eds.), *International review of industrial and organizational psychology 1992* (pp. 1–53). Chichester, UK: John Wiley.

Karasek, R. A., Jr. (1979). Job demands, job decision latitude, and mental strain: Implications for job redesign. *Administrative Science Quarterly*, 24, 285–307.

Karasek, R. A., Jr., Gardell, B., & Lindell, J. (1987). Work and non-work correlates of illness and behaviour in male and female Swedish white collar workers. *Journal of Occupational Behavior*, 8, 187–207.

Karl, K. A., O'Leary-Kelly, A. M., & Martocchio, J. J. (1993). The impact of feedback and self-efficacy on performance in training. *Journal of Organizational Behavior*, 14, 379–394.

Katz, D., & Kahn, R. L. (1978). *The social psychology of organizations* (2nd ed.). New York: John Wiley.

Katzell, R. A., & Austin, J. T. (1992). From then to now: The development of industrial-organizational psychology in the United States. *Journal of Applied Psychology*, 77, 803–835.

Keenan, A., & Newton, T. J. (1985). Stressful events, stressors and psychological strains in young professional engineers. *Journal of Occupational Behavior*, 6, 151–156.

Keenan, T. (1995). Graduate recruitment in Britain: a survey of selection methods used by organizations. *Journal of Organizational Behavior*, 16, 303–317.

Keller, R. T. (1989). A test of the path-goal theory of leadership with need for clarity as a moderator in research and development organizations. *Journal of Applied Psychology*, 74, 208–212.

Keller, R. T. (1997). Job involvement and organizational commitment as longitudinal predictors of job performance: A study of scientists and engineers. *Journal of Applied Psychology*, 82, 539–545.

Keller, R. T. (2006). Transformational leadership, initiating structure, and substitutes for leadership: A longitudinal study of research and development project team performance. *Journal of Applied Psychology*, 91, 202–210.

Kelloway, E. K., Mullen, J., & Francis, L. (2006). Divergent effects of transformational and passive leadership on employee safety. *Journal of Occupational Health Psychology*, 11, 76–86.

Khanna, C., & Medsker, G. J. (2007). 2006 income and employment survey results for the Society for Industrial and Organizational Psychology. *The Industrial-Organizational Psychologist*, 45(1), 17–32.

Kiefer, T. (2005). Feeling bad: Antecedents and consequences of negative emotions in ongoing change. *Journal of Organizational Behavior*, 26, 875–897.

Kirkman, B. L., & Mathieu, J. E. (2005). The dimensions and antecedents of team virtuality. *Journal of Management*, 31, 700–718.

Kirkpatrick, D. L. (1977). Evaluating training programs: Evidence versus proof. *Training and Development Journal*, 31, 9–12.

Klein, H. J. (1989). An integrated control theory model of work motivation. *Academy of Management Review*, 14, 150–172.

Klein, K. J., Conn, A. B., & Sorra, J. S. (2001). Implementing computerized technology: An organizational analysis. *Journal of Applied Psychology*, 86, 811–824.

Klein, H. J., & Kim, J. S. (1998). A field study of the influence of situational constraints, leader-member exchange, and goal commitment on performance. *Academy of Management Journal*, 41, 88–95.

Klein, H, J., Wesson, M. J., Hollenbeck, J. R., & Alge, B. J. (1999). Goal commitment and the goal-setting process: Conceptual clarification and empirical synthesis. *Journal of Applied Psychology*, 84, 885–896.

Kleinmann, M., & Strauss, B. (1998). Validity and application of computer-simulated scenarios in personnel assessment. *International Journal of Selection and Assessment*, 6, 97–106.

Kogan, N., & Wallach, M. A. (1964). *Risk taking: A study in cognition and personality*. New York: Holt, Rinehart & Winston.

Kohler, S. S., & Mathieu, J. E. (1993). Individual characteristics, work perceptions, and affective reactions: Influences on differentiated absence criteria. *Journal of Organizational Behavior*, 14, 515–530.

Koller, M., Kundi, M., & Cervinka, R. (1978). Field studies of shift work at an Austrian oil refinery: Vol. I. Health and psychosocial wellbeing of workers who drop out of shiftwork. *Ergonomics*, 21, 835–847.

Kompier, M. A. J., Aust, B., van den Berg, A., & Siegrist, J. (2000). Stress prevention in bus drivers: Evaluation of 13 natural experiments. *Journal of Occupational Health Psychology*, 5, 11–31.

Konradt, U., Schmook, R., & Mälecke, M. (2000). Impacts of telework on individuals, organizations and families: A critical review. In C. L. Cooper & I. T. Robertson (Eds.), *International review of industrial and organizational psychology 2000* (pp. 63–99). Chichester, UK: John Wiley.

Koppes, L. L. (1997). American female pioneers of industrial and organizational psychology during the early years. *Journal of Applied Psychology*, 82, 500–515.

Korsgaard, M. A., & Roberson, L. (1995). Procedural justice in performance evaluation: The role of instrumental and non-instrumental voice in performance appraisal discussions. *Journal of Management*, 21, 657–669.

Koslowsky, M. (2000). A new perspective on employee lateness. *Applied Psychology: An International Review*, 49, 390–407.

Koslowsky, M., Sagie, A., Krausz, M., & Singer, A. D. (1997). Correlates of employee lateness: Some theoretical considerations. *Journal of Applied Psychology*, 82, 79–88.

Kossek, E. E., & Ozeki, C. (1998). Work-family conflict, policies, and the job-life satisfaction relationship: A review and directions for organizational behavior-human resources research. *Journal of Applied Psychology*, 83, 139–149.

Koys, D. J. (2001). The effects of employee satisfaction, organizational citizenship behavior, and turnover on organizational effectiveness: A unit-level, longitudinal study. *Personnel Psychology*, 54, 101–114.

Kozlowski, S. W. J., & Bell, B. S. (2006). Disentangling achievement orientation and goal setting: Effects on self-regulatory processes. *Journal of Applied Psychology*, 91, 900–916.

Kozlowski, S. W. J., Chao, G. T., Smith, E. M., & Hedlund, J. (1993). Organizational downsizing: Strategies, interventions, and research implications. In C. L. Cooper & I. T. Robertson (Eds.), *International review of industrial and organizational psychology, 1993* (pp. 263–332). Chichester, UK: John Wiley.

Kravitz, D. A., Harrison, D. A., Turner, M. E., Levine, E. L., Chaves, W., Brannick, M. T., Denning, D. L., Russell, C. J., & Conard, M. A. (1997). *Affirmative action: A review of psychological and behavior research*. Bowling Green, OH: The Society for Industrial & Organizational Psychology.

Kravitz, D. A., & Klineberg, S. L. (2000). Reactions to two versions of affirmative action among whites, blacks, and Hispanics. *Journal of Applied Psychology*, 85, 597–611.

Kravitz, D. A., & Martin, B. (1986). Ringelmann rediscovered: The original article. *Journal of Personality and Social Psychology*, 50, 936–941.

Kristof, A. L. (1996). Person-organization fit: An integrative review of its conceptualizations, measurement, and implications. *Personnel Psychology*, 49, 1–49.

Kuhl, J., & Beckmann, J. (Eds.). (1994). Volition and personality: Action versus state orientation. Seattle, WA: Hogrefe & Huber.

Lamm, H., & Myers, D. G. (1978). Group-induced polarization of attitudes and behavior. In L. Berkowitz (Ed.), *Advances in experimental and social psychology*, 11 (pp. 145–195), New York: Academic Press.

Lance, C. E., Foster, M. R., Gentry, W. A., & Thoresen, J. D. (2004). Assessor cognitive processes in an operational assessment center. *Journal of Applied Psychology*, 89, 22–35.

Lance, C. E., Lambert, T. A., Gewin, A. G., Lievens, F., & Conway, J. M. (2004). Revised estimates of dimension and exercise variance components in assessment center postexercise dimension ratings. *Journal of Applied Psychology*, 89, 377–385.

Lance, C. E., LaPointe, J. A., & Stewart, A. M. (1994). A test of the context dependency of three causal models of halo rater error. *Journal of Applied Psychology*, 79, 332–340.

Lance, C. E., Lautenschlager, G. J., Sloan, C. E., & Varca, P. E. (1989). A comparison between bottom-up, top-down, and bidirectional models of relationships between global and life facet satisfaction. *Journal of Personality*, 57, 601–624.

Landy, F. J. (1997). Early influences on the development of industrial and organizational psychology. *Journal of Applied Psychology*, 82, 467–477.

Landy, F. J. (2005). Some historical and scientific issues related to research on emotional intelligence. *Journal of Organizational Behavior*, 26, 411–424.

Landy, F. J., Farr, J. L., & Jacobs, R. R. (1982). Utility concepts in performance measurement. *Organizational Behavior and Human Performance*, 30, 15–40.

Langan-Fox, J. (1998). Women's careers and occupational stress. In C. L. Cooper & I. T. Robertson (Eds.), *International review of industrial and organizational psychology 1998* (pp. 273–304). Chichester, UK: John Wiley.

Langfred, C. W. (2005). Autonomy and performance in teams: The multilevel moderating effect of task interdependence. *Journal of Management*, 31, 513–529.

Lapierre, L. M., Spector, P. E., & Leck, J. D. (2005). Sexual versus non-sexual workplace aggression and victims' overall job satisfaction: A meta-analysis. *Journal of Occupational Health Psychology*, 10, 155–169.

Larson, L. M., Rottinghaus, P. J., & Borgen, F. H. (2001). Meta-analyses of Big Six interests and Big Five personality factors. *Journal of Vocational Behavior*, 61, 217–239.

Latané, B., Williams, K., & Harkins, S. (1979). Many hands make light the work: The causes and consequences of social loafing. *Journal of Personality and Social Psychology*, 37, 822–832.

Latham, G. P. (1986). Job performance and appraisal. In C. L. Cooper & I. T. Robertson (Eds.), *International review of industrial and organizational psychology 1986* (pp. 117–155). Chichester, UK: John Wiley.

Latham, G. P., Skarlicki, D., Irvine, D., & Siegel, J. P. (1993). The increasing importance of performance appraisals to employee effectiveness in organizational settings in North America. In C. L. Cooper & I. T. Robertson (Eds.), *International review of industrial and organizational psychology 1993* (pp. 87–132). Chichester, UK: John Wiley.

Latham, G. P., & Wexley, K. N. (1977). Behavioral observation scales for performance appraisal purposes. *Personnel Psychology*, 30, 255–268.

Laughlin, P. R., Bonner, B. L., & Miner, A. G. (2002). Groups perform better than the best individuals on letters-to-numbers problems. *Organizational Behavior and Human Decision Processes*, 88, 605–620.

LeBlanc, M. M., & Kelloway, E. K. (2002). Predictors and outcomes of workplace violence and aggression. *Journal of Applied Psychology*, 87, 444–453.

Leck, J. D., Saunders, D. M., & Charbonneau, M. (1996). Affirmative action programs: an organizational justice perspective. *Journal of Organizational Behavior*, 17, 79–89.

Lee, K., & Allen, N. J. (2002). Organizational citizenship behavior and workplace deviance: The role of affect and cognitions. *Journal of Applied Psychology*, 87, 131–142.

Lee, K., Carswell, J. J., & Allen, N. J. (2000). A meta-analytic review of occupational commitment: Relations with person- and work-related variables. *Journal of Applied Psychology*, 85, 799–811.

Lefkowitz, J. (2000). The role of interpersonal affective regard in supervisory performance ratings: A literature review and proposed causal model. *Journal of Occupational and Organizational Psychology*, 73, 67–85.

Levenson, A. R., Van der Stede, W. A., & Cohen, S. G. (2006). Measuring the relationship between managerial competencies and performance. *Journal of Management*, 32, 360–380.

Levine, E. L., Ash, R. A., Hall, H., & Sistrunk, F. (1983). Evaluation of job analysis methods by experienced job analysts. *Academy of Management Journal*, 26, 339–348.

Levine, E. L., & Baker, D. P. (1987). Job analysis of deputy sheriff in the Pinellas County Sheriff's Office. Unpublished paper, University of South Florida, Tampa.

Liao, H., Joshi, A., & Chuang, A. (2004). Sticking out like a sore thumb: Employee dissimilarity and deviance at work. *Personnel Psychology*, 57, 969–1000.

Liden, R. C., Wayne, S. J., Jaworski, R. A., & Bennett, N. (2004). Social loafing: A field investigation. *Journal of Management*, 30, 285–304.

Lievens, F. (2001). Assessor training strategies and their effects on accuracy, interrater reliability, and discriminant validity. *Journal of Applied Psychology*, 86, 255–264.

Lievens, F., Chasteen, C. S., Day, E. A., & Christiansen, N. D. (2006). Large-scale investigation of the role of trait activation theory for understanding assessment center convergent and discriminant validity. *Journal of Applied Psychology*, 91, 247–258.

Lievens, F. & Klimoski, R. J. (2001). Understanding the assessment centre process: Where are we now? In C. L. Cooper & I. T. Robertson (Eds.), *International Review of Industrial and Organizational Psychology 2001* (pp. 245–286). Chichester, UK: John Wiley.

Lievens, F., & Sackett, P. R. (2006). Video-based versus written situational judgment tests: A comparison in terms of predictive validity. *Journal of Applied Psychology*, 91, 1181–1188.

Lim, B. C., & Klein, K. J. (2006). Team mental models and team performance: A field study of the effects of team mental model similarity and accuracy. *Journal of Organizational Behavior*, 27, 403–418.

Lim, B. C., & Ployhart, R. E. (2004). Transformational leadership: Relations to the five-factor model and team performance in typical and maximum contexts. *Journal of Applied Psychology*, 89, 610–621.

Lim, S., & Cortina, L. M. (2005). Interpersonal mistreatment in the workplace: The interface and impact of general incivility and sexual harassment. *Journal of Applied Psychology*, 90, 483–496.

Lindell, M. K., Clause, C. S., Brandt, C. J., & Landis, R. S. (1998). Relationship between organizational context and job analysis task ratings. *Journal of Applied Psychology*, 83, 769–776.

Liu, C., Spector, P. E., & Jex, S. (2005). The relation of job control with job strains: A comparison of multiple data sources. *Journal of Occupational and Organizational Psychology*, 78, 325–336.

Liu, C., Spector, P. E., & Shi, L. (2007). Cross-national job stress: A quantitative and qualitative study. *Journal of Organizational Behavior*, 28, 209–239.

Locke, E. A. (1980). Latham versus Komaki: A tale of two paradigms. *Journal of Applied Psychology*, 65, 16–23.

Locke, E. A. (2000). Motivation, cognition, and action: An analysis of studies of task goals and knowledge. *Applied Psychology: An International Review*, 49, 408–429.

Locke, E. A., & Henne, D. (1986). Work motivation theories. In C. L. Cooper & I. T. Robertson (Eds.), *International review of industrial and organizational psychology 1986* (pp. 1–35). Chichester, UK: John Wiley.

Locke, E. A., & Latham G. P. (1990). A theory of goal setting & task performance. Englewood Cliffs, NJ: Prentice Hall.

Loher, B. T., Noe, R. A., Moeller, N. L., & Fitzgerald, M. P. (1985). A meta-analysis of the relation of job characteristics to job satisfaction. *Journal of Applied Psychology*, 70, 280–289.

Lord, R. G., Binning, J. F., Rush, M. C., & Thomas, J. C. (1978). The effect of performance cues and leader behavior on questionnaire ratings of leadership behavior. *Organizational Behavior and Human Performance*, 21, 27–39.

Lord, R. G., & Maher, K. J. (1989). Cognitive processes in industrial and organizational psychology. In C. L. Cooper & I. T. Robertson (Eds.), *International review of industrial and organizational psychology 1989* (pp. 49–91). Chichester, UK: John Wiley.

Lowin, A., & Craig, J. R. (1968). The influence of level of performance on managerial style: An experimental object-lesson in the ambiguity of correlational data. *Organizational Behavior and Human Performance*, 3, 440–458.

Ludwig, T. D., & Geller, E. S. (1997). Assigned versus participative goal setting and response generalization: Managing injury control among professional pizza deliverers. *Journal of Applied Psychology*, 82, 253–261.

Luthar, H. K., & Pastille, C. (2000). Modeling subordinate perceptions of sexual harassment: The role of superior-subordinate social-sexual interaction. *Human Resources Management Review*, 10, 211–244.

Lyness, K. S., & Thompson, D. E. (1997). Above the glass ceiling? A comparison of matched samples of female and male executives. *Journal of Applied Psychology*, 82, 359–375.

Lyness, K. S., & Thompson, D. E. (2000). Climbing the corporate ladder: Do female and male executives follow the same route? *Journal of Applied Psychology*, 85, 86–101.

Machin, M. A., & Fogarty, G. (2003). Perceptions of training-related factors and personal variables as predictors of transfer implementation intentions. *Journal of Business and Psychology*, 18, 51–71.

Mack, D. A., Nelson, D. L., & Quick, J. C. (1998). *Applied Psychology: An International Review*, 47, 219–232.

MacKenzie, S. B., Podsakoff, P. M., & Fetter, R. (1991). Organizational citizenship behavior and objective productivity as determinants of managerial evaluations of salespersons' performance. *Organizational Behavior and Human Decision Processes*, 50, 123–150.

Maertz, C. P., Jr., & Griffeth, R. W. (2004). Eight motivational forces and voluntary turnover: A theoretical synthesis with implications for research. *Journal of Management*, 30, 667–683.

Majchrzak, A., & Borys, B. (1998). *Computer-aided technology and work: Moving the field forward*. In C. L. Cooper & I. T. Robertson (Eds.), *International review of industrial and organizational psychology 1998* (pp. 305–354). Chichester, UK: John Wiley.

Major, V. S., Klein, K. J., & Ehrhart, M. G. (2002). Work time, work interference with family, and psychological distress. *Journal of Applied Psychology*, 87, 427–436.

Man, D. C., & Lam, S. S. K. (2003). The effects of job complexity and autonomy on cohesiveness in collectivistic and individualistic work groups: A cross-cultural analysis. *Journal of Organizational Behavior*, 24, 979–1001.

Mannix, E., & Neale, M. A. (2005). What differences make a difference? The promise and reality of diverse teams in organizations. *Psychological Science in the Public Interest*, 6, 31–55.

Marcus, B. (2003). Attitudes towards personnel selection methods: A partial replication and extension in a German sample. *Applied Psychology: An International Review*, 52, 515–532.

Marion-Landais, C. A. (1993). A cross-cultural study of leader-member exchange quality and job satisfaction as correlates of intra-dyadic work-value congruence. Unpublished master's thesis, University of South Florida, Tampa.

Marks, M. L., Mirvis, P. H., Hackett, E. J., & Grady, J. F., Jr. (1986). Employee participation in a quality circle program: Impact on quality of work life, productivity, and absenteeism. *Journal of Applied Psychology*, 71, 61–69.

Martins, L. L., Gilson, L. L., & Maynard, M. T. (2004). Virtual teams: What do we know and where do we go from here? *Journal of Management*, 30, 805–835.

Maslach, C., & Jackson, S. (1981). *The Maslach Burnout Inventory*. Palo Alto, CA: Consulting Psychologists.

Maslow, A. H. (1943). A theory of human motivation. *Psychological Review*, 50, 370–396.

Mastrangelo, P. M., & Popovich, P. M. (2000). Employees' attitudes toward drug testing, perceptions of organizational climate, and withdrawal from the employer. *Journal of Business and Psychology*, 15, 3–18.

Mathieu, J. E., & Kohler, S. S. (1990). A cross-level examination of group absence influences on individual absence. *Journal of Applied Psychology*, 75, 217–220.

Mathieu, J. E., Martineau, J. W., & Tannenbaum, S. I. (1993). Individual and situational influences on the development of self-efficacy: Implications for training effectiveness. *Personnel Psychology*, 46, 125–147.

Maurer, T. J., Mitchell, D. R. D., & Barbeite, F. G. (2002). Predictors of attitudes toward a 360 degree feedback system and involvement in post-feedback management development activity. *Journal of Occupational and Organizational Psychology*, 75, 87–107.

Maurer, T. J., Solamon, J. M., Andrews, K. D., & Troxtel, D. D. (2001). Interviewee coaching, preparation strategies, and response strategies in relation to performance in situational employment interviews: An extension of Maurer, Solamon, and Troxtel (1998). *Journal of Applied Psychology*, 86, 709–717.

May, G. L., & Kahnweiler, W. M. (2000). The effect of a mastery practice design on learning and transfer in behavior modeling training. *Personnel Psychology*, 53, 353–373.

Mayer, R. C., & Davis, J. H. (1999). The effect of the performance appraisal system on trust for management: A field quasi-experiment. *Journal of Applied Psychology*, 84, 123–136.

McBride, J. R. (1998). *Innovations in computer-based ability testing: Promise, problems, and perils*. In M. D. Hakel (Ed.), *Beyond multiple choice: Evaluating alternatives to traditional testing for selection*. (pp. 23–39). Mahway, NJ: Lawrence Erlbaum Associates.

McCormick, E. J., Jeanneret, P. R., & Mecham, R. C. (1972). A study of job characteristics and job dimensions as based on the position analysis questionnaire (PAQ). *Journal of Applied Psychology*, 56, 347–368.

McCulloch, S. (1993). Recent trends in international assessment. *International Journal of Selection and Assessment*, 1, 59–61.

McFarland, L. A., Ryan, A. M., Sacco, J. M., & Kriska, S. D. (2004). Examination of structured interview ratings across time: The effects of applicant race, rater race, and panel composition. *Journal of Management*, 30, 435–452.

McGlynn, R. P., McGurk, D., Effland, V. S., Johll, N. L., & Harding, D. J. (2004). Brainstorming and task performance in groups constrained by evidence. *Organizational Behavior and Human Decision Processes*, 93, 75–87.

McGregor, D. M. (1960). *The human side of enterprise*. New York: McGraw-Hill.

McIntire, S. A., & Levine, E. L. (1991). Combining personality variables and goals to predict performance. *Journal of Vocational Behavior*, 38, 288–301.

McKay, P. F., & McDaniel, M. A. (2006). A reexamination of black-white mean differences in work performance: More data, more moderators. *Journal of Applied Psychology*, 91, 338–354.

McMahan, G. C., & Woodman, R. W. (1992). The current practice of organization development within the firm. *Group and Organization Management*, 17, 117–134.

McManus, M. A., & Ferguson, M. W. (2003). Biodata, personality, and demographic differences of recruits from three sources. *International Journal of Selection and Assessment*, 11, 175–183.

McManus, M. A., & Kelly, M. L. (1999). Personality measures and biodata: Evidence regarding their incremental predictive value in the life insurance industry. *Personnel Psychology*, 52, 137–148.

McNeely, B. L., & Meglino, B. M. (1994). The role of dispositional and situational antecedents in prosocial organizational behavior: An examination of the intended beneficiaries of prosocial behavior. *Journal of Applied Psychology*, 79, 836–844.

Meglino, B. M., DeNisi, A. S., & Ravlin, E. C. (1993). Effects of previous job exposure and subsequent job status on the functioning of a realistic job preview. *Personnel Psychology*, 46, 803–822.

Meglino, B. M., Ravlin, E. C., & DeNisi, A. S. (2000). A meta-analytic examination of realistic job preview effectiveness: A test of three counterintuitive propositions. *Human Resources Management Review*, 10, 407–434.

Melamed, S., Ben-Avi, I., Luz, J., & Green, M. S. (1995). Objective and subjective work monotony: Effects on job satisfaction, psychological distress, and absenteeism in blue-collar workers. *Journal of Applied Psychology*, 80, 29–42.

Melamed, S., Fried, Y., & Froom, P. (2001). The interactive effect of chronic exposure to noise and job complexity on changes in blood pressure and job satisfaction: A longitudinal study of industrial employees. *Journal of Occupational Health Psychology*, 6, 182–195.

Melamed, S., Shirom, A., Toker, S., Berliner, S., & Shapira, I. (2006). Burnout and risk of cardiovascular disease: Evidence, possible causal paths, and promising research directions. *Psychological Bulletin*, 132, 327–353.

Merchant, J. A., & Lundell, J. A. (2001). *Workplace violence: A report to the nation*. University of Iowa: Iowa City.

Meyer, J. P., Allen, N. J., & Smith, C. A. (1993). Commitment to organizations and occupations: Extension and test of a three-component conceptualization. *Journal of Applied Psychology*, 78, 538–551.

Meyer, J. P., Bobocel, D. R., & Allen, N. J. (1991). Development of organizational commitment during the first year of employment: A longitudinal study of pre- and post-entry influences. *Journal of Management*, 17, 717–733.

Meyer, J. P., Stanley, D. J., Herscovitch, L., & Topolnytsky, L. (2002). Affective, continuance, and normative commitment to the organization: A meta-analysis of antecedents, correlates, and consequences. *Journal of Vocational Behavior*, 61, 20–52.

Mitchell, K. K., Alliger, G. M., & Morfopoulos, R. (1997). Toward an ADA-appropriate job analysis. *Human Resource Management Review*, 7, 5–26.

Mitra, A., Jenkins, G. D., Jr., & Gupta, N. (1992). A meta-analytic review of the relationship between absence and turnover. *Journal of Applied Psychology*, 77, 879–889.

Mohammed, S., & Angell, L. C. (2004). Surface- and deep-level diversity in workgroups: Examining the moderating effects of team orientation and team process on relationship conflict. *Journal of Organizational Behavior*, 25, 1015–1039.

Mohammad, S., & Dumville, B. C. (2001). Team mental models in a team knowledge framework: Expanding theory and measurement across disciplinary boundaries. *Journal of Organizational Behavior*, 22, 89–106.

Moorhead, G., Ference, R., & Neck, C. P. (1991). Group decision fiascoes continue: Space shuttle Challenger and a revised groupthink framework. *Human Relations*, 44, 539–550.

Morgeson, F. P., & Campion, M. A. (1997). Social and cognitive sources of potential inaccuracy in job analysis. *Journal of Applied Psychology*, 82, 627–655.

Morgeson, F. P., Campion, M. A., & Maertz, C. P. (2001). Understanding pay satisfaction: The limits of a compensation system implementation. *Journal of Business and Psychology*, 16, 133–149.

Morgeson, F. P., Delaney-Klinger, K., Ferrara, P., Mayfield, M. S., & Campion, M. A. (2004). Self-presentation processes in job analysis: A field experiment investigating inflation in abilities, tasks, and competencies. *Journal of Applied Psychology*, 89, 674–686.

Morgeson, F. P., Reider, M. H., & Campion, M. A. (2005). Selecting individuals in team settings: The importance of social skills, personality characteristics, and teamwork knowledge. *Personnel Psychology*, 58, 583–611.

Morin, L., & Latham, G. P. (2000). The effect of mental practice and goal setting as a transfer of training intervention on supervisors' self-efficacy and communication skills: An exploratory study. *Applied Psychology: An International Review*, 49, 566–578.

Morrow, C. C., Jarrett, M. Q., & Rupinski, M. T. (1997). An investigation of the effect and economic utility of corporate-wide training. *Personnel Psychology*, 50, 91–119.

Moscoso, S., & Salgado, J. F. (2004). Fairness reactions to personnel selection techniques in Spain and Portugal. *International Journal of Selection and Assessment*, 12, 187–196.

Moser, K. (2005). Recruitment sources and post-hire outcomes: The mediating role of unmet expectations. *International Journal of Selection and Assessment*, 13, 188–197.

Mount, M., Ilies, R., & Johnson, E. (2006). Relationship of personality traits and counterproductive work behaviors: The mediating effects of job satisfaction. *Personnel Psychology*, 59, 591–622.

Mount, M. K., Witt, L. A., & Barrick, M. R. (2000). Incremental validity of empirically keyed biodata scales over GMA and the five factor personality constructs. *Personnel Psychology*, 53, 299–323.

Mowday, R. T., Steers, R. M., & Porter, L. W. (1979). The measurement of organizational commitment. *Journal of Vocational Behavior*, 14, 224–247.

Moyle, P., & Parkes, K. (1999). The effects of transition stress: A relocation study. *Journal of Organizational Behavior*, 20, 625–646.

Mueller-Hanson, R., Heggestad, E. D., & Thornton, G. C., III. (2003). Faking and selection: Considering the use of personality from select-in and select-out perspectives. *Journal of Applied Psychology*, 88, 348–355.

Mullarkey, S., Jackson, P. R., Wall, T. D., Wilson, J. R., & Grey-Taylor, S. M. (1997). The impact of technology characteristics and job control on worker mental health. *Journal of Organizational Behavior*, 18, 471–489.

Mumford, M. D. (1999). Construct validity and background data: Issues, abuses, and future directions. *Human Resources Management Review*, 9, 117–145.

Munene, J. C. (1995). 'Not-on-seat': An investigation of some correlates of organisational citizenship behaviour in Nigeria. *Applied Psychology: An International Review*, 44, 111–122.

Münsterberg, H. (1913). *Psychology and industrial efficiency*. Boston: Houghton Mifflin.

Murphy, K. R. (1988). Psychological measurement: Abilities and skills. In C. L. Cooper & I. T. Robertson (Eds.), *International review of industrial and organizational psychology 1988* (pp. 213–244). Chichester, UK: John Wiley.

Murphy, K. R. (2000). Impact of assessments of validity generalization and situational specificity on the science and practice of personnel selection. *International Journal of Selection and Assessment*, 8, 194–206.

Murphy, K. R., Cronin, B. E., & Tam, A. P. (2003). Controversy and consensus regarding the use of cognitive ability testing in organizations. *Journal of Applied Psychology*, 88, 660–671.

Murphy, K. R., Gannett, B. A., Herr, B. M., & Chen, J. A. (1986). Effects of subsequent performance on evaluations of previous performance. *Journal of Applied Psychology*, 71, 427–431.

Murphy, K. R., Jako, R. A., & Anhalt, R. L. (1993). Nature and consequences of halo error: A critical analysis. *Journal of Applied Psychology*, 78, 218–225.

Murphy, L., Gershon, R. M., & DeJoy, D. (1996). *Stress and occupational exposure to HIV/AIDS*. In C. L. Cooper (Ed.), *Handbook of stress, medicine, and health*. (pp. 177–190). Boca Raton, FL: CRC Press.

Narayanan, L., Menon, S., & Spector, P. E. (1999). A cross-cultural comparison of job stressors and reactions among employees holding comparable jobs in two countries. *International Journal of Stress Management*, 6, 197–212.

Nathan, B. R., & Lord, R. G. (1983). Cognitive categorization and dimensional schemata: A process approach to the study of halo in performance ratings. *Journal of Applied Psychology*, 68, 102–114.

Nathan, B. R., & Tippins, N. (1990). The consequences of halo "error" in performance ratings: A field study of the moderating effect of halo on test validation results. *Journal of Applied Psychology*, 75, 290–296.

National Institute of Occupational Safety and Health (1997). Violence in the workplace, [Online] Available: www.cdc.gov/niosh/violfs.html.

National Safety Council (1992a). *Sound sense*. Itasca, IL: Author.

National Safety Council. (1992b). *Blood pathogens*. Itasca, IL: Author.

National Safety Council (2005–2006). *Injury Facts, 2005–2006 edition*. Itasca, IL: Author.

Neal, A., & Griffin, M. A. (2006). A study of the lagged relationships among safety climate, safety motivation, safety behavior, and accidents at the individual and group levels. *Journal of Applied Psychology*, 91, 946–953.

Neuman, G. A., Edwards, J. E., & Raju, N. S. (1989). Organizational development interventions: A meta-analysis of their effects on satisfaction and other attitudes. *Personnel Psychology*, 42, 461–483.

Neuman, J. H., & Baron, R. A. (1997). Aggression in the workplace. In R. A. Giacalone, & J. Greenberg (Eds.), *Antisocial behavior in organizations* (pp. 37–67). Newbury Park, CA: Sage.

Newell, S., & Tansley, C. (2001). International uses of selection methods. In C. L. Cooper & I. T. Robertson (Eds.), *International review of industrial and organizational psychology 2001* (pp. 195–213). Chichester, UK: John Wiley.

Newton, T., & Keenan, T. (1991). Further analyses of the dispositional argument in organizational behavior. *Journal of Applied Psychology*, 76, 781–787.

Ng, T. W. H., Butts, M. M., Vandenberg, R. J., DeJoy, D. M., & Wilson, M. G. (2006). Effects of management communication, opportunity for learning, and work schedule flexibility on organizational commitment. *Journal of Vocational Behavior*, 68, 474–489.

Nicholson, N., & Johns, G. (1985). The absence culture and the psychological contract: who's in control of absence? *Academy of Management Review*, 10, 397–407.

Nielson, T. R., Carlson, D. S., & Lankau, M. J. (2001). The supportive mentor as a means of reducing work-family conflict. *Journal of Vocational Behavior*, 59, 364–381.

Noe, R. A., & Schmitt, N. (1986). The influence of trainee attitudes on training effectiveness: Test of a model. *Personnel Psychology*, 39, 497–523.

Northhouse, P. G. (2004). *Leadership theory and practice* (3rd ed.). Thousand Oaks, CA: Sage.

O'Connell, C. E., & Korabik, K. (2000). Sexual harassment: The relationship of personal vulnerability, work context, perpetrator status, and type of harassment to outcomes. *Journal of Vocational Behavior*, 56, 299–329.

O'Connor, E. J., Peters, L. H., Rudolf, C. J., & Pooyan, A. (1982). Situational constraints and employee affective reactions: A partial field replication. *Group & Organization Studies*, 7, 418–428.

O'Driscoll, M. P., & Beehr, T. A. (1994). Supervisor behaviors, role stressors and uncertainty as predictors of personal outcomes for subordinates. *Journal of Organizational Behavior*, 15, 141–155.

Oldham, G. R., Cummings, A., Mischel, L. J., Schmidtke, J. M., & Zhou, J. (1995). Listen while you work? Quasi-experimental relations between personal-stereo headset use and employee work responses. *Journal of Applied Psychology*, 80, 547–564.

Ones, D. S., & Anderson, N. (2002). Gender and ethnic group differences on personality scales in selection: Some British data. *Journal of Occupational and Organizational Psychology*, 75, 255–276.

Ones, D. S., & Viswesvaran, C. (1998). Gender, age, and race differences on overt integrity tests: Results across four large-scale job applicant data sets. *Journal of Applied Psychology*, 83, 35–42.

Ones, D. S., & Viswesvaran, C., & Schmidt, F. L. (1993). Comprehensive meta-analysis of integrity test validities: Findings and implications for personnel selection and theories of job performance. *Journal of Applied Psychology*, 78, 679–703.

Organ, D. W., & Konovsky, M. (1989). Cognitive versus affective determinants of organizational citizenship behavior. *Journal of Applied Psychology*, 74, 157–164.

Osborn, A. F. (1957). *Applied imagination* (Rev. ed.). New York: Scribner.

Osgood, C. E., Tannenbaum, P. H., & Suci, G. J. (1957). *The measurement of meaning*. Urbana: University of Illinois Press.

Ouchi, W. G. (1981). *Theory Z*. New York: Avon.

Palliser, C. R., Firth, H. M., Feyer, A. M., & Paulin, S. M. (2005). Musculoskeletal discomfort and work-related stress in New Zealand dentists. *Work & Stress*, 19, 351–359.

Parasuraman, S., & Purohit, Y. S. (2000). Distress and boredom among orchestra musicians: The two faces of stress. *Journal of Occupational Health Psychology*, 5, 74–83.

Parker, C. P., Baltes, B. B., & Christiansen, N. D. (1997). Support for affirmative action, justice perceptions, and work attitudes: A study of gender and racial-ethnic group differences. *Journal of Applied Psychology*, 82, 376–389.

Paronto, M. E., Truxillo, D. M., Bauer, T. N., & Leo, M. C. (2002). Drug testing, drug treatment, and marijuana use: A fairness perspective. *Journal of Applied Psychology*, 87, 1159–1166.

Pasmore, W., Francis, C., Haldeman, J., & Shani, A. (1982). Sociotechnical systems: A North American reflection on empirical studies of the seventies. *Human Relations*, 12, 1179–1204.

Paulus, P. B. (2000). Groups, teams, and creativity: The creative potential of idea-generating groups. *Applied Psychology: An International Review*, 49, 237–262.

Paunonen, S. V., Rothstein, M. G., & Jackson, D. N. (1999). Narrow reasoning about the use of broad personality measures for personnel selection. *Journal of Organizational Behavior*, 20, 389–405.

Pearce, J. A., II, & Ravlin, E. C. (1987). The design and activation of self-regulating work groups. *Human Relations*, 40, 751–782.

Pearlman, I., Schmidt, F. L., & Hunter, J. E. (1980). Validity generalization results for tests used to predict job proficiency and training success in clerical occupations. *Journal of Applied Psychology*, 65, 373–406.

Pearn, M. A. (1989). *Fairness in employment selection: A comparison of UK and USA experience*. In

M. Smith & I. T. Robertson (Eds.), *Advances in selection and assessment* (pp. 155–163). Chichester, UK: John Wiley.

Pearson, C. A. L., & Chong, J. (1997). Contributions of job content and social information on organizational commitment and job satisfaction: An exploration in a Malaysian nursing context. *Journal of Occupational and Organizational Psychology*, 70, 357–374.

Pedalino, E., & Gamboa, V. U. (1974). Behavior modification and absenteeism: Intervention in one industrial setting. *Journal of Applied Psychology*, 59, 694–698.

Penfield, R. D. (2006). Applying Bayesian item selection approaches to adaptive tests using polytomous items. *Applied Measurement in Education*, 19, 1–20.

Penney, L. M., & Spector, P. E. (2005). Job stress, incivility, and counterproductive work behavior (CWB): The moderating role of negative affectivity. *Journal of Organizational Behavior*, 26, 777–796.

Pervin, L. A. (1993). *Personality: Theory and research* (6th ed.). New York: John Wiley.

Peters, L. H., Hartke, D. D., & Pohlmann, J. T. (1985). Fiedler's contingency theory of leadership: An application of the meta-analysis procedures of Schmidt and Hunter. *Psychological Bulletin*, 97, 274–285.

Peters, L. H., & O'Connor, E. J. (1980). Situational constraints and work outcomes: The influences of a frequently overlooked construct. *Academy of Management Review*, 5, 391–397.

Peterson, N. G., Mumford, M. D., Borman, W. C., Jeanneret, P. R., Fleishman, E. A., Levin, K. Y., Campion, M. A., Mayfield, M. S., Morgeson, F. P., Pearlman, K., Gowing, M. K., Lancaster, A. R., Silver, M. B., & Dye, D. M. (2001). Understanding work using the Occupational Information Network (O*NET): Implications for practice and research. *Personnel Psychology*, 54, 451–492.

Petrides, K. V., & Furnham, A. (2000). On the dimensional structure of emotional intelligence. *Personality and Individual Differences*, 29, 313–320.

Phillips, J. S., & Lord, R. G. (1982). Schematic information processing and perceptions of leadership in problem-solving groups. *Journal of Applied Psychology*, 67, 486–492.

Pierce, J. L., & Dunham, R. B. (1992). The 12–hour work day: A 48–hour, eight-day week. *Academy of Management Journal*, 35, 1086–1098.

Pillai, R., Schriesheim, C. A., & Williams, E. S. (1999). Fairness perceptions and trust as mediators for transformational and transactional leadership: A two-sample study. *Journal of Management*, 25, 897–933.

Podsakoff, P. M., Ahearne, M., & MacKenzie, S. B. (1997). Organizational citizenship behavior and the quantity and quality of work group performance. *Journal of Applied Psychology*, 82, 262–270.

Podsakoff, P. M., MacKenzie, S. B., Ahearne, M., & Bommer, W. H. (1995). Searching for a needle in a haystack: Trying to identify the illusive moderators of leadership behaviors. *Journal of Management*, 21, 422–470.

Podsakoff, P. M., MacKenzie, S. B., Paine, J. B., & Bachrach, D. G. (2000). Organizational citizenship behaviors: A critical review of the theoretical and empirical literature and suggestions for future research. *Journal of Management*, 26, 513–563.

Porath, C. L., & Bateman, T. S. (2006). Self-regulation: From goal orientation to job performance. *Journal of Applied Psychology*, 91, 185–192.

Potosky, D., & Bobko, P. (2004). Selection testing via the internet: Practical considerations and exploratory empirical findings. *Personnel Psychology*, 57, 1003–1034.

Powell, G. N., & Butterfield, D. A. (1994). Investigating the "glass ceiling" phenomenon: An empirical study of actual promotions to top management. *Academy of Management Journal*, 37, 68–86.

Powell, G. N., & Butterfield, D. A. (2002). Exploring the influence of decision makers' race and gender on actual promotions to top management. *Personnel Psychology*, 55, 397–428

Powell, G. N., Butterfield, D. A., & Parent, J. D. (2002). Gender and managerial stereotypes: Have the times changed? *Journal of Management*, 28, 177–193.

Premack, S. L., & Wanous, J. P. (1985). A meta-analysis of realistic job preview experiments. *Journal of Applied Psychology*, 70, 706–719.

Prewett-Livingston, A. J., Feild, H. S., Veres, J. G., III, & Lewis, P. M. (1996). Effects of race on interview ratings in a situational panel interview. *Journal of Applied Psychology*, 81, 178–186.

Probst, T. M. (2004). Safety and insecurity: Exploring the moderating effect of organizational safety climate. *Journal of Occupational Health Psychology*, 9, 3–10.

Raabe, B., & Beehr, T. A. (2003). Formal mentoring versus supervisor and coworker relationships: Differences in perceptions and impact. *Journal of Organizational Behavior*, 24, 271–293.

Rafferty, A. E., & Griffin, M. A. (2006). Perceptions of organizational change: A stress and coping perspective. *Journal of Applied Psychology*, 91, 1154–1162.

Raggatt, P. T. (1991). Work stress among long-distance coach drivers: A survey and correlational study. *Journal of Organizational Behavior*, 12, 565–579.

Rain, J. S., Lane, I. M., & Steiner, D. D. (1991). A current look at the job satisfaction/life satisfaction relationship: Review and future considerations. *Human Relations*, 44, 287–305.

Raju, N. S., Burke, M. J., & Normand, J. (1990). A new approach for utility analysis. *Journal of Applied Psychology*, 75, 3–12.

Ralston, D. A. (1989). The benefits of flextime: Real or imagined? *Journal of Organizational Behavior*, 10, 369–373.

Randle, C. W. (1956). How to identify promotable executives. *Harvard Business Review*, 34, 122–134.

Rayner, C., & Keashly, L. (In press). Bullying at work: A perspective from Britain and North America. In S. Fox & P. E. Spector (Eds.), *Counterproductive work behavior: Investigations of actors and targets*. Washington, DC: APA Press.

Ree, M. J., & Carretta, T. R. (1998). General cognitive ability and occupational performance. In C. L. Cooper & I. T. Robertson (Eds.), *International review of industrial and organizational psychology 1998* (pp. 159–184). Chichester, UK: John Wiley.

Reilly, R. R., & Israelski, E. W. (1988). Development and validation of minicourses in the telecommunication industry. *Journal of Applied Psychology*, 73, 721–726.

Reilly, R. R., Henry, S., & Smither, J. W. (1990). An examination of the effects of using behavior checklists on the construct validity of assessment center dimensions. *Personnel Psychology*, 43, 71–84.

Rentsch, J. R., & Klimoski, R. J. (2001). Why do 'great minds' think alike?: Antecedents of team member schema agreement. *Journal of Organizational Behavior*, 22, 107–120.

Rice, R. W., Phillips, S. M., & McFarlin, D. B. (1990). Multiple discrepancies and pay satisfaction. *Journal of Applied Psychology*, 75, 386–393.

Richman, W. L., Kiesler, S., Weisband, S., & Drasgow, F. (1999). A meta-analytic study of social desirability distortion in computer-administered questionnaires, traditional questionnaires, and interviews. *Journal of Applied Psychology*, 84, 754–775.

Rickett, B., Orbell, S., & Sheeran, P. (2006). Social-cognitive determinants of hoist usage among health care workers. *Journal of Occupational Health Psychology*, 11, 182–196.

Rischall, J. (2001, March 1). Integrated approach to the knowledge worker. Paper presented at Electronic Human Resources 2001 conference, Tampa, FL.

Robbins, T. L., & DeNisi, A. S. (1994). A closer look at interpersonal affect as a distinct influence on cognitive processing in performance evaluations. *Journal of Applied Psychology*, 79, 341–353.

Robert, C., Probst, T. M., Martocchio, J. J., Drasgow, F., & Lawler, J. J. (2000). Empowerment and continuous improvement in the United States, Mexico, Poland, and India: Predicting fit on the basis of the dimensions of power distance and individualism. *Journal of Applied Psychology*, 85, 643–658.

Robertson, I. T., & Downs, S. (1989). Work-sample tests of trainability: A meta-analysis. *Journal of Applied Psychology*, 74, 402–410.

Robertson, I. T., & Kandola, R. S. (1982). Work sample tests: Validity, adverse impact and applicant reaction. *Journal of Occupational Psychology*, 55, 171–183.

Robinson, D. D., Wahlstrom, O. W., & Mecham, R. C. (1974). Comparison of job evaluation methods: A "policy-capturing" approach using the position analysis questionnaire. *Journal of Applied Psychology*, 59, 633–637.

Rodgers, R., & Hunter, J. E. (1991). Impact of management by objectives on organizational productivity. *Journal of Applied Psychology*, 76, 322–336.

Roethlisberger, F. J. (1941). *Management and morale*. Cambridge, MA: Harvard University Press.

Roethlisberger, F. J., & Dickson, W. J. (1939). *Management and the worker*. Cambridge, MA: Harvard University Press.

Rohrer, D., Taylor, K., Pashler, H., Wixted, J. T., & Cepeda, N. J. (2005). The effect of overlearning on long-term retention. *Applied Cognitive Psychology*, 19, 361–374.

Rosenthal, R. (1991). *Meta-analytic procedures for social research* (Rev. ed.). Newbury Park, CA: Sage.

Rospenda, K. M., Richman, J. A., & Shannon, C. A. (2006). Patterns of workplace harassment, gender, and use of services: An update. *Journal of Occupational Health Psychology*, 11, 379–393.

Roth, P. E., & Campion, J. E. (1992). An analysis of the predictive power of the panel interview and pre-employment tests. *Journal of Occupational and Organizational Psychology*, 65, 51–60.

Roth, P. L., Bobko, P., & Switzer, F. S. III (2006). Modeling the behavior of the 4/5ths rule for determining adverse impact: Reasons for caution. *Journal of Applied Psychology*, 91, 507–522.

Rowson, A. (1998). Using 369 degree feedback instruments up, down and around the world: Implications for global implementation and use of multi-rater feedback. *International Journal of Selection and Assessment*, 6, 45–48.

Russell, C. J., Colella, A., & Bobko, P. (1993). Expanding the context of utility: The strategic impact of personnel selection. *Personnel Psychology*, 46, 781–801.

Russell, C. J., & Domm, D. R. (1995). Two field tests of an explanation of assessment centre validity. *Journal of Occupational and Organizational Psychology*, 68, 25–47.

Ryan, A. M., McFarland, L., Baron, H., & Page, R. (1999). An international look at selection practices: Nation and culture as explanations for variability in practice. *Personnel Psychology*, 52, 359–391.

Saari, L. M., Johnson, T. R., McLaughlin, S. D., & Zimmerle, D. M. (1988). A survey of management training and education in U.S. companies. *Personnel Psychology*, 41, 731–743.

Sagie, A., & Koslowsky, M. (1994). Organizational attitudes and behaviors as a function of participation in strategic and tactical change decisions: An application of path-goal theory. *Journal of Organizational Behavior*, 15, 37–47.

Salgado, J. F. (2003). Predicting job performance using FFM and non-FFM personality measures. *Journal of Occupational and Organizational Psychology*, 76, 323–346.

Salovey, P., & Mayer, J. D. (1990). Emotional intelligence. *Imagination, Cognition and Personality*, 9, 185–211.

Sanchez, J. I. (2000). Adapting work analysis to a fast-paced and electronic business world. *International Journal of Selection and Assessment*, 8, 207–215.

Sanchez, J. I., & Fraser, S. L. (1992). On the choice of scales for task analysis. *Journal of Applied Psychology*, 77, 545–553.

Sanchez, J. I., & Levine, E. L. (1994). The impact of raters' cognition on judgment accuracy: An extension to the job analysis domain. *Journal of Business and Psychology*, 9, 47–57.

Sanchez, J. I., & Levine, E. L. (2000). Accuracy or consequential validity: Which is the better standard for job analysis data? *Journal of Organizational Behavior*, 21, 809–818.

Sarafino, E. P. (1990). *Health psychology: Biopsychosocial interactions*. New York: John Wiley.

Sauter, S. L., Lim, S. Y., & Murphy, L. R. (1996). Organizational health: A new paradigm for occupational stress research at NIOSH. *Japanese Journal of Occupational Mental Health*, 4, 248–254.

Savery, L. K., & Wooden, M. (1994). The relative influence of life events and hassles on work-related injuries: Some Australian evidence. *Human Relations*, 47, 283–305.

Scandura, T. A., & Lankau, M. J. (1997). Relationships of gender, family responsibility and flexible work hours to organizational commitment and job satisfaction. *Journal of Organizational Behavior*, 18, 377–391.

Scandura, T. A., Von Glinow, M. A., & Lowe, K. B. (1999). When East meets West: Leadership "best practices" in the United States and the Middle East. In W. H. Mobley, M. J. Gessner, & V. Arnold (Eds.), *Advances in global leadership*, Vol. 1 (pp. 235–238). Stamford, CT: JAI.

Schaubroeck, J., & Jones, J. R. (2000). Antecedents of workplace emotional labor dimensions and moderators of their effects on physical symptoms. *Journal of Organizational Behavior*, 21, 163–183.

Schaubroeck, J., & Kuehn, K. (1992). Research design in industrial and organizational psychology. In C. L. Cooper & I. T. Robertson (Eds.), *International review of industrial and organizational psychology 1992* (pp. 99–121). Chichester, UK: John Wiley.

Schein, V. E., Mueller, R., Lituchy, T., & Liu, J. (1996). Think manager--think male: A global phenomenon? *Journal of Organizational Behavior*, 17, 33–41.

Schippers, M. C., Den Hartog, D. N., Koopman, P. L., & Wienk, J. A. (2003). Diversity and team outcomes: The moderating effects of outcome interdependence and group longevity and the mediating effect of reflexivity. *Journal of Organizational Behavior*, 24, 779–802.

Schippmann, J. S., Ash, R. A., Battista, M., Carr, L., Eyde, L. D., Hesketh, B., Kehoe, J., Pearlman, K., Prien, E. P., & Sanchez, J. I. (2000). The practice of competency modeling. *Personnel Psychology*, 53, 703–740.

Schleicher, D. J., Watt, J. D., & Greguras, G. J. (2004). Reexamining the job satisfaction-performance relationship: The complexity of attitudes. *Journal of Applied Psychology*, 89, 165–177.

Schmidt, F. L., & Hunter, J. E. (1977). Development of a general solution to the problem of validity generalization. *Journal of Applied Psychology*, 62, 529–540.

Schmidt, F. L., Hunter, J. E., McKenzie, R. C., & Muldrow, T. W. (1979). Impact of valid selection procedures on work-force productivity. *Journal of Applied Psychology*, 64, 609–626.

Schmidt, F. L., Mack, M. J., & Hunter, J. E. (1984). Selection utility in the occupation of U.S. park ranger for three modes of test use. *Journal of Applied Psychology*, 69, 490–497.

Schmidt, F. L., & Rader, M. (1999). Exploring the boundary conditions for interview validity: Meta-analytic validity findings for a new interview type. *Personnel Psychology*, 52, 445–464.

Schmidt, F. L., & Zimmerman, R. D. (2004). A counterintuitive hypothesis about employment interview validity and some supporting evidence. *Journal of Applied Psychology*, 89, 553–561.

Schmit, M. J., Ryan, A. M., Stierwalt, S. L., & Powell, A. B. (1995). Frame-of-reference effects on personality scale scores and criterion-related validity. *Journal of Applied Psychology*, 80, 607–620.

Schmitt, N., & Chan, D. (1998). *Personnel selection: A theoretical approach*. Thousand Oaks, CA: Sage.

Schmitt, N., Gilliland, S. W., Landis, R. S., & Devine, D. (1993). Computer-based testing applied to selection of secretarial applicants. *Personnel Psychology*, 46, 149–165.

Schmitt, N., Gooding, R. Z., Noe, R. A., & Kirsch, M. (1984). Meta-analyses of validity studies published between 1964 & 1982 and the investigation of study characteristics. *Personnel Psychology*, 37, 407–422.

Schmitt, N., & Oswald, F. L. (2006). The impact of corrections for faking on the validity of noncognitive measures in selection settings. *Journal of Applied Psychology*, 91, 613–621.

Schneider, K. T., Hitlan, R. T., & Radhakrishnan, P. (2000). An examination of the nature and correlates of ethnic harassment experiences in multiple contexts. *Journal of Applied Psychology*, 85, 3–12.

Schneider, K. T., Swan, S., & Fitzgerald, L. F. (1997). Job-related and psychological effects of sexual harassment in the workplace: Empirical evidence from two organizations. *Journal of Applied Psychology*, 82, 401–415.

Schriesheim, C. A., Powers, K. J., Scandura, T. A., Gardiner, C. C., & Lankau, M. J. (1993). Improving construct measurement in management research: Comments and quantitative approach for assessing the theoretical content adequacy of paper-and-pencil survey-type instruments. *Journal of Management*, 19, 385–417.

Schriesheim, J. F. (1980). The social context of leader-subordinate relations: An investigation of the effects of group cohesiveness. *Journal of Applied Psychology*, 65, 183–194.

Schwab, D. P., & Grams, R. (1985). Sex-related errors in job evaluation: A "real-world" test. *Journal of Applied Psychology*, 70, 533–539.

Scott, W. D. (1903). *The theory of advertising*. Boston: Small, Maynard.

Shackleton, V., & Newell, S. (1991). Management selection: A comparative survey of methods used in top British and French companies. *Journal of Occupational Psychology*, 64, 23–36.

Shechtman, Z. (1992). A group assessment procedure as a predictor of on-the-job performance of teachers. *Journal of Applied Psychology*, 77, 383–387.

Shields, M. (2006). Unhappy on the job. *Health Reports*, 17, 33–37.

Shirom, A. (1989). *Burnout in work organizations*. In C. L. Cooper & I. T. Robertson (Eds.), *International Review of industrial and organizational psychology 1989* (pp. 25–48). Chichester, UK: John Wiley.

SHRM (2003). SHRM/CNN*fn* job satisfaction survey says more employees satisfied with benefits at large organizations versus small. [On-line]. Available: www.shrm.org/press_published/CMS_006538.asp [2004. March 18]

Simon, S. J., & Werner, J. M. (1996). Computer training through behavior modeling, self-paced, and instructional approaches: A field experiment. *Journal of Applied Psychology*, 81, 648–659.

Sinclair, R. C. (1988). Mood, categorization breadth, and performance appraisal: The effects of order of information acquisition and affective state on halo, accuracy, information retrieval, and evaluations. *Organizational Behavior and Human Decision Processes*, 42, 22–46.

Sitzmann, T., Kraiger, K., Stewart, D., & Wisher, R. (2006). The comparative effectiveness of Web-based and classroom instruction: A meta-analysis. *Personnel Psychology*, 59, 623–664.

Siu, O., Lu, L., & Cooper, C. L. (1999). Managerial stress in Hong Kong and Taiwan: A comparative study. *Journal of Managerial Psychology*, 14, 6–25.

Slaughter, J. E., Sinar, E. F., & Bachiochi, P. D. (2002). Black applicants' reactions to affirmative action plans: Effects of plan content and previous experience with discrimination. *Journal of Applied Psychology*, 87, 333–344.

Smith, C. A., Organ, D. W., & Near, P. J. (1983). Organizational citizenship behavior: Its nature and antecedents. *Journal of Applied Psychology*, 68, 653–663.

Smith, J. E., & Hakel, M. D. (1979). Convergence among data sources, response bias, and reliability and validity of a structured job analysis questionnaire. *Personnel Psychology*, 32, 677–692.

Smith, M. J., Hurrell, J. J., Jr., & Murphy, R. K., Jr. (1981). Stress and health effects in paced and unpaced work. In G. Salvendy & M. J. Smith (Eds.), *Machine pacing and occupational stress* (pp. 261–267). London: Taylor & Francis.

Smith, P. C., & Kendall, L. M. (1963). Retranslation of expectations: An approach to the construction of unambiguous anchors for rating scales. *Journal of Applied Psychology*, 47, 149–155.

Smith, P. C., Kendall, L. M., & Hulin, C. L. (1969). *Measurement of satisfaction in work and retirement*. Chicago: Rand-McNally.

Smither, J. W., London, M., Flautt, R., Vargas, Y., & Kucine, I. (2003). Can working with an executive coach improve multisource feedback ratings over time? A quasi-experimental field study. *Personnel Psychology*, 56, 23–44.

Smith-Jentsch, K. A., Mathieu, J. E., & Kraiger, K. (2005). Investigating linear and interactive effects of shared mental models on safety and efficiency in a field setting. 90, 523–535.

Society for Industrial and Organizational Psychology. (1985). *Guidelines for education and training at the doctoral level in industrial/organizational psychology*. College Park: University of Maryland.

Solomonson, A. L., & Lance, C. E. (1997). Examination of the relationship between true halo and halo error in performance ratings. *Journal of Applied Psychology*, 82, 665–674.

Somech, A. (2006). The effects of leadership style and team process on performance and innovation in functionally heterogeneous teams. *Journal of Management*, 32, 132–157.

Somers, M. J., & Birnbaum, D. (2001). Racial differences in work attitudes: What you see depends on what you study. *Journal of Business and Psychology*, 15, 579–591.

Sonnentag, S. (1998). Expertise in professional software design: A process study. *Journal of Applied Psychology*, 83, 703–715.

Sparks, K., Cooper, C., Fried, Y., & Shirom, A. (1997). The effects of hours of work on health: A meta-analytic review. *Journal of Occupational and Organizational Psychology*, 70, 391–408.

Spector, P. E. (1982). Behavior in organizations as a function of employees' locus of control. *Psychological Bulletin*, 91, 482–497.

Spector, P. E. (1985). Measurement of human service staff satisfaction: Development of the Job Satisfaction Survey. *American Journal of Community Psychology*, 13, 693–713.

Spector, P. E. (1986). Perceived control by employees: A meta-analysis of studies concerning autonomy and participation at work. *Human Relations*, 11, 1005–1016.

Spector, P. E. (1992). *A consideration of the validity and meaning of self-report measures of job conditions*. In C. L. Cooper & I. T. Robertson (Eds.), *International review of industrial and organizational psychology 1992* (pp. 123–151). Chichester, UK: John Wiley.

Spector, P. E., Brannick, M. T., & Coovert, M. D. (1989). Job analysis. In C. L. Cooper & I. T. Robertson (Eds.), *International review of industrial and organizational psychology 1989* (pp. 281–328). Chichester, UK: John Wiley.

Spector, P. E., Cooper, C. L., Sanchez, J. I., O'Driscoll, M., Sparks, K., Bernin, P., Büssing, A., Dewe, P.,

Hart, P., Lu, L., Miller, K., Renault de Moraes, L., Ostrognay, G. M., Pagon, M., Pitariu, H., Poelmans, S., Radhakrishnan, P., Russinova, V., Salamatov, V., Salgado, J, Shima, S., Siu, O. L., Stora, J. B., Teichmann, M., Theorell, T., Vlerick, P., Westman, M., Widerszal-Bazyl, M., Wong, P., & Yu, S. (2001). Do national levels of individualism and internal locus of control relate to well-being? An ecological level international study. *Journal of Organizational Behavior*, 22, 815–832.

Spector, P. E., Dwyer, D. J., & Jex, S. M. (1988). Relation of job stressors to affective, health, and performance outcomes: A comparison of multiple data sources. *Journal of Applied Psychology*, 73, 11–19.

Spector, P. E., Fox, S., Penney, L. M., Bruursema, K., Goh, A., & Kessler, S. (2006). The dimensionality of counterproductivity: Are all counterproductive behaviors created equal? *Journal of Vocational Behavior*, 68, 446–460.

Spector, P. E., & Jex, S. M. (1991). Relations of job characteristics from multiple data sources with employee affect, absence, turnover intentions, and health. *Journal of Applied Psychology*, 76, 46–53.

Spector, P. E., & Jex, S. M. (1998). Development of four self-report measures of job stressors and strain: Interpersonal Conflict at Work Scale, Organizational Constraints Scale, Quantitative Workload Inventory, and Physical Symptoms Inventory. *Journal of Occupational Health Psychology*, 3, 356–367.

Spielberger, C. D., (1996). *State-Trait Anger Expression Inventory, research edition: Professional manual*. Odessa, FL: Psychological Assessment Resources.

Spychalski, A. C., Quiñones, M. A., Gaugler, B. B., & Pohley, K. (1997). A survey of assessment center practices in organizations in the United States. *Personnel Psychology*, 50, 71–90.

Stajkovic, A. D., & Luthans, F. (2003). Behavioral management and task performance in organizations: Conceptual background, meta-analysis, and test of alternative models. *Personnel Psychology*, 56, 155–194.

Stauffer, J. M., & Buckley, M. R. (2005). The existence and nature of racial bias in supervisory ratings. *Journal of Applied Psychology*, 90, 586–591.

Staw, B. M., Bell, N. E., & Clausen, J. A. (1986). The dispositional approach to job attitudes: A lifetime longitudinal test. *Administrative Science Quarterly*, 31, 56–77.

Staw, B. M., & Cohen-Charash, Y. (2005). The dispositional approach to job satisfaction: More than a mirage, but not yet an oasis. *Journal of Organizational Behavior*, 26, 59–78.

Steiner, D. D., & Gilliland, S. W. (1996). Fairness reactions to personnel selection techniques in France and the United States. *Journal of Applied Psychology*, 81, 134–141.

Stevens, M. J., & Campion, M. A. (1999). Staffing work teams: Development and validation of a selection test for teamwork settings. *Journal of Management*, 25, 207–228.

Stewart, G. L. (2006). A meta-analytic review of relationships between team design features and team performance. *Journal of Management*, 32, 29–54.

Stogdill, R. M. (1963). *Manual for the Leader Behavior Description Questionnaire—Form XII*. Columbus: Ohio State University.

Stokes, G. S., & Reddy, S. (1992). Use of background data in organizational decisions. In C. L. Cooper & I. T. Robertson (Eds.), *International review of industrial and organizational psychology 1992* (pp. 285–321). Chichester, UK: John Wiley.

Stokes, G. S., & Searcy, C. A. (1999). Specification of scales in biodata form development: Rational vs. empirical and global vs. specific. *International Journal of Selection and Assessment*, 7, 72–85.

Stokes, G. S., Toth, C. S., Searcy, C. A., Stroupe, J. P., & Carter, G. W. (1999). Construct/rational biodata dimensions to predict salesperson performance: Report of the U.S. Department of Labor study. *Human Resources Management Review*, 9, 185–218.

Storms, P. L., & Spector, P. E. (1987). Relationships of organizational frustration with reported behavioural reactions: The moderating effect of locus of control. *Journal of Occupational Psychology*, 60, 227–234.

Straus, S. G., Miles, J. A., & Levesque, L. L. (2001). The effects of videoconference, telephone, and face-to-face media on interviewer and applicant judgments in employment interviews. *Journal of Management*, 27, 363–381.

Strauss, A., & Corbin, J. (1990). *Basics of qualitative research*. Newbury Park, CA: Sage.

Strube, M. J., & Garcia, J. E. (1981). A meta-analytic investigation of Fiedler's contingency model of leadership effectiveness. *Psychology Bulletin*, 90, 307–321.

Sturman, M. C. (2003). Searching for the inverted U-shaped relationship between time and performance: Meta-analyses of the experience/performance, tenure/performance, and age/performance relationships. *Journal of Management*, 29, 609–640.

Sundvik, L., & Lindeman, M. (1998). Performance rating accuracy: Convergence between supervisor assessment and sales productivity. *International Journal of Selection and Assessment*, 6, 9–15.

Sweeney, P. D., & McFarlin, D. B. (1997). Process and outcome: Gender differences in the assessment of justice. *Journal of Organizational Behavior*, 18, 83–98.

Sy, T., Tram, S., & O'Hara, L. A. (2006). Relation of employee and manager emotional intelligence to job satisfaction and performance. *Journal of Vocational Behavior*, 68, 461–473.

Sygnatur, E. F., & Toscano, G. A. (2000). Work-related homicides: The facts. *Compensation and Working Conditions*, Spring, 3–8.

Taylor, F. W. (1911). *Scientific management*. New York: Harper & Row.

Taylor, M. S., Tracy, K. B., Renard, M. K., Harrison, J. K., & Carroll, S. J. (1995). Due process in performance appraisal: A quasi-experiment in procedural justice. *Administrative Science Quarterly*, 40, 495–523.

Taylor, P. J., Russ-Eft, D. F., & Chan, D. W. L. (2005). A meta-analytic review of behavior modeling training. *Journal of Applied Psychology*, 90, 492–709.

Tepper, B. J. (2001). Health consequences of organizational injustice: Tests of main and interactive effects. *Organizational Behavior and Human Decision Processes*, 86, 197–215.

Tesluk, P. E., & Mathieu, J. E. (1999). Overcoming roadblocks to effectiveness: Incorporating management of performance barriers into models of work group effectiveness. *Journal of Applied Psychology*, 84, 200–217.

Tett, R. P., & Burnett, D. D. (2003). A personality trait-based interactionist model of job performance. *Journal of Applied Psychology*, 88, 500–517.

Tett, R. P., & Meyer, J. P. (1993). Job satisfaction, organizational commitment, turnover intention, and turnover: Path analysis based on meta-analytic findings. *Personnel Psychology*, 46, 259–293.

Tett, R. P., Steele, J. R., & Beauregard, R. S. (2003). Broad and narrow measures on both sides of the personality-job performance relationship. *Journal of Organizational Behavior*, 24, 335–356.

Tharenou, P. (1993). A test of reciprocal causality for absenteeism. *Journal of Organizational Behavior*, 14, 269–290.

Thomas, L. T., & Ganster, D. C. (1995). Impact of family-supportive work variables on work-family conflict and strain: A control perspective. *Journal of Applied Psychology*, 80, 6–15.

Thorndike, E. L. (1913). *Educated psychology: The psychology of learning* (Vol. 2). New York: Teachers College Press.

Three die in postal shootings in Michigan, California. (1993, May 7) *The Atlanta Journal/The Atlanta Constitution*.

Timmerman, G., & Bajema, C. (2000). The impact of organizational culture on perceptions and experiences of sexual harassment. *Journal of Vocational Behavior*, 57, 188–205.

Totterdell, P., Spelten, E., Smith, L., Barton, J., & Folkard, S. (1995). Recovery from work shifts: How long does it take? *Journal of Applied Psychology*, 80, 43–57.

Towler, A. J., (2003). Effects of charismatic influence training on attitudes, behavior, and performance. *Personnel Psychology*, 56, 363–381.

Treiman, D. J. (1979). *Job evaluation: An analytical review* (Interim Report to the Equal Employment Commission). Washington, DC: National Academy of Sciences.

Trevor, C. O. (2001). Interactions among actual ease-of-movement determinants and job satisfaction in the prediction of voluntary turnover. *Academy of Management Journal*, 44, 621–638.

Trevor, C. O., Gerhart, B., & Boudreau, J. W. (1997). Voluntary turnover and job performance: Curvilinearity and the moderating influences of salary growth and promotions. *Journal of Applied Psychology*, 82, 44–61.

Triandis, H. C. (2003). The future of workforce diversity in international organisations: A commentary. *Applied Psychology: An International Review*, 52, 486–495.

Triplett, N. (1897). The dynamogenic factors in pacemaking competition. *American Journal of Psychology*, 8, 507–533.

Trist, E. L., & Bamforth, K. W. (1951). Some social and psychological consequences of the longwall method of coal-getting. *Human Relations*, 4, 3–38.

Tubre, T. C., & Collins, J. M. (2000). Jackson and Schuler (1985) revisited: A meta-analysis of the relationships between role ambiguity, role conflict, and job performance. *Journal of Management*, 26, 155–169.

Turban, D. B., & Cable, D. M. (2003). Firm reputation and applicant pool characteristics. *Journal of Organizational Behavior*, 24, 733–751.

U.S. Bureau of Labor Statistics (1998). *Workers on flexible and shift schedules in 1997 summary*, [Online] Available: www.bls.gov/news/release/flex.new.htm [1998, April 8].

U.S. Bureau of Labor Statistics (2006). *News*. USDL 06–1860, Friday, October 27, Author.

U.S. Department of Labor. (1977). *Dictionary of occupational titles* (4th ed.). Washington DC: U.S. Government Printing Office.

U.S. Department of Labor. (1991). *Dictionary of occupational titles* (5th ed.). Washington DC: U.S. Government Printing Office.

U.S. Department of Labor (1998). *O*NET98 Data Dictionary Release 1.0*. Washington DC: U.S. Department of Labor Employment and Training Administration.

Underhill, C. M. (2006). The effectiveness of mentoring programs in corporate settings: A meta-analytical review of the literature. *Journal of Vocational Behavior*, 68, 292–307.

Uniform guidelines on employee selection procedures. (1978, August 25). *Federal Register*, 43, Section 60–3, 38295.

Valacich, J. A., Dennis, A. R., & Nunamaker. J. E., Jr. (1992). Group and anonymity effects on computer-mediated idea generation. *Small Group Research*, 23, 49–73.

Van Breukelen, W., Van Der Vlist, R., & Steensma, H. (2004). Voluntary employee turnover: Combining variables from the "traditional" turnover literature with the theory of planned behavior. *Journal of Organizational Behavior*, 25, 893–914.

Van Daalen, G., Willemsen, T. M., & Sanders, K. (2006). Reducing work-family conflict through different sources of social support. *Journal of Vocational Behavior*, 69, 462–476.

Van De Water, T. J. (1997). Psychology's entrepreneurs and the marketing of industrial psychology. *Journal of Applied Psychology*, 82, 486–499.

Van Der Vegt, G., Emans, B., & Van De Vliert, E. (2000). Team members' affective responses to patterns of intragroup interdependence and job complexity. *Journal of Management*, 26, 633–655.

Van der Vegt, G. S., & Janssen, O. (2003). Joint impact of interdependence and group diversity on innovation. *Journal of Management*, 29, 729–751.

Van Eerde, W. (2000). Procrastination: Self-regulation in initiating aversive goals. *Applied Psychology: An International Review*, 49, 372–389.

Van Eerde, W., & Thierry, H. (1996). Vrooms's expectancy models and work-related criteria: A meta-analysis. *Journal of Applied Psychology*, 81, 575–586.

Van Fleet, D. D., & Griffin, R. W. (1989). Quality circles: A review and suggested future directions. In C. L. Cooper & I. T. Robertson (Eds.), *International review of industrial and organizational psychology 1989* (pp. 213–233). Chichester, UK: John Wiley.

Van Iddekinge, C. H., Eidson, C. E., Jr., Kudisch, J. D., & Goldblatt, A. M. (2003). A biodata inventory administered via interactive voice response (IVR) technology: Predictive validity, utility, and subgroup differences. *Journal of Business and Psychology*, 18, 145–156.

Van Iddekinge, C. H., Taylor, M. A., & Eidson, C. E., Jr. (2005). Broad versus narrow facets of integrity: Predictive validity and subgroup differences. *Human Performance*, 18, 151–177.

Van Rooy, D. L., Alonso, A., & Fairchild, Z. (2003). In with the new, out with the old: Has the technological revolution eliminated the traditional job search process? *International Journal of Selection and Assessment*, 11, 170–174.

Van Rooy, D. L., & Viswesvaran, C. (2004). Emotional intelligence: A meta-analytic investigation of predictive validity and nomological net. *Journal of Vocational Behavior*, 65, 71–95.

Van Vianen, A. E. M., & Fischer, A. H. (2002). Illuminating the glass ceiling: The role of organizational culture preferences. *Journal of Occupational and Organizational Psychology*, 75, 315–337.

Vandenberghe, C., Bentein, K., & Stinglhamber, F. (2004). Affective commitment to the organization, supervisor, and work group: Antecedents and outcomes. *Journal of Vocational Behavior*, 64, 47–71.

Verquer, M. L., Beehr, T. A., & Wagner, S. H. (2003). A meta-analysis of relations between person-organization fit and work attitudes. *Journal of Vocational Behavior*, 63, 473–489.

Vigoda, E. (2002). Stress-related aftermaths to workplace politics: The relationships among politics, job distress, and aggressive behavior in organizations. *Journal of Organizational Behavior*, 23, 571–591.

Vinchur, A. J., Schippmann, J. S., Smalley, M. D., & Rothe, H. F. (1991). Productivity consistency of foundry chippers and grinders: A 6-year study. *Journal of Applied Psychology*, 76, 134–136.

Viswesvaran, C., Ones, D. S., & Schmidt, F. (1996). Comparative analysis of the reliability of job performance ratings. *Journal of Applied Psychology*, 81, 557–574.

Viswesvaran, C., Schmidt, F. L., & Ones, D. S. (2005). Is there a general factor in ratings of job performance? A meta-analytic framework for disentangling substantive and error influences? *Journal of Applied Psychology*, 90, 108–131.

Vroom, V. (1964). *Work and motivation*. New York: John Wiley.

Vroom, V. H., & Jago, A. G. (1988). *The new leadership: Managing participation in organizations*. Englewood Cliffs, NJ: Prentice Hall.

Vroom, V. H., & Yetton, P. W. (1973). *Leadership and decision-making*. Pittsburgh: University of Pittsburgh Press.

Wagner, J. A., III. (1994). Participation's effects on performance and satisfaction: A reconsideration of research evidence. *Academy of Management Review*, 19, 312–330.

Wall, T. D., Corbett, J. M., Martin, R., Clegg, C. W., & Jackson, P. R. (1990). Advanced manufacturing technology, work design, and performance: A change study. *Journal of Applied Psychology*, 6, 691–697.

Wall, T. D., & Davids, K. (1992). *Shopfloor work organization and advanced manufacturing technology*. In C. L. Cooper & I. T. Robertson (Eds.), *International review of industrial and organizational psychology 1992* (pp. 363–398). Chichester, UK: John Wiley.

Wall, T. D., Jackson, P. R., & Davids, K. (1992). Operator work design and robotics system

performance: A serendipitous field study. *Journal of Applied Psychology*, 77, 353–362.

Wall, T. D., Jackson, P. R., Mullarkey, S., & Parker, S. K. (1996). The demands-control model of job strain: A more specific test. *Journal of Occupational and Organizational Psychology*, 69, 153–166.

Wall, T. D., Kemp, N. J., Jackson, P. R., & Clegg, C. W. (1986). Outcomes of autonomous workgroups: A long-term field experiment. *Academy of Management Journal*, 29, 280–304.

Wallace, J. C., Popp, E., & Mondore, S. (2006). Safety climate as a mediator between foundation climates and occupational accidents: A group-level investigation. *Journal of Applied Psychology*, 91, 681–688.

Walsh, B. R., & Clarke, E. (2003). Post-trauma symptoms in health workers following physical and verbal aggression. *Work & Stress*, 17, 170–181.

Walumbwa, F. O., Wang, P., Lawler, J. J., & Shi, K. (2004). The role of collective efficacy in the relations between transformational leadership and work outcomes. *Journal of Occupational and Organizational Psychology*, 77, 515–530.

Wanberg, C. R., & Banas, J. T. (2000). Predictors and outcomes of openness to changes in a reorganizing workplace. *Journal of Applied Psychology*, 85, 132–142.

Wanek, J. E. (1999). Integrity and honesty testing: What do we know? How do we use it? *International Journal of Selection and Assessment*, 7, 183–195.

Wanek, J. E., Sackett, P. R., & Ones, D. S. (2003). Towards an understanding of integrity test similarities and differences: An item-level analysis of seven tests. *Personnel Psychology*, 56, 873–894.

Wanous, J. P. (1989). Installing a realistic job pre-view: Ten tough choices. *Personnel Psychology*, 42, 117–133.

Warr, P. (2001). Age and work behaviour: Physical attributes, cognitive abilities, knowledge, personality traits and motives. In C. L. Cooper & I. T. Robertson (Eds.), *International review of industrial and organizational psychology 2001* (pp. 1–36). Chichester, UK: John Wiley.

Warr, P., & Payne, R. (1983). Affective outcomes of paid employment in a random sample of British workers. *Journal of Occupational Behavior*, 4, 91–104.

Wasti, S. A. (2005). Commitment profiles: Combinations of organizational commitment forms and job outcomes. *Journal of Vocational Behavior*, 67, 290–308.

Wasti, S. A., Bergman, M. E., Glomb, T. M., & Dragsow, F. (2000). Test of the cross-cultural generalizability of a model of sexual harassment. *Journal of Applied Psychology*, 85, 766–778.

Watson, D., Pennebaker, J. W., & Folger, R. (1986). Beyond negative affectivity: Measuring stress and satisfaction in the workplace. *Journal of Organizational Behavior Management*, 8, 141–157.

Wayne, J. H. (2000). Disentangling the power bases of sexual harassment: Comparing gender, age, and position power. *Journal of Vocational Behavior*, 57, 301–325.

Wayne, J. H., Musisca, N., & Fleeson, W. (2004). Considering the role of personality in the work-family experience: Relationships of the Big Five to work-family conflict and facilitation. *Journal of Vocational Behavior*, 64, 108–130.

Wayne, S. J., Shore, L. M., Bommer, W. H., & Tetrick, L. E. (2002). The role of fair treatment and rewards in perceptions of organizational support and leader-member exchange. *Journal of Applied Psychology*, 87, 590–598.

Weber, M. (1947). *The theory of social and economic organization* (A. M. Henderson & T. Parsons, Trans. and Eds.). New York: Oxford University Press.

Weiss, D. J., Dawis, R., Lofquist, L. H., & England, G. W. (1966). *Instrumentation for the theory of work adjustment* (Minnesota Studies in Vocational Rehabilitation: XXI). University of Minnesota, Minneapolis.

Werner, J. M. (1994). Dimensions that make a difference: Examining the impact of in-role and extrarole behaviors on supervisory ratings. *Journal of Applied Psychology*, 79, 98–107.

Werner, J. M., & Bolino, M. C. (1997). Explaining U.S. courts of appeals decisions involving performance appraisal: Accuracy, fairness, and validation. *Personnel Psychology*, 50, 1–24.

West, J., & Karas, M. (1999). Biodata: Meeting clients' needs for a better way of recruiting entry-level staff. *International Journal of Selection and Assessment*, 7, 126–131.

West, M. A., Borrill, C. S., & Unsworth, K. L. (1998). *Team effectiveness in organizations*. In C. L. Cooper & I. T. Robertson (Eds.), *International review of industrial and organizational psychology 1998* (pp. 1–48). Chichester, UK: John Wiley.

Westman, M., & Eden, D. (1997). Effects of a respite from work on burnout: Vacation relief and fade-out. *Journal of Applied Psychology*, 82, 516–527.

Wiesner, W. H., & Cronshaw, S. F. (1988). A meta-analytic investigation of the impact of interview format and degree of structure on the validity of the employment interview. *Journal of Occupational Psychology*, 61, 275–290.

Wilk, S. L., & Cappelli, P. (2003). Understanding the determinants of employer use of selection methods. *Personnel Psychology*, 56, 103–124

Williams, C. R. (1999). Reward contingency, unemployment, and functional turnover. *Human Resources Management Review*, 9, 549–576.

Williams, M. L., McDaniel, M. A., & Nguyen, N. T. (2006). A meta-analysis of the antecedents and consequences of pay level satisfaction. *Journal of Applied Psychology*, 91, 392–413.

Willness, C. R., Steel, P., & Lee, K. (2007). A meta-analysis of the antecedents and consequences of workplace sexual harassment. *Personnel Psychology*, 60, 127–162.

Wilson, M. A., Harvey, R. J., & Macy, B. A. (1990). Repeating items to estimate the test-retest reliability of task inventory ratings. *Journal of Applied Psychology*, 75, 158–163.

Winterton, J. (1994). Social and technological characteristics of coal-face work: A temporal and spatial analysis. *Human Relations*, 47, 89–118.

Witt, L. A., Andrews, M. C., & Carlson, D. S. (2004). When conscientiousness isn't enough: Emotional exhaustion and performance among call center customer service representatives. *Journal of Management*, 30, 149–160.

Witt, L. A., & Nye, L. G. (1992). Gender and the relationship between perceived fairness of pay or promotion and job satisfaction. *Journal of Applied Psychology*, 77, 910–917.

Wofford, J. C., & Liska, L. Z. (1993). Path-goal theories of leadership: A meta-analysis. *Journal of Management*, 19, 857–876.

Wong, C., Hui, C., & Law, K. S. (1998). A longitudinal study of the job perception–job satisfaction relationship: A test of the three alternative specifications. *Journal of Occupational and Organizational Psychology*, 71, 127–146.

Woolley, R. M., & Hakstian, A. R. (1993). A comparative study of integrity tests: The criterion-related validity of personality-based and overt measures of integrity. *International Journal of Selection and Assessment*, 1, 27–40.

Wright, T. A., & Cropanzano, R. (2000). Psychological well-being and job satisfaction as predictors of job performance. *Journal of Occupational Health Psychology*, 5, 84–94.

Yang, H., Schnall, P. L., Jauregui, M., Su, T. C., & Baker, D. (2006). Work hours and self-reported hypertension among working people in California. *Hypertension*, 48, 744–750.

Yearta, S. K., Maitlis, S., & Briner, R. B. (1995). An exploratory study of goal setting in theory and practice: A motivational technique that works? *Journal of Occupational and Organizational Psychology*, 68, 237–252.

Young, A. M., & Perrewé, P. L., (2000). The exchange relationship between mentors and protégés: The development of a framework. *Human Resources Management Review*, 10, 177–209.

Yukl, G. A. (1989). *Leadership in organizations*. Englewood Cliffs, NJ: Prentice Hall.

Yukl, G. A., & Latham, G. P. (1975). Consequences of reinforcement schedules and incentive magnitudes for employee performance: Problems encountered in an industrial setting. *Journal of Applied Psychology*, 60, 294–298.

Yun, G. J., Donahue, L. M., Dudley, N. M., & McFarland, L. A. (2005). Rater personality, rating format, and social context: Implications for performance appraisal ratings. *International Journal of Selection and Assessment*, 13, 97–107.

Zajonc, R. B. (1965). Social facilitation. *Science*, 149, 269–274.

Zapf, D. (2002). Emotion work and psychological well-being: A review of the literature and some conceptual considerations. *Human Resources Management Review*, 12, 237–268.

Zickar, M. J. (2003). Remembering Arthur Kornhauser: Industrial psychology's advocate for worker well-being. *Journal of Applied Psychology*, 88, 363–369.

Zohar, D., & Luria, G. (2005). A multilevel model of safety climate: Cross-level relationships between organization and group-level climates. *Journal of Applied Psychology*, 90, 616–628.

Zottoli, M. A., & Wanous, J. P. (2000). Recruitment source research: Current status and future directions. *Human Resources Management Review*, 10, 353–382.

Glossary

360-degree feedback: A performance-appraisal technique that provides feedback from several perspectives, including peers, subordinates, supervisors, and self.

Ability test: A test designed to assess a person's abilities or aptitudes.

Ability: The capability of developing a skill or learning a task; a person's aptitude for learning.

Achievement test: A psychological test designed to assess a person's level of knowledge or skill; also called a knowledge and skill test.

Action process: From action theory, a series of steps describing the process by which a person translates desire for something to behavior.

Action theory: A motivation theory that links a person's goals to his or her behavior.

Action/state orientation: A personality variable concerning a person's ability to carry out a sequence of activities to accomplish a goal. An action-oriented individual is able to self-regulate behaviors to achieve goals, whereas a state-oriented person has difficulty doing so.

Actual criterion: The way the theoretical criterion is assessed; the operationalization of a construct.

Additive task: A task in which a group's performance is the sum of individual members' performances. For example, total sales for a group of salespeople in a store are the sum of each person's individual sales.

Adverse impact: Unfairness in the treatment of minority group or protected class members. In hiring it occurs if the protected class's selection ratio is less than four-fifths of the nonprotected class's selection ratio.

Affective commitment: Type of organizational commitment in which the person has an emotional attachment to the organization.

Affirmative action: A program designed to increase the number of minority or protected-class members in an organization.

Analysis of variance (ANOVA): A statistical test used to compare group means.

Application form: A form completed by a job applicant; asks for background information.

Apprenticeship: An on-the-job training method. The trainee learns by assisting an experienced employee; most often used to teach a skilled trade, such as carpentry or plumbing.

Arithmetic mean: The sum of scores divided by the number of scores.

Assessment center: A series of assessment exercises, including simulations of work tasks, that are used to assess a person's potential for a job. They are most frequently used to determine an employee's suitability for promotion into a management position.

Audiovisual instruction: A training method that uses pictures and sound to present material.

Autoinstruction: Any self-taught method of training.

Automaticity: A skill or task that is so well learned that a person can do it automatically with little conscious monitoring or thought. Professional athletes achieve this level of task performance.

Autonomy: The extent to which an employee is able to decide how to do his or her job.

Baserate: How often something occurs. In selection it is the proportion of people hired who will be successful on the job.

Behavior criteria: Methods of evaluating training by assessing changes in trainee behavior on the job.

Behavior Observation Scale (BOS): A behavior-based job performance instrument. Raters are given a list of behaviors and indicate how often the ratee performs each one.

Behaviorally Anchored Rating Scale (BARS): A behavior-based job performance instrument. Raters are given several behaviors shown on a scale and are asked to indicate which one is most characteristic of the ratee's performance.

Big Five: The five dimensions considered to represent the major factors of human personality.

Biographical inventory: A selection tool in which the job applicant provides extensive background information.

425

Blended learning: A training course or program that combines an e-learning method with a traditional method of classroom delivery, such as lecture.

Brainstorming: A group method whereby individuals meet to generate solutions to a problem.

Bureaucracy: A highly structured organizational form having the characteristics outlined in Max Weber's bureaucracy theory.

Burnout: An aversive emotional state that is thought to be the result of job stress. It is characterized by a lack of enthusiasm for the job and a lost sense of the importance of the job.

Cadre: A term from leader-member exchange (LMX) theory that refers to individuals who are favored by their supervisors.

Cafeteria benefits: Employee benefit program in which individuals are allowed to customize their fringe benefits by choosing several from a long list of benefits, such as different types of insurance plans.

Career ladder: A system in an organization that defines a progression of promotion opportunities, such as ranks in the military.

Carpal tunnel syndrome: A repetitive strain injury of the wrist brought on by continually performing the same motions.

Categorical measurement: A measurement technique in which numbers represent arbitrary categories of a variable rather than positions along an underlying continuum.

Central tendency error: The tendency for a rater to give everyone mid-range ratings across all dimensions of performance.

Chain of command: In bureaucracy theory, the idea that directives flow down the organization from supervisor to subordinate.

Change agent: The person (or persons) who implements the changes in organizational development plans.

Charismatic leader: A leader who has an unusual amount of influence on followers and can change their attitudes and beliefs.

Circadian rhythm: Physical body changes throughout the day involving hormone levels and temperature.

Classical measurement theory: States that a measure is composed of a true score component and an error component.

Coercive power: Power based on the use of punishments.

Cognitive ability tests: Tests that assess cognitive or mental abilities, such as mathematical or verbal reasoning. The most commonly used cognitive ability tests are intelligence tests.

Cohesiveness: The attraction that group members have toward the group; the importance of the group to group members.

Collectivism: A cultural value referring to the focus a person has on others rather than the self. It is the opposite of individualism.

Combination Job Analysis Method (C-JAM): A job analysis technique that involves several methods, including interviews and questionnaires.

Comparable worth: The idea that jobs having equivalent value to an organization should be paid the same; refers to differences in pay levels between jobs held predominantly by men and jobs held predominantly by women.

Compensable factors: In job evaluation, the variables that are used as the basis of the analysis.

Competency system: An organizational practice in which critical competencies (KSAOs) for a job are identified, and employee progress toward developing those competencies is tracked.

Computer Adaptive Testing: The use of a computer to administer a tailored test where the difficulty of items administered is determined by an individual's ability to answer prior items correctly.

Computer supported cooperative work, CSCW: Work involving two or more people that is done through the use of computers and other similar technologies, often from remote locations.

Concurrent validation study: A validation strategy in which the predictor and criterion are assessed at the same time.

Conference: A training method in which trainees meet to discuss the material.

Confounding: A state that occurs when two or more variables are tangled up such that conclusions about either one alone cannot be made.

Consideration: A supervisory style characterized by concern with the well-being of subordinates. One of the dimensions of the Leader Behavior Description Questionnaire that was developed during the Ohio State Leadership Studies.

Construct validity: The ability to confidently interpret the meaning of an instrument and the ability to conclude that we understand what it is that an instrument actually measures.

Content validity: A characteristic of a test that adequately covers the entire domain intended. For a final examination, content validity would mean that the entire curriculum has been included, as opposed to only a small part.

Contextual performance: Behavior that is not required of employees but benefits the organization. Also called organizational citizenship behavior.

Continuance commitment: Type of organizational commitment based on the investments an individual has in the organization, such as pensions and seniority.

Continuous measurement: A measurement technique in which numbers represent an underlying continuum of a variable from low to high.

Control group: A comparison group in an experiment; often a group that did not receive the treatment of interest.

Control: Any of a number of research procedures that eliminate the possibility that unwanted variables caused the results.

Correlation coefficient: A statistic that indicates the strength of association between two variables.

Correlation: The association between two variables.

Counterproductive work behavior (CWB): Employee behavior that hurts the organization or employees of the organization.

Criterion contamination: The extent to which an actual criterion assesses something other than the theoretical criterion.

Criterion deficiency: The extent to which a theoretical criterion is not assessed by the actual criterion.

Criterion relevance: The extent to which the actual criterion assesses the theoretical criterion.

Criterion: A standard of comparison. For performance appraisal, it is the definition of good performance.

Criterion-related validity: The instrument in question is related to a criterion to which it is theoretically expected to relate.

Critical incident: An example of either good or poor job performance; often used to conduct job analysis.

Cross-sectional design: A design for a study in which all data are collected at the same time.

Cross-validate: To replicate the results of one sample with those of another sample.

Cutoff score: A score that serves as the threshold for selection. Individuals who reach the cutoff are hired, whereas those who are below the cutoff are not.

CWB: Counterproductive work behavior. Employee behavior that hurts the organization or employees of the organization.

Decibel (dB): A measure of sound intensity.

Delegation of authority: From bureaucracy theory, the principle that each manager should assign the responsibility for portions of work to subordinates.

Demand/control model: A model of job stress that suggests how control can reduce the negative effects of job stressors.

Dependent variable: In an experiment, the variable that changes as a result of manipulating the independent variable.

Descriptive statistics: Statistics that summarize a distribution of scores, such as means and standard deviations.

Descriptive theory: An organizational theory that explains how organizations operate.

Dictionary of Occupational Titles (DOT): A book that contains descriptions of more than 20,000 jobs in the United States.

Distal motivation theory: A motivation theory that deals with variables that are remote from behavior, such as needs.

Distributive justice: The form of justice concerning a fair division of rewards among people.

Division of labor: Principle from bureaucracy theory that suggests how work should be divided into a series of tasks assigned to different individuals.

Dynamic criterion: The idea that job performance changes over time.

E-learning: The use of electronic technology such as the Internet to deliver training.

Emotional dissonance: A state a person experiences when having to pretend he or she is experiencing one emotion while actually experiencing an incompatible emotion, such as acting happy when sad.

Emotional Intelligence (EI): A cluster of abilities involving the control and recognition of emotions in oneself and others.

Emotional labor, also called emotion work: A requirement of a job to exhibit a particular emotion, most frequently enthusiasm and happiness. Common with customer-service jobs, such as sales.

Empirical biographical inventory: A biographical inventory developed statistically by conducting analyses of a large number of items to see which ones predict job performance.

Engineering psychology: The branch of psychology concerned with the interaction of people and technology; also called ergonomics or human factors.

Equity theory: A theory that bases work motivation on the balance between perceived contributions (inputs) and rewards (outcomes).

Ergonomics: The branch of psychology concerned with the interaction of people and technology; also called engineering psychology or human factors.

Error variance: Variability among subjects in the same experimental condition.

Error: According to classical test theory, the part of an observed score that does not represent the construct of interest.

Essential function: The idea that certain job tasks are necessary for an employee to perform.

Executive coaching: A training technique in which a high level executive or manager is paired with a consultant who provides one-on-one training to enhance managerial skills.

Expectancy theory: A theory that bases work motivation on a person's expectancy that behavior will lead to desired rewards.

Expectancy: The belief that effort will lead to good job performance.

Experiment: A research design in which subjects are randomly assigned to conditions or treatments created by the researcher.

Expert power: Influence based on the perceived expertise of the individual.

Face validity: What a measure appears to assess.

Facet: A dimension of job satisfaction, such as pay or supervision.

Factorial analysis of variance (ANOVA): A statistical technique for analyzing data from experiments with more than one independent variable.

Factorial design: An experimental design for a study that has two or more independent variables.

Fairness theory: A theory suggesting that people make judgments about situations as fair or unfair based on negative outcomes that are seen as purposeful and unreasonable.

Feedback: Information given to a person about his or her performance.

Fiedler's contingency theory: A theory that considers leader effectiveness to be a joint outcome of the leader and the leadership situation.

Field experiment: An experiment conducted in the setting in which the behavior in question naturally occurs.

Field setting: A research setting in which behavior naturally occurs.

Flextime: A work schedule that allows employees to choose some of their work hours.

Force: The term in expectancy theory that represents the level of motivation to engage in a behavior.

Formal role: An established role in an organization, such as supervisor.

Four-fifths rule: The threshold for adverse impact.

Frame of reference training: A form of training for raters who conduct performance appraisal in which they are given a common and consistent frame of reference upon which to base judgments.

Functional Job Analysis (FJA): Method of job analysis that produces scores on common dimensions; used to compile the Dictionary of Occupational Titles.

Galatea effect: A type of self-fulfilling prophecy in which an individual's belief in being able to do something well results in better performance. It is similar to self-efficacy.

General principles: A general overview of the area being trained that should be given to trainees.

Generalizability: The extent to which findings in a study can be extended to other settings.

Glass ceiling: The phenomenon that minorities and women can progress only to a certain level in organizations.

Goal orientation: An individual's focus on either enhancing knowledge and skill (learning orientation) or enhancing performance on job tasks (performance orientation).

Goal-setting theory: A motivation theory that considers motivation to be enhanced by the setting of goals.

Graphic rating form: A performance-appraisal technique in which employees are rated on dimensions of performance, such as work quality or work quantity.

Group cohesiveness: *See* Cohesiveness.

Group polarization: The tendency of a group to take more extreme positions than the mean of individuals' positions.

Group test: A psychological test administered to groups of individuals at the same time.

Groupthink: Poor decision making that results from certain group processes.

Growth need strength (GNS): A personality variable from job characteristics theory that concerns the level of a person's need for things that can be gotten from complex work, such as recognition and sense of accomplishment.

Halo error: The tendency for a rater to give an individual the same rating across different dimensions of performance.

Hawthorne Effect: Study results that are produced by the subjects' knowledge that they are research participants.

Health circle: An organized group of employees who meet to formulate recommendations to improve employee health and well-being.

Hired hands: In leader-member exchange (LMX) theory, the individuals who are not favored by the supervisor.

Human factors: The branch of psychology concerned with the interaction of people and technology; also called engineering psychology or ergonomics.

Hygiene factors: In two-factor theory, the job factors that fall outside the nature of the work itself, such as pay and other rewards.

Hypothesis: A researcher's guess about the outcome of a study.

Identical elements: In training, the correspondence between responses made in training and responses necessary on the job.

In-basket exercise: A simulation exercise used in an assessment center; asks the assessee to show what he or she would do with a series of items that might be found in a manager's in-basket.

Incentive system: A compensation system in which employees are paid for their level of productivity.

Incivility: When employees treat one another in a demeaning and rude way. A mild form of mobbing or bullying.

Independent variable: The variable in an experiment that is manipulated by the researcher.

Individual test: A psychological test administered to only one person at a time.

Individualism: A cultural value referring to the focus a person has on the self as opposed to others. It is the opposite of collectivism.

Industrial/organizational (I/O) psychology: Applied branch of psychology that is concerned with understanding people in organizations.

Inferential statistics: Branch of statistics that is concerned with generalizing results from the data at hand to all possible cases. It relies on statistical tests that are based on probability.

Informal role: A role not intended by the organization that develops in a work group.

Informed consent form: Explains a study to a potential subject before he or she agrees to participate.

In-group: *See* Cadre.

Initiating structure: A leadership style characterized by concern with task accomplishment; one of the dimensions of the Leader Behavior Description Questionnaire from the Ohio State Leadership Studies.

Inputs: In equity theory, the contributions made by an employee.

Instrumentality: In expectancy theory, the belief that performance will lead to rewards.

Integrity test: A paper-and-pencil test designed to predict employee counterproductive behavior.

Internal consistency reliability: The agreement among multiple items in a test or multiple ratings by different raters.

Inter-rater reliability: The association between the ratings of two (or more) raters who rate the same subject on the same variable.

Interview: A face-to-face meeting between two or more people for the purpose of sharing information; used for data collection and employee selection.

Job analysis: A method for describing jobs and characteristics necessary for jobs.

Job characteristics model: A model that relates employee motivation and satisfaction to job characteristics.

Job Components Inventory (JCI): A method of job analysis that matches job requirements to characteristics of people.

Job Descriptive Index (JDI): A five-facet measure of job satisfaction.

Job evaluation: A mathematical procedure for determining the relative value of a job to an organization.

Job in General (JIG) scale: A measure of overall job satisfaction.

Job satisfaction: A person's attitudes and feelings about his or her job and facets of the job.

Job strain: A physical or psychological reaction to a stressful job condition.

Job stressor: A stressful job condition.

Job-oriented job analysis: Any job analysis method that focuses on the content of jobs.

Joint optimization: The concept from sociotechnical systems theory that the social system and technical system of an organization must be designed to complement one another.

Knowledge and skill test: A psychological test designed to assess a person's knowledge or skills; also called an achievement test.

Knowledge: What it is necessary to know for a job.

KSAOs: The knowledge, skills, abilities, and other personal characteristics necessary for good job performance.

Laboratory setting: Research setting in which the behavior of interest does not naturally occur.

Law of effect: The psychological principle that a rewarded behavior will be more likely to reoccur and a punished behavior will be less likely to reoccur.

Leader Behavior Description Questionnaire (LBDQ): Scale to assess leadership style, including consideration and initiating structure.

Leader Match: A procedure based on Fiedler's contingency theory that trains leaders to modify situations to match their personal characteristics.

Leaderless group exercise: An assessment center exercise in which assessees are placed in a group without a leader to observe their interpersonal behavior.

Leader-member exchange (LMX) theory: A theory that views leadership from the perspective of individual leader-subordinate pairs.

Learning criteria: Measures that indicate how much trainees have learned from training.

Learning orientation: A goal orientation that focuses attention on enhancing knowledge and skill.

Least Preferred Coworker (LPC) scale: A measure used to assess a personality characteristic of a leader. The LPC is an important component of Fiedler's contingency theory.

Lecture: A training method in which trainees listen to a presentation.

Legitimate power: Influence based on followers' beliefs that a person has the right to ask for compliance, usually based on rank or title.

Leniency error: The tendency for a rater to give everyone high ratings across dimensions of performance.

Life satisfaction: A person's attitudes about his or her overall life.

Locus of control: A personality variable that refers to people's tendencies to attribute rewards to themselves (internals) or to other people or things (externals).

Longitudinal design: A design for a study in which data are collected at different times.

Management by objectives (MBO): An organizational change technique that involves setting interrelated goals throughout an organization.

Masculinity: A cultural value reflecting an emphasis on achievement as opposed to the well-being of others.

Massed training: Training that is done all at one time; the opposite of spaced training.

Mean: A measure of the center of a distribution; the sum of observations divided by the number of observations.

Measurement: The process of assigning numbers to characteristics of people or things.

Median: A measure of the center of a distribution; the middle score in a rank-ordered group of observations.

Mediator variable: A variable that intervenes in the process by which two variables are related and explains that relationship.

Mental model: A person's conception or cognitive representation of something, such as how a computer works.

Mentoring: The form of workplace relationship in which experienced employees assist less experienced employees in career development.

Merit pay: Pay based on level of job performance.

Meta-analysis: A mathematical summary of the results of several samples or studies of the same phenomenon.

Minnesota Satisfaction Questionnaire (MSQ): A 20-facet job satisfaction scale.

Mixed Standard Scale (MSS): A behavior-based performance appraisal method.

Mobbing, also called bullying: When one or more employees harass and mistreat an individual at work.

Modeling: A training method in which the trainee first observes someone executing a behavior and then practices it.

Moderator variable: A variable that affects the relation between two other variables.

Motivation Potential Score (MPS): From job characteristics theory, the overall complexity or scope of a job.

Motivation: The underlying force that explains why people engage in a behavior.

Motivator factors: In two-factor theory, the job factors that are inherent in the job itself.

Motor task: A task that involves body movements, such as placing pegs in holes or walking.

Multiple hurdle: A selection method whereby applicants must achieve a certain score on each predictor to be hired.

Multiple regression: A statistical procedure for combining several predictors to forecast a criterion.

Musculoskeletal disorder (MSD): An injury to the muscles, bones, and connective tissue caused either by an acute episode (e.g., lifting) or repetitive strain.

Need hierarchy theory: Considers motivation to be based on a hierarchy of five basic human needs.

Negative affectivity (NA): A personality variable that refers to a tendency to experience negative emotions across many different situations.

Nominal group: Several noninteracting people who serve as a comparison to an interacting group in group research.

Norm: A standard of behavior in a group of people.

Normative commitment: Type of organizational commitment in which a person feels obligated to the organization out of a sense of obligation or values.

Objective test: A test that has fixed response choices that the test taker picks for each item.

Observational design: A research design in which people are observed on the job.

Obtrusive method: A data collection method in which subjects are aware that they are being studied.

OCB (organizational-citizenship behavior): Behavior that is not required of employees but benefits the organization. Also called contextual performance.

Occupational commitment: Attachment to one's occupation or profession regardless of employer or organization.

Occupational health psychology (OHP): Interdisciplinary subfield of psychology concerned with employee health, safety, and well-being.

Occupational Information Network (O*NET): The U.S. Department of Labor's extensive database on jobs and worker requirements for jobs.

OHP (occupational health psychology): Interdisciplinary subfield of psychology concerned with employee health, safety, and well-being.

On-the-job-training: A training method in which the trainee learns the job while doing it.

Open system theory: A theory that describes organizations as having all the features of an open system.

Open-ended test: A test that requires the test taker to write out his or her answers, such as an essay examination.

Organizational citizenship behavior (OCB): Behavior that is not required of employees but benefits the organization. Also called contextual performance

Organizational commitment: The attachment that a person has for a job. *See also* Affective, Continuance, and Normative commitment.

Organizational constraints: Conditions in an organization that prevent employees from performing well.

Organizational development (OD): One of a family of methods used to improve the functioning of organizations.

Other personal characteristics: Characteristics of people relevant to jobs other than knowledge, skill, or ability.

Other: In equity theory, the person used for comparison of inputs and outcomes.

Outcome: In equity theory, the rewards a person gets from a job.

Out-group: *See* Hired hands.

Overlearning: Training that continues after a trainee first reaches a criterion of learning the skill.

Paper-and-pencil test: A written test that requires either indicating the correct answer from several choices or writing an answer to an open-ended question.

Part training: Training of individual subtasks one at a time; the opposite of whole training.

Path-goal theory: A leadership theory that emphasizes how leaders can enhance subordinate motivation by clarifying the paths between behavior and rewards.

Pearson product-moment correlation: The most frequently used measure of association between two continuous variables.

Performance appraisal: The formal procedures that an organization uses to assess job performance of employees.

Performance orientation: A goal orientation that focuses attention on enhancing performance on specific job tasks.

Performance test: A test that requires the test taker to perform tasks involving manipulation of objects.

Performance-level criteria: Measures that indicate how well training transfers to the job.

Personality test: A test designed to assess people's patterns of behavior or feelings.

Personality trait: The tendency of a person to engage in certain types of behavior or respond to situations in particular ways.

Person-oriented job analysis: Any job analysis method that focuses on characteristics necessary for a job.

Piece rate system: A system that pays employees for each unit of productivity.

Political skill: The skill in being able to influence others to accomplish either personal or organizational objectives.

Position Analysis Questionnaire (PAQ): A job analysis method that describes jobs and necessary job characteristics along common dimensions.

Power distance: A cultural value of tolerance for large power and status differences among levels in an organization.

Power test: A test without a time limit.

Power: The ability to influence other people.

Predictive validity study: A study in which predictor information is used to forecast a criterion that is assessed at a later time.

Predictor: A variable that is used to forecast a criterion.

Prescriptive theory: An organizational theory that explains how an organization should function.

Pretest-posttest design: A research design in which the same criterion variable is assessed before and after the treatment occurs.

Procedural justice: The fairness of a process by which rewards are allocated.

Process loss: Time spent by group members that is not devoted to task accomplishment.

Programmed instruction: A training method in which trainees work at their own pace.

Protected class: Group of people who are given special legal protection because of past discrimination against them.

Proximal motivation theory: A motivation theory that deals with variables that are closely linked to behavior, such as goals or intentions.

Psychological test: A sample of behavior assessed under standardized conditions to measure characteristics of people.

Psychomotor ability test: A psychological test designed to assess physical abilities, such as eye-hand coordination.

Qualitative method: Research that minimizes the use of quantitative and statistical methods.

Quality circle: A group of employees who meet to discuss ways to improve their work.

Quasi-experimental design: A research design that has some but not all the features of an experiment. For example, there might not be random assignment of subjects to conditions.

Questionnaire: A paper-and-pencil instrument used to collect information; can be completed by respondents themselves.

Random assignment: Placing subjects into treatment conditions in an experiment so that each subject has an equal chance of being in each condition.

Random selection: Choosing subjects for a study so that every possible subject has an equal chance of participating.

Rater error training (RET): A training program designed to familiarize individuals who rate performance with rating errors and techniques to avoid them.

Rational biographical inventory: A biographical inventory based on theory and research concerning the prior experiences that would be expected to relate to job performance.

Reactions criteria: Measures of trainee reactions to training.

Realistic job preview (RJP): Information given to job applicants to let them know what the job and organization are like.

Reasonable accommodation: A principle from the Americans With Disabilities Act that requires organizations to provide reasonable assistance or modifications to the job or workplace so that people with disabilities can perform the job.

Referent power: Influence based on the subordinate's liking for the supervisor.

Regression equation: A mathematical equation that allows the prediction of one variable from another.

Reinforcement theory: A motivation theory that considers behavior to be a function of rewards.

Reliability: The consistency of a measure; how well scores on the same subject are replicable across repeated measurements of the same variable.

Repetitive strain injury: An injury brought on by making the same motion continuously, such as typing on a computer keyboard.

Research design: The structure of a research study.

Response rate: The percentage or proportion of contacted people who participate in a survey.

Results criteria: Measures of training impact on the organization, such as profits.

Reward power: Influence based on giving rewards.

Role ambiguity: Employee uncertainty about what is expected of him or her on the job.

Role conflict: Incompatible demands placed on an employee.

Role play: A training technique that involves having the trainee pretend to perform a task.

Role: A person's position in a group or team.

Salary survey: A survey of employers to determine salary levels for certain jobs.

Sample: The subjects chosen for a study.

Schemata: Cognitive categories or frames of reference.

Scientific Management: The application of scientific principles to managing people's job performance; developed by Frederick Winslow Taylor.

Scope: The complexity of a job.

Selection ratio: The proportion of job applicants who are hired for a job.

Self-efficacy theory: A motivation theory based on the idea that people perform well when they believe they are capable of doing the job.

Self-efficacy: The belief a person has in his or her ability to perform a task well.

Severity error: In performance appraisal, the assignment of low ratings to all ratees.

Sexual harassment: Behavior of a sexual nature that adversely affects a person's ability to do his or her job.

Simulation: A training method that allows people to practice a skill in an artificial and controlled situation.

SIOP: *See* Society for Industrial and Organizational Psychology.

Skill variety: A dimension of the job characteristics model that involves the number of skills required to do a job.

Skill: How well a person is able to do a task.

Social facilitation: The improvement in a person's performance that sometimes occurs in the presence of other people. Research has shown that simple or well-learned tasks are facilitated by the presence of others, whereas performance on complex or new tasks is inhibited. *See* Social inhibition.

Social inhibition: The decline in performance that sometimes occurs in the presence of other people. Research has shown that complex or new tasks are inhibited by the presence of others, whereas performance on simple or well-learned tasks is facilitated. *See* Social facilitation.

Social loafing: A group phenomenon whereby the larger the group, the less effort on a task is made by each member.

Society for Industrial and Organizational Psychology (SIOP): Division of the American Psychological Association that is the world's largest association of I/O psychologists.

Sociotechnical systems theory: A theory stating that organizations should consider both the human and the technological demands of tasks in designing work environments.

Spaced training: Training in which sessions are spread out over time; the opposite of massed training.

Span of control: A principle of bureaucracy theory concerned with the number of people a supervisor can oversee.

Speed test: A test with a time limit.

Standard deviation: A measure of dispersion for a distribution of scores; the square root of the variance.

Statistical significance: A rule of thumb for evaluating the results of a statistical test.

Statistical test: A quantitative procedure based on probability that allows for the interpretation of study outcomes.

Stress: Physiological and psychological responses to demands that are perceived to be challenging or threatening.

Structured interview: An interview in which the questions are standardized across interviewees.

Subject matter expert: A person who is knowledgeable about a topic.

Survey design: A design in which subjects are asked to answer questions, usually with an interview or questionnaire.

Survey feedback: An organizational change technique in which employees are surveyed and the survey information is fed back to all levels of the organization.

Tailored testing: A testing procedure that adjusts the level of item difficulty to the test taker's ability.

Task identity: A dimension from the job characteristics model that identifies the extent to which a person does an entire job.

Task inventory: A job analysis technique that produces a detailed list of the tasks for a job.

Task significance: A dimension from the job characteristics model that represents the extent to which a particular job affects other people.

Team building: A procedure used to improve the functioning of work teams.

Team commitment: The attachment a person has to his or her team and teammates.

Team mental model: The cognitive conception a team member has about the various tasks each member of the team has and how the various tasks interrelate.

Telecommute: Work at home while communicating with work-related people via modem and the telephone.

Test-retest reliability: The consistency of a measure when it is repeated over time.

T-group: An organizational change technique that has employees attend training sessions over a period of days to learn interpersonal skills.

Theoretical criterion: The conceptual definition of what constitutes good job performance.

Theory X/Theory Y: A theory proposing that how a manager views subordinate characteristics affects his or her approach to supervision.

Theory Z: The Japanese style of management for large organizations that assumes employees will spend their entire careers with one organization.

Time and motion study: An analysis of task performance involving the observation and timing of subject motions. The purpose is to determine ways to eliminate or modify motions to make performance more efficient.

Training-level criteria: Measures of how well a trainee does in training.

Transfer of training: The application of what was learned in training to the job.

Transformational leader: *See* Charismatic leader.

True halo: The extent to which a person's performances across different dimensions are at the same level.

T-test: A statistical test used to compare two means.

Turnover: An employee's quitting his or her job.

Two-factor theory: A theory that considers job satisfaction and dissatisfaction to be separate factors rather than opposite ends of the same continuum.

Type A/B personality: A personality variable; a person can be hard driving and impatient (Type A) or easygoing and relaxed (Type B).

Uncertainty avoidance: A cultural value reflecting tolerance for ambiguity and uncertainty; reflected in the tendency to be rule oriented.

Uniform Guidelines on Employee Selection Procedures: A document produced by the U.S. government that describes appropriate and legally defensible selection procedures.

Unit control of variances: A principle of sociotechnical systems theory that recommends allowing employees who encounter problems to solve them.

Universal Precautions: Suggested safety procedures for healthcare workers to reduce chances of accidental exposure to infectious diseases such as AIDS/HIV or hepatitis B.

Unobtrusive method: A method of research in which subjects do not know they are being studied.

Utility analysis: The analysis of the financial benefits to an organization of taking a course of action, such as implementing a particular selection system.

Valence: In expectancy theory, the value or worth a person gives to an outcome.

Validation study: A study undertaken to determine whether a predictor is related to a criterion.

Validity generalization: A principle stating that if a predictor is a valid indicator of a criterion in one setting, it will be valid in another, similar setting.

Validity: The interpretation given to the meaning of a measure.

Variable: A characteristic of a person or thing that varies.

Variance: The degree to which scores differ among individuals in a distribution of scores.

Virtual team: Two or more individuals with interdependent tasks and separate roles who interact remotely via e-mail, telephone, and other technologies.

Vocational interest test: A test that matches the interests of test takers to people in various professions.

Vroom-Yetton model: A model that indicates the best approach to making decisions that involve subordinates.

Whole training: Training that focuses on an entire task at one time rather than on parts of the task; the opposite of part training.

Work group: Two or more individuals who interact and share common task goals.

Work sample: A test that includes tasks from a job.

Work team: A work group in which members have interdependent tasks and individual task-related roles.

Work-family conflict: A form of role conflict in which family demands and work demands conflict.

Name Index

Subject Index